STUDY GUIDE TO ACCOMPANY
SAMUELSON AND NORDHAUS
ECONOMICS

STUDY GUIDE TO ACCOMPANY
SAMUELSON AND NORDHAUS
ECONOMICS
TWELFTH EDITION

GARY W. YOHE

Wesleyan University

McGRAW-HILL BOOK COMPANY

New York St. Louis San Francisco Auckland Bogotá Hamburg
Johannesburg London Madrid Mexico Montreal New Delhi
Panama Paris São Paulo Singapore Sydney Tokyo Toronto

STUDY GUIDE TO ACCOMPANY
SAMUELSON AND NORDHAUS: ECONOMICS

Copyright © 1985, 1980, 1976, 1973, 1970, 1967, 1964, 1961, 1958, 1955
by McGraw-Hill, Inc. All rights reserved. Copyright 1952 by
McGraw-Hill, Inc. All rights reserved. Copyright renewed 1980, 1983
by Paul A. Samuelson and Romney Robinson. Printed in the United
States of America. Except as permitted under the United States
Copyright Act of 1976, no part of this publication may be reproduced or distributed in any form or by any means, or stored in a data
base or retreival system, without the prior written permission of the
publisher.

3 4 5 6 7 8 9 0 WEBWEB 8 9 8 7 6

ISBN 0-07-054687-8

This book was set in Highland by Automated Composition Service, Inc.
The editors were Patricia A. Mitchell, Elisa Adams,
and Peggy Rehberger;
the designer was Merrill Haber;
the production supervisor was Joe Campanella.
New drawings were done by J & R Services, Inc.
Cover photograph by Photo Researchers.
Webcrafters, Inc., was printer and binder.

For Linda, Marielle, and Courtney

Contents

vii

PART FIVE: WAGES, RENT, AND PROFITS: THE DISTRIBUTION OF INCOME

PART SIX: EQUITY, EFFICIENCY, AND GOVERNMENT

PART SEVEN: ECONOMIC GROWTH AND INTERNATIONAL TRADE

To the Student

This *Study Guide* has one specific objective: to help you to master the fundamentals of economic analysis as presented in the twelfth edition of *Economics* by Paul A. Samuelson and William D. Nordhaus. It has been prepared in close consultation with these authors to cover the material presented in the text and to involve you in deciphering that material. It is hoped that your work in the *Guide* will lead you to a deeper understanding of not only the content of each chapter of the text, but also of the rationale for anyone's ever worrying about such things. It will, however, accomplish this goal only if your reading of the *Guide* is an active process. If you simply read the pages of the *Guide* as you would any other text, you will see another presentation of the same material, but nothing more. Your passive reading will have caused you to lose most of the value of your supplementary purchase. If, however, you read the pages more slowly with pencil in hand and work through the various questions that they will pose, your active participation in exercising the fundamentals of economic analysis will generate a deeper understanding of what is going on and, I hope, a higher grade in your economics class.

Each chapter of the *Guide* begins with a list of learning objectives. These lists have been prepared to outline the major points of each chapter and appendix. After reading the text chapter, match them with a list that you draw up to see whether you (or I) have missed anything. You will, at that point, have a good idea of the material that the remainder of the chapter will exercise.

The second major part of each chapter in the *Guide* amounts to a collection of questions and problems designed to enhance your understanding of the learning objectives. Working through them one at a time (*before* looking at the answers provided in small print after each question) will test and extend your knowledge as you apply to different cicumstances what the text has taught you. The process is much like the one by which you might learn a new language. You can go to class and read textbooks to be exposed to the fundamentals of a new language, but it sinks in and becomes part of you only if you practice. With enough practice, you begin to think in the new language, and further progress becomes easier. Working through the question section of the *Guide*, you will similarly practice what you have learned in class and in the text, and eventually you might even begin to think like an economist.

Each chapter in the *Guide* concludes with a series of multiple choice quiz questions, with the answers provided at the end of the book. These are designed to tell you whether or not you have really mastered the chapter's content. You should, as you work through the questions, select one of the five alternative answers. It should be the answer that makes the *most* sense in context. Some answers are correct statements but are irrelevent to the question being posed. Other answers are simply wrong. Still others are almost right, but nonetheless inferior to an alternative choice. The answer listed in the back represents the *best* selection, and it is the one you should search for.

One of the most successful ways of mastering the fundamentals of economic analysis is to try to summarize the material of each chapter or unit in successively shorter outlines. The prose that surrounds the questions in the middle of each *Guide* chapter represents a first cut at such an outline. The list of learning objectives can, perhaps, represent a final stage. In the process of synthesizing text material down to the lists of objectives, use the *Guide* to look for threads of common thought and rationalization. When you have reached the point of needing only the objectives lists to recall content, make sure that you have a firm understanding of their connection to each other. Having accomplished that understanding, you will be able to apply your knowledge to unfamiliar problems and contexts.

The real lessons of economics are ones of process—insights into the methods by which economists try to identify logically the essentials of a particular circumstance from a multitude of data. Equipped with insight into these processes and methods, you will be ready to proceed to subsequent economics courses and do well. Perhaps more importantly, though, you will be equipped with the mental skills necessary to deal with the myriad of economics-related issues and decisions that will face you all of your life. You may forget what marginal cost is, but you should continue to be able to identify essential tradeoffs and weigh them accordingly.

ACKNOWLEDGMENTS

Preparation of this *Guide* would not have been accomplished on schedule without the assistance of many people. I would like to formally recognize their contributions and express my gratitude.

My family, which missed a summer of my attention but supported my efforts anyway, certainly deserves a heartfelt "thanks." Their support certainly made the project worthwhile.

Many people at McGraw-Hill also deserve grateful acknowledgment. Patricia Mitchell, Peggy Rehberger, and Kathy Harris certainly fall into that category. A special thanks must, however, be extended to Elisa Adams. Her excellent work, good humor, and constant encouragement were above and beyond.

Finally, I express my gratitude for the opportunity, education, and friendship offered by Bill Nordhaus—over the past decade as much as the past year.

Gary W. Yohe

PART ONE
BASIC CONCEPTS

CHAPTER 1
INTRODUCTION

This introductory chapter is, above all, one which should be read with a view toward perspective. It has been designed to provide a rough outline of what the discipline of economics is all about. You need not worry terribly about the few details that are presented. Try, instead, to get the "lay of the land." Try to get an idea of why people would ever want to concern themselves with the study of economics and how, in broad and general terms, such a study should be conducted. Having kept this in mind, you should be able to meet the following objectives after studying the text chapter and working through the Study Guide questions. (Each chapter in this guide will begin with a similar list of objectives. These lists should serve both as preliminary outlines of the material that you are about to cover and, once you have completed the chapter, review outlines of the points that you should have mastered. They will serve you best, therefore, if you read them at least twice—once as a preview of coming attractions and again as a review of past material.)

LEARNING OBJECTIVES

1. Explain (in general terms) why, in the text's summary definition of economics, the word "choice" (the choice between this alternative and that) is emphasized.

2. Distinguish between "gross national product" and "net economic welfare."

3. Distinguish between "economic description" (or "economic analysis") and "economic policy."

4. Contrast economics (regarded as a social science) with physics (as one of the natural sciences) in the matter of (a) controlled experiment, (b) the establishment of "laws," and (c) the "subjective element of perception" of raw data received by the senses.

5. Explain carefully (a) the "*post hoc, ergo propter hoc*" fallacy, and (b) the "fallacy of composition."

6. Explain why economists disagree. Find a source of current disagreement among economists in the newspaper or on the TV news and explore both sides of the argument. Is their argument based on issues of normative or positive economics? With whom do you agree? (Put your answer to this aside and reconsider the debate at the end of the course. You will be surprised to see how the study of economics, even at an introductory level, will help you to grasp the issues involved in the debate and to make a more informed answer to the "whose side are you on?" question.)

Five alternative definitions of economics are cited in the text before a single umbrella definition is advanced: "Economics is the study of how people and society choose to employ scarce productive resources that could have alternative uses to produce various commodities and to distribute them for consumption, now or in the future, among various persons and groups in society "

1. Review the five more specialized definitions and try to see how each fits under the general umbrella. With all six notions in mind, which of the following seem to fall correctly (C) within the scope of economic analysis and which seem to fall outside (O) the general umbrella?

a. The first objective of economics as a science is to study human performance in producing and selling goods in order to indicate how business can perform these activities more efficiently. .... (C / O)

b. Economics is closely associated with the particular activities in which money is involved—the purchase and sale of goods and of securities, the employment of labor, and so on. .... (C / O)

c. Economics is a study of the activities by means of which a nation acquires a high standard of income and of consumption. .... (C / O)

d. In economics, we look at the processes of producing and selling goods, and of buying and consuming goods, in order to develop some theory with respect to such behavior. . . . . *(C / O)*

e. Economics is a study of how people in a society decide what commodities and services they are going to produce, now and in the future, and how those commodities and services are to be distributed among members of the population. . . . . *(C / O)*

---

a. O **b.** C **c.** C **d.** C **e.** C

2.   a. Some 40 years ago, the concept of gross national product (GNP) was developed. It is an estimate of the nation's total annual output of goods (commodities) and services expressed in money terms; it summarizes the whole of a nation's economic activity across the entire population for an entire year.

In complex, interdependent societies such as ours, there has always been a steady demand for information on "how well the economy is doing." In major part, this demand asks: What is happening to total output? Is business improving, or not? In pre-GNP days, such questions had to be answered by piecing together data on total steel production, total freight-car loadings, and other bits of available information. The task of devising methods by means of which a reliable one-figure estimate of total production could be obtained was not easy. But once developed, the GNP measure was a vast improvement.

A single GNP figure is meaningless. (Does it enlighten you greatly to learn that GNP in the United States for 1980 is estimated at around $2500 billion?) But things are different if you have two or more GNP figures for comparison. (In the material following, where part of the sentence consists of two or more alternatives within parentheses and in italics, circle that one alternative which you think makes the sentence correct.) Year-to-year figures (properly adjusted for price changes) *(will / cannot)* indicate whether or not total output is increasing; and if increasing, at what rate. You *(can / cannot)* use GNP figures to compare (at least roughly) the sizes (economic sizes, not geographic) of the United States and the Soviet Union, and how those sizes are changing. You *(can / cannot)* use trends in GNP figures to assess the general employment outlook of an economy—how difficult or easy it will be for an individual of certain characteristics to find a job. You *(can / cannot)* even try to use recent movement in GNP to try to predict what will happen in the near future.

b. The gross national product idea was so useful that, after it had become part of everyday economic language, some people began to interpret it as conveying information it was never intended to carry. The rate of increase in GNP was taken as a measure of the improvement in human welfare, even of the increase in "happiness." This distortion set off, as might have been expected, a counter attitude which denounced even the computation of GNP as crass materialism at its worst. In point

of fact, the gross national product should be regarded simply as a measure that is useful for specific purposes, and is subject to particular limitations.

In response to this debate, James Tobin and William Nordhaus have produced a second, derivative measure. Its construction begins with the notion of GNP, but tries to adjust that notion to correct for the positive and negative influences of various parts of reality that are not captured in the GNP calculation. It tries, in that way, to be a more accurate indicator of genuine changes in the well-being of human beings. It does not purport to measure happiness, though; even economists agree that the measurement of happiness lies beyond the competence of economists, sociologists, philosophers, and New York City cabbies. Its name is _____

The GNP figure (simplifying it slightly) for any year is in principle an adding up of everything produced during that year, each item valued at the money price at which it sold. (Thus there is an underlying assumption that the "money worth" of any good is the market price that people do pay in order to buy it. If you dislike this assumption—and there are at least occasional instances that prompt one to wonder about it—remember that the world awaits your better—but workable—definition of worth.) The Tobin-Nordhaus NEW measure tries to take account of factors that do affect material welfare, but are not caught within the GNP's market price net. One example would be *(atmospheric and other pollution / changes in market prices)*. Another would be *(the appearance of new commodities / shorter working hours, hence more leisure time)*.

Like GNP, the NEW measure is a single money figure. So it must place a money value (minus or plus) on each correction of GNP it deems necessary. In most instances, there is no market price measure of this adjustment. So its money size must be estimated. That makes the computation of NEW, in principle, much more difficult than the computation of GNP.

c. Ponder, for a moment, why NEW should exceed GNP during the Great Depression of the 1930s and fall so short of GNP during the past few decades.

---

a. will; can; can; can **b.** new economic welfare; atmospheric and other pollution; shorter working hours, hence more leisure time **c.** Recall that the cost of pollution is subtracted from GNP and the value of leisure time is added to GNP in the NEW computation. The Great Depression provided many people with lots of leisure time—is that an appropriate addition? Recent experience has produced many pollution problems and shortened workweeks.

3.   Economics is a social science; it studies human behavior on both an individual and a collective level. The essential characteristic of most society is (in John Donne's words) that "no man is an island, entire of itself; every man is a piece of the continent, a part of the main." No individual and no group within a society can act without that action having its impact, direct or indirect, upon other individuals or groups. This quality of *interdependence* is one of the major factors that makes the true outcome of behavior difficult to explore, and that calls for special analysis of that behavior. As a result, economics borders and sometimes encroaches over its border with a wide range of other disciplines. Indicate which of the following are germane to the study of economics:

a. psychology .... (*Y / N*)

b. physics .... (*Y / N*)

c. political science .... (*Y / N*)

d. sociology .... (*Y / N*)

e. music .... (*Y / N*)

f. anthropology .... (*Y / N*)

g. astronomy .... (*Y / N*)

---

a. Y **b.** N **c.** Y **d.** Y **e.** N **f.** Y **g.** N

---

4. Physical scientists have learned, slowly and painfully, that things are not what they seem to be. They will tell you that the solid chair on which you sit, and the solid desk at which you work, are not firm, compacted material at all. Each is in fact composed of incredibly tiny atoms of matter: each atom has a nucleus that is positively charged electrically, with negatively charged electrons spinning in orbit around it. The proper analysis of material substances is a business of incredible complexity. It calls for theory: reaching beyond what at first seems to be obvious.

One's first inclination is to think that economics—the study of a particular area of human behavior—is different. Simple observation, and the exercise of ordinary judgment, should suffice to describe and to explain what happens among human beings. Not so, unfortunately. In economics, as in physical science, things are not what they seem to be. Again, we need theory: reaching beyond what at first seems to be obvious.

The nature of theory is overwhelmingly difficult to describe. Yet we can say with some confidence that it is the discovery of *patterns* in behavior. Once the pattern is discovered, behavior which hitherto had seemed incomprehensible or aimless is suddenly revealed as conforming to this pattern.

While the theory may seek to furnish some explanation of why the pattern exists, this is not the first order of business. The essential task is to discover that the pattern is *there*, and to describe it.

This raises the matter of the relation between theory and practice, or theory and reality. Which of the following correctly (C) repeat what the text has to say on this, and which are incorrect (I)?

a. Theory must correspond with reality in the sense of illuminating behavior observed in reality. Failing in this, it is not appropriate theory. .... (*C / I*)

b. In construction of theory, it is necessary to "stand back" from actual behavior a little, much as a referee stands back at a football game, in order to observe what is really happening. This observation involves "abstraction." .... (*C / I*)

c. Of necessity, theory simplifies. It ignores what is irrelevant or unimportant, in order to isolate the *pattern* in behavior. .... (*C / I*)

d. It is the failure of a theory to give a meaningful account of real behavior that marks it as false or incomplete. Yet if it is the best theory available, it may survive. Poor theories are more likely to be killed off by better theories than they are by lack of conformity with facts. .... (*C / I*)

e. As a general process, the development of economic knowledge is an evolutionary progression passing from theory through hypothesis through empirical testing to finish with validation. It mimics the classical scientific method of the pure sciences.

All statements correct (C).

---

5. We cannot establish whether or not a particular theory is in accord with reality until we have established what "the facts" of reality are. This is by no means always easy. The raw elements of experience which our senses carry to the brain are meaningless until the brain organizes them into a pattern (i.e., "theorizes" about them). The brain's disposition is always to fit the material, if possible, into a familiar pattern—even though, in the new situation, that pattern may be a false one.

If this difficulty arises in physics or in chemistry, where controlled experiments are so often possible, it becomes far more acute where the behavior observed is that of human beings.

Where the ordinary business of living requires us to do so, we are forced to develop some workably valid interpretations of the behavior around us. In everyday experience, we can often discover quickly whether or not our conclusions are workably accurate. Interpret a person's behavior falsely, act on your conclusion—and you may soon learn that your interpretation was incorrect. However, there is a broader range of human experience where this element of immediate verification is lacking, or where the degree of verification is uncertain. It is here that part **d** of the preceding question is applicable: When the verification of a theory is difficult, the familiar theory may survive regardless of its veracity until it can be supplanted by a clearly superior theory. The risk involved in this process should be clear. If an unsatisfactory theory is used so frequently that it becomes entrenched in the canonical view of the world, then the development of a new, potentially superior theory will become highly unlikely—nobody will think to question an ingrained theory, so nobody will try to develop a new one.

Which of the following seem to repeat correctly (C) what the text says on this topic, and which are incorrect (I)?

a. The basic requirement in seeking to develop a theory

about observed behavior is ordinary, levelheaded common sense. .... (C / I)

b. Common sense is a dangerous starting point, because it really means a reliance on familiar interpretation; on this account, common sense may on occasion be nonsense. .... (C / I)

c. Study and experience are needed if one is to attempt to construct theory on economic matters. .... (C / I)

d. Long experience is dangerous if familiarity leads to take-it-for-granted interpretations, or if overlong experience from a particular point of view persuades the observer to forget that there are other relevant points of view. .... (C / I)

e. If participants in the economic world—say, businesspeople—are to do their job efficiently, they must necessarily do the best they can to understand the relevant economic theory of what they are doing. .... (C / I)

f. The economist's approach and objective differ from that of anyone engaged in business. It is like the referee and the team player at a football game: The good referee would not necessarily make a good player, and vice versa .... (C / I)

---

a. I **b.** C **c.** C **d.** C **e.** I **f.** C

6. In physics, or in chemistry, theory means uncovering the laws which dictate the behavior of inanimate matter, and describing the quantitative properties of those laws. Is the task of economic theory to uncover comparable laws of human behavior—to which people rigidly and mechanically conform?

On this, the text's view is that individuals (*do / do not*) conform exactly to behavior patterns. But people in large groups, taken as a group, (*still do not conform / show considerable conformity, once the pattern is isolated*).

Sometimes there is a pattern even in the nonconformity. In Figure 1-3 in the text, a straight line with a slope is roughly equal to the relationship between personal consumption expenditure and disposable income. This representation means that, on the average, people consistently spent 95 cents of the last dollar they earned on consumption and saved the remaining nickel. It does not, however, mean that everyone behaved that way. Figure 1-1 recorded here suggests one way in which text Figure 1-3 might be correct even while many people spent more or less than 95 cents on the last dollar. Notice in Figure 1-1 that some people spend 97 cents on the dollar, some spend 93 cents, some spend 91 cents, and a few even spend 101 cents. All that is required to support Figure 1-3 is that these propensities to spend average 95 cents on the dollar. Figure 1-3 tells us that that is the case, not just for a single year, but for most years over the past half century.

---

do not; show considerable conformity, once the pattern is isolated.

7. The text chapter closes with a short section on *the fallacy of composition*. Spend a little time now learning the meaning of

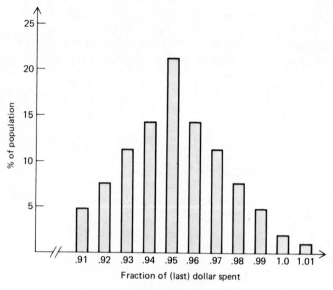

Figure 1-1

this idea, for you will meet it again later. For each statement below, put C in the space if the fallacy of composition seems involved. Put P if the fallacy of *post hoc, ergo propter hoc*.

a. The American economy remains essentially competitive as a result of diligent application of the antitrust laws. ..... ( )

b. All theories in social science are forced to simplify the real and complex world; because of this simplification, the conclusions of any such theory are inevitably distorted and inaccurate explanations. .... ( )

c. Workers in any single industry will benefit from higher wages; hence workers in all industries would benefit from a comparable wage increase. .... ( )

d. Advertising on a large scale is responsible for the present high standard of living in the United States. .... ( )

e. The more the human brain masters a subject in social science such as economics, the less room it has for comprehension of any quite different subject, such as physics. .... ( )

f. If one firm in an industry benefits from a large-scale advertising campaign, this is an indication that if all firms in that industry were to advertise, they would all obtain comparable increases in sales. .... ( )

g. I can gain 15 minutes by driving my car to work instead of using public transportation; if everyone in my community were to follow my example, the total gain in time would run into hundreds of hours each day. .... ( )

---

a. P **b.** N **c.** C **d.** P **e.** N **f.** C **g.** C

8. A distinction was raised in the text between normative and positive economics. Positive economics is descriptive—a relating of facts and circumstance based upon observation.

Normative economics is prescriptive—a relating of solutions and actions based upon ethics and value judgment. Economists disagree (*more / less / about the same*) on issues of positive economics than they do on issues of normative economics. Indicate which of the following are statements of normative (N) or positive (P) character.

a. Taxes should be progressive. . . . . ( )

b. Taxes discourage work effort. . . . . ( )

c. Inflation tends to be high when unemployment is low. . . . . ( )

d. Inflation is less harmful than unemployment. . . . . . ( )

e. Pollution restraints cost jobs. . . . . ( )

f. Pollution restraints are worth the cost. . . . . ( )

---

more; **a.** N **b.** P **c.** P **d.** N **e.** P **f.** N

The above should not be construed as a statement that economists agree an all issues of positive economics. There could, for example, be considerable debate over whether periods of low inflation need to be accompanied by high unemployment. This would be a different debate from the one over whether or not inflation is as harmful to the economy at large as unemployment.

APPENDIX:
How to Read and Understand Graphs

Economics makes extensive use of graphs and charts. They appear in every chapter of the text, and the Appendix to Chapter 1 is included to provide the reader with a basic review of their foundation. This associated Appendix amplifies that review.

Despite their importance, graphs and charts are not the content of a course in economics. A student can, in fact, receive an A in an introductory economics course without ever drawing a graph. But that would be difficult to do. Graphs and charts are tools with which the fundamental notions of economic reasoning can be illustrated, exercised, and stretched. They provide an easy context within which to explore many economic phenomena that would otherwise require pages of prose. To proceed without a minimal understanding of graphs would be to proceed with a great disadvantage; it would be like fighting a championship fight with one arm tied behind your back. This Appendix is designed to present both a brief review of the basics of graphical analysis and some small insight into its usefulness.

▶ A graph is always an illustration picturing how two sets of figures are related to one another.

First Example: Study Hours and Leisure Hours

Suppose you decide to plan your working day. A considerable part of each 24 hours must be given over to sleep, meals, and class attendance. Suppose these matters take up 14 hours per day. This leaves the remaining 10 hours to divide between study on the one hand, leisure and recreation on the other.

That 10 hours could be divided in an infinite number of ways. At one extreme would be 10 hours for leisure and 0 hours for study. This particular time allocation must be considered unsatisfactory in the sense that its pursuit tends to lead to unpleasant interviews with the dean of students or similar people of limited imagination.

At the other extreme would be 10 hours for study and 0 for leisure and recreation, or the week-before-examinations allocation. Among the possible choices are these:

Table 1A-1

	A	B	C	D	E	F	G
Leisure hours	10	8	7	6	4½	2½	0
Study hours	0	2	3	4	5½	7½	10

What we have is two sets of numbers. One set gives the number of possible study hours; the other gives the corresponding number of leisure hours (given a total of 10 hours to allocate between leisure and study). The numbers are, in other words, inexorably tied to one another; each study-hour number is paired with a leisure-hour figure. It is this type of pairing process that a graph always illustrates.

The leisure-study tradeoff provides a perfect example. All the pairs in Table 1A-1 are characterized by one relationship: The sum of the hours spend studving and the hours spent relaxing must always equal 10. All such points are captured somewhere along line *AG* in Figure 1A-1 (assuming that negative numbers of hours are not allowed). The details of this mapping will be covered shortly. For now, it is enough to note that the graph drawn in Figure 1A-1 illustrates a particular linking rule between pairs of points.

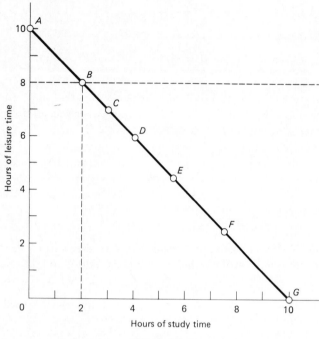

Figure 1A-1

east dimension is called the _____

or the _____. The south-north measuring line

is the _____

or the _____.

3.   In Figure 1A-1, point *B* stands for the combination of 2 *(study / leisure)* hours and 8 *(study / leisure)* hours. In Figure 1A-1, leisure hours are measured *(vertically / horizontally)* and study hours *(vertically / horizontally)*. Point *D* stands for

_____ leisure hours and _____ study hours; 9 study hours and 1 leisure hour would be a pair indicated by a point between points *(A and B / D and E / F and G)*.

4.   The rate at which study hours can be turned into leisure time is _____ hour(s) for every 1 hour of study time sacrificed.

---

1.   extreme left; very bottom

2.   horizontal axis; *X* axis; vertical axis; *Y* axis

3.   study; leisure; vertically; horizontally; 6; 4; *F* and *G*

4.   1

Economics is crammed with topics in which this linking together of two sets of numbers is important. Graphs are useful because they so readily illustrate the nature of the relationship involved.

In Figure 1A-1, the vertical line at the left and the horizontal line at the bottom are the axes against which the pairwise linkage is to be charted. Each is divided off with a number scale, and the meaning of these numbers is indicated by the labels: "Hours of study time" (horizontally) and "Hours of leisure time" (vertically).

The slanting line carrying points labelled *A* through *G* has already been identified as the actual graph of the leisure-study relationship. Each point identified along that line corresponds to a pair in Table 1A-1. Take point *B*, for example. Point *B* in Table 1A-1 pairs 2 hours of study with 8 hours of leisure time. The dashed lines in Figure 1A-1 do the same thing. Passing down from point *B* to the study-time/horizontal axis, note that 2 hours is associated with point *B*; moving left to the leisure-time/vertical axis, similarly note that 8 hours is associated with point *B*. Table 1A-1 and Figure 1A-1 illustrate the same thing, for point *B* and every other point along the line.

1.   In the horizontal or west-east dimensions, a figure of 0 would be recorded on the line at *(extreme left / extreme right / very bottom / very top / exact center)*. In the vertical dimension, 0 would be recorded on the line at *(extreme left / extreme right / very bottom / very top / exact center)*.

2.   The measuring line used to position numbers in the west-

Second Example: Money, Apples, and Oranges

Suppose that someone particularly interested in either apples or oranges were to decide that he would allocate $40 to the purchase of one or the other. Let apples cost $2 per bushel and let oranges cost $1 per dozen. Table 1A-2 records a few possible combinations of apples and oranges that this person might consider. Notice, for example, that devoting the entire $40 to apples would allow him to bring 20 bushels of apples home (point *A* in Table 1A-2). Devoting the entire $40 to oranges would allow him to bring 40 dozen oranges home (point *G* in Table 1A-2). Other intermediate combinations, designated elsewhere in Table 1A-2, would also be possible and should not be ignored. It is likely, in fact, that these intermediate points would be preferred to "specializing" exclusively in the consumption of one fruit or the other.

Table 1A-2

	A	B	C	D	E	F	G
Bushels apples	20	18	15	10	5	2	0
Dozen oranges	0	4	10	20	30	36	40

Drawing a Graph   If you are to recall what you know about graphs, then you must practice drawing graphs. Figure 1A-2 is blank save for a series of vertical and horizontal "grid lines," used to help locate the point that matches up with any given pair of numbers.

On Figure 1A-2, draw a graph that illustrates the points in Table 1A-2. First label your axis lines. Then pick a scale

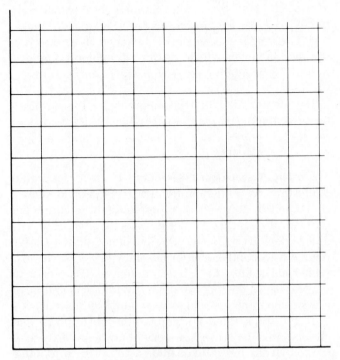

Figure 1A-2

for each of the axes; i.e., choose how much distance you are going to use to represent 1 bushel of apples and 1 dozen oranges. With these scales in mind, plot the seven points of Table 1A-2 and label each with its letter identification. They should all lie along a straight line much like the one drawn in Figure 1A-1. After you have satisfied yourself that they do, draw the entire line by connecting the points; it represents all the points that you could have marked off if you had had the time and patience—all of the combinations of oranges and apples (including fractions) that could be purchased with $40.

This last idea bears repeating. You cannot, in Figure 1A-1, possibly find any add-up-to-10 combination that does not appear somewhere on *AG*. *AG* includes every possible pair that satisfies this linking rule. Moreover, *AG* can be trusted in another respect. It has no point that does not meet the linking rule. In other words, *AG* is an exact graphical representation of the add-up-to-10 rule in the sense that (1) it includes *all* points that satisfy this rule, and (2) it includes *only* points that satisfy this rule. Similarly, the line that you drew in Figure 1A-2 includes all combinations of apples and oranges that cost $40 and only combinations that cost $40.

5. In the apples-oranges example, our fruit lover would have loved to have purchased 20 dozen oranges and 20 bushels of apples. He *(could / could not)* do that because he had *(more than enough / not enough)* money. That combination would cost

_____.

6. In the study-leisure example, the rate of exchanges be-

tween study time and relaxation time was _____ hour studying for every 1 hour of forgone relaxation. In the apples-

oranges example, the tradeoff was _____ dozen oranges for every bushel of forgone apples.

7. Take any point inside the triangle formed by the three lines of Figure 1A-1 (the *AG* line and the two axis lines). The pair of measurements for any such point:

a. must together total more than 10

b. must together total less than 10

c. must together total 10

d. may total more than 10 or less than 10

8. Which alternative in question 7 correctly describes the pair of measurements belonging to any point outside *AG* (above and to the right)? .... *(a / b / c / d)*

9. If we redid this example by assuming that there was a total of 11 hours rather than 10 to allocate, what would happen to *AG* (as the line indicating all possible combinations)?

a. It would move outward—i.e., upward and to the right—remaining parallel to the present line.

b. It would move inward—i.e., downward and to the left—remaining parallel to the present line.

c. Its position would not change.

d. It would pivot or rotate outward on point *A*.

---

5. could not; not enough; $60 **6.** 1; 2 **7. b.** For example, take any point—other than *B*—on the vertical broken line running between *B* and the 2 mark on the horizontal axis. This is a typical point inside the triangle. That point must stand for 2 study hours and—because it is below *B*—less than 8 hours of leisure time, or a total of less than 10.) **8. a.** **9. a.**

Third Example: The Guns-or-Butter Diagram

One of the first graphical diagrams that you will encounter in the text is the guns-or-butter chart of Chapter 2. As the following table (reproduced from the text) shows, it involves pairs of figures once again.

Table 1A-3

	A	B	C	D	E	F
Butter (millions of pounds)	0	1	2	3	4	5
Guns (thousands)	15	14	12	9	5	0

The background of the guns-or-butter case is this: The economy has only a limited and fixed stock of machinery, labor, and all the other things needed to produce such items as guns or butter. Some of these resources can be used in the production of either commodity. Labor, for instance, can be transferred from the production of guns to the production of butter, or vice versa (with due allowance for the training time that might be required to make labor proficient in its new location). If labor were switched from, say, work on guns to work on butter, the result would be an increase in the output of butter and a corresponding reduction in the output of guns. If resources were fully employed, the inevitable cost of getting more of one commodity must, by extension of this example, always be a reduction in the supply of another.

(The "guns or butter" metaphor first arose in Nazi Germany. By the late 1930s, Hitler's government had turned so much of German industry toward rearmament that there were shortages of some civilian goods, butter among them. The late and generally unlamented Hermann Goering made a famous speech in which he sought to appease the public's complaints by declaring, "We must choose between guns and butter!")

As a further exercise in graph drawing, draw the guns-or-butter diagram for yourself in Figure 1A-3. Use the figures in the preceding table. As before, first label your two axes. Measure quantity of guns in the vertical dimension (as the text does) and quantity of butter horizontally. Ordinarily, you want to make use of all the space available on a graph. In Figure 1A-3, the maximum butter quality to be recorded is 5 (million pounds); so put 5 at the bottom right-hand corner. There are 15 little squares sitting on the horizontal axis line; if 5 goes below the end of the fifteenth square, then 1 must go below the end of the third one, 2 below the end of the sixth, and so on. As to guns, your maximum is 15 (thousand); so put 15

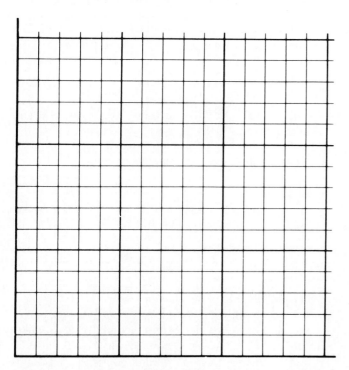

Figure 1A-3

at top left, with the smaller numbers correspondingly below. Notice that (in the matter of graph distances) your two number scales can be different. Here, the same distance in inches which measures 5 million pounds of butter (horizontally) records 15 thousand guns (vertically).

Having put labels and numbers on your axes, indicate on the graph the six points in the table. (This is known as *plotting* the points.) Identify them by letter and join them with a smooth curve.

The Utility of Graphical Illustrations   If a text uses graphs as illustrations, the assumption is that you, as student, will be helped by this means of presentation. If unfamiliar with graphs, you are not yet sufficiently advanced to be able to decide for yourself whether or not this illustrative device is worth the trouble. To show that it is, we now look briefly into the subject matter of Chapter 2 to illustrate what the tool can bring to our understanding of a basic economic question—the question of scarcity.

At this stage, the major point of the illustration is that all economies face an entire series of problems that are all derived from the fundamental scarcity of productive agents—machinery and tools, workers and raw materials. These productive agents are the source of finished consumer goods and services, and they are scarce in the sense that they cannot produce a sufficient quantity of such goods and services to satisfy fully everybody's wants for everything. One of the economy's problems is accordingly that it must decide *What* to produce; the guns-or-butter example is intended to reveal the nature of this problem and of the decision it demands. Matters are simplified to the point of assuming that there are only two final consumer goods wanted (by someone, not necessarily you) and producible. This represents an abstraction, a simplification to be sure, but it does not cost very much. If resources are scarce for the production of two goods, they are surely even more scarce for the production of 10 goods, or 20 goods, or 10,000 goods.

Each pair of figures in the gun-butter table is assumed to represent a combination which the resources in the economy could produce per period of time (*a*) when fully employed and (*b*) when employed to the best possible advantage—i.e., when the best possible use is made of the gun-producing and butter-producing technologies known in the economy.

The use of a graphical illustration is intended to bring out more clearly at least four points:

1.   The area of the graph above and to the right of the *ABCDEF* line represents more desirable but unattainable territory. Points therein represent larger gun-butter combinations than those represented by *ABCDEF*. But they are unattainable—unless or until the economy acquires more productive agents or develops better techniques for using what it has. The process of eco-

nomic growth can be represented as a gradual pushing outward of the *ABCDEF* line.

2. The graph area below and to the left of *ABCDEF* is fully attainable. But if the economy's actual gun-butter production were to be represented by a point in this area, it would signify (*a*) that the economy was not fully using all its available resources, or else (*b*) that although it was employing them, it was somehow failing to use them to the best advantage. We assume that the economy can reach any point on the *ABCDEF* line without disrupting its social order and without undue strain on its productive agents; and its people will want production to reach this line, since both of the two commodities are scarce relative to the desire for them. If actual production lands at some point in the area below *ABCDEF*, it means there has been some failure in the area of economic or social organization. In this sense, the area below *ABCDEF* is undesirable.

3. If both the unattainable area above the curve and the undesirable area below the curve were removed, then only the line *ABCDEF* would remain. The decision which people in this economy (or their leaders) must somehow make about *What* to produce can thus be represented as the problem of deciding which point along line *ABCDEF* to choose. To describe this as a "guns or butter" decision can be a bit misleading; it suggests (all) guns or (all) butter. If both guns and butter were desirable, though, it is most likely that points *A* and *F* would both be rejected in lieu of some intermediate point like *C* or *D*.

4. In actual life, decisions on *What* to produce have somehow been made for a long time; they are still being made. A decision of this nature is not something that need be made only once and can then be forgotten, for tastes change and so do productive conditions. It is a little more realistic, then, to think of an economy which is currently operating at some point such as *D*, and which might, for example, be disposed to move toward having a little more butter. This would mean a shift away from *D* toward *E*, a shift that is really two distinct actions:
a. First, there is a movement away from *D* horizontally and to the right, of a distance equal to the contemplated increase in butter production—say, ¼ million pounds.
b. The movement in part *a* takes the economy into unattainable territory. So it must be followed by another movement, vertically downward, of sufficient length to get back to the *ABCDEF* line. (On Figure 1A-3, starting at the *D* point, draw a short horizontal line to the right. This is the desired increase in butter production, and the move into unattainable territory. From the end of this line, draw another, this time vertical and downward, to reach the *ABCDEF* line. This is the reduction in gun production needed in order to get back to "attainable output.")

Dissecting a simple movement along a curved line into two right-angled sections might appear at first to be making something difficult out of something easy. That may be your first impression, but the dissection makes one essential point: the lengths of the side of the little right-angle triangle indicate precisely the "terms of the tradeoff" between the two goods—how much of one must be sacrificed to get one more unit of the other. The horizontal side in the guns-butter graph measures the contemplated increase in butter; the vertical side measures the required reduction in gun output. Whether or not an extra 250,000 pounds of butter is really worth having depends upon whether or not it is considered to be worth the sacrifice of (roughly) 1000 guns.

10. The figures in the guns-and-butter table represent (*maximum / minimum*) combinations of these two commodities which some imaginary community could produce per unit of time. The figures stand for (*money values / physical quantities*) of guns and butter. The economic reasoning behind these (*upper / lower*) limits on production (given the state of technology) is this: _____

_____

_____

11. If all available resources or inputs were devoted to butter production, butter output would be _____ million pounds and gun output would be _____ thousand guns. If the economy wished to have 9 thousand guns per period, butter output could not exceed _____ million pounds.

12. Suppose the community is producing a total of 1 million pounds of butter. It wants to increase this by a further 1 million pounds. The required decrease in gun production would be

_____ thousand. If the community were producing 4 million pounds of butter and wanted to increase this by 1 million (to a total of 5 million), the required decrease in gun production would be _____ thousand.

13. Suppose the community is currently producing 15 thousand guns and is considering a reduction to 14 thousand. The change would make possible a butter increase of _____ million pounds. Alternatively, if the community currently produces 9 thousand guns and decides on a reduction to 5 thousand, a butter increase of _____ million pounds would be possible. If gun production were to be increased from 9 thousand to 10 thousand, this 1-thousand increase would call for a reduction in butter output of approximately _____ million pounds.

---

10. maximum; physical quantities; upper; a limit on the total available supply of resources **11.** 5; 0; 3 **12.** 2; 5 **13.** 1; 1; ¹⁄₃

Notice that your answers in 12 varied with those at the starting point—the cost of butter in terms of guns changed as more butter was produced. This notion will be important later.

The Direction of the Line   There is an obvious similarity between all three illustrations presented thus far. All demonstrate the need for choice and decision necessitated by the hard fact that if you want more of one thing, you generally have to put up with less of another.

Graphically, this shows up as the line that falls as it proceeds to the right. The desire for more study time is illustrated in Figure 1A-1 by a horizontal movement to the right. To make that desire a reality, though, there must also be a downward movement along the graphed line—a movement to indicate that some leisure time must be sacrificed. The increase in one member of the linkage pairings must, in other words, be matched by a decrease in the other. The very same observation applies, of course, to the apples-oranges example in Figure 1A-2; even the guns-butter illustration in Figure 1A-3 shows the identical tradeoff in its downward movement.

In the study-leisure case, the "terms of trade" between study and leisure were constant. A 1-hour increase in study time always necessitated a sacrifice of exactly 1 hour of leisure time. Graphically, this constant tradeoff meant that the relationship between study time and leisure time had to be represented by a straight line falling to the right. In the apples-oranges case, the "terms of trade" were again constant but not equal to 1. A 1-bushel increase in the quantity of apples purchased (requiring an additional expenditure on apples of $2) always produced a 2-dozen reduction in the purchase of oranges. A different tradeoff was achieved, therefore, but still along a straight line sloping downward to the right.

In the butter-gun case, though, the story is different; the terms of trade were not constant. To see why, start at the left side of the graph—start at point A. Consider the horizontal movement indicating an increase of 1 million pounds of butter. This must be matched by a vertical movement signifying 1000 guns—the movement from A to B. But at the other extreme, E to F also signifies an increase of 1 million pounds of butter. Yet the required vertical movement is 5000 guns, or 5 times as large.

This variation in the tradeoff generates a curved line—here one that is bowed out away from the origin. In the parlance of mathematics, it is concave when viewed from the origin. A straight line with its constant "terms of trade" will, in other words, not come close to describing the butter-gun linking relationship.

Despite this difference, though, the common trait of all three examples bears repeating. Each of the cases involves an inverse relationship between two sets of points—a linking rule that requires that any increase (positive change) in one magnitude must be accompanied by a decrease (negative change) in the other.

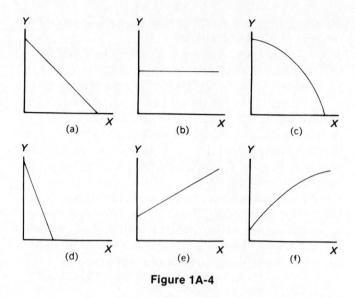

Figure 1A-4

Figure 1A-4 contains six different graphs. In each, X signifies the magnitude being measured horizontally, and Y the magnitude being measured vertically. Circle the correct letter or letters below.

14.   Diagrams *(a / b / c / d / e / f)* illustrate an inverse relation (positive change in one accompanied by negative change in the other) between X and Y.

15.   In one case, Y's response to a change in X is zero, namely, in diagram *(a / b / c / d / e / f)*.

16.   The X-Y relation is positive rather than inverse (i.e., plus change is accompanied by plus change) in diagram(s) *(a / b / c / d / e / f)*.

17.   Among the diagrams illustrating an inverse relation like study-leisure or butter-guns, the terms of trade are constant in diagram(s) *(a / b / c / d / e / f)* and they vary in diagram(s) *(a / b / c / d / e / f)*.

18.   To illustrate the relation between an adult's daily food intake in calories (measured along X axis) and his or her weight (measured along Y axis), the diagram best suited would be (either of two) *(a / b / c / d / e / f)*.

19.   The relationship between one's age (X) and one's height (Y) would probably be illustrated best by *(a / b / c / d / e / f)*.

20.   The most probable relation between number of study hours you put in before a given examination (X axis) and examination grade earned (Y axis) is illustrated by (or is supposed to be illustrated by) *(a / b / c / d / e / f)*.

21.   In diagram (d), assume the graph line meets the Y axis at measurement 10 and the X axis at 5. (Write these figures on the diagram.) The X-Y swapping terms are then as follows: A 1-unit increase in X must be accompanied by a *(0 / ½ / 1 / 2 / 4 / 10)* unit *(increase / decrease)* in Y. These swapping terms *(are constant / vary according to the position on the line)*.

22. In diagram (b), let the graph line meet the *Y* axis at measurement 4. Then, when the *X* value is 0, the *Y* value must be *(0 / 1 / 2 / 4 / can't tell)*. When the *X* value is 10, the *Y* value must be *(0 / 1 / 2 / 4 / can't tell)*.

23. In diagram (e), let one point on the graph line represent the values *X* = 0, *Y* = 4. This point on the diagram would be *(at extreme left / near center / at extreme right)*. Let another point on the graph line represent the values *X* = 3, *Y* = 5. These two points indicate an underlying linking rule as follows: for every increase of 1 in the *X* value, there must be *(an increase / a decrease)* in the *Y* value of *($^1/_4$ / $^1/_3$ / 1 / 3 / 4)*.

NOTE: If you find yourself stuck on any of these questions, or if you have answered incorrectly, do not be too concerned; the unfamiliar is seldom easy. Go back and review earlier material if necessary, until you are reasonably sure you understand why each answer is correct.

14. a, c, d **15.** b **16.** e, f **17.** a and d; c **18.** e or f **19.** f

20. f [Although e would be reasonably correct, presumably the payoff for continued investment in study hours tapers off, as indicated by the bend in (f)'s graph line. If you thought (a) was correct, you have some justification to provide in this semester's examinations!]

21. 2; decrease; are constant [Start with the point at the *Y* axis, where *X* = 0, *Y* = 10. From here, a 5-unit increase in *X* (from 0 to 5) would have to be matched by a 10-unit decrease in *Y* (from 10 to 0). Swapping terms are constant because the line is straight; and 5 for 10 is equivalent to 1 for 2.]

22. 4; 4 (A horizontal line means that the *Y* value stays the same, no matter what the *X* value is.)

23. At extreme left; an increase; $^1/_3$ (A 3-unit increase in *X*, from 0 to 3, is matched by a 1-unit increase in *Y*, from 4 to 5, 3 to 1 is equivalent to 1 to $^1/_3$.)

Summary Thus Far

1. When you meet any graph, always look first to see what is being measured on the horizontal axis and what is being measured on the vertical axis.

2. The line on the graph illustrates some form of relationship between the two items measured. Behind the line are two sets of figures linked together, pair by pair.

3. Which way does the line run? If it rises to the right, it means that as one figure in the pair rises, the other figure rises also. If the line falls as it moves to the right, then the paired numbers move inversely: one up, the other down.

This behavior of the line—whether it rises or falls as it moves to the right—is extremely important. Often, for purposes of the economics being illustrated, it is not important to know the exact pairs of numbers corresponding to particular points on the line; it is, instead, enough sometimes to reflect on the direction and shape of the line being discussed. The previous set of questions illustrates just this point. How did you answer those questions? You looked at whether the line was rising or falling. You looked to see if it was straight or curved. And you thought about what your observations told you. Do grades go up when study time goes down, for example?

Not usually. If *X* is study time and *Y* is grade point average, then panels (a), (b), (c), and (d) in Figure 1A-4 cannot possibly represent the linking rule. Not because they are curved or straight, but because they move in the wrong direction. Only panels (e) and (f) have the appropriate direct, positive relationship, and we know that without any idea of the scales that are implicitly recorded along the two axes.

Slope: Straight Lines One way that works in describing a straight-line linking rule that joins some *X* variable to some other *Y* variable is this: *X* and *Y* are linked together in such a way that any given change in *X* necessarily generates a certain and constant change in *Y*. That is how, in reality, problems and relationships are often presented. Starting with *X* and *Y* occupying some initial positions, we often ask "What would happen to *Y* if *X* were to change its position (i.e., its value)?" Put a more useful way, perhaps we might ask "What change in *Y* would be forthcoming if *X* were to increase by 1 unit?"

In the study-leisure case, an immediate and unqualified answer shows up. The required change in *Y* would be minus one, or in number symbols, −1. The butter-gun case is more complicated. The answer is always a minus quantity, but whether it is −1 or −2 or −5 depends on whether your starting position is *A* or *B* or *E*. The difference is that one line is straight, the other curved.

Consider the simple straight-line case first. Think of starting somewhere on a straight-line linkage graph and making little movements to the right in two stages—the same two stages outlined above. Think, in particular, first about making a strictly horizontal movement of sufficient length to indicate a 1-unit increase in the *X* value. Since the move was horizontal, the *Y* value will not have changed. Then think about a vertical movement up or down to signify a change in *Y* of a very special dimension: a vertical distance precisely equal to the amount of movement required to return to the linkage graph. For example, in either of the two little diagrams composing Figure 1A-5, the true path traced out is *ABDE*. But the movement from *B* to *D* can be considered as (1) a probing movement from *B* to *C* (the 1-unit change in *X* which takes the point momentarily off its true path),

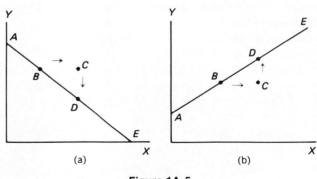

(a)   (b)

Figure 1A-5

followed by (2) a correcting movement from *C* to *D* (the required matching change in *Y*). If *BC*'s length indicates a 1-unit increase in *X*, then *CD*'s length must indicate the rate at which *Y* must change in response to *X* to stay on the straight line. On the graph, this measure of the change is called the slope of the line *ABDE*.

Several points about the slope of a line should now be clear:

1.   Slope is always a number that measures change. It is the amount by which *Y* must change in response to a 1-unit change in *X* if we are to stay on the same straight line.

2.   If the graph line is straight, one single number measures its slope at any and all points thereon. This is just another way of saying that a straight line is one whose direction does not change.

3.   The slope always assumes a negative value if the *X*-*Y* relation is an inverse one—one in which a positive increase in *X* requires a reduction in *Y*. Both the study-leisure and the apples-oranges examples qualify, and both straight lines drawn above to reflect them have negative slopes. In terms of what we draw, therefore, the slope is negative if the graph falls down to the right. The slope is, conversely, positive if the line climbs up toward the right.

Now consider a little more fully the technique for measuring or illustrating graphically the slope of a straight line. We have said with respect to Figure 1A-5 that the slope of the graph line *ABDE* is measured by the length of *CD*. This assumes that *BC* is of a length equal to 1 *X* unit.

We could equally well have said that slope is measured by the fraction *CD/BC*, with the lengths of *CD* and *BC* representing the numbers for which they stand. Since *BC* corresponds to the number 1, *CD/BC* reduces to *CD* anyhow. The only objection to naming slope as *CD/BC* is that at first it seems needlessly clumsy.

But measuring slope as *CD/BC* is a reminder that the *Y* movement (*CD*) can be considered only relative to the amount of *X* movement (*BC*). Look at Figure 1A-5. *BC* and *CD* form with the graph line itself a right-angled triangle, of which the graph line is the hypotenuse (the side opposite the right angle). Look particularly at diagram (b), in which this triangle is suspended below the graph line. *Any* right-angled triangle so hung can be used to measure slope, regardless of its size. All such triangles would be proportionate; that is to say, (*CD/BC*) = (*C'D'/BC'*). Thus, in Figure 1A-6, the slope of the line *ABCD* is one-half ($+\frac{1}{2}$). Any one of several triangles shown can measure that slope: *AEB*, *AFC*, *AGD*, *CHD*. The fraction made up of vertical side over horizontal side is ½ for all these triangles. (The triangle's sides must of course be exactly in the vertical and horizontal dimensions.)

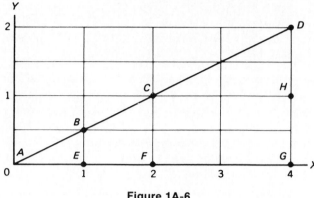

Figure 1A-6

If the graph line falls as its path runs rightward, you can still use a right-angled triangle hung below it. Or you can use one sitting atop the line, like that in diagram (a) of Figure 1A-5. As before, slope is measured by the fraction vertical side over horizontal side. But remember that a falling line means an inverse *X*-*Y* relation, hence a negative slope value.

Some people find it helpful to think of slope as "the rise over the run." "The rise" is the vertical distance involved; in Figure 1A-5 terms, the rise is *CD*. "The run" is the horizontal distance; it is *BC* in Figure 1A-5 terms. So the rise over the run would in this instance be *CD* over *BC*.

It is tempting to associate the measure of slope with the steepness with which the graph line rises or falls, so that a steeply tilted line is taken as one with a high slope value, positive or negative. And sometimes this conclusion is valid—but don't overlook the fact that the steepness with which a graph line rises or falls depends in part on the scale chosen for the graph. Diagrams (a) and (b) in Figure 1A-7 both portray exactly the same linking relation, and either is a perfectly respectable illustration. Notice in (b), however, that the horizontal scale has been stretched out in comparison with that used in (a). The slope of the line in both parts of Figure 1A-7 is $+\frac{1}{2}$. The trick is that relative steepness accurately reflects relative slope only when the scales are the same. When you have two lines on the same graph, therefore, you can certainly say that the steeper line has the larger slope, in absolute value—more negative if the two lines are negatively sloped and downward-sloping and more positive if the two lines are positively sloped and upward-sloping. In Figure 1A-7(c), for example, line I has a slope of 4, line II has a slope of 2, 4 is greater than 2, and I is clearly steeper than II. In Figure 1A-7(d), line I has a slope of −4, line II has a slope of −2, 4 is still greater then 2, −4 is more negative than −2, and I is again steeper than II.

Finally, one small point. We have been talking throughout in terms of a 1-unit increase in *X*. The slope measure

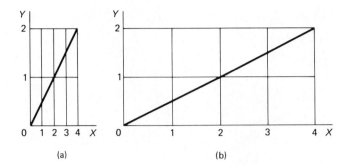

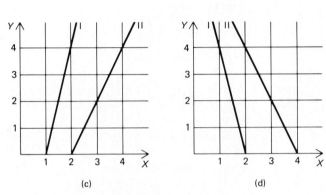

Figure 1A-7

would work equally well for a decrease. Suppose that two positions traced by the moving point are these:

	Point A	Point B
X	4	5
Y	10	15

Slope value is 5, since the 1-unit rise in X from 4 to 5 occasions a 5-unit rise in Y. But we could equally well speak of a 1-unit decrease in X, from 5 to 4, accompanied by a 5-unit decrease in Y, from 15 to 10. Here again, the convenience of putting things in the form of a fraction (vertical side over horizontal side, or Y change over X change) becomes evident. For the fraction is either

$$\frac{+5}{+1} \quad \text{or else} \quad \frac{-5}{-1}$$

depending on whether you start with an increase or a decrease in X; the result is 5, or +5, either way. (For practice, graph these points, plot the line, and verify a positive slope of 5.)

24. Slope is a measure of the rate at which the Y value—i.e., the magnitude we are measuring along the Y axis—changes for each change of *(0 units / 1 unit / the same number of units)* in the X value.

25. A graph line has the same slope value throughout when that line is *(curved / rising / straight / falling)*.

26. Graphically, we can illustrate or measure slope in terms of a right-angled triangle below the graph line. Slope is the fraction or ratio obtained by putting the length of the *(vertical / horizontal)* side of the triangle over the length of the *(vertical / horizontal)* side.

27. When the X-Y relation is an inverse one, then its graphical illustration can be considered the path of a point which *(falls / rises)* as it moves to the right. The slope value of such a relation is *(positive / zero / negative)*.

28. In diagram (b) of Figure 1A-4, the slope of the line illustrated is *(positive / negative / zero / impossible to tell)*.

29. Two positions of X on a straight graph line are 5 and 7. What is the value of slope if the corresponding Y positions are:
a. 5 and 7? ....*(−3 / −2 / −1 / 0 / 1 / 2 / 3 /infinity)*
b. 4 and 2? ....*(−3 / −2 / −1 / 0 / 1 / 2 / 3 /infinity)*
c. 2 and −2? ....*(−3 / −2 / −1 / 0 / 1 / 2 / 3 /infinity)*
d. 4 and 4? ....*(−3 / −2 / −1 / 0 / 1 / 2 / 3 /infinity)*
e. −2 and −8? ......*(−3 / −2 / −1 / 0 / 1 / 2 / 3 /infinity)*
f. −8 and −2? ......*(−3 / −2 / −1 / 0 / 1 / 2 / 3 /infinity)*

---

24. 1 unit **25.** straight **26.** vertical; horizontal **27.** falls; negative **28.** zero
29. a. 1 **b.** −1 **c.** −2 **d.** 0 **e.** −3 **f.** 3

The Slope of Curved Lines A curved line is one whose direction continually changes. The amount of Y change required by a 1-unit X change varies according to the position from which this change begins.

Consider the curved line $ABCDEF$ in Figure 1A-8. Suppose we are at point B. If we know the exact X and Y values associated with every point on this line—i.e., if we know the underlying linking rule which it illustrates—then we should have no difficulty in learning what the Y change would be as a result of a shift from B to E. Moreover, we could put the usual right-angled triangle underneath, with corners at B and E, and from it develop a slope value. But this would not in a true sense be the

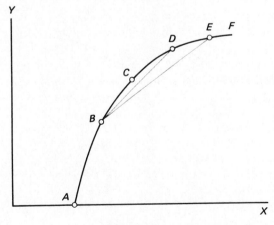

Figure 1A-8

slope of the curved line itself; it would really measure the slope of the straight line running between B and E. We would get a different and somewhat higher slope figure if we dealt similarly with a change from B to D, and a still different figure for a change from B to C.

For some purposes, it is quite sufficient to know what the actual Y change would be in consequence of moving from B to E, or to D, or to C. But for other problems it is useful or even necessary to ask: What is the slope of the curved line exactly at some point, such as B?

To ask this question is to pose another one: Does it make sense to speak of the slope of a line precisely at a single point?

Certainly point B, considered in isolation, has no slope, no direction. But point B considered as part of the line $ABCDEF$ is another matter. The slope of the line is a measure of the direction in which it runs, reckoned in terms of the scales on the two axes. Think for the moment of $ABCDEF$ as the path traced by a moving automobile. The direction of movement of that automobile changes continually, since it follows a curved path. But can we say that at the exact moment when it passes over point B, the automobile is headed in some given direction? Certainly we can do so, in the sense that a compass mounted aboard would at that exact moment give an exact reading, such as northeast or east by north.

How is this direction at B to be indicated? The accepted answer is this: by a tangent drawn to the curved line at point B. The tangent to a curved line is itself by definition a straight line; it does not cross the curved line but touches it only, and it touches it at one point only. By inspection of Figure 1A-9(a), it is easy to see how the slope of the tangent line FJ is considered as measuring the slope of the curved line at point B; and GH does the same for point D. To each such straight line we can apply our usual right-angle measuring technique.

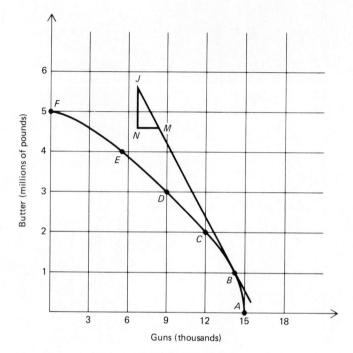

Figure 1A-9(b)

But what does this slope mean? Figure 1A-9(b) redraws the guns-and-butter line from before. At point B, a tangent line is drawn, and its slope, $-(JN/MN)$, represents the slope of the guns-and-butter schedule at point B. It is, intuitively, a reflection of how many guns need to be sacrificed to increase the production of butter not by 1 million pounds, but by 1 pound—a much smaller number. In reality, the slope of line BJ is the sacrifice in guns required to finance a minuscule change in butter production; and after all, 1 pound is a small quantity when it is compared to 1 million pounds.

Circle each correct alternative below.

30. Figure 1A-10 consists of eight separate diagrams, each illustrating a small segment of a graph line. In each, the numbers indicate the length of the adjacent straight-line segment. What is the slope of each AB line? Where AB is curved, it is the slope at point C that is desired.

a. (-4 / -3 / -2 / -1 / 0 / 1 / 2 / 3 / 4 / 10 / *infinity*)
b. (-4 / -3 / -2 / -1 / 0 / 1 / 2 / 3 / 4 / 10 / *infinity*)
c. (-4 / -3 / -2 / -1 / 0 / 1 / 2 / 3 / 4 / 10 / *infinity*)
d. (-4 / -3 / -2 / -1 / 0 / 1 / 2 / 3 / 4 / 10 / *infinity*)
e. (-4 / -3 / -2 / -1 / 0 / 1 / 2 / 3 / 4 / 10 / *infinity*)
f. (-4 / -3 / -2 / -1 / 0 / 1 / 2 / 3 / 4 / 10 / *infinity*)
g. (-4 / -3 / -2 / -1 / 0 / 1 / 2 / 3 / 4 / 10 / *infinity*)
h. (-4 / -3 / -2 / -1 / 0 / 1 / 2 / 3 / 4 / 10 / *infinity*)

---

a. -4 **b.** 3 **c.** 10 **d.** 2 **e.** 0 **f.** -2 **g.** -2 **h.** -1

Two or More Lines on a Graph So far our discussion has run in terms of the interpretation of a single line on a

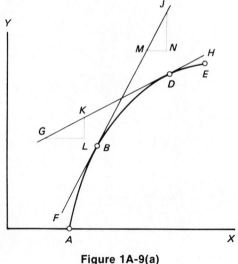

Figure 1A-9(a)

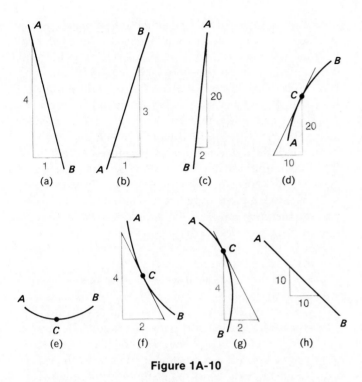

Figure 1A-10

graph. But most text diagrams include two lines, usually intersecting at one point on the graph. Some students will even joke about the "fundamental theorem of economics": whenever two lines intersect, it is more likely than not that the economics instructor will spend two class periods describing something "essential."

The supply-and-demand diagram of Chapter 4 is a good example. The demand line, or demand curve, is drawn as usual—from two sets of figures paired together. Here is one example of a demand curve:

	Price of Wheat per Bushel	Quantity Demanded (Million Bushels per Month)
A	$5	9
B	4	10
C	3	12
D	2	15
E	1	20

This is a "demand schedule." It is a schedule of the quantities of wheat that buyers in some market would demand (i.e., be prepared to buy) if the price were to stand at any one of five possible levels.

It does not matter whether this is a real market or an imaginary one. The precise figures in the table are not especially important. What this schedule is intended to illustrate is the reasonable (and important) fact that as the price of anything falls, buyers probably will want to buy a larger total amount than they did before. In other words, quantity of wheat bought is inversely related to

the price of wheat. If the price were to change, therefore, so would the quantity (in the opposite direction!).

Now this schedule indicates what buyers of wheat are prepared to do, at various prices. It is also possible to prepare another schedule, indicating what sellers of wheat (the producers of wheat, the suppliers of wheat) are prepared to do. In this case, it seems reasonable to assume that if the price were to go up, then suppliers would try to supply a larger quantity because the higher price would generate a higher return on their efforts. Alternatively, if the price were to fall, then they would choose to supply less. Below is a representative supply schedule. Note that it illustrates what has just been said— the higher the price, the greater the quantity offered for sale. Again, though, the actual numbers are not really important; it is the sign of the slope of the line that tells the story of the negative correlation between price and quantity to be expected along a demand curve and a positive correlation between price and quantity to be expected along a supply curve.

	Price of Wheat per Bushel	Quantity Supplied (Million Bushels per Month)
A	$5	18
B	4	16
C	3	12
D	2	7
E	1	0

At this stage, it is not particularly essential that you fully understand the ideas conveyed by the demand and/or supply schedules. What matters for the moment is that you recognize something familiar in the construction: The demand curve consists of two sets of inversely related figures, neatly paired one with the other; the supple curve consists of two sets of positively related figures, equally neatly paired with each other. This means that either can be depicted as a line on a graph— even together on the same graph.

Why? Despite their differences, there is a fundamental similarity between the two schedules. Although they represent the attitudes or the intentions of two entirely different groups of people, the two schedules match one another in that one column refers to price and the other to quantity. It is only because they match in this respect that both can be depicted on the same graph. If we are to make any sense out of two or more lines on the same graph, these lines must refer to the same kinds of things, measured in the same kinds of units.

In Figure 1A-11, draw the lines corresponding to these two schedules. (Plot the five points for each schedule and join them with a smooth curve.) Label your demand curve *DD* and your supply curve *SS*.

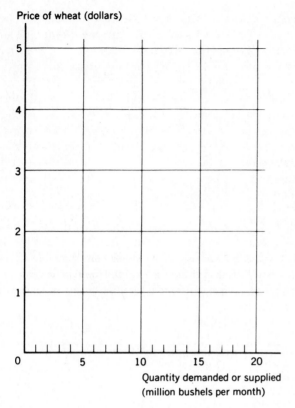

Figure 1A-11

Your two lines should cross at one point, and one point only. That is the point signifying a price of $3 and a quantity of 12 million bushels. Its significance is that at this level of price, and no other, the intentions of buyers and the intentions of sellers match. In these circumstances, the price of $3 will be called an "equilibrium price," and the quantity of 12 million bushels an "equilibrium quantity."

Once you have grasped the idea of demand schedules and supply schedules, Figure 1A-11 becomes a very simple illustration, and you can understand it with little trouble. In fact, you may wonder why a graph is necessary at all. If the object is just to find equilibrium price and quantity, and if you have to draw the graph yourself, it would be quicker just to hunt through the two schedules until you find a pair of figures in one that matches a pair of figures in the other.

The text will, however, not ask you to draw graphs; they will, instead, generally be supplied for you. In all cases, a graph will be only an illustration. It will never tell you anything that you could not have acquired by other means if you were sufficiently determined. The graph may, however, tell you what you want to know much more quickly. The text will supply you with the essential diagrams at the critical points not because they are essential economics, but because they are the quickest and simplest way of making, illustrating, and extending economic insights of fundamental importance.

Consider Figure 1A-11 again, for instance. To the trained eye (by now that means, of course, *your* eye), this diagram tells a good deal more than just the equilibrium price and quantity. It tells how such an equilibrium level is possible. Take any price above the equilibrium level, say, $4 or $5. At any such price, the quantity supplied would not match the quantity demanded. More specifically, the quantity supplied would exceed the quantity demanded. But if the price were permitted to fall, then this excess supply would diminish. Why? Because as the price fell, the corresponding quantity demanded would insist on moving to the right (increasing). And as the price fell, the quantity supplied would also insist on moving, but this time to the left (decreasing the quantity). Both pressures move the excess supply down toward (and eventually reaching) zero.

The point on the graph at which the two lines intersect is a unique and important point. But to consider it as the only point of importance or interest would be to miss the whole purpose of using graphs as illustrations. Certainly the intersection or "equilibrium" point has no special significance unless there is some tendency for the price which it illustrates actually to become established. And if so established, this is because of the situation that would prevail—and which the graph illustrates with particular clarity—at other prices. At prices above the equilibrium level, for example, the graph indicates that the quantity that suppliers would like to sell would exceed the quantity that buyers would be willing to purchase. Inventories would build, and suppliers would send the word to distributors to sell their stuff at a lower price. This "market" pressure on the price is precisely what the graph illustrates—a natural tendency exhibited by the market to push prices down to the equilibrium level where desired demand matches desired supply.

A similar argument applies to prices below the equilibrium level. Again, such prices could prevail, at least temporarily; and once again, we need the rest of the graph to explain why the intersection point has particular significance.

Conclusion   Graphs were made for lazy people who want to grasp the idea with as little expenditure of time and effort as possible. But if you want to take advantage of this device, you must learn the rules; you musk ask the right questions:

1. What does the graph measure on each axis? What are the labels on the axes? Each line on a graph indicates some kind of relation or linking rule between these two sets of numbers.

2. Which way does the line run? Does it fall to the right or rise to the right? If it falls, then the relation between the two sets of numbers is an inverse one—as one rises, the other falls. If it rises to the right, the two sets of numbers move in the same direction.

3. Is the line straight or curved? If it is straight, the ratio of change in Y to change in X is constant. If the line curves, this ratio varies.

4. If there are two or more lines on a graph, then there are two or more schedules in the background. What kind of relationship is involved in each schedule, and why is it important to bring them together on the same graph? Usually the two lines cross one another at some point, and usually this intersection is important because at this point the two schedules match one another. Why is this matching important?

Review   Complete as before.

31.   One point on a graph indicates an X value of 4, a Y value of 10. Another point indicates an X value of 5, a Y value of 8. If these two points are joined by a straight line, the slope of that line is _____.

32.   The slope of a straight line is −3. If movement from one point to another along that line results in an increase in Y from 10 to 16, what change in X must have taken place? It will have (*risen / fallen*) by (6 / 3 / 2 / 1 / $^1/_2$).

33.   A line on a graph appears as the upper half of a circle: It starts out at the origin of the graph, rises, and then falls, until finally it drops to the horizontal axis from which it started. Which of the following correctly describes the slope value of this line?

a. It will have a changing slope value, but a figure which is positive throughout.

b. It will at first have a negative slope-value figure (toward the left-hand side) and this slope value will grow larger; then, as the line proceeds to the right, the slope-value figure will become positive.

c. It will at first have a positive slope-value figure (toward the left-hand side) and this slope value will grow larger as the line proceeds to the right; then the slope-value figure will become negative.

d. It will at first have a positive slope-value figure (toward the left-hand side), but this slope value will diminish in value as the line proceeds to the right; it will reach a value of zero, and then become a negative figure.

34.   In Figure 1A-11, the *DD* curve has a (*negative / positive*) slope value. This figure is a (*constant / changing*) one. The SS curve in this figure has a (*negative / positive*) slope value. This figure is a (*constant / changing*) one.

---

31. −2   **32.** fallen; 2   **33.** d.   **34.** negative; changing; positive; changing

CHAPTER 2
BASIC PROBLEMS OF ECONOMIC ORGANIZATION

Most of this chapter is organized around a series of fundamental ideas and concepts. They are all related, but they are all distinct. They are important as a group because they define the essence of the economic problem. They are important individually because they introduce tools for and methods of thinking about the world that will be carried throughout the text. It is essential, therefore, that you grasp each of them before you proceed.

When you have finished, you should be able to meet the following objectives.

LEARNING OBJECTIVES

1. State (a) the three basic economic problems that confront all societies, regardless of the manner of their political organization, and (b) the single underlying fact that gives rise to these problems.

2. Show how the "production-possibility curve" illustrates one of these three basic economic problems. Explain how this curve (if it is concave relative to the graph's origin) illustrates the "law of increasing (relative) costs."

3. Explain (a) why it is impossible for a nation to move "outside" (i.e., to the northeast of) its given production-possibility curve, and (b) how it *is* possible, over time, for this curve to move "outward" (i.e., to the northeast).

4. Explain why it is undesirable (in material terms) for a nation to operate "inside" its production-possibility curve. Outline the circumstances that might produce this result.

5. Define carefully the law of diminishing returns. Describe the Malthusian application of this law in predicting the world's future. Outline the (presumed) reasons why this prediction has not (as yet, at any rate) been fulfilled.

6. Distinguish between the diminishing-returns law and the principle of "increasing returns to scale" (economies of scale, or mass-production economies).

▶ The basic ingredients from which our material wants for goods and services are satisfied are: labor, capital goods, and land. What we consume comes from the labor effort of men and women, using tools and machinery, mainly to process raw materials obtained from the land.

These real productive inputs—not money—are the items genuinely needed to satisfy life's material demands. Money plays a crucial part in the production process; it will be considered at length in due course. Money is not, however, one of the basic real inputs upon which an economy is built. It is something else—special, but different. It is the device with which the cooperative employment of real inputs can be effectively arranged. It is a kind of lubricating oil that allows the machinery of an economy to operate with a minimum of friction.

▶ Every society has only a finite supply of productive inputs—the real sources of economic value. There is, as a result, a physically imposed limit on the total output of goods and services which any one society can produce. Goods of economic value are, in other words, scarce.

▶ Even in societies relatively well endowed with productive inputs, the total demands of consumers outrun total productive capacity.

In sum, even in rich societies, it is impossible to produce enough to satisfy everybody's desire for everything. Today, many poor economies are still hard pressed to turn out enough in the way of elemental food and shelter for their populations. The richer societies are easily capable of covering life's basic necessities for all their members. But our interest here is not with necessities alone; it is with consumers' *total* demands. Once necessities have been met, consumer wants pass quickly to comforts and to luxuries. In this sense, even rich societies face the *law of scarcity*: total consumer demands outrun total productive capacity.

1. **a.** The text sets out three basic social problems which arise out of this law of scarcity, namely, _____, _____, and _____ goods shall be produced. _____ is sometimes a fourth question.

b. If the total input stock is limited, then the more of this stock that is devoted to production of good A, the less there remains for production of goods B, C, D, etc. The problems of *how much* of A to produce, *how much* of B, *how much* of C, and so on (in the light of this limit on the overall input stock), is the (*What / How / For Whom*) problem.

c. An output restricted by the fact of a limited input supply must somehow be shared out or rationed among society's members; this is the (*What / How / For Whom*) problem.

The problem of *How* goods shall be produced is a little trickier. It is the problem of the exact mix of resources to be used in the manufacture of any given commodity.

It may strengthen your grasp of both *What* and *How* problems to consider instances in which they would not arise at all. The *What* problem emerges because resources are versatile, because they have more than one possible use or occupation. Suppose, however, that a particular kind of labor or machine is not versatile, that it is useful only for producing good A; it is useless for B, C, or D. And suppose (however unlikely) that all resources are specialized in this way. They can make only A, only B, only C, or only D. Hence there is no opportunity to swap less of A for more of B. Then there is no problem of *What* to produce, because there is only one bill of goods that can be produced. Each resource works on the sole commodity it is capable of helping to produce.

Similarly, the *How* problem arises because A, B, C, and D can ordinarily be made in more than one way. But suppose there is only one fixed recipe for making A: there is no opportunity to substitute more of input X (say, machinery) for less of input Y (say, labor). And suppose this fixed-recipe rule applies throughout. Then there is no problem of *How* goods shall be produced; each good will be made in the one and only way it *can* be made.

The more general situation is that in which there is more than one known productive technqiue (e.g., workers can be substituted for machines, and vice versa). If so, then *How* exists as a social problem. (Typically, the *How* problem appears to students less clear than *What* and *For Whom*, or as a problem less vital, less universal. But remember that such a question as "to adopt automatic processes or not to automate" is a particular illustration of *How*. And Chapter 3 will make it clear that in capitalist societies *How* ranks along with *What* and *For Whom* as a matter for the pricing system to settle.)

_____

a. *What, How, For Whom; When* **b.** *What* **c.** *For Whom*

2. The nature of all four questions can be explored more fully by means of a *production-possibility schedule* and its graphical counterpart, the *production-possibility curve*. Because a graph has only two dimensions, the *What* problem must then be set out as one involving the choice between two goods only (in the text example, the choice between guns and butter). The principles are the same whether the total number of goods is 2, 20, or 20,000. Ultimately, the problem is that of the terms of choice between a little more of this and a little less of that.

The *How* question is subsumed in the definition of the schedule itself. If new technology or clever insight were to bring forth a new production technique for, say, butter, then the schedule and the curve would change because the economy could produce more butter with fewer inputs. It could, in other words, produce more of both guns and butter if it wanted to. It follows, then, that the schedule captures the best the economy can do. *How* does the economy produce its goods? With the most efficient techniques available. Insight into the *For Whom* question can also be gleaned from a production-possibility graph, but only very indirectly. It does not show up in the construction of the schedule; it is, instead, picked up as an inference of the point on the schedule actually chosen. If the economy picks a point that indicates a strong concentration in the type of good that only a particular group of people favors, we need not look very far to find out "for whom the bell tolls." It tolls for them.

Finally, a redefinition of the axes to reflect the choice between investment goods and consumption goods can be used to represent how an economy answers the *When* question. A relatively strong leaning toward investment goods would indicate that "later" is the answer; a strong leaning toward consumption goods would, conversely, indicate that "now" is the economy's choice.

The production-possibility schedule is simply a listing of some of the alternative output combinations which a given input stock could produce weekly, or monthly, or using whatever time unit is convenient.

The production-possibility curve (e.g., Figure 2-2 in the text) is the graphical illustration of this schedule. (NOTE: If you are weak on graphs, study of the Orientation chapter in this Study Guide is strongly recommended. The production-possibility diagram is discussed there, on pages 8–11.)

a. Along the axes of a production-possibility diagram are measured (pick one):

(1) Quantities of productive inputs or resources

(2) Quantities of finished commodities

(3) Values of finished commodities

Each and every point on the entire surface of this diagram (whether on the curve or off it) stands for some combination of the two goods involved (e.g., so many guns produced and so much butter produced per unit of time). With a given input stock, some of these points would be attainable, others would not. Specifically, with respect to production, the economy could operate (pick one):

(1) Anywhere on the curve, and only on the curve

(2) Anywhere on the curve or anywhere inside it (below and to the left)

(3) Anywhere on the curve, inside it, or outside it

b. In order to operate outside the curve (above and to the right of it), the economy would have to (pick one or both):

(1) Somehow increase its stock of inputs

(2) Discover some new production techniques enabling any given input stock to produce more output than before

(3) Remove some incompetent bureaucrats from their jobs

(4) Eliminate the sources of significant abuse of monopoly power

If the economoy did somehow add to its input stock, or did discover new production techniques, the production-possibility curve would thereupon (pick one):

(1) Remain unchanged

(2) Move appropriately inward and to the left

(3) Move appropriately outward and to the right

c. If there is a law of scarcity, then the economy will want to make good use of its limited input supply—that is, it will want to operate *on* the production-possibility curve, not inside it. (That is why the text speaks of this curve as the "production-possibility frontier.") Should the economy be operating inside the curve, this would be attributable to some inefficiency or breakdown in economic organization. Specifically (pick one or both):

(1) Some part of the input supply must be unemployed.

(2) The input supply, if fully employed, is somehow being used improperly. The best available production technques are not being used, or some inputs are in the wrong jobs.

---

a. (2); **(2)**   **b. (1)** and **(2)**; **(3)**   **c. (1)** and **(2)**

---

3. The production-possibility frontier in text Figure 2-2 is curved. Specifically, it is concave as viewed from the left and below. A full account of the background reasons for this concavity would be complicated, and relatively unimportant at this early stage. However, one background factor deserves careful study: the *law of diminishing returns.*

The nature of this law is most easily illustrated by assuming that only two inputs, say, A and B, are needed for production of some commodity X. Input A (which in the text example is land) is available in some fixed and limited quantity only. Input B (labor, in the text example) can be varied in quantity employed. The question with which the diminishing-returns law deals is this: We would like to have more of X. The supply of input A, which is essential for X production, is limited. To what extent can we get more X by adding more of input B to the fixed A quantity?

The diminishing-returns law gives the following answer: Up to a point, more B will yield more X. But the cost of getting additional X, in terms of the additional B quantity required, will steadily *(increase / decrease)*. Or, to say the same thing differently, the "payoff" from each extra unit of B employed, in terms of the number of extra units of X resulting, will *(increase / decrease)*. In fact, a point will ultimately be reached at which—because of the restricted supply of A—the payoff from an extra unit of B employed would be *(zero / infinity)*.

Notice that this law runs in physical quantities of A, B, and X—that is, it runs in *(money / "real")* terms.

For illustrative purposes, it is convenient to use an example involving two inputs only. Most actual productive processes involve more than two (e.g., tools, equipment, and seed grain in addition to labor and land). Where more than two inputs are involved, then, for the diminishing-returns law to apply, *(all the inputs / at least one input, but not all inputs / one input and one only)* must be fixed in available supply.

---

increase; decrease; zero; "real"; at least one input, but not all inputs

---

4. This question uses a specific, illustrative example to develop more fully the relation between the production-possibility curve, the shape of that curve, and the diminishing-returns law.

A certain economy produces only two consumer goods, X and Y. For manufacture of these goods, it has three kinds of resources: (1) a fixed stock of resources useful only in the production of X; (2) a similarly fixed stock of different resources useful only in the production of Y; and (3) a fixed labor force of 100 workers capable of working in either occupation. Table 2-1 indicates the amounts of X and Y producible daily when various quantities of labor work with the specialized resources.

Table 2-1

Number of Workers	Daily X Production	Number of Workers	Daily Y Production	Corresponding X Production
0	0	0	0	600
10	40	10	5	_____
20	105	20	12	_____
30	200	30	20	_____
40	300	40	28	_____
50	390	50	36	_____
60	450	60	43	_____
70	500	70	49	_____
80	550	80	54	_____
90	580	90	58	_____
100	600	100	60	_____

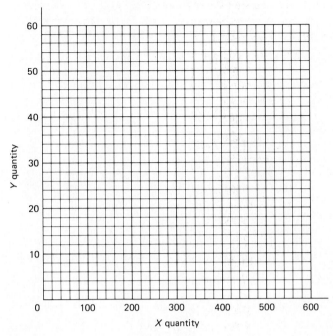

Figure 2-1

The economy's labor force of 100 workers—if fully employed—must be distributed between the two occupations: if there are 100 workers in X production (yielding an X output of 600), then there must be zero workers in Y production (hence zero Y production); if there are 40 workers in X production (producing 300 X), then there must be 60 workers in Y production (producing 43 Y). Hence, corresponding to each figure in the "Daily Y Production" column there must be an appropriate X-production figure. Fill in the blanks in the extreme right-hand column in Table 2-1 with the proper X figures.

In Figure 2-1, draw the production-possibility curve—i.e., show the varous X-Y combinations which can be produced. [Your curve should have the same "bulged-out" shape as those in the text, with anchor points at (X = 600; Y = 0) and (X = 0; Y = 60).]

580, 550, 500 etc.—the figures in the "Daily X Production" column inverted because only labor not devoted to Y can be released to the production of X.

5. a. According to the table, diminishing returns first appears in X production when the total of workers employed rises to *(10 / 20 / 30 / 40 / 50 / 60 / 70 / 80 / 90 / 100)*.

b. The corresponding diminishing-returns point in Y production is at *(10 / 20 / 30 / 40 / 50 / 60 / 70 / 80 / 90 / 100)*.

c. This diminishing-returns phenomenon occurs because, as output and employment are increased:

(1) The competence or skill of the workers later employed is less than that of the workers first employed.

(2) Each worker has proportionately less of the fixed or specialized resource to work with.

(3) The product must sell for a lower price.

---

a. 50 **b.** 60 **c.** (2)

---

6. There is no conflict between the law of diminishing returns and the idea of *mass-production economies* or *increasing returns to scale*. A large-scale automobile plant, built to assemble 1000 cars daily, may illustrate mass-production economies of scale because, when it is operated at capacity, the cost of each car produced is less than it would be in a smaller plant.

Suppose a rush of orders prompts the company to try to produce daily output in excess of 1000 cars by hiring more workers, running machines faster, etc. The probable result will be an output increase that is less than proportionate to the work-force increase. If so, this *(confirms / denies / has no application to)* the diminishing-returns law. The company will find that at some output such as 1100 cars daily, perhaps even 1001 cars daily, further output is impossible no matter how many extra workers are hired. If so, this *(confirms / denies / has no application to)* the diminishing-returns law. Here, the limiting input comparable to land in the text examples is *(labor / materials / equipment)*.

---

confirms; confirms; equipment

---

7. The law of diminishing returns appraises the cost of getting more and more extra output of a good in terms of the extra inputs (e.g., work-hours) required. The *law of increasing (relative) costs*, although related to the diminishing-returns law, is different.

Suppose more corn is to be produced, so that more labor inputs are required. If resources are fully employed, the needed inputs must be taken away from production of some other good. So the "cost" can be stated not only in terms of the extra inputs needed but also in terms of the amount of some other good that must be sacrificed. That is how the increasing-cost law runs.

Using question 4 data, suppose that production is 600 X units daily and zero Y. If it is decided to produce 5 Y units daily, this requires a sacrifice of *(zero / 5 / 20 / 40 / 600)* X units. Each of the 5 Y units will cost *(4 / 8 / 20 / 40 / 600)* X units.

Suppose, instead, that X output is 500 units, so that Y output can be *(zero / 4 / 5 / 10 / 20)* units daily. To raise this Y quantity to 28 would require reduction of X output to *(zero / 100 / 250 / 400 / 450)*—a drop of *(zero / 10 / 20 / 50 / 100)* units. Each extra Y unit would thus cost *(1 / 5½ / 6¼ / 8 / 10)* X units.

The greater the amount of total Y output happens to be, the *(higher / lower)* would be the cost of obtaining further Y output, measured in terms of X given up.

Whenever a production-possibility curve "bulges out," as in Figure 2-1, instead of being a straight line, the increasing-cost

law automatically applies. Each additional unit of either good will cost slightly more (in terms of sacrifice of the other good) than its predecessor did. Each 1-unit increase in Y means a small, vertical, upward movement on the graph. To stay on the curve, this requires a *(leftward / rightward)* movement to compensate—a *(decrease / increase)* in X. If we want further increases in Y—i.e., if we continue along the curve, moving approximately northwest—these compensating *(leftward / rightward)* movements (the required decreases in X) grow larger.

The curve "bulges out" because of the figures in question 4's table. Had the additional quantity of X per each additonal 10 workers been fixed, with extra Y quantities similarly fixed (i.e., no diminishing returns), the production-possibility curve would have been a straight line. Thus the diminishing-returns law here accounts for the increasing-cost phenomenon (although it is not the only source of increasing cost).

20; 4; 20; 450; 50; 6¼; higher; leftward; decrease; leftward

8. In a model in which there exists only one discretionary input (i.e., one input that can be employed in the production of either X or Y), it is easy to get the idea that the law of diminishing returns is the only thing operating to produce the law of increasing (relative) cost—the concave, outward bending of the production-possibility curve. This problem will present an example for investigation in which relative costs are constant despite the existence of diminishing returns in both X and Y for two distinct, discretionary inputs.

Table 2-2 summarizes the production of either X or Y for various combinations of capital (K) and labor (L). It shows, for example, that 28 units of X (or Y) would be produced if 10 units of capital and 10 units of labor were employed. If 10 units of labor were combined with 30 units of capital, 48 units of X (or Y) would be produced. And so on. Suppose throughout this exercise that the economy is endowed with 30 units of capital and 15 units of labor. Both inputs can be employed in either industry. Fill in the blanks in Table 2-3 on the basis of Table 2-2 and the endowment constraints; assume full employment of both capital and labor. Plot points A through G on Figure 2-2 and draw the production-possibility frontier.

Table 2-2
Production Schedule for Either Good X or Good Y

Labor Employment (Units of X or Y)	Capital Employment			
	0	10	20	30
0	0	0	0	0
5	0	20	28	32
10	0	28	40	48
15	0	32	48	60

Table 2-3

Case	X Production			Y Production		
	Capital	Labor	Output	Capital	Labor	Output
A	0	0	0	30	15	60
B	___	___	___	0	0	0
C	10	___	___	___	10	___
D	10	10	___	___	___	28
E	20	___	40	___	___	___
F	20	___	___	___	___	28
G	___	___	___	10	15	___

a. For any level of employment of labor, X and Y *(do / do not)* display diminishing returns. For 10 units of labor, for example, the output of X increases by _____ as capital employment increases from 0 to 10 units, by _____ as capital employment increases from 10 units to 20, and by _____ as capital employment rises from 20 units to 30. Per unit of capital, the return to the employment of capital is therefore _____, _____, and _____, respectively, for the three increments just noted.

b. For any level of employment of capital, X and Y *(do / do not)* display diminishing returns. For 30 units of capital, the per unit return to labor is _____, _____, and _____ as labor employment climbs from 0 to 5, 5 to 10, and 10 to 15, respectively.

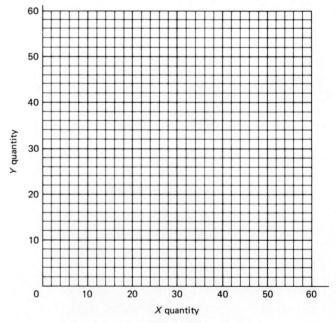

Figure 2-2

c. The production-possibility frontier drawn in Figure 2-2 is (*concave, convex, a straight line*) because _____

_____

_____

B: 30, 15, 60; C: 5, 20, 20, 40; D: 28, 20, 5; E: 10, 10, 5, 20; F: 5, 28, 10, 10; G: 20, 0, 0, 32; **a.** do; 28; 12; 8; 2.8; 1.2; 0.8 **b.** do, 6.4; 3.2; 2.4 **c.** a straight line; inputs are always used in the same proportion regardless of whether they are employed in the production of X or the production of Y

9. a. In question 4, suppose the number of workers rises from 100 to 200 (the fixed amounts of X resources and Y resources remaining unchanged). The production-possibility curve would then move outward (pick one):

(1) Until its end points indicated 1200 X, 120 Y

(2) By a greater amount than stated in alternative (1)

(3) By a much lesser amount than indicated in (1)

(4) Not at all

b. Suppose X is a necessity (say, food) and Y is a luxury. Every worker (or family) must have at least 3½ units of X daily in order to live. The population still consists of only 100 workers, and they choose to produce 450 of X, 28 of Y. (Mark this point on Figure 2-1.) If output is equally distributed, this means each worker gets daily 4½ X units and a little more than ¼ Y unit.

Now let the number of workers rise from 100 to 200. An extended X-production table indicates that 200 workers can produce 700 X. If all workers are to remain alive, what quantities of X and Y will be produced?

(1) 700 X plus about the same amount of Y per worker as before

(2) 700 X and no Y at all

(3) More than 700 X and about the same amount of Y per worker as before

(4) Impossible to tell from information given

c. If X is food, what idea discussed in the text does this illustrate? _____

_____

_____

a. (3) b. (2) c. Malthusian theory of population growth

10. The following questions will investigate your understanding of "Pictures in an Exhibition."

a. Consider the production-possibility curves drawn in Figure 2-3.

(1) An economy produces only two goods, and employs all inputs in exactly the same proportion. Which of the alternatives drawn in Figure 2-3 most accurately reflects this circumstance?

(2) An economy produces only two goods, and one of those goods displays increasing returns to scale. Which panel in Figure 2-3 most accurately reflects this circumstance?

(3) An economy produces only two goods. All of the inputs are entirely specialized for the production of one good or the other; i.e., the X inputs would be useless in the production of Y and the Y inputs would be useless in the production of X. Which alternative most accurately reflects this circumstance?

b. Consider the production-possibility curves drawn in Figure 2-4. In each, the shaded schedule represents an original curve; solid schedules represent what happens to the frontier after something has changed the economy.

(1) Suppose that scientific invention increased the productivity of resources used only in the production of X. Which panel most accurately reflects this development?

(2) Many scientists believe that we are exhausting our natural resources. Assume that there are two inputs, labor and natural resources, used to produce one of two goods, X and Y, but assume that resources are employed only in the production of Y. Which of the alternatives in Figure 2-4 most accurately reflects what would happen if the scientists were correct and there were no improvement in the technology involved in producing Y?

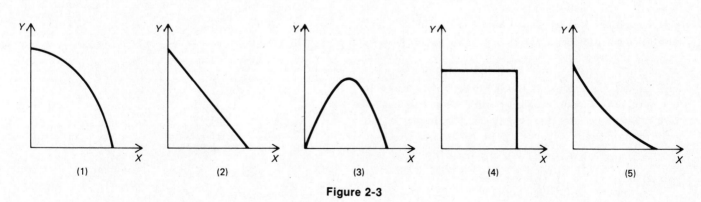

Figure 2-3

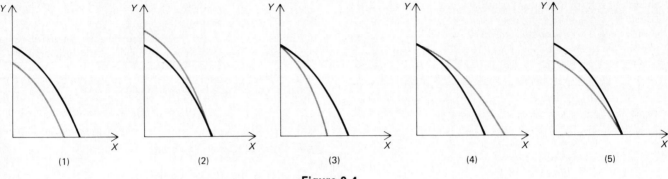

Figure 2-4

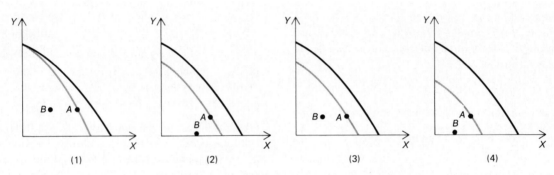

Figure 2-5

(3) Now assume that technology improves the efficiency of resources in the production of Y in **(2)**. Which alternative might then be appropriate?

c. Let X represent consumption goods and Y represent investment goods. Suppose that an economy were in full employment and operating at point A in Figure 2-5. Which panel in Figure 2-5 represents the growth result most accurately? Now suppose that the economy were suffering through a period of unemployment that discouraged investment (high unemployment corresponds to low demand, excess capacity, and thus no need to invest in new equipment or technology). Which panel would now be most appropriate?

---

a. (1) 2; **(2)** 5; **(3)** 4   **b. (1)** 3; **(2)** 2; **(3)** 5;   **c.** 4, 2

---

11. We can illustrate the "linear programming" technique referred to in footnote 4 of the text to elucidate Stigler's least-cost-diet program. Suppose that each unit of milk (*M*) and beans (*B*) has, respectively, (1, 8) calories and (4, 2) vitamins. Suppose that each unit of the two goods costs $1 and $2, respectively. If you must buy at least 120 calorie units and 180 vitamin units per month, show by experiment that the least-cost combination is 40 units of milk (i.e., M = 40) and 10 units of beans (B = 10) costing $60. The linear programmer would write this problem:

$$\text{Minimize } Z = \$1M + \$2B$$

subject to
$$1M + 8B \geqslant 120$$
$$4M + 2B \geqslant 180$$
$$M \geqslant 0 \quad \text{and} \quad B \geqslant 0$$

The experimental method is trial and error; you are on your own. The programming problem can be solved geometrically, and doing so will illustrate the technique involved in solving problems of this sort. Points satisfying each of the two constraints are labelled in Figure 2-6; points satisfying both constraints simultaneously are indicated by the shaded region. The solution must lie within that region. Schedule C in Figure 2-6 represents one possible cost line—combinations of milk and beans that cost a certain amount of money. Unfortunately, they do not cost enough because no point along schedule C lies within

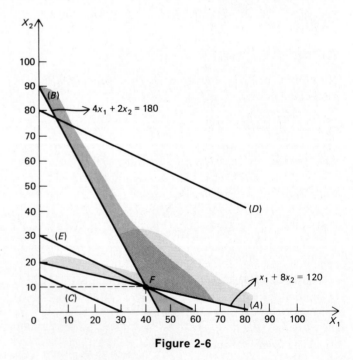

Figure 2-6

the shaded constraint region; nowhere along *C* is there a combination of milk and beans that simultaneously provides 120 calories and 180 vitamin units. Schedule *D* does contain points that satisfy both constraints, but there exist other points that cost less. Points along Schedule *E*, for example, all cost less, and one point—point *F*—satisfies both constraints. Point *F*, then, is the solution with $M = 40$, $B = 10$, and total expenditure equaling $1(40) + $2(10) = $60.

QUIZ: Multiple Choice

1. When production is subject to the influence of the law of diminishing returns—but it is still possible to increase total product—then, in order to obtain successive increases in output of 1 extra unit:

(1) smaller and smaller amounts of the variable input will be needed.

(2) adding more of the variable input will do more harm than good, because it must diminish total output instead of increasing it.

(3) the cost of hiring each additional unit of the variable input must steadily increase.

(4) greater and greater amounts of the variable input will be needed.

(5) none of the above is necessarily true.

2. The three economic problems of *What, How,* and *For Whom* goods shall be produced apply:

(1) mainly to totalitarian or centrally planned societies, wherein the problem of planning arises directly.

(2) only or principally to free enterprise or capitalist societies, wherein the problem of choice is most acute.

(3) only or almost entirely to the less developed societies, since development is largely a question of meeting these three problems.

(4) to all societies, regardless of stage of development or form of political organization.

(5) to none of the above necessarily, since they are problems for the individual business firm or family, not for society.

3. There cannot be a problem of *What* goods shall be produced if:

(1) the supply of productive resources is small, so that it must be devoted to the production of necessities.

(2) production has not yet reached the stage at which the law of diminishing returns begins to operate.

(3) the supply of productive resources is sufficiently large to make possible the production of some luxury goods.

(4) every productive input is so specialized that it can be used only in the production of one good and no other.

(5) production can be carried on under conditions of decreasing or constant cost, rather than increasing cost.

4. If the law of diminishing returns is to apply, the following condition must be satisfied: the increase in output:

(1) must come from a proportionate increase in all inputs.

(2) comes from an increase in some inputs, but at least one input must remain fixed in quantity.

(3) must come from an increase in one input only, all others remaining fixed in quantity.

(4) must grow less because of a decline in the competence or skills of inputs later applied.

(5) may be proportionate in physical quantity to the increase in inputs, but the *value* of that extra output must decline.

5. The economic problem of *What* goods shall be produced:

(1) may be a problem for any individual firm seeking to make a profit, but is not in any sense a problem for society as a whole.

(2) can be illustrated as the problem of choosing a point on the production-possibility curve.

(3) is a problem whose nature is illustrated by the law of diminishing returns.

(4) arises only when the stock of productive resources is very small, so that it must be devoted to the production of necessities.

(5) arises only when all productive inputs are so specialized that each can be used only in the production of one good and no other

6. The economic problem of *How* to produce goods does not exist:

(1) if the required proportions of inputs are fixed for all commodities, so that substitution of input B to replace part of input A in production is impossible.

(2) provided production has not been carried to the point where the law of diminishing returns has begun to set in.

(3) where the economy's stock of capital is small relative to its labor force.

(4) in a technically advanced society, since proper technology will then have established the best possible method of producing each good.

(5) in any circumstances—the problem of how to produce goods is an engineering problem throughout and not an economic problem.

7. A production-possibility diagram illustrates the limit on the amount of finished goods that can be produced, as imposed by the limited supply of productive inputs or factors. On the axes of this diagram are measured:

(1) quantities of productive inputs.

(2) prices of productive inputs.

(3) quantity of inputs on one axis, value of finished goods on the other.

(4) money value of finished goods.

(5) quantities of finished goods.

8. On the heavy production frontier drawn in Figure 2-7, which point corresponds to the economy's valuing food most heavily (i.e., at which point would you expect to find the price of food to be the largest relative to the price of clothing)?

(1) *A*.

(2) *B*.

(3) *C*.

(4) *D*.

9. The heavy curved line in Figure 2-7 illustrates a country's production-possibility curve. A shift in this curve to the position

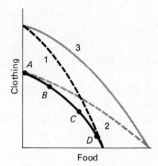

Figure 2-7

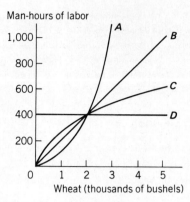

Figure 2-8

indicated by the line marked 1 would be appropriate to illustrate:

(1) a change in the tastes of the population whereby its members want more food produced and less clothing.

(2) the appearance of some new resources useful only in the clothing industry.

(3) an improvement in technology applicable to both occupations.

(4) a change in production involving an increase in clothing output and a decrease in food output.

(5) the development of a better technology in the food industry.

10. Which alternative in question 9 would apply had the heavy curve shifted to position 2?

(1).

(2).

(3).

(4).

(5).

11. Which alternative in question 9 would apply had the heavy curve shifted to position 3?

(1).

(2).

(3).

(4).

(5).

12. Figure 2-8 shows outputs of wheat obtainable on a fixed plot of land by varying the input of labor. The curve that would correctly illustrate application of the law of diminishing returns, as the graph is drawn, would be:

(1) *A.*

(2) *B.*

(3) *C.*

(4) *D.*

(5) either *A* or *C.*

13. A production-possibility (transformation) curve is intended to show:

(1) the exact amounts of two goods that an economy will decide to produce.

(2) the most valuable combination of two goods that an economy can produce.

(3) the alternative combinations of products available from a given quantity of resources.

(4) when the law of diminishing returns first begins to take effect.

(5) none of the above.

14. If, with respect to the guns-and-butter production-possibility diagram used in the text, actual output is marked by a point inside (to the southwest) of this curve, this means that:

(1) it is impossible to produce more guns without the sacrifice of some butter output.

(2) either all available resources are not being fully employed or they are not being employed to the best advantage.

(3) the law of diminishing returns cannot be in operation.

(4) the diagram illustrates something which could not possibly happen.

(5) the phenomenon of "increasing returns to scale" must be in operation.

15. If all inputs in a productive process are increased in amount by 100 percent, and the result is an increase in output of 120 percent, this would:

(1) illustrate the law of diminishing returns.

(2) contradict the law of diminishing returns.

(3) illustrate increasing returns to scale.

(4) contradict the principle of increasing returns to scale.

(5) contradict the law of scarcity.

16. An economy can produce 200 of good X and 300 of good Y—i.e., this is one point on its production-possibility frontier. Another point on this frontier is 240 of X and 290 of Y. The "law of increasing (relative) costs" would be illustrated by the following third point on the frontier:

(1) 280 of X, 270 of Y.

(2) 160 of X, 310 of Y.

(3) 280 of X, 280 of Y.

(4) 160 of X, 315 of Y.

(5) 280 of X, 285 of Y.

CHAPTER 3
PRICE FUNCTIONING IN A MIXED ECONOMY

This chapter introduces you to the workings of a price system in a mixed economy. When you have covered the material in the text and this guide, you should be able to satisfy the following objectives.

LEARNING OBJECTIVES

1. Describe what Adam Smith meant by the *invisible hand*. Indicate the particular system of political and economic organization that Smith was advocating when he introduced this phrase.

2. State the requirement that must be satisfied if the *invisible hand* is really to function just as Smith said it would.

3. Describe briefly how a market system (system of money and prices) settles each of the three basic problems of *What*, *For Whom*, and *How* goods shall be produced. Explain as fully as you can (recognizing that the approach here is an introductory one) what the text means in saying that the resolution of these problems is an interdependent process, or that the system is a "general-equilibrium" one.

4. Outline what the text means by a "mixed economy," indicating the major elements of a free enterprise system present therein, and those of a communist (socialist) system.

5. Describe three roles that government might play in a mixed economy and indicate how each might influence the economy's answers to the fundamental questions of *What*, *How*, and *For Whom*.

6. Explain carefully what is meant by "capital," as the word is used in this chapter. Explain also why, in discussing capital, the text speaks of "time-consuming indirect methods," and of "the need to forgo present consumption."

7. Define or explain briefly (*a*) imperfect competitor, (*b*) capitalism (not capital), (*c*) specialization (division of labor), (*d*) interdependence in production.

A "free private enterprise society" permits (for the most part) individual ownership of capital goods and land in the belief that this encourages initiative and productivity. It tolerates inequality of incomes, since the lure of a higher income presumably encourages introduction of new and better commodities and improved production techniques. The notion behind free enterprise is perhaps best described in the terms of Adam Smith's notion of the *invisible hand*. In his words, cited even before the text chapter begins, "Every individual endeavors to employ his capital [physical and human] so that its produce may be of greatest value . . . [intends] only his own security, only his own gain . . . being led by an invisible hand to promote an end which was no part of his intention . . . that of society more effectually than when he really intends to promote it [society's]." The present author added the brackets to, in part, emphasize that people contribute all their assets—their possessions and their skills—to a degree that they alone control in the pursuit of their own individual well-being.

Socialist societies, in contrast, bar or sharply restrict private ownership of capital goods or land, on the grounds that such ownership yields an unfair distribution of income. Equality or near-equality of income is commonly a first principle among socialist thinkers. This is not, however, to say that income equality is a condition which normally prevails among socialist societies. It is a philosophical ideal.

1. The text lists four principal characteristics of free enterprise societies (other than the ownership and income features noted above). List them below, citing first the characteristic upon which major emphasis is placed.

a. _____

b. _____

c. _____

d. _____

a. Use of money pricing system **b.** Use of an extensive stock of capital goods **c.** Specialization, or division of labor **d.** Use of money

Chapter 2 said that the three basic economic problems confronting every society are those of *What, How,* and *For Whom*. As problems of choice, they require decisions. The system of markets, money, and prices (in brief, "the pricing system") is the primary mechanism by which a "capitalist" or "free enterprise" system makes these decisions.

The pricing system is essentially one of exchange. Each person specializes (usually in cooperation with others) in producing some commodity or service. Each good thus produced is sold for a money price. These money proceeds are shared among those who helped in production. Each person's money share is his or her claim on the commodities and services that have been produced.

2. a. Thus, one vital part of the pricing system is *the market for consumer goods*. But the text speaks of the *two* market fronts on which consuming families face business enterprises. There is a second vital part of the pricing system, a second market with which families must deal. This is the market for

_____ .

b. In the market for finished goods, the individual consumer (or family) is a *(buyer / seller)*. In the market for productive inputs, the individual consumer is a *(buyer / seller)*. By contrast, the business firm whose task it is to manufacture consumer goods or to ready them for sale is a *(buyer / seller)* in the consumer-good market, and a *(buyer / seller)* in the productive-input market.

_____

a. productive inputs (notably labor)　**b.** buyer; seller; seller; buyer

3. No society, no matter how "free-enterprise-oriented," ever relies solely on the pricing system for its decisions on *What, How,* and *For Whom*. There is always some government intervention; that is what makes it a "mixed society." Governments in socialist countries intervene to a greater extent. But these socialist countries also rely heavily upon the pricing mechanism. In this respect, the difference between "capitalist" and "socialist" is one of degree. The role of government is outlined a bit more fully in section B of this chapter and in subsequent chapters. This *Study Guide* will return to consider that role when it is appropriate.

The working of the pricing system is best understood by considering a completely laissez-faire system—i.e., one in which government exists only to provide an outer framework of law and order. The ideal laissez-faire world is one of *pure* (or *perfect*) *competition*: one in which all monopolistic and other disruptive elements are completely absent. No buyer or seller is sufficiently important to be able to affect market price. And prices are notably "flexible"—i.e., responsive to even small changes arising either on the demand (buying) or the supply (selling) side of the market. (REMEMBER: This is an outline of how an *ideal* laissez-faire society would work, not an accurate description of how any real society actually functions.)

a. A system of perfect competition resolves the question of What goods to produce by the following process:

Consumers use their "dollar votes" (their money incomes available for spending) to buy the goods they want most. If they wish some of these goods badly enough, their bidding may push up the prices of such goods. One of the precepts of perfect competition is, however, that no single individual can influence a market price. An increase in your individual demand for wall posters will not, by itself, increase the price that distributors and stores charge for posters. An increase in the demand for posters by all college students could, however, do the trick. Prices can rise in response to widespread changes in the desirability of particular items. Suppliers observe market conditions and pay special attention to prices. They will move to produce commodities whose prices are high (relative to production costs), and to reduce or cut down entirely on production of goods whose prices are similarly low. In this way, the problem of *(What / How / For Whom)* goods shall be produced is settled. Producers are consciously trying to *(earn profits / satisfy consumer preferences)*—i.e., this is their primary objective—but in so doing, they are also *(earning profits / satisfying consumer preferences)*.

b. The same "ideally competitive" laissez-faire pricing system of part **a** operates to settle the question of *For Whom* goods shall be produced, as follows:

Productive inputs or factors such as labor (skilled or unskilled), land, and machinery also carry prices. These prices—wage rates, salary rates, rental rates, etc.—*(count / do not count)* as part of "the pricing system."

The size of a consumer's money income is governed (pick one):

(1) By the market price(s) of the input(s) and the input quantities the consumer owns
(2) Only by the price the input commands, not by its quantity
(3) Only by the input quantity the consumer owns, not by its price

The *For Whom* problem is that of distributing (fairly or unfairly) the available consumer-good supply among society's members. The size of my money income, relative to your money income, settles the *For Whom* problem between you and me. And the sizes of these two incomes, as indicated above, are governed by (1) the distribution of input ownership, and (2) *(input / consumer-good)* prices. Thus, given the ownership distribution, the relation of my income to yours is a matter of the prices my inputs can command relative to yours.

According to the myopic behavior of individuals postulated by Adam Smith, one person's view of the ideal *For Whom* solution would give that person somewhat more and give someone else an inconsequential trifle less. A second person might possibly disagree. When the phrase "ideally competitive" (or perfectly competitive) is used concerning a laissez-faire distribution system, it means simply those conditions under which individual prejudices of this sort are dwarfed by the more global interactions of society; the outcome that determines relative position is left to the impartial verdict of the marketplace. (This marketplace verdict indicates the collective decision of the society of which we are both members.) Overall, in one set of conditions, that verdict might result in substantial inequality of incomes; in another set, in approximately equal incomes. So the marketplace verdict may or may not conform to other measures of justice. What can be said on behalf of the market's decision is that—if that market is really free of monopolistic and other imperfections—it is an impartial justice.

c. The "ideally competitive" pricing system settles the question of *How* goods are to be produced as follows: suppose a given quantity of some good can be made either (1) with 2 units of capital and 10 units of labor, or (2) with 10 units of capital and 2 units of labor. For simplicity, assume these two are the only possible combinations.

The *How* problem is that of choosing between these two methods. To make the choice properly, producers must know *(the price of the finished good / which of them is more efficient / the prices of labor and capital)*. "The most efficient method" is that method which costs *(less / more)* than any other method. The *How* question persists until *(input / finished-good)* prices are known, and it is settled by reference to these prices. For example, if capital costs $2 per unit and labor costs $3, then method *(1 / 2)* above is preferable. If capital costs $3 and labor $2, then method *(1 / 2)* is preferable.

---

a. *What*; earn profits; satisfying consumer preferences **b.** count; **1**; input
c. the prices of labor and capital; less; input; 2; 1

In a laissez-faire system, producing business firms try to make all the profit they can. But the ability to earn profits is restrained by competition from other firms. Were you to operate a firm that earned enormous profits, for example, perfect competition would allow other firms to be attracted by those profits and enter into competition with you. These other firms would produce the same stuff, sell it to some of your customers at a lower but nonetheless profitable price, and cost you some business. To stay in business, in fact, you would have to lower your price to theirs, and your profits would be squeezed down to a reasonable level. Without this discipline of competition, "the profit motive" cannot be expected to work to the benefit of consumers.

Throughout, the important behavior is marketplace behavior. This governs the interdependent decisions on *What, How,* and *For Whom.* Suppose a nation puts a tariff on imported oil (departing from laizzes-faire because it wants to reduce its dependence on such oil). This could easily change the *What* decision. It is reasonable to expect, for example, that there would now be more domestic coal production. Coal producers would then have larger money incomes (relative to the rest of the population), and their desires would receive a correspondingly higher weight in a system in which money

"votes." Should the tastes of coal producers happen to differ even slightly from those whose incomes have (in relative terms) been reduced, the pattern of overall consumer-good spending and production would have to change accordingly. A change in the *What* decision could, in other words, work through the *For Whom* decision to create a secondary adjustment in the *What* decision. The *How* decision could be influenced, as well, because gradually increasing oil and coal prices goad producers to look for alternative energy sources.

4. **a.** Given the existing supply of any input (a kind of machine, a type of land or labor), the price that input can receive will depend on the demand for it. The strength of this demand, in turn, will depend on (pick one):

(1) The usefulness or "productivity" of that input in producing various kinds of consumer goods
(2) The price commanded by each of the various consumer goods which the input can help to manufacture
(3) Both the productivity of the input in making various kinds of consumer goods and the prices for which those consumer goods can be sold

b. Thus, if input A's productivity in making consumer good X is very high, that would tend to make the price of A *(high / low)*; if X can be sold only for a very low price, that would portend a *(high / low)* price for A. Consumer-good prices therefore *(have / do not have)* an influence over input prices. The *For Whom* problem is most immediately settled by the relation between input prices (the fact that some are high and some are low), but because input prices are influenced by consumer-good prices, the disposition for this *For Whom* problem is also influenced by the relation between consumer-good prices. The whole apparatus is an exercise in the complications of what economists call "general equilibrium."

---

a. (3) **b.** high; low; have

---

5. **a.** We can say that the money price system acts as a set of guideposts to consumers because (pick one only):

(1) A high price on consumer good X is a persuasion to buy in small quantities or not at all; a low price on Y is a persuasion to buy in large quantities.
(2) If there is only a small supply of consumer good X, it goes to the highest bidders.
(3) A low price on input B is a persuasion to use B as fully as possible; a high price on input A is a persuasion to use A only to the extent necessary.
(4) If there is only a small supply of input A, it goes to the highest bidders.

b. The pricing system also furnishes guideposts to producers, as indicated by alternative *(1 / 2 / 3 / 4)* above.

c. The pricing system also serves to ration out whatever supply of consumer goods is available, as indicated by alternative *(1 / 2 / 3 / 4)* above.

d. Similarly, money prices ration out the supply of inputs or factors—see alternative *(1 / 2 / 3 / 4)* above.

---

a. (1)   b. (3)   c. (2)   d. (4)

---

6.   Consider the five types of people whose relevant attributes are described:

A: Owns a coal mine; likes ice cream; hates fancy dessert yogurt

B: Works in a coal mine; likes yogurt and ice cream

C: Owns fancy yogurt company; hates dessert

D: Works at yogurt factory; hates dessert

E: Works at ice cream plant; hates dessert

Assume that there are enough of each type of person so that changes in their economic condition could affect a market price.

a.   If an oil embargo increased the demand for coal, would the following *(increase / decrease / stay the same / you can't tell from the information given)*

(1) A's earnings

(2) B's wages

(3) C's earnings

(4) D's wage

(5) E's wage

b.   If a nationwide mineworkers settlement increased B's wage without extending A's market, would the following *(increase / decrease / stay the same / you can't tell from the information given)*

(1) A's earnings

(2) C's earnings

(3) D's wage

(4) E's wage

---

a. All answers—increase (This problem has some further general-equilibrium aspects to it. Someone beyond the indicated set of people should have been hurt by higher energy prices; even, say, B might have been hurt if his house were energy-wasteful)   **b. (1)** decrease **(2)** increase **(3)** increase **(4)** cannot tell

---

7.   Could supply and demand work out to give salespeople with a "gift of gab" twice the income of skilled scientists? Could it give surgeons the same incomes as accountants and plumbers and 5 times that of butchers?

Yes and yes, in the short run at least. One should expect, though, that a "supply response" could undermine any of these comparisons. If, for example, some butchers felt that they could do plumbing, they might change professions. That would reduce the supply of butchers (presumably increasing the earnings of the butchers that remain butchers) and increase the supply of plumbers (presumably reducing the earnings of plumbers).

Section B of the text chapter introduces the various roles that government might play in very broad terms. These roles are catalogued according to the equity, efficiency, and stability difficulties that typically plague an economy left to its own devices. The existence of monopolies, or other forms of significant market imperfection, creates inefficiency that government might try to ameliorate. So do externalities, good or bad, and public goods that need societal support to be financially viable. Competitive laissez-faire solutions do not necessarily produce fair or just distributions of income, and governments sometimes try to use devices like progressive income taxation and social safety nets to diminish inequities. Fiscal and monetary policies have, since the 1930s, been used to try to shave off the peaks of economic boom and fill in the troughs of economic bust. The experience of the 1930s, in fact, is strong historical evidence that we cannot rely on laissez-faire policy to avoid dramatic turns in the long-term business cycle.

It should be noted, however, that government intervention need not be the best solution. Many times, the medicine of government policy is worse than the economic disease that it was intended to cure. We should, in short, avoid the error of the monarch who awarded a medal for singing talent to the second of two contestants after hearing only the first contestant sing.

8.   This question will explore the potential roles of government in a mixed economy.

a.   If monopoly power allowed the owner of a firm to produce too little, to charge too high a price, to earn an extraordinary rate of profit, and to ignore competitive pressures of potential competitors, would it alter society's answers to the three fundamental questions?

(1) Would the answer to *What* change? *(yes / no / probably)*

Why? _____

_____

_____

(2) Would the answer to *How* change? _____

Why? _____

_____

(3) Would the answer to *For Whom* change? _____.

Why? _____

_____

b.   If freedom to dump pollution into the air allowed a polluter to produce too much and charge too little regardless of competitive pressures, would answers to the questions change?

(1) Would the answer to *What* change? _____

Why? _____

_____

(2) Would the answer to *How* change? _____

Why? _____

_____

(3) Would the answer for *For Whom* change? _____ .

Why? _____

c. If instability in the business cycle increased risk so that the price charged for a given good had to be higher than otherwise would have been appropriate and production were therefore smaller than appropriate, would answers to the questions change?

(1) Would the answer to *What* change? _____

Why? _____

_____

(2) Would the answer to *How* change? _____

Why? _____

_____

(3) Would the answer to *For Whom* change? _____

Why? _____

_____

d. If policy were enacted to redistribute income, would answers to the questions change?

(1) Would the answer to *What* change? _____

Why? _____

_____

(2) Would the answer to *How* change? _____

Why? _____

_____

(3) Would the answer to *For Whom* change? _____ .

Why? _____

_____

e. Listed below are three policy options that a government might consider:

(1) A minimum-wage law prohibits the payment of any hourly wage rate below $3.35.

(2) A new toll-free highway is built.

(3) Taxation on incomes reduces the spending power of rich citizens.

Item *(1 / 2 / 3)* illustrates an influence directly exerted on the decision as to *What* goods shall be produced. Item *(1 / 2/ 3)* illustrates a similar influence on *How*, and item(s) *(1 / 2 / 3)* on *For Whom*.

---

a. (1) Yes; Too little of one good also means too much of another **(2)** Probably; The most efficient process is probably not used **(3)** Yes; The monopolist is earning relatively more than otherwise **(b) (1)** Yes; Too much of one good also means too little of another **(2)** Yes; The process chosen makes more pollution than it would if the polluter had to pay to pollute **(3)** Probably; Never say never in general equilibrium **c.** The answers of **a** apply except that the income distortion would probably not weigh heavily in **(3)** **d. (1)** Probably; The people receiving the income would probably want different things than the wealthier people, and giving them more dollar "votes" would cause the market system to accommodate **(2)** Probably; The scales of various industries might change and thereby change the most appropriate production process **(3)** Yes; This is the point of the policy **e.** 1; 1 and 3, though indirect effects on all three questions could be expected from each.

9. Listed below are several examples of how a government might try to modify the workings of an automatic price system:

a. pure food and drug laws _____

b. minimum wage laws _____

c. pollution limitations _____

d. free penicillin _____

e. rent controls _____

f. military draft _____

g. unemployment compensation _____

Write in the blanks which of the three motives for government action—efficiency concerns, equity concerns, and stability concerns—is closest to the rationale that might underlie each policy.

---

a. efficiency **b.** equity **c.** efficiency **d.** equity **e.** equity **f.** equity and/ or efficiency **e.** a toss-up between equity and stabilization

Section C of the text chapter discusses the subject of *capital*. "Capital" is a word with too many meanings: you must understand the particular meaning here involved. Capital here does not mean money. It means manufactured productive inputs. It includes durable items like blast furnaces, factory buildings, machine tools, electric drills, tack hammers, etc. It includes stocks of semi-finished goods; such goods are on the way to becoming consumer goods, but they are still manufactured inputs to be used in later stages of the production process.

Capital is important only because it "pushes back" the law of scarcity; it makes possible the output of more consumer goods. Every nation would like to become "capitalist" in the sense of having a large stock of capital relative to its population. However, there is a cost involved in the production of capital goods. The same resources that make these goods also make consumer goods; there is a choice to be made between capital and consumer goods. Recall the production-possibility curves drawn in text Chapter 2 between consumption goods and investment goods. Countries that climbed farther on the frontier away from the consumption axis found themselves on a higher curve the next year, but enjoyed less consumption in the current year.

Once the capital goods are finished, we can have more consumer goods. But if resources are fully employed, then during the time it takes to make the capital goods, we must give up some consumer goods. The production of capital goods demands waiting, the sacrifice of present consumption.

10. **a.** Circle all the following that qualify as "capital"—as the word is used in this chapter.

(1) An oil refinery
(2) An issue of General Motors stock
(3) Cash in a business owner's safe
(4) A screwdriver
(5) Money borrowed by a business firm from a bank to expand its operations
(6) A steel-ingot inventory held by a steel company
(7) Unsold automobiles held by an auto manufacturer
(8) An inventory of groceries held by a supermarket

b. Money *(is / is not)* counted as part of "capital" (as the word is used in this chapter) because (pick one):

(1) It is essential to production.
(2) It has no part to play in production.
(3) It is not actually useful in production, although it is essential to have money in order to buy the real inputs that are needed for production.

c. To qualify as "capital" (still using the word as in this chapter), the item in question *(must be / need not necessarily be)* an input that is useful or necessary at some stage of production. And the item must be *(of a type found only in highly developed economies / a primary factor of production / manufactured)*.

---

a. (1), (4), (6), (7), and (8)   **b.** is not; (3)   **c.** must be; manufactured

---

11. **a.** Remember two elementary but essential things about capital, or "capital goods":

1. In the final reckoning, only consumer goods are important. Capital goods have no merit in themselves. They are produced only because they are roundabout ways of producing consumer goods.

2. Because any item of capital takes time to make, the effort devoted to making it is production for tomorrow's consumption use. The resources employed in constructing that item of capital could have been used to satisfy today's consumption demands.

Any developed nation, whether "capitalist" or not, possesses a large stock of capital, and much of each day's productive effort goes into maintenance and expansion of that stock. Consequently, in such nations today's productive effort is largely going to satisfy *(yesterday's / today's / tomorrow's)* needs, while the consumer goods actually enjoyed today result from *(yesterday's / today's / tomorrow's)* effort.

b. Circle as many of the following as are correct:

(1) The larger the available stock of capital, the larger the output of consumer goods that is possible.
(2) In terms of Chapter 2's production-possibility curve, additions to the stock of capital push that curve upward and outward.
(3) A decision to produce or not produce more capital goods is not part of the decision on *What* goods to produce.
(4) In a fully employed economy, a decision to produce more capital goods is a decision to produce fewer consumer goods in the immediate future.

c. When reference is made to "a capitalist economy," what is probably contemplated is any economy (pick one or more):
(1) In which most capital goods are privately owned
(2) In which the stock of capital is large relative to the population of that economy
(3) Not under communist or socialist direction

---

a. tomorrow's; yesterday's   **b.** (1), (2), and (4)   **c.** (1), (2), and (3) [Note that there is room for dispute concerning properties (2) and (3). A dictionary definition of capitalism may not specify that the stock of capital must be large relative to the country's size or population; nevertheless, the "capitalist" countries are typically those in which the stock is large. However, even a communist country may be "capitalist" in the sense of having a large capital stock relative to its population, and wanting to have an even larger stock.)

---

12. Specialization (or division of labor) is rampant in a modern economy because it increases the output obtainable from a given resource supply. The consequences of specialization include (circle as many as are correct):

a. Exchange of goods

b. Use of money

c. Social interdependence

d. An intensified law of scarcity

e. Possibly a sense of alienation on the part of members of the society involved

---

a, b, c, and **e**

QUIZ: Multiple Choice

1. Capital (considered as a factor of production, or as one of the three major inputs of "land, labor, and capital") means:
(1) manufactured productive inputs.
(2) undeveloped natural resources, such as iron ore not yet mined.
(3) the financial assets of producing businesses.
(4) the same thing as the nation's total money stock.
(5) none of these things.

2. One vital reason why indirect, or "capital-using," methods

of production have not displaced direct methods in economically less developed nations is that:
(1) the governments of such nations have not issued enough money to finance indirect production methods.
(2) people do not realize that indirect methods would produce more consumption goods.
(3) there are no indirect methods that would actually produce more consumption goods.
(4) such areas lack a properly functioning price system.
(5) the introduction of such indirect methods would involve a sacrifice of present consumption.

3.   The economic problem of *How* goods shall be produced is solved in capitalist societies:
(1) through the decisions of consumers in the marketplace, as these appear in the form of finished-good prices.
(2) by means of the profit motive impelling producers, which prompts them to try to keep their costs of production at a minimum.
(3) by means of extensive use of capital goods.
(4) by means of extensive specialization, which may or may not involve large-scale use of capital goods.
(5) in none of the above ways, since *How* to produce goods is not a basic problem in capitalist societies.

4.   The economic problem of deciding *What* goods to produce requires or includes, among other things:
(1) the necessity of deciding the degree to which specialization is to be employed in the manufacture of goods.
(2) a decision as to the quantity of advertising that should be used to encourage the sale of whatever has been produced.
(3) the choice between the production of consumer goods and the production of capital goods.
(4) the establishment of a central government, since all decisions on *What* are ultimately made by such governments.
(5) the establishment of a system of pure (or perfect) competition.

5.   We speak of "land, labor, and capital" as the basic grouping of the factors of production. Which of the following is correct with respect to whether or not money, stocks, and/or bonds should be counted as "capital"?
(1) All three (money, stocks, and bonds) count.
(2) Stocks and bonds count, but money does not.
(3) Money counts, but stocks and bonds do not.
(4) Money and stocks count, but bonds do not.
(5) None of the three counts.

6.   A major social problem to which specialization and division of labor give rise is:
(1) the need to use paper money.
(2) the need to use capital.
(3) interdependence.
(4) the need to learn economics.
(5) none of these.

7.   In economics, the term "imperfect competitor" is applied to a seller who:
(1) operates outside the system of specialization and money pricing.
(2) supplies a sufficiently large quantity of the good involved to be able to affect its price.
(3) seeks to distort the pattern of consumer tastes (through advertising campaigns and the like).
(4) knowingly or unknowingly uses inferior production methods.
(5) is not correctly described by any of these descriptions.

8.   Figure 3-1 depicts a production-possibility curve involving

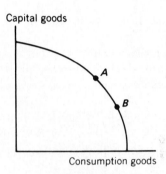

Figure 3-1

capital goods and consumer goods. The significance of points *A* and *B* is this:
(1) they indicate possible demands for capital goods and consumer goods—*A* representing capital-good demand and *B* consumer-good demand.
(2) they represent possible and alternative combinations of maximum output which the economy in question could produce.
(3) they indicate the maximum possible quantities of capital goods and consumer goods which could be produced—*A* indicating maximum possible capital-good output and *B* maximum possible consumer-good output.
(4) the movement from *A* to *B* indicates the growth of output resulting from the use of capital goods.
(5) no significance at all, since production-possibility diagrams refer to consumer goods only, not to capital goods.

9.   In Figure 3-1, operation at a point such as *A* indicates production of some capital goods. Assuming this is more than sufficient to replace capital goods currently being worn out, then continued operation at *A* should result in:
(1) an inward movement of the whole curve.
(2) no change in the curve, but a move from *A* to *B*.
(3) no change necessarily either in the position of the curve or in the operation of the economy at *A*.
(4) no change in the curve, but a move from *A* to a point inside the curve.
(5) an outward movement of the whole curve.

10.   Figure 3-2 depicts a production-possibility curve with respect to consumer goods X and Y. The economy involved

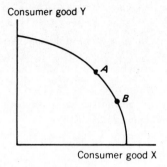

Consumer good Y

Consumer good X

Figure 3-2

makes full use of a money pricing system. The significance of such points as *A* and *B* is this:

(1) either is a possible operating point, and if selected, it indicates a verdict on *What* to produce with respect to X and Y, settled by consumer preferences as expressed through the price system.

(2) either is a possible operating point, but it will have been reached quite independently of the operation of the price system, since the curve in question refers to production, not prices.

(3) if either is chosen as an operating point, it will indicate the combination of X and Y having maximum money value, but it is not necessarily a point in any way related to consumer preferences.

(4) each is a typical point on the curve, and the position of the entire curve (all points thereon) is established by consumer preferences as expressed through the price system.

(5) either is a possible operating point, but a money pricing system is bound to show that *A* is a point preferable to *B*.

11.   In a money-using, capitalist society, the economic problem of *For Whom* goods shall be produced is primarily settled as follows:

(1) each producer looks for the type of consumer or market most likely to be interested in the product offered, then tries to tailor that product so that it is particularly appealing to the consumer or market.

(2) consumers bid up the prices of those goods they most want to have, and refuse to bid, or bid only a low price, for goods they find less attractive.

(3) business firms bid for the services of productive inputs according to their usefulness in production, thus giving each input supplier a money income that can be used to buy goods.

(4) competition operates so as to keep down profits, hence to keep prices at a level which consumers can afford to pay.

(5) income is distributed in keeping with the needs of individual consumers.

12.   Which alternative in question 11 best describes the process by which the problem of *What* goods shall be produced is primarily settled, in a society which relies on the mechanism of money and prices?

(1).

(2).

(3).

(4).

(5).

13.   If it is true that most of the goods a certain society consumed today were produced in the past, and that most of its production today is intended for future consumption, then from these facts it must be true that this society makes extensive use of:

(1) specialization and division of labor.

(2) money.

(3) a money pricing system.

(4) advertising.

(5) capital.

14.   In a decentralized, capitalist society, the use of a money pricing system is not expected to help settle the following economic problem, that of:

(1) distributing money incomes among the members of the society.

(2) helping a consumer with given tastes and a limited income to decide how best to spend that income.

(3) deciding how much of the available resource supply is to be occupied in making any given consumer good.

(4) choosing the particular kinds of inputs (factors of production) that should be used for the manufacture of any given consumer good.

(5) determining the particular output of goods and services which the society really needs, regardless of the tastes of any or all individual consumers therein.

15.   The government role that significantly effects the question *For Whom* is:

(1) promotion of equity.

(2) promotion of efficiency.

(3) promotion of stabilization.

(4) all the above.

CHAPTER 4
THE BARE ELEMENTS OF SUPPLY AND DEMAND

There is a common expression among people who think about economic issues: "its all a matter of supply and demand." There is a lot of truth to this refrain, and this chapter provides the reader with his or her first systematic exposure to what it means to economists. By the end, the following objectives should be in reach.

LEARNING OBJECTIVES

1. Define "demand schedule" and "supply schedule."

2. Explain the difference between a demand schedule and a demand curve.

3. Describe "the law of downward-sloping demand."

4. Explain the three background "effects" that account for the law of downward-sloping demand.

5. Explain why the supply schedule is normally sloped upward.

6. Describe equilibrium price (in a competitive market). Explain how the market manages to reach that price.

7. Explain what is meant by "other things equal" with respect to demand schedules (curves) or supply schedules (curves). What factors are held constant in the construction of a demand schedule? A supply schedule?

8. Explain precisely how changes in the factors identified in objective 7 change market equilibria.

9. Identify the kind of market to which the supply-and-demand analysis of this chapter strictly applies. Identify the kinds of markets to which it does not apply.

10. Explain the difference between "partial-equilibrium" and "general-equilibrium" analysis.

Many forces operate to drive the price of any given commodity high or to push it low: people's tastes, the amount of income they have to spend, the prices at which substitute commodities are selling, what it costs to produce that commodity, and so on.

If we are to explain a commodity's actual price, there are a few essential starting points that must be thoroughly understood.

The enormous collection of forces which influence the price of a commodity can be divided into two distinct groups:

▶ One group of forces operates through its influence on the behavior of buyers of the commodity. We sum up what buyers want to do through the device of a demand schedule, or demand curve. The demand curve is concerned exclusively with buyer attitudes—not with sellers.

▶ The second group of forces operates through its influence on the behavior of sellers. This we represent by means of the supply schedule, or supply curve. The supply curve reflects solely seller (not buyer) attitudes.

The division between these two groups is nearly absolute. Its importance cannot be overemphasized if we are to correctly analyze the workings of even the simplest of markets. Economic forces, in all but a few very special cases, influence either the demand side of a market, or the supply side of a market, but never both.

1. This question will explore the forces that play on the demand side.

a. The text notes that the demand curve is, typically, downward-sloping. To support this slope, list three reasons why the quantity demanded should increase as the price of some good falls:

(1) _____

(2) _____

(3) _____

b. The text also identifies four economic forces that determine precisely where a demand curve must be located; i.e., four factors other than price were identified as determinants of the quantity demanded. Changes in these factors shift the entire demand curve. List them:

(1) _____

(2) _____

(3) _____

(4) _____

a. (1) New buyers enter **(2)** More purchased by existing consumers **(3)** New uses might become economical **b. (1)** Income **(2)** Size of the market **(3)** Prices of substitute or complementary goods **(4)** Tastes

2.   We will now explore the forces that play on the supply side.

a. The text notes that the supply curve is, typically, upward-sloping. To support this slope, list one important reason why suppliers must be paid a steadily increasing price to increase the quantity that they are willing to sell; explain how it works.

_____

_____

_____

_____

b. The text also identifies five economic forces that determine precisely where a supply curve must be located; i.e., five factors other than price were identified as determinants of the quantity supplied. Changes in these factors shift the entire supply curve. List them:

(1) _____

(2) _____

(3) _____

(4) _____

(5) _____

a. Law of diminishing returns; to increase output, more and more of some variable inputs will have to be added to work with relatively fixed supplies of other inputs; they become increasingly less productive **b. (1)** Costs of production **(2)** Technology **(3)** Taxes and/or subsidies **(4)** Market structure **(5)** Uncertainties

3.   Each of the 10 prices (*P*) below is associated with a particular quantity (*Q*). In Figure 4-1, mark the 10 points corresponding to these *PQ* pairs. Join them with a smooth curve.

P:	$10	$9	$8	$7	$6	$ 5	$ 4	$ 3	$ 2	$ 1
Q:	1	2	3	5	8	12	15	20	25	40

a. In this schedule, the lower the price, the *(lower / higher)* the quantity. These figures therefore suggest a *(supply / demand)* curve.

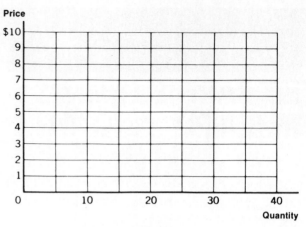

Figure 4-1

b. Also record the following 10 pairs in Figure 4-1.

P:	$10	$ 9	$ 8	$ 7	$ 6	$ 5	$ 4	$ 3	$2	$1
Q:	26	25	24	22	20	18	15	10	0	0

This would represent a *(supply / demand)* curve.

a. higher; demand **b.** supply

4.   a. Given the data of question 3, what would be the *equilibrium price?* .. *$(10 / 9 / 8 / 7 / 6 / 5 / 4 / 3 / 2 / 1)*

b. Why would this be the equilibrium price?

(1) It is about midway in the total schedule of prices.
(2) It is the price sellers have decided should be charged for this commodity.
(3) It is the only price at which the quantity buyers want to purchase just equals the quantity sellers want to supply.

a. 4 **b.** (3)

5. If (still using question 3 data) price stood temporarily at a level of $6, what would be the situation? (Pick one.)

(1) Quantity offered for sale would exceed quantity demanded. Competition among sellers would drive price higher.

(2) Quantity demanded would exceed quantity offered for sale. Competition among buyers plus seller awareness of shortages would drive price higher.

(3) Quantity demanded would exceed quantity offered for sale. Competition among sellers plus buyer awareness of shortages would drive price lower.

(4) Quantity demanded would be less than quantity offered for sale. Competition among sellers would drive price lower.

b.   If price stood temporarily at a level of $3, which alternative in part **a** would apply? .... *(1 / 2 / 3 / 4)*

a. (4) **b.** (2)

6. When the text speaks of the *law of downward-sloping demand*, it is referring to a particular kind of behavior among buyers, with so few exceptions that it is designated as a "law" of behavior. Circle as many of the following as correctly describe or illustrate this law.

a. If the price of X falls, at least some X buyers will increase the quantity they purchase by at least some small amount.

b. When people have more income to spend, they normally increase their purchases of any commodity.

c. Demand curves normally slope downward as they run to the right—i.e., their general direction is between northwest and southeast.

d. The quantity of any commodity bought ultimately tends to decline as it goes out of style or is superseded by something of better quality.

e. When the price of X rises significantly, people tend to reduce the quantity of X that they purchase.

f. If the price of butter falls considerably, the drop will tend to reduce purchases of oleomargarine.

a, c, e (The "law of downward-sloping demand" has to do with the influnece of price on quantity demanded. Item **b** does not illustrate this law because it refers to an income change; changes in income shift the entire demand curve in or out for all prices. In item **d**, the change in purchases is not set set off by a price change; tastes change, to be sure, but the entire curve shifts when they do, regardless of the price. Item **f** does refer to a price change, but it is a change in the price of another commodity. Like items **d** and **b**, this change generates a shift in the entire curve for each and every price.)

7. If the price of any good falls, the quantity buyers want to purchase will rise because (*a*) new buyers are attracted, and/or (*b*) existing buyers increase their purchases. The text cites two background reasons for such increases: the *substitution effect* and the *income* effect.

a. First, if X's price were to fall, buyers may substitute X for Y. Even though the price of Y were unchanged, Y would then be relatively more expensive. This would be (*an income / a substitution*) effect, and would apply to (*only old / only new / both old and new*) buyers. Similarly, if X's price were to rise, (*only old / only new / both old and new*) buyers may substitute Y for X because Y would then be relatively (*more / less*) expensive.

b. The second reason applies only when expenditure on X bulks large in the total budget, so that any rise in X's price provokes a budget crisis, whereas a fall in that price calls for celebration. A fall in X's price resembles an increase in income, for the same amount of X can now be bought, with money left over. With this "increase in income," buyers may want to purchase more of various goods—including good X. This is (*a substitution / an income*) effect, and it applies (*only to old / only to new / to both old and new*) buyers.

c. These two effects apply (*only for price reduction / only for price increases / for both price reductions and increases*).

a. a substitution; both old and new; only old; less (only current consumers can substitute away from a commodity) **b.** an income; only old **c.** for both price reductions and increases

8. Put S in the space below if the description suggests the "substitution effect" of question 5; put I if the "income effect" is indicated; put N if neither is appropriate.

a. A family decides its guests cannot tell the difference between butter and oleomargarine; consequently it switches some of its purchases from butter to margarine. ...... ( )

b. A sharp increase in rents forces the family to move to a smaller apartment. .... ( )

c. Butter prices go up, and the family switches more of its purchases from butter to oleomargarine. .... ( )

d. The family receives a considerable increase in income and therefore buys, among other things, more butter and more apartment space. .... ( )

a. N **b.** I **c.** S **d.** N (These two "effects" are intended to apply to the consequences of a price change only. In cases **a** and **d**, the behavior change was not set off by a price change.)

It is essential to keep in mind that a demand curve is a conditional schedule; it answers an "if _____, then _____" type of question. It shows, in particular, that if the price of some good were to stand at some specified level, then consumers would be willing to purchase the indicated quantity.

In Figure 4-2, the demand curve indicates that if the price were equal to $A0$, then consumers would want to buy a quantity AF (or $0C$). Should the price fall to $B0$, then the quantity demanded (willingly) by consumers would rise to BG (or $0E$).

When equilibrium in the marketplace has been worked out, there will be just one price for which the quantity willingly demanded will equal the quantity willingly supplied. The essential feature of the demand curve is

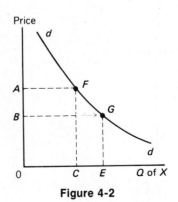

Figure 4-2

that that equilibrium is just one possibility covered by the curve; the curve itself covers all the possibly relevant prices, and only from the demand side. The quantity read from the curve does not depend at all upon whether or not that quantity is feasible to supply at the given price. It reflects only the desires of consumers who worry only about their own preferences.

Remember, too, that price is not the only factor that influences the consumers' decisions to buy. The income that they receive, the prices of other goods, and their own tastes also have an effect. Rather than try to capture all there effects in one curve, economists have historically favored charting the price effect on the quantity demanded under the assumption that the other factors do not change. Buyer behavior for one good is thus insulated against disturbances arising from other sources, and we can indicate how this behavior changes solely in response to changes in the price of the good in question. This is the "other things equal" or "other things constant" assumption.

These other factors do, of course, change. These changes are recognized by a shift in the entire demand curve to an appropriate new position; each price is, in other words, associated with a new quantity demanded.

In Figure 4-3, for example, the *dd* demand curve is shown as shifting to an entirely new position, *d'd'* — because, say, buyer incomes have increased. Demand curves are always drawn on an *other things equal* assumption. These "other things" include consumers incomes; if this factor changes, then the demand curve must change position accordingly. If good X's price had been *A*0, then the consumers would have been buying quantity 0*C*. Now, with higher incomes, they want to increase their purchases to 0*E*. Mind you, this doesn't mean they will succeed in buying quantity 0*E* at price *A*0. The supply curve will have something to say about that. But our concern for the moment is with demand, not supply; it is with what buyers want to do. The point is that at each and any price, because of the income rise, consumers will want to buy a larger quantity than they would previously have wanted.

What has just been said about the demand curve applies equally to the supply curve.

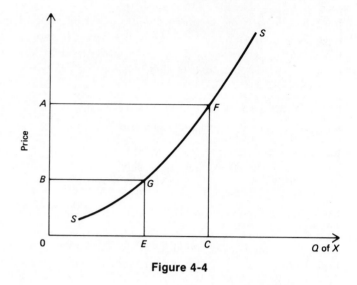

Figure 4-4

A supply curve is a conditional schedule, as well. It shows that if the price of some good were to stand at some specified level, then suppliers would be willing and able to sell the indicated quantity.

In Figure 4-4 the supply schedule indicates that if the price were equal to *A*0, then a quantity *AF* (or 0*C*) would be supplied. If the price fell to 0*B*, then the quantity supplied would fall to *BG* (or 0*E*). These quantities depend only upon the parameters of the suppliers' decision, and not on the willingness of consumers to purchase the indicated quantities at the prescribed price. Again, equilibrium will identify one price, but the supply schedule represents the suppliers' response to all possible prices.

▶ Price is not the only factor which influences the disposition of suppliers to sell. For example, if costs of production go up, this will change the amount suppliers would want to sell at any given price. For any particular price, they will be disposed to sell less than they did before; at certain low levels of price, they may no longer want to sell any amount at all. Technological advance that lowers cost, would, of course, have the opposite effect. Taxes, market structure, and production uncertainties all influence the supply response to any specified price.

▶ That is, a supply curve, just like a demand curve, is an "other things equal" curve. It assumes all factors which influence supplier decisions other than price are given or fixed. If any of these "other things" (e.g., production costs) changes, then the entire supply curve must shift to an appropriate new position.

9. Figures 4-5 through 4-8 illustrate these ideas. In each, one curve, demand or supply, has shifted in position because of the change in some influencing factor other than price. The solid line indicates the former position; the broken line, the new. In Figure 4-5, for example, the demand curve has shifted to the right (or upward) from position *dd* to position *d'd'*.

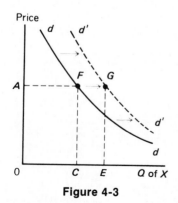

Figure 4-3

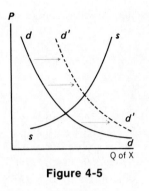

Figure 4-5

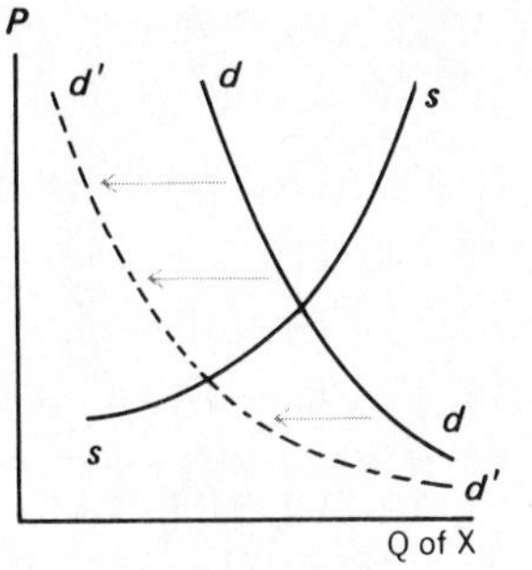

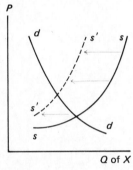

Figure 4-6

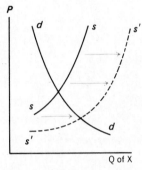

Figure 4-7

Figure 4-8

a. With respect to change in price, the result of each of the shifts indicated by these four figures would be:

(1) In Figure 4-5, *(an increase / a decrease)*.
(2) In Figure 4-6, *(an increase / a decrease)*.
(3) In Figure 4-7, *(an increase / a decrease)*.
(4) In Figure 4-8, *(an increase / a decrease)*.

b. Each of the seven events outlined below could reasonably be expected to change the position of the demand curve for commodity X, or the supply curve of X, or possibly both the demand and supply curves. That is, each event could be illustrated by one or more of Figures 4-5 through 4-8. Fit each event into one or more of these figures.

In answering, use "5" as an abbreviation for Figure 4-5, "6" for Figure 4-6, and so on. If you think that both the demand curve and the supply curve would shift by reason of the event in questions, answer by inserting two numbers.

The "leftward" and "rightward" shifts in these figures might equally have been shown as upward or downward; e.g., in Figure 4-8, we could equally well say that the supply curve has shifted upward to position *s's'*.

(1) Costs of manufacturing commodity X increase. ... ( )
(2) Consumer tastes shift away from X and in favor of other commodities. .... ( )
(3) The price of Y, another commodity that can readily be produced by the suppliers of X, rises considerably. .... ( )
(4) A recession reduces income of X buyers. .... ( )
(5) A widespread inflation increases both money incomes of X buyers and the costs of producing X. .... ( )
(6) The price of Y, another commodity which consumers regard as a good substitute for X, rises considerably. .. ( )

(7) The government removes a heavy tariff on imports of X so that foreign producers of X are now able to offer supplies on a domestic market. .... ( )

---

a. (1) an increase **(2)** a decrease **(3)** a decrease **(4)** an increase **b. (1)** 8 **(2)** 6 **(3)** 8 **(4)** 6 **(5)** 5 and 8 **(6)** 5 **(7)** 7 [Notes: As to item **b(3)** the higher price for Y will attract producers into production of Y, and so they will reduce their production of X. As to item **b(6)**: if Y is a substitute of X, then X is a substitute for Y, and consumers will switch their buying from Y to X.]

---

10. a. Fill in the blanks in Table 4-1 with

(1) the most appropriate graphical representation from among Figures 4-5 through 4-8
(2) an explanation of your answer to part **(1)**
(3) the direction that the equilibrium price would move (+ = up and − = down)
(4) the direction that the equilibrium quantity would move (same convention)

The first row of the table is filled in to help elucidate the directions.

b. In general, an increase in supply will *(lower / raise)* the equilibrium price and *(lower / raise)* the equilibrium quantity. A decrease in supply will *(lower / raise)* the price and *(lower / raise)* the quantity.

c. In general, an increase in demand will *(lower / raise)* the equilibrium price and *(lower / raise)* the equilibrium quantity. A decrease in demand will *(lower / raise)* the price and *(lower / raise)* the quantity.

---

a. Table 4-1, B: 4-8, production more expensive, +, −; C: 4-5, market size increased, +, +; D: 4-6, substitute out of X, −, −; E: 4-8, cost of production increased, +, −; F: 4-5, income increased, +, +; G: 4-7, cost of production diminished, −, + **b.** lower, raise, raise, lower **c.** raise, raise, lower, lower

---

Table 4-1

Change in Condition	(1) Figure	(2) Rationale	(3) Price	(4) Quantity
A Good X is clothing that has gone out of style.	4-6	change in taste moves *dd* in	−	−
B Pollution tax on supplier.	___	___	___	___
C Opening of market to foreign buyers.	___	___	___	___
D Price of substitute good falls.	___	___	___	___
E Market structure requires more advertising.	___	___	___	___
F A 10% across-the-board income tax cut.	___	___	___	___
G Robot makes production more efficient.	___	___	___	___

11. When either the demand or the supply curve shifts in position, things are thrown "out of equilibrium," and a new equilibrium price and quantity must be established. It is easy to draw supply and demand curves upon a page or blackboard, but the market does not have such pretty little diagrams laid out for its inspection. The market has to fumble its way toward its new equilibrium. Without knowing the curves, how does it get there? Question 5 has already touched upon this matter; now it is examined in a little more detail.

a. Figure 4-9 reproduces Figure 4-5; i.e., it depicts one possible shift in one of the two curves. Specifically, note the arrow and the new broken-line position. It shows (*an increase / a decrease*) in (*supply / demand*).

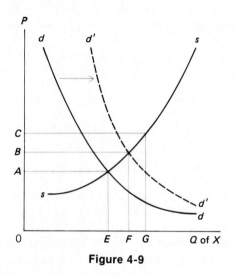

Figure 4-9

Before this change, equilibrium price was *AO*, and quantity bought and sold was *OE*. Now demand has increased—again, let's say, because of an increase in consumer incomes. At the *AO* price, buyers would now like to buy the larger quantity (*OE / OF / OG*). But this buyer wish does not match the supplier wish. To furnish this larger quantity in full, suppliers would require the price (*CO / BO / AO*). This in turn does not match consumer wishes. So the new equilibrium must be a compromise in which price is (*CO / BO / AO*) and quantity bought and sold is (*OE / OF / OG*). This compromise is the new equilibrium position.

b. How is this new equilibrium reached? What the market can discern, without the provision of supply and demand curves, is that at the old *AO* price, quantity demanded now (*exceeds / falls short of*) quantity supplied. Buyers find it (*difficult / easy*) to buy all they want to buy; suppliers find it (*difficult / easy*) to sell what they want to sell at the *AO* price. Thus, on both buying and selling sides, the pressure is toward a (*higher / lower*) price. This pressure persists so long as the price holds at any level at which quantity demanded exceeds quantity supplied. This disequilibrium pressure ends when—with the demand curve at its *d'd'* position—price reaches the level of (*CO / BO / AO*).

In the opposite situation—a decrease in demand or an

increase in supply—the mechanism just outlined works in reverse.

---

a. an increase, demand; *OG*; *CO*; *BO*; *OF*   **b.** exceeds; difficult; easy; higher; *BO*

---

12. Figures 4-10 and 4-11 show special cases of possible demand or supply curves: a horizontal line in Figure 4-10, a vertical line in Figure 4-11. As a demand or as a supply curve, what would such a line mean? (Never mind whether such a curve would be reasonable or not. The question is: What is the information which such a line would convey?)

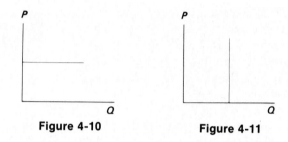

Figure 4-10   **Figure 4-11**

a. A demand curve indicating desire to buy some fixed quantity at any price (at least within the range of prices indicated by the length of the line drawn), but no intention whatever of buying any greater quantity; no matter how low price might fall, would be illustrated by Figure 4- (*10 / 11*).

b. A supply curve indicating that any quantity (at least up to the quantity indicated by the length of the line drawn) would be supplied at the indicated price, but no quantity at all at any lower price, would be illustrated by Figure 4- (*10 / 11*).

c. A demand curve indicating willingness to buy any quantity (at least up to the quantity indicated by the length of the line drawn) at the indicated price, but refusal to buy any quantity at any higher price, would be illustrated by Figure 4- (*10 / 11*).

d. A supply curve indicating willingness to supply some fixed quantity, regardless of price (even at zero price), but refusal to supply any greater quantity, no matter how high the price (at least within the range of prices indicated by the length of the line drawn), would be illustrated by Figure 4- (*10 / 11*).

---

a. 11   **b.** 10   **c.** 10   **d.** 11

---

13. This chapter explains how "equilibrium price" emerges at the intersection of "other things equal" demand and supply curves. Toward the chapter's close is a discussion of *general equilibrium*—which is distinguished from "partial equilibrium." How does this discussion relate to the principal topic of the chapter? (Pick one or more).

a. It is a reminder that prices are closely interrelated. It is useful to single out commodity X and explain its price in "partial-equilibrium" terms—that is, in terms of "other things equal" demand and supply curves. But in the real world, other things may not stay equal. The demand curve has many strings linking it to other elements in the economy; so has the supply curve. Hence we cannot think of X's price, and after that, Z's price—because the position of X's demand and/or supply curves may be influenced by what Y's price is, and so on.

b. It is a particular way of stating the fact that both supply and demand play their parts in price determination. Equilibrium price must be a "general" equilibrium in the sense that it strikes a balance between demand forces and supply forces.

c. It is an interesting statement about the manner of price determination, but it has no special significance as a warning with respect to topics discussed earlier in the chapter.

a. (b does not indicate correctly the meaning of "general equilibrium.")

14. Identify whether each of the following involves a shift in the demand curve or a change in the quantity demanded:

a. Auto sales rise as consumer incomes rise.

b. Fish prices fall after the Pope allows Catholics to eat meat on Friday.

c. A gasoline tax lowers the consumption of gasoline.

d. A disastrous wheat blight causes bread sales to fall.

e. The wheat blight causes peanut butter and jelly sales to fall.

a. demand curve shifts as income rises   **b.** must be a quantity demanded effect caused by an exaggerated supply response to the Pope's announcement   **c.** quantity demanded   **d.** quantity demanded; demand curve shifts as the price of complement good changes (refer to part **d**)

15. This question will explore your preliminary understanding of the notion of general equilibrium. In each, you are asked to trace the effects of some change in economic circumstances onto other markets. Are the following statements true or false and why?

a. Failure of Brazil's coffee crop will lower the prices of coffee, tea, lemon, and cream. _____

b. A fad for long skirts will lower the price of wool and raise the price of salt. _____

c. A new yen for meat will lower the prices of grain and raise the prices of hide and horn. _____

d. Development of the sugar beet raised the rents paid on tropical cane lands. _____

a. F; Failure means short supply, higher prices for coffee, higher prices for coffee substitutes (tea), and lower prices for coffee and tea complements (cream and lemon)   **b.** F; Longer skirts mean higher demand and thus higher prices for wool, but no effect on salt (unless skirts are a large portion of the consumers' budgets)   **c.** F; Higher demand for meat will increase the demand and thus the price of what cows eat (grain) but also increase the supply and thus lower the prices of joint products (hide and horns)   **d.** F; Sugar beets lowered the demand for cane sugar and thus the demand and the price paid for cane lands

The text identified three pitfalls of incorrect logic that must by avoided when we conduct supply-and-demand analysis of various markets. The first two are closely related: (1) care must be taken to remember what is being assumed constant and (2) care must be taken to determine whether the market adjustment to be studied shifts a demand, a supply curve, or does something else. If the adjustment occurs in one of the forces that is normally assumed to be held constant (income, tastes, other prices, etc. on the demand side and costs, technology, market structure, taxes, etc. on the supply side), then a shift in one schedule or the other is appropriate. The final pitfall warns us to remember that demand and supply curves reflect quantities that people are willing to purchase and supply, respectively, at any given price. Equilibrium will involve a single price, but demand and supply curves cover the entire domain of possible prices.

16.   a. Consider the following statement: "A simultaneous increase of demand and decrease of supply is statistically and logically impossible. Demand and supply are identically the same thing." Into which pitfall has the speaker fallen? _____ What would happen to equilibrium price and quantity and quantity if demand rose and supply fell at the same time? _____

b. Now consider Figure 4-12. What is the equilibrium price if *dd* and *ss* represent demand and supply schedules, respectively? .... Now let supply move to *s′ s′*. This represents a

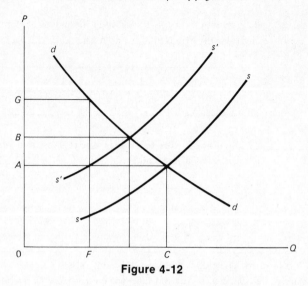

Figure 4-12

(contraction / expansion) of supply. Suppose that the government imposed a price ceiling at *OA* so that the price could not climb. The market clearing quantity would be _____ read from *(supply curve ss / supply curve s's' / demand curve dd)*.

There would be a *(shortage / surplus)* equal to _____

because the quantity demanded would be _____ read from *(supply curve ss / supply curve s's' / demand curve dd)*. If a black market arose for X in which people who possessed some of the good could sell it at an illegally high price, what price would clear the market? _____ What price would clear the

market if the government had not interfered? _____ What

would be the effect of the government's action? _____

_____

_____

a. All three. The speaker missed the interpretaiton that things normally held fixed must have changed requiring shifts in the demand and supply curves. The speaker also presumed that equilibrium always exists when price questions are answered by quantities along supply and demand curves   **b.** *OA*; contraction; *OF*; supply curve *s's'*; *FC*; *OC*; demand curve *dd*; *OG*; *OB*; a larger contraction in the quantity supplied than necessary, and a higher than necessary market clearing price

QUIZ: Multiple Choice

1. The following is a complete and correct definition of the demand curve for commodity X. (Select the best alternative.) It shows, for a given market:

(1) how much of X would be bought at the equilibrium price.

(2) how, as people's incomes rise and they have more money to spend, their purchases of X would increase and by how much.

(3) how the amount of money people spend to purchase X changes as the price they must pay for it changes.

(4) the amount of X that would be bought each period, at each and any price, assuming other factors influencing demand (income, tastes, etc.) remain constant.

(5) the amounts of X to be supplied in each period, at each and any price, assuming other factors influencing sale remain constant.

2. The law of downward-sloping demand says that:

(1) an excess supply over demand will cause a reduction in price.

(2) as people's incomes increase, they normally buy more of a commodity.

(3) when a demand schedule is illustrated graphically, it generally runs from northeast to southwest.

(4) when price falls, quantity bought normally increases.

(5) the quantity bought of any good will ultimately decline as it goes out of style or is replaced by something of better quality.

3. One reason given in the text for the law of downward-sloping demand is that:

(1) when the price of something we buy falls, we are slightly better off; it is as though our incomes have risen slightly, and so we buy a little more.

(2) most commodities over a sufficiently long period of time, tend to lose their markets in favor of newer and more attractive goods.

(3) the law of scarcity permits us to consume only so much of a commodity, no matter how much of it we may wish to have

(4) in the case of many commodities, a fall in price will bring in very few new buyers, or none at all.

(5) the producers of a given commodity will not offer any quantity for sale at all if its price falls below some critical level.

4. The government declares that it is prepared to purchase any and all gold supplied to it by domestic gold mines at a price of $500 an ounce. Which—if any—of the four diagrams within Figure 4-13 would illustrate this demand situation? (The labels *P* and *Q* on the axis lines refer respectively to price and to quantity.)

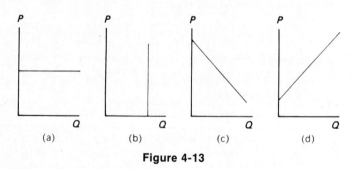

Figure 4-13

(1) *(a)*.

(2) *(b)*.

(3) *(c)*.

(4) *(d)*.

(5) None of them.

5. A patient must purchase some given quantity of a given drug (but not more than that quantity) and will pay any price, if necessary, in order to obtain it. Which—if any—of the four diagrams within Figure 4-13 could be used to illustrate this situation?

(1) (*a*).

(2) (*b*).

(3) (*c*).

(4) (*d*).

(5) None of them.

6. I can buy sugar in a supermarket at a fixed price of 90 cents per pound. This price applies to any quantity—1 pound, 5 pounds, 100 pounds. The store is so obliging that it will even sell me fractions of a pound at the same price per pound—e.g., 45 cents for a half-pound. Which—if any—of the four diagrams within Figure 4-13 can be used to illustrate this supply situation?

(1) (*a*).

(2) (*b*).

(3) (*c*).

(4) (*d*).

(5) None of them.

7. An increase in consumers' money incomes prompts them to demand a greater quantity of consumer good X. Which—if any—of the four diagrams within Figure 4-13 could be used to illustrate this situation?

(1) (*a*).

(2) (*b*).

(3) (*c*).

(4) (*d*).

(5) None of them.

8. At any given price, the producers of commodity X are willing to supply some given quantity. If they are to supply a larger quantity, they must be persuaded to do so through the offer of a higher price. Which—if any—of the four diagrams within Figure 4-13 can be used as shown to illustrate this situation?

(1) (*a*).

(2) (*b*).

(3) (*c*).

(4) (*d*).

(5) None of them.

9. Which—if any—of the four diagrams within Figure 4-13 could illustrate "the law of downward-sloping demand"?

(1) (*a*).

(2) (*b*).

(3) (*c*).

(4) (*d*).

(5) None of them.

10. If the demand curve for commodity X shifts its entire position to the left (or downward), one reasonable explanation for this shift would be:

(1) the available supply of X has for some reason decreased.

(2) the price of X has increased, and in consequence people have decided to buy less of it than they did before.

(3) consumer tastes have shifted in favor of this commodity, and they want to buy more of it than they did before at any given price.

(4) the price of X has fallen, and in consequence people have decided to buy more of it than they did before.

(5) none of these events.

11. Four of the five events described below might reasonably be expected to shift the demand curve for beef to a new position. One would not shift that demand curve. The single exception is:

(1) a rise in the price of some good which consumers regard as a substitute for beef.

(2) a fall in the price of beef.

(3) an increase in the money incomes of beef consumers.

(4) a widespread advertising campaign undertaken by the producers of a product competitive with beef (e.g., pork).

(5) a change in people's tastes with respect to beef.

12. The phrase "other things equal," or "others things constant" when applied to the demand for commodity X, means this:

(1) the price of X is held constant.

(2) both buyer incomes and the price of X are held constant.

(3) buyer incomes, tastes, and the price of X are held constant.

(4) all factors that might influence the demand for X, including the price of X, are held constant.

(5) none of the above.

13. An increase in the cost of materials needed to produce commodity X causes:

(1) the demand curve to move upward (or to the right).

(2) the supply curve to move upward (or to the left).

(3) both demand curve and supply curve to move upward.

(4) the supply curve to move downward (or to the right).

(5) none of the above—no reason why this change need occasion a shift of either curve.

14. In prosperous times, the price of commodity X may go up, and consumption of X may go up also. This situation:

(1) is one of the few recognized exceptions to the law of downward-sloping demand.

(2) is precisely what the law of downward-sloping demand says can be expected.

(3) is the consequence of a demand curve running from southwest to northeast.

(4) cannot be explained by means of ordinary supply-curve and demand-curve analysis.

(5) is not correctly described by any of the preceding.

15. Beef supplies are sharply reduced because of drought in the beef-raising states, and consumers turn to pork as a substitute for beef. In the beef market, this would be described, in supply-and-demand terms, as:

(1) a leftward (or downward) shift in the demand curve.

(2) a leftward (or upward) shift in the supply curve.

(3) a rightward (or upward) shift in the demand curve.

(4) a rightward (or downward) shift in the supply curve.

(5) both a leftward (or downward) shift in the demand curve and a leftward (or upward) shift in the supply curve.

16. Which alternative in question 15 would be correct with respect to the events described, had that question referred to the pork market?

(1).

(2).

(3).

(4).

(5).

17.   If the price of a good is $5 (in a competitive market), and if at that price buyers wish to purchase 4000 units weekly and sellers wish to sell 5000 units weekly, then.

(1) price will tend to fall below $5 and suppliers will tend to offer less than 5000 units.

(2) price will tend to rise above $5 and suppliers will tend to offer more than 5000 units.

(3) price will tend to fall below $5 and buyers will tend to buy less than 4000 units.

(4) price will tend to rise above $5 and suppliers will tend to offer less than 5000 units.

(5) something is wrong—this could not occur in a competitive market.

18.   Supply curves are typically "positively sloped"—i.e., they run approximately between southwest and northeast. The meaning conveyed by any such curve is this:

(1) any increase in costs of production will result in a higher price.

(2) the lower the price, the larger the supply that consumers are prepared to buy.

(3) the higher the price, the larger the quantity suppliers will wish to sell.

(4) the larger the quantity suppliers have to sell, the lower the price they will have to quote in order to dispose of it.

(5) none of the preceding.

PART TWO

MACROECONOMICS:
FLUCTUATIONS OF
OUTPUT AND PRICES

CHAPTER 5

OVERVIEW OF MACROECONOMICS: AGGREGATE SUPPLY AND DEMAND

The study of macroeconomics is the study of the "big picture." It is the study of how entire economies move through time. It ponders the sources of growth, inflation, unemployment, and business cycles. It ponders the ability of governments to help (or hinder) their economies by manipulating any of a number of macroeconomic policy instruments. It wonders why some policies work and why some fail. It wonders why the same policy works sometimes and not others. It wonders how to assess this success, and it is frustrated that many policy objectives seem to be mutually incompatible— objectives that are admirable when considered on their face value, but which are damaging to other objectives of debatably equal importance when pursued too strenuously.

Having completed your work on this overview, you will not have many answers. You will, instead, have collected a multitude of questions whose answers will be addressed over the course of the next 13 chapters. Your working through this list of questions without answers will not, however, be an exercise in futility. In noting the significance and the context of each, you will have accomplished the following objectives even without the answers.

LEARNING OBJECTIVES

1. Identify the major goals of macroeconomic policy: output, employment, price stability, and foreign-trade balance.

2. Identify the major policy instruments available to the macroeconomic policymaker: fiscal policy (spending and taxes), monetary policy, incomes policies, foreign-trade policies.

3. Recognize the existence of tradeoffs between policy objectives (e.g., price stability versus high employment, rapid growth versus present consumption, etc.).

4. Note two or three major events in the history of active governmental macroeconomic policy.

5. Understand the difference between policy, exogenous, and endogenous variables.

6. Understand the difference between the short run and long run, particularly in the context of the determinants of potential and actual output.

7. Understand the basics of aggregate supply and aggregate demand and apply them to illustrate the distinction between the long run and the short run, potential sources of stagflation, and accommodative policy.

There are four major goals of economic policy: high output, high employment, price stability, and foreign balance. The first four questions will deal with each one in turn.

1. Output is usually denoted by gross national product, its most comprehensive measure. GNP is the *(market / discounted / stable)* value of all goods and services produced during any given year. When measured at current prices, this measure is termed *(nominal / real / potential)* GNP. When measured after correcting for inflation, it is termed *(nominal / real / potential)* GNP. When measured in terms of high employment, it is termed *(nominal / real / potential)* GNP. The correct measure for the target for high employment upon which this last measure is based *(is / is not)* 0 percent unemployment. It is based upon the notion of the natural rate of unemployment that is currently around *(0 percent / 6 percent / 7.5 percent)*. During the 1970s, periods of high inflation caused real GNP to *(exceed potential GNP / exceed nominal GNP / fall short of nominal GNP)*. Periods of high unemployment during the same decade caused nominal GNP to *(exceed potential GNP / fall short of potential GNP / fall short of real GNP)*.

---

market; nominal; real; potential; is not; 6 percent; fall short of nominal GNP; fall short of potential GNP

2. The objective of high employment is usually conceptualized from the other side of the coin: the objective of a low rate of unemployment. The rate of unemployment has, on average since 1950, *(climbed from / fallen from / remained steady at)* roughly _____ percent. From 1950 to 1970, this pattern persisted despite a *(falling / growing / constant)* rate of labor-force participation *(at roughly 60 percent / through 60 percent by 1970)*. Since 1970, this picture *(has / has not)* changed. In that decade, participation rates *(fell / rose / remained steady)*.

---

climbed from; 3 to 4 percent; constant; at roughly 60 percent; has; rose (to almost 65 percent)

3. Price stability, as a goal of macroeconomic policy, does not mean absolute stability of all prices. Absolute stability would eliminate the natural role of changes in relative prices in allocating goods and services. Price stability is, instead, an objective stated in terms of a price index like the *(DAR / CIA / CPI)* that *(ignores price movement across goods and services / averages price movement across goods and services / weights only price increases across goods and services)*. Inflation, then, is measured as *(the rate of change in the index / the absolute value of the price index / the absolute price levels of a representative number of goods)*. In the last decade, inflation peaked in *(1973 and 1979 / 1972 and 1973 / 1973 and 1976)* because of *(energy-price increases / wage increases tied to the cost of living / shortages of agricultural goods)*.

CPI; averages price movements across goods and services; the rate of change in the index; 1973 and 1979; all the above

4. Stability in external economic affairs is the last major goal. It is important because disruptions in import and export markets disrupt not only mutually beneficial international markets, but also domestic, internal markets. A highly valued dollar in the early 1980s caused a higher rate of *(inflation / unemployment / growth)* and a lower rate of *(inflation / unemployment / growth)* in the United States that would have otherwise been observed. The source of these changes was a *(decline / expansion / explosion)* in the U.S. exporting sector.

---

unemployment; inflation and growth; decline

5. Policy tools available to the policymaker are varied. They fall under four general rubrics: fiscal policy (FP), monetary policy (MP), incomes policy (IP), and trade policy (TP). In the spaces provided, match each of the following more specific policy with its general classification; use the abbreviations noted in parentheses to signify your answer.

a. federal income taxes .... _____

b. increase in the money supply .... _____

c. tariff on German cars .... _____

d. tax penalty on high wage settlements .... _____

e. domestic content legislation that specifies a minimum percentage of domestically produced inputs that must be used in production .... _____

f. higher defense spending .... _____

g. interest-rate deduction against taxable income .. _____

a. FP **b.** MP **c.** TP **d.** IP **e.** TP **f.** FP **g.** FP

6. The text notes that the Employment Act of 1946 had some positive effect on the ability of the United States to achieve stability in its macroeconomic circumstance and that the Humphrey-Hawkins Bill of 1978 did not. Explain this statement in light of Figure 5-1, in which annual rates of growth in GNP are plotted for the United States from 1901 to the mid-1970's.

The variation in the rate of growth has declined markedly since 1946—the year in which Congress declared that government would take an active role in trying to steer the macroeconomy of the United States

Figure 5-2 plots unemployment against inflation for two periods of recent experience: 1960–1969 and 1976–1979. One issue of some current debate among macroeconomists is whether or not these and other points display enough evidence to support the existence of what is known as a Phillips curve. If they do not, then the proposed tradeoff between inflation and unemployment is cast under a shadow of doubt. If they do, then certain issues of policy and the contradictory nature of high employment and price stability are clarified. The next question will explore this doubt by noting not one, but two tradeoff curves among the points of Figure 5-2.

7. Draw a smooth line that connects the points from 1960 through 1969. Above 4 percent unemployment, each percentage point of increased unemployment seems to be associated with a(n) *(reduction / increase)* of inflation of *(5 / .5 / 0)* percentage points. Below 4 percent unemployment, each reduction of unemployment of one percentage point seems to be associated with a(n) *(reduction / increase)* in inflation of *(5 / .5 / 0)* percentage points. The natural rate of unemployment in the 1960s—the rate of unemployment below which the economy of the United States could not fall without experiencing significantly higher inflation—was therefore around *(2 percent / 4 percent / 8 percent)*.

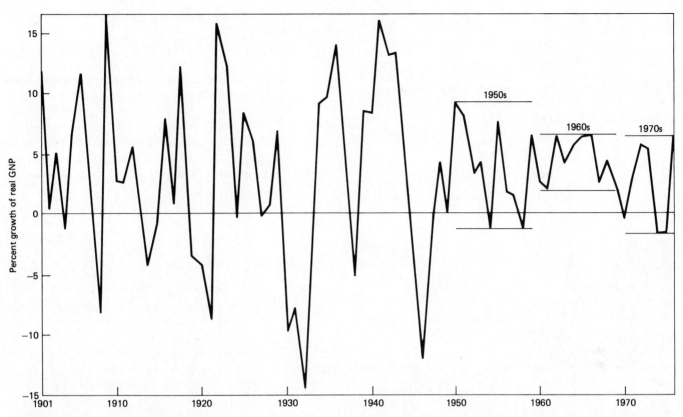

Figure 5-1 (Source: M. N. Baily: Stabilization Policy and Private Economic Behavior, *Brookings Papers on Economic Activity,* vol. 1, 1978.)

Now draw a line through the 1976–1979 points. Inflation rates associated with 3.5 percent unemployment in the 1960s were associated with unemployment rates of *(3.5 percent / 6 percent / 10 percent)* in the late 1970s. The tradeoff *(had / had*

not) worsened. The natural rate of unemployment had climbed to approximately *(4 percent / 6 percent / 8 percent)*. Meanwhile, the curve to the right of the natural rate had apparently *(grown steeper / grown much flatter / remained sloped as before)*, signifying that increases in unemployment had apparently *(become more / become less / remained equally)* effective in slowing inflation.

---

reduction; .5; increase; 5; 4 percent; 6 percent; had; 6 percent; grown steeper; become more

8. Which of the following are policy variables (*P*), exogenous variables (*EX*) that may shock the economy from beyond its confines, and endogenous variables (*EN*) that are determined by the economy. Identify each by recording the appropriate abbreviation in the spaces provided.

a. money supply . . . . _____

b. wars . . . . _____

c. the price level . . . . _____

d. government spending . . . . _____

e. sunspots . . . . _____

f. population growth . . . . _____

g. imports . . . . _____

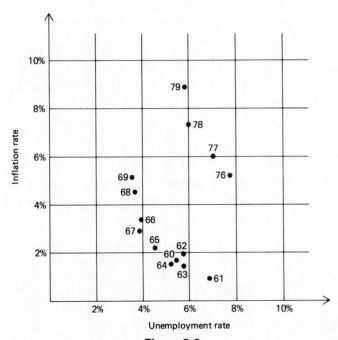

Figure 5-2

h. tax deductions .... _____

i. interest rates .... _____

j. employment levels .... _____

a. *P* **b.** *EX* **c.** *EN* **d.** *P* **e.** none of the above (they do not affect economies) **f.** *EX* **g.** *EN* **h.** *P* **i.** *EN* (though some might argue that they are policy variables) **j.** *EN*

9.   The text makes a careful distinction between the long run and the short run. In the long run, the performance of the economy is determined primarily by the sources of growth in (*nominal / real / potential*) GNP. In the short run, the economy is determined primarily by (*imports / spending / exogenous variables*). Identify each of the following variables as determinants primarily of either the short run (SR) or the long run (LR) by recording the appropriate abbreviation in the spaces provided.

a. labor growth .... _____

b. oil prices .... _____

c. availability of resources .... _____

d. fiscal policy .... _____

e. rate of growth of technology .... _____

f. monetary policy .... _____

Short-run performance is measured in terms of (*actual GNP / unemployment / inflation*).

potential; spending (though exogenous shocks do play some role); **a.** LR **b.** SR **c.** LR **d.** SR **e.** LR **f.** SR all the above (each of the variables recorded in the numbered list has impacts in both the long and the short runs; the answers indicate the arena of the larger effect)

Aggregate supply and demand curves are presented in the text to apply the tools of Chapter 4 to the workings of the macroeconomy. They have the familiar axes of price and quantity, but these terms take on new meaning in a macro setting. The quantity measured is not the quantity of some particular good; it is, instead, the total quantity of goods and services produced across the economy. It is, in short, GNP. The price is not the unit cost of purchasing some particular good; it is, instead, a price index reflecting the overall level of prices across the economy. It is, in short, something like the CPI.

These changes in the interpretations of the axes mean that the curves, while they have familiar shapes, assume those shapes for different reasons, too. The *AD* curve is, on the one hand, downward-sloping not because of tastes and budget constraints, but because of an asymmetry in the effect of lower prices on goods and assets. As prices fall, assets become more valuable, people feel wealthier, and they therefore want to buy more stuff—they demand more.

The *AS* curve, on the other hand, is upward-sloping in the short run only because higher prices for final products make increasing output a profitable enterprise until input prices catch up. When input prices eventually climb in the long run to keep up with output prices, however, that enterprise loses its appeal, output is contracted, and the curve becomes vertical at the level of potential output. The following two questions will explore the application of *AS* and *AD* to questions of policy and implication.

10.   Figure 5-3 uses aggregate supply and demand to illustrate four possible reactions, in the short run, to changes in the macroeconomic environment. In each panel, *AD* and *AS* represent initial positions of aggregate demand and aggregate supply, respectively. In panels (a) and (b), *AS'* represents a new position; in panels (c) and (d), *AD'* represents a new position. In Table 5-1, record in column (2) the letter identification of the panel in Figure 5-3 that most appropriately illustrates the change noted in column (1). Note in columns (3) and (4) the direction of the effect on the price level and GNP, respectively; (+) should signify an increase and (−) should signify a reduction.

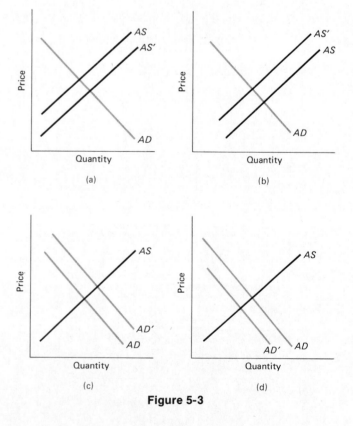

Figure 5-3

Table 5-1
Changes in the Macroeconomic Evnironment

Condition (1)	Panel (2)	Price (3)	Output (4)
A. Increase in defense spending	_____	_____	_____
B. Sudden energy crisis	_____	_____	_____
C. Large cut in personal taxes	_____	_____	_____
D. Increase in interest rates	_____	_____	_____
E. Large reduction in government taxation of inputs	_____	_____	_____

For the changes indicated in rows A, C, and D, passing to the long run would cause *(the price effect / the output effect / neither effect)* just noted for the short run to be exaggerated.

Reading across the rows of the table: A: c; +; + B: b; +; − C: c; +; + D: d; −; − E: a; −; + the price effect (because the long-run supply curve is vertical)

11. Suppose that Figure 5-4 were to illustrate the short-run effect of a sudden energy shock. *AD* represents the preshock aggregate demand curve, (*AS₁* / *AS₂*) represents the preshock aggregate supply curve, and (*AS₁* / *AS₂*) represents the post-

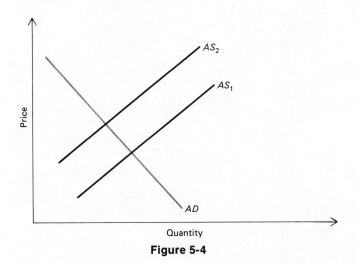

Figure 5-4

shock aggregate supply curve. *(An increase / A decrease / No change)* in aggregate demand would be required in the short run to accommodate the shock and keep output at its preshock level. If this accommodation were kept in place in the long run, however, the appropriate shift in the aggregate supply curve would be to *(leave a vertical supply curve unchanged / shift a short-run supply curve back down)*, and the accommodation just prescribed would produce the *(increase / reduction)* in prices that it was intended to avoid.

AS₁; AS₂; An increase; leave a vertical supply curve unchanged; increase

QUIZ: Multiple Choice

1. The study of macroeconomics includes, among other topics, which of the following?
(1) The sources of inflation, unemployment, and growth.
(2) The microeconomic foundations of aggregate behavior.
(3) Reasons why some economies succeed and some fail.
(4) Policies that can be enacted to improve the likelihood of success.
(5) All the above.

2. The practice of directing policy to support the macro-economic health of the United States was initiated formally in:
(1) the Humphrey-Hawkins Act of 1978.
(2) the Nixon wage-and-price controls.
(3) the Full Employment and Balanced Growth Act of 1946.
(4) the election of FDR in 1932.
(5) none of the above.

3. The objective of stable prices can, in the view of at least some of the world's economists, be tackled by adjustments in:
(1) fiscal policy.
(2) monetary policy.
(3) incomes policies.
(4) all the above.
(5) none of the above.

4. Policies directed at stimulating exports can influence:
(1) the employment picture.
(2) price stability.
(3) growth of actual GNP relative to potential GNP.
(4) the foreign-trade balance.
(5) all the above.

5. Which of the following pairs of objectives seem to be mutually contradictory?
(1) Low inflation and low unemployment.
(2) Low unemployment and high rates of growth in actual GNP.
(3) High rates of growth in actual GNP and balance in the foreign-trade balance.
(4) Price stability and balance in the foreign-trade balance.
(5) Price stability and rapid growth in potential GNP.

6. The aggregate supply curve is positively sloped in the short run because of:
(1) increasing costs of production.
(2) decreasing returns to scale.
(3) uneven short-run distributions of high output prices and high input prices.
(4) the potential for high unemployment.
(5) none of the above.

7. The aggregate supply curve is vertical in the long run because:
(1) wealth effects in the quantity demanded cancel out.
(2) it is determined by potential output.
(3) of decreasing returns to scale in the extreme.
(4) of policy adjustments that constrain total output below a certain level.
(5) of the Phillips curve tradeoff.

8. Unemployment, inflation, and the rate of growth of actual GNP are all examples of
(1) policy variables.
(2) exogenous variable.
(3) international variables.
(4) endogenous variables.
(5) none of the above

9. Which of the following is a determinant of potential output in the long run?
(1) Taxes.
(2) Money.
(3) Technology.
(4) Tax penalties for excessive wage demands.
(5) War in the Persian Gulf.

10. The effect of increased defense spending that is not accommodated by increased taxation could be:
(1) higher prices and higher GNP.
(2) higher prices and lower GNP.
(3) lower prices and lower GNP.
(4) lower prices and higher GNP.
(5) lower prices and the same GNP.

11. Accommodation of the OPEC oil shock would have:
(1) preserved prices and GNP.
(2) preserved output with higher prices.
(3) increased output with lower prices.
(4) lowered domestic oil prices.
(5) none of the above.

12. The orchestrated rise in interest rates in the United States in the early 1980s can be illustrated in an *AS-AD* graph by:
(1) a shift upward of the *AS* curve.
(2) a shift downward in the *AS* curve.
(3) a shift upward in the *AD* curve.
(4) a shift downward in the *AD* curve.
(5) no shift in either the *AD* or *AS* curve.

CHAPTER 6
MEASURING NATIONAL OUTPUT

This chapter is important. It must be approached carefully and patiently. You will, however, discover that there is really only one basic idea being presented here. It is surrounded by a sequence of complications, to be sure, but the point of this chapter is singular: the accounting procedure with which a nation measures its total output in any one year is to add up the market value of all the goods and services that it produces. This procedure will be presented here in its simplest form before each of the complications will be confronted in sequence and alone. Taken together, the complications look imposing and impenetrable; taken individually, they can be handled.

National-income accounting is concerned with one basic notion: The computation of an economy's national product is defined to be the measure of that nation's total output for 1 year. Every nation uses its limited stock of labor, machines, and materials to produce commodities and services. The money value of the resulting mix of total output valued at the market price for which each component is sold (or would have been sold) constitutes the national product for the period—the year in question. You should ignore the difficulties that are certainly involved in a computational exercise of this magnitude. Your job is not to do the counting. Your job, instead, is to understand the rules that govern the counting. Having completed your work in this chapter, you will have achieved the objectives listed below. Without this achievement, you will find it almost impossible to understand what economists mean when they talk about growth, unemployment, and inflation.

LEARNING OBJECTIVES

1. Describe briefly what each of the following concepts is intended to measure: (*a*) gross national product, (*b*) net national product, (*c*) national income, (*d*) disposable income.

2. Explain why net national product and national income are (almost) identical, or "two sides of the same coin." State the one element that results in a difference between them, in the statistics.

3. List the three types of production that make up gross or net investment.

4. List the four items that must be subtracted from national income in moving from this measure toward disposable income.

5. List the three items that must be added to national income in moving from this measure toward disposable income.

6. Explain the distinction between "real and money GNP," recognizing the fact that all GNP figures are unavoidably money figures. Describe the process of "deflating" a money GNP.

7. Explain why there is a danger of "double counting" in the estimation of GNP or NNP, and how the "value-added" approach avoids this danger.

1. Suppose, for example, that the national output consists of only two commodities: X, a consumer good, and Y, a capital good (some form of machine or tool needed in production). In 1980, just 500 units of X were produced and sold to consumers at a price of $2. Twenty units of Y were produced and sold to business firms, at a price of $10. Then the national product for 1980 would be $(*500 / 800 / 1000 / 1200 / 1500 / 2000*).

1200

2. This figure is *gross national product.* To produce this total output, the nation's existing stock of capital goods must have been to some extent used up or worn out during the year—that is, depreciated. Suppose the nation began the year with a stock of 100 Y machines (assuming, for simplicity, that there is just one kind of capital good involved). By the year's end, some few of these machines, the oldest, will have become completely worn out. And all the others will have moved just a little closer to the scrap heap.

Suppose the best possible estimate of this 1980 depreciation (still using the question 1 example) is $50. There is no cash expenditure by the producing firm in question in a depreciation figure; it is just an estimate of the extent of "wearing out" during the year. With the price of a new Y machine being $10, it is *as though* 5Y machines, brand new at the year's beginning, had been completely worn out by the year's end in the production of 1980 national product.

The 1980 national-product figure of $1200 included the value of the 20 new Y machines produced. But to make these machines, and to make also the 500 units of consumer good X, the equivalent of 5 new Y machines was totally used up. So the nation was not "better off" at the year's end by 20 machines— only by *(5 / 10 / 15)* machines.

With *gross* meaning "no allowance for depreciation," and *net* meaning "after allowance for depreciation," then this nation's gross national product (GNP) for 1980 was $1200, and its *net national product* (NNP) was $*(1000 / 1050 / 1100 / 1150 / 1200)*.

In the statistics for national product and national income, the phrase *capital consumption allowance* may be used instead of the word "depreciation."

15; 1150

These first two questions have identified two fundamental measures of national income:

▶Gross national product (GNP) is a measure of the total output of goods and services produced in a given time period, usually 1 year, all valued at their market prices, without any allowance for depreciation.

▶Net national product (NNP) is GNP minus a suitable allowance for depreciation (capital consumption).

3.   There are certain distinctions that are made among the goods that comprise either GNP or NNP. The most basic of these distinctions is the division between (*a*) goods that were produced to be consumed during the year in question and (*b*) goods that were produced during the year not to be consumed but to be additions to the existing stock of capital. This is precisely the difference noted in question 1 with X representing a consumption good and Y representing an investment good.

The consumption-goods total is the same figure in both GNP and NNP. The investment-goods figure in GNP is gross investment: total production of new capital goods without depreciation allowance. The investment figure in NNP is net investment: value of new capital goods produced after a deduction for depreciation. In the example above, the GNP of $1200 would divide between consumption of $*(200 / 800 / 1000 / 1150 / 1200)* and gross investment of $*(zero / 100 / 150 / 200 / 250 / 300)*. The NNP of $1150 would divide between consumption of $*(200 / 800 / 1000 / 1500 / 1200)* and net investment of $*(zero / 100 / 150 / 200 / 250 / 300)*.

There are one or two other important divisions of the GNP and NNP totals. In particular, we must recognize that both

also include a "government purchases" figure (the same figure in both). Such matters can be set aside just long enough to gain a little more overall perspective on national-product and national-income measures.

1000; 200; 1000; 150

Like all developed nations, the United States relies overwhelmingly on the price-and-market mechanism. The commodities and services produced normally reach consumers by being sold for a market price. Indeed, that is what makes possible single dollar-value totals for GNP and NNP. In less developed countries, though, many goods do not pass through a market pricing mechanism. The value of these goods must be estimated, therefore, and the money figures for GNP and NNP in these countries are necessarily subject to more uncertainty; they are simply made less precise by the absence of markets. Even in developed economies, precise measurement is impossible. Why? Because even in developed countries like the United States there are many goods and services that do not pass through a pricing mechanism.

Two notatable examples of this type of good or service come to mind easily:

1.   "Social" or "public" goods purchased or produced by an agency of the government and provided to the population are frequently not sold in the marketplace. People pay for them, instead, by paying their taxes, and it is hard to measure their value. How much is a submarine worth? In terms of its contribution to national defense, who knows? We know only how much it costs to build and operate.

2.   A housewife supplies her family members with goods and services of great value. But ordinarily, even on her more difficult days, she does not think of charging a market price for each service that she furnishes.

To master the basics of national-income accounting, though, it is best to set these and other exceptions aside and to concentrate instead on the easy cases—the cases in which each and every good and service supplied is given a money price in a market and supplied through that market according to that price.

The price of any such item is the exact amount available for dividing up among all those who helped to produce and sell it. Because incomes are earned by making some contribution to production, the total value of what is produced ought to be the total value of incomes earned—the value of *national income*. Hence:

▶To a first approximation, net national product is also national income. The two figures are opposite sides of the same coin.

We must say "to a first approximation," because a particular kind of government taxation causes the national-product and national-income totals to differ slightly. But we have been setting aside the complications produced by government. And with such complications removed, NNP will equal national income (*NI*).

This idea needs fuller development. There are just five earning categories within *NI*:

1. Wages and salaries—by far the biggest item.
2. Interest paid by business. (Anyone who has helped to finance a producing firm by lending it money is considered as having contributed to production. The amount of interest paid by the producing firm to the lender is the amount of income earned by that lender.)
3. Rental income—received by supplying land or other property to producing firms. The principle here is the same as with interest payments.
4. Profit remaining after paying wages and salaries, interest, and rents, consisting of:
   a. Corporation profits (belonging to corporation shareholders).
   b. Profits from unincorporated businesses— what the statisticians call "proprietors' income."

GNP and NNP can thus be computed (with the government still set aside) as either the sum of the total output produced and supplied to someone by business firms or equivalently the total amount of money that these firms had to pay for their factors of production. This is the point of Figure 6-2 of the text, reproduced here as Figure 6-1. "Business firm," in this context, simply means anything from an enormous corporation to a single individual with a tiny business in his or her garage. Each firm will, in the course of business, record its total sales for a given year on an income statement where it will be balanced by its payments in wages, salaries, interest, material costs, and so on (see the Appendix to Chap-

ter 20 for a more complete description of income statements; the simple ones presented here are sufficient for our present purposes). The income statement is thus the business-level equivalent of the national-income account. It is useful, as a result, to examine that relationship: the similarities between GNP, NNP, *NI*, and the ordinary income statement.

4. **a.** A firm's income statement begins with the value of its sales for a given period—say, year 1980, sales amount $800. All costs incurred in making and selling these goods are then listed: depreciation, wages and salaries, interest paid, rents paid. Suppose depreciation to be $25, and the total of the other three items $650. What's left after deducting all such costs from the sales total is profit—in this instance, $(*zero / 25 / 50 / 75 / 100 / 125 / 150*).

The initial sales figure of $800 was this firm's contribution to GNP. Deduct depreciation, and its NNP contribution is $(*700 / 725 / 750 / 775*). The *NI* figure is the total of wages and salaries, interest paid, and profit remaining. So the *NI* figure here is $(*700 / 725 / 750 / 775*). Hence *NI* is (*less than / equal to / greater than*) NNP.

b. Notice that profit is the residual item which makes things come out even. Had our firm paid out wages, interest, and rents totaling $775, its profit (allowing for depreciation) would have been $(*zero / 25 / 50 / 70 / 100*). *NI* would (*still / no longer*) be $775. That is, *NI*, would (*still / no longer*) equal NNP.

---

a. 125; 775; 775; equal to **b.** zero; still; still

Our first rapid survey of the national-income and -product accounts is completed. Various complications remain to be recognized—mostly arising out of government expenditure and taxation. With all such government items set aside, what has been said is summarized in Figure 6-1. Its three columns correspond to the three measures discussed: GNP, NNP, and *NI*. The GNP column divides between "Gross investment" and "Consumption"; NNP between "Net investment" and "Consumption"; and *NI* divides into the five income categories. NNP differs from GNP only by the measure of depreciation. *NI* is exactly the same as NNP—although when we come to recognize taxation, we shall find that one set of taxes causes *NI* to fall short of NNP, just as (because of depreciation) NNP falls short of GNP.

Study Figure 6-1 and the preceding material until you feel you have a fair grasp of the ideas involved. We turn now to the complications that you need to master. They can seem painfully difficult unless you recognize them for what they are: adjustments required (most of them fairly small) to make the basic idea work in practice.

Figure 6-2 is an extended version of Figure 6-1. You have already mastered almost half of this larger (and seemingly involved) diagram: its three left-hand columns

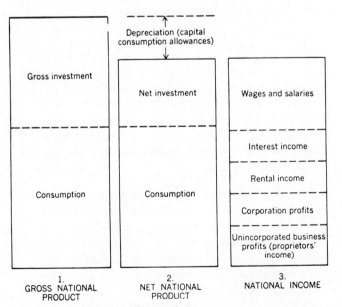

Figure 6-1

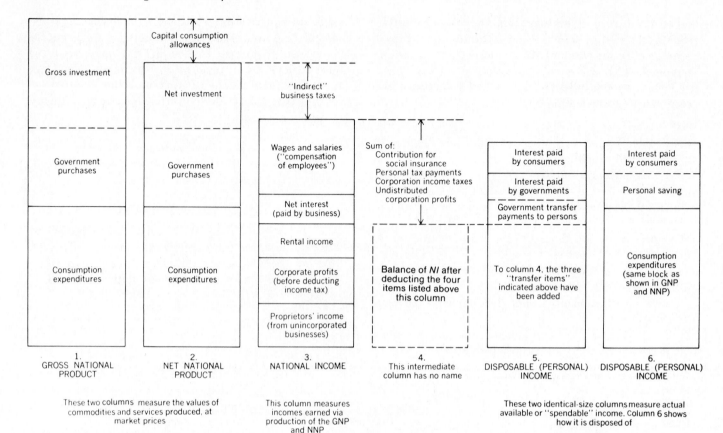

Figure 6-2

correspond to those of Figure 6-1—save for only two changes: GNP and NNP now include a "Government purchases" block, and *NI* now falls short of NNP by reason of "'Indirect' business taxes."

5. a. All goods and services purchased for the public through the agency of government (federal, state, or local) count in GNP and NNP—assuming they were produced within the year in question. Many such goods will have gone through the market system in that they were produced by a private firm and sold to a government. Except for a few items like *(national defense / post office services)*—they are not sold to the public for a price per unit. They are "social goods"; the public *(gets them entirely free / pays for them via taxation)*.

b. All these goods and services enter the GNP and NNP totals valued at the price the goverment pays for them. A judge's legal services are valued at the salary paid that judge; the production of a new typewriter is valued at the price the government paid the typewriter-manufacturing firm.

Incomes earned via production of such government-purchased goods and services are *(counted / not counted)* in *NI*: as the GNP and NNP columns grow by reason of goverment purchases, the *NI* column *(grows also / does not grow)*.

You can well argue that GNP and NNP do not need this third

component, since every cent of "Government purchases" should count either as consumption (e.g., services furnished by a police officer in protecting the public) or as investment (e.g., construction and purchase of some long-lived item like a new highway). But the "Government-purchases" category is kept separate, because government statistics are not kept in a way that makes a meaningful division between consumption and investment within this category possible.

c. For inclusion in GNP and NNP, there must be a good or a service currently produced. Hence, one important category of federal expenditure (and to a lesser degree, of state and local expenditure) is not included: payments under the Social Security program and other "transfer payments" through which the government takes money from some people and gives it to others. The recipient of such a transfer payment, by definition *(must give something / does not give anything)* concurrently in return.

d. Suppose that, in addition to the $1200 in private purchases of question 1, we had to recognize government expenditure on goods and services totaling $400, and health and welfare expenditures (payments made to social security beneficiaries) of $100. If depreciation were still $50, then GNP would now be $*(1200 / 1250 / 1550 / 1600 / 1700)*, and NNP would be $*(1200 / 1250 / 1550 / 1600 / 1650)*. The required increase (from the original GNP of 1200) would be *(GNP only / GNP and NNP, not NI / all of GNP, NNP, and NI)*, and the amount of this increase would be $*(100 / 400 / 500)*.

---

a. post office services; pays for them via taxation **b.** counted; grows also **c.** does not give anything **d.** 1600; 1550; all of GNP, NNP, and *NI*; 400

6. Consider now the " 'Indirect' business taxes" which, in Figure 6-2 cause *NI* to fall short of NNP.

There are two kinds of taxes. One is epitomized by the personal income tax. It is levied on, and paid out of, income; and there is little doubt that the burden of this tax rests on the person who must pay it. There are, however, other taxes whose burdens are not as easily defined. Consider, for example, a property tax levied on a business's buildings or land. Is this tax ultimately paid by the owners of that business, through a reduction in the profits that they earn? Probably not. It is far more likely, though not certain, that at least some of the tax is paid by the firm's customers through an increase in the price charged by the firm. What about the excise tax on cigarettes once advocated by Reagan Budget Director David Stockman? He argued from experience that a smoker would pay the tax and not reduce his or her habit. The cigarette manufacturer might collect the tax, but the consumer would pay most of it if Mr. Stockman were right.

The important point here is that the items entering into GNP and NNP are valued at market price. Most taxes levied on business—property taxes, excise taxes—almost certainly do elbow their way into market price, at least in part. The GNP and NNP totals are intended as the measure of a certain volume of real production, valued at its market price. This market-price value must *(be less than / exceed)* the total of money incomes earned from that volume of real production, because of the business taxes which work their way into market price. Apart from depreciation, already taken account of in NNP, it is almost exactly correct to say that such "indirect taxes" mark the only difference between the dollar value of what is produced and the dollar total of what is earned. ("Almost exactly correct," and not "exactly correct," because if you look in the *Survey of Current Business*, the monthly publication in which the Commerce Department reports all the national-product and -income figures, you will find three small items which differentiate *NI* from NNP.[1] They are of minor importance, and should be disregarded completely in a first approach to this detail-filled subject.)

---

[1]They are:

a. The "statistical discrepancy." The Commerce Department collects its figures from both production and earnings sides; they do not come out exactly equal. Considering the obvious difficulties in collecting complete and accurate data, it is remarkable that this discrepancy should be so small in comparison with the totals involved.

b. "Business transfer payments," to make an allowance for such things as uncollectible debts.

c. "Subsidies less current surplus of government enterprises," an adjustment needed because of such things as the post office, where the price charged for services does not necessarily match the cost of providing those services.

The national-income statisticians count any tax levied on a business firm—with one important exception—as an "indirect business tax" which marks a difference between total NNP and total *NI*. Such taxes are assumed to be "shifted" by the business firm, via an increase in market price.

The one important exception is the corporation income (profits) tax. This is treated as a tax *not* shifted, as a tax on shareholder income.[2] Hence it *(is / is not)* included among the "indirect business taxes."

---

exceed; is not

National income is a useful concept. For example, the figures within it will give you at least a rough comparison between the total of incomes earned through personal effort and the total of those obtained through ownership of property. But for many purposes, national income is less interesting than *disposable income:*

▶Disposable income is a measure of the total incomes which people can actually dispose of (spend or save) as they wish.

In strict Department of Commerce terminology, it is "disposable personal income" *(DPI)*. But it has become customary to abbreviate this, as the text does, to "disposable income" *(DI)*.

National income (*NI*) and disposable income (*DI*) are closely related, but they differ for two basic reasons:

(1) National income is total earned income. Your take-home pay (which is pretty much the idea that "disposable income" seeks to convey) will be less than your total earnings. There will be several deductions from your wage or salary check. All major deductions of this nature must be subtracted from the *NI* total in order to reach *DI*.

(2) National income includes only earned income. There may exist some money payments that contribute to spendable income but which are not payments for having helped to make some part of the national product. These payments are not included in *NI;* they must be added to *NI* if we want to reach *DI*.

Unfortunately, there are (in all) no less than seven of these adjustments to make: four subtractions (question 7), and three additions (question 8).

7. The four required deductions are listed above column 4 in Figure 6-2. The first two (Contribution for social insurance"

---

[2]This handling is open to dispute; the burden may be shifted to consumers, employees, or shareholders. We simply do not know. The preparation of statistics cannot, however, be held up until all the truth becomes available. The rule that must be adopted in any decision-making situation is this: You balance the available evidence pro and con as best you can, then you make a decision. All such decisions have their arbitrary element; there is always some contrary evidence that must be ignored.

and "Personal tax payments") are obvious: your salary check will be less than your total earnings by reason of such deductions. ("Personal tax payments" include not only the federal income tax but other taxes levied on individuals—e.g., local government property taxes.)

The third and fourth deductions pertain entirely to corporation profits: they bring such profits down to the level of dividends actually received by shareholders. This dividend total is less than the profits total for two reasons: (*a*) the corporate income tax must be paid out of profit; (*b*) corporations do not distribute all of their after-tax profit as dividends. (Undistributed profits are the "Additions to retained earnings" of Chapter 6 Appendix.)

If before-tax corporation profits were $100, if the total corporation tax were $50, and dividends were $20, then undistributed corporate profits must have been $(*10 / 20 / 30 / 40 / 50*). Disregarding social insurance contributions and personal taxes, the amount to deduct from *NI* in moving toward *DI*—that is, the total amount to be deducted from before-tax corporate profits in order to get *DI* in the form of dividends—would be $(*40 / 50 / 60 / 70 / 80 / 90*).

If *NI* were $600, social insurance contributions were $15, personal tax payments were $120, and corporate taxes and undistributed profits were as stated above, then the size of column 4 in Figure 6-2 would stand for a figure of $(*285 / 315 / 385 / 420 / 495*).

30; 80; 385

8. What's left, after deduction from *NI* of the four items just discussed, is column 4 in Figure 6-2.

To reach disposable income, we need only stack three blocks of "nonearned income" or "transfer payments" on the top of column 4. The result is column 5; it is *DI*.

a. Begin with the bottom added block (in column 5): "Government transfer payments to persons."

A typical item here would be a $200 social security check paid to a retired worker. Such an expenditure by government *(would / would not)* be included in the "Government purchases" sector or block of GNP and NNP. It *(would / would not)* be included in the *NI* total. (Remember: *NI* is "earned income," income paid for some contribution to current production.)

Nevertheless, the recipient of this $200 check certainly considers it income; most or all of it will be spent on consumer goods.[3] So it must be included in *DI* (the total of "spendable income") regardless of whether it was earned income or not.

[3]Don't get mixed up by thinking that if this $200 is spent on consumption goods, the transfer payment really does sneak into GNP and NNP, through the back door of "consumption." Keep your transactions separate. One transaction is the transfer payment by government to the individual; it doesn't count at all in GNP and NNP. *Another* transaction, following this payment, is the consumption expenditure. This *does* count; $200 in GNP and NNP as the purchase of part of the current output of consumption goods; $200 (or something less than $200) in *NI* as the earnings of those who produced those consumption goods.

Thus, to the dollar figure represented by the size of column 4 in Figure 6-2, we must *(add / subtract)* the total of all such government transfers.

b. The next block included in column 5 is: "Interest paid by governments."

If you receive interest on money loaned, you will count that interest as part of your spendable (i.e., disposable) income. If that loan was made to finance any part of production (i.e., if it was money loaned to a corporation or an unincorporated business), it is already counted. It is within the second block ("Net interest paid by business") of column 3, and what remains of that interest income after personal taxes is in column 4 and in the large bottom block of column 5, the *DI* column.

But suppose your interest comes from a government bond. This is not chalked up in the statistics as "earned income" (i.e., as part of *NI*). It *(is / is not)* in column 3 or 4. It is considered a transfer payment from government to you. It *(does / does not)* count as part of *DI*, and so it must be added in when moving from *NI* to *DI*.

This handling of government-paid interest is open to some dispute. The somewhat paradoxical result which emerges is that interest paid you on a corporation bond is counted within *NI* (it is "earned income"); interest paid you on a government bond is not.

The reasoning here is that the total amount of government debt, and thus the total amount of interest paid out by governments, bears little relation to the amount of goods and services produced through the agency of government. The best supporting argument is the federal debt. Much of this was first incurred during World War II; the debt grew enormously during that war and doubtless contributed to production at that time. But the war is now part of history. A good case can be made that the total debt had little effect on either GNP or the level of government spending from 1945 through 1981.

That historical case could become considerably weaker when it is applied to the 1980s, though, because of the record size of the yearly deficits run up by the Reagan administration. Deficits in the recent past have been so large that many economists fear that they might dampen the rate of growth of GNP by increasing interest rates and slowing investment. Interest payments on the debt had, for example, risen so far by 1983 that the nearly $100 billion required to finance the debt exceeded the total revenue collected from American corporations through the corporate income tax by a factor of over 250 percent. Should these fears be correct and contributions to the debt succeed in slowing investment and growth, they will generate higher levels of unemployment and even larger deficits (each point of unemployment costs the federal treasury roughly $30 billion in lower taxes and higher compensation). In the face of these expanded deficits, governments will necessarily try to lower program spending in an effort to try to "stem the tide of red ink." The size of the debt could, quite conceivably, reverse itself and play a major role in the reduction of total purchases of goods and services by the government in the very near future.

When statistics must be published, rules must be set for their construction. Sometimes these rules contain an arbitrary element (as already noted regarding the corporation income tax). On your first approach, complications such as this one are of minor importance. Just note that any receipt of interest paid by a business firm *(is / is not)* considered part of earnings from production; if a government pays interest (or if a consumer does—an item still to be considered), it is a transfer payment. Notice, though, that government's interest payments are, in the statistics, kept separate from the other government transfers. That is, there are two "Government transfer payment" blocks in column 5. It is almost as though the Commerce Department's conscience were not entirely clear on this issue; it segregates such interest payments from the other transfers.

c. Finally, the remaining block in column 5: "Interest paid by consumers."

The reasoning here is much the same as that just outlined in part **b.** You may receive interest on a loan made, not to any business, not to any government, but to an individual or family, to finance a consumer purchase (e.g., a new automobile). In such a case, the loan did nothing to assist production,[4] and the interest payment does not show up in column 3 or 4. Nevertheless, it is still disposable income. So the total of such consumer-loan interest payments is included in the *DI* total.

Question 7 used at its close an example in which *NI* was $600 and the four deductions from *NI* were specified. Using the same figures, and assuming the totals of "Interest paid by consumers," "Interest paid by governments," and other "Government transfer payments" to be $20, $15, and $25, respectively, then the amount of *DI*—column 5—would be $(*445 / 480 / 490 / 500 / 505*).

---

a. would not; would not; add **b.** is not; does; is **c.** 445

---

9. Column 5 depicted the total of disposable income received: the remainder of national income after deductions, plus the three transfer items.

Column 6 also shows *DI;* it is exactly the same column as column 5. But it shows what people do with their disposable incomes. Basically, there are just two things to do with it: spend it on consumption goods, or save it. (Strictly, there are three things to do with *DI*; we'll get to the third in a moment.)

The bottom "Consumption expenditures" block in column 6 is exactly the same block as appeared in columns 1 and 2. If you like, appearance of this block in the first two columns records the production and sale of all these consumer goods and services; its appearance in column 6 records the purchase of these same items.

[4] If you are tempted to argue that the loan did assist production, because the automobile wouldn't have been sold without it, consider further. Doubtless the loan helped to sell the car, and its purchase price will have been included within the "Consumption expenditures" block of columns 1 and 2 (for the period within which it was sold). But nothing about the making of that consumer loan actually helped in the process of converting iron ore, plastics, and other materials into a shiny new automobile.

"Personal saving," the second block in column 6, is—by definition—that part of *DI* which is not spent on consumption goods or services (or not used to pay interest on consumer loans, the remaining column 6 block).[5]

That leaves the top block, "Interest paid by consumers." It is exactly the same block as appeared in column 5, and you may wonder why it is making a second appearance. The first thing to keep in mind is that this item really isn't very important—not on a first approach to the intricacies of national-product and national-income accounting, at any rate. You can probably lead a reasonably happy and prosperous life without having paid lavish attention to this statistical item.

Nevertheless, the logic of the entry is simple. One part of the public lends money (for the financing of consumer-good purchases) and receives interest thereon. Another part of the public borrows that same money, and pays that same amount of interest on it. Column 5 recorded the receipt of interest; column 6 records the payment.

You may reasonably argue that this is just a private transfer of funds from one sector of the consuming public (borrowers) to another sector (lenders); it could be left completely out of these statistics, thereby dispensing with one complication faced by the beginning student. The Commerce Department felt otherwise. Credit buying is now widespread, and with the marked increase in interest rates that has developed in recent years, the total of consumer interest payments has risen sharply. It is a statistic of interest; the Commerce Department wanted to include it (its inclusion is a recent change) and this was the only way to get it in.

This question asks you to compute (for three different situations GNP, NNP, *NI*, and *DI* totals by fitting together bits and pieces of information. They key is Figure 6-2. Every line in the table following matches an item within that diagram. Your task is to find enough figures that you can build one complete column (GNP, NNP, *NI* or *DI*) then work to other columns.

The figures are billions of dollars, and refer to some year such as 1980. An "x" opposite any item means that its value is not given you.

	Problem		
	a	b	c
Capital consumption allowances	10	25	10
Consumption expenditures	100	180	x
Contributions for social insurance	0	10	5
Corporation income taxes	15	15	10
Corporate profits before taxes	x	x	50
Gov't. purchases of goods and services ...	50	x	50
Gov't. transfer payments to persons (other than interest payments)	5	15	15
Gross investment	x	x	55

[5] The statistics do not record, and are not intended to record, what people do with their saving—e.g., buy securities with it, put it in the bank, hide it in the mattress, etc. We shall meet this topic in the next few chapters.

	Problem		
	a	**b**	**c**
Indirect business taxes	20	30	40
Interest paid by consumers	10	5	5
Interest paid by governments	5	10	5
Net interest (paid by business)	x	x	10
Net investment	50	x	x
Personal saving	x	40	30
Personal tax payments	15	25	20
Proprietors' income (from unincorporated business)	x	x	20
Rental income	x	x	20
Undistributed corporation profits	10	5	10
Wages and salaries	x	x	250

For each problem, compute:

	a	b	c
Gross national product	_____	_____	_____
Net national product	_____	_____	_____
National income	_____	_____	_____
Disposable (personal) income .	_____	_____	_____

a. The only row you can immediately fill is NNP; for this you have consumption (100), government (50), and net investment (50). The total of these makes an NNP of 200. Add depreciation (10) to reach GNP. The various items needed to move from NNP to *NI* and to *DI* are all given   **b.** Here you can start only with *DI*; but you have consumption (180), personal saving (40), and consumer interest payments (5); so *DI* is 225. From here, work backward to *NI*, NNP, and GNP   **c.** This one requires you to start with *NI*; you have all the five categories of "earnings" needed to fill out this column. Precise answers are recorded below.

	a	b	c
Gross national product	210	305	400
Net national product	200	280	390
National income	180	250	350
Disposable income	160	225	330

10. Using the same data furnished in question 19, compute where possible the total of the following (if the data supplied are insufficient and you cannot compute it, put an x in the space):

a. Personal saving (out of *DI*) in problem **a** . . . _____

b. Consumption expenditure in problem **c** . . . . _____

c. Gross investment in problem **a** . . . . _____

d. Net investment in problem **b** . . . . _____

e. Dividends paid out by corporations in problem **c** _____

f. Government surplus or deficit in problem **c** . . _____

(NOTE: Government's surplus or deficit here is simply the difference between total tax collections and other receipts and total money outlays. Remember that "Contributions for social insurance" count as a government receipt.)

a. 50 **b.** 295 **c.** 60 **d.** x **e.** 30 **f.** surplus of 5. [If part **e** gave you trouble, remember that the total corporation profits can be divided in three ways only: corporation taxes, dividends, and addition to retained earnings (this last meaning the same thing as "undistributed profits"). So if you know the total and any two of three, you can compute the third]

11. One statistical problem is: How is the dividing line between consumption and investment drawn? What goes into the "Consumption expenditures" category of GNP and NNP, and what into "Gross (or Net) investment"?

Ideally, the consumption figure should measure the goods and services not only produced during that year, but actually consumed during the year (so that they were gone by the year's end). but there is no possible way of measuring this "true consumption." The statisticians must content themselves with recording what consumers bought. Clothing, for example, may last much more than a year, but purchase of a new dress or suit is still treated as consumption during the year in which it was made and bought.[6]

Items consumed immediately or almost immediately after purchase (bread, for example) pose no problem. Regarding those which last, say, 2 or 3 years, the interpretation of consumer purchases as "true consumption" still works fairly well, assuming that what is bought is pretty much a replacement for what is worn out through use. One item demands different treatment: housing. A house is far and away the longest-lived item a consumer ordinarily buys; it is typically the biggest purchase a person ever makes. It would be ridiculous to say that a house built in 1980 is fully "consumed" by the end of 1980.

The statisticians handle this by saying: A house is an investment good, not a consumer good. It is a kind of machine for providing consumer services. What *should* be counted as consumption in 1980 GNP and NNP is the service which the house supplies—and indeed, if the house is rented, there is a market price measure of the value of this service.[7]

With every house treated as a service-producing machine, the services supplied by that house are thus counted as consumption within GNP and NNP, valued at the market price of such services (rental value) for each year of its life that it is occupied. In the year it was built, the full construction value of

[6]Consumer items made during the year but not bought are dealt with in question 12.

[7]If the house is owner occupied, the rental value of its services must be estimated. (This is another exception to the general rule that goods and services go through the market mechanism.) Such an estimate of the total value of housing services for owner-occupied houses goes into each year's "Consumption expenditures" for GNP and NNP.

the house is counted, but as an investment item, not as consumption.[8]

a. Suppose a house is built in the first half of 1980 and sold for $90,000. It is rented for the remainder of the year, total rental for the 6 months being $6000. Depreciation for this same period is estimated at $600. In the 1980 statistics, the proper entries for this house would be:

Gross investment, $(*zero / 600 / 6000 / 89,400 / 90,000*);
Net investment, $(*zero / 600 / 6000 / 89,400 / 90,000*);
Consumption expenditures, $(*zero / 600 / 6000 / 89,400 / 90,000*).

b. Hence the total entries in 1980 GNP and NNP, with respect to construction and use of this house, would be:
GNP: $(*89,400 / 90,000 / 95,400 / 96,000*);
NNP: $(*89,400 / 90,000 / 95,400 / 96,000*).

---

a. $90,000; $89,400; $6000   **b.** $96,000; $95,400 (The GNP figure must be "Gross investment" plus "Consumption"; the NNP figure, "Net investment" plus "Consumption.")

---

12. There are three categories within "investment goods." (A fourth category, of lesser importance, is left aside.[9] These three are:

1. New business and industrial buildings, machinery, and equipment produced
2. New housing constructed (private residences and apartment houses)
3. Increases in inventories of raw materials and partly or wholly finished goods

Category (1) is what we ordinarily think of as "investment goods." Category (2) has been covered in question 11.

If any firm has a bigger physical inventory of its product (partly or wholly finished) at the end of the year than it had at the year's beginning, then the value of its additional inventory must count as part of investment for the year.

Suppose a shirt manufacturer had a $3000 inventory of shirts on hand at the start of 1980 and a $4000 inventory at its close. (No problem of style or price change is involved; the firm just has more shirts on hand, as yet unsold, than it had a year ago.) The fact that its inventory is up by $1000 means that this firm must have (*sold more than it manufactured / manufactured*

more than it sold). (In the extreme case, you could think of the firm as, in 1980, making shirts worth $1000 and not selling one.)

The essence of investment in all its various forms is that it is production for future benefit. A newly finished machine tool yields no direct consumer satisfaction whatsoever. It is built to yield future benefit; it is expected to contribute toward consumer-good production in the future, throughout its coming 5-year or 10-year life. A new house counts within investment for the same reason.

Our shirt firm's additional inventory must receive the same treatment. It made $1000 worth of shirts in 1980 which it hadn't yet sold. The shirts it did sell count as part of consumption in the regular way. The shirts it made but didn't sell must also go into GNP and NNP (because they were made in 1980). but (because they weren't sold) they do not go into consumption. They are included in investment because they will be consumed in the future, presumably *next* year.

This inventory rule must work both ways. Had this firm's beginning inventory been $4000 and its closing inventory $3000, then we would include a figure of (*minus / plus*) $(*1000 / 3000 / 4000*) within (*consumption / investment*).

Note that this is the same "beginning and closing inventory" matter discussed in the course of the Chapter 20 Appendix on business accounting.

---

manufactured more than it sold; minus; 1000; investment

---

13. a. Could a country's net investment for any given period ever turn out to be a negative figure? If you can think of any reason why it could, don't write down the reason; just check the "Yes" box below. If you cannot think of any reason, check the "No" box . . . . Yes( ) No( )

b. Could a country's gross investment ever turn out to be a negative figure? . . . . Yes( ) No( )

Answers are given in question 15's answers. Do 14 and 15 before checking your response to this one.

14. You are given the following data for a certain country:

	Year 1	Year 2
New buildings produced	5	5
New equipment produced	10	10
Consumer goods produced	110	90
Consumer goods consumed	90	110
Estimated depreciation on existing buildings during year	10	10
Estimated depreciation on existing equipment during year	10	10
Inventories of consumer goods at beginning of year	30	50
Inventories of consumer goods at close of year	50	30

---

[8]Is it double counting to include in the figures both the original purchase value of the new house and the value of the services that it supplies? Yes and no. The same is true of any other investment—a machine or a factory building. (The rent of a factory building works its way into the market price of the item produced therein. The use of a machine inside the factory does the same thing.) The key factor here is depreciation. Gross national product, which makes no allowance for depreciation, does double-count. However, in net national product, the original value of the house is gradually subtracted from the national product, year by year, using depreciation, until (at the end of its life) the entire original purchase value of the house has been deducted. All that remains is the total value of the services which that house supplied.

[9]This minor item is "foreign investment." The Commerce Department treats this as a separate (and fourth) block within GNP and NNP, calling it "Net exports of goods and services," or "Net foreign investment."

These figures are complete; there is no government sector of GNP or NNP.

a. The difference, in year 1, between 110 consumer goods produced and 90 consumer goods consumed is explained by *(an increase / a decrease)* in inventories on hand at the *(beginning / end)* of the year.

The difference, in year 2, between 90 consumer goods produced and 110 consumer goods consumed is explained by *(an increase / a decrease)* in inventories on hand at the *(beginning / end)* of the year.

b. Compute the following for the 2 years:

	Year 1	Year 2
Gross national product	**(1)** _____	**(7)** _____
Breakup of GNP into:		
Consumption	**(2)** _____	**(8)** _____
Gross investment	**(3)** _____	**(9)** _____
Net national product	**(4)** _____	**(10)** _____
Breakup of NNP into:		
Consumption	**(5)** _____	**(11)** _____
Net investment	**(6)** _____	**(12)** _____

a. an increase; end; a decrease; end **b. (1)** consumption + buildings + equipment + change in inventories = 90 + 5 + 10 + (50 − 30) = 125 **(2)** 90 **(3)** 35 **(4)** GNP − building depreciation − machinery depreciation = 125 − 10 − 10 = 105 **(5)** 90 **(6)** 15 **(7)** 105 **(8)** 110 **(9)** −5 **(10)** 85 **(11)** 110 **(12)** −25

15. To summarize question 14: in the national-product statistics, a negative net investment figure *(could / could not)* appear if total depreciation exceeded the total value of new buildings and equipment produced. A negative net investment figure *(could / could not)* appear if (leaving depreciation aside) the value of inventory reduction exceeded the total value of new buildings and equipment produced.

A negative gross investment figure *(could / could not)* appear if total depreciation exceeded the total value of new buildings and equipment produced. A negative gross investment figure *(could / could not)* appear if the value of inventory reduction during the year exceeded the total value of new buildings and equipment.

could; could; could not [Hence answer to both parts of question 13 is: Yes (if you were fooled by the gross-investment part, console yourself with the fact that you have plenty of good company)]; could

16. A common use of national-product figures is to compare total real output as between 2 years. If prices have changed in the interim, however, the comparison is meaningless unless a proper price adjustment is made.

a. Consider this problem: NNP (in billions) was $500 in 1975, $650 in 1980. The price index was 100 in 1975 and 125 in 1980—i.e., prices had risen by 25 percent by 1980, as compared with 1975. Was 1980's real output higher than 1975's, and if so, by how much?

For the moment, set aside completely the question just posed. We'll start with an easier problem, then use it to answer the actual problem. Suppose, instead, that 1980's real output had been exactly the same as that of 1975 ($500). That 1980 real output would, in 1975 prices of course, have to be $500. But again, the 1975 and 1980 price indices were 100 and 125; i.e., prices rose by 25 percent over that period. Allowing for this inflation, the 1980 NNP, expressed in 1980 prices, would have to be

$$\$500 \times \frac{125}{100}$$

That would make the 1980 NNP (in 1980 prices) $*(500 / 550 / 575 / 625)*.

If we wanted to *deflate* this 1980 NNP (in 1980 prices), to get it down to 1975 prices (and so make it comparable with the actual 1975 NNP), we would do in reverse what was just done. That is, we would start with the $625 NNP and multiply it by a deflating factor of $^{100}/_{125}$. The result would be $500.

Still assuming for convenience, a 25 percent price increase, we can apply this deflating factor of $^{100}/_{125}$ to bring any 1980 NNP down to a 1975 price level. Suppose, for example, that real output in 1980 had been twice the 1975 NNP of $500. That 1980 NNP would accordingly have to be twice $500, or $1000—measured in 1975 prices. Since prices were up by 25 percent by 1980, the actual 1980 NNP would be $1250. The same deflating factor would bring that $1250 down to $1000.

To get finally to the problem posed at the start of this question (i.e., to get the actual 1980 NNP of $650 in terms of 1975 prices and so make it comparable in real terms with the 1975 NNP), we multiply by $^{100}/_{125}$. The resulting deflated figure is $*(500 / 520 / 580 / 625)*—i.e., real output in 1980 was *(4 / 8 / 12 / 100)* percent *(higher / lower)* than in 1975.

Another way of making a proper comparison would be to inflate the 1975 NNP of $500 by 25 percent, thus making it comparable with 1980. That is, the 1975 NNP, at 1980 prices, would be $625. Comparing this with the actual 1980 NNP of $650, we get *(a lower increase than / the same 4 percent increase as / a higher increase than)* before.

b. Sometimes this kind of problem is complicated by asking: What happened to per capita income (income per person, total income divided by total population)? Suppose, for example that with the same pair of NNPs as before, total population fell by 5 percent between 1975 and 1980. What was the rise in per capita income?

Real NNPs, in 1975 prices, were $500 in 1975, $520 in 1980. But the latter total was shared among a smaller population. Suppose the 1975 population was 100 people. If so, then given a 5 percent drop, it must have been 95 in 1980. If these were the two population figures, then real income per person was $5 in 1975 ($500 divided by 100), whereas in 1980 ($520 divided by

95) it was approximately $(5.0 / 5.5 / 6.0 / 6.5). Comparing $5 per person in 1975 with about $5.5 in 1980, you will find the result is that 1980 real per capita income rose by about 10 percent over 1975. (To compute the percentage change in per capita income, it doesn't make any difference what pair of population figures you use, just so long as they are in the proper ratio. Try it with 200 people and 190, or with 1000 and 950; you get exactly the same percentage increase.)

---

a. 625; 520; 4; higher; the same 4 percent increase as   **b.** 5.5

---

17. The text notes one implication of the national-income accounting identity that GNP equals the sum of consumption, investment, government spending, and the difference between exports and imports: actual saving always equals actual investment. This does not, however, mean that actual saving always equals intended investment. This question will explore the implications of this distinction.

In question 14, there is no government and no foreign sector. In that question, therefore,

GNP = _____ + _____

If the difference between GNP and consumption represents saving (that part of income which is not spent), then this equation can be rewritten as

_____ = investment

This is the purported accounting identity.

Continuing now with question 14, suppose that, in each year, business wanted to maintain inventories at the beginning of the year level throughout the year; that is, assume that intended inventories were 30 for the end of year 1 and 50 for the end of year 2. Another way of stating this assumption is to say that the intended level of investment in inventories in both years was zero. Suppose, additionally, that investment on building and machinery proceeded as intended in both years. Fill in the blanks of the following table with numbers drawn from question 14.

	Year 1	Year 2
Intended building investment	_____	_____
Intended equipment investment ...	_____	_____
Intended inventory investment	_____	_____
Total intended investment	_____	_____
Actual building investment	_____	_____
Actual equipment investment	_____	_____
Actual inventory investment	_____	_____
Actual saving	_____	_____

From the table, it is clear that, in year 1, actual saving (*exceeded / equalled / fell short of*) intended investment by

_____. Inventories were (*increasing / decreasing*) faster than intended, and the likely response of the firm owner would be to (*speed up / slow down / leave unchanged*) the level of his or her production and employment. By the same token, actual saving (*exceeded / equalled / fell short of*) intended investment by _____ in year 2. Inventories were, in the second year, (*increasing / decreasing*) faster than intended, and the likely response of the owner would be to (*speed up / slow down / leave unchanged*) the level of his or her production and employment.

---

consumption; investment; saving   Table entries by column: (year 1) 5; 10; 0; 15; 5; 10; 20; 35; (year 2) 5; 10; 0; 15; 5; 10; −20; −5   exceeded; 20; increasing; slow down; fell short of; 20; decreasing; speed up

---

18. A nation's GNP was $260 billion in 1975 and $325 billion in 1985. Both figures were computed as usual in terms of market prices for the year involved. The index prices rose from 100 in 1975 to 130 in 1985.

a. As compared with 1975, did real output increase or decrease in 1985?

b. In terms of 1985 prices, what would the 1975 GNP be?

c. In terms of 1975 prices, what would the 1985 GNP be?

---

decrease; $338; $250

---

19. A house is built and sold in the first 6 months of 1960 for a price of $50,000. It is rented for the next 20 years, beginning July 1, 1960. Annual rent is $3000 per year ($1500 for the last half of 1960, $1500 for the first half of 1980). The house lasts for just 20 years. Depreciation is charged at the rate of $2500 per year ($1250 for each of the 2 half-years involved, 1960 and 1980).

What figures enter the national-product accounts with respect to the building and rental of this house? Answer by completing the columns below.

	1960	1961 or Any Later Year through 1979	1980	Total of All Years Combined
Gross investment	_____	_____	_____	_____
Net investment	_____	_____	_____	_____
Consumption	_____	_____	_____	_____

By column (1960): $50,000; $48,750; $1500   (1961–1979): 0; −$2500; $3,000 (1980): 0; −$1250; $1500   (Total): $50,000; 0; $60,000

---

20. In the accompanying table are three sets of statistics relating to national product and income. Some figures have been omitted, but in each case there are just enough to permit computation of the accounts. For each of the three sets of figures:

1. Compute GNP, NNP, and *DI*, showing your figures in the spaces at bottom of each column.

	Problem		
	a	**b**	**c**
Business and industrial plant equipment constructed	105	60	100
Capital consumption allowances (depreciation)	45	____	____
Consumption expenditures	380	275	____
Corporation dividends	20	15	25
Corp'n. income (profit) after tax	____	____	____
Corp'n. income (profit) before tax	65	55	____
Corp'n. income (profit) undistributed	____	15	30
Government purchases of goods and services	120	____	140
Gov't. transfer payments (excluding interest payments) to individuals	25	10	45
Housing constructed	40	25	60
Increase in inventories of commodities accumulated during year	−10	5	−5
Interest paid: By business (net) ..	20	25	60
By consumers	10	20	25
By governments ...	25	10	30
Investment (total gross)	____	90	____
Investment (total net)	____	65	130
Proprietor's income (from unincorporated business)	30	____	50
Rental income	15	30	35
Saving (by consumers, out of *DI*)	____	50	105
Taxes: Corporation income	30	25	45
Indirect business	35	30	30
Personal	90	60	95
Social insurance contributions	25	40	40
Wages and salaries	____	300	450
Gross national product	____	____	____
Net national product	____	____	____
Disposable income	____	____	____

2. Fill in all the blanks within each column; e.g., "Corporation income (profit) after tax" in problem **a**, and so on.

HINT: These are essentially "jigsaw puzzle" problems. The key diagram for their solution is Figure 6-2, page 58. Note that there are just three things to be done with corporation income (or profit): taxes must first be paid; dividends are paid out of after-tax profit; and what's left is undistributed profit (addition to retained earnings). The total of corporation taxes, dividends,

and undistributed profit must be corporation income before taxes.]

	a	**b**	**c**
Capital consumption allowances		$ 25	$ 25
Consumption expenditures			445
Corporation income (profit) after tax	$ 35	30	55
Corporation income (profit) before tax ...			100
Corporation income (profit) undistributed .	15		
Government purchases of goods and services		135	
Investment (total gross)	135		155
Investment (total net)	90		
Proprietor's income		35	
Saving (by consumers, out of *DI*)	65		
Wages and salaries	425		
Gross national product	635	500	750
Net national product	590	475	725
Disposable income	455	345	585

QUIZ: Multiple Choice

1. In GNP and NNP statistics, "investment" includes:

(1) any durable product produced through the agency of government, such as a new road.

(2) any purchase of a new common-stock issue.

(3) any increase in the amount of year-end inventories over their year-beginning amount.

(4) any commodity bought by a consumer but not fully consumed by the year-end.

(5) none of these items.

2. In GNP and NNP statistics, the value of housing services, where the houses are occupied by their owners, is treated as follows. It is:

(1) not counted, since property services are not considered "production."

(2) not counted, since such property services are included in the value of the house itself.

(3) not counted in GNP and NNP, using an arbitrary estimate of rental value.

(4) counted in both GNP and NNP, using an arbitrary estimate of rental value.

(5) counted in GNP, but not in NNP, using an arbitrary estimate of rental value.

3. To compute a firm's contribution to GNP on a value-added basis, we must deduct from the value at market price of the goods it has produced:

(1) all indirect business taxes paid.

(2) any undistributed profits.

(3) depreciation.

(4) all sales to other business firms.

(5) none of the above.

4. In GNP and NNP statistics, a negative gross investment figure:

(1) could never occur.

(2) could appear if the total of depreciation on buildings and equipment were sufficiently large.

(3) would automatically occur if there were no production of buildings or equipment during the year.

(4) could be caused by a sufficiently large reduction in inventories during the year.

(5) means simply that the economy has produced more than it has consumed.

5. There would be double counting in either GNP or NNP computations if statisticians were to add together:

(1) net value added by the iron-mining industry and net value added by the steel-manufacturing industry.

(2) net increase in inventories of flour mills and net increase in inventories of bakeries.

(3) total output of iron ore and total output of iron.

(4) value added by bakers and value of the baker's salespeople's services.

(5) total consumer services purchased and total of investment goods produced.

6. Subtract (*a*) corporation income taxes and (*b*) undistributed corporation profit from the total of corporation profit before taxes, and the remainder must equal:

(1) indirect business taxes.

(2) addition to retained earnings.

(3) dividends.

(4) bond interest.

(5) disposable income.

7. Among the five items listed below, one is not in the same class as the other four for purposes of national-income accounting, namely:

(1) corporation income (or profits).

(2) government transfer payments.

(3) net interest payments by business.

(4) rental income.

(5) wages and salaries.

8. If you know the NNP figure, and from it want to compute disposable personal income, one thing you must not do is to:

(1) deduct depreciation.

(2) add government transfer payments.

(3) deduct indirect business taxes.

(4) deduct social security levies.

(5) deduct undistributed corporation profits.

9. In computing the "government" sector of GNP for a particular period:

(1) all governmental expenditures on commodities and services are counted.

(2) all governmental expenditures on commodities are counted; those on services are not.

(3) all governmental expenditures on final commodities and services are counted; those on intermediate items are not.

(4) all governmental expenditures on consumption items are counted, whether commodities or services; other are not.

(5) none of the above is correct.

10. "National income" (*NI*), as this term is used in the national-product and national-income statistics, means specifically:

(1) NNP (net national product) plus all taxes not considered taxes paid out of income—i.e., NNP plus "indirect business taxes."

(2) NNP minus all taxes that are considered taxes paid out of income, such as the personal and corporation income taxes.

(3) NNP plus all taxes that are considered taxes paid out of income, such as the personal and corporation income taxes.

(4) NNP minus all taxes not considered taxes paid out of income—i.e., NNP minus "indirect business taxes."

(5) none of the preceding.

11. If NNP was $360 (billion) in 1975, as measured in 1975 prices, and if the price level had risen by 20 percent from 1970 to 1975, the 1975 NNP, measured in 1970 prices, would be (in billions):

(1) $300.

(2) $320.

(3) $340.

(4) $360.

(5) $432.

12. In computing the national-income and national-product accounts, it would be incorrect to add together the following two items:

(1) consumption expenditure and personal saving.

(2) net investment and consumption expenditures.

(3) corporate profits and net interest paid by business.

(4) government purchases and consumption expenditures.

(5) government purchases and wages and salaries.

CHAPTER 7
CONSUMPTION AND INVESTMENT

This chapter begins a two-chapter review of the intellectual core of "Keynesian economics." The tools developed here first appeared in *The General Theory* published by Keynes more than 50 years ago, but their application in contemporary thought about macroeconomic issues has certainly changed over the intervening years. In its purest form, therefore, the Keynesian core no longer applies directly to the way economics is currently practiced. It is, nonetheless, useful to study the old Keynesian model for at least two reasons. First, a careful review of the Keynesian foundations builds an understanding of the antecedents of modern macroeconomic theory. Without such an understanding, much of modern economic theory is so isolated that it can be virtually impenetrable. Second, it is equally important to understand the evolutionary process that brought us to our current state of economic awareness. To do this, we need a point of departure—a historical benchmark against which the reasons behind the changes that have occurred in the conventional wisdom can be cast. The pure Keynesian model is an excellent starting point, and the integration of money into that model is an equally good example of the type of change that has occurred over the past half-century.

This initial chapter on investment and consumption begins to define the Keynesian benchmark. In addition to starting the process of understanding that benchmark, your work here should allow you to accomplish the following objectives.

LEARNING OBJECTIVES

1. Define consumption (by families), saving (by families), and investment (by businesses). Contrast this view of investment with a common usage of "investment" that does not apply to macroeconomic analysis of real (as opposed to financial) assets.

2. List four or more factors that influence the total amount of investment spending within an economy.

3. List factors that influence the total amount of saving done by families within an economy.

4. Contrast the two lists generated in objectives 3 and 4 to understanding the "cleavage between saving and investment."

5. Define (*a*) the propensity to consume, (*b*) the marginal propensity to consume, (*c*) the propensity to save. Explain carefully the difference between (*a*) and (*b*). Explain also the relationship between (*a*) and (*c*).

If an economy is to produce at its full-employment level of output, then the total of its aggregate demand must be maintained at the proper level. If the flow of money spending for goods and services pouring into the marketplace is insufficient to buy what can be produced at full employment (given the prevailing price level), then unemployment of people and machines may be expected as a result. If this flow is too large, greater in magnitude than the total available supply of goods (valued at current prices), then we can expect that prices will rise. This price increase would bring the money value of available supply into equality with the demand flow.

"The flow of money spending" means an expenditure stream with three components: consumer spending, investment spending, and governmental spending—the three components of GNP and NNP outlined in Chapter 6. If we disregard expenditure by foreigners to buy U.S. goods, then every currently produced good or service is supplied to meet one of these three demand categories. The nation's economic well-being requires that their sum total be just right, neither too high nor too low.

In point of fact, this total flow is frequently off the mark. It can shrink to produce a recession, or expand to produce an inflation. To understand how these disruptions occur, we must understand the forces that influence and control each of the three flows.

In our first approach, we set government spending and taxation (and also foreign transactions) aside. Later, the role of government must be considered at length; but it simplifies the analysis to begin with a situation in which only private spending decisions—consumption (*C*) spending and investment (*I*) spending— are important.

The Consumption Flow Two factors govern the amount of *C* spending undertaken by a family or a community:

▶ **1.** The amount of income received by that family or community.

▶ **2.** The way the family or community chooses to divide that income between consumption and saving.

"Income received" means, of course, disposable income—*DPI*, or *DI*. By definition, saving ("personal saving") is that part of *DI* not spent on consumption.[1]

Figure 7-1 illustrates this division of income for a community. The total amount paid out by producing firms in the forms of wages and salaries, rental payments, dividends, and so on, appears at top left. It flows to individuals and families as earned income. They divide it between *C* and *S*. That part of the income flow used for *C* spending is obviously directed back toward producing firms. We'll consider in due course what happens to both the *S* flow and the *C* flow after it leaves Figure 7-1.

We come now to a simple but vitally important concept: *the propensity to consume.* We'll approach it in

[1] This ignores the fact that, in Department of Commerce terms, part of *DI* goes to interest payments by consumers, now officially regarded as neither consumption expenditure nor saving. This is quite unimportant here; just assume that there are no such interest payments.

The Commerce Department's official wording is "disposable personal income" (*DPI*). But "disposable income" (*DI*) is shorter and more convenient.

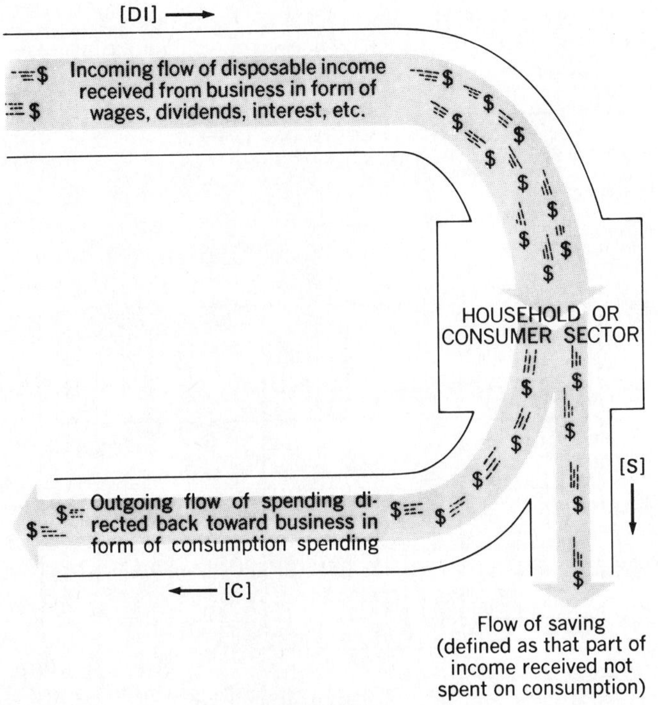

terms of the single family, although it can be used just as much (and will be) with respect to the community.

▶ The propensity to consume, for any family, records the amount of *C* spending that family will undertake, at each and any level of *DI*. It is sometimes called the consumption function.

In Figure 7-1 terms, the propensity to consume indicates how much of the incoming *DI* flow (whatever its amount) will be sent through the *C* spending "loop" at bottom left.

1. a. The propensity-to-consume idea needs careful development. Suppose a certain family's weekly expenditure on consumption is governed by this rule: spend $100 plus one-half of weekly *DI*. Hence its *C* spending and its saving at various income levels would be (fill in the blanks):

DI	C	S	DI	C	S
$ 0	$ _____	$ _____	$300	$ _____	$ _____
100	_____	_____	400	_____	_____
200	_____	_____	500	_____	_____

(Remember that S must be the difference between *DI* and *C*. So at low income levels, S will be a negative amount.)

b. In Figure 7-1 terms, if the incoming income flow were $400, then the outgoing flow of *C* spending at bottom left would be $*(400 / 300 / 200)*, and the flow through the *S* "drain" $ *(300 / 200 / 100)*. Should income rise from $400 to $500, the flow of *C* spending would rise by $*(200 / 100 / 50)*, to $*(500 / 450 / 400 / 350)*.

a. *C*: 100, 150, 200, 250, 300, 350; *S*: −100, −50, 0, 50, 100, 150 **b.** 300; 100; 50; 350

2. a. In Figure 7-2, plot the points relating to *C* and *DI* for the six *DI* values of question 1. Join these points with an appropriate line.

The figures you have completed in question 1 illustrate a propensity to consume. So does the graph you have drawn above. Notice that although the detail of the figures is different, the line you have drawn corresponds in general shape and direction to the consumption curve of Figure 7-2 in the text. The text line has a little curvature to it, and it is not carried far enough to the left to show consumption for very low levels of income. The case developed here is, nonetheless, sufficient to illustrate the fundamental points raised in the text.

b. In Figure 7-2, also, draw a diagonal line from bottom-left corner to top-right corner. (Use, if possible, a different color, to distinguish this line from the propensity-to-consume line.) Note that the text's Figure 7-2 carries a similar 45° "helping line" or "convenience line."

This particular diagram is used extensively in Chapters 7 through 9 (and indeed in many places later in the text as well). It

[DI] ⟶

Incoming flow of disposable income received from business in form of wages, dividends, interest, etc.

HOUSEHOLD OR CONSUMER SECTOR

[S]

Outgoing flow of spending directed back toward business in form of consumption spending

⟵ [C]

Flow of saving (defined as that part of income received not spent on consumption)

Figure 7-1

Consumption [C]

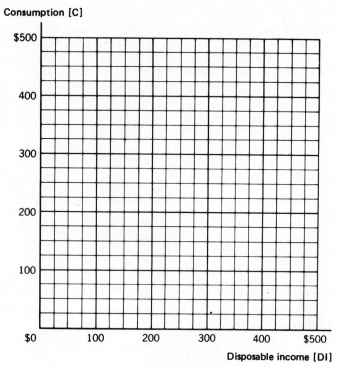

Figure 7-2

is therefore important to grasp the usefulness and significance of the 45° line. In this particular diagram, the same dollar scale is used on both vertical and horizontal axes. This means that

▶ The 45° line runs through all the equal-value points.

For example, the line you have just drawn on Figure 7-2 runs through the point marking off $100 of *DI* and $100 of *C*; through the point marking $200 *DI* and $200 *C*; through $300 *DI* and $300 *C*; and so on. *All* the points where *DI* and *C* are equal are found on this line, and all points on this line have *DI* and *C* equal. In fact, the 45° line can be represented algebraically by *C = DI* (consumption equals disposable income).

One thing that the 45° line tells us, then, is the particular *DI* level at which the family just "breaks even"—spends on *C* an amount just equal to its *DI*. This is where the 45° line and the propensity to consume intersect: in our Figure 7-2, it is at a *DI* of $*(100 / 200 / 300 / 400)*.

To the *left* of this intersection point, the propensity-to-consume line lies *(above / below)* the 45° line. The significance of this is that within this range of incomes—from $0 to $200—the family spends on *C (more / less)* than its *DI*.

To the *right* of the intersection point, the propensity-to-consume line lies *(above / below)* the 45° line. That is, in this income range, the family would spend *(more / less)* than its *DI*; that is, it would save part of its *DI*.

---

b. 200; above; more; below; less

The point made immediately above is a simple one, but be sure you have grasped it: to the left of the intersection between the two lines, the family spends more than

its income; at the intersection, it just "breaks even"; to the right it spends less than its income (and saves the remainder).

Now something related to the above, and equally important;

▶ The vertical distance from the propensity-to-consume line up to the 45° line marks the amount of saving.

This is so because the 45° line marks off equal values horizontally and vertically.

3.   **a.** For example, at $400 *DI* (at the 400 mark on the horizontal axis of Figure 7-2), the vertical distance up to the 45° line is $*(500 / 400 / 300)*. The vertical distance up to the propensity-to-consume line is $*(500 / 400 / 300)*; this is the amount of *C* spending. The difference of $100—the vertical distance between the two lines—is the amount of *S*.

b. Similarly, Figure 7-2 indicates, with the aid of the 45° helping line, that at *DI* of $300 the family would *(save / "dissave")* an amount of $*(0 / 50 / 100 / 150)*. At *DI* of $100, the family would *(save / "dissave")* an amount of $*(0 / 50 / 100 / 150)*. When the propensity-to-consume line is above the 45° line, there is "dissaving" or "negative saving." This means simply that if the family's income should happen to be temporarily at a low level such as $100, it would draw on past savings, or borrow, in order to supplement *DI* currently received, for *C* spending.

c. The amount of *S* can of course be plotted directly on a saving-*DI* graph. Record the same six points of question 1 on Figure 7-3, and join them.

What you have drawn on Figure 7-3 is a graph of the *propensity to save*. If you are given a family's propensity to consume *(then you know / this does not necessarily tell you)* its propensity to save.

---

a. 400; 300   **b.** save; 50; "dissave"; 50   **c.** then you know

---

Saving [S]

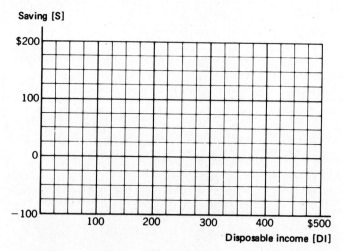

Figure 7-3

The propensity-to-consume (or "consumption function") idea says this: income governs spending (and saving). If you know a family's income you can estimate reasonably well what its total expenditure on consumer goods will be. Not precisely, of course, because families differ. Out of the same income, one family will spend more than another. Some are more freehanded with money; some have more children to support. There are many families, and many possible reasons for different spending patterns. So income is by no means the only factor to influence consumer spending. But it is the primary control. Propensities to consume will vary among families; yet they will show the same general construction.

We can speak also of the *community* propensity to consume—the community being the aggregate of its individual members. There are one or two analytic problems in aggregating individual-unit consumption functions to get the community propensity to consume, but they turn out to be fairly unimportant. Despite differences in spending patterns from family to family, the statistical evidence indicates a remarkably consistent pattern between total community *DI* and total *C* spending. The text's Figure 7-5 shows how closely, over the years, in the United States, the actual relationship between total disposable income and total consumer expenditures has matched the "fitted consumption schedule."

From the propensity-to-consume idea, we can say that a given *change* in *DI* is likely to produce a given change in *C* spending. Here, we reach a most important concept: the *marginal propensity to consume*. (Again: Be careful. The idea of the marginal propensity is simple, but be sure you have grasped what it is and what it is not, for it is used extensively later on.)

To approach the marginal-propensity idea, let's turn back to the family consumption function, and use some hypothetical figures:

Yearly *DI*	Yearly *C*	Increase in *C*
$12,000	$11,600	
		$640
13,000	12,240	
		590
14,000	12,830	

These figures say that if this family's disposable income were to rise by $1000, from $12,000 to $13,000, its total consumer expenditures would rise from $11,600 to $12,240—an increase, not of $1000, but of $640. (The other $360 would go to extra saving.) If *DI* were to rise by another $1000 from $13,000 to $14,000, *C* spending would rise to $12,830—an increase, not of $1000 and not of $640, but of $590.

▶ The marginal propensity to consume (*MPC*) is the ratio between extra *C* spending and extra *DI*.

The next page or so of the Study Guide is devoted fully to this "marginal-propensity" idea. If you wonder why it gets so much space, here is a rough indication: look again at Study Guide Figure 7-1. Suppose the incoming flow of *DI* (at the top of this diagram) rises or falls—rises, let's say. It is the marginal propensity, and *only* the marginal propensity, which dictates how much of this extra *DI* will go into extra *C* spending, and how much of it into extra saving. (And this disposition of extra income, as Chapter 8 will indicate, often turns out to be very important.)

The careful reader will have noted that Figure 7-1 dealt with the entire community while the material of the example dealt with individual families. The key to passing from individuals to community lies in the careful aggregation of individual behavior over the entire population. If the community were, for instance, composed of two families who earned $12,000 and $13,000, respectively, then an aggregate measure of the marginal propensity to consume based on the above example might be:

$$.5 \times .64 + .5 \times .59 = .615$$

Expanding this type of procedure to a more realistic community of any size with advanced statistical techniques allows economists to use the notion of the marginal propensity to consume to describe the consumption behavior of an entire community in the same way that they describe consumption behavior of an individual. Figure 7-5 in the text shows the result of this type of aggregation technique applied to consumption.

There are four essential facts that you need to grasp concerning the *MPC*:

1. As income rises, in real experience, the *MPC* typically falls. (Note how it fell from .64 to .59 in the table above.) If we were being very precise, we would not speak of a single *MPC* figure for an income change as big as $1000; we would have to recognize the slight change in *MPC* produced by a *DI* rise of $100 or even $10. But the difference would be almost imperceptible; and so we speak of "the" *MPC* for an income change of $1000.

Text Chapters 8 and 9 assume, in fact, a constant *MPC*. For some analytical purposes, particularly when distributive issues are to be explored, this would be an unwarranted distortion of reality. But for others, particularly those aggregate issues that the text will explore, it is an appropriate procedure that greatly simplifies the analysis without doing significant "violence to reality."

2. The *MPC* is concerned solely with the ratio between a change in *DI* and the resulting change in *C*. In the table above, the family's *C* spending at a *DI* of $12,000 is $11,600. The ratio of $11,600 to $12,000 is .9667—that is, the family is spending 96.67 percent of its total income on consumption, at this income level. This is the average propensity to consume (*APC*). It is *not* the *MPC*. The *MPC* tells what extra consumption spending will go with any extra income (i.e., any increase or decrease in income); and the *MPC* in the vicinity of *DI* = $12,000 is about .64 (a little higher, if we allow for the fact that this .64 figure is spread across a full $1000 income range).

3.   Graphically, the *MPC* is the slope of the propensity-to-consume line. (The idea of slope was reviewed in the Appendix to Chapter 1.) If you have had any training in calculus, this will tell you that the *MPC* is really the derivative of the consumption function; if you have not, understanding the notion of *MPC* might help you when you do take calculus. Meanwhile, the average propensity to consume is simply the slope of a line connecting a point on the propensity-to-consume line and the origin. (On the basis of the Appendix to Chapter 1, can you show why?)

4.   There is also a *marginal propensity to save* (*MPS*). We know already that a family must always decide to allocate any increase in *DI* (positive or negative) between extra *C* and extra *S*. If the *MPC* stands for the fraction of an extra dollar of income devoted to *C*, then the remaining fraction (*MPS*) must go to saving. Always, that is:

$$MPC + MPS = 1$$

4.   Review question 1 gave the following propensity to consume: spend on *C* one-half of weekly *DI* plus $100. Given this consumption function, complete the blanks below to indicate the change in *C* spending resulting from the indicated change in *DI*. Complete also the *MPC* column (ratio of extra *C* to extra *DI*):

Change in *DI*	Change in *C*	*MPC*
From $0 to $1 (+$1)	_____	_____
From $399 to $400 (+$1)	_____	_____
From $400 to $401 (+$1)	_____	_____
From $400 to $410 (+$10)	_____	_____
From $410 to $400 (−$10)	_____	_____
From $400 to $399 (−$1)	_____	_____

Change in *C*: +50¢, +50¢, +50¢, +$5, −$5; −50¢, *MPC*: ½ throughout

5.   **a.** What is the slope of the propensity-to-consume line of Figure 7-2 (the propensity to consume of review questions 1 through 4)? _____.

Slope, as measured by the rule above, would indicate the ratio of change in (*DI* / *C* / *S*) to change in (*DI* / *C* / *S*). That is, it would measure the value of the (marginal / average) propensity to consume.

b. The *MPC*, in this instance as *DI* rises, (falls / remains constant / rises). Graphically, this propensity to consume is a (straight / curved) line. Its slope does not change; hence neither does the *MPC*.

By contrast, the propensity to consume illustrated in the text's Figure 7-2 "bends over." Its slope (increases / remains constant / decreases) as the *DI* level increases. Correspondingly, the *MPC* involved (increases / remains constant / decreases) as *DI* increases.

a. ½; *C*; *DI*; marginal   **b.** remains constant; straight; decreases; decreases

6.   Show, for the income levels given, the fraction of total income spent on consumption, and the marginal propensity to consume, for the family in questions 1 through 5.

	DI	Fraction of *DI* Spent on *C*	*MPC*
	$100	_____	_____
	200	_____	_____
	300	_____	_____
	400	_____	_____
	500	_____	_____

The figures you have entered in the middle column above represent a series of (marginal / average) propensities to consume. They deal with total *DI* and total *C*, whereas the *MPC* deals with extra or additional amounts.

DI fractions: $\frac{3}{2}$, 1, $\frac{5}{6}$, $\frac{3}{4}$, $\frac{7}{10}$; *MPC*: ½ throughout   average

A final point regarding the propensity to consume—and again an important one in terms of material to follow in the text. If a family increases its *C* spending, a likely explanation—but not the only possible one—is that its *DI* has increased. If the imaginary family of the preceding questions were to increase its *C* spending from $300 to $350 weekly, the increase could well be attributable to a rise in *DI* from $400 to $500. But this change could occur for other reasons. The family might (with an unchanged *DI*) be changing the distribution of its *DI* between *C* and *S*. It might have decided that its saving for future needs was close to sufficient; or it might be increasing its *C* spending because of greater optimism about the level of its future income. There are plenty of conceivable explanations.

Note this carefully:

▶ If the amount of money habitually spent on consumption changes for any reason other than a change in *DI*, then the propensity-to-consume line has shifted to a new position.

▶ To put the same idea in different words, any nontransitory change in the distribution of *DI* between *C* and *S* means a change in the position of the propensity-to-consume line.

The situation is precisely analogous to the demand curve analysis of Chapter 4. A demand curve shows how quantity purchased will increase if price falls. But price is not the only factor influencing quantity of purchases. Purchases may change because of a change in tastes, a rise in the price of substitute goods, or for other reasons. If some factor such as this—anything other than a change in the price of the good involved—is responsible, then we must show the demand curve as moving to a brand-new position.

The same reasoning applies to our propensity-to-consume line. It shows how *C* expenditure will change with any change in *DI*—other factors held constant. If some one of these other factors changes (thus producing a change in *C* for some reason other than a change in *DI*), then we must show the whole propensity-to-consume curve as having moved to an appropriate new position.

7. a. The family of earlier questions has a *DI* of $450 weekly (so that its *C* expenditure is $325). One family member now leaves home to get married, and so the propensity-to-consume schedule changes. It now becomes: one-half of *DI*, plus $75.

If family *DI* is unaltered, its weekly *C* spending will henceforth be $*(300 / 325 / 350 / 375)*. On a propensity-to-consume graph such as Figure 7-2 above, this change would be represented as (pick one):

(1) A movement downward along the existing curve.

(2) A movement upward along the existing curve.

(3) A shift of the entire propensity-to-consume curve upward to a new position.

(4) A shift of the entire propensity-to-consume curve downward to a new position.

Is the value of the marginal propensity to consume changed? *(No / Yes, it has risen / Yes, it has fallen)*

b. Suppose the new propensity-to-consume schedule had been: spend two-fifths of *DI*, plus $75. If so, as compared with the previous schedule, the value of the *MPC* would *(fall / remain unchanged / rise)*.

---

a. 300; (4); No **b.** fall (*Note:* When the propensity-to-consume schedule changes, the *MPC* may change, or may not. The *MPC* is strictly concerned with a given propensity to consume, and with the ratio between extra *C* and extra *DI*, given that propensity to consume)

---

8. a. The solid line *CC* in Figure 7-4 illustrates a community's propensity-to-consume schedule. One possible level of total *DI* is indicated by the horizontal measure *OA*, and total consumption expenditure out of that particular *DI* by the vertical measure *DO*.

The community's total *C* expenditure now rises from *DO* to *EO*. This increase could be the consequence of (pick one):

(1) Only an increase in *DI* from level *OA* to level *OB*.

(2) Only some factor other than a *DI* increase—a factor causing the propensity-to-consume line to shift upward to a new position indicated by the broken line *C'C'*.

(3) Either of (1) or (2)—an increase in *DI*, or else a decision to spend more prompted by some factor other than an increase in *DI*.

b. A respected economic authority predicts a coming recession. His prediction is influential, and people decide that they should spend less and save more as a precaution against coming hard times (even though *DI* has not fallen—not yet, at any rate). If this decision were to be illustrated in Figure 7-4 terms, it would imply (pick one):

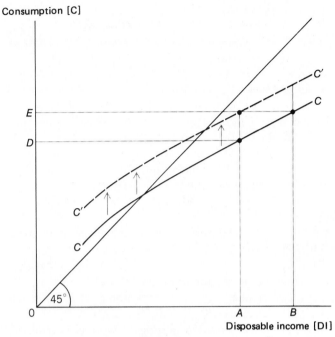

Consumption [C]

Disposable income [DI]

Figure 7-4

(1) A movement downward and to the left along a given propensity-to-consume line, say, the solid *CC* one, to indicate the reduced *C* spending.

(2) An upward movement of the entire propensity-to-consume line—say, from the position indicated by the solid *CC* line upward to the broken *C'C'* line.

(3) A downward movement of the entire propensity-to-consume line—say, from the position indicated by the broken *C'C'* line downward to the solid *CC* line.

c. Which of the following would cause the propensity-to-consume line to shift up? _____. To shift down? _____.

(1) An anticipated downturn in business conditions that leads everybody to worry that they might lose their jobs.

(2) A reduction in the interest rate paid by banks that makes saving less attractive to everyone.

(3) A reduction in taxes so that people retain more of their income after taxes.

(4) An actual contraction in the economy that causes a reduction in the availability of outside or overtime employment.

---

a. (3) **b.** (3) **c.** up; (d); down: (1) [Answers (3) and (4) are incorrect because they imply movement along the propensity-to-consume curve rather than shifts in the curve itself. Answer (3), for example, implies an increase in disposable income and not an increase in the marginal propensity to consume. The careful reader might object to this because Figure 7-2 in the text indicates some sensitivity in the marginal propensity to consume to changes in income. Figure 7-2 illustrates, however, one individual's behavior. Figure 7-5 shows that, when things are aggregated, the marginal propensity to consume is remarkably insensitive to income. The key, therefore, is that (1) and (2) produce changes in the level of consumption at any level of disposable income while (3) and (4) produce only changes in the level of disposable income.

The Investment Flow   Finally, we are able to turn to the second component of the spending flow: investment. In the main, investment spending is spending by business firms for the purchase of new capital goods—new buildings, new machinery, and so on. Changes in the levels of inventories count, too.

We cannot isolate any one factor that dominates in explaining the flow of investment. Investment spending is undertaken in the hope of making some profit relative to the cost. It is, therefore, influenced by a wide range of economic and psychological variables. First, of course, is the cost of the investment, both for the physical equipment or material involved and for the money required to finance the expenditure. The rate of interest charged by the financing institution is thus critical. This is true whether or not the business is borrowing to finance the investment or using its own money. Why? When the investing firm is considering what to do with its money, it has no particular allegiance to anything. It will put its money where it will earn the highest return. If that highest return is earned by putting the money in a bank or some government bond, then so be it. The proposed physical investment project will go by the boards.

The second determinant of the flow of investment is the anticipated stream of income that the investment would generate. Would the project pay off quickly, or would it take a long time? Can business conditions in the future be expected to support the increased activity that the project would generate, or would the project appeal to a market that is already saturated by competition? Critical here, of course, is the anticipated health of the entire economy. If a weak economy were anticipated, then an investment project that would try to sell a new product or more of an old product would not be as attractive as it would be if a vigorous, growing economy were forecast.

The result of all this anticipation is that investment spending is extremely volatile and extremely hard to predict. It is, in fact, much harder to predict than the consumption flow. Investment is, nonetheless, one of the keys to disturbances in the growth of GNP and NNP. Its full significance will be revealed in Chapter 8.

We can begin to piece together the parts of the puzzle even before then, however, by joining the two flows of spending: consumption and investment. They are both flows of money toward producing firms—firms producing consumption goods and/or firms producing investment goods. Both flows generate production and employment to meet a demand. Their only fundamental difference lies in their respective origins. We know now that the consumption flow originates with consumers. It is a flow represented in Figure 7-5 by the path entering from the bottom right. The investment flow originates with businesses, meanwhile, and is portrayed in Figure 7-5 along a second path entering from the bottom left. Without government in the picture, these are the only two sources of earned income for the business sector with

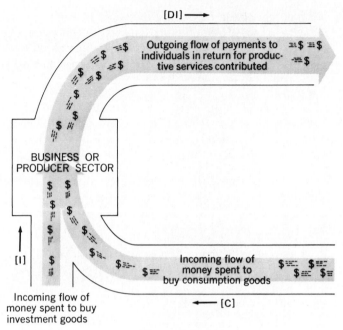

Figure 7-5

which it can finance its payment of wages, dividends, and other factor costs.

Now look at Figure 7-6; it is a carefully constructed composite of Figures 7-1 and 7-5. Study it carefully. It depicts the central money flow of a typical capitalistic economy and previews the analysis of Chapters 8 and 9. It shows a clockwise flow of money incomes and spending. This circular flow is continually being depleted by the outward "drain" of consumer saving. It is continually being replenished by the inflow of new investment spending.

Examining Figure 7-6, you may at first feel a strong inclination to tidy it up or complete it by linking the S drain with the I inflow, so as to make a closed loop through which saved money flows into investment spending. But be careful! We are, in this chapter, stressing the cleavage between saving and investment—the fact that one group (business firms seeking to buy new capital goods) does most of the investing, while another group (consumers) does much of the saving.[2] In Figure 7-6 terms, this means we cannot take it for granted that the dollar amount of the I inflow (lower left) will automatically equal the dollar amount of the S outflow (lower right). Much of the theory of income determination to follow turns on the question of what it means to the economy if the relation between I and S is disturbed. Suppose I and S have been equal in amount. Now let the I flow suddenly grow smaller (because some business firms decide that they have added enough new plant and

[2] A substantial amount of saving is done by corporations. "Corporate saving" means the same thing as "undistributed corporation profits," or the total of "additions to retained earnings." Since most of this "saving" is used to finance investment projects, it is an exception to the "different groups" idea. Begin by assuming that such corporate saving is zero. It can easily be fitted into the analysis after you have mastered the all-important basic relationships.

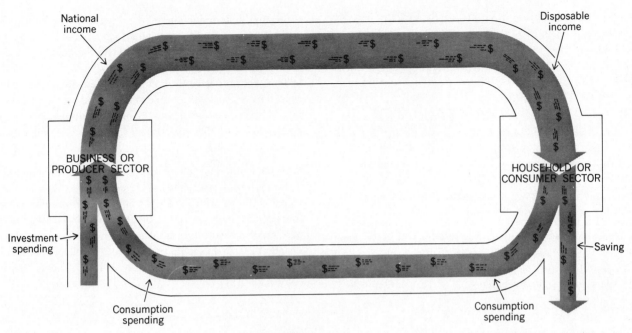

Figure 7-6

equipment for the time being). The *S* decision makers (households) cannot be expected to change their plans because of a change in *I* decisions about which they were not consulted, and did not even know about. A shrinkage in the planned *I* flow does not occasion an immediate and equal shrinkage in the planned *S* flow. We must allow for the possibility of differences beween the two intended flows. (And if the *I*-spending inflow is reduced, with the *S* outflow remaining unchanged, the level of incomes received must fall.)

Thus it would be wrong to finish off Figure 7-6 by making a closed loop between the *S* outflow and the *I* inflow. To do this would be to imply that the *I* inflow could never be anything different in amount from the *S* outflow. It would imply that the *I* flow could never decrease except as the result of a prior decrease in the *S* flow—and similarly for *I* increases.

Yet it is true that personal saving does flow into investment through borrowing or the sale of new corporation stock. An open reservoir, as in Figure 7-7, pro-

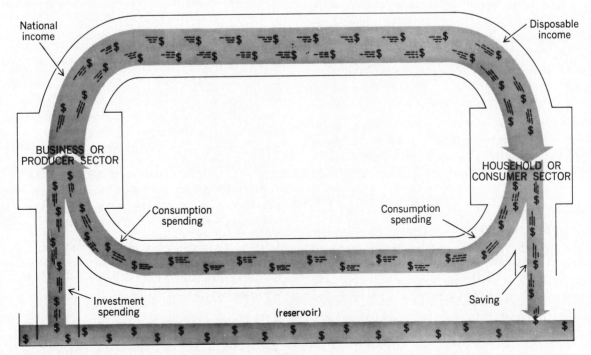

Figure 7-7

vides the needed connection between S and I. But it gives the I flow some freedom to increase or decrease without prior change in the S flow; and a change in the S flow does not mechanically force an identical change in the I flow.

9.   Investment, as the term is used in economics (e.g., a firm purchases a new machine tool or an addition to its existing plant), generates employment while the investment item in question is being built, and results in income earned for those so employed. In terms of Figures 7-6 and 7-7, it is a flow of money expenditure to the firms which produce such investment goods. In this sense, do the following constitute investment?

a. Having a contractor build a new house for you. . . . .

. . . . *(Yes / No)*

b. Buying a house built a year ago. . . . . *(Yes / No)*

c. Buying Du Pont stock on the stock market. . . *(Yes / No)*

d. Buying stock in a newly formed corporation, where the money proceeds from stock sale are to be used to build a new factory building. . . . . *(Yes / No)*

e. Using money obtained from the bond or stock issue of item **d** to build a new factory building. . . . . *(Yes / No)*

---

a. Yes; **b., c., d.,** No; **e.** Yes (*Note:* The answer cannot be Yes for both **d** and **e**, or else there would be double counting. The sale of stock may be a necessary prerequisite to investment, but it is only a transfer payment from the stock buyers to the new corporation. Actual investment takes place only when money is in fact spent for the purpose defined as investment)

---

10.   **a.** A firm is considering building a new plant to add to its output capacity. To do this sensibly, it must try to evaluate the future market for its product to be sure there is likely to be sufficient demand to justify that plant. This requires it to estimate, among other things, the likely degree of competition from rival firms, and coming "general business conditions"—i.e., probable future course of GNP. True or False? . . . .

. . . . *(T / F)*

b. This means, then, that the flow of expenditure through the "investment intake" of Figures 7-6 and 7-7 is governed by many considerations frequently having to do with forecasts about the future. . . . . *(T / F)*

c. A large corporation which has been steadily adding new plant and equipment may stop doing so because it feels it has "caught up" with probable demand for its product for the time being. If it stops, the flow through the "investment intake" of Figures 7-6 and 7-7 will be correspondingly reduced. . . . .

. . . . *(T / F)*

d. Such investment plans may be postponed or canceled because the firm is fearful of a recession—a drop or pause in GNP. This would again mean a drop in the flow of investment spending. . . . . *(T / F)*

e. If any such reduction in the investment-spending flow occurs, it is reasonable to assume that there will at once be a matching reduction in the flow of personal saving. . . . *(T / F)*

f. The economy goes through a period of high interest rates caused by a variety of internal and external factors. The result should be a reduction in both the investment financed through borrowing *and* the investment financed through retained earnings . . . . *(T / F)*

g. After a period in which every economist in the country had a different forecast of future economic activity, the nation enters a period during which there is rough consensus among major forecasters (there will *never* be absolute consensus about the past much less the future) that a period of reasonable and sustainable growth should be expected to pull an economy out of a slump. The result should be an immediate increase in investment activity. . . . . *(T / F)*

All true except **e** and **g**. Plans to save are, in general, made quite independently of plans to invest; **e** is, therefore, false. After a recession, investment does not increase even with the expectation of recovery until capacity idled by the recession is more fully utilized and the need for investment to increase or improve capacity is more completely known. The result: **g** is also false

---

11.   **a.** Money saved by a family and hidden in the family mattress is money withdrawn from the income stream; it creates no income or jobs for anyone so long as it remains in the mattress. . . . . *(T / F)*

b. Money saved by a family and promptly used to buy a new house is money put right back into the income stream. Because (by the definitions of Chapter 6) any consumer expenditure for the construction of a new house counts as investment expenditure, these actions would count as both saving and investment.

. . . . *(T / F)*

c. Money saved by a family and promptly used to buy General Motors stock would count as both saving and investment.

. . . . *(T / F)*

d. Money saved and deposited in a savings account in a bank counts as saving. This is not investment in the national-income sense. So long as this money stays deposited, it can be used for investment spending only if the bank lends it to some borrower, or if the bank uses the money itself. . . . . *(T / F)*

e. Much investment spending is financed by use of other people's money, i.e., financed by borrowing from a bank or by sale of bond or stock issues. . . . . *(T / F)*

f. Those who are in a position to lend money must consider (1) the honesty of the would-be borrower, and (2) his or her ability to repay the borrowed money, i.e., the prospects for profitable use of such money. . . . . *(T / F)*

g. If business conditions seem particularly uncertain, people with money to spare may hesitate to lend it, feeling that would-be borrowers are likely to get into trouble and be unable

to make repayment. Thus, even though there are mechanisms for converting saving into investment, this does not mean that all saved money is automatically transformed into investment.
.... *(T / F)*

All true except **c** [*Note 1:* Money spent to buy a stock or a bond does not count as investment; see parts **(3)** and **(4)** of question 9. *Note 2:* When a family spends money to have a new house built, we must think of this money, in Figure 7-6 and 7-7 terms, as passing through the "saving drain," going at once through the saved-money reservoir, and up through the "investment-spending intake." It would be easier to think of it as simply passing through the consumption loop, like any other consumer expenditure; but we can't do that because the national-product definitions say that any new housing purchase is the one consumer expenditure item which must be classified as investment. No great analytic issue is involved; it's just a matter of respecting the definitions.]

Having spent the effort in exploring the reasons why saving might not match investment, it seems reasonable to spend a little extra effort in anticipating the answer to the "So what?" question that will be addressed over the next several chapters. The key lies in Figure 7-7 and the recollection that spending flows generate business activity and thus employment. Suppose, for the sake of illustration, that *S* were to exceed *I*. Then, in terms of Figure 7-7, the money leaving through the *S* "drain" would not be matched by an identical quantity of money entering through the *I* "faucet." The circular pool on the top would, therefore, necessarily shrink, thereby supporting less business activity and fewer jobs. Unemployment should, as a result, be expected to rise.

But what of the accounting identity that demands that actual investment always equal actual saving? How can the measured investment be brought up to the level of saving in the example just described? The answer lies in inventory investment. Less business, fewer jobs, and more unemployed workers mean a smaller circular pool in Figure 7-7; they mean lower-than-expected demand for products in the real economy. Unsold products therefore accumulate on shelves and create higher-than-expected accumulation of final product inventories. Since these accumulations are part of actual investment, they swell actual investment beyond the intended level and up to the level of actual saving.

12. There are 100 families in an economy. Half have an *MPC* of ½; half have an *MPC* of ¾. If this economy's *DI* rises by $10,000, and all this goes to the first group, then *C* spending will rise by $(*zero / 2500 / 5000 / 7500 / 10,000*). If, instead, all the additional *DI* goes to the second group, then *C* spending will rise by $(*zero / 2500 / 5000 / 7500 / 10,000*).

Thus, even if we know the exact propensity to consume of each family, we *(cannot / can)* predict the exact *C* increase that would follow any given *DI* increase. If different families have different marginal propensities, then for such a prediction, we would have to know how the *DI* increase was distributed—i.e., which families got the extra *DI*.

Or suppose every family has exactly the same propensity to consume, but there is some curvature in the propensity-to-consume line, as in text Figure 7-2. Such a curvature means that *MPC* *(increases / remains constant / decreases)* as *DI* increases. If there is some inequality in the distribution of income, then we *(could / could not)* predict the exact amount of change in *C* associated with any given *DI* change.

In sum, there are analytic difficulties in moving from an individual-family to a whole-community propensity to consume. But note (see text) that the relationship between *DI* and *C* for the whole economy is still remarkably consistent.

5000; 7500; cannot; decreases; could not

---

13. There are 200 families in a community. Each of these families spends exactly $100 plus one-half its income each week on consumption. (Review question 1 uses this propensity to consume.) Half (100) these families are "poor"; they each receive weekly incomes of $200. The other 100 families are "rich"; they receive $400 apiece weekly.

It is desired to increase total consumption spending in this community. (Reasons for wishing such an increase can be disregarded.) It is proposed to increase total spending by taxing rich families $100 apiece weekly, giving the tax proceeds to poor families to spend. Thus, each and every family would have a net weekly income of $300.

This proposal is justified as follows: poor families spend 100 percent of their incomes on consumption; they receive $200, and they spend $200. Rich families spend only 75 percent of their income; they receive $400, but they spend only $300. So the total of consumption spending would be increased by redistribution of income.

a. Would such a proposal, if adopted, increase total consumption spending? Explain your answer in terms of the marginal propensity to consume.

b. Are there any circumstances in which such a redistribution-of-income proposal would increase consumption spending? Again answer in terms of the *MPC*.

c. Explain two circumstances in which a redistribution of income through this tax scheme might actually lower consumption spending. (This is a hard question; think beyond the *MPC* notion that was sufficient to answer part **b**.)

---

a. No. Their *MPC*s are identical **b.** Yes, if the *MPC* for the lower-income people were higher than the *MPC* for the upper-income people **c.** One clearly is the opposite case of the one described in **b**. A second takes note of how hard people work. If the wealthier people worked less and were paid correspondingly less, total spending might fall because total output fell.

QUIZ: Multiple Choice

1. The "marginal propensity to consume" means:
(1) at any income level, ratio of total consumption to total income.

(2) at any income level, change in consumption spending caused by an income change (increase or decrease).

(3) for each and all income levels, a schedule showing amount of consumption spending at that level.

(4) at any income level, and concerning a small change in that level, the ratio of resulting change in consumption to change in income level.

(5) none of these things.

2.   The volume or magnitude of investment opportunities in the American economy (using "investment" in its national-product sense), according to the text, is governed primarily by:

(1) the total amount of saving available for investment users.

(2) the level of prevailing interest rates.

(3) the state of the stock market.

(4) the rate at which new and commercially exploitable inventions are appearing from laboratories.

(5) none of the above, there being no such single dominant factor.

3.   The relation between the marginal propensities to consume and to save is that:

(1) their total must equal 1, since some fraction of extra income must go to extra consumption spending, and the remaining fraction to extra saving.

(2) the ratio between them must indicate the "average propensity to consume."

(3) their total must indicate the current total of disposable income received, since *DI* must divide between consumption and saving.

(4) the point at which they are equal must be the "breakeven" level of income.

(5) their total must equal zero.

4.   "Personal saving," as the term is used in connection with national-income and national-product analysis, means explicitly:

(1) the total of all assets held by families.

(2) income received within the period in question and not spent on consumption.

(3) the total of all assets held by families minus the total of their liabilities.

(4) income received within the period in question but used only to buy a security or deposited in a bank.

(5) income received within the period in question, not spent on consumption and not used to buy a security nor deposited in a bank.

5.   If people do not consume all their income, but put the unspent amount into a bank or buy a security with it, in national-income and -product terms they are:

(1) saving but not investing.

(2) investing but not saving.

(3) both saving and investing.

(4) neither saving nor investing.

(5) saving, but investing only to the extent that they buy securities.

6.   Which of the following would be regarded as investment by economists concerned with national product and income?

(1) Any purchase of a corporation bond.

(2) Any amount saved out of income and not "hoarded."

(3) Any purchase of a new corporation bond.

(4) Any productive activity resulting in present consumption.

(5) None of the preceding.

7.   The "breakeven point" on a family's propensity-to-consume schedule is at the point where:

(1) its saving equals its income.

(2) its income equals its consumption.

(3) its saving equals its consumption.

(4) its consumption equals its investment.

(5) the marginal propensity to consume equals 1.

8.   In Figure 7-8, the solid line *CC* is the propensity to consume for some family or community. If the total amount of consumption expenditure is *EA*, then the amount of disposable income must be:

(1) *AB*.

(2) *FD*.

(3) *FA*.

(4) *DA*.

(5) none of the preceding.

9.   Alternatively, given the total amount of consumption expenditure *FA* in Figure 7-8, then the amount of disposable income must be:

(1) *EA*.

(2) *GB*.

(3) *ED*.

(4) *OA*.

(5) none of the preceding.

10.   In Figure 7-9, if the solid propensity-to-consume line *CC* were to shift upward to the broken-line position *C'C'*, this would be appropriate to illustrate:

(1) an increase in consumption expenditure resulting from a rise in disposable income.

(2) a decision on the part of the family or community involved to consume more and save less out of any given disposable income.

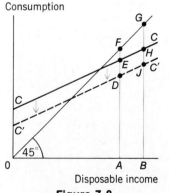

Figure 7-8

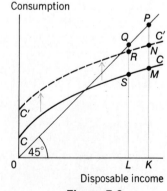

Figure 7-9

(3) a decrease in consumption expenditure resulting from a fall in disposable income.

(4) a decision on the part of the family or community involved to consume less and save more out of any given disposable income.

(5) none of these events.

11. The difference between Figures 7-8 and 7-9, both propensity-to-consume diagrams, is that:

(1) in Figure 7-8, the *MPC* (marginal propensity to consume) is constant; in Figure 7-9, the *MPC* decreases as income increases.

(2) in Figure 7-8, the *MPC* decreases as income increases; in Figure 7-9, the *MPC* is constant.

(3) in Figure 7-8, the *MPC* increases as income increases; in Figure 7-9, the *MPC* is constant.

(4) in Figure 7-8, the *MPC* is constant; in Figure 7-9, the *MPC* increases as income increases.

(5) in both instances, the *MPC* falls as income increases, but it falls more rapidly in the case of Figure 7-9.

12. In Figure 7-9, if the propensity-to-consume line is the solid line *CC*, and the amount of disposable income is *OK*, then the amount of saving out of that disposable income *OK* must be:

(1) *PK*.

(2) *MK*.

(3) *PM*.

(4) *NM*.

(5) none of the preceding.

13. If, again in Figure 7-9, the amount of disposable income were to change from *OK* to *OL*—the solid *CC* line still indicating the propensity-to-consume line—the amount of saving out of income would become:

(1) *SM*.

(2) *QR*.

(3) *PQ*.

(4) *RS*.

(5) *QS*.

14. In Figure 7-8, a change in consumption expenditure from *HB* to *EA* would be the result of:

(1) a decision to spend more and save less at each level of income.

(2) a decrease in disposable income from *OB* to *OA*.

(3) a decision to spend less and save more at each level of income.

(4) an increase in disposable income from *OA* to *OB*.

(5) none of the preceding.

15. The "propensity to consume" means, or refers to:

(1) the level of income at which consumption spending just equals income.

(2) the inclination on the part of some consumers to "keep up with the Joneses" in their consumer spending.

(3) the fraction of extra income that will be spent on consumption.

(4) a schedule showing the amount a family (or community) will spend on consumption at different levels of income.

(5) the fact that, at low incomes, families spend more on consumption than the amount of their incomes.

16. The statistical evidence suggests that the typical American family behaves as follows with respect to spending out of income:

(1) an increasing proportion of income is spent on consumption as income increases.

(2) the same proportion of income is spent on consumption at all except very low income levels.

(3) the same proportion of income is spent on consumption at all income levels.

(4) a decreasing proportion of income is spent on consumption as income increases.

(5) the same proportion of income is spent on consumption at all except very high income levels.

17. A family saves $2000 out of a disposable income of $10,000. Its propensity to consume can be represented by the solid line in Figure 7-8. At the $10,000 income level its marginal propensity to consume should be:

(1) less than ⅕.

(2) ⅕.

(3) less than ⅘, but not necesarily ⅕ or less.

(4) none of the preceding.

18. Which factor complicates the determination of the community's overall "propensity to consume?"

(1) The amount of consumption expenditure out of any given income total varies very substantially from one year to another.

(2) For the whole community, consumption and disposable income must be one and the same thing.

(3) Families save more money at higher income levels, which means that they save a larger fraction of their total incomes.

(4) Families save more money at higher income levels, which means that they save a smaller fraction of their total incomes.

(5) The total of consumption expenditure out of any given income total may vary according to how income is distributed among the members of that community.

19. Among the following five statements, four repeat ideas stressed in Chapter 7. The fifth is not a proper statement of any idea in this chapter. Which statement is incorrect?

(1) Much of the saving in today's society is done by one group, and much of the investment by a different group.

(2) Undistributed corporation profits (addition to retained earnings) constitute one case in which both saving and investment are undertaken by the same economic unit.

(3) The total amount of investment spending is capable of varying considerably from year to year.

(4) In today's society, people will not choose to save whenever there are few or no opportunities for investment.

(5) The total amount of personal saving is governed by the

amount of disposable income and by the propensity to consume.

20.   A family spends $2000 on consumption when its income is zero, and $6000 on consumption when its income is $6000. Graphically, its propensity to consume is a straight line, as in Figure 7-8. At this family's $6000 income level, its marginal propensity to consume is:

(1) ⅔.

(2) ¾.

(3) ⅘.

(4) 1.

(5) greater than 1.

21.   "Investment" and "consumption," as these terms are used in national-income and -product analysis, have which feature in common?

(1) Both activities are undertaken by the same group (i.e., households), although not always for the same reasons.

(2) Both are demands calling for the current use or employment of the economy's stock of productive inputs.

(3) Both are components of disposable income.

(4) In both instances, the only factor of major consequence which governs them is the level of national product or disposable income.

(5) None of the preceding.

CHAPTER 8

THE THEORY OF OUTPUT DETERMINATION

Previous chapters have introduced you to the fundamental concepts of macroeconomic analysis: aggregate supply, aggregate demand, GNP, price indices, consumption, saving, and investment. It is now time to learn how to use these concepts to develop an understanding of how a macroeconomy works. What, in particular, can an understanding of how these concepts interact teach us about our ability to manipulate a large economy? Can we learn what sort of policies might help us to avoid overheated periods of unacceptably high inflation? Or sluggish times of unacceptably high unemployment? Or stagnant times marked by unacceptably high levels of both? Or is the die cast beyond our control?

Chapter 8 will begin your investigation into these questions, and it will quickly lead you into an area of enormous controversy. The first part of the chapter will use the simple notions of aggregate supply and demand to contrast two fundamentally different schools of thought. On the one hand will be the classical view of the world that will be summarized, in an oversimplified way, by drawing a vertical aggregate suppy curve. Classicists believe that prices and wages adjust so quickly and completely that output and employment are determined only by the potential of an economy. There will not, for any significant length of time (in the absence of artificial interference by the government), exist involuntary unemployment of any productive resources. Changes in aggregate demand, classicists believe, do nothing but create changes in prices and wages, and so there is neither the need nor the ability for policies to be written to move aggregate demand one way or the other in the hopes of influencing GNP.

Keynesians take a different approach. They note many reasons why wages and prices do not always respond to periods of either excess demand or (more importantly) excess supply. Wages do not, the Keynesians argue for example, fall very quickly when the supply of labor exceeds the demand for labor (as in a recession or depression). Their simplified aggregate supply curve is therefore horizontal, and the equilibria that they envision can occur anywhere with any level of employment. Equilibrium can, in particular, occur well below the potential output of the economy in question, and persist there for a long time. Keynesians also believe, however, that the manipulation of aggregate demand can be used to move equilibrium up toward potential GNP when it is required to reduce unemployment.

The second part of the chapter presents the simple Keynesian model and shows how the multiple equilibria are computed. Imbedded in this computation is the observation that a given change in consumption or investment expenditure will cause a greater change in the equilibrium level of GNP. This amplification is known as the multiplier effect, and it will serve as a focal point of the discussion of fiscal policy to be conducted in Chapter 9. The concluding section to Chapter 8 will, however, emphasize that this multiplier result depends critically upon the Keynesian assumption about wages and prices. A reduction in aggregate demand must not be associated with lower wages and prices if GNP is to fall. An enlarged aggregate demand must, similarly, be accommodated by some unemployed resources that have been idled by an existing equilibrium falling well below potential GNP; otherwise, the stimulus of higher demand will simply be vented in the form of higher prices.

It will serve you well to carry the caution of this concluding section with you as you proceed through the coming chapters on macroeconomic policy. Having completed even this first chapter in output determination, though, you will have accomplished the following objectives.

LEARNING OBJECTIVES

1. Understand that the classical view of the world envisions wages and prices responding so quickly that an economy's performance is determined almost exclusively by its potential

GNP. In the simplified arena of aggregate supply and demand, this view is represented by a vertical aggregate supply curve at potential GNP.

2.   Understand that the Keynesian view of the world envisions wages and prices responding so slowly that an economy can be in equilibrium well below its potential. In the aggregate supply and demand arena, this view is represented by a horizontal aggregate supply curve up through potential GNP.

3.   Derive the classicists' results that (*a*) there exists no involuntary unemployment and (*b*) policy designed to manipulate aggregate demand will affect neither GNP nor employment.

4.   Derive the Keynesian results that (*a*) there can exist involuntary unemployment even in what appears to be equilibrium and (*b*) policy designed to manipulate aggregate can affect both output and employment.

5.   State the two algebraic equations by means of either of which the "equilibrium level" of GNP can be defined. Explain briefly what is meant by "equilibrium" in GNP.

6.   Describe briefly what happens when the total dollar amount which business firms plan to invest (*a*) falls short of or (*b*) exceeds the amount which consumes wish to save out of income. Sketch diagrams if necessary to illustrate your descriptions.

7.   Explain why an equilibrium level of GNP is reached when the amount of planned investment spending is just equal to the amount of saving indicated by the propensity to save for that particular GNP level. If necessary, sketch a diagram to illustrate your explanation.

8.   Explain why a state of equilibrium can be expressed in terms of GNP = *C* + *I* (assuming the *C* in this equation corresponds to that dictated by the propensity to consume for this particular GNP). If necessary, sketch a diagram to illustrate your explanation.

9.   Describe what happens to GNP if there is a "downward shift" in the community's propensity to consume (i.e., if at each and any level of *DI* or GNP, the amount the public plans to spend on consumption is decreased). Describe similarly the consequences of an "upward shift" in the propensity to consume.

10.   Understand why the Keynesian view of the world can be considered only when there exist unemployed resources in an economy operating well below its potential.

This list of objectives is uncommonly long. Its length speaks graphically to the importance of this chapter, though, so it is presented in its entirety without apology. Chapter 8 is simply a critical juncture in your journey through the foundations of modern macroeconomics—critical for two very good reasons. First, the tools and concepts developed here will prove to be the essential building blocks for what follows. You will be using the tools presented in Chapter 8 to contemplate answers to

questions of policy and practice for the next 10 chapters. Without a thorough understanding of the foundation laid in Chapter 8, you will be lost. Second, and new to this edition, the very heart of the policy controversy that rages throughout the free world today is accurately identified in this chapter in the simplest possible terms. As you work through the various parts of this chapter, the bare essentials of the debate will be laid before you. You will, as you begin to study the debate, be laying your own groundwork for understanding the sources of the controversy, perceiving the relative merits of both sides, and making up your own mind about which view is more reasonable. You will use the simplicity of this chapter later to see and assess the need for the theoretical middle ground that is so elusive. The time that you spend here will, quite clearly, pay large dividends later.

1.   Consult Figures 8-1 and 8-2. On both are depicted aggregate supply schedules based upon a potential output of $1000 (billion). Identify the indicated figure with either the classical or the Keynesian view of the economic world in the spaces provided below:

a. Figure 8-1: _____

b. Figure 8-2: _____

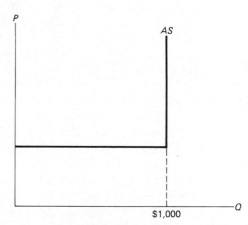

Figure 8-1

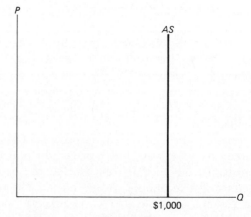

Figure 8-2

The (*Keynesian / classical*) view holds that a reduction in aggregate demand will cause no significant change in GNP because there will be (*an immediate / no significant*) change in prices. The appropriate representation of the aggregate supply curve is therefore (*a horizontal line up to / a vertical line directly above*) potential output. The (*Keynesian / classical*) view meanwhile holds that a reduction in aggregate demand will cause GNP to fall by more than the initial reduction in demand because there will be (*an immediate / no significant*) change in prices. The appropriate representation of the aggregate supply curve is therefore (*a horizontal line up to / a vertical line directly above*) potential output.

---

a. Keynesian **b.** classical; classical; an immediate; a vertical line directly above; Keynesian; no significant; a horizontal line up to

2. The classical view of the economic world is based upon the immediate responsiveness of wages and prices to disequilibrium. Belief in this responsiveness was dealt a severe blow by (*World War II / the stock market crash of 1929 / the Great Depression*). A persistent unemployment rate of about (*8 percent / 25 percent / 34 percent*) during the early 1930s cast serious doubt on the ability of wages to fall in response to excess supply of labor. Even today, many reasons why wages appear to be sticky, at least "sticky-down," can be advanced; the text lists at least four:

a. _____

b. _____

c. _____

d. _____

If you accept the stickiness of wages, as the Keynesians do, then it (*is / is not*) possible for an equilibrium to persist with a high rate of unemployment of not only labor, but also other productive resources. In response to this situation, a Keynesian would prescribe (*nothing, because nothing would work / some kind of increase in aggregate demand / some kind of reduction in aggregate demand*) that would increase equilibrium GNP and thus employment. A classicist would prescribe (*nothing because nothing is required / some sort of increase in aggregate demand / some sort of reduction in aggregate supply*); he or she would remark either that the existing unemployment was voluntary or that artificial barriers had prevented the necessary movement of wages down to equilibrium.

---

the Great Depression; 25 percent **a.** three-year contracts **b.** cost of living clauses **c.** regulated prices **d.** the price-setting inertia of large corporations is; some kind of increase in aggregate demand; nothing, because nothing is required

3. In the spaces provided in the table below, indicate what a Keynesian and a classicist would expect to be the effect on GNP and prices of the following events. Indicate only the direction of the expected effect by recording a (+) for "up," (−) for "down," and (o) for "no change." It may be useful (as it always seems to be) to represent the event on the graph with the appropriate aggregate supply curve drawn beforehand. Graphs hardly ever generate any news, but they frequently make it easier to apply something that we already know. Assume no effect other than the direct effect of the event noted on one curve.

    A.   An increase in potential output

    B.   A large increase in aggregate demand

    C.   An increase in interest rates that depresses aggregate demand

    D.   An increase in OPEC oil prices that depresses the demand for other goods and services

    E.   A major catastrophe that reduces potential output by 25 percent

Case	Keynesian		Classicist	
	Price	Output	Price	Output
A	_____	_____	_____	_____
B	_____	_____	_____	_____
C	_____	_____	_____	_____
D	_____	_____	_____	_____
E	_____	_____	_____	_____

Reading across rows: A: (o); (o); (−); (+); B: (+); (+); (+); (o); C: (−); (−); (−); (o); D: (−); (−); (−); (o); E: (o) though perhaps (+) if potential output is now less than demand; (o) though perhaps (−) if potential output is now lower than the old equilibrium; (+); (−)

We now turn to a more thorough development of the simple Keynesian model of output determination. The notion behind the Keynesian determination of output is one of equilibrium. Although it might look different in the geometry of consumption, investment, and GNP, the Keynesian equilibrium is really the very same equilibrium as the earlier one that equates aggregate supply with aggregate demand in the usual geometry of price and quantity axes. To a Keynesian, though, equilibrium is much more than the intersection of two lines or the equating of quantities supplied and demanded. To a Keynesian,

▶ The characteristic of an equilibrium GNP level is that it is one at which GNP has no tendency to rise or fall in value, because none of its components has any disposition to rise or fall in value.

Moreover,

▶ The actual level of GNP is not necessarily its equilibrium level. But if GNP is out of equilibrium, then it must be rising or falling in value as time proceeds. GNP is thereby seeking out its equilibrium value, and it will continue to rise or fall until it reaches that equilibrium level.

Finally,

▶ Equilibrium GNP does not necessarily mean full-employment GNP.

It is quite possible, in the Keynesian view, for GNP to be in equilibrium just where resources are (reasonably) fully employed with no undue pressure on prices. But it is also possible for GNP to be in equilibrium at a level much below full employment, so that the economy is stuck in conditions of recession or depression.

Similarly, GNP might be out of equilibrium even though its current disequilibrium level is one of full employment. It might be trying to reach an unattainable equilibrium, because that equilibrium is above the full-employment-of-resources level, given current prices. The outcome is then an upward price movement.

In sum, the fundamental Keynesian insight is that there is no automatic tendency for GNP to gravitate toward a level that is either needed or desired. It is the task of the remainder of this chapter to explain how that can be so.

To simplify matters, Chapter 8 presumes that government spending and taxation are so small relative to GNP that they can be ignored (i.e., treated as zero). Before you stop laughing, you should be warned that this is an assumption that will lapse in the very next chapter. For the time being, though, treating an economy with no government will make our lives as simple as they would be if the assumption were, in actual fact, true. Chapter 8 also handles depreciation in like fashion. Thus GNP is virtually the same thing as NNP. NNP is made up of C plus I (there being no G), and (because the items which cause the two totals to differ, mainly government items,[1] have been discarded) NNP is the same thing as DI (disposable income). This stripping-down process, clearing away a lot of detail, greatly simplifies the analysis; yet it does not significantly distort the reasoning involved or the ideas to be grasped. Chapter 9 tackles the same ideas with government brought back in again.

Chapter 7 noted that C spending is governed primarily by disposable income. In Figure 8-3, we show C as varying with GNP rather than DI; it is the level of GNP we want to explain, and the simplifying process just outlined has assured us that GNP and DI are pretty much the same thing. Figure 8-3's propensity-to-consume curve is a straight line (another simplification; it would complicate the analysis to give it a little real-life curvature, but it wouldn't alter the basic conclusions in any significant respect).

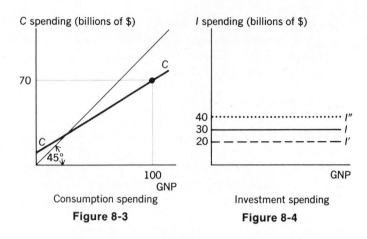

Consumption spending

Figure 8-3

Investment spending

Figure 8-4

Figure 8-4 refers to investment spending. This I spending is measured vertically, just as C spending is measured in Figure 8-3. Horizontally, we measure the level of GNP, just as Figure 8-3 does.

The fact that the I-spending line (the solid line) is shown as horizontal, at a height of 30, signifies that I is assumed to be $30 (billion) regardless of the GNP level. This is unrealistic because a GNP rise or fall is one of the factors likely to affect I spending. But we start with this assumption for convenience, then change it later on.

Remember that Chapter 7 taught us that I spending is influenced by many factors; it can readily change to a different level. For reasons quite apart from the level of GNP, for example, it may drop to $20 (indicated by the broken I' line); or it may rise to $40 (the dotted I'' line).

We begin, however, with I spending of $30 (billion) per period—and we begin, deliberately, with an equilibrium situation. We make GNP $100 (billion) per period. Figure 8-3's propensity to consume says that at this GNP level, the public will want to spend $70 on C, and save the other $30.

There are various ways of grasping why these figures fit together to produce "equilibrium." (Always use the way which seems to you to afford the most insight into the way things work in a real economy.) One method is to glance back to Study Guide Figure 7-7, the circular-income-flow diagram. If the inflow of money expenditure on investment projects is $30 and if the outflow of saved money is also $30 (i.e., if $30 is the amount that the public wants to save out of a GNP of $100), then nothing is happening that would cause the level of incomes (here, GNP), the amount of C, or the amount of S to change. (Remember, I is deliberately being held steady at $30.)

Equilibrium can be identified by *the saving-investment equality:*

▶ In equilibrium, the total of saving equals the total of investment.

The fact that S and I are both $30 does not happen automatically, remember. Business firms are doing most

---

[1]This means we also assume undistributed corporation profits to be zero. This item is likewise quite readily picked up at a later stage, when the essentials have been mastered.

or all of the investment, but consumers (a different group) are doing the saving.

The second characteristic by which equilibrium can be identified is less obvious.

▶The total of incomes earned is just equal to total expenditure to buy goods and services.

Sometimes this alternative measure of "equilibrium" is more convenient than the first, but it is no more than a different way of saying exactly the same thing. You can check this out if you wish by referring once again to Study Guide Figure 7-7. Given investment spending steady at $30, if incomes earned (the total clockwise flow through the upper loop in that diagram) come to $100, and the propensity to consume says that families want to spend $70 of that $100 on consumer items (saving the other $30), then total expenditure to buy goods and services will be $100: $70 on consumption products plus $30 on investment products. This equals total incomes earned of $100.

Once you have grasped the equilibrium relationships set out above between income, consumption, saving, and investment, you may ask: Is there much in all this that is worth studying? Absolutely. GNP can easily be pushed "out of equilibrium."

It isn't necessarily undesirable for a GNP equilibrium to be disrupted. If that equilibrium happened to be a deep-depression GNP, we would want it changed. In any event, when GNP is shoved out of equilibrium, whether this happens to be desirable or not, we get an interesting set of consequences.

The symptom of a disequilibrium GNP is that it is changing in value. It is moving up or down, seeking a new equilibrium at which it can settle.

In the simple model that we are using for the moment, only two things could throw GNP out of equilibrium: a decision to change I spending, or a decision to change C spending. In terms of Figures 8-3 and 8-4, the I line must shift in position, or the C line must shift.

Because of the inherent variability of investment-spending plans, these disturbances of equilibrium are usually (and most easily) outlined in terms of a change in the I-spending level. Nonetheless, the propensity to consume can also change, thereby throwing GNP out of equilibrium. An example of a change in consumer spending plans and its results follows later in this chapter.

4. Figures 8-5 (propensity to consume) and 8-6 (investment) below are similar in construction to Figures 8-3 and 8-4.

a. Consider Figure 8-6. (Disregard for the moment the broken I' line at height RO.) The solid I line at height BO is horizontal. To draw this line horizontally is to say that if the level of GNP were to rise, the amount of investment spending would (*rise* / *remain unchanged* / *fall*); if the level of GNP were to fall, I spending would (*rise* / *remain unchanged* / *fall*).

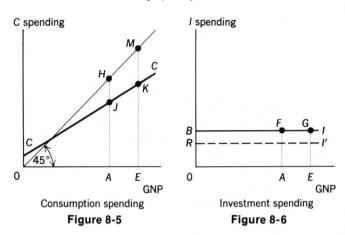

Figure 8-5
Consumption spending

Figure 8-6
Investment spending

b. Consider Figure 8-5. It says that if the amount of GNP were to be OE, the amount of consumption spending would be (*HA* / *JA* / *ME* / *KE*). With GNP at OE, the amount of saving would be (*HA* / *JA* / *MK* / *KE*).

If, however, GNP were to be at the lower level OA, then C spending would be (*HA* / *JA* / *ME* / *KE*), and S would be (*HJ* / *JA* / *MK* / *KE*).

---

a. remain unchanged; remain unchanged **b.** *KE*; *MK*; *JA*; *HJ*

---

5. If GNP is to be "in equilibrium," the amounts of S and I must be equal. Measure the two S amounts indicated on Figure 8-5 (*HJ* and *MK*), and compare them with the investment amount indicated by the solid I line (*BO*, *FA*, or *GE*) in Figure 8-6. The S value that would match this I value would be (*HJ* / *MK*).

That is to say, S and I will be equal when S has climbed to level MK. This would call for a GNP level of (*OA* / *OE*).

Given the I level BO (or FA or GE) and the propensity to consume of Figure 8-5, the equilibrium GNP level must be OE. This is the only GNP value at which C-spending plans and I-spending plans "fit together" properly. (Examples of figures which do not fit together properly follow in question 6.)

Notice that this equilibrium can be measured in either of the two ways earlier noted:

either as $\qquad S - I \qquad$ (i.e., $MK - GE$)

or else at $\quad$ GNP $- C + I \quad$ (i.e., $OE - KE + GE$)

MK; *OE*

---

6. a. Alternatively, suppose the total of investment spending is indicated in Figure 8-6 by level RO (the broken I© line) and not by BO. What would the equilibrium value of GNP then be? Again measuring S against I, it follows that saving would have to be (*HJ* / *MK*). Saving would be this amount only if GNP were at the corresponding level, namely, (*OA* / *OE*).

Notice in passing one interesting consequence: if the I-spending level were to drop from BO to RO, then in the resulting new equilibrium, C spending would (*also have dropped / remain unchanged / have risen*). The point will be considered in a moment.

b. Suppose that GNP has been holding steady at an equilibrium level of *OE*, with investment spending at *BO*. Now let *I* spending suddenly drop to the lower level of *RO*, and stay there. (Business firms have become less optimistic about the future; or the volume of just-beginning investment projects simply happens to be less than the volume of just-finishing projects.)

The impact of this cut in *I* spending does not occur instantaneously. At the moment it occurs, the last installment of GNP income payments made at the older and higher *I* level is still wending its way toward consumers, and they are still spending accordingly. So we have a situation in which GNP (*OE*) is not equal to the sum of *C* spending (*KE*) and *I* spending (*RO*). GNP is out of equilibrium. Because of the drop in *I* spending, it is going to (*fall / rise*). (The consequences of this are outlined in the next question.)

c. Below are three sets of values based on Figures 8-5 and 8-6. In at least one, the situation is "out of equilibrium." Which one, or which ones?

Case	GNP	C	I	S
(1)	OA	JA	RO	HJ
(2)	OA	JA	BO	HJ
(3)	OE	KE	BO	MK

a. *HJ*; *OA*; also have dropped   **b.** fall   **c.** (2)

It should be clear, by now, that investment spending can call the tune in determining the level of GNP. We must, therefore, explore more fully what happens when the level of this *I* spending changes.

For this, we use the figures (in billions) associated with Figures 8-3 and 8-4. GNP has been in equilibrium at a level of $100, with *I* spending at $30 and *C* spending at $70. But, as in question 3 above, suppose that *I* spending drops. Suppose, in particular, that it drops from $30 to $20, and that it stays at $20. The horizontal *I* line of Figures 8-4 and 8-6 drops to a new and lower position at *I'*.

The flow of money spending directed toward producers has dropped from $100 to $90 because the *I*-spending component of this flow has dropped. It will take a little time before consumers begin to feel the impact of this. But when business was paying out $100 in wages and salaries, interest and dividend payments, it was simply passing on money it received from the buyers of consumption goods and of investment goods. When (because of the drop in investment spending) this incoming flow drops to $90, then the earnings flow (wages and

salaries, dividend payments, etc.) must drop correspondingly. There is no alternative source which could maintain it at the old $100 level. Some workers will be laid off, or required to work short time; the total of profits earned by incorporated and unincorporated businesses will fall. Specifically, the flow of earned income reaching consumers must likewise drop from $100 to $90. But note: this is not the end of the process at all.

7.   a. When income (which here we are measuring in the form of GNP) drops, *C* spending will (*drop also / remain constant / rise*); this is what the propensity to consume says.

By how much will *C* drop if income (GNP) has dropped by $10? For this, we must know the (*average / marginal*) propensity to consume. [Now you can begin to understand why we lavished so much time on the *MPC* in Chapter 7. The *MPC* will tell you the change (rise or fall) in *C* that goes with any given change (rise or fall) in income received.]

Suppose the *MPC* is .6, or %10. This means that the reduction in *C* spending following a $10 reduction in income will be $(*0 / 6 / 10*). That is, with income now at $90 rather than $100, *C* spending, instead of being $70, will be $(*10 / 64 / 70 / 90 / 100*). And the amount saved out of this income of $90, rather than being $30, will be $(*0 / 6 / 10 / 26 / 30 / 36*).

b. Investment spending, remember, has dropped to $20 and stays at $20 After the cut in *C* just reviewed, is *S = I*? (*Yes / No*). Is GNP at an equilibrium level? (*Yes / No*).

a. drop also; marginal; 6; 64; 26   **b.** No; No

8. We now reach a point in the analysis which must be grasped. Although *C* spending has fallen from $70 to $64 in response to the $10 drop in GNP, we are still nowhere near a new equilibrium GNP level. The fact that GNP is still out of equilibrium is evident from the fact that *S* ($26) is still not equal to *I* ($20).

The all-important point is that any drop in consumption spending has exactly the same effect on production and on incomes earned as a drop in investment spending. Consumption spending has fallen from $70 to $64. To producers, this means that the demand for consumer goods has fallen off: a smaller volume of such goods produced and sold means a smaller total of incomes earned.

a. If the total of incomes earned by producing and selling consumer goods drops by $6, this means a drop of $(*3 / 6 / 10*) in GNP. Note that this is in addition to the initial drop of $10 set off by the reduction in *I* spending. So GNP, which first fell from $100 to $90, drops further to $(*60 / 80 / 84 / 88*).

b. To review the sequence of events thus far, and to extend it:

Event 1: Investment spending falls from $30 to $20. GNP consequently falls from $100 to $90. This means a drop in employment, and a $10 drop in incomes earned, for the firms and the individuals producing investment goods.

Event 2: With lower incomes, the people in these investment-good industries must reduce their consumption spending—specifically, the income drop being $10 and the *MPC* being .6, by $6. That is, total consumption drops from $70 to $64. Saving (which had been $30) drops by .4 times $10, to $26. GNP falls again, this time from $90 to $84.

Note exactly what we did in event 2: We recognized the immediate (not full) consequences of event 1, the $10 drop in *I* spending. These consequences were: *C* spending down $6, GNP down $6, *S* down by $4.

Event 3: This reduction of $6 in investment-worker spending (event 2) means a drop of $6 in incomes for the business firms and individuals engaged in producing consumer goods. So a different group is hit. But the overall effects are similar: a further drop in employment and incomes. The income cut being $6, the consumption spending cut is .6 times $6, or $3.6. Adding this to the initial drop of $6, total *C* spending is now down from its original level of $70 to $(50.6 / 56.4 / 58.6 / 60.4 / 64.0). Saving is correspondingly down. Its original level was $30; it dropped first by $4, and has now fallen by .4 times $6, or $2.4. So its level is now $(20.0 / 21.6 / 22.4 / 23.0 / 23.6). GNP has fallen again; its level is now $(80.4 / 80.6 / 82.0 / 86.4 / 90.0).

What we have done in event 3 is to recognize the immediate (not full) consequences of event 2, a reduction in *C* spending and in GNP of $6. (Event 3 will in turn set off event 4.)

Notice the roles played by the fall in *C* and by the fall in *S* in this around-and-around process. It is the drop in consumer spending that precipitates another drop in incomes earned (since what you call expenditure is really income on the other side) and hence a further (but smaller) drop in such consumer buying. It is the drop in saving that indicates we are drawing closer to a new equilibrium. We assume (for simplicity; this is not necessarily indicative of how it would behave in real life) that investment spending, once having dropped from $30, holds steady at $20. By the close of event 3 (and by comparison with its original level), total saving has moved (and is moving) *(closer to / farther away from)* this new and lower investment spending level.

Event 4: This of course repeats event 3, but on a still smaller scale. It concerns the results of a drop in GNP and *C* spending of $3.6—i.e., still another reduction in such spending, this time of .6 times $3.6, and a corresponding reduction in saving, this time of .4 times $3.6.

We need hardly pursue this sequence through events 5, 6, 7, ... The process will gradually peter out, ending when (with investment at $20) *(GNP has fallen to zero / saving has fallen to zero / saving has fallen to $20).*

Here is a test of your grasp of the ideas. Throughout the "events" of this question, GNP was "out of equilibrium." To see why, consider what happened when GNP first fell to $90 before consumption spending had begun to drop by its initial level of $70.

By the *S* = *I* test, of course, this could not have been equilibrium because saving was $30 and investment was $20. But what of the consumption side of the analysis; did total spending match supply? Does not, in particular, a $90 GNP conform with consumption of $70 and investment of $20? Sure, but only if consumption is really $70 when GNP is $90. And this is not the case. We can expect *C* to be $70 if and only if GNP is $100. It was precisely because GNP fell to $90 that we had to move to event 2, reducing *C* from $70 to $64.

Thus if you are using the GNP = *C* + *I* test, make sure that the *C* figure on the right-hand side of this equation matches up with the GNP figure on the left—i.e., that the *C* figure is what it should be, according to the propensity to consume, given that particular GNP.

---

a. 6; 84 **b.** 60.4; 23.6; 80.4; closer to; saving has fallen to $20

Question 8 outlined an around-and-around sequence of income reduction. Each of them was .6 times its predecessor—assuming, for convenience, a universal *MPC* of .6.

Mathematically, this kind of sequence is known as a convergent geometric progression—an elegant phrase, and one that is useful for impressing your friends (or some of them) on social occasions, if you can manage to work it into the conversation. All you need to know about such a progression is that its sum has a finite limit. That is, GNP does not keep dropping until it collapses to zero or below. The sequence here involved is as follows: 10 + 6 + 3.6 + (.6 times 3.6) + · · · etc. The sum of this sequence, fully extended, is 25, not infinity. The full GNP drop will be $25, and GNP, upon dropping from its original value of $100, will stop when it reaches a new equilibrium at $75.

Don't worry overmuch at this stage about the detail of mathematics. Instead, study question 8 until you have a reasonable grasp of the process involved. It is *the multiplier process:*

▶ Any change in spending which disturbs the equilibrium level of GNP will set off a chain reaction such that the final change in GNP is much larger than—is a multiple of—the initial change.

In our example, equilibrium is disturbed by a cut in investment spending of $10. But in the resulting new equilibrium, GNP fell, not just by $10, but by $25.

If you find that it strengthens your grasp of the process involved, refer once again to the circular-flow diagram of the previous chapter. The flow of spending through the "investment intake" (at lower left) shrinks by $10; this reduces the flow of incomes through the upper loop by $10. So both *C* spending and saving must fall. A $6 shrinkage in the money flowing through the lower "Consumption spending" loop means a further reduction in GNP of $6; this means a further cut in incomes of $6—and so on.

Thus, GNP can be "out of equilibrium" much of the time (perhaps virtually all of the time, because of continuing changes in I). Still, the idea of an equilibrium position is still vitally important: if GNP is out of equilibrium, then it is changing in value, seeking out an equilibrium goal. That goal may of course be replaced before it is reached, by reason of a further change in investment. Yet even if no equilibrium were ever reached, the idea would retain its importance in explaining the direction in which GNP is currently moving.

The diagrams typically used to illustrate this analysis are "short-cut" analytical tools. They do not bother with the intermediate, out-of-equilibrium process. They show only some original equilibrium GNP level, and the new equilibrium which would result from some change in decisions on the part of I spenders (or C spenders). The saving-investment diagram is an example of such a tool.

9. In equilibrium, saving equals investment, so we must be able to use a saving-investment diagram to illustrate equilibrium GNP.

If we know the propensity to consume, we can develop from it a propensity-to-save schedule showing the amount saved at each GNP level. In Figure 8-7, the SS line is such a propensity to save; it corresponds to Figure 8-3's propensity to consume.

The solid I line in this figure repeats that of Figure 8-4. The intersection of SS and I curves, at GNP = $100, indicates the equilibrium GNP level, because it is the only GNP level at which S and I are equal.

a. The broken I' line shows what happens if I spending drops from $30 to $20. The new equilibrium GNP must be $*(20 / 30 / 60 / 75 / 90 / 100)*, for the same reason as before. If I spending is to be $20, then S must be $20 also; $75 is the only GNP level at which S is $20.

b. Also shown in Figure 8-7 is a dotted I'' line, at level $40. If I spending were to rise to this level, the diagram indicates that the resulting GNP equilibrium level would be $*(75 / 100 / 110 / 125 / 150)*. (CAUTION: Should full-employment GNP happen to

be in the vicinity of $100, the applicability of the Keynesian model lapses and this equilibrium GNP might be unattainable. Chapter 9 explores this matter.)

---

a. 75   **b.** 125

---

10. As question 5 noted, there are two possible algebraic statements of the equilibrium requirement, $S = I$, or GNP = $C + I$. Each has its corresponding diagram. (Be sure you understand that the two diagrams are simply two alternative ways of illustrating exactly the same set of relationships.)

The figure corresponding to GNP = $C + I$ is the now-familiar 45° diagram, already used in this chapter as Figures 8-3 and 8-5. (At the close of question 8, you were warned to be sure when using GNP = $C + I$ that the C and the GNP "match" in the particular sense of satisfying the requirements of the propensity to consume. The 45° diagram takes care of this automatically, since the propensity to consume is an integral part of that diagram.)

a. In Figure 8-8, the line CC is the same propensity to consume we have already used in Figures 8-3 and 8-5. Remember: The amount of C spending, for any given GNP level, is measured vertically. At the GNP level indicated by OG in Figure 8-8, C spending would be DG. If the GNP level were OH, then C spending would be *(KD / DG / LM / MH)*.

For GNP purposes, our interest is in total spending—in C spending plus I spending. There is no reason why we cannot add I spending on this diagram, thus showing total spending. We draw the line TT above CC, and we make the vertical distance between these two lines the amount of I spending. The TT line thus reflects aggregate demand for any level of GNP.

To explain more fully, suppose we take the same level of I spending assumed when Figure 8-3 was first used, namely, $30. In Figure 8-8, the vertical distance between TT and CC lines would then be $30. That is, the distance between K and D, marked off by the arrow line, would be $30. So would the distance similarly marked off between L and M.

b. This means that the vertical distance from any point on TT down to the axis line now measures total spending, $C + I$. At GNP level OG, the I spending would be KD, the C spending would be DG, and total spending, $I + C$, would be KG—i.e., KD plus DG.

Similarly, if the GNP level were OH, the amount of I spending would be indicated by *(LM / DG / MH)*. C spending would be measured by *(LM / DG / MH)*. Total spending would be measured by *(LM / KG / MH / LH)*.

This material may be unfamiliar, but it is not complicated. Be sure you understand it reasonably well before you pass on to part **c**.

c. Figure 8-9 is basically the same as Figure 8-8. The same CC and TT lines appear. We have simply added a 45° "helping line."

Now remember the special property of this 45° line: it marks off all the equal-value points. Given any point on the 45° line,

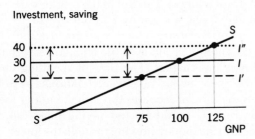

Figure 8-7

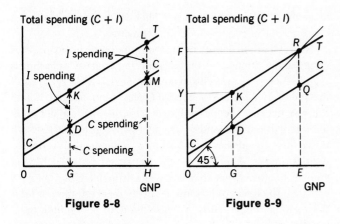

Figure 8-8   Figure 8-9

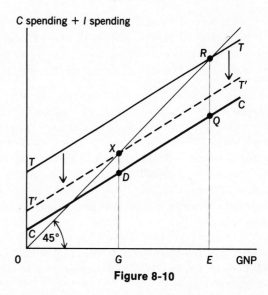

Figure 8-10

distances to vertical and horizontal axes will be equal. Take any point *off* this line and the distances to the two axes will be unequal.

Recall our equilibrium GNP condition: GNP = C + I.

Pick any GNP at random. Given the particular propensity-to-consume and investment schedules involved, would this GNP be an equilibrium one?

For example, take a GNP of *OG* in Figure 8-9. Total spending, C + I, would then be *KG*. But point *K* is off the 45° line. So *KG* is not equal to *OG*. (That is, GNP would *not* be equal to C + I.) Thus the equilibrium GNP level can only be at the point where the total-spending line, *TT*, cuts across the 45° line. This is at point *R*, indicating a GNP of *OE*. Here, total spending of *RE* *(is / is not)* just equal to GNP of *OE*.

d. If the two equilibrium conditions come to one and the same thing, then it ought to be true that the equilibrium GNP of *OE* depicted in Figure 8-9 marks an S = I position, and it does. Saving at any GNP level is the vertical distance from the propensity-to-consume line up to the 45° line. Hence at GNP of *OE*, saving must be *RQ*. This *(is / is not)* the same as investment.

At any GNP lower than (to the left of) *OE*, S would be *(less than / equal to / greater than)* I. At any GNP higher than (to the right of) *OE*, S would be *(less than / equal to / greater than)* I.

---

a. *MH* **b.** *LM*; *MH*; *LH* **c.** is **d.** is; less than; greater than

---

11. Suppose there is a sudden and drastic drop in the level of *I* spending: it falls, say, from $30 (billion) per period to $10. In terms of Figure 8-9, this would mean a *(rise / drop)* in the total-spending line *TT*.

Figure 8-10 shows this event. The *TT* line drops from its former position (the solid black line) to the level *T'T'* (the broken line). The new total-spending line will cut the 45° line at point *(X / R / D / Q)*, and the new equilibrium level of GNP indicated will be *(OG / OE)*. That is, the drastic drop in investment spending has produced an even more drastic reduction in incomes and employment.

---

drop; *X*; *OG*

12. **a.** Remember that any such change in *I* spending has a magnified or "multiplied" effect on the GNP level because it sets off a series of C changes (as earlier outlined).

If the multiplier figure is 3, and *I* spending rises by $10 billion, then GNP will *(rise / fall)* by $*(10 / 20 / 30 / 40 / 50)* billion. If *I* spending rises by $10 billion with a multiplier of 4, then GNP will *(rise / fall)* by $*(10 / 20 / 30 / 40 / 50)* billion.

The multiplier formula given in the text is:

$$\frac{1}{1 - MPC} \quad \text{or} \quad \frac{1}{MPS}$$

This means that if the *MPC* is .6, the multiplier is *(1 / 2 / 2½ / 3 3½ / 4)*. If the *MPC* is .8, the multiplier is *(1 / 2 / 2½ / 3½ / 4 / 5)*.

b. Suppose there is a change in investment (either rise or fall) of $10. If the *MPC* is .6, the resulting change in GNP (rise or fall) will be $*(10 / 20 / 25 / 30 / 50)*. If the *MPC* is .8, the resulting change in GNP (rise or fall) will be $*(10 / 20 / 25 / 30 / 50)*.

(NOTE: The multiplier formula given above holds only in the simplified conditions used in this chapter. In Chapter 9, we will incorporate some complications, and the multiplier formula will be changed accordingly.)

---

a. rise; 30; rise; 40; 2½; 5 **b.** 25; 50

---

13. An equilibrium GNP will not be disturbed unless either the *II* line or the *CC* line shifts to a new position. (That is, it will not be disturbed unless there is some change either in investment-spending plans or in consumer-spending plans. We are of course still assuming the influence of government spending and taxation to be entirely absent.)

Thus far, we have considered only disturbances in equilibrium GNP produced by a change in investment spending (a shift in the *II* line of Figure 8-4). Changes in GNP are most commonly attributed to changes in *I* spending.

Nevertheless, changes in the propensity to consume can occur. Any such change will upset equilibrium GNP just as an *I* change would. Here, you should recall Study Guide questions 7 and 8 from Chapter 7 which pointed out that the *CC* line (the propensity to consume) can shift up (or down) if, for some reason, consumers decide to spend more (or less) money out of a given *DI* (here, a given GNP).

We begin with the same set of figures as before: GNP is in equilibrium at $100, *C* spending is $70, and *I* spending is $30. Saving is likewise $30.

For some reason, consumers decide to become more thrifty. They plan to spend $10 less on consumption, and to save $10 more, at each and any GNP level. Since GNP is currently $100, this means they plan to spend $60 on consumption and to save $40.

Figure 8-11 shows the same propensity to consume we have already used. The consumer decision to save more and spend less will cause the *CC* line to shift downward to the position *C′C′* (the broken line).

The total-spending line, *TT* in Figure 8-12, is the sum of *C + I*. If *CC* is displaced vertically downward by $10 as in Figure 8-11, the same must hold for *TT*. It must shift downward to position *T′T′* (also a broken line).

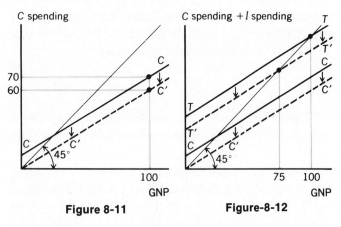

Figure 8-11   **Figure-8-12**

This *(affects / does not affect)* equilibrium GNP. GNP will *(fall / rise)*. The resulting new equilibrium level of GNP indicated in Figure 8-12 is $ _____ .

(Notice that this initial change in *C* spending has the same multiplier effect as a change in *I* spending would have: an initial change of $10 causes equilibrium GNP to change by $25.)

affects; fall; 75

14. The point finally to be discussed is a tricky one. Don't tackle it until you have a pretty fair grasp of the material preceding. If you find it puzzling, you will not be the first.

The text emphasizes "scheduled" or "planned" investment. It is possible also to have "unscheduled" or "unintended" investment. Investment of this latter kind is symptomatic of disequilibrium in GNP.

Consider question 13's reduction in *C* spending. When this first occurs, department stores and other firms involved in retail trade may be taken by surprise. Their inventories pile up as a consequence of reduced consumer buying.

Now Chapter 6 told us that any increase in inventories counts as investment. So, temporarily, the drop in *C* spending is matched by a rise in *I*. This makes it appear as if GNP were still in equilibrium because the total of *C* plus *I* is unchanged. In fact it is not, because the inventory pile-up (the increase in *I*) was unintended and unwanted. The stores will proceed to work down their inventories by canceling or reducing their orders to their suppliers. That is how the impact of reduced buying spreads to other firms; that is how the drop in incomes begins.

When the new equilibrium is finally reached, there is *(still some / no longer any)* "unscheduled," "unintended," investment.

The same words "unscheduled," "unintended," or "unplanned" may also be applied to saving. Again, the reference is to a situation of disequilibrium GNP, when the various figures for investment, consumption, and saving do not mesh together properly, so that GNP is moving toward a new equilibrium level.

In the statistical sense, but not in the analytic sense of this chapter, the statistics for *S* and *I* always show up as equal in total. This does not mean that GNP is always in equilibrium; it just means that the statisticians have counted the "unscheduled" *S* and *I* along with the "scheduled" or "planned" *S* and *I*. They have no way of knowing which is which. The important thing about the "unscheduled" figures is that they are about to change in amount, thus affecting the GNP level.

no longer any

15. You are given the following propensity to consume for a community: Consumption spending for each and any level of GNP will be $20 (billion) plus three-fifths of that GNP.

a. What will consumption be if GNP is $40? _____ .

If GNP is $60? _____ . If GNP is $100? _____ .

b. Draw this propensity to consume in Figure 8-13.

c. Suppose that investment spending will be $20, at each and all levels of GNP. Draw in Figure 8-13 a total-spending line (assuming government spending to be zero). What will be the resulting equilibrium value of GNP? _____ .

a. $44.00; $56.00; $80.00   **c.** $100

16. You are given the following information:

1. The full-employment level of GNP in a certain economy is estimated at $100 billion.

2. The amount of consumption spending to be expected at this full-employment GNP level is $80 billion.

3. The marginal propensity to consume is .8.

4. The amount of planned investment spending will be $10 billion, regardless of the GNP level.

Spending: consumption, investment

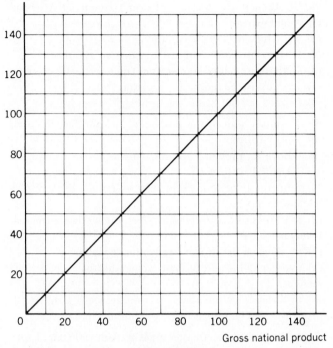

Gross national product

Figure 8-13

a. Assuming all government items (spending and taxation) to be zero, then the equilibrium level of GNP will be (pick one):
(1) $100 billion
(2) $90 billion
(3) less than $90 billion

b. The increase in investment spending, if any, needed to bring GNP up to its full-employment, $100 billion level would be (pick one):
(1) zero
(2) $10 billion
(3) $20 billion
(4) more than $20 billion

---

a. (3) **b.** (2)

17. The following figures (billions of dollars) indicate an economy's propensity to consume out of GNP:

GNP:	130	150	170	190	210	230	250	270	290	310
C:	112	126	140	154	168	182	196	210	224	238

a. If the amount of investment spending is 60, and if government spending of all types is zero, what is the equilibrium level of GNP? . . . . _____ .

b. If the total of this investment spending should drop by 30, what would be the new resulting equilibrium level of GNP?

. . . . _____ .

a. $270   **b.** $170

18. Consult Figure 8-14. The top panel there will present equilibrium in the consumption-investment geometry of the Keynesian model; the bottom panel will present equilibrium in the aggregate supply–aggregate demand geometry of earlier chapters. Note that the shape of the aggregate supply curve drawn there conforms to the shape identified with the Keynesian view in the first part of the chapter.

Draw, first of all, an aggregate demand curve on the lower panel that would support the same equilibrium level as curve TT in the upper panel.

Now let investment increase to I' so that $T'T'$ becomes the appropriate representation of total spending. Draw a second aggregate demand curve on the bottom panel to illustrate the same new equilibrium. Reading from the vertical and horizontal axes, it would appear that a $10 increase in investment has produced a $*(5 / 10 / 15 / 30)* increase in GNP; the multiplier would, therefore, appear to be _____ .

Now consider $T''T''$ in the upper panel. It would appear,

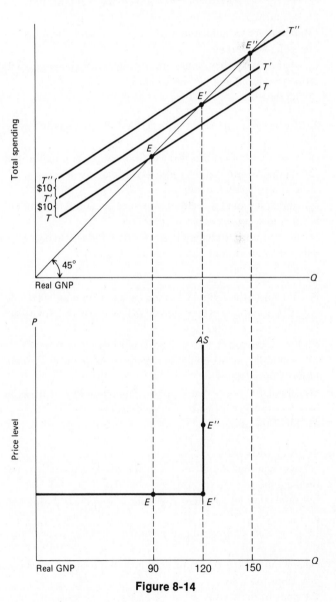

Figure 8-14

given the geometry of the upper panel, that the second $10 increase in investment should, by producing $T''T''$, cause GNP

to increase by another $ _____ . This will, however, not be the case because $T'T'$ had already brought GNP up to its maximum potential. The second increase in I will simply cause (*prices / employment / output*) to rise. Show this by drawing a third aggregate demand curve on the lower panel.

---

downward-sloping through E; downward-sloping through E'; 30; 3; 30; prices; *downward-sloping through E''* (*Note:* Italicized phrases give descriptions of demand curves to be drawn on the bottom panel of Figure 8-14)

QUIZ: Multiple Choice

1.   Keynes, in the "general theory," suggested:
(1) that wages and prices were unresponsive to disequilibrium in economic markets.
(2) a structure that can be summarized in its simplist form as a horizontal aggregate supply curve.
(3) that macroequilibrium could include massive numbers of unemployed workers.
(4) that active policy to manipulate aggregate demand could influence output and employment.
(5) all the above.

2.   By way of contrast, the classical view of macroeconomics is that:
(1) wages and prices are always responsive to disequilibrium.
(2) the aggregate supply curve is vertical at a level of GNP indicated by potential output.
(3) unemployment was either voluntary or caused by artificial barriers to wage necessary adjustments.
(4) active policy to change aggregate demand would influence only prices and not output or employment.
(5) all the above.

3.   Which of the following might be a reason why wages do not fall very rapidly in the face of high levels of unemployment?
(1) Three-year contracts.
(2) Cost of living clauses in labor contracts.
(3) Unemployment compensation that cushions the immediate blow of losing a job.
(4) Regulated prices that keep wage demands high among the negotiating labor officials who have seniority.
(5) all of the above.

4.   A classicist will:
(1) worry about stabilizing the economy through active economic policy.
(2) think that government spending is fine even during full employment.
(3) worry about government spending crowding out productive investment.
(4) encourage the government to invest in projects that business finds too risky.
(5) none of the above.

5.   Suppose that business firms change their plans and increase the total of their spending new plant and equipment. As a result, we would expect:
(1) no change in GNP, necessarily.
(2) GNP to rise, and consumer spending to also rise.
(3) GNP to rise but consumer spending to be unaffected.
(4) GNP to rise but consumer spending to fall.
(5) GNP to fall but consumer spending to rise.

6.   If, on a graph of the propensity to consume, the entire propensity-to-consume line shifts to a new and different position above its previous position, this means that consumers have decided:
(1) to increase the amount of their saving (S) because of an increase in income.
(2) to increase S because of some factor other than an increase in income
(3) to reduce S because of a reduction in income.
(4) to reduce S because of some factor other than a reduction in income.
(5) to do none of the above necessarily, since a shift in the propensity to consume affects consumption, not saving.

7.   In the Keynesian circumstances spelled out in this chapter, if the value of the marginal propensity to consume is .8, then the value of the multiplier must be:
(1) 1.6.
(2) 2.5.
(3) 2.8.
(4) 4.
(5) 5.

8.   If the amount of investment (*I*) spending should suddenly fall, then the Keynesian model predicts that:
(1) GNP will begin and will continue to fall, but the ultimate fall will be less than the *I* fall.
(2) GNP will fall immediately by an amount much greater than the *I* fall.
(3) GNP will fall immediately by an amount less than the *I* fall, but will show no further tendency to fall.
(4) it is more likely that GNP will rise rather than fall.
(5) GNP will begin and will continue to fall, until it has fallen by an amount considerably greater than the *I* fall.

9.   A change in the total of consumer spending can have the same effect upon GNP (throwing it from equilibrium into disequilibrium, and so changing the GNP value by a multiplied amount) that a change in the total of investment spending would have:
(1) only if that *C*-spending change is set off by some factor other than a change in GNP.
(2) only if that *C*-spending change is itself set off by a change in GNP.
(3) regardless of the circumstances that set off the *C*-spending change.
(4) with respect to increases in *C* spending only, not with respect to decreases.
(5) in no circumstances, since disequilibrium GNP results only from changes in *I* spending.

10. The "equilibrium" level of GNP is related to the "full-empoyment" level of GNP as follows. It:

(1) is the same thing as full-employment GNP.

(2) definitely is not full-employment GNP.

(3) normally means full-employment GNP, except in special disequilibrium circumstances.

(4) may or may not be the same thing as full-employment GNP.

(5) means a future level of GNP above the present full-employment level.

11. If an equilibrium level of GNP is altered by a decrease in planned investment spending, then we would expect:

(1) GNP to fall, but saving (S) to rise.

(2) GNP to fall, but no change in S.

(3) GNP to fall, and S to fall also.

(4) GNP to remain unchanged, but S to fall.

(5) none of the preceding.

12. Which alternative in question 11 would be correct had it spoken, not of a decrease in planned investment spending, but of a decision on the part of consumers to save more and to spend less upon consumption?

(1).

(2).

(3).

(4).

(5).

13. On a 45° diagram, such as is used extensively in both the text and the Study Guide for this chapter, the intersection of the propensity-to-consume and 45° lines has the following significance with respect to GNP. It indicates:

(1) the GNP level at which net investment spending (I) first rises above zero.

(2) equality of consumption (C) and I.

(3) equilibrium GNP.

(4) equality of C and saving.

(5) nothing in particular, unless I happens to be zero.

14. We say that GNP is above its equilibrium level whenever:

(1) the amount that consumers plan to withdraw from the "income stream" as saving (S) exceeds the amount business firms and others plan to pump into that income stream as investment spending (I).

(2) the total of planned consumption spending (C) exceeds the total of planned I.

(3) there is no unscheduled or unplanned I.

(4) GNP has moved temporarily above the "breakeven" point on the propensity to consume.

(5) the total of planned I plus the total of planned C exceeds the current level of GNP.

15. Which alternative in question 14 would be correct had that question referred to a GNP below its equilibrium level?

(1).

(2).

(3).

(4).

(5).

16. Before a particular Christmas, shoppers decide to spend considerably less than retail stores anticipated, leaving those stores with considerable unsold inventories of goods. This situation is an example of:

(1) planned investment.

(2) unscheduled saving.

(3) a rise in GNP.

(4) unscheduled investment.

(5) none of the preceding.

17. If GNP falls by reason of a fall in investment spending, we would expect as a consequence that:

(1) both consumption (C) and saving (S) would rise.

(2) both C and S would fall.

(3) C would rise but S would fall.

(4) C would fall but S would rise.

(5) neither C nor S would necessarily change in value.

18. One way of specifying the requirement that must be satisfied for an equilibrium level of GNP is to say that:

(1) the total of incomes earned must just equal the total that consumers are planning to spend out of that income plus the total they are planning to save.

(2) the total of consumer spending must be just equal to the "breakeven" level of income.

(3) the total of GNP must be just equal to the total of planned saving plus the total of planned investment.

(4) the total of incomes earned must just equal the total consumers are planning to spend out of that income plus the total of planned investment.

(5) the total of spending must be just enough to bring production to its full-employment level.

19. The current level of GNP is $500 (billion), and out of this, consumers wish to spend $390 (billion) on consumption. The total amount of investment spending planned is $120 (billion). These figures indicate:

(1) that GNP is out of equilibrium and will fall in value.

(2) that GNP is out of equilibrium and will rise in value.

(3) that GNP is out of equilibrium, although whether it will rise, fall, or remain at its present level is indeterminate.

(4) that GNP is in equilibrium.

(5) none of the above necessarily, since from the information given, GNP may be in equilibrium or out of it.

20. If the marginal propensity to save is .3 (i.e., $3/10$), and investment spending rises by $6 billion, we can expect this to increase the level of equilibrium GNP by:

(1) $2 billion.

(2) $6 billion.

(3) $18 billion.

(4) $20 billion.

(5) $60 billion.

21. In a certain country, (*a*) full employment implies a GNP of $200 billion; (*b*) consumption expenditure at this full-employment level of GNP would be $170 billion; (*c*) total investment expenditure will be $20 billion regardless of the

level of GNP; and (*d*) the community's *MPC* is ¾. Given these facts the equilibrium level of GNP will be:
(1) more than $200 billion.
(2) $200 billion.
(3) $190 billion.
(4) less than $190 billion.
(5) impossible to compute from information given.

22. With respect to the preceding question, the increase in investment spending needed to restore the economy to full employment would be:
(1) more than $10 billion.
(2) $10 billion.

(3) less than $10 billion but a positive amount.
(4) zero.
(5) impossible to compute from information given.

23. The Keynesian multiplier applies:
(1) whenever investment increases.
(2) only when investment increases in any economy in which there exist unemployed resources.
(3) only when some economic variables like investment changes in either direction, thereby either creating or putting to work unemployed resources.
(4) only to changes in government finance.
(5) none of the above.

CHAPTER 9
FISCAL POLICY IN THEORY AND PRACTICE

Chapter 8 presented all the essential elements of the Keynesian theory of output determination. It was also noted explicitly that the Keynesian view of the world represents only one polar vision of the workings of an economy that should always be tempered by a recognition of the contrasting, classical picture. Chapter 9 applies the fundamentals of that chapter to the study of fiscal policy—the expenditure of public funds and the collection of government taxes. It should be no surprise to discover that one's expectations about the effects of fiscal policy will depend critically upon one's sympathies in the Keynesian/classical controversy and your understanding of this point will plant the seeds of understanding the synthesis of "modern mainstream theory."

Chapter 9 also explores what has become known as the "paradox of saving"—the counterintuitive notion that an increase in saving by everyone in an economy can actually reduce that economy's level of output and thus its source of well-being. The Keynesian/classical controversy will be seen to be important here, as well. You will, in fact, begin to see why macroeconomists with different feelings vis à vis the shape of the aggregate supply curve hardly ever agree on anything. When the chapter closes with a review of empirical estimates of the multiplier, you should, therefore, not be surprised by the wide range of disagreement. Economists who estimate multipliers face not only the uncertainties of dealing with an enormously complex economy, but also the ramifications of different academic and philosophical traditions.

Even if one accepts the Keynesian view of the world, fiscal policy is not the panacea for inflation, unemployment, and the vagaries of the business cycle that some students of introductory economics think. Problems associated with automatic and discretionary changes in tax and spending policies are also noted in Chapter 9 to explicitly dispel any feeling that solutions to all an economy's potential ills are well in hand.

Having worked through this chapter, you will have not only begun to understand the wide-ranging implications of the Keynesian/classical debate, but also accomplished the following objectives.

LEARNING OBJECTIVES

1. Outline the effect of (*a*) a change in government spending and (*b*) a change in tax rates on the level of GNP.

2. Understand why a change in spending has a larger effect, dollar for dollar, on GNP than a change in tax collections.

3. Describe what happens to the effects outlined in objective 1 when the strict Keynesian model does not apply.

4. Describe the paradox of thrift and explain why one's belief in its conclusion depends upon one's sympathies in the Keynesian/classical debate.

5. Explain the theory behind the "lean against the economic winds" view of fiscal policy.

6. Describe the roles and consequences of the various automatic and discretionary components of fiscal policy as practiced in the United States in the 1980s.

7. Understand why there is so much discord among economists when they discuss the size of the fiscal-policy multiplier (non-defense government spending).

Chapter 8 described how fluctuation in aggregate demand might be translated into fluctuation in GNP. Depending upon the difference between potential and actual GNP, an economy might be afflicted by unemployment, inflation, or both. Chapter 9 notes that while the simple Keynesian model has trouble explaining the simultaneous appearance of both ailments, it can be used to suggest both the need and the appropriate direction for adjustment in a fiscal policy designed to "lean against the winds" of either unemployment or inflation.

1. Refer to Figure 9-2 in the text for enough information to be able to record in the following table whether you would expect unemployment or inflation to have been the dominant economic illness during the periods noted. Also record, in the spaces provided, whether a "lean against the wind" policy would have been stimulative or contractionary.

Time Period	Unemployment or Inflation	Policy Prescription
1958–1962	_____	_____
1965–1970	_____	_____
1973–1975	_____	_____
1975–1977	_____	_____
1981–1983	_____	_____

There is, of course, more to the design of fiscal policy than the simple comparison of actual and potential GNP. There are issues of monetary policy; these will be discussed in future chapters. There are issues of outside shocks and the need to fight unemployment and inflation at the same time; these, too, will be addressed later. The point of this question was not, therefore, to provide an illustration of a methodology for setting fiscal policy. It was, instead, included only to provide some exercise in the meaning of "leaning against the wind."

1958–1962: unemployment; stimulative   1965–1970: inflation; contractionary
1973–1975: inflation; contractionary   1975–1977: unemployment; stimulative
1981–1983: unemployment; stimulative

2. The pure Keynesian model envisions, in its simplest form, a *(vertical / horizontal)* aggregate supply curve. As a result, any adjustment in aggregate demand created by an adjustment in either taxes or government spending produces *(no / a dollar-for-dollar / a multiplied)* effect on GNP and *(no / a dollar-for-dollar / a multiplied)* effect on prices. On the other extreme, the classical view holds that fiscal policy will produce *(no / a dollar-for-dollar / a multiplied)* effect on GNP and *(a significant / absolutely no)* effect on prices. In between these two extremes, changes in fiscal policy can be expected to affect *(both prices and GNP / only GNP / only prices)*.

Record in the spaces provided in the table below the ex-

pected effects of the policy changes indicated. Denote "up" by (+), "down" by (−) and "no change" by (o). Take care to note that you must answer according to the specified philosophy.

horizontal; a multiplied; no; no; a significant; both prices and GNP; reading across rows: (A): (o); (−); (−); (o); (−); (−)   (B): (o); (+); (+); (o); (+); (+)   (C): (o); (+); (+); (o); (+); (+)   (D): (o); (−); (−); (o); (−); (−)

3. With respect to its effect on employment and income, government spending (*G*) on goods and services *(is / is not)* in the same category as *C* spending and *I* spending.

Figures in Chapter 8 showed how, on a 45° diagram, *I* spending could be added to *C* spending to produce a total-spending line. *G* spending is handled in precisely the same way: it is added vertically above *I* + *C* so that the total-spending line is now a *G* + *I* + *C* line.

An increase in *G* would *(push up / pull down)* (vertically) the total-spending line. A decrease in *G* would *(push it up / pull it down)* (vertically).

A change in *G* spending *(would / would not)* have multiplier effects similar to any change in *I* or *C* spending.

is; push up; pull it down; would

4. Thus far in Chapters 8 and 9, we have been able to work entirely in terms of GNP, using this figure as a measure both of total production and of total income earned from production. But once we get into the matter of taxes, and the effect of taxes on income and spending, we must reintroduce some of the more refined measures employed in Chapter 6. Specifically, we must bring back (*a*) national income, which is the measure of total income earned in producing the GNP and NNP, before any taxes[1] and (*b*) disposable income, which is income earned after taxes.

a. Suppose that the government suddenly imposes a personal income tax. The immediate effect of this tax will be that national income (*NI*)—which, remember, is before-tax income—

[1]Other than "indirect business taxes"—see Chapter 10.

Policy Change	Keynesian View		Classical View		Intermediate	
	Price	Output	Price	Output	Price	Output
A. Increase in taxes	___	___	___	___	___	___
B. Increase in spending	___	___	___	___	___	___
C. Reduction in taxes	___	___	___	___	___	___
D. Reduction in spending	___	___	___	___	___	___

is *(unchanged / lowered)*. However, disposable income (*DI*)—which is after-tax income—will be *(unchanged / lowered)*.

b. When *DI* is reduced, we must expect consumption spending to *(rise / remain unchanged / fall)*. If *C* spending is reduced, then production, and the incomes earned thereby, are likewise reduced. That is, GNP and *NI* will *(rise / remain unchanged / fall)*.

---

a. unchanged; lowered **b.** fall; fall

5. At least to a first approximation, then, government spending (*G*) and taxation tend to cancel one another in their effects upon GNP. Any increase in *G* tends to raise GNP; any increase in taxation, to lower GNP. Strangely enough, however, *equal* increases in spending and taxes may not cancel each other exactly. To see why this might be so, suppose that spending and personal taxes were both increased by $30 billion. One's inclination is to say that in combination these two increases would "net out" to zero, leaving GNP unchanged. That expectation is wrong. A given amount of extra *G* has slightly more upward leverage on GNP than the same amount of extra personal taxation has by way of downward leverage.

The crucial point involves the exact amount by which such a personal tax increase "pulls down" the propensity-to-consume line on a 45° diagram showing *C* spending at various GNP levels. It turns out that the tax pulls the *CC* line down by an amount less than the tax increase. This is the point we must explore.

a. We assume that personal taxes are increased by a flat $30 billion.[2] As an immediate result, GNP *(is unchanged / falls by $30)*. (GNP changes only when *C*, *I*, or *G* changes. GNP is going to fall in a moment, to be sure, because higher personal taxes cut the public's disposable income. That will reduce *C* spending, but by how much? That is the real question.)

What *does* happen when the extra $30 (billion) in personal taxes is imposed is that *DI* (disposable income, after-tax income) will *(remain unchanged / at once fall by $30)*.

Now suppose the community's *MPC* is ⅔, or .67. If so, then by reason of the fall in *DI*, consumption spending is going to *(remain unchanged / fall by $20 / rise by $20)*.

So planned consumption is about to drop by $20—not because GNP has fallen, but because consumers are being hit by higher taxes, and even at the old, as-yet-unchanged GNP, they feel they must cut their spending by $20.

Now, finally, we recognize that when *C* is cut (by $20), GNP will begin to fall. This cut of $20 will have the usual multiplier effects on GNP. But note carefully: this multiplier process is going to begin working from a base of $20 and not $30. The tax increase was $30, but consumers adjusted to this increase by cutting their consumption by only $20. (The other $10 was made up by a cut in saving.)

[2]For simplicity, we assume the dollar amount of the tax increase to be fixed and to not change with any change in incomes.

b. In sum, the initial *C* reduction which starts off the multiplier reduction in the level of GNP will be *(less than / the same as / greater than)* the amount of the tax increase.

That is, the public is most likely to adjust to any increase in personal taxes by cutting its *C* spending (pick one):
(1) By the full tax amount.
(2) By less than the full tax amount, the balance of the adjustment being made by a reduction in saving.
(3) Not at all, the entire adjustment being made in *S*.

The *CC* line's downward displacement is illustrated in Figure 9-1. Note that the amount by which consumers cut their spending, with an unchanged GNP, equals the amount of the tax cut multiplied by the _____.

---

a. is unchanged; at once fall by $30; fall by $20 **b.** less than; **(2)**; *MPC*

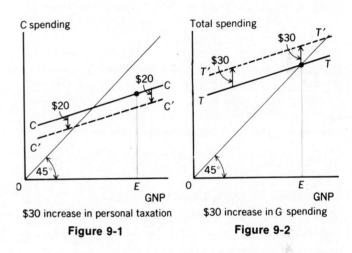

Figure 9-1   Figure 9-2
$30 increase in personal taxation $30 increase in G spending

6. Now consider what happens if the government spends the full $30 (billion) of its additional tax proceeds for the purchase of goods and services. This will push up the total-spending line, as shown in Figure 9-2, by $*(10 / 20 / 30 / 40)*.

Finally, combine the two effects: (*a*) levying of the tax, and consequent downward shift of the *C* component of the total-spending line and (*b*) spending of tax proceeds, and consequent upward shift of the *G* component of the total-spending line.

The overall effect on this total-spending line will be (pick one):
a. To push it up somewhat higher than before.
b. To push it down somewhat lower than before.
c. To leave it in its original position.

$30; **a.**

7. Chapter 8 set out two alternative "equilibrium conditions" for an equilibrium level of GNP:

1. $S = I$ (made use of in saving-investment diagram)
2. $GNP = C + I$ (made use of in 45° diagram)

These two conditions are still valid. They must simply be modified to take account of the expansions of analysis introduced in this present chapter. For example, the second condition obviously now becomes:

$$GNP = C + I + G$$

The S-I equality requires a little more amplification. This condition really says that for equilibrium, the total of all "inflows" to the GNP circuit must just equal the total of all "drains" from the circuit. (Inflows and drains are to be interpreted in terms of a diagram like Figure 7-7.)

In Chapter 8, there was just one inflow (I spending) and just one drain (personal saving, S).

Chapter 9 has introduced new inflows and drains. G spending is an inflow (and so would be government transfer payments, although they are not mentioned in this chapter). Taxes are a drain. So are undistributed corporation profits ("corporate saving").

In an introductory course, there is no reason why you need be much concerned about this expansion of the S-I equilibrium condition. But remember: don't expect that the equality of I spending and personal S will necessarily indicate an equilibrium level of GNP if you are considering a case in which elements like taxation and undistributed profits are present.

If you are curious about the full expansion of the S-I equilibrium condition, it is this:

Personal saving + corp'n. saving + tax total
      $= G$ spending $+ I$ spending $+$ gov't. transfers

Consolidate the various government items in this equation to show that it can be reduced to:

Gov't. surplus + personal saving + corp'n. saving $= I$

8. The following annual figures (in billions of dollars) pertain to a particular economy. The three right-hand columns indicate

GNP	Consumption	Investment	Government
$200	$275	$ 0	$55
225	285	0	55
250	295	0	55
275	305	0	55
300	315	0	55
325	325	0	55
350	335	4	55
375	345	8	55
400	355	12	55
425	365	16	55
450	375	20	55
475	385	24	55
500	395	28	55

the amount of planned consumer, investment, and governmental expenditure at the particular GNP level indicated (e.g., if GNP is $200 billion, C spending will be $275, I zero, G $55).

a. What is the equilibrium value of GNP? ..... $_____

b. What is the marginal propensity to consume (out of GNP)?

.... _____

c. Suppose the amount of government spending were to drop from $55 to $33 annually. What would be the resulting new equilibrium GNP (assuming no change in the given relations of C spending and of I spending to GNP?   ..... $_____

d. What is the value of the multiplier? .... _____

a. $450   **b.** .4   **c.** $400   **d.** $^{25}/_{11}$

9. You are given the following data with respect to a certain economy (the figures being billions of dollars):

1. The amounts of investment spending to be expected at various levels of GNP are:

GNP:	$150	160	170	180	190	200	210	220	230	240	250
I:	17	20	23	26	29	32	35	38	41	44	47

2. When GNP is $180, consumption spending to be expected is $160.
3. The community's marginal propensity to save (constant throughout the range of GNPs considered) is $\frac{2}{5}$.
4. Government spending and taxation are both zero.

a. In the spaces below, show the community propensity to consume from GNPs of $150 to $250.

GNP:	$150	$160	$170	$180	$190	$200
C:	____	____	____	____	____	____

GNP:	$210	$220	$230	$240	$250
C:	____	____	____	____	____

b. What is the equilibrium level of GNP?   ..... $_____

a. $142; $148; $154; $160; $166; $172; $178; $184; $190; $196; $202   **b.** $240

10. The "paradox of thrift" is a fancy name for the observation that while increased saving might make an individual wealthier in the long run, higher saving can actually make an economy poorer. It is a classic example of the *(fallacy of correlation not causality / fallacy of composition / application of irrelevant alternatives)*.

One place to illustrate the paradox is the usual Keynesian graph that plots total spending against GNP. Figure 9-3 provides such a graph. As it stands, equilibrium GNP is $1000 (billion). Now suppose that everyone saves more so that, for any level of GNP, total saving is always $10 higher than before. Draw the new total-spending curve; it shows a new equilibrium GNP that is *(higher than / exactly equal to / lower than)* the original. If the marginal propensity to consume were .6, government spending and taxes were fixed, and investment did not

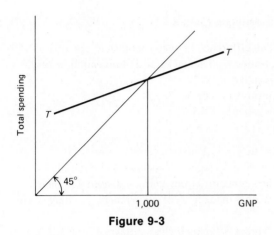

Figure 9-3

change, then the new equilibrium would, in fact, be $_____.
To maintain equilibrium at $1000, an increase in government

spending of $ _____ or a reduction in tax collections of

$ _____ would be required.

The paradox is decidedly a *(Keynesian / classical)* phenomenon. Show, on both panels of Figure 9-4, aggregate demand curves that would support equilibrium at $1000. Now draw new aggregate demand curves to reflect an increase in saving. On the Keynesian panel, GNP *(rises / stays the same / falls)* while prices *(rise / stay the same / fall)*. On the classical panel, meanwhile, GNP *(rises / stays the same / falls)* while prices *(rise / stay the same / fall)*. For an intermediate view somewhere between the Keynesian and classical extremes, we should expect that higher saving would cause GNP to *(rise / stay the same / fall)* and prices to *(rise / stay the same / fall)*.

fallacy of composition; lower than; 975; 10; 16.67; Keynesian; *drawn downward-sloping, cutting AS above $1000; drawn downward-sloping, cutting AS to the left of $1000;* falls; stay the same; stays the same; fall; fall; fall (*Note:* Italicized answers describe schedules to be drawn in Figure 9-4)

11. The text identifies two distinct types of fiscal policy: automatic policy, which comes into play simply because the economy behaves in a certain way, and discretionary policy, which must be devised and implemented by conscious action.

Two examples of automatic policies with significant stabilizing properties were listed. One was the *(proportional income tax of the state of Pennsylvania / progressive federal income tax / proposed national sales tax)*. In times of recession, the revenue collected from this tax would *(fall / stay the same / rise)* and thereby *(increase / have no effect on / decrease)* disposable income and consumption. Consumption being part of aggregate demand, the net effect would be *(stimulative / insignificant / contractionary)* just at the time when a deepening recession was to be short-circuited.

Unemployment insurance and welfare transfers compose a second set of automatic policies identified in the text to have built-in abilities to stabilize GNP. During a period of boom when employment is growing and fewer people need public assistance, expenditure on these programs *(falls / remains the same / increases)* and automatically provides some of the needed *(expansionary / contractionary)* adjustment in overall fiscal policy.

Both these policies work in reverse when the need arises, of course. Revenues collected from the progressive income tax increase during a boom and thereby provide part of the fiscal restraint needed to slow the growth of aggregate demand. Similarly, transfers swell during times of recession and maintain at least part of the needed support for aggregate demand.

progressive federal income tax; fall; increase; stimulative; falls; contractionary

12. All is not, however, roses. The automatic stabilizing abilities of these policies also serve to *(diminish / increase)* the multiplier effects of changes in investment and changes in discretionary fiscal policy. Policy is thus *(more / less)* effective in moving GNP around.

To see this, suppose that the marginal propensity to consume were .8 and a public-works program involving the expenditure of $1 billion were undertaken. Without built-in stabilizers and assuming the availability of sufficient unemployed resources to make the Keynesian model appropriate, the result should be an increase in equilibrium GNP of

$ _____ billion. If, however, this result were accompanied by an increase in tax collections of $400 million and a

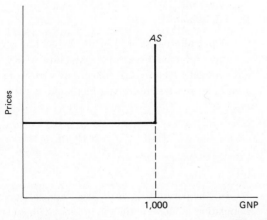 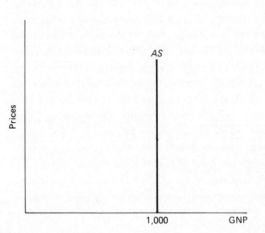

Figure 9-4

reduction in unemployment expenditure of $100 million, then the increase in GNP would be diminished by $ _____ billion and $ _____ billion, respectively. The net effect would, in other words, be an increase in GNP of $ _____ billion, or _____ % of the original increase.

In short, then, built-in stabilizers work to reduce part of any fluctuation in GNP, regardless of its source, but they do not eradicate the entire disturbance. What to do about the part of the disturbance that remains is the problem facing the authors of discretionary fiscal (and monetary) policy.

diminish; less; 5; 1.6; .5; 2.9; 42

13. Four types of discretionary fiscal policy are listed in the text; list them in the spaces provided:

a. _____

b. _____

c. _____

d. _____

Problems with discretionary policies include the length of time involved to get them geared up (a spending program or tax program designed nominally to help stimulate an economy out of recession might finally get off the ground 3 years later in the middle of a boom when the stimulus is counterproductive), the tenuous connection between employment in the public domain and subsequent employment in the private sector, and the reluctance to initiate larger welfare expenditure in times of recession for fear that it will be difficult to call it back when the recession is over.

public works; public employment; transfers and welfare payments; tax-rate adjustments

14. Estimates of the dynamic multiplier for non-defense government expenditure differ widely. Consulting Figure 9-8 in the text, it is apparent that most models compute a multiplier in the range of *(.5 / 1 / 2)* after about 4 to 6 months. The *Wharton* model climbs above *(2 / 3 / 4)* and never falls; the *DRI* model reaches a peak of about *(.5 / 1.2 / 1.8)* after about 12 months and then declines; and the St. Louis Federal Reserve model falls to *(0 / .2 / .4)* in a little over a year's time. One reason behind the declines is *(that all the money leaves the country by the end of 2 years / the effect of monetary accommodation or the lack thereof / that no investment is created by non-defense spending)*. The reasons behind the differences of opinion include *(the inherent uncertainties in predicting economic behavior / the different economic philosophies of various researchers that dictate different models / the innate desire of researchers to differentiate their product / differences in the assumed type of non-defense expenditure)*.

1; 2; 1.8; 0; the effect of monetary accommodation or the lack thereof; the inherent uncertainties in predicting economic behavior (and) the different economic philosophies of various researchers

QUIZ: Multiple Choice

1. The difference between actual and potential GNP was:
(1) positive (i.e., actual exceeded potential) in 1982.
(2) negative in 1975.
(3) positive in 1961.
(4) negative in 1973.
(5) positive in 1968.

2. In the pure Keynesian view of the world:
(1) prices and wages are assumed to be sticky.
(2) the aggregate supply curve is assumed to be flat.
(3) changes in the level of government spending can influence GNP.
(4) changes in tax policy can influence GNP.
(5) all of the above.

3. If the Keynesian prescription for correcting recession is applied but the aggregate supply curve has some finite slope to it, then:
(1) GNP should climb while prices fall.
(2) GNP should climb while prices hold steady.
(3) prices should climb along with real GNP.
(4) real GNP should not change while prices soar.
(5) none of the above.

4. If people suddenly decide to spend less at every level of income, then the total-spending line on the usual Keynesian graph should be drawn:
(1) higher and to the right.
(2) lower and to the right.
(3) higher and to the left.
(4) lower and to the left.
(5) none of the above

5. If (*a*) GNP is initially in equilibrium, (*b*) the government then increases its total expenditure on goods and services by $2 billion, (*c*) there is no increase at all in tax collections, (*d*) the marginal propensity to consume is .75, and (*e*) the marginal propensity to invest is zero, then (assuming no price-inflationary consequences) in the new equilibrium thus produced, GNP will have risen by:
(1) zero—i.e., not at all.
(2) $2 billion.
(3) $6 billion.
(4) $8 billion.
(5) $10 billion.

6. Which alternative in question 5 would be correct, had that question referred to a total reduction of $2 billion in the government's income tax collections with its expenditure on goods and services not being increased at all?
(1).
(2).
(3).
(4).
(5).

7. In "the paradox of thrift," the result of an attempt by the population to increase the total of its saving is as follows:

(1) all of GNP, *C* (consumption), *S* (personal saving), and *I* (investment) unchanged.

(2) all of GNP, *C*, *S*, and *I* increased.

(3) GNP and *C* unchanged, *S* decreased, *I* increased.

(4) GNP decreased, *C* and *I* unchanged, *S* decreased.

(5) all of GNP, *C*, *I*, and *S* decreased.

8. The moral of the paradox of thrift is this:

(1) A decrease in saving during low-employment periods may temporarily increase consumption, but only at the cost of lower GNP later on.

(2) an increase in the amount of saving is always a desirable thing in terms of its influence upon GNP.

(3) a decrease in the amount of saving is always a desirable thing in terms of its influence upon GNP.

(4) attempts to increase saving may actually increase consumption also, since saving provides the funds to finance investment.

(5) none of the above.

9. If GNP is in equilibrium, then:

(1) consumption must be just equal to investment.

(2) business receipts from consumption spending must just equal national income.

(3) any increase in spending must result in an inflationary gap.

(4) the overall budgets of federal, state, and local governments must be just balanced.

(5) none of the above is necessarily correct.

10. GNP is in equilibrium at its full-employment level. The federal government finds it necessary to increase its expenditures on goods and services by $10 billion. It wants to increase taxes sufficiently so that there will be no more serious threat of inflation—i.e., it wants the net change in the equilibrium level of GNP to be zero. The probable increase in tax collections needed will be:

(1) more than $10 billion.

(2) $10 billion.

(3) less than $10 billion, although not zero.

(4) zero.

(5) less than zero—i.e., tax collections can be reduced.

11. An equilibrium level of GNP (below full employment) is disturbed by an autonomous rise in planned investment spending of $10 billion. The marginal propensity to consume is .6. In the new equilibrium GNP will have risen (in billions) by:

(1) $10.

(2) $25.

(3) $60.

(4) $80.

(5) $100.

12. The text chapter says that there is a small but significant difference between the multiplier effect of an increase of, say, $10 (billion) in government spending and that of a decrease of $10 in personal taxes levied. This is because:

(1) government spending, by increasing income earned, increases consumption spending.

(2) a $10 reduction in taxation has a significantly greater effect on the government surplus or deficit than has a $10 increase in government spending.

(3) a tax reduction affects consumer income and spending directly, whereas the effect of an increase in government spending on consumers is only indirect.

(4) a $10 reduction in personal taxes does not produce a $10 increase in consumer spending, since part of this reduction goes into extra saving.

(5) of none of the above reasons.

13. Whenever total planned investment exceeds the total of planned saving (personal plus corporate), then:

(1) GNP will fall below potential GNP.

(2) GNP will rise above potential GNP.

(3) **GNP will rise if initially below potential GNP.**

(4) GNP will fall only if initially at potential GNP.

(5) there is no reason to expect any change in GNP, either up or down, nor any reason to expect, as a necessary result, any change in potential GNP.

14. The paradox is a perfect example of the "fallacy of composition" if you accept:

(1) the pure Keynesian model.

(2) the pure classical model.

(3) a model somewhere in between the Keynesian and the classical models.

(4) items 1 and 2 only.

(5) items 1 and 3 only.

15. According to the classical model, an increase in saving should:

(1) lower real GNP.

(2) lower potential GNP.

(3) affect only the rate of growth of future potential GNP.

(4) leave nominal GNP unaffected.

(5) none of the above.

16. Automatic policies tend to be built-in stabilizers because they automatically:

(1) provide fiscal restraint in times of boom.

(2) provide fiscal stimulus in times of recession.

(3) come into play without the conscious action of any policy maker.

(4) are sometimes the accidents of other policy objectives (e.g., the progressive income tax is a mechanism designed to distribute at least part of the burden of financing government equitably).

(5) all the above.

17. Public-works projects tend to be passed over as discretionary fiscal policies designed to promote stability because:

(1) the transition to private employment is difficult.

(2) they take too long to enact.

(3) they take too long to get under way.

(4) they tend to perpetuate themselves.

(5) they are viewed as effecting temporary changes in disposable income and are therefore not as effective as they would be if they were viewed as permanent.

18. Which answer to question 17 would have been correct if it had addressed a problem with public employment programs?
(1).
(2).
(3).
(4).
(5).

19. Which answer to question 17 would have been correct if it had addressed a problem with amendments in welfare transfer programs?
(1).
(2).
(3).
(4).
(5).

20. Estimates of the non-defense spending multiplier vary significantly from researcher to researcher because:
(1) of inherent uncertainties and philosophical differences.
(2) different researchers use different data to make their estimates.
(3) different researchers want to make certain that readers distinguish their work from the work of others.
(4) the estimation procedures are so complex that errors necessarily distort the results beyond belief.
(5) none of the above.

CHAPTER 10
AGGREGATE SUPPLY AND BUSINESS CYCLES

Previous chapters have explored the determinants of aggregate demand; it is now time to turn our attention to a careful examination of aggregate supply. What are the determinants of aggregate supply? What are the sources of growth in potential GNP? What are supply-side policies and how are they supposed to work? What is the connection between the interaction of aggregate supply, aggregate demand, and the level of (un)employment?

These are all theoretical issues, to be sure, and they occupy our full attention in the first part of Chapter 10. They would, however, be empty theoretical issues if their importance were not supported by empirical evidence and recent observation. That evidence is presented in the second part of the chapter before we turn briefly to the question on everyone's mind: Can we, by clever design of economic policy, avoid the ups and downs of the business cycle? The short answer to that question will be "probably not," but the qualification to that answer is that we should be able to reduce the size of the swings.

Having completed your work in this chapter, you should have accomplished the following objectives.

LEARNING OBJECTIVES

1. Identify the sources of growth of potential GNP and illustrate it graphically as a shift in the aggregate supply curve.

2. Explain the turning points and phases of the business cycle in terms of shifts in aggregate demand.

3. Understand the import of Okun's Law in relating unemployment levels and actual GNP.

4. Explain the three major components of supply-side policy as practiced by the Thatcher and Reagan administrations, and evaluate their likely effectiveness in different phases of the business cycle.

5. Distinguish internal and external theories of business cycles, including the notion of the political business cycle.

6. Explain the operation of the acceleration principle in creating swings in business activity.

7. Confront the question of whether or not business cycles

are avoidable, totally beyond our control, or somewhere in between.

Evidence of the existence of the business cycle can be found in the periodic fluctuation of almost all the major macroeconomic variables that we study: prices, employment, output, interest rates, etc. To understand where the cycle might come from, though, we cannot simply jump into the cycle and look around; we need first to understand why potential GNP grows and what that growth does to the aggregate supply curve.

1. From 1948 through 1981, potential GNP grew at an annual rate of approximately *(1.2 percent / 3.3 percent / 4.5 percent)*. Of that growth, *(.5 / .9 / 1.4)* percentage points have been attributed to growth in the labor force, *(.9 / 1.6 / 2.1)* percentage points have been attributed to growth in the capital stock, *(.3 / .7 / 1.0)* point has been attributed to technological advancement, and the rest is unexplained. It is, however, estimated that the rate of growth of potential output fell to *(2.3 percent / 2.7 percent / 3.0 percent)* during the period from 1981 to 1984.

Now consult Figure 10-2 in the text. It shows that growth in potential GNP shifts the aggregate supply curve *(up / down)* and to the *(right / left)* because wages and other costs of production tend to *(climb / fall)* over time. The figure also shows a flat curvature *(only below / in a small neighborhood on both sides of / only above)* estimated potential GNP. Prices appear to be sticky through potential GNP until they begin to become "unstuck." When the curves turn up, though, they turn up quickly.

Could equilibrium have moved from point A in Figure 10-2 to point B without an increase in aggregate demand? _____. If aggregate demand had decreased between 1981 and 1984, potential output would have *(still grown / fallen)*, actual GNP would have *(grown / fallen)*, and prices would have *(climbed / fallen)*.

3.3; .9; .9; 1.0; 2.7; up; right; climb; in a small neighborhood on both sides of; No; still grown; fallen; climbed

2. Figure 10-1 shows, in two separate panels, shifts in aggregate demand from AD to AD'. Panel **(a)** illustrates a shift that would cause *(recession / expansion)* because equilibrium GNP would *(fall / climb)* and price inflation would *(accelerate / slow)*. Panel (b) shows the opposite, of course—*(a recession / an expansion)* with *(accelerating / braking)* prices and *(expanding / contracting)* GNP. Formally, a recession is an economic downturn during which *(real / nominal)* GNP declines for *(1 / 2 / 3)* successive calendar quarters. To the first people to be laid off, however, the technical definition is not important; it is a recession as soon as they lose their jobs.

---

recession; fall; slow; an expansion; accelerating; expanding; real; 2

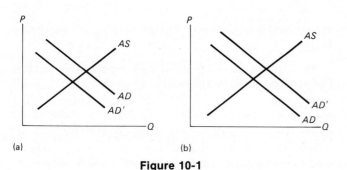

(a)   (b)

Figure 10-1

3. Okun's Law is one of those miracles of statistics—a simple rule that fits reality extremely well. Okun's empirics tell us that every time that actual GNP falls 2 percent relative to potential GNP, unemployment *(increases / decreases)* by *(1 / 2 / 3 / 4)* percentage point(s). In application of this result, we now know that if potential GNP is growing at X percent per year, then real GNP will have to grow at *(less than X percent / X percent / more than X percent)* to keep unemployment from climbing.

Other computations are also possible. In completing the following table, you will not only practice those computations, but also confirm the accuracy of the law by comparing your answers with observed unemployment rates. Record, in particular, your prediction for the actual unemployment rate for the years indicated by applying Okun's Law to the data provided. The actual rates, listed down the column, were 6.7 percent, 3.8 percent, 4.9 percent, 8.5 percent, 9.8 percent.

Starting Year	Ending Year	Rate of Growth of		Unemployment Rate	
		Potential GNP, %	Actual GNP, %	Initial, %	Predicted
1960	1961	3.3	2.2	5.5	_____
1965	1966	3.3	6.0	4.8	_____
1970	1971	3.3	−.2	3.5	_____
1975	1976	3.3	−1.1	5.6	_____
1981	1982	2.7	−1.3	7.5	_____

increases; 1; X percent; 6.0; 3.5; 5.3; 7.8; 9.5 (the fit is not bad, is it?)

4. There were three components of the "supply-side" recovery packages enacted in the early 1980s by the Reagan administration in the United States and the Thatcher administration in the United Kingdom. The first was a retreat from the short-run stabilization prescriptions of the Keynesian model. This retreat was supported by a view that the aggregate supply curve was *(nearly vertical / nearly horizontal)* so that any recession that might be forthcoming would be short and mild. Prices and wages would, in particular, *(quickly / slowly)* adjust to any excess supply in the labor market.

The second was a set of tax incentives designed to move the aggregate supply curve up and (mostly) out by boosting potential GNP as shown in Figure 10-2 by the shift from AS to AS'. The effectiveness of this policy also depends upon the shape of the aggregate supply curve. If the curve were vertical (or if the economy were represented by AD_1 on the vertical portion of the AS supply curve), then the shift would be effective in *(increasing / reducing)* actual GNP and *(lowering / increasing)* prices. If the curve were horizontal (or the economy represented by AD_2 on the flat portion of AS'), though, the supply shift would *(increase actual GNP slightly / reduce actual GNP slightly / still be effective in increasing GNP substantially)* and actually *(increase / reduce)* prices. Again, support for the program was based upon a rejection of the horizontal AS curve of the Keynesian model.

The third arm of the program was a substantial reduction in personal income taxes. The effect of this reduction would, of course, influence *(aggregate demand / aggregate supply)*. As such, one should have expected that it would increase actual GNP with stable prices only if the aggregate supply schedule were *(nearly vertical / nearly horizontal)*. Otherwise, the increase in aggregate demand would be vented almost exclusively in *(prices / potential GNP/output)*. In supporting this final component of the program, it would appear that the architects of the program were not ready to discard Keynes entirely. Indeed, the Reagan people campaigned for the program by comparing it favorably with the Kennedy round of tax cuts of the early 1960s—the beginning of the high point for Keynesians in making federal policy.

---

nearly vertical; quickly; increasing; lowering; reduce actual GNP slightly; increase; aggregate demand; nearly horizontal; prices

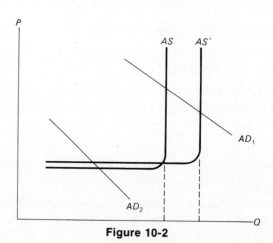

Figure 10-2

Business cycles are, at the same time, all different and all the same. Each one has its own cause, its own length of time, its own degree of severity, and its own trajectory. Despite all these differences, though, they all seem to follow the same general pattern: decline into recession, bottom out; climb into recovery; continue into boom; peak; fall toward price stability; decline into recession; and so on. The differences are confounding, but the similarities suggest the possibility that some equally general pattern of policy might reduce the severity of the cycle.

5. Record in the blanks provided the phase of a business cycle during which you would expect to observe the indicated events; denote recession by (*R*) and boom by (*B*).

a. an increase in business investment .... (————)

b. profits falling .... (————)

c. tax receipts climbing .... (————)

d. demand for labor rising .... (————)

e. stock prices falling .... (————)

f. accelerating inflation .... (————)

g. unemployment insurance payments increasing ....
.... (————)

h. interest rates falling .... (————)

a. *B* b. *R* c. *B* d. *B* e. *R* f. *B* g. *R* h. *R*

6. Chapters 12 and 13 suggest that recessions (or depressions) most commonly arise from a (*drop / rise*) in (*consumption / investment / government*) spending. Because of the "multiplier effect," this initial (*drop / rise*) has magnified consequences—i.e., total spending drops (*even more / somewhat less*) than the initial drop in (*C / I / G*) spending.

Among the following time series, the greatest cyclical fluctuation is typically found in (*wholesale prices / production of capital goods / production of basic materials such as anthracite coal / expenditure on consumer goods*).

drop; investment; drop; even more; *I*; production of capital goods

7. If we believe the population level to be in no way influenced by economic conditions, a theory that business cycles result from changes in total population would be an (*external / internal*) theory of the cycle.

If we go to the other extreme, considering population changes to result entirely from economic conditions (e.g., because people cannot afford to get married or have children during depressions), then such a theory would be an (*external / internal*) theory of the cycle.

external; internal

The *acceleration principle* is one theoretical explanation of business cycles. It is simply stated:

▶ The argument of the acceleration principle is that investment spending will take place when GNP is going up.

Notice that the acceleration principle says there will be investment because GNP is rising. It is not a low GNP that sets off investment; nor is it a high GNP. It is the fact that GNP is rising from a lower to a higher level.

Here is the logic behind the acceleration principle: net investment spending (that is, investment which is more than sufficient to compensate for the current wearing-out of presently existing capital goods) adds to the economy's total capital-goods stock. To produce a GNP of, say, $800 (billion), a certain capital-goods stock is needed. (If you had less than that given stock, you couldn't produce an $800 GNP. If you had more than that stock, you would have more than enough for an $800 GNP.)

Similarly, there is a particular capital stock that "just goes" with a GNP of $1000. Assuming the same price level, this will be a bigger stock than that associated with the $800 GNP.

Once the economy has built the capital-goods stock appropriate to an $800 GNP, and is operating at an equilibrium level of $800, then no further capital goods are needed. That is, net investment spending will be zero so long as GNP remains at $800. The same would be true of a $1000 GNP: no net investment spending so long as the capital stock appropriate to that GNP has been built, and GNP is in equilibrium at that level.

But if the economy starts to move from an $800 GNP toward a $1000 GNP, then it needs more capital goods—the extra capital goods required for the higher GNP level. As a result, there will be positive net investment spending.

8. a. You are sales representative for a machine-tool firm. One of your customers is a firm which has 10 machines, identical except for age. Each machine has a 10-year life, and they are nicely staggered in age, so that each year one machine is ready for the scrap heap; there will be one machine 9 years old, one 8 years old, and so on. The plant has just enough business to keep its machines steadily occupied.

As seller of these machines, you visit the plant once yearly, expecting an order for one machine to replace the machine currently wearing out. Assuming, for simplicity, that each new machine costs $10, your order each year will be for $10. In national-product terms, gross investment will be $(*100 / 10 / zero*), and net investment $(*100 / 10 / zero*)

Suddenly, the demand for this firm's product jumps. Sales rise by 30 percent and stay at this higher level. The firm must expand its equipment (its capital-goods stock) to allow for this extra production. On your annual visit (which is happily timed to coincide with the sales jump), you receive an order for (*5 / 4 / 3 / 2 / 1 / 0*) machine(s). That is, gross investment (at the $10 price) is $(*50 / 40 / 30 / 20 / 10*), and net investment is $(*40 / 30 / 20 / 10 / zero*).

One year passes. Again you visit the plant, knowing in advance that the firm's sales are still holding at their 30-percent-higher level. The firm expects them to remain steady at that level. What will your order be this time? It will be for *(5 / 4 / 3 / 2 / 1 / 0)* machine(s). That is, gross investment is $*(50 / 40 / 30 / 20 / 10 / zero)*, and net investment is $*(40 / 30 / 20 / 10 / zero)*.

This is a small-scale example of the acceleration-principle idea. Net investment is not a matter of the absolute level of output. It takes place when output is rising.

b. Suppose the level of GNP (or of consumption, which is the major component within GNP) is for 4 successive years as follows: year 1, $500; year 2, $600; year 3, $650; year 4, $650. The acceleration principle would say that net *I* spending would be (pick one):

(1) A positive but different amount in each of the 4 years
(2) Positive between years 1 and 3, zero in year 4
(3) Zero in the first 2 years, but positive and increasing in the last 2

c. It is hard to say how far the acceleration-principle idea has been verified in experience. Even its most zealous proponents would hardly argue that this principle affords a complete account of net *I* spending. But some economists think it carries an important element of truth.

Its critics point out that most *I* spending is undertaken by business firms in the hope of profit. Even if GNP is presently in equilibrium at a certain level, but if business firms think (rightly or wrongly) that that GNP is going to rise, so that there will be an increased demand for output, they *(will / will not)* be encouraged to undertake new investment spending.

Conversely, if GNP is presently rising but if firms are inclined to believe that this rise will be small and of short duration, they *(will / will not)* be encouraged to undertake *I* spending.

---

a. 10; zero; 4; 40; 30; 1; 10; zero   **b.** **(2)**   **c.** will; will not

---

9. Both the following statements repeat ideas in the text:

1. The level of *C* spending is influenced by the level of *I* spending, because *C* spending depends considerably on the level of GNP, and the level of GNP depends considerably on the level of *I* spending.

2. The level of *I* spending is influenced by *C* spending—specifically, by the rate at which the level of *C* spending is increasing.

a. Which of the above is a statement of the acceleration principle? . . . . *(1 / 2 / neither)*

b. Which is a statement of the theory of income determination found in Chapter 9 . . . . *(1 / 2 / neither)*

In other words, *I* spending and *C* spending interact with one another, each influenced by the other, so that both may be changing as they seek out mutually compatible levels. In the

process, GNP (which is principally the sum of *C* and *I* spending) must change also. That is, the ups and downs of GNP that we call the business cycle are to at least some degree the result of this interaction.

When the acceleration-principle idea is introduced, the interaction becomes a complicated one. You should understand the acceleration-principle idea. You should understand that that there is an interaction between *C* and *I*; you should grasp its general nature. But an introductory course cannot outline in full detail how *I*, *C*, and GNP would interact in an acceleration-principle world.

---

a. 2   **b.** 1

QUIZ: Multiple Choice

1. Compared with the experience of the United States between 1948 and 1975, the rate of growth of potential GNP has, in early years of the 1980s:
(1) climbed dramatically by more than 50 percent.
(2) climbed slightly by about 18 percent.
(3) remained at the historical level.
(4) fallen by about 18 percent.
(5) fallen by more than 25 percent.

2. Business cycles seem to be caused:
(1) exclusively by external factors.
(2) exclusively by internal factors.
(3) by factors of any type that mostly influence aggregate demand.
(4) by factors that mostly influence aggregate supply.
(5) entirely by the vagaries of the political seasons.

3. According to Okun's Law, if potential GNP rose by 9 percent between 1979 and 1982 but actual GNP did not change, then unemployment should have climbed from 5.8 percent in 1979 to:
(1) 6.1 percent.
(2) 10.3 percent.
(3) 11.2 percent.
(4) 8.8 percent.
(5) 9.7 percent.

4. Which of the following statements are true about the supply-side program for recovery offered by the Reagan administration in 1981?
(1) It represented a retreat from belief in the Keynesian model of macroeconomic behavior.
(2) It represented a belief that price and wage adjustments would keep any recession short.
(3) It included a prescription to increase potential output that depended upon a nearly vertical aggregate supply curve to be most effective.
(4) It included a prescription to increase aggregate demand by cutting personal taxes, which depended upon a nearly horizontal aggregate supply curve to be most effective.
(5) All of the above.

5. Which of the following would you not expect to see during a period of recession?
(1) Lower business investment on durable equipment.
(2) Lower stock prices; lower demand for labor.
(3) Lower tax receipts.
(4) Lower corporate profits.
(5) Lower unemployment compensation payments.

6. Which of the following time frames was marked by the most severe period of recession?
(1) 1969–1970.
(2) 1982–1983.
(3) 1974–1975.
(4) 1960–1961.
(5) 1953–1954.

7. Which of the following time frames was marked by the most energetic period of economic boom?
(1) 1983–1984.
(2) 1973–1974.
(3) 1938–1939.
(4) 1955–1956.
(5) 1967–1968.

8. The implication of the theory of political business cycles is that:
(1) anti-inflationary medicine is generally administered early in an administration.
(2) the year after an election is frequently a year of austerity.
(3) the year of an election is frequently a year of growth and prosperity.
(4) the timing of elections can dictate the timing of the business cycle.
(5) all of the above.

9. In the United States the major business cycle:
(1) has been much less pronounced than in European economies, with the single exception of the 1930s.
(2) strikes very sharply at certain limited sectors of the economy, but leaves major sectors almost totally unaffected.
(3) shows a remarkably uniform and symmetrical pattern in the sequence of prosperity, peak, slump, and depression, once "random" elements have been removed.
(4) has been more intense than in European economies, at least with respect to the degree of variation in total employment.
(5) is not correctly described by any of these statements.

10. According to the text, if we look to any particular kind of spending as a key factor in accounting for the major business cycle, we find it in:
(1) net investment spending, specifically spending on inventories.
(2) net investment spending, specifically spending on durable goods.
(3) consumer spending.
(4) variations in spending by state and local governments.
(5) none of the above, the point stressed being that no single type of spending plays any key role.

11. The multiplier and the acceleration principle are related in what way?
(1) They both seek to explain how changes in the level of investment spending come about.
(2) The multiplier seeks to explain how a condition of full-employment GNP can be maintained, and the acceleration principle seeks to explain how a condition of depression may come about and may persist despite efforts to increase spending.
(3) The multiplier shows how a change in the level of GNP, particularly an upward change, may give rise to net investment, and the acceleration principle shows how a given change in spending (e.g., in investment) can result in a larger change in the level of GNP.
(4) The multiplier shows how a given change in spending (e.g., in investment) can result in a larger change in the level of GNP, and the acceleration principle shows how a change in the level of GNP, particularly an upward change, may give rise to net investment.
(5) In none of the ways described above.

12. The role of consumer spending in the business cycle, according to U.S. experience described, is that:
(1) changes in consumer durable purchases may occasionally set off an upswing or downturn, and changes in consumer spending will intensify the effect of any disturbance originating outside the consumer sphere, via the multiplier.
(2) consumer spending and investment spending seem to have approximately equal parts to play in the cycle, although the two are so intermixed that it is difficult to separate one from the other and to analyze the role of either.
(3) changes in consumer spending on nondurables most commonly initiate the downturn in a major business cycle, whereas increases in consumer durable purchases are most likely to start the upturn, as replacement of worn-out durable items becomes necessary.
(4) changes in consumer spending are most often the initial disturbing factor, and the impact then spreads to investment spending, thus intensifying the original disturbance.
(5) consumer spending has no part to play in the cycle, which (except for wartime disturbances) is almost entirely due to investment-spending changes.

13. In economics, "capital formation" means specifically:
(1) the purchase of any new commodity.
(2) net investment.
(3) the borrowing of money.
(4) the sale of any new stock issue.
(5) none of these activities.

14. According to the acceleration principle, spending on net investment will take place:
(1) when GNP or consumption is at a high level.
(2) when GNP or consumption is at a low level.
(3) when GNP or consumption is rising.
(4) when GNP or consumption is falling.
(5) perhaps in any of the above situations, since no such link with GNP or consumption is assumed.

15.   The theory of the multiplier:

(1) is an external theory of the business cycle.

(2) is a theory of the business cycle based on the fact of "replacement waves" in the construction of capital goods.

(3) while not a theory of the business cycle, is a useful addition to any cycle theory, since it explains how changes in investment spending can occur.

(4) while not a theory of the business cycle, is a useful addition to any cycle theory, since it explains how small fluctuations in spending can have magnified effects on GNP.

(5) bears no relationship to the problem of business cycles or their explanation.

16.   Four of the five following statements are reasonably correct as to the nature of the "acceleration principle." Identify the incorrect statement. This theory says, with respect to acceleration-principle-induced net investment, that the amount of expenditure thereon:

(1) is related to the growth of GNP or of consumption, rather than to the absolute level of either of them.

(2) may be very large even though it may be set off by a comparatively small change in GNP or consumption.

(3) will be zero if and when GNP reaches an equilibrium level.

(4) is explainable in terms of the fact that a particular level of total output requires a particular quantity of capital goods in order to produce that output.

(5) tends to increase as more money is injected into the economy through the medium of the banking system.

17.   Statistically, the widest swings between peak and bottom of the major business cycle (according to the test) are to be found in:

(1) the supply of consumer services.

(2) the production of inventories.

(3) the production of durables—i.e., capital goods.

(4) wholesale rather than retail goods.

(5) export and import goods.

Experimental Exercise

18.   Find three dice. Roll the three together 20 times in succession and record the numbers that emerge in column (1) of the table provided below. Record, in column (2) of the table, the moving average of the current and four previous rolls, and plot that average on Figure 10-3. [Note, for a sequence of 7, 4, 10, 3, 7, 11, 7, 2, 9, etc., the sequence of appropriate moving averages would start $(7 + 4 + 10 + 3 + 7)/5 = 6.2$; $(4 + 10 + 3 + 7 + 11)/5 = 7$; and so forth.]

Now repeat the same procedure in columns (3) and (4) and in Figure 10-3 (using a different color) for a sequence of rolls conducted according to the following rules:

1.   Roll three dice on the first roll.

2.   On subsequent rolls, roll:

a. Two dice if the previous value was less than 9

b. Two dice if the previous roll achieved a value greater than 12

c. Three dice otherwise

Roll Number	(1) Roll	(2) Average	(3) Roll	(4) Average
1	_____		_____	
2	_____		_____	
3	_____		_____	
4	_____		_____	
5	_____	_____	_____	_____
6	_____	_____	_____	_____
7	_____	_____	_____	_____
8	_____	_____	_____	_____
9	_____	_____	_____	_____
10	_____	_____	_____	_____
11	_____	_____	_____	_____
12	_____	_____	_____	_____
13	_____	_____	_____	_____
14	_____	_____	_____	_____
15	_____	_____	_____	_____
16	_____	_____	_____	_____
17	_____	_____	_____	_____
18	_____	_____	_____	_____
19	_____	_____	_____	_____
20	_____	_____	_____	_____

The variation simulating a sequence of business cycles should be smaller for the second sequence than the first. The rules that governed the second sequence serve the function of the automatic stabilizers of Chapter 9.

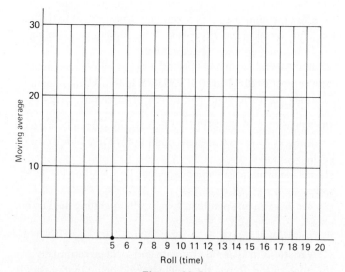

Figure 10-3

CHAPTER 11

UNEMPLOYMENT

Unemployment is, to some, the major macroeconomic issue of the past two decades; to others, it is simply a measure of how many people do not want to work at the going wage. Chapter 11 explores both these points of view, as well as the multitude of opinions that fall somewhere in between. A precise definition of unemployment will be presented, both in terms of economic content and statistical expedience. Interpretation of the scope and the texture of the problem of involuntary unemployment will also command some of our attention. In closing, though, the discussion will not turn to the macro policies that might help reduce unemployment by pushing output higher; those are the topics of past and future chapters. We will, instead, mention briefly the types of employment-focused micro policies that might be designed specifically to alleviate the problem, on the one hand, and the social safety net programs that might actually aggravate it, on the other.

Having worked your way through the chapter, therefore, you will have accomplished the following objectives.

LEARNING OBJECTIVES

1. Understand the dimension of the economic and social consequences of unemployment.

2. Explain how the unemployment rate is estimated and the problems associated with that procedure.

3. Delineate the difference between voluntary and involuntary unemployment, and understand the necessity of observing some Keynesian-styled wage stickiness to adequately explain the existence of the latter.

4. Recognize the uneven distribution of unemployment over classifications of workers, the more even impact of recession across the same classifications, and the relationship between the overall macroeconomic health of an economy and the average duration of a spell of unemployment.

5. Differentiate frictional, structural, and cyclical unemployment, and explain how the first two types help build a natural rate of unemployment that is currently estimated to be 6 percent.

6. Understand that the natural rate of unemployment is not an optimal rate of unemployment. It is, instead, a rate consistent with stable prices, and it has been growing over the past two decades.

7. Explore the role of policy in the growth of the natural rate and suggest other policies that might turn the trend around.

Economists are quick to remember Okun's Law when they are asked to evaluate the costs of unemployment. The joblessness that plagued the United States from 1975 through 1984 cost us $1200 billion, or 37 percent of then current GNP. That number is astronomical compared with the efficiency costs of monopoly and other forms of imperfect competition, the costs of strict environmental controls, or even the Grace Commission's estimate of waste in government. Nonetheless, it misses the human cost: the homes that are broken by the strain; the kids that sell their bikes to buy milk for their baby sisters; the anguish of 10,000 unemployed workers that show up to interview for 40 openings at a tanning factory. Unemployment is one of those topics that brings the dismal science out of its tower of numbers and makes it a social science.

1. When the unemployment rate is measured every month, *(10,000 / 30,000 / 60,000)* households are sampled to determine their employment status. There are three categories: employed, unemployed, and not in the labor force. Indicate the category into which people who find themselves in the following circumstances would be classified; designate employed by (E), unemployed by (U), and not in the labor force by (N).

a. A laid-off autoworker .... (———)

b. A laid-off autoworker employed part time at Wendy's .....

.... (———)

c. A lawyer too sick to work .... (_____)

d. An unemployed steel worker too discouraged to look for a job .... (_____)

e. A full-time college student .... (_____)

f. A car mechanic going to college at night .... (_____)

g. An executive on leave to go to law school ... (_____)

h. A housewife who works full time at home .. (_____)

i. A housewife who works part time at the library ....

.... (_____)

j. A housewife who volunteers part time at the library ......

.... (_____)

60,000 **a.** *U* **b.** *E* **c.** *N* **d.** *N* **e.** *N* **f.** *E* **g.** *N* **h.** *N* **i.** *E* **j.** *N*

Many of the entries in the list recorded in question 1 were constructed to illustrate one problem or another with the measurement procedure. The procedure does not, for example, count as employed some people who work full time; housewives who work at home are "not in the labor force." It counts some people who are "underemployed" as employed; i.e., people who can find only part-time work are "employed." It does not count people who have been unemployed for so long that they have become discouraged as unemployed; they, too, are no longer "in the labor force."

These are not simply academic curiosities designed to interest the scholar and confound the bureaucrat. In December of 1982 when the unemployed rate rose above 10 percent for the first time since the 1930s, the unemployed rate reflected over 11 million people who are officially out of work. At the same time, though, there were 2 to 3 million discouraged workers who were officially "out of the labor force" and another 3 million underemployed workers who were officially "employed." No "small change" there. The procedure can even produce anomalies like recording lower unemployment rates even as the number of people officially counted as employed declines. Question 2 produces a quick illustration of how that might happen.

2. The formula for the unemployment rate is simply:

$$\text{Unemployment rate} = \frac{U}{U + E} \times 100\%$$

where U and E represent the number of people counted as unemployed and employed, respectively. Suppose, to begin with, that $U = 10$ million and $E = 90$ million; in that case, the unemployment rate would be _____ percent. Now let 1 month pass during which .5 million of the 90 million who had jobs are laid off and 1 million of the 10 million who were officially unemployed get discouraged and officially leave the labor force. One month later, in other words, $E =$ _____ million, $U =$ _____, and the unemployment rate has (*risen / fallen*) to _____ percent.

10; 89.5; 9.5; fallen; 9.6

3. Entirely separate from the statistical characterization of worker status, economists differentiate between voluntary and involuntary unemployment. People are voluntarily unemployed if they choose not to work at the offered wage; people are involuntarily unemployed if they would like to work at the going wage but cannot find work.

To explore this second distinction, consult Figure 11-1. Curve *SS* there represents a typical supply schedule for labor, with *LL* indicating the size of the available labor force. Curve *DD* meanwhile reflects the (derived) demand for labor. Accordingly, the equilibrium wage is $_____, with _____ people desiring and finding employment and _____ people choosing not to work. The number of people voluntarily unemployed is therefore _____; the number of people involuntarily unemployed is _____.

Now suppose that demand conditions deteriorate so that $D'D'$ represents the demand for labor. If the wage could fall, then the new equilibrium wage would be $_____, total employment would be _____, total involuntary unemployment would be _____, and total voluntary unemployment would be _____. If the wage could not fall, though, then total employment would be _____, total involuntary unem-

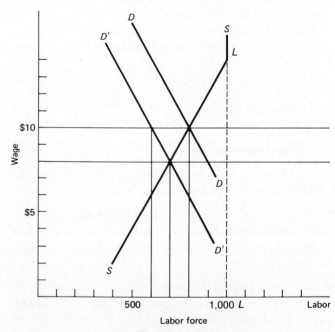

Figure 11-1

ployment would be _____ , and total voluntary unemployment would be _____ .

The important point to note from this exercise is that the existence of involuntary unemployment depends critically upon the inability of the wage to fall in response to excess supply in the labor market. Quite simply, no one who wanted to work at the going wage would be unable to do so if wages were sufficiently flexible. This *(is / is not)* to say that total employment would not fall if the demand for labor were to fall; it is simply a statement about the ability of people who want to work even at the lower wage to find a job.

10; 800; 200; 200; 0; 8; 700; 0; 300; 600; 200; 200; is not

---

4. Table 11-3 in the text records unemployment rates for various demographic groups for 1973, a boom year, and 1982, a year of severe recession. Several points can be gleaned by studying the numbers recorded in this table. It is clear, first of all, that unemployment hits *(all / most / only some)* demographic groups *(in exactly the same degree / differently)*. Nonetheless, comparing the experience of the United States in 1973 and 1982 suggests that recession *(is / is not)* fairly even-handed in its effect on unemployment rates. While the overall unemployment rate in 1982 was roughly twice as large as it was in 1972, teenage unemployment *(more than / almost exactly / less than)* doubled; black unemployment *(more than / almost exactly / less than)* doubled; white unemployment *(more than / almost exactly / less than)* doubled; and so on. The only real exception was male unemployment. The numbers recorded in the table prompted Senator Kennedy of Massachusetts to quip that recession of 1982 advanced the cause of equal rights for women because it brought the male unemployment rate up to the level of the female unemployment rate.

The effect of recession on the duration of unemployment was also noted in the text in Figure 11-4. Glancing at the picture, it becomes clear that recession tends to *(increase / decrease)* the average duration of unemployment by *(reducing / increasing)* the proportion of unemployed who are out of work for less than 5 weeks and *(increasing / decreasing)* the proportion who are out of work for more than 15 weeks.

Finally, text Figure 11-5 shows us that recession tends to increase the unemployment rate by increasing the percent of the labor force that is unemployed because it has *(reentered the labor market / lost its job / left its job voluntarily / entered the labor market for the first time)*.

---

all; differently; is; almost exactly; almost exactly; almost exactly; increase; reducing; increasing; lost its job

---

Economists have, after decades of study, identified three different sources of unemployment. Frictional unemployment, caused by the usual turnover of some workers, reentry of others, and migration by still others, is the first major category. It is generally viewed as a lubricant for the overall labor market because it improves that market's economic efficiency. Structural unemployemt meanwhile arises from the contraction of some industries whose time has come and is now going; even in a growing economy, some industries contract as the demand for their products contracts and must therefore lay workers off. Finally, cyclical unemployment is the natural manifestation of the business cycle in the labor market; an overall contraction in business activity means that fewer people are required to produce the desired level of output, and employment must therefore fall.

The distinction between the three categories is critical because their different sources indicate different degrees of concern and different policy prescriptions. If frictional unemployment improves efficiency, for example, then we need not worry terribly about it. If structural unemployment can be associated with a particular industry or group of industries, then specific policies targeted at the people who used to work for them may be appropriate. If cyclical unemployment is most troublesome, finally, then policies targeted at macro stabilization may be most appropriate.

5. Identify each of the following scenarios with the type of unemployemt that it most closely exemplifies. Denote structural employment by (*S*), frictional unemployment by (*F*), and cyclical unemployment by (*C*).

a. A graduating senior who cannot find a job .. (_____)

b. A steel worker who loses his job because of permanent foreign competition .... (_____)

c. An autoworker who loses her job in a recession .... (_____)

d. An executive who loses her job because higher oil prices cause aggregate demand to fall .... (_____)

e. An executive who loses his job because higher oil prices cause the demand for oil burners to fall .... (_____)

f. A spouse who quits a job because the family had to move .... (_____)

g. A member of the garment union who loses his job because U.S. wages cannot fall in the face of inexpensive foreign labor .... (_____)

---

a. *F* **b.** *S* **c.** *C* **d.** *C* **e.** *S* **f.** *F* **g.** *S*

---

6. The natural rate of unemployment has a variety of nearly equivalent definitions. One of the most operative is the lowest rate consistent with stable prices. At the natural rate, therefore, upward and downward pressures on prices would be exactly balanced across the various sectors of an economy. It is greater than zero primarily because of the contribution of *(frictional / structural / cyclical)* unemployment to the overall rate. From Figure 11-5 in the text, in fact, it can be seen that new entrants and reentrants into the labor force, typically account for *(1 to 2 / 2 to 3 / 4 to 5)* percentage points of unemployment. Quits account for another *(1 / 2 / 3)* point(s), so that the unemployment rate would hover around *(2 to 3 percent / 3 to 4 percent / 4 to 5 percent)* even without anyone losing a job.

Most scholars put the natural rate around *(5 percent / 6 percent / 8 percent)* in the early 1980s, though, so there must be more to it than efficient frictional components. The natural rate *(is / is not)* therefore an optimal rate. There has, in particular, been a growing structural component over the past few decades. Additionally, the labor force has accumulated a larger proportion of teenage and female participants over the past few decades, and their underlying rates of unemployment seem to be *(higher / the same / lower)* than the rate associated with the historical composition.

Finally, some have blamed social policies for the growing natural rate. The growth of unemployment compensation can, for example, be blamed for easing the pain of being unemployed. Unemployed workers might, therefore, search for a new job with *(less / greater)* urgency and stay unemployed for a *(longer / shorter)* period of time. The minimum wage has, in addition, been blamed for making it *(more / less)* difficult for new entrants to find work.

---

frictional (although structural unemployment does play a role, and business cycle downturns can accelerate the decline of industries contributing to structural unemployment); 2 to 3; 1; 3 to 4 percent; 6 percent; is not; higher; less; longer; more

7. The text identifies four different types of employment policies that might be effective in reducing the level of structural unemployment and thus reverse the upward trend in the natural rate. List them below.

a. _____

b. _____

c. _____

d. _____

---

job matching; training; public employment; removal of governmental obstacles (these were mentioned; others are possible)

QUIZ: Multiple Choice

1. A computation based on Okun's Law would put the cost in forgone output of the 1974–1983 period of high unemployment at:
(1) $2100 billion.
(2) $40 billion.
(3) $1200 billion.
(4) $3000 billion.
(5) an amount roughly comparable to the deadweight loss created by the abuse of market power.

2. Based on the research of Dr. Harvey Brenner, unemployment caused by the loss of a job:
(1) ranks among the top five items in a list of most stressful events in one's life.
(2) ranks below getting married as a stressful event in one's life.
(3) ranks above the death of a spouse as a stressful event.
(4) has no effect on one's life expectancy.
(5) all of the above.

3. A person who is waiting to be recalled to a job would be classified as:
(1) employed.
(2) unemployed.
(3) not in the labor force.
(4) underemployed.
(5) a discouraged worker.

4. Which answer to question 3 would have been correct if it had asked for the classification of a person who was too sick to work?
(1).
(2).
(3).
(4).
(5).

5. Because of the treatment of discouraged workers, the official unemployment statistics:
(1) overestimate the proportion of the labor force that is out of work.
(2) can actually climb even as the number of people with jobs falls.
(3) can actually fall even as the number of people with jobs falls.
(4) are not at all controversial.
(5) none of the above.

6. The existence of involuntary unemployment:
(1) depends critically on the Keynesian assumption that wages do not rise in response to excess demand in the labor market.
(2) depends critically upon the Keynesian assumption that wages do not fall in response to excess supply in the labor market.
(3) is accepted even by classical economists.
(4) plays a small role in the overall unemployment statistics.
(5) none of the above.

7. Which of the following statements is most accurate?
(1) Unemployment rates are generally different for different demographic categories of people.
(2) Unemployment rates tend to move in parallel as the economy proceeds through the business cycle.
(3) The duration of unemployment tends to increase during recession.

(4) Unemployment does not increase during recession because the number of reentrants rises.
(5) All the above.

8. Someone who loses his or her job because of a recession would fall under the category of:
(1) frictionally unemployed.
(2) structurally unemployed.
(3) cyclically unemployed.
(4) permanently unemployed.
(5) none of the above.

9. Which of the answers to question 8 would have been correct if the person in question had lost employment because of the decline of the U.S. steel industry?
(1).
(2).
(3).

(4).
(5).

10. Which of the answers to question 8 would have been correct if the person in question had just entered the labor force?
(1).
(2).
(3).
(4).
(5).

11. The natural rate of unemployment:
(1) has been growing over the past few decades.
(2) has a base of 3 to 4 percent because of frictional components.
(3) is not an optimal rate of unemployment.
(4) is the lowest rate that is consistent with stable prices.
(5) all the above.

CHAPTER 12
INFLATION: DEFINITIONS AND COSTS

Earlier chapters have concentrated on how changes in economic conditions can move real GNP up or down. They have conducted the analysis of these changes both in the prices-quantities geometry of aggregate supply and demand and in the total-spending geometry of the Keynesian model. With the exception of the classical model, however, they have implicitly assumed stable prices. With a flat aggregate supply curve, in particular, it has been a simple matter to show that a change in aggregate demand can change real GNP and, by application of Okun's Law, employment. This analysis might be appropriate during a depression, but we now live in a world in which prices move as well as output. During the recession year of 1982, for example, unemployment rose above 10 percent, real GNP fell at an annual rate of 2 percent, and prices still increased at an annual rate of 6 percent. An increase in aggregate demand in that environment might increase nominal GNP, but it is not a simple matter to determine whether that nominal increase would be the result of higher real output or higher prices. To be useful in the present context, therefore, it is clear that the previous analysis must be amended to allow prices to move.

Chapter 12 begins our progress toward that amendment. The history and necessary conceptualization of inflation are presented in advance of Chapter 13's treatment of the modern theories of price determination and control. As you begin Chapter 12, therefore, you are beginning an exploration of some of the central policy issues of today. What is stagflation, where does it come from, and what can be done about it? Why has history recorded an occasional episode of hyperinflation, and what can be done to guard against its recurrence? What are the costs of inflation, and are they at all dependent upon economic circumstance?

Having completed your work in this chapter, you will have achieved not only some understanding of the answers to these questions, but also the following more specific learning objectives.

LEARNING OBJECTIVES

1. Define the general notion behind and the precise measurement of inflation (and deflation).

2. Understand the conceptual and economic difficulties involved in constructing the price indices with which inflation is measured.

3. Generate an awareness of the inflation experiences of the United States and the United Kingdom.

4. Understand the differences between moderate, galloping, and hyperinflation and cite the incidence of each through history and throughout today's world economy.

5. Decipher the distinction between anticipated and unanticipated inflation, on the one hand, and balanced and unbalanced inflation, on the other. Why does the impact of inflation depend critically upon these distinctions?

6. Relate recent inflationary episodes in the United States to the distinctions of objective 5, and understand that one major cost of increasing inflation is the expense associated with the policies required to turn the time trend around.

Inflation is measured as a rate of change in a price index from one period (e.g., 1 year) to the next. If P_t represents the price index recorded in period t and P_{t+1} represents the index recorded in period $(t + 1)$, then inflation between period t and period $(t + 1)$ would be:

$$\frac{P_{t+1} - P_t}{P_t} \times 100\%$$

A major issue, therefore, must be how the price indices are constructed. Questions 1 and 2 will focus your attention on that construction.

1. Inflation is not an increase in all prices. It is, instead, an increase in the general level of prices and costs. Deflation is exactly the opposite circumstance. One commonly quoted price index upon which inflation computations are made is the

(DRI / CPI / CIA). It is based on the cost of a market basket of goods computed across 265 major groups in 85 cities. Based on the equation quoted in the text, record in the blanks provided below the weights associated with the indicated major components of the market basket:

a. food .... _____ percent

b. shelter .... _____ percent

c. transportation .... _____ percent

d. medical expenses .... _____ percent

e. clothing .... _____ percent

These weights represent *(the share of income devoted to the indicated category / the ratio of prices across the indicated categories / selected probabilities for inflation in the indicated categories)* in the year *(1957 / 1972 / 1981)*.

A second index that is widely used is the producer price index (the PPI). It is based upon the *(retail / world / wholesale)* prices of *(1000 / 3400 / 6200)* products. The GNP deflator is a third index. It has the advantage of being based on *(a sample of the current product mix of an economy / all the goods and services produced in an economy / a weighted average of the production of the world's industrial economies)*, but it is difficult to compute contemporaneously.

_____

CPI; 19; 43; 18; 5; 7; the share of income devoted to the indicated category; 1972; wholesale; 3400; all the goods and services produced in an economy

2. Price indices can easily suffer from two major deficiencies. They do not, for one thing, take *(quantity / quality / the rest of the world)* into account. Better products that cost more cause any price index to *(fall if the improvement is worth more than the higher price / rise in response to the higher price regardless of the improvement)*.

Price indices with fixed weights do not, moreover, reflect the substitution out of more expensive items that we might usually expect to diminish the impact of product specific inflation. Columns (1) and (2) in the table below record hypothetical price indices for the five major categories of goods noted in 2 successive years. Columns (3) and (4) indicate the proportions of income allocated to the five categories in the 2 years in response to those prices. Based upon the CPI formula using year 1 weights, the price index for year 1 would be _____. Based upon the CPI formula using year 1 weights, again, the price index for year 2 would be _____; an inflation rate of _____ percent would therefore be announced on the basis of this calculation. Now suppose that the year 2 price index were computed on the basis of year 2 weights. The index would then be _____, with the resulting inflation rate *(rising / falling)* to _____ percent. If year 2 weights were used to compute the index for year 1, moreover, then the year 1 index would be _____, and the quoted rate of inflation would again be _____ percent.

The point of this exercise is not that one index is correct and the others are wrong. It is, instead, that the selection of weights can be critical in the computation of inflation. Based on the substitution that occurred, though, it can be said that the computation that used year 1 weights for both years probably *(overestimated / underestimated / correctly estimated)* the effect of inflation on the real well-being of the population.

Category	Underlying Price Indices		Underlying Income Shares	
	Year 1 (1)	Year 2 (2)	Year 1, % (3)	Year 2, % (4)
Food	100	110	20	20
Clothing	100	150	20	5
Fuel	100	100	20	35
Medical	100	110	20	15
Transport	100	105	20	25

_____

quality; rise in response to the higher price; 100; 115; 15; 107.25; falling; 7.25; 100; 7.25; overestimated

3. Figures 12-2 and 12-3 in the text trace the inflationary experiences of the United States and the United Kingdom. Several lessons can be gleaned from the trends that they portray even without getting into the specifics of the numbers recorded there. First of all, it is clear from plotting wages versus prices that inflation *(necessarily / does not necessarily)* imply a reduction in real income. Wages have, over the long term of history, risen *(faster than / slower than / at the same rate as)* prices. In England, for example, a 350-fold increase in a market basket of grain, meat, dairy products, drink, fuel, and cloth since the year 1300 has been supported by *(100-fold / 3000-fold / 5000-fold)* increase in wages. Real wages have, as a result, *(fallen 250-fold / increased 2650-fold / increased 4650-fold)* over the course of seven centuries.

Second, the United States experience includes a marked increase in the *(rate of increase of / stickiness of / rate of reduction of)* prices since World War II. If prices rise in good times and remain stable in bad times, inflation cannot do anything but *(persist / collapse / accelerate)*.

_____

does not necessarily; faster than; 3000-fold; increased 2650-fold; stickiness of; persist

4. Three "strains" of inflation, distinguished by their virulence, are identified in the text; they are:

a. _____

b. _____

c. _____

Use Figure 12-4 in the text to diagnose the strain infecting each of the following countries for the years indicated. Record the approximate rates of inflation for each country in the smaller spaces.

(1) United States (1970s) _____% _____

(2) Germany (1922) _____% _____

(3) Germany (1923) _____% _____

(4) Israel (1970s) _____% _____

(5) United Kingdom (1980) _____% _____

(6) Brazil (1970s) _____% _____

(7) Argentina (1970s) _____% _____

Despite the occasional occurrence of hyperinflation throughout history, it is happy news that even galloping inflation does not necessarily accelerate to unmanageable levels in the absence of heroic anti-inflationary policy measures. Moderate inflation, meanwhile, does not seem to be terribly troublesome because relative prices are not terribly distorted, people do not spend too much time and energy in managing their money balances to avoid losses in real purchasing power, and inflationary expectations are fairly stable and predictable. Expectations of moderate inflation can, in fact, be self-fulfilling prophesies if they generate moderate wage settlements.

---

a. moderate (less than 10 percent) **b.** galloping (up to 150 percent or so) **c.** hyperinflation (upward to 1 million percent per year) **(1)** 7 to 9 percent; moderate **(2)** 500; (the beginnings of) hyperinflation **(3)** over 20,000,000; the throws of hyperinflation! **(4)** 90 to 95; galloping **(5)** 15 to 20; (the border of) galloping **(6)** 120 to 150; (maintained) galloping **(7)** 120 to 150; (maintained) galloping

Chapter 12 has taught you that the costs of unemployment are easily identified and documented. They are costs that can be seen in the faces of unemployed workers standing in long lines to apply for new jobs. They can be seen in the faces of the children of unemployed workers who worry about their younger brothers and sisters. They can be computed in terms of forgone GNP. They can even be seen in the pattern of government expenditure and the magnitude of federal tax revenues. Given the aversion that most people, politicians, and governments have to inflation, you might expect that the same type of clear documentation would be possible when we now turn to consider the costs of inflation. That is, however, not the case. The remaining questions will consider that documentation.

5. Consider, first of all, the impact of inflation on GNP. On the first three panels of Figure 12-1, draw a new aggregate demand curve that would illustrate the potential that higher demand (caused by, for example, higher government spending or a tax cut) might cause inflation. In each case, *AS* indicates the aggregate supply curve, and *AD* represents aggregate demand before the increase. It is clear from this geometry that higher aggregate demand is most likely to produce higher prices when equilibrium GNP is *(nearly equal to / far above / far below)* potential GNP. Moreover, GNP can be expected to *(rise / fall / hold roughly constant)* when inflation is most likely. When an intermediate increase in prices is expected, though, real GNP might actually *(fall / rise)*.

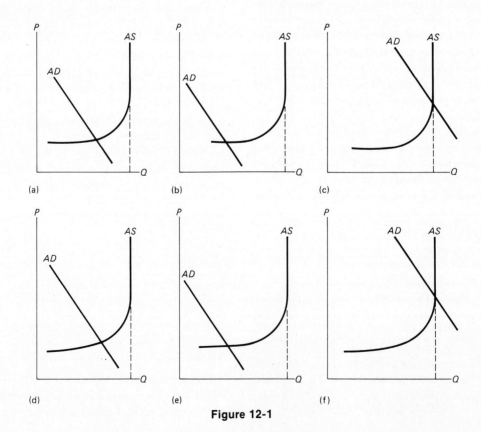

Figure 12-1

Now record on the remaining three panels of Figure 12-1 the change in aggregate supply that might produce inflation as the result of an outside price shock that leaves potential GNP fixed. In each case, GNP can be expected to *(fall / rise)*. Contrasting the six possible cases, therefore, an inflationary episode can be associated with *(an unambiguous increase in GNP / an ambiguous increase or reduction in GNP depending upon the source of the inflation / an unambiguous reduction in GNP)*.

---

draw higher AD curves in the first three panels; nearly equal to; hold roughly constant; rise; draw higher AS curves turning vertical at potential GNP and a higher price level; fall; an ambiguous increase or reduction; (Note: Italicized answers indicate instructions for drawing new AD and/or AS curves in Figure 12-1)

6. Inflation can cause two general types of effects. The first surrounds the distribution of wealth and income; the second concerns the efficiency of relative prices and the information that they contain. The text argues that the incidence of these effects can be expected to depend critically upon whether or not the inflation is (*a*) anticipated or unanticipated and (*b*) balanced or unbalanced.

If all prices were to increase at the same rate, for example, then the resulting inflation would be _____. It *(would / would not)*, as a result, be expected that the inflation would produce "winners and losers" depending upon what types of goods and services individuals and institutions purchased or produced. There *(would / would not)*, in other words, be troublesome efficiency losses created by the inflation. If the prices of some goods rose disproportionately, though, some people could win at the expense of others. People might therefore spend *(more / less)* time managing their money to avoid becoming locked into a disadvantageous financial position. The information contained in relative prices would, meanwhile, be *(increased / decreased)* because they would change so quickly that nobody could keep up.

If balanced inflation were fully anticipated, there would be *(almost no / surely a significant)* cost. The inflation would look like a situation of stable prices to everyone who could insulate themselves from the rising prices. This insulation would, in particular, include such things as the indexing of transfer payments like social security and the adjustment of nominal interest rates to preserve the desired real rate. If 10 percent inflation were expected, for example, then banks that wanted a 3 percent real return would charge _____ percent. If the inflation were unanticipated, though, then *(distributional / governmental)* effects would be expected even if it were balanced.

Borrowers would, for instance, be *(worse off / better off / unaffected)* because they could pay off their debt with currency that was *(worth more / worth less)*. Lenders would experience the opposite effect. Under conditions of high inflationary risk, therefore, lenders can be expected to hedge against unanticipated inflation by charging *(higher / lower / exactly the same)* interest rates on new loans. Alternatively, they might try to shift the risk to the borrower through *(policy lobbying / offering no loans / offering adjustable-rate loans)*.

In the table below, summarize these potential costs by noting the correlations between the following combinations of potential costs and the character of inflation. Record the letter identifying the appropriate cost structure in the boxes provided.

a. no cost

b. efficiency losses

c. distribution losses

d. both efficiency and distribution losses

	Balanced Inflation	Unbalanced Inflation
Anticipated inflation		
Unanticipated inflation		

The general conclusion to be reached is that the costs of inflation may or may not appear, they may or may not be associated with lower GNP, and they can be expected to be randomly distributed across an economy even if higher GNP results. It all depends upon where people are economically and how flexible their situation is when unanticipated inflation strikes.

---

balanced; would not; would not; more; decreased; almost no; 13; distributional; better off; worth less; higher; offering adjustable-rate loans; (reading by row) no cost; efficiency losses; distribution losses; both efficiency and distribution losses

7. The following statements have been made about inflation. Indicate by (*T*) those that are true and by (*F*) those that are false.

a. "Inflation is just big oil companies ripping off the little people." .... (_____)

b. "Inflation is theft. Government can increase their taxes without passing a tax bill." .... (_____)

c. "Inflation lowers our living standards by raising the cost of living." .... (_____)

d. "The only cost of inflation is the unemployment that follows as government tries to lower inflation." .... (_____)

---

a. *F* (Even if oil companies try to rip people off, oil price are not the only source of inflation; they kept inflation down in the early 1980) **b.** *F* (Theft presumes intent, and governments do not create inflation to increase taxes) **c.** *F* (This is a tautology, not a statement of truth) **d.** *F* (The total cost of inflation depends upon its character, but one major cost of inflation is certainly the unemployment cost of reducing it)

8. Fill in the inflation rates for the years noted in the following table in the spaces provided. Notice that high rates of inflation seem to be associated with *(high / low)* rates of interest. Do you see any evidence that recent interest rates include a hedge against the possibility that inflation might be unexpectedly rekindled? _____ .

Year	CPI (1967 = 100)	Inflation Rate, %	Nominal Rate of Interest, %
1977	181.5		5.5
1978	195.4	_____	7.6
1979	217.4	_____	10.0
1980	246.8	_____	11.4
1981	272.4	_____	13.8
1982	289.1	_____	11.1
1983	298.4	_____	8.8
1984	312.7	_____	9.8

high; yes; (reading down the column) 7.7; 11.3; 13.5; 10.4; 6.1; 3.2; 4.8

QUIZ: Multiple Choice

1. The consumer price index is based upon the share of income devoted to which of the following major categories?
(1) Shelter.
(2) Food.
(3) Medical expenses.
(4) Transportation expenses.
(5) All the above.

2. Inflation measured in terms of annual changes in the CPI using 1972 weights might overestimate the impact of inflation on individual purchasing power because:
(1) it ignores the likely substitution out of expensive categories.
(2) it ignores the depressing effect of world prices on American goods.
(3) it ignores the effects of unemployment on aggregate demand.
(4) it inaccurately includes the price effects of improved production technology.
(5) all the above.

3. Since the 1983 index price for medical care was 357, it is true that the 1983 value for the CPI:
(1) must have been greater than 357.
(2) must have been less than 357.
(3) must have been exactly equal to 357.
(4) could have been anything because medical expenses are not included in the CPI.
(5) none of the above.

4. Prices in the United States:
(1) became less flexible after World War II.
(2) have stabilized since World War II.

(3) have increased faster than wages since World War II.
(4) have increased since World War II only because of the Vietnam war and the OPEC oil shock.
(5) none of the above.

5. Moderate inflation:
(1) is characterized by less than double-digit rates.
(2) is characterized by relatively stable relative prices.
(3) does not seem to cause people to spend excessive amounts of time and energy managing their account balances.
(4) creates fairly stable inflationary expectations.
(5) all the above.

6. Inflation in Israel in the 1970s was lower than the rate experienced during the 1970s by:
(1) the United States.
(2) the United Kingdom.
(3) Brazil.
(4) Italy.
(5) all the above.

7. Inflation seems to be associated with:
(1) increasing GNP more often than not.
(2) increasing or decreasing GNP, depending upon its source.
(3) decreasing GNP more often than not.
(4) increasing GNP only when the economy is operating at its full potential.
(5) none of the above.

8. One of the potential costs of unanticipated inflation is:
(1) the redistribution of wealth from lenders to debtors.
(2) the redistribution of wealth from debtors to lenders.
(3) the redistribution of wealth from the government to those who have helped finance its debt.
(4) the indexing of transfer payments to inflation.
(5) the elimination of variable-rate mortgages.

9. In response to the potential risks of unanticipated inflation, you should expect:
(1) that banks will charge a risk premium on loans that they write.
(2) that the government will try to index transfer payments to people on fixed incomes.
(3) that banks will try to sell variable-rate mortgages to home buyers.
(4) the stock market will stagnate in expectation of the anti-inflationary policies that might be forthcoming.
(5) all the above.

10. Unbalanced and unanticipated inflation usually causes:
(1) no harm.
(2) efficiency losses.
(3) the redistribution of income and wealth.

(4) efficiency losses accompanied by the redistribution of income and wealth.

(5) none of the above.

11. One potential cost of anticipated and balanced inflation is:

(1) the economic cost of overmanagement of money.

(2) the loss of employment required to lower the inflation rate for political reasons.

(3) the excessive inflation of real-estate prices.

(4) a reduction in the flow of imports into the country.

(5) none of the above.

12. In 1979, most people expected inflation to run at 7 percent. Inflation actually proceeded at 12 percent, with a reduction in the real wage of 3 percent. The major cost associated with the experience was:

(1) slower growth resulting from high real interest rates.

(2) reduced imports caused by higher U.S. prices.

(3) deadweight losses resulting from repeated gasoline shortages.

(4) the dramatic increase in unemployment in 1980 and again, more severely, in 1982.

(5) all the above.

13. Which of the following is a hedge that you might expect to see an individual pursue in an effort to protect only himself from the risk of unanticipated inflation?

(1) Negotiate a cost of living clause in a long-term wage contract.

(2) Accept an adjustable-rate mortgage whose rate of interest would be expected to climb with inflation.

(3) Offer a friend a loan at a rate of interest lower than that charged by a hedging bank.

(4) Start a new business whose cash needs would be covered by borrowing from a bank.

(5) All the above.

CHAPTER 13

INFLATION: CAUSES AND CURES

Chapter 12 probed the measurement and history of inflation in the United States and elsewhere. It is now time to explore the potential of an economy to enjoy the simultaneous blessings of low inflation and low unemployment. We need, more specifically, to explore the purported tradeoff between unemployment and inflation. Is an economy forever doomed to endure high levels of one or the other, or can fiscal and monetary policy be employed to reduce the severity of the tradeoff? If not, are there other policy options that might help? Can, in particular, some type of incomes policies be exploited to, for example, lower inflation without creating intolerable levels of unemployment? And finally, can the cost of reducing inflation by enduring high levels of unemployment be assessed in either the short run or the long run?

Having worked through this chapter, you will have achieved some preliminary insight into not only these fundamental questions, but also the following more specific learning objectives.

LEARNING OBJECTIVES

1. Differentiate inertial, cost-push, and demand-pull inflation, and understand how shocks to an economy can change the underlying rate of inertial inflation.

2. Illustrate the occurrence of each of the three types of inflation in the geometry of aggregate demand and aggregate supply.

3. Understand the dimensions and the significance of the modern Phillips curve, particularly within a discussion that tells a story in the short run that is different from the story that it tells in the long run.

4. Outline precisely the roles of the natural rate of unemployment and the inertial rate of inflation in the definition of short-run and long-run Phillips curves.

5. Use the long-run-short-run distinction in the Phillips curve construction to produce the spiral pattern of unemployment-inflation combinations that has emerged since 1970.

6. Produce an estimate, based on the Phillips curve construction, of the cost of reducing inflation by enduring high rates of unemployment.

7. Understand why indexing can lead to greater instability in prices.

8. Define the general rubric of incomes policies, outline the range of potential structure that they might assume, and discuss their necessity (or lack thereof).

The rate of inertial inflation is a bit of a misnomer. The rate itself has some inertia—a tendency not to move unless pushed—only because prices have a consistent momentum that translates into a stable rate of increase. Inertial inflation therefore reflects an internal rate of inflation with which an economy seems to be comfortable. Individuals expect it, and those expectations tend to become self-fulfilling prophesies. Policies are written in acceptance of those expectations. Interest rates include premiums to accommodate those expectations. Transfer payments are amended to keep up. And so on. Inertial inflation has the potential to be both balanced and anticipated, but only because prices display a clear, well-defined momentum. Question 1 explores how that can happen in a very simple example.

1. Suppose that labor is the only productive factor available to an economy so that it has only one type of production cost—the wage paid to the labor that it employs. Let the rate of growth of labor productivity be zero and assume that labor expects prices to climb over the next year at a rate of 5 percent. When they negotiate their contracts for that year, therefore, they demand and receive a 5 percent raise. The result must be a _____ percent increase in the average cost of production, a _____ percent increase in the price of output, and thus a _____ percent rate of inflation. Labor's inflationary expectations are thereby *(exceeded / met exactly / found to be excessive)*.

Reinforced by this experience, labor should be expected to demand a second-year raise that would be *(higher than / identical to / lower than)* the first-year raise that initiated the process. *(Declining / Stable / Increasing)* price and wage inflation could therefore be perpetuated in the absence of any outside shocks.

Now suppose that the economy suffers an outside shock that produces an additional 5 percent increase in prices so that the overall rate of inflation in year 2 is 10 percent. If labor expects that year 2 inflation to continue into year 3, then labor will demand a *(5 percent / 10 percent / 15 percent)* raise for year 3 that would support a *(5 percent / 10 percent / 15 percent)* wage-based inflation rate in year 3 even without another outside shock. Once again, labor's expectations would be *(exceeded / met exactly / found to be excessive)*, and the inertial rate of inflation would have *(increased / remained the same / decreased)*.

5; 5; 5; met exactly; identical to; Stable; 10 percent; 10 percent; met exactly; increased

Notice two things about question 1. First, the pattern that you discovered in question 1 would, if it were graphed against time, look a lot like the pattern for the inertial rate of inflation for the 1960s and 1970s that is depicted in Figure 13-8 in the text. The inertial rate "ratcheted" up during that period because the outside shocks suffered by the U.S. economy all pushed prices up. The Vietnam war spending of the late 1960s, the OPEC oil shock of 1973–1974, and the Iran-Iraq war of 1978 all produced inflationary pressures that were reflected not only in wage negotiations that were settled shortly thereafter, but also in wage negotiations that were conducted well into the future.

Second, it should be clear that the expectations story need not be followed down to the last letter to produce this "ratchet" effect. Cost of living clauses in existing contracts can produce the same effect even without active wage negotiation based upon inflationary expectations. Those expectations can probably be identified as the source of the cost of living clause designed to protect wage earners from inflation, but the clauses themselves can produce the identical pattern.

2. Label each of the three panels of Figure 13-1 according to the type of inflation that it illustrates. On the basis of that labelling, notice one fundamental difference between cost-push inflation and demand-pull inflation. Demand-pull inflation occurs, in particular, only when the economy is operating *(at or above its potential / below its potential)* and usually produces *(an increase / almost no change / a reduction)* in real GNP. Cost-push inflation, on the other hand, can occur when the eco-

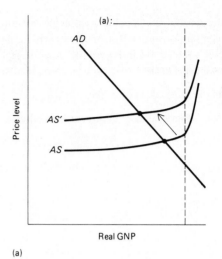

(a)

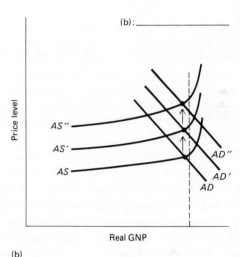

(b)

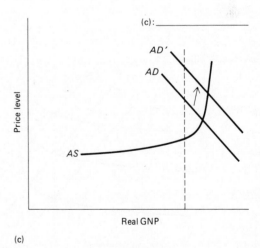

(c)

Figure 13-1

nomy is operating *(above / at / below)* its potential and produces *(an increase / no change / a reduction)* in real GNP. *(Cost-push / Demand-pull)* inflation can, therefore, be identified as one source of "stagflation"—the simultaneous occurrence of rising prices and rising unemployment.

Turning now to the specific sources of cost-push and de-mand-pull inflation, indicate in the spaces provided which type of inflation each of the following is more likely to create. Denote cost-push with a (*C*) and demand-pull with a (*D*).

a. a dramatic increase in oil prices .... (_____)

b. a dramatic increase in government expenditure to finance a war .... (_____)

c. an automatic wage increase produced by a cost of living clause .... (_____)

d. a sudden reduction in the saving of an entire population .... (_____)

e. a wage settlement that increases the cost of steel .... (_____)

f. a sudden and large reduction in personal income taxes .... (_____)

Panel (**a**): cost-push; panel (**b**): inertial; panel (**c**): demand-pull; at or above its potential; almost no change; below; a reduction; Cost-push **a.** *C* **b.** *D* **c.** *C* **d.** *D* **e.** *C* **f.** *D*

3.   Refer now to Figure 13-2. Three aggregate supply curves are drawn there. AS_1 represents aggregate supply at the beginning of year 1; AS_2 represents aggregate supply at the beginning of year 2 (the end of year 1) and AS_3 represents aggregate supply at the beginning of year 3 (the end of year 2). The

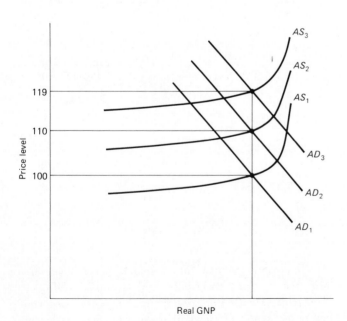

Real GNP

Figure 13-2

corresponding aggregate demand curves are indicated by AD_1, AD_2, and AD_3. The rate of inflation during year 1 was, there-fore, _____ percent, while the rate of inflation during year 2 was _____ percent. If potential GNP were growing at 4 per-cent per year throughout this 2-year period, then an initial unem-ployment rate of 6 percent would, by application of Okun's Law, *(grow / fall)* to _____ percent by the end of year 1 and _____ percent by the end of year 2.

10; 8; grow; 8; 10

4.   Question 3 produced some numbers that would lie along a *(short-run / long-run)* Phillips curve. Because the experience illustrated there pushed the unemployment rate *(above / below)* the natural rate, it can be expected that the rate of inertial inflation would *(rise / fall)* in year 3 to put the economy onto a *(lower / higher)* Phillips curve. Should the economy then expand past the natural rate in subsequent years, it would be expected that the rate of inertial inflation would then (*in-crease / decrease*) and push the economy back toward the original Phillips curve. The time trend would thus look like the (*vertical straight line / nearly horizontal curved line turning at the natural rate / spiral pattern around the natural rate*) that has characterized the past two decades.

---

short-run; above; fall; lower; increase; spiral pattern around the natural rate

5.   The geometry of the Phillips curve can be displayed with either price inflation or wage inflation on the vertical axis. This arithmetic equivalence can be supported by a markup theory of pricing that equates the difference between the rate of wage inflation and the rate of price inflation with (*a constant 2.45% / the rate of growth of labor productivity / the rate of conservation of scarce energy resources*). On the basis of this equality, complete the following table.

Rate of Wage Inflation, %	Rate of Price Inflation, %	Rate of Productivity Growth, %
10	_____	3
10	_____	0
3	5	_____
_____	7	2
_____	150	0

---

the rate of growth of labor productivity; (reading each row down the table in sequence) 7; 10; −2; 9; 150

6. Assume that labor has a long-term contract guaranteeing that wages will climb by 80 percent of the rate of increase of prices during the previous year. Using the equation that you recorded in question 5, complete the following table given a constant rate of growth of labor productivity of 2 percent per year and an initial rate of price inflation of 20 percent.

Year	Rate of Wage Inflation, %	Rate of Price Inflation, %
1	_____	_____
2	_____	_____
3	_____	_____
4	_____	_____

For year 1, wage inflation equals .8 × 20 percent = 16 percent and price inflation equals 16 − 2 percent = 14 percent; continuing down the columns, wage inflation would be 11.2; 7.4; 4.3 and price inflation would be 9.2; 5.4; and 2.3.

7. Repeat the process in question 6 with the additional assumption that a price shock adds 10 percent to the inflation rate that occurs in year 2.

Year	Rate of Wage Inflation, %	Rate of Price Inflation, %
1	_____	_____
2	_____	_____
3	_____	_____
4	_____	_____

The numbers are identical for year 1; in year 2, wage inflation based on 80 percent of year 1 price inflation is still 11.2 percent, but price inflation combines the 9.2 percent wage-based increase with the 10 percent shock for a total of 19.2 percent; in year 3, then, wages climb by .8 × 19.2 percent = 15.4 percent and prices climb by 15.4 percent − 2 percent = 13.4 percent; year 4 thus has wage inflation at 10.7 percent and price inflation at 8.7 percent.

8. Now repeat question 7 under an assumption that the outside price shock causes productivity growth to fall to zero percent per year in year 2 and beyond.

Year	Rate of Wage Inflation, %	Rate of Price Inflation, %
1	_____	_____
2	_____	_____
3	_____	_____
4	_____	_____

The experience of year 1 is unchanged; the 19.2 percent price inflation of year 2 produces a 15.4 percent rate of price and wage inflation in year 3, and a .8 × 15.4 percent = 12.3 percent rate of price and wage inflation in year 4.

There are two points to questions 6, 7, and 8. First, the rate of growth of labor productivity is a buffer between wage and price inflation that can serve to reduce inertial inflation over periods of time in which an economy is insulated from outside shocks. Question 6 shows this with an 80 percent cost of living clause, but the decline in inflation would have proceeded at a rate of 2 percentage points per year even with a 100 percent cost of living clause. Second, no indexation scheme in the world will allow the standard of living to increase faster than real output—the rate of growth of labor productivity in these questions.

9. Figure 13-3 shows four panels. Each panel corresponds to either a boom cycle, an austerity cycle, an inflationary supply shock, or a complete political business cycle. The 6 percent level indicates the natural rate of unemployment, and the dots along the schedules indicate years (dot 1 for year 1, dot 2 for year 2, etc.).

Identify each panel with its most appropriate cycle in the spaces provided in the upper right-hand corners of the graphs. Record a brief chronicle of what each panel portrays in the spaces of the table provided below. Also record on the table a period in the past two decades whose pattern exemplifies the experience illustrated by the indicated panel.

Panel	Description of Events Portrayed	Sample Period
(a)	_____	_____
(b)	_____	_____
(c)	_____	_____
(d)	_____	_____

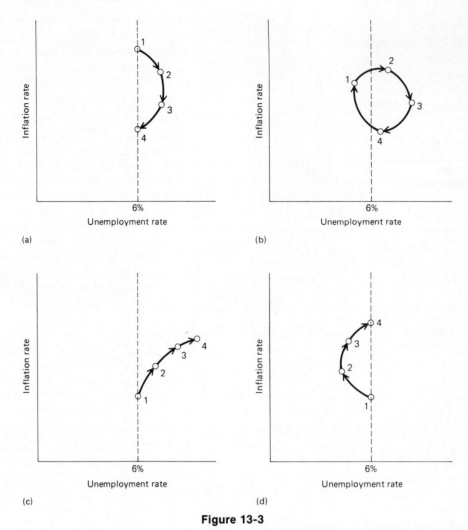

Figure 13-3

(a): austerity cycle **(b):** political business cycle **(c):** supply shock **(d):** boom cycle **(a):** unemployment rising above the natural rate along a short-run Phillips curve until inertial inflation falls and employment can recover; 1981–1983 **(b):** expansion during election year, austerity to reduce resulting inflation, employment recovery and postering for next election; 1980–1984 **(c):** upward shock to aggregate supply curve producing higher prices and lower real GNP and thus higher unemployment; 1978–1979 **(d):** expansion of past potential GNP causing demand-pull inflation; 1965–1968

Incomes policies are devices whose very design reflects an attempt by policymakers to curb inertial inflation by reducing the effect of inflationary expectations on future rates of inflation without the economy suffering the severe costs associated with dramatically higher unemployment. That is, of course, an enormously difficult task to accomplish, and it must be stated that this difficulty has lead to a widespread reluctance to give incomes policies a try.

One attempt was made to employ an extreme form of incomes policies, but the results were not very encouraging. The Nixon administration enacted strict wage-and-price controls in the early 1970s, but they did not work. Pressure against the rigidity of these strict controls caused the system to collapse before it could convince anyone that anything substantive had happened. Everyone thought that the controls were temporary and that inflation would return to its old rate as soon as they were lifted. The controls *were* temporary, they *were* lifted quickly, and inflation *did return* to its former level of virulence.

The other extreme, voluntary wage-and-price guideposts have also been attempted, but with only limited success. In between these extremes, the Carter administration announced in the late 1970s an insurance program that would have protected the real purchasing power of individuals who accepted wage settlements at or below a specific guidepost by adjusting their income tax liabilities in April of the following year. This idea was, however, one of those proposals that never got through Congress, so we do not know how it would have worked.

As difficult as history has been on incomes policies, though, the basic notion behind their operation is easily explained. Question 10 will explore that notion.

10. Suppose that there were an economy with 1000 workers. In the absence of any growth in their productivity and any outside shocks, suppose further that any wage increase that they all received would be passed on, percentage point for percentage point, to the price of the economy's output. Thus, an X percent rate of wage inflation would always be translated into an X percent rate of price inflation.

If these workers expected inflation to be 10 percent in the following year, then they would demand a 10 percent wage increase to preserve their real standards of living. That would,

of course, produce a _____ percent rate of inflation.

If one worker were to realize that his or her wage increase would contribute to inflation, then he or she could, of course, refuse the offer of a 10 percent wage increase in the interest of being a "good citizen." In that case, his or her real wage would

(rise / fall / remain the same) by _____ percent, but the rate of inflation would *(rise / fall dramatically / remain almost exactly the same)* because the increase in the average cost of production would *(rise / fall dramatically / fall ever so slightly)*.

If, by way of contrast, everyone were to realize that his or her wage settlement contributed to inflation and demanded only a 5 percent wage increase, then inflation would *(rise / fall)*

to _____ percent. If they agreed to no wage increase, in fact, then inflation in this simple economy would *(rise / fall)* to

_____ percent.

The key, therefore, is to get everyone to adjust their wage demands at the same time. Nobody would want to be alone in taking a lower wage settlement, but something that would encourage everyone to react in the same moderating way could have a moderating effect on price inflation. It would be the purpose of an incomes policy to provide the incentive for everyone to behave in that way.

10; fall; (very nearly) 10; remain almost exactly the same; fall ever so slightly; fall; 5; fall; 0

QUIZ: Multiple Choice

1. Inertial inflation:
(1) can usually be traced to some sort of supply-side price shock.
(2) can usually be traced to some sort of increase in aggregate demand.
(3) reflects an expected rate of inflation to which the major institutions of an economy have adjusted.
(4) is highly volatile and unpredictable at best.
(5) none of the above.

2. Which answer to question 1 would have been correct if it had referred to cost-push inflation?
(1).
(2).
(3).
(4).
(5).

3. Which answer to question 1 would have been correct if it had referred to demand-pull inflation?
(1).
(2).
(3).
(4).
(5).

4. The inertial rate of inflation is reflected in:
(1) interest rates.
(2) wage settlements.
(3) long-term price specifications.
(4) federal macroeconomic-policy specifications.
(5) all the above.

5. Consult Figure 13-4. AS_1 and AS_2 depicted there represent aggregate supply curves for 2 successive years; AD_1 and AD_2 depict the corresponding aggregate demand curves. In moving from year 1 to year 2:
(1) prices climb in classic illustration of cost-push inflation.
(2) prices climb illustrating inertial inflation.
(3) prices are stable but GNP falls.
(4) prices climb in illustration of demand-pull inflation.
(5) prices are stable, but real GNP falls in response to lower aggregate demand.

6. The occurrence of stagflation can be explained as a consequence of:
(1) a cost-push inflationary episode caused by a supply shock.
(2) inertial inflation that lowers the rate of growth of actual GNP below the rate of growth of potential GNP.
(3) a demand-push inflationary episode caused by an increase in aggregate demand.
(4) answers 1 and 3.
(5) answers 1 and 2.

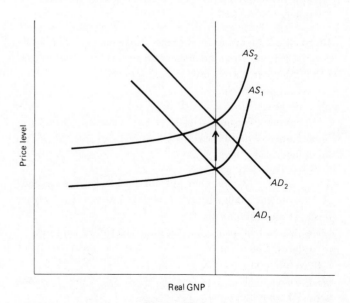

Figure 13-4

7. The short-run Phillips curve tradeoff might be made favorable by:
(1) a policy that lowers export competition.
(2) an incomes policy that reduces inertial inflation.
(3) a trade policy that deflects inflationary price shocks from abroad.
(4) a Constitutional amendment that mandates that the fraction of GNP supported by government spending cannot climb.
(5) none of the above.

8. Which of the following correctly states the correlation between the natural rate of unemployment and the rate of inertial inflation?
(1) Any inertial rate of inflation can be maintained at the natural rate of unemployment as long as non-labor costs increase at the same rate as labor costs.
(2) If the rate of unemployment falls below the natural rate, then the inertial rate of inflation can be expected to climb, and vice versa.
(3) If the rate of unemployment is driven above the natural rate, then the inertial rate of inflation can be expected to climb, and vice versa.
(4) Answers 1 and 2.
(5) Answers 1 and 3.

9. Suppose that an economy were initially operating at its full potential with an unemployment rate of 6 percent. If inflation were initially 10 percent and policymakers were to choose to engineer a recession of 1 year's duration to lower it to 9 percent, then unemployment would have to climb:
(1) approximately 8 percent at a cost of something in the neighborhood of $160 billion in GNP.
(2) approximately 8 percent at a cost of something in the neighborhood of $80 billion in GNP.
(3) approximately 7 percent at a cost of something in the neighborhood of $160 billion.
(4) approximately 6.5 percent at a cost of less than $45 billion.
(5) none of the above.

10. Consult Figure 13-5. The natural rate is 6 percent and the dots indicated correspond to successive years (i.e., dot 1 to year 1, dot 2 to year 2, etc.). Figure 13-5 reflects:
(1) an austerity cycle.
(2) a boom cycle.
(3) a complete business cycle.
(4) a supply-side price shock.
(5) none of the above.

11. In Figure 13-5, movement from dot 1 to dot 2 represents:
(1) movement along a short-run Phillips curve toward higher levels of unemployment.
(2) a shift in Phillips curves caused by increased supplies.
(3) a shift in Phillips curves caused by a reduction in the rate of inertial inflation.
(4) movement along a short-term Phillips curve toward lower levels of unemployment.
(5) movement along a long-run Phillips curve.

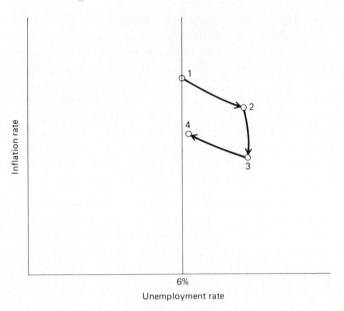

Figure 13-5

12. Which answer to question 11 would have been correct if it had referred to movement from dot 2 to dot 3?
(1).
(2).
(3).
(4).
(5).

13. Which answer to question 11 would have been correct if it had referred to movement from dot 3 to dot 4?
(1).
(2).
(3).
(4).
(5).

14. The point of an incomes policy would be to:
(1) lower inertial inflation without the country suffering a period of high unemployment.
(2) simultaneously moderate the wage demands of as many workers as possible.
(3) lower the inflationary expectations of bankers so that the inflationary premiums built into interest rates might fall.
(4) facilitate a monetary policy designed to support a lower rate of inflation without creating unemployment.
(5) all the above

15. One of the paradoxes of the study of inflation is that
(1) lower unemployment is sometimes associated with higher inflation and sometimes not.
(2) indexing an economy to protect it from inflation tends to make inflation worse.
(3) inflationary expectations are sometimes more important than anything going on in a contemporaneous market.
(4) foreign trade is entirely unaffected by rates of domestic inflation.
(5) all the above.

PART THREE

MACROECONOMICS:
MONEY, INTEREST RATES,
AND DEFICITS

CHAPTER 14
MONEY AND COMMERCIAL BANKING

Up until this point, the determination of output has been accomplished in the total absence of money. It is now time to correct that omission. Money is perhaps the most powerful instrument of modern stabilization policy, and to continue to omit it from consideration would be an enormous mistake. As you progress through the next three chapters, though, it will become clear that the previous omission was a matter of exposition. The models that have been presented thus far can easily accommodate the inclusion of money. It therefore made sense to develop them fully before the complications of money were introduced.

Recall that under the Keynesian model, a change in government spending, for example, had an immediate effect on aggregate demand that led to a change in GNP. Even in the classical extreme, a change in government spending had an immediate effect on the price level. The connection between changes in the money supply is far more indirect and tortured. An adjustment in the money supply affects real variables only because it affects the rate of interest. Since the rate of interest is critical in determining the level of investment, the money supply is linked to aggregate demand, but only through the mysteries of interest-rate correlation between the supply of money and the demand for money. The next three chapters will explore that correlation.

Chapter 14 begins with a discussion of the evolution of money and its associated financial institutions. Of some interest there are the components of the various measures of the money supply. Part of the mystery in the interest-rate correlation with aggregate demand can be found in the problem of defining precisely what is meant by "the money supply." The second part of the chapter begins your exploration into the mechanics of the correlation— the nuts and bolts of the monetary system. It will be shown that the banking system as a whole creates money because of the fractional reserve system upon which it is based. No single bank creates money, mind you, but all

of them operating together are perfectly capable of multiplying the quantity of reserves issued by a central bank by a factor of 2, or 3, or 10.

Your learning objectives for this chapter are therefore centered around achieving a firm understanding of the workings of the banking system. They include, in particular, the following more specific objectives.

LEARNING OBJECTIVES

1. Outline the highlights of the evolution of a monetary system from barter to the system of fiat money with which we are all presently comfortable.

2. Relate the differences among the various definitions of the money supply starting with M_1 (coins, currency, and demand deposits) and progressing through the wide variety of "near-monies" that are now available. Understand, though, that there is no one, single "right" definition.

3. Outline the evolution of the banking system from the neighborhood goldsmith to the array of financial intermediaries that now want to manage your money.

4. Describe precisely the process by which a banking system can create money from central bank reserves if it operates under a practice of fractional reserves.

5. Support the mathematics of the money multiplier, but understand the two qualifications upon which its precise determination is critically dependent.

1. **a.** In a state of total self-sufficiency, there are (by definition) no exchanges of goods or services of consequence. As soon as specialization in production begins, exchanges begin. Barter, the most obvious exchange method, becomes impossibly clumsy as soon as the variety of items exchanged grows large. You must, for each commodity, work out the swapping terms with every other one (for two commodities, there is just one rate to settle; but for three commodities there are three

129

rates; for four there are six; for five, there are ten; and so on). And there is a further difficulty: if you have good A, and want to exchange it for B you must (before even thinking about haggling over terms) find someone who both has B and wants A.

The text has a phrase for this; it is called _____ .

b. So money evolved because money was essential for large-scale exchanges. It began as "commodity money." (This was the transition from barter: people began to measure values in terms of one suitable commodity.) In due course, one special commodity often assumed the money role: gold (or in some instances, silver). Now gold has (except for international settlements) lost its association with money.

Today, we have three kinds of money. Ranking them by importance (as measured by total amount within the present money supply), they are:

(1) _____

(2) _____

(3) _____

c. Why do we use three different kinds of money? Why not simplify by having just one single kind?

_____

_____

---

a. the double coincidence of wants **b. (1)** demand (or checking) bank deposits; **(2)** paper currency; **(3)** coins **c.** Because each has its particular convenience for particular kinds of transactions.

Today, virtually all money is "fiat" money; the government decrees that it is money, so it is. People accept it and conduct business with it. But what is it, really? The answer that applies to the strict M_1 definition associates money with anything that, by convention, is immediately spendable. A store will readily give you merchandise in exchange for part of your checking bank account. (If you propose to pay by check, the only thing the store will want to make sure of is that you really have a bank account of at least the required amount; if you pay by coins or bills, this problem does not arise.)

Anything not immediately spendable is never part of the money supply, strictly defined. However, there are certain classes of assets which are very close to being money; their owners think of them as money because conversion is ordinarily such a quick and simple process. For example: a time deposit with a commercial bank. You cannot spend such a deposit, under normal circumstances, but the bank will ordinarily exchange your deposit for money in a matter of minutes.

2. a. It has become conventional, in tables listing the money supply, to make the distinction between "M_1" and "M_2." Items within M_1 are exclusively the three strictly defined money

items. The M_2 category takes account of the very-close-to-being-money items. It consists of the total of *(these "very close" items alone / the "very close" items plus the M_1 items)*.

A basic problem with the "very-close-to-being-money" idea is: How close is very close? The "official" definition of M_2 includes only time deposits in commercial banks and money market funds. Why not federal government bonds? The market for such bonds is so well organized that ordinarily they can be converted into money very rapidly indeed. However, if such bonds are included, then why not other easily marketed securities?

As in all such cases, the decision is necessarily an arbitrary one. The M_2 category consists of M_1 plus commercial-bank time deposits and money market funds. Other time deposits, and government bonds, are lumped into a category called *("convertible money" / "non-money" / "near-money"/ "high-grade money")*. In brief: The boundary around M_1 is logical. It's money if you can readily make payments with it. This excludes time deposits, for you cannot write checks—which are transfers of money for purposes of payment—against them. The boundary around M_2 is arbitrary. And just what truly constitutes "near-money" is a topic you can debate endlessly, if you have the time and inclination.

b. Which of the following would count as money strictly defined—i.e., as part of M_1?

(1) Any deposit in a commercial bank on which checks may be issued
(2) Any deposit in a commercial bank, regardless of whether or not checks may be issued against it
(3) A deposit in a mutual savings account or in a credit union.
(4) A high-grade corporation bond
(5) A check drawn on a commercial-bank checking account

---

a. The "very close" items plus the M_1 items; "near-money" **b. (1)** only [Note for **(5)**: For many students, the temptation to argue that a check drawn on a bank account is money is almost overwhelming. You can hand a $10 bill across a store counter, or you can use a $10 check. But consider: if the total in your deposit at the bank has been counted in the money supply, you can't count any check drawn on that account in addition. To do so would involve double counting. The check is just an order to your bank, instructing it to transfer part of your account to someone else.]

3. Banks and other firms that offer banklike services are engaged in "financial intermediation." They are in the business of making money by facilitating the flow of your money to those people, businesses, and governments who are willing to pay higher interest rates to borrow it. You could do the same thing, but you would quickly wind up with the barter problem of coincidence. Moreover, unless you have a lot of money to lend you could not spread the risk of bad loans across many borrowers with the same efficiency that these financial intermediaries achieve.

In the spaces below, list five major types of firms that engage in financial intermediation.

a. _____

b. _____

c. _____

d. _____

e. _____

commercial banks; savings and loans; life-insurance companies; pension funds; money market funds

The questions to follow begin with a situation in which there is no "bank money." They trace the development of such money through lending activity on the part of banks.

These questions concern an isolated community which uses initially only gold coins as money. The local goldsmith has a storage vault for gold. He is prepared to store money for others in this vault, charging a small fee. He chooses to list such deposits as an asset on his balance sheet, matched by a "deposit liability" of equal amount.[1] His balance sheet, with respect to such deposits, reads:

Assets	Liabilities
Gold coins in vault $10,000	Deposits—payable to customers on demand $10,000

4. a. A. Pennywise, a customer of the goldsmith, is asked for payment by one of his creditors. The goldsmith's shop having already closed for the day, Pennywise gives his creditor a note reading as follows:

> *To: Ye Gold Shoppe.*   Pay B. Poundfoolish $5
> *from my deposit.*   (Signed) A. Pennywise.

What is the name given to such a note? _____ .

b. Poundfoolish presents the note the next morning, but instead of taking coins, he asks the goldsmith to keep the money stored in his name. Is any change necessary in the goldsmith's balance sheet? If so, explain.

_____

_____

_____

a. A check   **b.** Total of deposits unchanged; only ownership of deposits need be changed

5. a. If this practice of writing notes to the goldsmith

[1] Of course, the goldsmith could omit both asset and liability items from his balance sheet entirely. If his obligation were to pay back those identical gold coins which the depositor left with him, he doubtless would do so. But if his obligation were simply to pay back gold coins of equal value, there would be no reason why he should not list them as shown.

becomes general, does it involve any increase in the total money supply? .... *(Yes / No)*

b. If we define money as something which can be spent immediately, which should count as money: gold coins in the vault or demand deposits? .... *(Coins / Deposits / Both)*

a. No   **b.** Deposits (Gold coins must be withdrawn before they can be spent thus destroying the corresponding deposits.)

6. Suppose (*a*) all money transfers are now handled by checks. (*b*) Ye Gold Shoppe is the only place for storage of gold, and (*c*) all members of the community keep their entire gold supply in this vault, the total being $10,000. Will the asset figure of $10,000 in gold on the balance sheet ever change? Why or why not?

_____ .

No, because gold is never withdrawn

7. Most transactions are now handled by check. Occasionally a depositor withdraws gold to make a payment, but the person receiving payment usually deposits it once again, since the vault is the safest place for gold storage and checks can always be drawn against such deposits.

A responsible merchant now asks the goldsmith for a loan of $2000. The goldsmith has no gold free of deposit claims, only the $10,000 deposited with him. Is there any reason why he should nonetheless consider making the loan?

_____ .

Yes, most of the $10,000 gold is not being used

8. The loan is made. The merchant is given $2000 in gold. The goldsmith's balance sheet (insofar as these transactions are concerned) now reads:

Assets	Liabilities
Gold $8,000	Demand deposits $10,000
Loans 2,000	

a. If the person receiving the gold redeposits it with the goldsmith, how will his balance sheet then appear?

Assets	Liabilities
Gold ...... $_____	Demand deposits .... $_____
Loans .... _____	

b. Has the money supply (the total of "spendable stuff") increased? *(Yes / No)*. By how much? _____ .

a. Gold: $10,000; Loans; $2000; Demand deposits: $12,000   **b.** Yes; By $2000

9. Suppose the borrower, instead of taking $2000 in gold, simply asks for a $2000 deposit account against which he can draw checks. How will the balance sheet appear before the loan is spent? (NOTE: In actual practice, this is how bank loans are normally handled.)

Assets	Liabilities
Gold ...... $_____	Demand deposits .... $_____
Loans ...... _____	

Same answer as in question **8a**

10. After the borrower has spent his $2000 loan (making payment to people whose custom is to keep a deposit with the goldsmith) how will this balance sheet look?

Assets	Liabilities
Gold ...... $_____	Demand deposits .... $_____
Loans ...... _____	

Same answer as in question **8a**

11. Provided (*a*) the custom of using checks for payment is followed and people rarely withdraw gold coins from the vault, and (*b*) we disregard any inflationary consequences of the money-supply increase, what is the limit on the amount of loans the goldsmith could make: (NOTE: There is no legal reserve requirement.)

_____

_____ .

_____

Almost no limit, except insofar as an increase in total *M* tends to increase amount of gold circulating hand to hand

12. Below is the relevant part of the goldsmith's balance sheet after he has made loans of $20,000, at a time when $2000 of the community's total gold stock is not stored with him but is in hand-to-hand circulation:

Assets	Liabilities
Gold .... $ 8,000	Demand deposits $28,000
Loans 20,000	

a. The total money supply (*M*) is now $_____ , consisting of

$_____ bank money (demand deposits) and $_____ in gold hand-to-hand circulation.

b. Should the $8000 gold in vault count as part of *M*?

_____

_____ .

c. When the goldsmith makes such loans, will his action influence *I* spending or GNP? Why or why not?

_____

_____ .

a. 30,000; 28,000; 2000   **b.** No; it must be withdrawn before it is spendable, and withdrawal would reduce bank money by same amount   **c.** Yes; borrowers borrow for spending, typically *I* spending

We want to examine the situation when the community has grown to accept the use of "bank money," as modern economies have come to do.

We assume, therefore, that the money expansion developed in previous questions has not had adverse effects: the process of expansion has been gradual, and the extra spending has put unemployed resources to work on investment projects. Hence, the *M* increase has generally matched as well as having contributed to an expansion of the community's productive capacity.

It is essential, of course, that there be confidence in the goldsmith's establishment. Given this confidence, there is no reason why any large number of the community's members should want to switch from bank money to gold money all at the same moment. The new bank-account money will then function just as effectively as gold money did.

13. **a.** Starting with question 13's balance sheet, depositors withdraw $2000 in gold coins as suitable gifts to students at graduation time. Show the new balance sheet.

Assets	Liabilities
Gold ..... $_____	Demand deposits .... $_____
Loans .... _____	

b. Does this withdrawal change the total of *M*? The composition of *M*?

_____

_____ .

c. What two events are likely, following these graduation gifts?

(i) _____ .

(ii) _____ .

a. Gold; $6000; Loans: $20,000; Demand deposits; $26,000   **b.** Total *M* is unchanged, but its composition is now: bank money $26,000, coin money $4000   **c.** (i) The gold will probably be spent; (ii) Those who receive it in payment for goods will redeposit most or all of it with the goldsmith

14. **a.** From what fear can the goldsmith never fully escape?

_____ .

b. If he were faced with immediate demands for gold in excess of his supply, could he meet the crisis by demanding immediate repayment from all his borrowers?

_____

_____ .

c. At a time when the community's entire gold stock of $10,000 happens to be on deposit with the goldsmith, a panicky demand for gold develops. Can the goldsmith meet this demand by saying: "Only $10,000 of my deposits stands for true deposits of gold. All the other deposits represent loans. I will pay off the $10,000 in the 'real deposits.' The rest of you are just borrowers and have no right to demand gold." Why or why not?

_____

_____

_____ .

d. As protection against the danger of a panic and bank run, the authorities issue this decree: "All deposits with Ye Gold Shoppe are insured. The public's deposits are protected." If the public has confidence in this proclamation (whatever its meaning), this (*will / will not*) lessen the possibility of a bank run.

a. From the fear that he will be lynched because people demand more gold than he possesses **b.** No; he will only bankrupt borrowers. The total gold supply is only $10,000 **c.** No; most or all borrowers will have spent their deposits, which thus pass into the hands of other depositors. Most deposits are indistinguishable one from another **d.** will

The authorities now require the goldsmith to maintain a gold reserve of at least 20 percent of his demand deposits. That is, he is expected to restrain his total loans sufficiently that his total demand deposits are not more than 5 times the gold amount he is holding. For every $1 in gold on hand, he must have not more than $5 in demand deposits.

The community's total gold supply is $10,000. On the average, $8000 of this is deposited in the bank. The other $2000 is held by people in "hand-to-hand circulation." This $8000 to $2000 ratio varies somewhat. People continually withdraw small gold amounts from the bank for one purpose or another; at the same time, others are bringing small gold amounts in for deposit. A few people may prefer gold coins to bank-deposit money; some transactions are perhaps more conveniently made by gold coins. Some gold coins are collected in piggy banks; but this accumulated gold is spent from time to time, thus finding its way back to the bank.

As a consequence of this variation in gold deposited, the 20 percent gold-reserve ratio is not applied on a strict hour-to-hour or day-to-day basis. The goldsmith is expected to hold down his loans and deposits sufficiently that on the average of, say, each week's transactions, his gold on hand is at least 20 percent of his demand deposits.

But he is not in trouble just because, by the accident of one day's withdrawals, he is down to a 19 percent gold reserve. Next day's deposits will probably restore him to 20 percent.

If, however, enough gold is withdrawn into hand-to-hand circulation that the ratio between gold and deposits persists at a ratio below 20 percent, then the goldsmith must take action. Perhaps he can persuade the public to deposit more gold with him—but that may not be easy to do. Failing this, he must reduce his loans, or sell some of them to another goldsmith for gold. He will not be enthusiastic about doing this, for it will reduce the total of his interest earnings. But a reduction in loans will reduce his demand deposits. That will bring the required ratio of gold to deposits back into line.

15. a. Show the goldsmith's balance sheet if he has $8000 in gold on deposit and is fully "loaned out," allowing for the legal reserve requirement.

Assets		Liabilities	
Gold .... $_____		Demand deposits .... $_____	
Loans .... _____			

b. The community's total *M* at this point is $_____ , made up of $_____ in bank money and $_____ in gold in hand-to-hand circulation.

a. Gold: $8000; Loans: $32,000; Deposits: $40,000 **b.** 42,000; 40,000; 2000

16. a. The balance sheet is as in question 15a. A depositor now withdraws $100 in gold. Show the resulting balance sheet.

Assets		Liabilities	
Gold .... $_____		Demand deposits .... $_____	
Loans .... _____			

b. Will this withdrawal force the goldsmith to reduce loans? .... (*Yes / No*)

a. Gold: $7900; Loans: $32,000; Deposits: $39,900 **b.** No. This is a typical day-to-day withdrawal. The same $100, or another $100, will probably be redeposited tomorrow. No loan reduction is needed unless the gold-deposits ratio stays below 20 percent

17. a. A storekeeper brings in $500 in gold coin, the proceeds of Christmas sales, for deposit. How does this change question 16a's balance sheet?

Assets		Liabilities	
Gold .... $_____		Demand deposits .... $_____	
Loans .... _____			

b. This storekeeper has a loan of $1000 outstanding at the bank. By now, he has more than $1000 in his deposit account. He asks that his loan be paid off. His deposit is reduced by $1000, and he is given back his IOU. How will the balance sheet now look? (Disregard interest on the loan.)

Assets	Liabilities
Gold .... $_____	Demand deposits .... $_____
Loans .... _____	

c. When the loan is paid off, does this affect the community's total money supply, M? If so, by how much?

_____ .

a. Gold: $8400; Loans: $32,000; Deposits: $40,400 **b.** Gold: $8400; Loans: $31,000; Deposits: $39,400 **c.** Yes, it reduces total M by $1000 (*Note:* Any increase in the bank's total loans increases M; any decrease in total loans decreases M)

We have assumed thus far, that there is just one goldsmith in town; i.e., just one bank. Now an event of crucial importance in the economic history of the community occurs: a second goldsmith sets up business in competition with Ye Gold Shoppe.

There are now two very important points which you must grasp, and which the questions to follow develop:

▶ Neither bank will have as much freedom to increase loans as was true in the one-bank case. If either bank has sufficient reserves to permit a loan increase, it must allow for the fact that any loan increase will cause some of its reserves to "spill over" to the other bank.

▶ Yet "the banking system" (the two banks taken together) has exactly the same power to expand loans, on the basis of any given amount of reserves, as the one-bank system did.

18. The new goldsmith is willing to store gold and to handle checks as a means of transferring deposits from one customer's account to another. But he does not wish to engage in lending.

A few customers of goldsmith No. 1, finding the new location more convenient, transfer their accounts. They do so by issuing checks drawn on their accounts with No. 1, payable to No. 2. How does No. 2's balance sheet look immediately after he has received checks for $5000?

Assets	Liabilities
_____	_____
_____ $_____	_____ $_____

Checks drawn on Ye Gold Shoppe, $5000; Demand deposits, $5000

19. After protracted discussion between all concerned, the second goldsmith agrees to engage in lending. He is subject to the same 20 percent legal reserve requirement as goldsmith No.

1. How will the balance sheet of either look if each has $4500 in gold and is fully "loaned up"?

Assets	Liabilities
Gold .... $_____	Demand deposits .... $_____
Loans .... _____	

Gold: $4500; Loans: $18,000; Deposits: $22,500

20. A local boy who has made good abroad now returns home, bringing with him $3000 in new gold coins. These he deposits with goldsmith No. 2. Show the goldsmith's balance sheet immediately after this deposit has been made, i.e., before he has had any opportunity to increase loans.

Assets	Liabilities
Gold .... $_____	Demand deposits .... $_____
Loans .... _____	

Gold: $7500; Loans: $18,000; Deposits: $25,500

21. a. Goldsmith No. 2 now has "excess reserves." By simple application of the 1 to 5 ratio, it would seem that his $7500 in gold would support total deposits of $_____;—i.e., he could increase his loans by $_____ .

b. There are still reputable borrowers available. So No. 2— perhaps incautiously—does increase his loans by $12,000. He gives the new borrowers deposit accounts, against which they can issue checks. Show his balance sheet immediately after this expansion in loans and deposits, but before the borrowers have had time to spend any part of their newly created deposits.

Assets	Liabilities
Gold .... $_____	Demand deposits .... $_____
Loans .... _____	

c. At this stage, No. 2's reserve position is: (*Still has excess reserves / Just fully loaned up / Overexpanded*).

a. 37,500; 12,000 **b.** Gold: $7500; Loans: $30,000; Deposits: $37,500 **c.** Just fully loaned up

22. a. The combined balance sheet (billions of dollars) of all commercial banks appears (in part) below. The legal reserve requirement is 20 percent of deposits. The banks thus have excess reserves of $(*0 / 5 / 10 / 15 / 20 / 30*) billion.

Assets	Liabilities
Reserves (deposits with Federal Reserve and cash in vaults) $30	Demand deposits $100
Loans 70	

b. Show their balance sheet after they have taken full advantage of excess reserves to expand loans. All new money remains as demand deposits.

Assets	Liabilities
Reserves ..... $_____	Demand deposits .... $_____
Loans .... _____	

a. 10 **b.** Reserves: $30; Loans: $120; Deposits: $150 (When we have many banks, but work in terms of their combined balance sheet, the reasoning can be the same as in the one-bank Ye Gold Shoppe case)

23. The process of bank-money creation is most easily explained (perhaps can be explained only) in terms of deposit of cash in a bank. Bear in mind, though, that once the credit expansion process is completed and banks are fully loaned up, most deposits made with banks do not permit any further loan expansion at all.

In the two cases following, assume the banking system to be fully "loaned up." The reserve requirement is 20 percent.

a. I deposit $1000 cash in my bank. Which description is more correct?
(1) This $1000 will permit the banking system to expand loans by $4000.
(2) Unless the $1000 was a net addition to reserves, no loan expansion by the banking system is possible. The money may have been withdrawn from another bank (or even my bank) a day or two earlier.

b. I deposit a $1000 salary check in my bank. Again, pick the better description.
(1) This $1000 will permit the banking system to expand loans by $4000.
(2) My bank's reserves are increased, but at the cost of the reserves of some other bank. There has been no net addition to the entire banking system's reserves.

a. (2) b. (2)

24. It is frequently said that "banks lend out the money which people deposit with them." Circle as many of the following statements as seem to you correct.

a. Money deposited with a bank does not necessarily permit any expansion of loans by banks.

b. If the money deposited is cash, and if it constitutes a net addition to reserves, then the deposit will support a loan increase.

c. If a deposit does constitute a net addition to total banking system reserves, then it will permit a loan increase by the banking system of several times the deposit amount.

d. If the cash deposit does support a loan increase, the banks do not collectively "lend out" that cash. On the contrary, they keep it. They use it as a reserve to support the money they have newly created.

e. If I deposit $1000 in my bank, then I am the only person who can spend that deposit. If I choose not to spend it, it is as effectively "out of circulation" as if I had hidden the money at home.

f. If I withdraw $1000 in cash from my bank, and hide it at home, so that there is a net reduction in bank reserves, this will force a multiple contraction of loans. To this extent then, there is a difference between keeping money in a bank and keeping it at home.

All statements correct

25. In the United States, the public chooses to hold roughly one-fourth of the total money supply in coins and paper bills (about $99 billion in 1979), and the other three-fourths in bank demand (checking) accounts (about $255 billion in 1979).

These fractions are set by the public in keeping with needs and convenience. The public holds as much in the way of coins and bills as it finds convenient for the kinds of transactions coins and bills best handle. Usually, people keep the remainder of whatever money they possess, after the coin-and-bill need is satisfied, in a bank account. So any excess of coins and bills over the total "convenience" figure would typically be deposited in bank accounts and so converted into bank money (thus adding to the banking system's reserves).

Suppose the nation is recovering from recession. As part of this recovery, bank lending increases considerably. GNP rises, as does the total of deposit-account money. It is likely that the public, wanting to maintain the same convenient ratio between the two kinds of money, will convert some of the newly created bank money into coins and bills.

To the banking system, this means a "leakage" of reserves into hand-to-hand circulation. (This is the first of the "Two Qualifications to Deposit Creation" mentioned near the end of the text chapter with respect to the multiple expansion process: if deposits are expanded significantly, this may cause some part of the reserve base to "leak away.")

If the leakage is sufficiently large, and if the Federal Reserve does not take action to restore bank reserves (on this, see the next chapter), the banking system may be forced to cut back somewhat on loans.

Circle as many of the following as are correct:

a. Any sudden disposition on the part of the public to change the form of its assets in favor of coins or bills and against bank money (i.e., to convert bank money into coins or bills) will reduce bank reserves and may force a reduction in lending.

b. If we recognize "leakage into hand-to-hand circulation" as a consideration, this reduces the multiple factor by which the banking system could convert any amount of excess reserves into loans and deposit accounts.

c. If bank money comes to be used for transactions hitherto reserved for coins and bills (e.g., if gasoline purchases come to be paid for monthly by credit card, rather than by at-the-pump cash payments), this increases bank reserves and makes possible some expansion loans.

d. The banks cannot significantly alter the fraction of the total money supply which the public wants to keep in the form of coins and bills rather than as bank deposits (except insofar as they succeed in encouraging the use of credit cards and the like).

All statements correct

---

26. The reserve which a bank is legally required to maintain against its deposits *(may / must)* consists of *(a deposit with a Federal Reserve Bank exclusively / cash held on its own premises exclusively / both a Federal Reserve deposit and cash on its own premises).*

---

may; both an FR deposit and cash on its own premises

---

27. Suppose we define the total money supply *(M)* as the total of coins, paper bills, and bank demand-deposit accounts owned by the public, excluding any coins or bills held within the banks as reserves. Now the following events occur:

1. A single small bank receives a deposit of $1000 in coins and bills, money which hitherto had been hidden in a mattress.

2. Out of this deposit it makes a loan of $800 by giving the borrower credit for a deposit (checking) account of $800. (The remaining $200 is retained as a reserve against the original deposit.)

3. The borrower issues checks in order to spend his $800 loan. The deposit thus passes (via those to whom the checks are made payable) from the original bank to other banks.

a. Did event 1 change (increase or decrease) *M*? Explain.

b. Did event 2 change *M*? Explain

c. Did event 3 change *M*?

d. If your answer to **b** was yes, how can you reconcile it with the argument that no single bank can create money, since it only lends out part of what was deposited with it? If your answer to **b** was no, how can you reconcile it with the fact that the bank's demand deposits rose by $800?

e. Suppose the bank had given the borrower $800 in cash instead of a deposit account. How, if at all, would this change your answers to the preceding questions?

---

a. No; coin-and-bill money is down; bank money is up   **b.** Yes; bank money is up by $800; no change in coin-and-bill money   **c.** No   **d.** The single bank can create money (as we have here defined "the money supply")   **e.** Money supply would again be up by $800, just as in part **b**; but it would be an increase in coin-and-bill money, not in bank money

---

28. Assume that *(a)* commercial banks are all subject to a legal reserve requirement of 20 percent; *(b)* they have no excess reserves of any kind, except that *(c)* they always keep an extra 5

percent of their demand deposits as vault cash or till money, in addition to the legal requirement; and *(d)* the total of demand deposits is $12 billion. If the legal reserve requirement is increased from 20 percent to 25 percent, by how much must demand deposits be changed, if at all?

Deposits must be reduced by $2 billion, assuming no change in money in hand-to-hand circulation

---

29. A commercial bank is one of three equal-sized banks in an area. It is subject to a 20 percent reserve requirement; i.e., for each dollar of its demand deposits, it must have at least 20 cents on its premises or on deposit with its Federal Reserve Bank.

This bank has excess reserves of $11,000.

What is the maximum amount by which it can expand its loans, if it calculates that (because it is one of three equal-sized banks) for each extra $3 that it lends, it will lose $2 in reserves to the other banks?

The answer to the question is which one of the following four figures: $*(8500 / 11,000 / 15,000 / 18,500).*

15,000 (When these loans are first made, its deposits liability will rise by $15,000. The borrowers will spend these deposits by drawing checks against them. Two-thirds of these checks will go to other banks, so that our bank's reserves and deposits will both fall by $10,000. That will leave a $1000 reserve against the remaining deposits liability of $5000)

QUIZ: Multiple Choice

1. Barter, the first step in the evolution of a monetary system above self-sufficiency, gave way to commodity money because:
(1) barter was an inefficient transaction mechanism involving high transaction cost incurred by the necessity of finding someone willing to trade what you have for what you want.
(2) it was inconvenient at best.
(3) barter stood in the way of the efficient division of labor unless the output was divisible.
(4) barter depended upon a double coincidence of wants that was unlikely.
(5) all the above.

2. Commodity money was a step toward efficiency, but was undermined frequently by:
(1) frequent relapse into barter.
(2) the vagaries of supply and demand for the commodity that altered the value of the money.
(3) the inability of communities to agree to one commodity.
(4) the inability of communities to find a commodity that was not perishable.
(5) none of the above.

3. The strictest definition of money, M_1, includes:
(1) coins, currency, and demand deposits.
(2) coins, currency, and time deposits.
(3) coins, currency, and all deposits in a bank.
(4) all currencies and near-monies.
(5) none of the above.

4. Financial intermediaries are institutions that:
(1) buy and sell all types of goods, including merchandise.
(2) include only international corporations that must have large holdings of various types of currency.
(3) accept the deposits of some people and institutions and use that money to support the borrowing needs of others.
(4) are not really necessary in the United States because of the size of the federal debt.
(5) all the above.

5. Commercial banks are the largest category of financial intermediaries; others include:
(1) life-insurance companies.
(2) pension funds.
(3) savings and loan institutions.
(4) money market funds.
(5) all the above.

6. In a "fractional-reserve" banking system, such as that of the United States, the reserve requirements imposed on commercial banks:
(1) are primarily intended to set a limit on the total money supply rather than to serve as adequate protection against bank runs.
(2) are in excess of what is normally required, but are sufficient to cover what would be needed if for any reason people became uneasy over the safety of bank deposits.
(3) are essentially an average of the amounts needed to meet the public's demands in good times and bad.
(4) are now obsolete, according to the text, and will shortly be replaced by a 100 percent reserve requirement.
(5) are not correctly described by any of the above.

7. Which of the following is not a correct statement with respect to gold and its relationship to (or use as) money?
(1) Gold backing is essential if paper money is to retain its value over the long term.
(2) United States citizens may now own gold, but it is unrelated to the money supply, and the price at which they buy and sell it is a free (unregulated) market price.
(3) There is no longer any U.S. money which citizens can present to the government and receive gold in exchange.
(4) Historically, gold coins have not been much used as a medium of exchange, since they would have been too small for use in most everyday transactions.
(5) The intent of a legal requirement that a government must redeem paper money for gold upon demand is to prevent overissue of that paper money.

8. The essential difference between "money" and "near-money" is that:
(1) money is directly spendable whereas near-money is not.
(2) near-money includes all deposits in bank accounts, whereas money includes none of these.
(3) the velocity of circulation of money is rapid, while that of near-money is slow.
(4) near-money is "fiat money," whereas money is not.
(5) near-money is made up of any and all items that can be marketed for a money price.

9. There is a group of assets which is categorized as "near-money." As to this asset category, the text says that U.S. government bonds are:
(1) included to the extent that such bonds were purchased with part of the actual money supply, but not otherwise.
(2) excluded, since these bonds do not constitute spendable money.
(3) included, since the income from such bonds is paid in cash.
(4) excluded, since only assets which count as legal tender are included in the near-money category.
(5) included, since people's spending habits are influenced in much the same way, whether their assets are held in such bonds or in actual money.

10. If you write a check on your bank account, that check counts, or does not count, as part of the total money supply as follows. It:
(1) counts, provided it is a valid check, i.e., there are funds in the bank to support it.
(2) counts, whether valid or not, provided the person to whom it is given accepts it.
(3) counts if used to buy goods and services, but not otherwise.
(4) does not count, since no bank account is considered part of the money supply.
(5) does not count—to count both it and the deposit account on which it is drawn would be double counting.

11. When money has been deposited in any private financial institution (e.g., a commercial bank, a savings and loan association, etc.), the critical factor in deciding whether that deposit should count as part of the money supply (M_1 or "money narrowly defined") is that:
(1) checks can be freely written against the deposit by its owner.
(2) the deposit has insurance or backing by the government or some public institution.
(3) the institution maintains 100 percent backing or reserve for the deposit—whether the backing is provided by government or not.
(4) the institution has a legal franchise which permits its deposits to be counted as money.
(5) so long as the money deposited consists of genuine bills or coins, then the deposit within any such institution must be counted as part of the money supply.

12. The commercial banking system (all banks taken together) lends money to business firms and consumers, normally by setting up demand deposits which the borrowers may spend. The effect of this lending activity upon the money supply is as follows. The total money supply is:
(1) decreased, by the total amount of all coins and bills deposited with the banking system for safekeeping.
(2) neither increased nor decreased.
(3) increased, by an amount somewhat less than the system's total coin-and-bill deposits, owing to the fraction it holds as reserves.
(4) increased, by an amount just equal to the system's total coin-and-bill deposits.

(5) increased, by an amount considerably greater than the system's total coin-and-bill deposits.

13. The principal assets of a commercial bank are its:
(1) Federal Reserve (FR) deposit, vault cash, government securities, and demand and time deposits made by customers.
(2) IOUs received from borrowers, vault cash, government securities, and capital stock.
(3) FR deposit, IOUs received from borrowers, government securities, and demand and time deposits made by customers.
(4) FR deposit, IOUs received from borrowers, vault cash, and capital stock.
(5) FR deposit, IOUs received from borrowers, vault cash, and government securities.

14. The economy's total money supply will increase whenever commercial banks:
(1) increase their deposits with a Federal Reserve Bank.
(2) increase their total loans to the public.
(3) increase their demand-deposit liabilities by receiving coins or bills from the public as a deposit.
(4) withdraw part of their deposits from a Federal Reserve Bank.
(5) reduce their demand-deposit liabilities by paying out part of these accounts in the form of coins or paper bills.

15. I deposit, in Bank X, $10,000 in paper currency which has for a long time been hidden and out of circulation. The legal minimum reserve requirement for banks is 25 percent of deposits. Bank X is one among many banks. This deposit should enable Bank X, if it wishes, to increase its loans by a maximum amount of:
(1) zero.
(2) $7500.
(3) $10,000.
(4) $30,000.
(5) more than $30,000.

16. Assuming that the loan increase does not set off any increase of coins and paper currency in hand-to-hand circulation, the deposit described in question 15 would enable the banking system to increase its loans by a maximum of:
(1) zero.
(2) $7500.
(3) $10,000.
(4) $30,000.
(5) more than $30,000.

17. In the circumstances of questions 15 and 16, if consideration is given to some increase of coins and paper currency in hand-to-hand circulation, the most probable maximum amount (among the five alternatives listed below) by which the banking system as a whole could increase loans would be:
(1) zero.
(2) less than $5000.
(3) between $20,000 and $30,000.
(4) between $30,000 and $40,000.
(5) more than $40,000.

18. Had Bank X been a "monopoly bank" (i.e., if there were no other banks in competition with it) but with all other circumstances as in question 15 (including zero hand-to-hand circulation leakage), the maximum amount by which this deposit would have enabled Bank X to increase its loans, if so disposed, would be:
(1) zero.
(2) $7500.
(3) $10,000.
(4) $30,000.
(5) more than $30,000.

19. If the legal reserve requirement had been 20 rather than 25 percent, but with all other circumstances as in question 15, the deposit would have enabled Bank X to increase its loans, if so disposed, by:
(1) zero.
(2) $2000.
(3) $8000.
(4) $10,000.
(5) $40,000.

20. If the deposit of question 15 had been a $10,000 check drawn on Bank Y, but with all other circumstances as in question 15, this deposit (considered in the isolation from all other deposits or withdrawals) would have enabled Bank X to increase its loans, if so disposed, by:
(1) zero.
(2) $7500.
(3) $10,000.
(4) $30,000.
(5) more than $30,000.

21. The deposit of question 20 would enable the entire banking system to increase loans, if so disposed, by:
(1) zero.
(2) $7500.
(3) $10,000.
(4) $30,000.
(5) more than $30,000.

22. Which one among the following five statements is incorrect (according to the text) with respect to "bank runs" and bank failures?
(1) The bank's predicament arises from the fact that it has turned most of its cash into "earning assets"—government securities, IOUs, and the like.
(2) The bank's depositors are simply trying to convert their assets from one form of money into another form of money
(3) The bank has been operating on a fractional-reserve basis.
(4) Membership in the Federal Reserve System is no guarantee against the possibility of a bank run.
(5) The bank must have been insolvent, or very nearly so, before the bank run began.

23. If the legal reserve requirement is a minimum of 30 percent of the amount of demand deposits, and if the banking system now has excess reserves of $15 million, then (disregard-

ing any resulting increase in hand-to-hand circulation) the banking system could increase demand deposits by a maximum of:
(1) zero.
(2) $10.5 million.
(3) $15 million.
(4) $35 million.
(5) $50 million.

24. The banking system can create deposits which are several times as large as reserves deposited with it. One element which limits the extent of the banking system's power to do this is the legal reserve requirement. Another limiting element is the fact that:
(1) no individual bank can really increase the money supply; it can only lend out a major fraction of any money deposited with it.
(2) all member banks must maintain a deposit with the Federal Reserve.
(3) a substantial increase in loans on the part of any single bank normally causes it to lose cash reserves to other banks.
(4) a substantial increase in the quantity of bank-deposit money usually causes part of that money to be converted into coins and bills.
(5) cash on the bank's own premises can no longer be counted as part of their reserves.

25. The federal Reserve System is owned by the:
(1) federal government and operated in keeping with the needs of the federal government.
(2) public, through the federal government, and operated in keeping with the needs of the public.
(3) commercial banks and operated in keeping with the wishes of the commercial banks.
(4) public, through the federal government, but operated in keeping with the needs and wishes of the commercial banks.

(5) commercial banks, but operated in keeping with the needs of the public.

26. The Federal Reserve System has many functions and responsibilities. Which among the following does not correctly describe the Fed?
(1) It seeks to make a system of small-unit banking workable in an advanced economic society.
(2) It controls the quantity of commercial-bank demand deposits, which make up the major part of the nation's money supply, in that it controls legal reserve requirements.
(3) It seeks to earn a profit for its member-bank owners.
(4) It considers itself primarily responsible to Congress rather than to the Treasury.
(5) It holds on deposit most of the "reserves" of member banks.

27. The "excess reserves" of a commercial bank consist of:
(1) assets which, although not money, can be quickly converted into money by the bank should the need arise.
(2) money and near-money assets possessed by the bank in excess of 100 percent of the amount of its demand deposits.
(3) cash which must be kept on hand, not because everyday bank needs require it, but because of a legal requirement.
(4) money held by the bank in excess of that fraction of its deposits required by law.
(5) the difference between the amount of its money assets and the amount of its demand deposits.

28. The money multiplier is the multiplicative inverse of the reserve requirement as long as:
(1) substantial currency leakages into circulation and/or foreign markets do not occur.
(2) banks do not frequently maintain excess reserves.
(3) the reserve requirements is far in excess of the reserves that banks think are prudent given the deposits that they hold.
(4) all the above.
(5) none of the above.

APPENDIX:
Stock Market Fluctuations

The main part of Chapter 14 examined the nature of money and credit. The Appendix focuses on the common-stock holdings that many Americans find so attractive. These are assets that, while they fall outside the technical definitions of M_1 and M_2, are nonetheless held in great quantity by thousands of households across the United States. Table 14A-1 in the text shows the magnitude of those holdings. They are down substantially from 1960, to be sure, but they still represent approximately one-quarter of the financial holdings of the American people.

In working through the Appendix, you will not only review the size of these holdings, but also gain some

insight into the workings of the stock market. Upon completing your work, therefore, you will have accomplished the following objectives.

LEARNING OBJECTIVES

1. Relate the distribution of wealth across the myriad of financial assets available to the individual and the distribution of holdings of common stock across the population.

2. Understand the basis of the "efficient-market" hypothesis and how it translates into a "random-walk" theory of stock market prices.

3. Glean some notion of what the efficiency of the stock market means to investment strategies in the market and your ability to "beat the market" by being very clever.

Holdings of common stock were very popular as late as the 1960s, but their popularity has declined dramatically since then. Nonetheless, they are still the form in which almost 25 percent of the wealth of the American population is held, and they gained renewed, if perhaps short-lived popularity during the market boom from August of 1982 through December of 1983.

1. In 1982, corporate equities represented a higher proportion of the total assets of American households than (circle as many as apply) *(currency / time deposits and money funds / pension funds / government securities)*. Measured in dollars, it is clear from Table 14A-1 in the text that over *($1.2 / $2.2 / $3.0)* billion in assets were held in the form of corporate equity in 1982. These holdings were up from nearly *($200 / $300 / $400)* billion in 1960 despite the decline in the relative popularity of stocks. Over *(35 million / 50 million / 75 million)* people own stock, with at least *(1 million / 2 million / 3 million)* of those earning less than $10,000 a year holding at least one share. For those low-income people, the average dividend payment is approximately $80.00 per year. On the other side of the distribution, more than *(25 percent / 35 percent / 50 percent)* of the outstanding corporate stock in the United States is owned by the wealthiest 1 percent of the population.

---

currency; pension funds; government securities; $1.2; $400; 35 million; 3 million; 50 percent

2. a. *Margin buying* on the stock market works as follows: you want to buy XYZ stock, currently selling at $40 per share; you think XYZ will rise to $50 or higher. You have only $1000 in cash; this will buy only 25 shares (disregarding the broker's commission and other incidental buying costs). But with a margin requirement of 25 percent, you can buy a larger number of shares. You do this by borrowing $3000 from your broker or, via the broker, from a bank or other lending agency. The loan proceeds plus your own cash will buy *(25 / 50 / 100 / 200)* shares. Of course you must put up some security against your loan. But you have this; you can furnish XYZ stock worth $*(1000 / 3000 / 4000)*. This is accepted as adequate security for your $3000 loan.

b. If XYZ goes to 50, you sell your stock, pay off principal and interest on your loan, and pocket the rest of your profit, happy at having taken an economics course. But if, instead, XYZ should drop below 40—say, to 35 or 34—you will get a call from your broker to report that the bank "wants more margin," for the value of the asset you have supplied as collateral is falling. You must put up some more security or else pay off part of the loan. If you fail to come across, the bank will sell your XYZ stock. If it sells at close to 30, the entire sale proceeds go to cover your loan, leaving you with the sad reminder that you should first have read beyond Chapter 4.

Note the unstable quality of a market heavily involved with margin buying. If prices begin to fall, this sets off a *(further wave of selling / wave of buying)*, as borrowers cannot furnish more margin and lenders sell to protect their loans. This pushes stock prices down even more.

---

a. 100; 4000   **b.** further wave of selling

3. a. A "bull" market is one in which most expectations are that stock prices are going to *(rise / fall)*. Most people with cash are accordingly inclined to *(buy / refrain from buying)* stocks. Most people holding stocks are inclined to *(continue to hold / sell)* them. The consequence of such expectations is that stock prices generally *(rise / fall)*.

b. A "bear" market is one in which most expectations are that stock prices are going to *(rise / fall)*. Most people with cash are accordingly inclined to *(buy / refrain from buying)* stocks. Most people holding stocks are inclined to *(continue to hold / sell)* them. The consequence of such expectations is that stock prices generally *(rise / fall)*.

---

a. rise; buy; continue to hold; rise   **b.** fall; refrain from buying; sell; fall

4. If you buy stock through your broker and through the New York Stock Exchange, the seller of that stock (pick one):

a. May have been some private holder, or may have been the corporation whose stock it is (i.e., it may have been stock newly issued by that corporation).

b. Must have been the corporation whose stock it is.

c. Must have been some private holder—i.e., it cannot normally have been the corporation whose stock it is.

---

c. (The NYSE, like other exchanges, is a place where "used" securities are exchanged. A corporation cannot use it to "float" a new issue of stock)

5. When you buy a stock, you do so either because you think its price will rise or else because you think the dividend yield is sufficiently high to make it worth buying. But remember: someone holds just the opposite opinion from yours—namely, whoever it was that sold you that stock. (In the stock market, you cannot know the identity of that "whoever it was." All transactions are anonymous.) This need not stop you from buying. Your judgment may be better than that of the anonymous somebody on the other side of your buying (or for that matter, selling) transaction.

This leads us into two topics discussed in the test: (a) the idea of an "efficient market," and (b) the "random-walk" hypothesis of stock market prices.

Today there are thousands of professionals whose job it is to scrutinize the background of all stocks listed on the New York, American, and lesser stock exchanges. (They look into "over-the-counter" stocks as well—stocks of smaller companies that are unlisted but do trade through less formal channels.) They have probed into everything that is to be known about all the companies involved; their balance sheet positions, the competence of their managers, their future sales and earning prospects, and so on. All this information has been passed on to stock buyers and sellers. This yields—in principle, at any rate—an "efficient market," one in which there are no underpriced stocks, and none overpriced.

Why? Because accurate information is quickly absorbed into the price. Suppose, for the sake of illustration, that you decide that you want to buy a few shares of stock in a firm that has suddenly become more profitable. The firm has just marketed a new product for which demand is unexpectedly high, or just developed a new technology that will dramatically lower its costs and improve its competitive position, or has just discovered an enormous oil deposit under its Texas plant. In any case, you are attracted to the stock because future earnings by that firm should be significantly *(higher / lower)* than had originally been expected. You and other investors will want to *(buy / sell)* stock in that firm. People who already own stock in that firm will, on the other hand, want to *(sell / hold onto)* those issues in the expectation that they will soon be worth *(less / more)*. The result will be an immediate *(increase / reduction)* in the price of that stock in response to *(higher / lower)* demand and *(higher / lower)* supply at the original market clearing price. By the time you get to the market and find someone who will be willing to sell you the shares that you want, therefore, the price will already include the increment in value of the newly announced profitability that you had hoped to cash in on.

The problem is that the efficient-market hypothesis means that the effects of foreseeable events are already included in the prices of stocks before you can get to them. You are therefore left with trying to predict unforeseeable events in your effort to "beat the market." As a result, if you invest in the stock market and accept the hypothesis, then you should (pick one or more):

a. Concentrate your purchases on a small number of stocks.

b. Buy a widely diversified collection of stocks.

c. Keep altering your portfolio—i.e., trade frequently.

d. Stick to your portfolio—i.e., trade infrequently.

higher; buy; hold onto; more; increase; higher; lower; **b** and **d**

QUIZ: Multiple Choice

1. Holdings in common stock:
(1) amount to about 10 percent of the assets held by American households.
(2) amount to about 50 percent of the assets held by American households.
(3) have fallen proportionately in the portfolios of American households but have risen absolutely since 1960.
(4) have risen proportionally in the portfolios of American households since the crash of 1975.
(5) have held remarkably steady as a proportion of the assets of the American household.

2. Holdings of common stock:
(1) are distributed over a wide range of income levels but are concentrated in the wealthiest 1 percent of the American population.
(2) are held exclusively by the wealthy.
(3) are confined to pension funds and insurance companies.
(4) are considerable, but less than holdings of currency.
(5) are dwarfed only by holdings of government securities needed to finance the federal debt.

3. The efficient-market theory:
(1) states that all public information is reflected almost immediately in the price of a share of common stock.
(2) implies that "beating the market" involves predicting unforeseeable events.
(3) implies that stock market prices move in the short run as if they were random numbers.
(4) diversification is a reasonable strategy for investing in the stock market.
(5) all the above.

4. The essential property of margin buying of a stock is:
(1) participation in stock buying during a period of price rise by inexperienced investors.
(2) trading in a stock in quantities that do not really exist.
(3) any purchase of a stock in anticipation of a rise in its price, provided the stock is held for a short period only.
(4) a stock purchase financed in part by use of borrowed money.
(5) none of the above.

5. As the result of some favorable news regarding a company, the price of its stock rises. If we were to use supply and demand curves to illustrate the nature of that price rise, we would say that it resulted from:
(1) solely a rightward or upward shift of the demand curve.
(2) solely a leftward or upward shift of the supply curve.
(3) both a rightward demand-curve shift and a leftward supply-curve shift.
(4) principally a rightward (or downward) shift of the supply curve.
(5) principally a rightward shift of both demand and supply curves.

6. Some profitable and well-regarded companies whose stocks are listed on the New York exchange pay no dividends at all (e.g., Crown Cork and Seal); profits are used entirely for expansion of plant and operations. A shrewd investor:
(1) might buy such stock in hope of capital gains, but not otherwise.
(2) might buy such stock in expectation of a "stock split," but not otherwise.
(3) might buy such stock in expectation of a dividend being declared in the near future, but not otherwise.
(4) might buy such stock when expecting stock prices to fall.
(5) would not buy it at all.

7. One group of stock market investors buys and holds for the long pull, disregarding short-term price fluctuations. This type of investor has the following overall effect on the market. He or she:

(1) destabilizes it in that his or her purchases keep tending to push price upward.

(2) stabilizes it by refusing to sell on price declines, but destabilizes it by making the market "thinner."

(3) stabilizes it by making it "thinner."

(4) destabilizes it by selling at times which have no relation to the current price of the stock.

(5) does none of these things, since his or her group is not of sufficient importance to have any impact.

8. The contribution of margin buying to the great stock market crash of 1929 was which of the following?

(1) Owners of stock were forced to sell that stock in order to raise the cash needed to buy the further stock which their margin commitment required them to buy.

(2) The small or marginal stock buyers grew panicky and dumped their stock for whatever price they could get.

(3) Margin buying had increased the volume of stock trading and thus intensified the fall in prices, but otherwise it played no special part in the crash.

(4) The lenders of money sold the stock they were holding as collateral security when stock prices began to fall substantially.

(5) Margin buyers made an unsuccessful attempt to stop the decline in stock prices by increasing the amount of their buying.

CHAPTER 15

THE FEDERAL RESERVE AND CENTRAL BANK MONETARY POLICY

Having come to understand how fractional reserves allow a banking system to create "bank money," it is now time to ponder the next logical question: "So what?" The present chapter will begin to answer that query by providing an initial discussion of how changes in the money supply can influence real economic variables. It will be seen to be an indirect influence, operating from a change in reserves through the resulting change in the money supply to effect a change in the interest rate and thus aggregate demand. Once aggregate demand changes, of course, the old stories that translate those changes into changes in real GNP, prices, and employment apply immediately, and we are done.

Having covered that long chain of indirect influence in its first part, Chapter 15 turns to consider how a central banking system actually works. With particular reference to the Federal Reserve System of the United States, you will see how a variety of tools can be used to adjust monetary policy. Since monetary policy is arguably the most important factor of modern macroeconomic stabilization policy, it is essential that you grasp precisely not only how each of the control mechanisms work in theory, but also how they are managed in the real world of policymakers.

Once you have completed your work on this chapter, therefore, you should have accomplished the following learning objectives.

LEARNING OBJECTIVES

1. Outline the six-step chain of events that translates a change in the quantity of reserves available to banks into a change in GNP, prices, and/or employment.

2. Understand the potential long-run evolution of a macroeconomy that can eventually move interest rates in a direction that is exactly opposite to the short-run movement caused by monetary policy.

3. Describe the operating structure of the Federal Reserve System of the United States.

4. Identify open-market operations, changes in the discount rate, and changes in the reserve requirement as the major policy instruments available to the Fed and relate how they are manipulated to set monetary policy.

5. Explain how each one of the major policy instruments identified in objective 4 works in theory and in practice.

6. Understand the strengths and weaknesses of the major policy instruments identified in objectives 4 and 5.

7. List the several minor instruments that the Fed can manipulate to exert some control over the money supply, and explain how they work.

8. Relate the difference between variables of monetary policy, intermediate target variables for that policy, and objective variables that help define the intermediate targets. Describe the October 1979 change in how the Fed has set its targets.

9. Understand the nature of the deregulation of financial institutions that was accomplished in the United States by the Banking Acts of 1980 and 1982 and their impact on (*a*) the independence of the Fed and (*b*) the ability of the Fed to control the money supply.

10. Relate the dimension of dollar holdings beyond the boundary of the United States and the effect that those holdings have on the ability of the Fed to exert the desired level of control by sterilizing international capital movements.

Careful attention to the content of this chapter will pay dividends in your understanding of subsequent material. The mechanics of monetary policy are important in their own right, of course, but their importance is amplified by their application to policy questions in the next few chapters. Chapter 15 presents, in particular, the supply side of the "money market." The demand side will be presented soon, and the details of the long policy-to-GNP linkage noted here will follow. It will be extremely difficult for you to follow that final line of reasoning if you have not mastered this material.

1. We begin with a chronicle of the path from some sort of adjustment in bank reserves to some sort of change in GNP and employment. Suppose, for the sake of illustration, that an open-market operation designed to lower inflation reduced the reserves available to the banking system. The result would be *(an expansion / a contraction)* in the quantity of bank money supplied to the economy. It should be expected, therefore, that interest rates would *(climb / fall)* and the supply of credit would *(contract / expand)*. Businesses would therefore find it *(easier / more difficult)* to finance new investment. Individuals would feel *(richer / poorer)* and would therefore *(increase / reduce)* their consumption expenditures. And so on. Aggregate demand would, in general, *(climb / fall)* and thus put pressure on GNP to *(climb / fall)*, prices to *(climb / fall)*, and/or unemployment to *(climb / fall)*.

If the policy were the result of trying to reduce inflation and it were successful, then the long-term effect on interest rates could actually be *(up / down)*. This is because interest rates include an inflation premium, and the policy-inspired *(increase / reduction)* in rates could be *(amplified / canceled)* by a reduction in the inflation premium. While investment should be expected to *(fall / increase)* in the short run, the long-run effect might therefore be *(movement in the opposite direction / an acceleration of the short-run effect)*.

The long-term effect just noted is not always good news. Some fear that while periods of expansionary monetary policy might cause interest rates to *(fall / climb)* in the short run, such policy might ultimately cause rates to *(climb / fall)* as inflation accelerates.

---

a contraction; climb; contract; more difficult; poorer; reduce; fall; fall; fall; climb; down; increase; canceled; fall; movement in the opposite direction; fall; climb

---

Monetary policy, in essence, means this: policy designed to make the borrowing of money easy or difficult, as conditions require. Those who borrow money do so in order to spend it. Consequently, if the amount of borrowing can be increased or decreased, so too can the total volume of spending. And as spending goes, so goes GNP.

The total of borrowing can be manipulated by the Federal Reserve System—the central bank of the United States. The Fed can significantly influence the borrowing total because of the power it can exercise over the reserves of the commercial banks.

2. a. To understand how monetary policy is conducted, it is necessary to have some familiarity with the various accounts on the Federal Reserve balance sheet. Begin by writing down the names of the three asset accounts (omitting miscellaneous assets) in text Table 15-1.

(1) _____

(2) _____

(3) _____

b. Omitting miscellaneous liabilities and capital accounts, write down the five items on the liabilities and net worth side of the Fed's balance sheet.

(1) _____

(2) _____

(3) _____

(4) _____

(5) _____

---

a. (1) gold certificates and other cash; **(2)** U.S. government securities; **(3)** discounts and loans **b. (1)** Federal Reserve notes; **(2)** bank reserve deposits; **(3)** U.S. Treasury deposits; **(4)** foreign and other deposits; **(5)** capital accounts

---

3. The Federal Reserve can operate monetary policy primarily because it is "a bank for bankers." Commercial banks keep most of their cash on deposit with the Fed. This means that on the balance sheet for the commercial banks (combined) there is *(an asset / a liability)* deposit with the Federal Reserve. On the Fed's balance sheet, there is a matching *(asset / liability)* account called

_____ .

This relationship between a commercial bank and the Federal Reserve corresponds exactly to the relation you have with your own (commercial) bank. You count as an asset whatever money you have on deposit there. Disregarding any checks you may have written but which have not yet worked their way back to your bank, exactly the same figure shows up on your bank's balance sheet as *(an asset / a liability)*. To the bank, it is money owed to you.

---

an asset; liability; bank reserve deposits; a liability

Commercial banks do not keep a deposit with the Fed just to demonstrate their faith in the banking principle. They do so because they are legally required to keep a reserve against their own customer deposit accounts, and a deposit with the Fed is the most convenient way of keeping most of it. This is particularly true because there are continually accounts to be settled with other banks.

Cash on the bank's own premises—"vault cash," or "till money"—may also be counted as part of this reserve. But the reserve must take one of these two forms: either a deposit with the Fed, or cash on hand.

If a bank is deficient in its reserve requirement (i.e., if its total reserve is less than the legally required percentage of its total customer deposits) then it must do one of two things: increase its reserve, or decrease its customer deposits.

Usually a bank can temporarily increase its reserve by

borrowing funds from another bank which happens to have excess reserves. (There is an active market in such transfers. It is the *Federal Funds market*, and the interest rate charged is the "Federal Funds rate." But these loans are made strictly on an overnight basis.)

Alternatively, the deficient bank might sell some of its security holdings to another bank with reserves in excess. Or it might borrow from the Federal Reserve. As will be noted shortly, though, this is simply one more short-term option of limited expedience.

If the reserve situation is tight throughout the entire banking system, and some banks are deficient in reserves, then the remedy will almost certainly have to be a reduction in demand deposits.

4. For reasons indicated in Chapter 14, the banks accomplish this demand-deposit reduction by means of a

_____ / _____ .

reduction in loans made to customers

5. a. So a bank that is deficient in reserves must, if the deficiency persists, curtail its loans. As old loans fall due and are paid off, the bank does not make corresponding new ones.

A bank's reduction in loans works to remedy a reserve deficiency because it is the opposite of the loan-expansion process examined in detail in Chapter 14. There, it was pointed out that a bank which increases its loans loses reserves to other banks. Now we deal with the same process in reverse. A business firm accumulates the money needed to pay off its bank loan by means of sales to customers. The checks received from customers, which the borrowing firm deposits in its bank, ordinarily come from other banks; and the receiving bank collects funds in settlement from these other banks. Hence, as funds for loan repayment accumulate, reserve funds tend to flow *(away from / toward)* the bank which earlier made this loan.

In sum, when a bank is deficient in reserves, it can remedy the deficiency by cutting its loans. This transfers the deficiency to other banks, and they too must curtail loans, unless they have excess reserves. A reduction in loans means *(a reduction / an increase)* in total deposits. So when the banking system reduces total loans, it is reducing deposits to the level which the specified reserve total will support.

b. If total reserves, in Federal Reserve deposits and cash on hand, were $20 (billion), total demand deposits owned by the public were $110, and the reserve requirement were 20 percent, then reserves would be *(in excess / deficient)*. The amount of reserve *(deficiency / excess)* would be $*(2 / 10)* billion.

c. In such a case, the banks may be able to supplement reserves by borrowing from the Fed. But there are limitations on this method, on both borrowing and lending sides. Banks are usually reluctant to borrow from the very agency which polices their overall activities. And even if the banks are prepared to borrow, there is no automatic guarantee that the Fed will lend.

The Fed's ordinary policy is to grant loans to deficient banks only for enough time to permit the adjustment to be made by other means without disrupting the economy. Ultimately, the banking system must *(increase / decrease)* its loans unless the Fed decides that a credit expansion is desirable and increases the reserve base by one of the methods outlined in this chapter.

Such a loan reduction would *(reduce / increase)* the demand-deposit total. It may also perhaps bring in some coins and bills hitherto in hand-to-hand circulation, which can be added to reserves.

d. In the situation described in *b* above, assuming no change in coins or bills in circulation, loans and deposits would have to be *(increased / decreased)* by $*(1 / 2 / 5 / 10 / 20)* billion.

a. toward; a reduction **b.** deficient; deficiency; 2 **c.** decrease; reduce **d.** decreased; 10.

6. Consider the $153.8 billion liability that appears on the March 1984 Federal Reserve balance sheet record in Table 15-1 of the text under "Federal Reserve Notes." Circle the letters identifying which of the following statements are correct.

a. This liability represents the bulk of the paper money circulating in the United States. It is, in fact, all such money except for a few bills of various types (silver certificates, U.S. notes) which date back to earlier generations. They are still held in small amounts by the public; but they are withdrawn whenever they come out of hiding and reappear in circulation.

b. This figure of $153.8 billion represents the total of all such Federal Reserve paper money existing outside the Fed itself, i.e., held by commercial banks and by the public.

c. This total of paper money is listed as a liability by the Federal Reserve because, in the last analysis, such bills are simply IOUs of the Fed and must be listed on its balance sheet, as any such IOU must be.

d. If any member commercial bank deposits a $10 Federal Reserve note with the Fed, then on the Fed's balance sheet the liability bank reserves rise by $10 and the liability Federal Reserve notes fall by $10 (since this particular IOU is no longer outstanding).

e. If a Federal Reserve employee receives a brand-new $10 Federal Reserve note as part of his or her salary, the Fed's liability Federal Reserve notes must rise by $10.

f. If any commercial bank withdraws $10 from its deposit with its Federal Reserve Bank, and takes this withdrawal in the form of a $10 Federal Reserve note, then the Fed's liability bank reserves must fall by $10, and its liability Federal Reserve notes must rise by $10.

g. Federal Reserve notes held by a commercial bank in its own vaults may be counted as part of its legal reserve.

h. The public can increase its holdings of Federal Reserve notes simply by withdrawing part of its demand-deposit accounts. This action would decrease the deposit-money total and increase the total of paper money held by the public.

All statements are correct. [*Note:* Some students have difficulty accepting the fact that any piece of paper money such as a $10 bill is really an IOU. It is; it is an IOU of the Federal Reserve. Like any other IOU, it must appear on the Fed's balance sheet as a liability. Any new Federal Reserve notes which the Fed pays out must increase that liability; any notes returned to the Fed (e.g., deposited by a bank for credit to its reserve) reduce that liability.]

The questions to follow deal with the operation of monetary policy in terms of Federal Reserve and commercial bank balance sheets. In these questions, assume that each bank is required to keep a *bank reserve* of at least 10 percent of its own total demand deposits (owned by its customers). Assume, as well, that the bank tries to keep this reserve as follows: 7.5 percent as a deposit with the Fed, and 2.5 percent as cash on its own premises—"vault cash."

We start with the following (incomplete[1]) balance sheets (in billions of dollars) for the Federal Reserve and the combined commercial banks.

Federal Reserve

Assets		Liabilities	
Gold certificates	$10	Federal Reserve notes	$15
Gov't. securities	35	Deposits:	
Loans	5	Government	5
		Member bank	30

Combined Commercial Banks

Assets		Liabilities	
Federal Reserve deposits	$ 30	Demand deposits	$400
Vault cash	10		
Loans	360		

7. This question outlines the working of the principal instrument which the Federal Reserve uses in conducting its monetary policy: *open-market operations.*

The Fed decides (for reasons that will shortly be evident) to buy government securities from the public. It enters the bond market and buys $10 (billion) of short-term government securities (bidding up the prices of these securities somewhat, if necessary, in order to obtain them).

(With rare exceptions, the Federal Reserve conducts its open-market operations by buying or selling short-term federal government IOUs: treasury bills, treasury certificates, treasury notes. "Bonds" are much longer-term government IOUs, and

---

[1]Some accounts which are of no interest for purposes of this exercise have been omitted; the remaining accounts have arbitrarily been made to balance between themselves. You can work these exercises just as though they were the complete balance sheets.

ordinarily the Fed does not deal in them for its open-market activities.)

The Fed pays for these bonds by means of checks drawn on itself. These checks pass through the following sequence:

1. Those who sold the securities—financial institutions, business corporations, individuals—and to whom the Fed's checks are payable, deposit these checks in their accounts in commercial banks.

2. The banks, to whom these claims on the Fed have now passed, return them to the Fed as increases in their reserve account deposits.

Hence, as a consequence of this bond purchase by the Fed, two significant account totals have increased:

1. The public now has an additional $10 in its total demand deposits with commercial banks.

2. The commercial banks likewise have an additional $10 in their deposits with the Federal Reserve.

Write out new balance sheets for the Fed and the banks, corresponding to those immediately preceding this question, but showing the changes just described. (As yet, the banks have changed neither their vault cash nor their loans.)

Federal Reserve

Assets		Liabilities	
Gold certs.	$_____	FR notes	$_____
		Deposits:	
Gov't. securities	_____	Gov't.	_____
Loans	_____	Banks	_____

Combined Commercial Banks

Assets		Liabilities	
FR deposits	$_____	Demand deposits	$_____
Vault cash	_____		
Loans	_____		

Fed: Gold certs. $10; Gov't. securities $45; Loans $5; FR Notes $15; Govt. deposits $5; Bank deposits $40; *Banks:* FR deposits $40; Vault cash $10; Loans $360; Demand deposits $410

---

8. The position of the commercial banks is now that they *(have excess reserves / are just fully "loaned up" / are deficient in their total reserve requirement).*

This means that they *(will want to increase / must decrease)* their total loans in order to increase their earnings.

Specifically, their total reserves are now $*(10 / 20 / 30 / 40 / 50)*, and this is sufficient to maintain demand deposits totaling a maximum of $*(150 / 200 / 250 / 275 / 300 / 350 / 400 / 450 / 500 / 550 / 600)*.

---

have excess reserves; will want to increase; 50; 500

9. Show balance sheets of both the Fed and the combined banks, after the banks have taken full advantage of this opportunity to increase their loans.[2]

Remember that both FR deposits and vault cash count as reserves: the banks want to keep them in a 3 to 1 ratio. Vault cash is increased by withdrawing part of the FR deposit. Assume that withdrawal is made in Federal Reserve notes.

Federal Reserve

Assets	Liabilities
Gold certs. ...... $_____	FR notes .... $_____
	Deposits:
Gov't. securities .. _____	Gov't. .... _____
Loans .... _____	Banks .... _____

Combined Commercial Banks

Assets	Liabilities
FR deposits .... $_____	Demand deposits $_____
Vault cash ...... _____	
Loans .... _____	

Fed: Gold certs. $10; Gov't. securities $45; Loans $5; FR notes $17.5; Gov't. deposits $37.5 *Banks:* FR deposits $37.5; Vault cash $12.5; Loans $450; Demand deposits $500

10. a. Assuming that the banks do so increase their loans, then the money supply has *(increased / decreased)*, altogether, by $*(0 / 20 / 40 / 60 / 80 / 100)*.

Would you expect this to affect the level of GNP?

b. In sum, if the Federal Reserve enters the securities market as a buyer (and remember, its purchase of securities set off the process explored in the previous questions) its objective would be to *(raise / restrain)* the GNP level by making credit *(easier / more difficult)* to obtain. This would be an *easy-money policy.* Interest rates, those on bank loans in particular, should *(rise / fall)*.

a. increased; 100; Yes, because increased lending by banks means increased spending by borrowers **b.** raise; easier; fall

[2]At the close of Chapter 14, it was pointed out that if the banks create a considerable amount of new "bank-account money," as in this case, the public may want to convert some of it into coins and bills. If this happens, the banks must provide the public with such coin and bill money by getting it from the Fed. This of course reduces their own deposits (reserves) with the Fed. Consequently, this reduces somewhat bank power to increase deposits on the basis of a given amount of new and excess reserves. But apart from this reduction in their expansion power, the process is unchanged. For simplicity assume (in this and subsequent questions) that the deposit increase causes no increase in the quantity of coins and bills held by the public.

11. a. Would the increase in the money supply indicated in the previous questions happen automatically or inevitably? What would stop it from happening?

b. If banks should refuse to increase their loans at all, will this open-market operation have increased the money supply at all? If so, how, and by how much?

a. No, if banks cannot find satisfactory borrowers or want to keep excess reserves because they are uneasy about expanding loans **b.** Yes, by the $10 created when the Fed bought securities

12. If the Federal Reserve wanted to tighten credit and to restrain the GNP level, then it would pursue a *tight-money policy.* It would work the open-market process of the previous questions in reverse.

a. That is, the Fed would enter the securities markets as a *(buyer / seller)*. If necessary, it would accept a price somewhat *(higher / lower)* than the previously existing market level in order to bring about its *(purchases / sales)* of government securities. The buyers of these securities (insurance companies, other financial institutions, business corporations, even individuals) would pay for them by means of checks drawn on their commercial bank accounts. The Fed would return these checks to the banks involved, and require settlement by *(increasing / reducing)* the reserve deposit which these banks kept at the Fed.

b. When the reserves of commercial banks decline then (unless they have excess reserves) they must *(increase / decrease)* their loans to customers. The effect of this tighter-money open-market operation is that the totals of commercial bank loans and demand deposits go *(up / down)*.

(If you wish, you can work all this out in detail, starting with the same pair of balance sheets provided above, and with a sale by the Fed of $10 of its government securities. Remember that if a bank has more Federal Reserve notes than needed to cover its 2.5 percent vault-cash requirement, it can return the excess to the Fed, thereby increasing the amount of its reserve deposit.)

c. Because money loaned by banks is ordinarily spent by the borrowers, and because so much of this spending goes to maintain or increase GNP, the overall effect of this tight-money operation is to *(restrain / increase)* the GNP level.

a. seller; lower; sales; reducing **b.** decrease; down **c.** restrain

13. Should the commercial banks happen to have excess reserves when the Fed begins a tighter-money open-market operation, then all this operation does is to soak up part of the excess. The banks are not under pressure to reduce their loans and deposits because of a shortage of reserves. The Fed must continue its operation until the banks do come under pressure.

The point of specifying high reserve requirements is to guarantee that this won't happen. The Fed can, in other words, assume that banks will operate close to the reserve requirement.

Notice a difference between easy- and tight-money policies. When an easy-money policy gives them more reserves, the banks *(must / may or may not)* then increase their loans to the fullest possible extent. If they don't like the credit prospects of the would-be borrowers standing in line, they may decide not to become "fully loaned up." Nothing the Fed can do can force them to change this decision.

The Fed can always push a tight-money operation until any excess reserves have been mopped up. Thereafter, the banks *(do not have any / still have some)* choice. They *(need not necessarily / must)* reduce their loans outstanding.

---

may or may not; do not have any; must

14. In a "tight-money" period, interest rates are generally going *(up / down)*. In such a period (pick the best alternative):

a. Borrowed money is hard to obtain because the total of loans granted is going down.

b. The total supply of borrowable money is small.

c. The total of loans granted may actually be increasing, but not so fast as the demand for such loans, so that to any borrower, money seems hard to obtain.

---

up; **c.**

15. a. The *discount rate* means the interest rate charged by the *(commercial banks / Federal Reserve)* for loans made to the *(public / commercial banks / Federal Reserve)*.

b. As indicated earlier, commercial banks can and do borrow from the Fed. But such borrowing is limited in amount and in scope. The Fed reserves the right to refuse the loan. And it will not permit a bank to maintain continuously part of its loans on the strength of reserves borrowed from the Fed. Such borrowing is intended primarily to tide the bank over a period of adjustment, since it cannot reduce its loans to customers overnight. Banks themselves are often reluctant to borrow from the Fed; there is a feeling among many banks that such borrowing is unwise or undesirable.

If banks did borrow continuously from the Fed as a means of obtaining reserves to increase their own loan total (which they do not), then an increase or decrease in the discount rate charged by the Fed could reasonably be expected *(to affect / not to affect)* the amount so borrowed. But since such borrowing is limited, a discount-rate change has little immediate effect. Such a change is really a kind of flag raised by the Fed to signal that it is continuing to move toward easier or tighter money and that its open-market operations will be conducted accordingly. Thus, an increase in the discount rate is most likely to indicate continued, or even increased, *(selling / buying)* of

bonds by the Fed in the open market; a decrease in the discount rate, greater *(selling / buying)* of bonds.

---

a. Federal Reserve; commercial banks **b.** to affect; selling; buying

16. In brief summary of earlier material, the money supply can change as business firms and families seek to borrow more or to borrow less. The Federal Reserve seeks to control this money supply (and interest rates), having as its goals the maintenance of a reasonably stable price level and avoidance of recession.

a. The text points out that the money supply can change also as a consequence of international reserve movements. The transactions here involved can be exceedingly complex. But the elements that need to be grasped for present purposes are simple.

The U.S. dollar has become something of an international currency. It is widely held by foreign central banks, financial institutions, and business firms. Any flow of these foreign-held dollars back to the United States may increase commercial bank reserves—and hence, the U.S. domestic money supply. An outflow of dollars (caused, say, by an excess of U.S. imports over U.S. exports) may have the reverse effect.

Consider how an inflow of foreign-held dollars increases U.S. commercial bank reserves. The effect is the same as if the Federal Reserve had conducted an open-market *(purchase / sale)* of securities. However, the Fed did not initiate this action. And (as the text points out) it can undertake offsetting action; i.e., it can sterilize the increase in reserves by means of an open-market *(purchase / sale)*.

b. To illustrate this matter of international reserve movements more fully, consider an altogether different example, one arising out of foreign trade. Suppose that Mercedes-Benz and Volkswagen have sold $100 million worth of their automobiles in the United States. These sales are not matched by U.S. sales abroad, so that the United States has imported $100 million more than she has exported.

The two German companies accordingly have $100 million in deposits in U.S. commercial banks. (For simplicity, assume that the entire sales amount accrues to them, disregarding the fact that some part would actually go to U.S.–owned automobile agencies.)

These companies, being German-based, want to convert their dollars into deutsche marks. So they sell their dollar accounts to the West German central bank, the Bundesbank, receiving the marks that they want in exchange.

The Bundesbank in turn sells these dollar accounts to the Federal Reserve. It doesn't matter here how the Fed makes payment to the Bundesbank; that is a matter of international settlements, a topic discussed later in the text. The point is that the Fed now owns the U.S. commercial-bank deposit accounts. In this respect, it is in exactly the same position as if it had conducted an open-market operation, *(buying / selling)* U.S. government securities. It has a claim on these banks.

If the Fed wishes, it can ask the banks to settle up. This will cause them to *(lose / gain)* reserves. In effect, the Fed would have conducted a *("tight-" / "easy-")* money operation. Of course, if the Fed considers that policy undesirable in the light of domestic conditions, it can keep the commercial-bank deposit accounts. Or it can conduct a countering *("tight-" / "easy-")* money operation.

---

a. purchase; sale **b.** selling; lose; "tight-"; "easy-"

17. Decisions about the direction of monetary policy are made by the Federal Open Market Committee. The FOMC has 12 members: the Federal Reserve chairman, six other members of the Board of Governors, and five presidents drawn from the regional Federal Reserve Banks.

The text points out that until around 1970, the FOMC's primary goal was (pick one):
(1) Maintaining an orderly bond market by trying to keep interest rates from moving up and down excessively.
(2) Control—short-term—over the money supply. That is, seeking to maintain a steady (but not excessive) growth in M from quarter to quarter.
(3) Control—longer-term—over the money supply. That is, paying somewhat less attention to short-term fluctuations in M, seeking instead to maintain a steady (but not excessive) long-term growth in M.

In the early 1970s, inflation first appeared as a serious problem, and the Fed ran into criticism. It was pointed out that the money supply had jumped up and down excessively (allegedly, at least in part, in consequence of the Fed's activity). Pressure from Congress forced the Fed into some revision of its objective. Which of the three alternatives above best indicates the primary goal then adopted? (1). (2). (3).

The Federal Reserve then ran into more difficulty. It was blamed (whether correctly or not) for having generated (or worsened) the 1973–1975 recession by tightening too much on the money supply and credit availability. Accordingly, there was some further reorientation of policy. Which of the three alternatives above best indicates it? (1). (2). (3).

---

(1); (2); (3)

Today, central banks everywhere seem to be acutely sensitive to the charge that they caused (or contributed significantly to) past inflation by excessive expansion of the money supply. Central bank presidents and monetary officials from around the world have responded to this sensitivity by becoming strongly inclined toward tight money. In 1980, the remarkably high levels of interest rates began to reflect this attitude. Blame for the subsequent worldwide recession of 1982 has been laid by many observers squarely on those interest rates. Although interest rates have fallen, in nominal terms, they still approximate historical highs in real terms; they con-

tinue to reflect a sensitivity to the potential of loose monetary policy to spark renewed inflation. It is especially revealing to note that most policy officials at the western economic summit conferences have called on the United States to lower its interest rates not by expanding the money supply, but by reducing the size of the federal deficit. But that is a story for another chapter.

18. The political independence of the Federal Reserve is an issue of enormous importance. As it stands now, the Fed belongs to the *(administrative / legislative / judicial / no single)* branch of government. It reports directly to *(Congress / the President)*, hears advice and criticism from *(Congress / the President / everyone)*, but makes up its own mind. The major movement in future years will probably be to open up the process to more public scrutiny, but a strong desire to preserve the ability of the Fed to resist contributing more to the political business cycle will probably preserve its independence.

---

no single; Congress; everyone

19. A second current issue of potentially extreme consequence is the effect of recent deregulation on the ability of the FED to control the money supply. Two significant acts of Congress in _____ and _____ greatly diminished the Fed's power. Nontransactions accounts were *(totally / partially)* deregulated so that, by 1986, there will be *(no / higher / lower)* interest rate ceilings and *(higher and substantial / lower and minimal)* reserve requirements applied to those accounts. These accounts include *(saving / checking / store-based credit)* accounts. Transactions accounts were *(totally / partially)* deregulated, as well, with interest-rate ceilings *(lapsing / being raised / being lowered)* by 1986, but with substantial reserve requirements remaining. The effects of these provisions are, as yet, still unknown.

In addition, deregulation has allowed a variety of institutions beyond the traditional sphere of the Federal Reserve System to offer banklike services. Because these institutions face *(large / small / no)* reserve requirements, the current ability of the Fed to control their contributions to "bank money" is *(high / small / zero)*. The one source of consolation is that all this is the product of legislation, and legislation can be changed if it is harmful.

1980; 1982; totally; no; lower and minimal; saving; partially; lapsing; no; zero

QUIZ: Multiple Choice

1. "Open-market operations" means specifically:
(1) the activity of commercial banks in lending to business firms and to consumers.
(2) the activity of the Federal Reserve in making loans to commercial banks.

(3) the effect on the level of interest rates caused by an increase or a decrease in the total of commercial bank loans.

(4) the total operations of the Federal Reserve designed to increase or to decrease the total of member-bank demand deposits.

(5) the activity of the Federal Reserve in buying or selling government securities.

2.   The principal assets on a Federal Reserve balance sheet are:

(1) gold certificates and cash, deposits by banks, and deposits by government.

(2) Federal Reserve notes, government securities, and loans.

(3) gold certificates and cash, bank deposits, and loans.

(4) gold certificates and cash, loans, and government securities.

(5) Federal Reserve notes, gold certificates and cash, and member-bank deposits.

3.   The text speaks of six steps in the process by which the Federal Reserve can affect the level of GNP. If the Fed seeks to increase GNP, one of the following is not among these steps, namely, to:

(1) increase investment spending so as to raise the level of total spending.

(2) increase interest rates to make lending more attractive to holders of cash.

(3) increase bank reserves so as to encourage the banks to increase their noncash assets.

(4) increase demand deposits.

(5) increase the availability of credit.

4.   Which among the following five combinations constitutes the tools of monetary policy used by the Federal Reserve in "day-to-day" or routine operations (i.e., excluding tools that might be employed in exceptional situations)?

(1) Discount-rate policy, control over stock-buying margin requirements, and moral suasion.

(2) Moral suasion and legal reserve-requirement changes.

(3) Open-market operations and discount-rate changes.

(4) Discount-rate policy and legal reserve-requirement changes.

(5) Open-market operations, legal reserve-requirement changes, and selective controls over consumer and mortgage credit.

5.   The total of Federal Reserve notes held by business and the public appears on the Federal Reserve balance sheet:

(1) as a liability, because these notes are IOUs of the Fed.

(2) as an asset, since these notes constitute part of the money supply; i.e., they are cash.

(3) as a liability, because they are part of reserves; i.e., they represent deposits made by commercial banks.

(4) within the capital accounts section, since this represents the money by means of which the Federal Reserve is financed.

(5) not at all—only notes not held by business or the public appear on this balance sheet.

6.   If the Federal Reserve System raises the discount rate, this act should be interpreted as part of a general policy intended, among other things, primarily to:

(1) reduce the total of commercial bank reserves.

(2) increase the amount saved out of income by the public.

(3) encourage increased borrowing from the Fed by commercial banks.

(4) increase the total of commercial bank reserves.

(5) do none of the preceding.

7.   Suppose the Federal Reserve System conducts a large-scale open-market purchase of government securities from the public. Which alternative in question 6 would be correct as the primary objective of this act?

(1).

(2).

(3).

(4).

(5).

8.   If a commercial bank deposits with the Federal Reserve a $20 Federal Reserve note, how will the Federal Reserve balance sheet will be affected?

(1) The asset discounts and loans will rise.

(2) The liability commercial bank demand deposits will fall.

(3) The asset U.S. government securities will rise.

(4) The liability Federal Reserve notes will rise.

(5) None of the preceding is correct.

9.   One reason why a reduction in the discount rate might have limited effectiveness as a tool of monetary policy is the fact that:

(1) the Fed, although it can increase the quantity of money held by the public, cannot force the public to spend that money, which is what is needed to increase GNP.

(2) the Fed no longer has the same statutory power it once had to change the discount rate.

(3) the Fed cannot control the quantity of discount borrowing, since banks borrow only in whatever amounts they choose.

(4) such a reduction is likely to be offset (have its effect canceled out) by an increase in member bank reserves.

(5) such a reduction is likely to drive down the prices of stocks and bonds.

10.   If the Federal Reserve sells a large quantity of U.S. government securities to the public, it would be reasonable to conclude that this action is intended to:

(1) increase the total of personal saving.

(2) decrease the total of loans made by commercial banks to their customers.

(3) increase the total of deposits of member banks with the Federal Reserve.

(4) decrease the general level of interest rates.

(5) increase the volume of Federal Reserve notes in circulation.

11.   If the Federal Reserve buys a large quantity of U.S. government securities from the public, then:

(1) the Federal Reserve liability in the form of bank reserve deposits will go up.

(2) the commercial bank liability demand deposits will go down.

(3) the total quantity of money held by the public will go down.

(4) the Federal Reserve asset discounts, loans, and acceptances will go up.

(5) the commercial bank asset loans and discounts will go down.

12. If the Federal Reserve wants to restrict the growth of the total money supply, its task is made more difficult if:

(1) it lacks legal power to reduce the reserve requirements of commercial banks.

(2) commercial banks are holding large excess reserves.

(3) the amount of personal saving out of income is very high.

(4) gold is being exported to other countries in large quantities.

(5) business firms and the public are anxious to buy more government bonds than they now hold.

13. The "discount rate," as this term is used in monetary-policy discussion, means:

(1) the degree of reduction in price required by the Federal Reserve when it purchases any government security.

(2) the degree of pressure exerted by the Federal Reserve upon commercial banks to reduce their loans to customers.

(3) the interest rate charged by the Federal Reserve on loans made to commercial banks.

(4) the extent to which the Federal Reserve is acting so as to increase the money supply and the level of GNP.

(5) none of the preceding.

14. A large-scale "easier-credit" operation conducted by the Federal Reserve through open-market operations will:

(1) raise the price of government securities.

(2) reduce the total of commercial bank reserves.

(3) lower the level of prices generally.

(4) lower the price of government securities.

(5) raise the legal reserve requirements imposed upon commercial banks.

15. If the Federal Reserve sells a large quantity of government securities in the open market, one of its purposes is normally to:

(1) make credit generally more easily available.

(2) discourage the public from buying government securities.

(3) increase the level of investment spending.

(4) decrease the discount rate.

(5) decrease the total quantity of money in circulation.

16. An increase in the discount rate will ordinarily:

(1) cause both stock and bond prices to rise in value.

(2) cause stock prices to rise but bond prices to fall in value.

(3) cause stock prices to fall but bond prices to rise in value.

(4) cause both stock and bond prices to fall in value.

(5) have none of these results.

17. The Federal Reserve System of the United States:

(1) is part of the judicial branch of government.

(2) is part of the administrative branch of government.

(3) is part of the legislative branch of government.

(4) is part of the regulative branch of government.

(5) none of the above.

18. The bank deregulation of the early 1980s has:

(1) reduced the ability of the Fed to control the money supply.

(2) begun a process to lift interest-rate ceilings from accounts in financial institutions.

(3) preserved the reserve requirement on transactions accounts.

(4) done nothing to undermine the legislative mandate to the Fed that it announce its policy objectives.

(5) all of the above.

CHAPTER 16
MONETARISM AND THE DEMAND FOR MONEY

Chapters 14 and 15 provided a detailed description of how banks and the Fed work to determine the money supply. It is now time to look to the other side of the money market to ponder the sources of the demand for money. Two underlying motives, demand for money to facilitate transactions and demand for money to round out a diversified financial portfolio, will be identified. Together with the supply of money, they will determine an equilibrium interest rate, a corresponding level of investment, a resulting level of aggregate demand, and finally, a supportable level of nominal GNP.

With that mechanism in place, a thorough discussion of monetarism will occupy the second part of the chapter. You will be introduced not only to the historical antecedents of modern monetarism (the crude quantity theory of money), but also to the power of its present incarnation. An Appendix will, in fact, bring you up to date with an exploration of the hypothesis of rational expectations. Even before you read the Appendix, though, you will be able to understand the crux of the recent monetarist—mainstream (or neo-Keynesian) policy debate by referring once more to the aggregate supply and demand geometry. The major tenets of modern monetarism can be represented there (in a way that you have already seen and which will now be reinforced) and contrasted with the current incarnation of mainstream thinking. The resulting policy differences will become clear in the process, as will the basis for the general conservative political view of monetarist economists. Finally, recent experience in the United States will be reviewed with an eye toward bringing the debate into practical, not overstated academic, focus.

Chapter 16 covers a lot of material, and understanding what it says is essential if you are to be able to apply what you have learned in the macro section of the text to events that you will see happening and that will be discussed in today's world. Your general learning objective here is, therefore, to develop sufficient feel for the various schools of thought to be able to sort through all their similarities and differences in practical as well as academic contexts. In addition, a long list of more specific learning objectives should be mastered.

LEARNING OBJECTIVES

1. Describe the three functions of money (medium of exchange, unit of account, and store of value) and explain how they are translated into a transactions demand for money and an assets demand for money.

2. Understand that the two motives for holding money generate an overall demand for money that increases when nominal GNP climbs and declines when nominal interest rates climb.

3. Describe the link between the supply of money and the interest rate in a supply-and-demand context that identifies the nominal interest rate as the price of currency.

4. Describe the resulting link between the supply of money and the level of nominal GNP that runs from the interest rate, through investment and aggregate demand, to the standard determination of GNP.

5. Explain again why a reduction in, say, the supply of money might cause nominal interest rates to climb in the short run but fall in the (very) long run.

6. Define the velocity of money and explain its role in (a) the classical (crude) quantity theory and (b) the modern monetarist view of macroeconomic policy. Critical here is the notion that velocity is either fixed or, at the very least, fairly stable; it is not, in either case, very sensitive to the interest rate.

7. Describe the reasoning behind the monetarist views that (a) the money supply is the major determinant of nominal GNP in the short run, (b) the money supply is the major determinant of prices in the long run, and (c) fiscal policy can do little but determine the mix in aggregate demand between public and private spending.

8. Relate why the monetarist view prescribes a targeted rate of growth of the money supply that should be maintained without regard for short-term economic performance, and why recent experience has suggested to some that the targeted growth in money be tied to a targeted rate of growth in GNP.

There has, throughout the macro chapters of the text, been an almost unstated differentiation between nominal and real variables. The distinction is always important, but it has not been emphasized—at least, not until now. Your work in Chapter 16 will be much easier if you take a great deal of care to see if the paragraph that you are reading is discussing real or nominal levels of interest rates, GNP, etc.

Money has three functions: (1) a medium of exchange, (2) a store of value, and (3) a unit of account. The first and the third functions are easily understood. As a medium of exchange, money is a device to avoid the inconvenience of barter. As a unit of account, money is simply a yardstick with which people measure how much things cost and how much things are worth. The second function, though, is a bit more complicated and deserves more than cursory mention.

In the early part of 1984, as Table 14-1 in the text indicates, the total money stock in the United States (the M_1 measure of coins, bills, and demand-deposit bank accounts) was over $520 billion. Each dollar of that stock had, and still has, an owner: an individual, a business, a financial institution. Why was this money being held?

At first this may seem a foolish question. Who wouldn't want to hold money? Despite inflation, you can buy things with it. Nevertheless, there are alternatives to holding money as an asset. If you hold any significant amount of money, you could buy a security with it. Most securities pay an interest or dividend return; money does not. If you reject the idea of buying any security, then you must have some reason for holding onto money instead. (If you buy the security, then you pass your money on to someone else—and the recipient must have some reason for wanting to hold it.)

What are the reasons, then, for holding money in preference to other assets that would yield some income return? Essentially, there are two. The first is simple. You need some money on hand because income does not arrive in a minute-by-minute flow. Instead, it comes at discontinuous intervals; wage or salary payments come each week, half-month, or month. Hence, people hold a cash balance which is gradually spent, until the next installment of income arrives.

The second reason is more complex, and its origins are varied. It is the desire to hold money as an asset, over and above the ordinary amount needed to tide you over until the next wage or salary payment reaches you. Why? Well, (1) you may want to keep some surplus cash against the possibility of some unexpected and cash-demanding emergency. Or, (2) having acquired your cash illegally, you may be shy about doing anything that would reveal you have it. Or, (3) you may be strongly convinced that security prices are going to fall so that the immediate purchase of any such security would be a bad idea.

1. The result of adding these two components together to compute the demand for money is significant. The first, the transactions demand for money, means that the demand for money will (*increase / be unaffected / decrease*) as income climbs. The more income that is available, the more people want to spend and the more money they will have to keep around to pay for those purchases. The second, the assets demand for money, emerges from portfolio theory to give the demand for money some (arguable, monetarists would say) sensitivity to the nominal interest rate. Why? Because the nominal interest rate is the price of holding wealth in money instead of in some interest-bearing asset. Thus, as the interest rate falls, the demand for money, through its assets demand component, should (*fall / remain the same / climb*).

In Figure 16-1, four panels show the quantity of money demanded changing from M to M'. Record in the spaces below which panel illustrates the indicated change in economic conditions.

a. an increase in nominal GNP that leaves interest rates fixed .... (_____)

b. an increase in the nominal rate of interest .... (_____)

c. a reduction in prices that is not yet reflected in nominal interest rates .... (_____)

d. a reduction in real interest rates that is not yet reflected in a change in aggregate demand .... (_____)

increase; climb **a.** a **b.** c **c.** d **d.** b

Figure 16-4 of the text is repeated here as Figure 16-2. It is especially important in understanding the link between changes in the money supply and changes in nominal GNP. It shows, in particular, that monetary policy can be expected to work as follows:

1. The quantity of money in an economy affects the nominal interest rate and thus the availability of credit. Specifically, the greater the quantity of money available, the lower the interest rate. This relationship is portrayed in panel (a) of Figure 16-2 by curve LL—the demand-for-money curve.

2. The interest rate influences investment spending in a similar fashion. The lower the interest rate, the more attractive is physical investment in, say, plant and equipment. This is one of the lessons of Chapter 7, and is portrayed in panel (b) of Figure 16-2 by $D_I D_I$—the demand-for-investment curve.

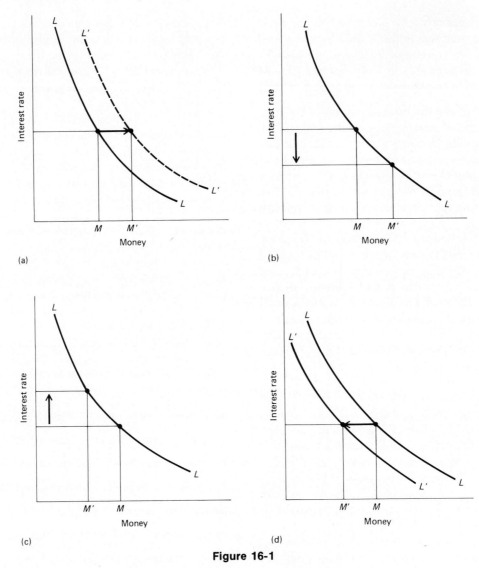

Figure 16-1

3.   The level of investment is one of the major determinants of GNP. The saving-investment equality that characterized equilibrium GNP in Chapter 8 is portrayed in panel (c) of Figure 16-2.

The effect of changing the money supply can now be illustrated in this simple framework. Should the money supply climb from S_AS_A to S_BS_B, the interest rate would fall from 8 percent to 4 percent, investment would climb from $100 to $200, and nominal GNP would climb from $3000 to $3300. This is a change in nominal GNP because the increase would be felt entirely in the price level if $3000 were equal to potential GNP.

2.   With the *LL* curve drawn as it is, this diagram says that if the interest rate were to go up, some people would decide that they ought to (*use some of their "idle" money to buy securities / sell some of their securities and hold money as an asset instead*).

Alternatively, if the interest rate goes down, then the total quantity of money which people will want to hold as an asset will (*increase / decrease*).

In sum, interest is the reward paid you for parting with money (parting with liquidity). If the interest rate falls, that reward is less, and the attractiveness of parting with money decreases; i.e., the demand to hold money becomes a stronger force.

---

use some of their "idle" money to buy securities; increase

3.   Figure 16-2 shows how the Federal Reserve will seek to push the economy out of a recession by raising the level of GNP.

We start, in terms of this diagram, at point *A*. The Fed now undertakes a large-scale open-market operation: It enters the securities market and buys government securities from the public—bidding up their price to the extent needed to persuade the public to sell them.

Suppose these open-market purchases have increased the total of the public's "asset money" from *A* to *B*. But *B*, in the text diagram, indicates a lower interest rate.

This interest-rate reduction comes about as follows: having more "asset money" than before, people begin to look for other interest- or dividend-yielding securities to replace those sold to the Fed; they look for corporation bonds and the like. When this

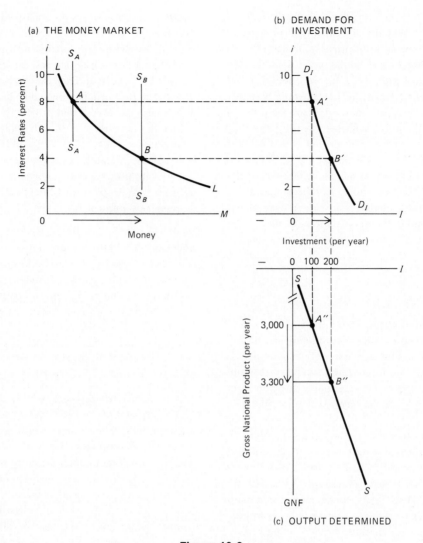

(a) THE MONEY MARKET

(b) DEMAND FOR INVESTMENT

(c) OUTPUT DETERMINED

Figure 16-2

money enters the market seeking securities (other than the government issues whose price the Fed has already bid up), its effect is to cause the prices of those other securities to go *(up / down)*. If the market price of securities goes up, then, for reasons already indicated in question 2, the market interest rate goes down.

So the sequence, in summary, is this: in an easy-money operation, the Fed enters the market to *(buy / sell)* government issues. This bids up their price, thus sending the effective interest rate on these issues *(up / down)*. The sellers of these issues look for other securities to buy with their newly acquired cash. This sends the prices of such securities *(up / down)* and their effective interest yield *(up / down)*. With *(lower / higher)* interest rates and easier credit conditions, borrowers with real investment projects in mind are *(discouraged / encouraged)* to undertake them.

---

up; buy; down; up; down; lower; encouraged

4. Look once again at the *LL* curve in text Figure 16-2. Suppose it were much steeper (closer to being vertical).

Such a steeper curve (as compared with the one drawn) would mean that any given change in interest rates—say, the reduction from 8 percent to 4 percent indicated—would produce a *(larger / smaller)* change in the "asset demand for money."

That is, starting from point *A*, but with a steeper *LL* curve than that shown, the Federal Reserve would have to pump a *(smaller / larger)* amount of extra money into the economy, to get the interest rate down from 8 to 4 percent.

Conversely, if the *LL* curve were flatter (closer to being horizontal) than shown, the Fed's task (for any desired reduction in interest rates) would be *(easier / more difficult)*.

If the *LL* curve were flatter, it would mean that asset holders were highly sensitive to interest-rate changes. Even a fairly modest reduction in interest rates would "turn them off" securities; they would want to sell securities in large quantities and to hold money instead.

Should the *LL* curve be very close to horizontal (i.e., highly elastic with respect to interest-rate changes), monetary policy may prove ineffective for we then have what some early Keynesians describe as "the depression model." In depression conditions, people are fearful of the risk which security holding involves; they dread the possibility of a calamitous price drop. (And when buyers are few, security prices quite naturally do drop.) In seeking to produce easier-money conditions, the Fed always must battle against preference for cash holdings. But this struggle is at its worst when the *LL* schedule is highly elastic. In such conditions, when the Fed raises the price of government securities, the public sells them readily. But they hold the cash proceeds as cash; they do not look for other securities to buy, because they are uneasy about the entire securities market. As a result, the extra money pumped into the economy does no good. The Fed wants to see this money move out of the hands of asset holders and into the hands of borrowers who will spend it. But in the depression model, the cash remains with the asset holders; it is idle, inactive money.

---

smaller; smaller; more difficult

5. All the preceding discussion of "asset demand for money" has dealt with the attitudes and behavior of lenders of money (the buyers of securities). That is, we have been considering people and financial institutions holding money saved out of income who would be interested in exchanging this money for securities (bonds or stocks) if the terms seemed sufficiently attractive.

Now we pass to the other side of the market—to the attitudes and behavior of sellers of securities. Some of these sellers may be people wanting to dispose of securities they bought earlier. Perhaps they want to sell because they need cash for some expenditure. Or perhaps their "asset demand for money" has risen because they think security prices are likely to fall.

The sellers also consist of business firms wanting to borrow money (to sell new IOUs) because they need financing for new investment projects, and this brings us to the demand for investment.

Any sensible firm contemplating a new investment project—say, the building of a new plant—must do its best to estimate (1) what it would cost to build that plant, and (2) what this plant would yield in the way of net income (income over and above operating costs), if built. Such estimates or forecasts, being clouded with uncertainty, are exceedingly difficult. But an intelligent decision requires the firm to make the best estimate it can.

This topic is discussed much later in the text. All you need know at this stage is that such an estimate can be summed up in the form of an interest rate. The firm must be able to say: We think the cost of building and establishing this projected new plant would be approximately X dollars. By a conservative estimate of the net income it would bring in, if and when built, the plant would yield us, say, 15 percent on the X dollars that would be tied up in it.

If money can be borrowed at 12 percent, and if the firm has been conservative in its cost and revenue estimates, then the plant *(would / would not)* be worth building. Even after pay-

ing the interest charges on borrowed money, there would be income left over. If money can be borrowed only at 20 percent, that plant *(still would / would not)* be worth building.

Suppose the market interest rate has been 20 percent. The plant will not be built. Then the market rate drops to 12 percent. It will now be worth borrowing the money to build this plant. It is a "marginal" investment project, worth building only if and when the market interest rate falls significantly below 15 percent.

Similarly, it can be expected that there will be other new investment projects to be tackled if—but only if—the market interest rate drops from 12 percent to 10 percent, or from 8 percent to 6 percent.

In sum, if the market interest rate decreases, some investment projects hitherto considered "extra-marginal" (just outside the boundary of profitable undertakings) will become *(more / less)* attractive to business firms, since their financing will have become *(cheaper / more expensive)*. Conversely, if the market rate rises, some planned investment projects will be *(undertaken / canceled)*.

---

would; would not; more; cheaper; canceled

6. In some few instances, supplying firms can make fairly close estimates of the likely "efficiency" of a proposed investment project. (For example, a power company can often make pretty good estimates of the likely increase in demand for electricity in its community over the next 10 years.) More commonly, there are so many uncertainties over future marketing conditions and the like that these "efficiency" estimates are very rough even at best. The firm will therefore include a big "safety factor" in its estimate before it goes ahead with an investment project.

Because precise estimates are difficult or impossible, some economists argue that the investment demand schedule will not show much responsiveness to any moderate change in interest rates. That is, a small change in the market rate will produce *(a very large / only a very small)* change in the total of investment spending.

Insofar as this is true, it would make the D_ID_I curve of Figure 16-2(b) very *(steep / flat)*. And it would make the Fed's task of altering the GNP level via changes in the money supply *(easier / more difficult)*.

---

only a very small; steep; more difficult

7. Part (c) of Figure 16-2 requires less attention, for it simply repeats material dealt with earlier in the text. It shows the relationship between investment and GNP: the higher investment spending is, the *(higher / lower)* will be GNP. Any rise or fall in investment spending will have a magnified effect upon GNP, by reason of the multiplier process outlined in Chapter 8.

---

higher

8. Figure 16-2 depends, in its final panel, on the Keynesian construction that determines GNP by the equality of saving and investment (in the absence of government spending and taxes). That dependence is not critical in excluding the Keynesian model to the modern mainstream construction. Figure 16-3 portrays the increase in investment that was depicted in panel (b) of Figure 16-2 as an increase in aggregate demand. In panel (a) of Figure 16-3, the story told by Figure 16-2 is repeated; the higher investment causes real GNP to climb because output was initially *(well below / almost equal to / far above)* potential GNP. In panel (b), though, the higher investment causes only nominal GNP to climb because *(real GNP / only prices)* climb. The key here, of course, is that GNP was initially *(far below / almost equal to / well above)* potential.

well below; only prices; almost equal to (actually, the same result would apply if GNP were initially well above potential, too)

9. The algebraic difference between the real interest rate and the nominal interest rate is the _____ . The demand for money depends on the *(nominal / real)* interest rate; the demand for investment depends upon the *(nominal / real)* interest rate. As a result, a reduction in the money supply can cause nominal interest rates to *(fall / climb)* in the long run even though they *(fall / climb)* in the short run. As the money supply contracts, in particular, the *(nominal / real / both)* interest rate(s) climb, causing investment to fall, aggregate demand to fall, and, eventually, price inflation to slow down. As a direct result of the slowdown in inflation, though, the *(nominal / real)* rate falls; it is supported by the slower growth in nominal GNP that causes the demand for money to shift *(to the right / nowhere / to the left)*. The problem with this scenario is, though, that *(it happens too fast for people to keep up / it happens too slowly to avoid the costs of high unemployment)*.

rate of inflation; nominal; real; fall; climb; both; nominal; to the left; it happens too slowly to avoid the costs of high unemployment

Modern monetarism, based on the evolution of the quantity theory of money among other things, has generated several propositions that impact directly upon policy. Monetarists believe, first of all, that the money supply is the major determinant of nominal GNP in the short run. They believe, moreover, that the money supply is also the major determinant of prices in the long run. Finally, they support maximum reliance on the market. These propositions lead them to espouse (1) the advisability of fixed policy rules for the sake of predictability, (2) the advisability of minimum intervention into the marketplace, and (3) the absolute futility of price and wage control programs.

10. In the space provided, record the quantity exchange equation.

According to the crude quantity theory, velocity and real GNP are assumed to *(vary proportionately / be fixed / be wildly variable)*. The result is, according to the crude theory, that any change in the money supply will be immediately reflected in *(prices / output / investment)*. While this is a reasonable explanation of *(recession / hyperinflation / hyperventilation)*, it is not very satisfactory in a world where the velocity of money has been *(climbing / falling)* for the past three decades.

$MV = PQ$ (i.e., the money supply multiplied by the velocity of money always equals nominal GNP); be fixed; prices; hyperinflation; climbing

11. The problems with the crude theory aside, modern monetarists use a fairly stable velocity and the quantity theory of money to make their points. Rough stability in V is all that they need.

Their first proposition is that the money supply determines nominal GNP in the short run. If V is fixed in the short run, then any change in the money supply will, by application of the

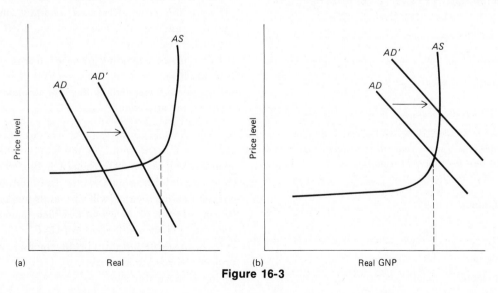
Figure 16-3

quantity equation, be *(proportionately / progressively)* reflected in *(nominal / real)* GNP.

Their second proposition is that the money supply determines prices in the long run. This follows from the quantity theory and their *(conservative political views / belief in the market responsiveness of wages and prices / belief in the proportional variation of velocity)*. In particular, market clearing sets real GNP at its *(potential / nominal level / second best optimum)* so that the quantity equation has, in effect, *(1 / 2 / 3)* constants, namely: _____

_____ .

Any change in the money supply is therefore translated directly into changes in prices.

As an aside, the quantity theory of modern monetarism still precludes the effectiveness of fiscal policy to move GNP around. There is, quite simply, no place in the quantity equation for either government spending or taxes to appear. The only role for fiscal policy is to determine the mix of spending between the public and private sectors.

proportionately; nominal; belief in the market responsiveness of wages and prices; potential; 2; potential real GNP and velocity

12. Belief in the quantity theory of money, based on the belief in a fairly stable velocity of money in the short run, depends on a belief in the lack of sensitivity of either the demand for money or the demand for investment to changes in the interest rate. Therein lies the rub of at least part of the current debate in academic circles. On a more practical level, the recent rise of the monetarist philosophy has led mainstream theorists (neo-Keynesians) to four conclusions. Record them, as listed in the text, below.

a. _____

_____

b. _____

_____

c. _____

_____

d. _____

_____

a. Money does matter   b. Money is not the only thing that matters   c. They were too optimistic about fine-tuning the economy, but they can "gross"-tune the economy   d. They were too cavalier about inflation

QUIZ: Multiple Choice

1. Money serves:
(1) as a medium of exchange.
(2) as a store of value.
(3) as a unit of exchange.
(4) all of the above.
(5) none of the above.

2. On the basis of the transactions demand component of the demand for money:
(1) the demand for money climbs as the nominal interest rate climbs.
(2) the demand for money climbs as the nominal interest rate falls.
(3) the demand for money falls as nominal income rises.
(4) the demand for money falls as nominal income falls.
(5) none of the above.

3. Which answer to question 2 would have been correct if it had referred to the assets demand component of the demand for money?
(1).
(2).
(3).
(4).
(5).

4. The demand curve for investment:
(1) parallels the demand curve for money in that high interest rates reduce demand.
(2) most precisely plots the real rate of interest against quantity demanded.
(3) is negatively sloped because high real interest rates cause marginal investment projects to be rejected.
(4) is a vital link between changes in the money supply and nominal GNP.
(5) all of the above.

5. A reduction in interest rates engineered by the Federal Reserve can reasonably be expected to:
(1) encourage investment (*I*) spending because it makes lending of money more attractive.
(2) discourage *I* spending because it makes borrowing of money less attractive.
(3) have little or no effect on *I* spending, since that is not its purpose—interest-rate changes are intended to alter security prices, not *I* spending.
(4) discourage *I* spending because it makes lending of money less attractive.
(5) encourage *I* spending because it makes borrowing of money more attractive.

6. The demand-for-investment schedule means:
(1) a schedule showing how the total volume of investment spending will change with changes in the interest rate.
(2) a schedule showing how the true rate of interest on an interest-bearing security will vary as its market price varies.
(3) an indicator of the extent to which changes in investment spending will change the level of GNP.
(4) an estimate of the rate of profit which any given investment project will yield to its owners.
(5) none of the above.

7. The "demand for money" means:
(1) the desire to hold securities which can readily be converted into money at a fixed or near-fixed price if necessary.
(2) the amount which businesses will wish to borrow at any given interest rate.
(3) the desire to save more money out of income as protection against the uncertainties of the future.
(4) the same thing as "asset demand for money."
(5) the same thing as the sum of "assets and transactions demand for money."

8. According to a monetarist, monetary policy and fiscal policy differ in what way?
(1) Monetary policy should be deliberately operated in the short run in an effort to keep GNP in the full-employment region, whereas fiscal policy cannot have anything but minor effects on the GNP level.
(2) Monetary policy deals with the amounts of money spent and collected by the government, whereas fiscal policy deals with interest rates.
(3) Monetary policy seeks to encourage or discourage investment (*I*) spending and consumption (*C*) spending by business firms and private citizens by influencing interest rates and credit availability, whereas fiscal policy operates directly upon the level of public spending through spending and taxation.
(4) Fiscal policy works principally through changes in the level of *I* spending, whereas monetary policy affects *I* spending little or not at all.
(5) There is no essential difference between them at all, since both objectives and techniques of operation are the same—they differ only in that they are administered by two different agencies.

9. Monetary policy is made somewhat less effective in restraining a period of excessive spending whenever:
(1) the "demand-for-investment" schedule is highly elastic.
(2) corporations rely heavily upon internal financing for their investment projects.
(3) the money demand schedule is highly inelastic.
(4) changes in interest rates tend to bring with them changes in the market value of securities.
(5) investment spending responds more to changes in credit availability than to changes in interest rates.

10. In terms of the "saving-investment" diagram used extensively in Chapters 7 and 8 of the text, the introduction of a tight-money policy by the Federal Reserve would be intended to:
(1) lower both the investment (*I*) and savings (*S*) schedules, hence lower GNP.
(2) raise the *I* schedule, hence lower GNP.
(3) raise the *I* schedule, hence raise GNP.
(4) lower the *S* schedule, hence raise GNP.
(5) lower the *I* schedule, hence lower GNP.

11. If the Federal Reserve conducts a large-scale easy-money open-market operation:

(1) government security prices will rise and interest rates will fall.
(2) interest rates will fall, but government security prices need not be affected.
(3) both government security prices and interest rates will fall.
(4) government security prices will fall and interest rates will rise.
(5) interest rates will rise, but government security prices may or may not change.

12. The Federal Reserve should slow down or halt a tight-money policy:
(1) as soon as interest rates have reached a sufficiently low level.
(2) when investment spending has been sufficiently increased.
(3) whenever the equilibrium level of GNP has been reached.
(4) when prices begin to rise sharply.
(5) in none of these situations.

13. The effectiveness of monetary policy in a recession will be reduced or destroyed if:
(1) interest rates cannot be forced down much because the level of borrowing is highly responsive to small changes in the level of the interest rate.
(2) the Fed finds that security prices start to go up as soon as it begins its easy-money operation.
(3) interest rates cannot be forced down much because money holders prefer to retain money rather than buy securities at any lower rate.
(4) the "asset demand" or "liquidity demand" for money is very low.
(5) the value of the "multiplier" is very high.

14. The effectiveness of monetary policy in a recession will be reduced or destroyed if:
(1) the public is principally interested in holding securities rather than money as assets.
(2) the Federal Reserve does not wish the prices of government securities to fall below their maturity value.
(3) the Federal Reserve is determined to maintain an easy-money rather than a tight-money policy.
(4) the current level of interest rates is very high.
(5) potential borrowers do not respond to reductions in the interest rate or to greater availability of credit.

15. If the Federal Reserve conducts a large-scale open-market sale of government securities, then we would expect:
(1) the demand for investment to decrease.
(2) the federal government's budget to move into surplus or at least into balance.
(3) the total quantity of money in circulation to increase.
(4) liquidity preference to decrease.
(5) none of the preceding to occur.

16. When fiscal policy and monetary policy are being operated in concert in order to combat a recession, we are likely to observe the combination of a:
(1) budget deficit and open-market security purchases.

(2) budget surplus and open-market security purchases.

(3) budget deficit and open-market security sales.

(4) budget surplus and open-market security sales.

(5) balanced budget and open-market security sales.

17.   A government bond is marketable; i.e., its owner may sell it freely in the bond market. The holder of this bond gets $70 per year in interest; the government will also pay back the principal amount of $1000 5 years from now. An increase in demand for these bonds engineered by the Federal Reserve drives up their price in the bond market to $1050. To a person who has paid this price, the "yield" (effective interest rate earned) is:

(1) zero.

(2) less than 7 percent but not zero.

(3) 7 percent.

(4) more than 7 percent but less than 10 percent.

(5) 10 percent or more.

18.   What will be the impact, if any, of the bond price change described in question 17 on new bonds being offered for sale by the federal government and by corporations?

(1) Both new government and new corporation bonds must be offered for sale at a somewhat higher interest rate.

(2) New government bonds can be offered for sale at a lower interest rate, but new corporation bonds must be offered at a higher rate.

(3) Both new government and new corporation bonds can be offered for sale at a somewhat lower interest rate.

(4) New government bonds can be offered for sale at a somewhat lower interest rate, but new corporation bonds will not be affected at all.

(5) There is no reason why the sale of either new government or new corporation bonds should be affected at all.

19.   Because the difference between real and nominal interest rates is the rate of inflation:

(1) nominal rates can fall, in the long run, in response to tight monetary policy.

(2) nominal rates must rise, in both the short and the long runs, in response to tight monetary policy.

(3) there is no difference between the demand for money and the demand for investment.

(4) the quantity theory of money is unquestionably true.

(5) none of the above.

20.   The crude quantity theory of money:

(1) assumed that both V and nominal GNP were fixed.

(2) assumed that both V and real GNP were fixed.

(3) assumed that only V was fixed.

(4) assumed that V and the price level were fixed.

(5) none of the above.

21.   Monetarists believe:

(1) the money supply determines nominal GNP in the short run.

(2) the money supply determines prices in the long run.

(3) fiscal policy is essentially ineffective.

(4) market forces will maintain potential GNP in the long run.

(5) all of the above.

22.   The lessons of the past decade or so include which of the following?

(1) Strict adherence to money-supply growth targets can cause substantial unemployment.

(2) The Keynesian view is entirely wrong.

(3) There is nothing to the monetarist view of the world that should be accepted in constructing policy.

(4) Money matters, but so does fiscal policy.

(5) Answers 1 and 4.

APPENDIX:
The Rational-Expectations Revolution

The mainstream neo-Keynesian policies that called upon governments to manipulate aggregate demand to smooth out business cycles were moderately successful in countries like the United States, Japan, and West Germany from 1950 through the early 1970s. Starting in 1973, though, a combination of outside shocks and "stop and go" policy adjustments worked to accelerate what was until then a gradual worsening of the Phillips curve trade-off between unemployment and inflation into a condition known as "stagflation." The latter half of the 1970s and the early 1980s were, in fact, marked by unacceptably high levels of both inflation and unemployment that were lowered only at the cost of a severe recession. Throughout this painful period, the natural-rate theories of Milton Friedman and Edmund Phelps that were so bitterly resisted in the 1960s gradually worked themselves into the mainstream of economic thought. They appeared, in fact, in the form of a vertical long-run Phillips curve and the resulting cycle pattern of unemployment and inflation noted in Chapter 16.

This acceptance does not, however, mean the end of debate. Monetarists and mainstream theorists still debate the effectiveness of fiscal policy. Beyond the mainstream, though, there is a new school of thought that debates the effectiveness of any policy. The "rational-expectations macroeconomics" of people like Lucas, Barro, Sargent, and Wallace question the ability of even monetary policy to affect a short-run change in GNP. These economists conclude, in fact, that the short-run Phillips curve is just as vertical as the long-run Phillips curve and that it is just misperception and confusion that makes it look otherwise. This Appendix is devoted to a brief overview of the roots of their conclusion.

Having completed your work on this Appendix, therefore, you will have accomplished the following objectives.

LEARNING OBJECTIVES

1. Understand the two fundamental assumptions of the rational-expectations macroeconomics: (*a*) people's expectations are efficiently and rationally formed and (*b*) prices and wages are extremely flexible.

2. Relate the reasoning that leads from the assumptions listed in objective 1 to the conclusion that predictable policy cannot move the unemployment rate from its natural level even in the short run.

3. Relate the criticisms leveled against the rational-expectations macroeconomics, and the responses to the criticisms of its proponents.

The rational-expectations theory holds that people make the best use of their limited information and their understanding of economic theory to undo any policy adjustment that the government might attempt. It follows that policy cannot fool anyone. If, for example, the government were to lower taxes in an attempt to increase aggregate demand, people would see that their taxes would have to increase later to pay for the current reduction. They would therefore save their tax savings in anticipation of that future increase in tax liability so that increased consumption would not provide the desired increase in aggregate demand.

The second assumption of the rational-expectations school is familiar; it presumes that wages and prices are sufficiently flexible to clear all markets in response to any outside shock. Prices and wages are, therefore, always in equilibrium (or at the very least, moving rapidly toward equilibrium).

1. It follows from the second assumption that most unemployment that is observed during a recession is *(voluntary / involuntary)*. Consider the supply and demand curves representing a labor market in Figure 16A-1; SS represents the supply curve and DD represents an initial demand curve. The initial

equilibrium wage is $ _____ with _____ people voluntarily unemployed; i.e., they *(are / are not)* willing to work for the going wage because *(it is too small / they cannot find a job)*. If the demand curve were to fall to *D'D'*, the rational-expectations theory would predict *(an immediate / a slow and tortured)* decline in the wage to $ _____ with _____ people in voluntary unemployment and _____ in involuntary un-

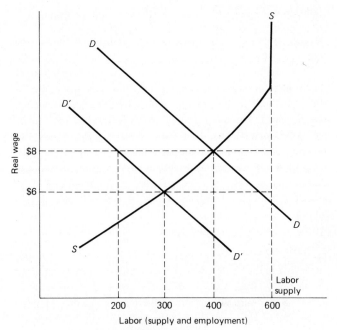

Figure 16A-1

employment. If the wage did not fall, though, _____ would be employed and _____ would be out of work—_____ voluntarily and _____ involuntarily.

---

voluntary; 8; 600 − 400 = 200; are not; it is too small; an immediate; 6; 300; 0; 200; 400; 200; 200

---

2. The proponents of rational-expectations macroeconomics hold that the observed slope in the short-run Phillips curve is the result of confusion and misperception. Consult Figure 16A-2.

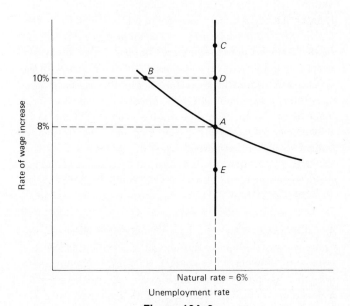

Figure 16A-2

Beginning at point *A*, wage inflation would be running at

_____ percent with unemployment holding at the natural rate of 6 percent.

Suppose, now, that government policy were initiated to try to stimulate employment and to move the economy along the short-run Phillips curve to a point like *B*. Rational-expectations theory states that unemployed workers would *(have to be offered higher real wage increases / have to be tricked into thinking that higher nominal wage increases were higher real wage increases)* to accomplish that move. Only if labor thought that the *(nominal / real)* wage were rising would they be attracted to work (remember, the 6 percent natural rate includes a significant number of voluntarily unemployed workers) so that the unemployment rate would fall. The

_____ percent wage increase noted at point *B* would, according to the theory, be exhausted by price inflation so that the real wage increase would be *(the expected positive increment / zero / actually negative)* and those who were voluntarily unemployed at point *A* would again leave the labor force. As a result, the economy would have moved to point *(C / D / E)* instead of *B*. Even in the short run, because labor would not have been so fooled in the first place, the policy stimulus would have been vented entirely in price and wage inflation and not in the intended reduction in the rate of unemployment. Notice that it *(does / does not)* matter whether or not the stimulus were the result of a change in monetary policy or a change in fiscal policy; the result *(would / would not)* be the same in either case—a short-run Phillips curve that is *(vertical / horizontal)* in the region directly above the *(current rate / natural rate)* of unemployment.

8; have to be tricked; real; 10; zero; *D*; does not; would; vertical; natural rate

---

3. If employment policy can (a) always be immediately undone and (b) can create bad things like inflation, then it follows that discretionary changes in policy *(should nonetheless be allowed because they are currently expected / should be discontinued because they are only harmful)*. The money supply should increase at a *(targeted / variable)* rate with the clear understanding that the velocity of money will *(be fixed / vary to preserve potential GNP)*. Fiscal policy should meanwhile be conducted according to a fixed rule that dictates *(the relative share of public and private spending / that the federal budget should be balanced)*.

should be discontinued; targeted; vary to preserve potential GNP; either of these (both, in fact, have been proposed)

---

4. Mainstream economists have attacked both of the assumptions that form the basis of the rational-expectations macroeconomics. In reviewing these countercriticisms, it is important to note that the policy conclusions derived from the rational-expectations theory depend upon both assumptions. If, for example, people form rational expectations about the future but markets do not clear immediately, then policy can still make a dent in the short run. There can, in particular, still exist involuntary unemployment that *(can / cannot)* be reduced by stimulus. If the 6 percent initial level of unemployment noted in Figure 16A-2 were *(above / below)* the natural rate, for example, then the stimulus might have achieved a reduction in the rate of unemployment. Inflation would have *(increased / decreased)*, to be sure, but the short-run Phillips curve *(would / would not)* have some slope to exploit.

On the other hand, disallowing the formation of rational expectations on the part of labor would, even in the presence of rapidly clearing markets, make the misperception story of the rational-expectations theorists right on target. Since that *(is / is not)* their explanation for the observed slope to the short-run Phillips curve, their conclusions about a vertical Phillips curve would not hold.

Prolonged periods of high unemployment do damage to *(both assumptions / only the expectations assumption / only the flexibility assumption / neither assumption)*, but they are "explained" to some degree by the practitioners of rational expectations in terms of (a) artificial impediments to market clearing and (b) confusing "stop and go" policies by the federal government.

can; above; increased; would; is; both assumptions

QUIZ: Multiple Choice

1. The basic assumptions of the rational-expectations macroeconomics include:
(1) a presumption that people form their expectations about the future efficiently and rationally.
(2) a presumption that prices are extremely flexible in both directions.
(3) a presumption that wages are extremely flexible in both directions.
(4) all of the above.
(5) choices 1 and 3 only.

2. It follows from the assumptions that:
(1) most unemployment is voluntary.
(2) monetary policy can work in the short run and not the long run.
(3) fiscal policy can affect the long term but not the short term because of delays in Congress.
(4) any policy might work depending upon the circumstance.
(5) none of the above.

3. It follows from the assumptions that a reduction in taxes to stimulate consumption:
(1) would work as advertised.
(2) would not work unless accompanied by accommodating monetary policy.

(3) would not work because people would save their tax break in anticipation of future higher taxes.

(4) might work unless there were substantial leakages into foreign markets.

(5) none of the above.

4. According to the rational-expectations macroeconomics, the short-run Phillips curve is:

(1) horizontal.

(2) positively sloped.

(3) vertical.

(4) negatively sloped.

(5) sloped in either direction depending upon conditions.

5. The observed slope in the short-run Phillips curve is explained by the rational-expectations macroeconomics in terms of:

(1) cost of living contracts.

(2) confusion and misperception.

(3) the effects of monetary policy only.

(4) the vagaries of the uncertain international market.

(5) all of the above.

6. Should an economy attempt to move up its short-run Phillips curve to reduce unemployment below the natural rate, the rational-expectations macroeconomist would expect that:

(1) people would not be fooled and only inflation would result.

(2) people would gradually find out that real wages had not climbed and turn the curve vertical in the long run.

(3) the economy would be successful in the short term, but successful in the long term only if there were substantial economic growth.

(4) the natural rate would indeed fall as potential output grew.

(5) none of the above.

7. The policy prescription of the rational-expectations macroeconomics includes:

(1) a notion that monetary policy rules should be constructed and followed no matter what.

(2) a notion that discretionary policy should be avoided at all cost.

(3) a notion that no policy adjustment would be required to help an economy over an oil crisis like the one that occurred in 1973.

(4) a notion that fiscal policy should determine the mix of public and private spending once and for all and then let it alone.

(5) all of the above.

8. The existence of periods of prolonged unemployment in our history does damage to:

(1) the expectations assumption only.

(2) the flexibility assumption only.

(3) both assumptions of the rational-expectations theory.

(4) either assumption depending upon conditions.

(5) neither assumption in any circumstance.

9. Without the flexibility assumption:

(1) periods of unemployment could exist.

(2) the short-run Phillips curve would have some slope.

(3) policy could be used to exploit the short-run tradeoff.

(4) the expectations hypothesis would be damaged but not necessarily destroyed.

(5) all of the above.

CHAPTER 17

THE FISCAL-MONETARY MIX AND GOVERNMENT DEFICITS

You have nearly completed your introduction to macro-economics. You have seen how the business cycle can produce periods of high inflation and low unemployment, periods of high unemployment and low inflation, and periods during which both inflation and unemployment are high or low. You have seen how monetary policy and fiscal policy can be used to combat these macroeconomic ills, and you have seen that there is a difference of opinion about the likely success of these policies in achieving their objectives. It is now time to look at fiscal and monetary policy together and to ponder their appropriate mix. The first part of this chapter will explore that question.

It is also time for you to confront one of the most controversial political and economic issues of our time: what to do about the federal deficit and the resulting federal debt. Are deficits recession or policy induced? Do their dimensions depend upon the fiscal-monetary policy mix? Are there burdens associated with deficits that should cause us to avoid them at all cost? These and other questions are the topics of the second part of Chapter 17.

Having completed your work in this chapter, therefore, you will have achieved the culmination of your study of macroeconomics. In addition to "putting it all together" in an exploration of these general questions about policy interaction and the federal debt, you will have accomplished the following objectives.

LEARNING OBJECTIVES

1. Differentiate between the old (classical) and modern views of the federal debt.

2. Differentiate between the structural, active component of the federal deficit (surplus) and the cyclical, passive component of the federal deficit (surplus).

3. Apply the distinction noted in objective 2 to differentiate between demand-management and policy-mix decisions within the structure of any one year's deficit, and apply this third distinction to hypothetical and realistic policy problems.

4. Understand that a policy mix that directs monetary policy to fight inflation and fiscal policy to control unemployment is likely to produce a low-investment, high-consumption, and high-deficit economy. Conversely, explain why a mix that directs monetary policy at employment objectives and fiscal policy at inflation objectives is likely to produce the opposite result: a high-investment, low-consumption, and budget-surplus economy.

5. Explain what is meant by crowding out and why it is a problem only with the structure component of the deficit. Show why monetarists worry about complete crowding out even in the short run, while others expect no crowding out during recessions and 100 percent crowding out only over the long run.

6. Provide a brief chronicle of the federal debt of the United States, with particular note to its recent unprecedented peacetime growth. Explain why predictions of large surpluses by 1985 turned into actual deficits of historic proportions.

7. Explain the errors involved in the myths about the debt that (a) people cannot run deficits forever so governments cannot either and (b) private debt is growing without concern so there is no reason to worry about public debt.

8. Explain the sources of true concern over the burden of the debt, particularly the possibility of capital displacement.

The old public finance policies were based on the belief that the federal budget should always balance, that debt of any size imposes a burden on future generations, and that public finance and private finance are one and the same. Modern public finance has turned each of these conclusions into a question. Budgets do not seem to balance, so why not? Does the policy mix have anything to do with it? What is the true burden of the debt? How is public finance different from private finance? Chapter 17 explores each of these questions in turn.

1. Two distinct components of the federal deficit were identified in the text. The first, the _____ deficit, involved active or discretionary changes in fiscal policy; the second, the _____ deficit, was passive and changed automatically with the business cycle. Automatic stabilizers built into our country's progressive tax structure and social infrastructure can thus contribute to the _____ deficit. For example, every point of unemployment above the natural rate that lasts a full year causes the deficit to *(increase / decrease)* by $*(25 / 35 / 45)* billion because tax revenues *(fall / rise)* and expenditures *(fall / rise)*. Because these cyclical changes happen automatically to help to ward off recession or slow inflation, it is essential to look at the _____ deficit when you are trying to tell whether discretionary fiscal policy is stimulative or contractionary.

In the spaces provided, record whether or not the indicated policy would affect the structural deficit (S), the cyclical deficit (C), or neither (N).

a. A reduction in tax rates of 25 percent .... (_____)

b. An increase in unemployment compensation during recession .... (_____)

c. An increase in defense spending of $50 billion .... (_____)

d. A reduction in social security tax rates ...... (_____)

e. An expansion of the money supply .... (_____)

f. An expansion in tax receipts during an economic upswing .... (_____)

g. A reduction in funding for Head Start and other welfare programs .... (_____)

structural; cyclical; cyclical; increase; 35; fall; rise; structural; **a.** *S* **b.** *C* **c.** *S* **d.** *S* **e.** *N* **f.** *C* **g.** *S*

2. In the spaces provided in the following table, indicate the likely short-term effects on the structural and cyclical deficits of the indicated changes in economic condition. Denote a reduction with a (−), an increase with a (+), and no change with a (0). Differentiate only on the basis of the active or passive character of an indicated policy change and on the basis of the short-run effect of a non-policy change.

Change in Condition or Policy	Structural Deficit	Cyclical Deficit
A A permanent tax cut	(_____)	(_____)
B A sharp increase in private investment	(_____)	(_____)
C Tighter monetary policy	(_____)	(_____)
D A corn blight	(_____)	(_____)
E An increase in welfare payments	(_____)	(_____)
F An increase in tax evasion	(_____)	(_____)

(reading across rows) A: +;− (or 0, depending upon the stimulus of the cut)   B: 0;− C: 0; +   D: 0; +   E: +;− (or 0, depending upon the stimulus of the spending)   F: +; + (because lower tax revenues increase both)

3. From 1979 through 1982, the actual deficit *(fell / rose)* in response to *(active fiscal policy / passive fiscal policy)*. The result was actually a(n) *(increase / reduction)* in the *(structural / cyclical)* deficit that signaled *(more stimulative / no change in the degree of stimulus applied by / less stimulative)* fiscal policy.

In 1982, though, the supply-side tax cuts and the massive defense buildup of the Reagan administration came on line. The result was fiscal *(stimulus / contraction)* reflected by a dramatic increase in the *(structural / cyclical)* deficit. In fact, from 1983 through early 1985, the cyclical deficit *(fell / rose)* while the structural deficit *(fell / rose)*.

Referring now to Table 17-1 in the text, a projected $138 billion surplus for 1985 turned into an actual $_____ billion deficit because of economic and technical changes, amounting to $_____ billion, and policy changes, amounting to $_____ billion. Note, in particular, that higher interest payments contributed $_____ billion to the economic component of the projection error. Why? Because the federal government turns over its entire debt about every 3 or 4 years so that large increases in current interest rates can have large effects on the cyclical deficit.

rose; passive fiscal policy; increase; cyclical; no change; stimulus; structural; fell; rose; 195; 221; 112; 65

4. Suppose, in the face of "secular stagnation," that the President wanted to stimulate recovery without adjusting monetary policy. You would, as adviser to the President, recommend a policy that would *(increase / decrease)* government spending and/or *(increase / decrease)* federal taxes. The immediate result of your recommendation would be a(n) *(reduction / increase)* in the size of the *(structural / cyclical)* deficit. If your policies were implemented and worked to stimulate recovery, the ultimate result would be a(n) *(reduction / increase)* in the *(structural / cyclical)* deficit. To bring the actual deficit down, though, you would have to also recommend *(the eventual cancellation of the active policy / no further change)*.

Facing the opposite problem, of course, you would recommend the opposite policies. If you were free to suggest changes in monetary policy to support the stimulus package that you proposed above, though, you would recommend *(a reduction / an increase)* in the money supply, probably instituted by *(an open-market operation / a reduction in the reserve requirement / an increase in the discount rate)*. The desired result would be a(n) *(increase / decrease)* in investment because of *(higher / lower)* interest rates and perhaps induced investment (crowding in).

---

increase; decrease; increase; structural; reduction; cyclical; the eventual cancellation of the active policy; an increase; an open-market operation; increase; lower

5.   The Reagan Program for Economic Recovery instituted in January of 1981 called for (*a*) substantial cuts in personal taxes, (*b*) substantial cuts in business taxes, (*c*) substantial increases in defense spending, and (*d*) moderate cuts in social spending. President Reagan also asked the Fed to pursue fairly tight monetary policy. The ultimate result was *(stimulative / contractionary)* fiscal policy reflected halfway through his first term in an increase in the *(cyclical / structural)* deficit but lower investment caused by high interest rates. Some contend that the recession of 1982 was caused in large part by the high interest rates.

The Carter administration tried to stimulate investment in the late 1970s by (*a*) increasing taxes, (*b*) maintaining government spending, and (*c*) encouraging expansionary monetary policy. The idea was to *(increase / reduce)* the structural deficit and thereby *(increase / decrease)* public saving, lower interest rates, and promote investment. Monetary policy turned out to be too tight, though, and investment did not climb. Combined with the oil shock of the Iran-Iraq war, a recession developed because the change in the *(structural / cyclical)* deficit actually signaled a move toward more *(contractionary / expansionary)* fiscal policy.

---

stimulative; structural; reduce; increase; structural; contractionary

6.   Actual experience in the United States, as illustrated in the preceding examples, has tended to target monetary policy at *(inflation / unemployment)* and fiscal policy at *(inflation / unemployment)*. Each successive recession has, therefore, produced employment-targeted spending and tax programs that have increased the structural deficit in ways that *(have seldom been / have generally been)* erased during the subsequent recovery. As a result, the actual deficit has been *(growing / falling)* over time, and monetary policy has had to become increasingly *(more / less)* contractionary. The overall trend in interest rates has thus been *(up / down)*, and the federal debt has been growing *(faster / slower)* than GNP. We have had, in short, a *(high- / low-)* investment, *(high- / low-)*

spending, *(high- / low-)* deficit experience over the past several decades.

One way to turn that around would be to target monetary policy at *(inflation / unemployment)* and fiscal policy at *(inflation / unemployment)*. Running structural surpluses over time would keep *(inflation / unemployment)* down, and quick adjustments in monetary policy could be left to deal with the business cycle. The cyclical component of the deficit would, of course, continue to help through the operation of its built-in stabilizers.

---

inflation; unemployment; have seldom been; growing; more; up; faster; low-; high-; high-; unemployment; inflation; inflation

7.   The basic mechanism behind the concern that government spending "crowds out" private investment is as follows. An increase in government spending initially causes GNP to *(rise / fall)*. As a result, the transactions demand for money *(rises / falls)* so that interest rates must *(rise / fall)* to engineer the change in the asset demand for money required to cancel the change in transactions demand. And because interest rates respond, investment must decline. The problem is particularly acute in the monetarist view of the world in which GNP does not increase with *G* because government spending replaces investment spending dollar for dollar. The economy is, by assumption, at its potential, and further increases in GNP are impossible. An increase in aggregate demand caused by an increase in government spending must, therefore, be matched by an equal reduction in investment.

The evidence on crowding out is mixed. The expansionary fiscal policy of the early 1960s did not cause any substantial crowding out, but that was not really a fair test. Why? Because during the 1960s, *(the natural rate of unemployment was lower / the Fed accommodated fiscal policy to keep interest rates constant / the Keynesian model was widely accepted)*. Recent evidence suggests that *(25 percent / 50 percent / 75 percent)* of the stimulative effects of increases in government spending are canceled in the short term, and that *(75 percent / 90 percent / 100 percent)* of the effects may disappear in the long term. That is because the long-run aggregate supply curve is *(horizontal / vertical)* over potential GNP.

Even in the long term, though, crowding out appears to be a problem associated only with the *(cyclical / structural)* deficit. There is reason to believe that an increase in government spending caused by automatic stabilizers during a recession might actually increase investment. How? If the spending does in fact promote recovery, then GNP will begin to rise, and *(higher / lower)* investment might be induced by the prospect of a more vigorous economy. By the time the potential for crowding out appears (i.e., by the time the economy approaches its level of potential GNP), the cyclical spending will have *(disappeared / accelerated)* and there will be *(nothing / even more spending)* to do the crowding.

---

rise; rises; rise; the Fed accommodated; 50 percent; 100 percent; vertical; structural; higher; disappeared; nothing

8. Indicate which of the following arguments for or against large deficit spending are valid (*V*) and which are invalid (*I*).

a. I can't run a deficit forever, so why can the government?

.... (_____)

b. The debt is internally held, so there is no problem ......

.... (_____)

c. There are efficiency losses associated with the taxes required to pay the interest .... (_____)

d. Private debt is high, too, and that is not a source of concern

.... (_____)

e. There is a significant likelihood that large deficits displace capital from private borrowers to public ones .. (_____)

f. If interest payments grow faster than GNP, then increasingly large proportions of GNP will have to be taxed away to pay for the debt service .... (_____)

---

a. *I* **b.** *I* **c.** *V* **d.** *I* **e.** *V* **f.** *V*

9. The basic trend over the past few years has been for the size of the debt measured as a proportion of nominal GNP to (*rise / fall*). More alarmingly, the proportion of GNP required to pay the interest on the debt has (*risen / fallen*), as well. To see why this is so alarming, consider the following exercise (problem 7 in the text).

Let the ratio of government debt to GNP be fixed and denote the rate of growth of nominal GNP and the nominal rate of interest by *g* and *i*, respectively. Starting in 1984, then, GNP produced *t* years into the future will be

$$(1 + g)^t$$

times larger than it was in 1984. With no further deficit spending, the federal debt will grow at a rate *i* over the foreseeable future because borrowing will have to proceed to pay for the interest due each year. The debt will, therefore, be

$$(1 + i)^t$$

times larger *t* years into the future than it was in 1984. The ratio of the debt to nominal GNP will therefore change at a rate given by the ratio of these two rates of change; i.e., it will change by $[(1 + i)/(1 + g)]$ each year, and it will be

$$\left[\left(\frac{1 + i}{1 + g}\right)\right]^t$$

times bigger or smaller *t* years into the future. Now, if *i* is bigger than *g*, as it has been recently, then this fraction climbs to infinity as *t* gets larger. It passes through 1, therefore, the point at which all of the year's GNP would have to go to paying off the interest on the debt.

---

rise; risen

QUIZ: Multiple Choice

1. Structural deficits:
(1) vary in size with changes in discretionary fiscal policy.
(2) vary in size with the sensitivity of the tax revenues to upswings in the economy.
(3) vary in size depending upon the latitude of welfare entitlement programs during economic downturns.
(4) are reflections of the degree of stimulus embodied in monetary policy.
(5) none of the above.

2. Cyclical deficits:
(1) are the products of discretionary fiscal policy.
(2) are the appropriate reflection of the stimulative character of fiscal policy.
(3) are dependent in part on the automatic stabilizers built into the macroeconomy.
(4) are never considered until strict monetary control raises the specter of crowding out.
(5) none of the above.

3. A $50 billion increase in defense spending is an example of:
(1) monetary policy directed at reducing inflation.
(2) fiscal policy directed at reducing inflation.
(3) fiscal policy that would contribute directly to increasing the structural deficit.
(4) fiscal policy that would contribute directly to increasing the cyclical deficit.
(5) none of the above.

4. Which answer to question 3 would have been correct if it had asked about an increase in tax revenues caused by a growing economy and a progressive income tax?
(1).
(2).
(3).
(4).
(5).

5. Which answer to question 3 would have been correct if it had asked about an open-market operation that purchased bonds?
(1).
(2).
(3).
(4).
(5).

6. Deficits in the early 1980s were enormous, in part, because the Reagan administration:
(1) pursued expansionary fiscal policy with high structural deficits.
(2) received the tight monetary policy that it wanted.
(3) suffered a recession that enlarged the cyclical deficit.
(4) all of the above.
(5) none of the above.

7. In the face of a stagnant economy, a government should:
(1) spend more, tax less, and pursue a contractionary monetary policy.
(2) spend less, tax less, and pursue an expansionary monetary policy.
(3) spend more, tax less, and pursue an expansionary monetary policy.
(4) tax more, spend less, and pursue an expansionary monetary policy.
(5) do nothing and rely on the ability of the economy to rapidly return to potential GNP that was apparent in the 1983 recovery.

8. Which of the following characterizes the Carter policy to stimulate investment that was tried in the late 1970s?
(1) Faster monetary growth, spending growth, and lower taxes.
(2) Lower spending, slower monetary growth, and lower taxes.
(3) Faster money growth, stable spending, and higher taxes.
(4) Faster money growth, lower spending, and lower taxes.
(5) None of the above.

9. A policy mix that targets monetary policy at inflation and fiscal policy at unemployment seems to produce high-consumption, low-investment, high-deficit economies because:
(1) monetary policy is ineffectual against inflation.
(2) fiscal stimulus during recession is never turned off so monetary policy must become increasingly contractionary over time.
(3) Congress never writes fiscal policy fast enough to avoid a recession.
(4) fiscal policy is ineffective in stimulating an economy past its potential GNP.
(5) none of the above.

10. Examples of the "ratcheting" of fiscal stimulus that is never fully repealed include:
(1) the temporary tax surcharge of 1968 following the 1962– ^64 tax cuts.
   the tax increases of 1983 that followed the supply-side cuts 1981–1983.
(3) the continuation of foreign-trade job benefits in 1984 well .fter the recovery of the automobile industry.
(4) the continuation of the investment tax credits through 1984 even after they did not stimulate investment.
(5) all of the above.

11. The linkage between government spending that could lead to the crowding out of private investment is best outlined by a causal connection from spending growth to:
(1) output growth to an increase in the assets demand for money to higher interest rates to lower investment.
(2) output contraction to an increase in the transactions demand for money to a lower assets demand for money to lower interest rates to higher investment.
(3) output growth to an increase in the transactions demand for

money to a lower assets demand for money because of higher interest rates that cause lower investment.
(4) output growth to higher investment with higher transactions and assets demand for money.
(5) none of the above.

12. Monetarists believe that the vertical aggregate supply schedule mandates that, for every dollar increase in government spending, private investment will fall:
(1) 50 cents.
(2) 75 cents.
(3) 90 cents.
(4) $1.
(5) none of the above.

13. Which answer to question 12 would have been correct if it had referred to the mainstream view of crowding out in the short run?
(1).
(2).
(3).
(4).
(5).

14. Which answer to question 12 would have been correct if it had referred to the mainstream view of crowding out in the long run?
(1).
(2).
(3).
(4).
(5).

15. Which of the following is a valid reason to be concerned about the size of the federal debt?
(1) It has been growing, recently, as a proportion of GNP.
(2) It has been growing, recently, so that interest payments are growing faster than GNP.
(3) High deficits may displace capital by distorting the financial markets.
(4) The taxes required to pay the interest are inefficient, as are most taxes.
(5) All of the above.

16. If federal budgets in the future were all balanced except for borrowing needed to pay the interest on the current debt and if GNP were growing at a rate that was smaller than the rate of interest, then:
(1) the interest payments required to keep the debt afloat would eventually grow larger than GNP, itself.
(2) the debt would remain at a constant proportion of GNP.
(3) the debt would gradually decline to a negligible fraction of GNP.
(4) the debt would remain at substantial levels, but fall as a fraction of GNP.
(5) none of the above.

APPENDIX:
Advanced Treatment of Monetary and Fiscal Policy

The classical view of the macroeconomic world was based upon a firm belief in Say's Law. Say's Law was, in turn, a result that depended in its demonstration upon a strong analogy between a barter economy and monetary economy so that workers would always be around to buy whatever was produced. Why? Because that analogy would support the notion that prices and wages would always adjust immediately to any disequilibrium so that the income that the workers earned would just exhaust the output of the economy. Overproduction would be impossible, therefore, and so would underproduction. There would, in the modeling presented in this text, then be a vertical aggregate supply curve directly over potential GNP. And classical economists would write at the height of the Great Depression that whatever involuntary unemployment happened to exist was the result of "frictional resistance" to market forces.

Modern macroeconomic theory has come a long way since that characterization of 25 percent unemployment was advanced, of course, and you have been introduced to much of that progress in the preceding 10 chapters. Now that you have worked through that material, however, you are capable of at least a passing knowledge of a more succinct analytical framework within which the workings of today's mainstream macroeconomic theory can be explored. This Appendix presents the skeleton of this framework with an eye toward not only its construction, but also its application to the policy debates that you have studied. Having worked through this Appendix, therefore, you will have accomplished the following objectives.

LEARNING OBJECTIVES

1. Understand how an *IS* schedule can be constructed to indicate combinations of real GNP and real interest rates that support equilibrium in the goods market (i.e., the equality of aggregate supply and aggregate demand).

2. Understand how an *LM* schedule can be constructed to indicate combinations of real GNP and real interest rates that support equilibrium in the money market (i.e., the equality of the quantity of money supplied and the quantity of money demanded).

3. Explain why intersections of *IS* and *LM* schedules indicate macroeconomic equilibria.

4. Understand how the monetarist and mainstream models are reflected in the shapes of the *IS* and *LM* schedules.

5. Describe precisely how changes in fiscal policy move the *IS* curve around, how changes in monetary policy move the *LM* curve around, and how *IS-LM* analysis can therefore be used to investigate the likely effects of certain policies or combinations of policies.

1. A simple statement of Say's Law is that "_____

_____ creates its own _____." If that were the case, then GNP would always converge quickly to (*actual / potential / real*) GNP and unemployment would correspondingly converge to its (*natural / actual / potential*) rate. The inflation rate, meanwhile, (*could proceed at any moderate rate / would have to fall to zero / would be expected to accelerate into hyperinflation if not controlled*).

---

supply; demand; potential; natural; could proceed at any moderate rate

---

2. Consult Figure 17A-1 to construct an *IS* curve from the familiar geometry of aggregate supply and demand. Panel (a) of Figure 17A-1 shows one aggregate supply curve *AS* and three aggregate demand curves AD_1, AD_2, and AD_3. Each successively higher demand curve corresponds to higher investment and thus (*higher / lower*) aggregate demand at every price; it is higher investment that must be caused by (*higher / lower*) interest rates. Judging from the rates identified along the vertical axis of panel (b), r_1 must therefore be associated with (AD_1 / AD_2 / AD_3) and thus an equilibrium level of real GNP given by (Q_1 / Q_2 / Q_3). Similarly r_2 must be associated with (Q_1 / Q_2 / Q_3) and r_3 must be associated with (Q_1 / Q_2 / Q_3). Connect these points in panel (b) and observe an *IS* curve with its usual (*negative / vertical / horizontal / positive*) slope.

---

higher; lower; AD_1; Q_1; Q_2; Q_3; negative [passing through points (Q_1, r_1), (Q_2, r_2), and (Q_3, r_3)]

---

3. Figure 17A-2 will accomplish a similar construction of an *LM* curve from the familiar confines of supply and demand in the money market. Panel (a) of Figure 17A-2 shows one money supply curve denoted *MS* and three money demand curves denoted MD_1, MD_2, and MD_3. Each successively higher demand curve corresponds to successively (*higher / lower*) levels of GNP so that (*higher / lower*) transactions demand for money can be canceled by (*higher / lower*) assets demand— lower assets demand caused by (*higher / lower*) equilibrium real interest rates. Given the three levels of GNP denoted on the horizontal axes of panel (b), MD_1 must correspond to (Q_1 / Q_2 / Q_3) and (r_1 / r_2 / r_3), MD_2 must correspond to (Q_1 / Q_2 / Q_3) and (r_1 / r_2 / r_3), and MD_3 must correspond to (Q_1 / Q_2 / Q_3) and (r_1 / r_2 / r_3). Plot these combinations on panel (b), connect

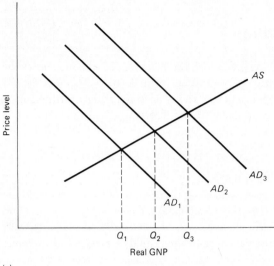

(a)

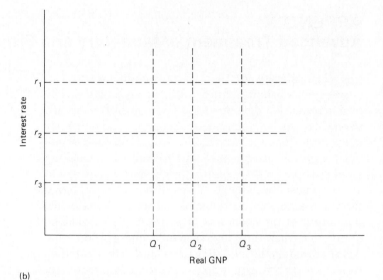

(b)

Figure 17A-1

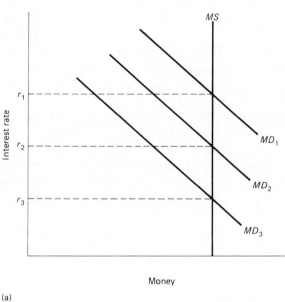

(a)

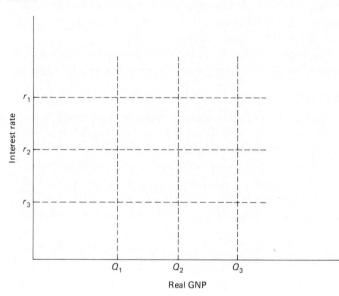

(b)

Figure 17A-2

them, and observe an *LM* curve with the usual (*vertical / negative / horizontal / positive*) slope.

---

higher; higher; lower; higher; Q_3; r_1; Q_2; r_2; Q_1; r_3; positive [passing through points (Q_1, r_3), (Q_2, r_2), and (Q_3, r_1)]

4. Now consider an economy initially in equilibrium at $r°$ and $Q°$ as shown in Figure 17A-3. In the spaces provided in the following table, indicate whether the specified policy change(s) would cause the *IS* curve or the *LM* curve or both to move. Record your answers by signifying an upward shift in either curve by (+), a downward shift in either by (−), and no shift at all by (0). Also indicate with the same notation the direction of the resulting movement in the equilibrium levels of real interest rates and GNP. Use (?) to denote an ambiguous effect when policies collide and cancel each other.

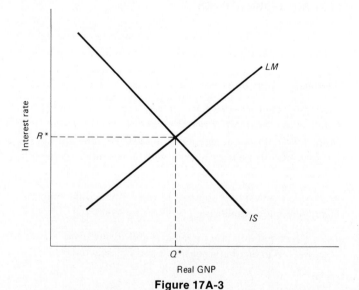

Figure 17A-3

Policy Change	Effect on IS Curve	Effect on LM Curve	Effect on r*	Effect on Q*
A An increase in government spending	_____	_____	_____	_____
B An increase in the money supply	_____	_____	_____	_____
C A reduction in the money supply	_____	_____	_____	_____
D A reduction in federal taxes	_____	_____	_____	_____
E An open-market operation that buys bonds plus a tax cut	_____	_____	_____	_____
F A reduction in the money supply and an increase in government spending	_____	_____	_____	_____

(reading across the rows) A: (+); (0); (+); (+)   B: (0); (+); (−); (+)   C: (0); (−); (+); (−)   D: (+); (0); (+); (+)   E: (+); (+); (?); (+)   F: (+); (−); (+); (?)

5. The monetarist view of the world postulates a *(vertical / horizontal) LM* curve. That assumption is based on the quantity theory of money in which the demand for money is *(infinitely sensitive / totally insensitive)* to changes in the interest rate; i.e., potential GNP is associated with *(any / only one)* price level and *(any / only one)* interest rate.

In the table below, redo the exercise of question 4 under the monetarist assumption. Be sure to note any changes in the predicted changes in GNP and interest rates that are the result of that assumption.

Policy Change	Effect on IS Curve	Effect on LM Curve	Effect on r*	Effect on Q*
A An increase in government spending	_____	_____	_____	_____
B An increase in the money supply	_____	_____	_____	_____
C A reduction in the money supply	_____	_____	_____	_____
D A reduction in federal taxes	_____	_____	_____	_____

Policy Change	Effect on IS Curve	Effect on LM Curve	Effect on r*	Effect on Q*
E An open-market operation that buys bonds plus a tax cut	_____	_____	_____	_____
F A reduction in the money supply and an increase in government spending	_____	_____	_____	_____

vertical; totally insensitive; any; any; (reading across rows) A: (+); (0); (+); (0)   B: (0); (+); (−); (+)   C: (0); (−); (+); (−)   D: (+); (0); (+); (0)   E: (+); (+); (?); (+)   F: (+); (−); (+); (?)

6. Crowding out is the circumstance in which government spending, whether for investment or not, replaces private investment in aggregate demand. Why? Because higher aggregate demand can cause interest rates to *(fall / climb)* and thus cause investment to fall. This effect is complete along the *(vertical / horizontal) LM* curve of the monetarists; interest rates climb so far that equilibrium GNP is maintained at potential GNP.

If the *LM* curve were *(horizontal / vertical)*, to assume the opposite Keynesian extreme, then there would *(still be some / be no / still be substantial)* crowding out because interest rates *(would / would not)* climb with the stimulated aggregate demand. Thus, one more distinction between the Keynesians and the monetarists: the _____ worry about crowding out, and the _____ do not. (Actually, mainstream theorists do too, to a lesser degree—unless deficits climb to unacceptably high levels.)

climb; vertical; horizontal; be no; would not; monetarists; Keynesians

QUIZ: Multiple Choice

1. Say's Law:
(1) formed the foundation of classical macroeconomics.
(2) stated that supply creates its own demand.
(3) depended upon an analogy between a monetary economy and a barter economy for its proof.
(4) is no longer part of the mainstream of modern macroeconomic thought.
(5) all the above.

2. The *IS* curve used to analyze macroeconomic policy:
(1) is derived from the workings of the money market.
(2) is derived from the workings of the aggregate goods market.
(3) is positively sloped because of the direct correlation between interest rates and GNP.

(4) is negatively sloped because of the inverse relationship between transactions and assets demands for money.
(5) none of the above.

3. The *LM* curve used to analyze macroeconomic policy:
(1) is derived from the workings of the money market.
(2) works with the representation of the goods market to illustrate macroeconomic equilibrium.
(3) is positively sloped because of the negative correlation between transactions and assets demand for money.
(4) all of the above.
(5) none of the above.

4. An increase in the money supply would cause:
(1) the *LM* curve to shift in.
(2) the *LM* curve to shift out.
(3) the *IS* curve to shift in.
(4) the *IS* curve to shift out.
(5) any of the above depending upon the circumstance.

5. Which answer to question 4 would have been correct if it had referred to a sale of bonds by the Fed in an open-market operation?
(1).
(2).
(3).
(4).
(5).

6. Which answer to question 4 would have been correct if it had referred to a reduction in the federal income tax?
(1).
(2).
(3).
(4).
(5).

7. Which answer to question 4 would have been correct if it had referred to a reduction in the discount rate charged by the Fed to borrowing banks?
(1).
(2).
(3).
(4).
(5).

8. Suppose that there were a sudden increase in the tax rates built into the federal income tax. You should expect, based on *IS* and *LM* curves with some appropriate slope, that:
(1) GNP and interest rates would both climb.
(2) GNP and interest rates would both fall.
(3) interest rates would climb, but the effect on GNP would be ambiguous.
(4) GNP would climb and interest rates would fall.
(5) GNP would fall but the effect on interest rates would be ambiguous.

9. Which answer to question 8 would have been correct if it had referred to a purchase of bonds by the Fed in an open-market operation?
(1).
(2).
(3).
(4).
(5).

10. Which answer to question 8 would have been correct if it had referred to a simultaneous contraction of the money supply and expansion of government spending?
(1).
(2).
(3).
(4).
(5).

11. In the monetarist model:
(1) the *IS* curve is horizontal.
(2) the *LM* curve is horizontal.
(3) the *IS* curve is vertical.
(4) the *LM* curve is vertical.
(5) answers 3 and 4.

12. If you were to analyze an increase in government spending from a monetarist perspective, you would expect the result to be:
(1) an increase in both interest rates and GNP.
(2) an increase in GNP and a reduction in interest rates.
(3) an increase in interest rates and no change in GNP.
(4) an increase in interest rates and an ambiguous effect on GNP.
(5) an ambiguous effect on interest rates and an increase in prices.

13. If you were a monetarist and you noted that an increase in government spending accompanied by an increase in the money supply produced a higher level of GNP, then you would conclude that:
(1) the fiscal policy did not really work; the result was due to the effect of the increase in the money supply.
(2) both policies worked to reinforce each other.
(3) the monetary policy helped bring down the inflation that would have been the result of the fiscal policy.
(4) crowding out was not a problem and the monetary policy was unnecessary.
(5) none of the above.

14. If you were a mainstream theorist and observed the happenings of question 13, which answer would have been correct?
(1).
(2).
(3).
(4).
(5).

PART FOUR

MICROECONOMICS:
Supply, Demand, and
Product Markets

CHAPTER 18

OUTPUT AND PRICE AS DETERMINED BY SUPPLY AND DEMAND

Before you concentrate on the new material presented here, you should make certain that you are in firm command of the material presented in Chapter 4. The foundation upon which most of microeconomics is built is laid in that final chapter of the introductory section. By referring to the learning objectives identified there, you should be able to determine the baggage that will be required to travel further. Paraphrasing them slightly, these objectives included:

1. An understanding of what demand schedules and supply schedules are (and are not), and how they can be used to conceptualize market equilibrium
2. An understanding of why demand is generally downward-sloping and why supply is usually upward-sloping
3. An understanding of what economic factors are and are not assumed to be held fixed in the construction of both schedules
4. An understanding of how changes in these factors alter one schedule or the other and thus equilibrium
5. An understanding of what types of markets can and cannot be represented by supply-and-demand modeling
6. An understanding of how markets that are out of equilibrium for some reason automatically tend toward equilibrium

Should any of these notions appear foreign to you, you should return to Chapter 4 for some review work.

The study of microeconomics is the study of relative prices. Why are cars so expensive? Why is sand so cheap? Why is gasoline now so expensive when it used to be so cheap? Why do doctors earn so much money? Why are some athletes paid even more? Are there really 150 taxes buried in the price of a suit (as one presidential candidate claimed in 1980)? And so on. The answers to these questions will be found in pitting individual tastes against the scarcity of resources. They are interesting to econo-

mists in their own right, but they also contribute to our understanding of macroeconomics, our understanding of the distribution of income, our understanding of the sources of judgmental tradeoffs between, for example, equity and efficiency, and much more. These understandings are the goals of our study of microeconomics.

Chapter 18 begins that study by covering two major topics: (1) the effects of changes in supply and demand and (2) the price elasticities of supply and demand. Applications of both are presented through a set of examples ranging from simple supply shocks to the equity-efficiency tradeoff in designing a tax structure. When you have completed this chapter, you should have mastered the following new objectives.

LEARNING OBJECTIVES

1. Describe the measure used to indicate the responsiveness of buyers to a change in the market price of any commodity. In quantitative or numerical terms, be able to calculate this responsiveness.

2. Relate market price to consumer purchasing patterns.

3. Relate market price to the behavior of sellers.

4. Explain how Alfred Marshall's notions of "momentary," "short-run," and "long-run" equilibrium relate to the responsiveness of suppliers to a price change.

5. Name the two categories which the text uses to distinguish between changes among any of the factors which may affect buyers in their decisions to purchase any given good (e.g., a change in price of that good, a change in the price of some competing or substitute good, and a change in buyer incomes or tastes). Explain the difference between these two categories in terms of the demand curve and its position on a graph.

6. Name the two categories which correspondingly apply to sellers and the quantity they wish to supply. Explain the difference between these two categories in terms of the supply curve and its position on a graph.

7. State a factor that may cause a price not to reach the equilibrium level described in this chapter.

8. Enumerate a variety of applications of supply-and-demand analysis.

The first major topic in this chapter is one that was introduced in Chapter 4: changes in demand or supply. To review the underlying idea in terms of demand: price is one important factor influencing the quantity of good X that will be bought, but it is by no means the only influencing factor. Others include the level of consumer incomes, consumer tastes or preferences for X, and the prices at which goods competing with X are selling.

The demand curve for X does not ignore these other factors; it assumes them held constant. If any other such factor changes, then the demand curve must be redrawn in an appropriate new position. If consumer incomes rise, for example, it is likely that the demand curve for X will shift to the right (or upward), as in Figure 18-1. This is just a particular way of saying that if consumers have more spendable income, they will want to buy more of X, at every price, than they did previously. (For a review of such shifts in demand—and supply—curves, see particularly Chapter 4, questions 9–11, Study Guide pages 40–42.)

In the Figure 18-1 case, the equilibrium quantity bought and sold rises from 0A to 0B; and the price goes up.

Now here is a point you must watch carefully. In Figure 18-2, alongside Figure 18-1, there has also been a change in the equilibrium position. Purchases have again risen from 0A to 0B—but price has fallen, not risen. This change was initiated by a shift of the supply curve.

▶Figure 18-1 illustrates an "increase in demand"—a shift of the entire demand curve to a new position.

▶Figure 18-2 illustrates an "increase in quantity demanded"—a movement along a demand curve from one point thereon to another. The position of the demand curve does not change.

Thus the phrases *increase in demand* and *increase in quantity demanded* have significantly different meanings. An "increase in demand" (Figure 18-1) occurs when some factor other than the price of good X changes, causing buyers to change their decisions; the entire demand curve shifts. An "increase in quantity demanded" (Figure 18-2) occurs when more of X is bought because its price fell. (Price fell because some background factor caused the supply curve to shift in position.)

1. a. A "change in quantity demanded" means precisely (pick one):

(1) A shift in the schedule of quantities that producers will offer for sale at each and any possible price, due to some change in background conditions such as an increase in production costs.
(2) A shift in the particular quantity which producers offer for sale, due to a change in market price.
(3) A shift in the particular quantity which consumers buy, due to a change in market price.
(4) A shift in the schedule of quantities that consumers will buy at each and any possible market price, due to some change in background conditions such as a change in tastes or consumer incomes.

b. Which alternative properly describes a "change in supply"? . . . . (1 / 2 / 3 / 4)

c. Which alternative properly describes a "change in demand"? . . . . (1 / 2 / 3 / 4)

d. Which alternative properly describes a "change in quantity supplied"? . . . . (1 / 2 / 3 / 4)

a. (3) **b.** (1) **c.** (4) **d.** (2)

2. a. As already noted, Figure 18-1 illustrates "an increase in demand." This figure also illustrates an ("increase in supply" / "increase in quantity supplied").

Barring the exceptional case of a perfectly flat supply curve, this increase in demand will (always / sometimes / never) set off a price increase.

Notice that the "increase in quantity supplied" in Figure 18-1 does not bring about any price reduction. It is just the supplier response to a higher price. All we can say is that insofar as there is some slope to the supply curve (i.e., insofar as a higher price elicits a larger supply quantity), it makes the price increase set off by the increase in demand less than it would otherwise have been.

Thus an "increase in quantity supplied" will (always / sometimes / never) result in a price reduction.

b. In contrast, Figure 18-2 depicts an "increase in quantity demanded." This increase came about only because of an ("increase in supply" / "increase in quantity supplied"). Such

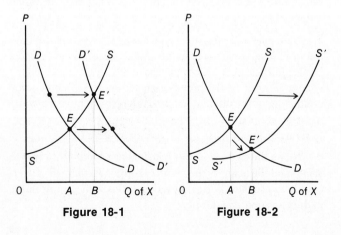

Figure 18-1   **Figure 18-2**

an increase in quantity demanded *(will always / might / would never)* be the reason for a price increase. It is simply the buyer response to a lower price.

This difference in the effect upon price in large part explains why all the tedious distinction between the two kinds of "increases" and "decreases" is necessary.

c. An example framed in terms of quantity reduction can cement this distinction. Suppose for the sake of illustration that the production of good X is disrupted by lengthy strikes. The supply quantity available is much reduced, and price rises in consequence. This would be an instance of *(a decrease / an increase)* in *(quantity supplied / supply)*, followed by *(a decrease / an increase)* in *(quantity demanded / demand)*. The price rise was set off by the decrease in *(demand / supply)*, and not by the decrease in quantity *(demanded / supplied)*.

a. "increase in quantity supplied"; always; never   **b.** "increase in supply"; would never   **c.** a decrease; supply; a decrease; quantity demanded; supply; demanded

The concept of *elasticity* was devised to indicate the degree to which quantity demanded (or supplied) would respond to any price change. Compare the two demand curves D_1 and D_2 drawn to the same scale in Figure 18-3 to reflect two potential demand curves for the same good X. Both curves satisfy the ordinary "law of demand," that any price reduction should produce an increase in the quantity demanded and purchased. D_2 is the more elastic of the two, though, because the quantity demanded is more responsive to any change in price. If the price were to fall from p_a to p_b, for example, the quantity demanded would grow by a larger amount along the D_2 curve; if the price were to rise from p_a to p_c, on the other hand, the quantity would shrink further along D_2.

3.   a. If we say that "demand in this situation is highly elastic with respect to price," we mean that any price reduction would produce a *(large / small)* *(decrease / increase)* in purchases, and that a price rise would yield a *(large / small)* *(decrease / increase)* in buying.

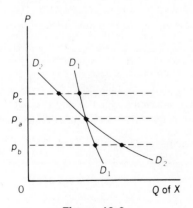

Figure 18-3

b. Although the elasticity idea is more commonly used concerning demand, it can be used also as to the responsiveness of supply. To describe supply as "decidedly inelastic with respect to price" would mean that any price increase would call out a *(large / small)* *(increase / decrease)* in quantity offered for sale, and that any price reduction would produce a *(large / small)* *(increase / decrease)*.

a. large increase; large decrease   **b.** small increase; small decrease

Terms like "highly elastic" or "decidedly inelastic" are imprecise. The task now is to give a more exact meaning to elasticity. The text defines the (price) elasticity of demand as

$$E_D = \frac{\% \text{ change in quantity demanded}}{\% \text{ change in price}}$$

The sign of this expression is assumed to be positive by convention. Given this numerical expression, three different possibilities emerge:

$E_D > 1$ representing elastic demand

$E_D = 1$ representing unitary elasticity

$E_D < 1$ representing inelastic demand

The importance of the distinction between these three cases will become increasingly clear as the text proceeds. The reader's first introduction to this importance comes in the linkage between demand elasticity and the sensitivity of revenue to changes in the price. If the price of some good were to increase by 10 percent, revenue generated by its sale could go up, remain the same, or go down depending upon the elasticity. To see why, take each case one at a time:

1.   If demand were elastic, then the 10 percent increase in the price would have to be associated with a reduction in the quantity demanded of more than 10 percent to get a number greater than 1 out of the elasticity formula. That would mean that quantity would be falling faster than price was rising, and revenue would fall *(recall that revenue is simply price times quantity)*.

2.   If demand displayed unitary elasticity, then the 10 percent increase in the price would be matched by a 10 percent reduction in the quantity demanded to get 1 out of the elasticity formula. That would mean that revenue would remain exactly the same.

3.   If demand were inelastic, then the 10 percent increase in the price would have to be associated with a reduction in the quantity demanded of less than 10 percent to get a number less than 1 out of the elasticity formula. That would mean that revenue would actually rise with the price.

The text also defines the elasticity of supply in a like manner:

$$E_s = \frac{\% \text{ change in quantity supplied}}{\% \text{ change in price}}$$

No adjustment in sign is required, in this case, because increases in prices are always matched with increases in quantities supplied along the usual upward-sloping supply curve. The same subsequent differentiation between elastic, unitary, and inelastic supply is made, as well, but the demand-side connection to revenue is not valid.

The next set of questions will explore and illustrate these points.

4. The table below shows demand for some commodity at prices from $10 to $1. Use these figures to draw a demand curve in the upper part of Figure 18-4.

Price	Quantity	Revenue	Price	Quantity	Revenue
$10	0	50	$5	20	100
9	4	36	4	24	96
8	8	64	3	28	84
7	12	84	2	32	64
6	16	96	1	36	36

Associated with each possible quantity bought (and hence with each possible price) will be a certain amount of revenue

received by sellers (i.e., expenditure by buyers). If price is $9, so that 4 units are bought, revenue will be $36. Show the proper revenue amounts in the 10 blanks above. Then complete the lower part of Figure 18-4 to show the quantity-revenue relation (e.g., with quantity 4, revenue is $36, etc.).

$0; $36; $64; $84; $96; $100; $96; $84; $64; $36 [demand curve is straight line from $(Q = 0; P = 10)$ through $(Q = 40; P = 0)$; revenue curve is parabola peaking at $(Q = 20; \text{Rev} = 100)$ and equaling zero at both $Q = 0$ and $Q = 40$]

---

5.   a. Notice the interesting behavior of revenue as we move down the length of this straight-line demand curve. As price falls, revenue (pick one):
(1) Remains the same at all quantities purchased.
(2) Falls throughout the entire price range.
(3) First rises, reaches a peak, then falls.
(4) First falls, reaches a minimum, then rises.

b. If price falls from $7 to $6, buyer expenditure (i.e., seller revenue) (*rises / stays constant / falls*). Any price fall brings with it a reduced-expenditure tendency, since the quantity that was bought at the higher price can now be had for less money. If price falls from $7 to $6, the 12 units which formerly cost $84 can now be bought for $72. But the price fall also produces a countertendency: a disposition to buy more. The rise in this case (from 12 to 16) (*is / is not*) sufficiently great to more than offset the reduced-expenditure tendency.

c. If price falls from $4 to $3, the increased-expenditure tendency (*again wins over / loses to*) the reduced-expenditure tendency.

---

a. (3)   **b.** rises; is   **c.** loses to

---

6. "Price elasticity" means the responsiveness or "stretch" of quantity to any given price change. We can reach a more explicit statement of what demand elasticity means with respect to price just by using the phenomenon noted in question 4—that revenue may, for a given price change, go up, go down, or remain constant.

If there is enough "stretch" in quantity demanded when price goes down to cause revenue to go up, then we designate this section of the demand curve as *elastic* (or as price-elastic). If revenue stays constant, it is *unit-elastic*. If revenue falls, it is *inelastic*. This means the demand curve of question 4 is elastic for prices from $_10_ to $_5_, and inelastic for prices from $_5_ to $_0_.

It happens that this demand curve does not conveniently illustrate unit elasticity. But the curve would be unit-elastic between prices $5 and $4 if the quantity associated with price $4, instead of being 24, were _25_.

10; 5; 5; 0; 25

---

7. If we say this demand curve is elastic between prices of $10 and $5, we speak of that segment of the demand curve, not just

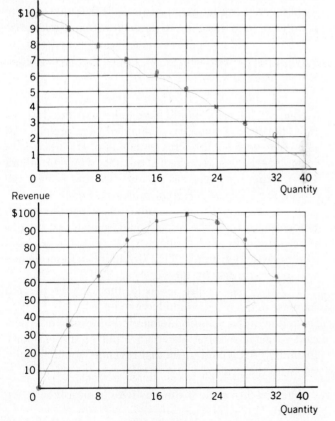

Figure 18-4

of one-way movements down the curve. As we go down the curve in this region, revenue increases. If we go up it from price $5 to price $10, revenue decreases. The degree of stretch (in this case, contraction) in quantity is here sufficiently powerful to cause revenue to decrease with any increase in price.

An elasticity definition must be a two-way street. If demand is elastic because the revenue associated with price $8 is $64 and that with price $7 is $84, then we must say it is elastic if either:

A price decrease brings a revenue increase, or
A price increase brings a revenue decrease.

The same applies to the unit-elastic and inelastic sections of the demand curve. (A quick rule is: demand is inelastic if price and revenue go in the same direction.)

Put *E* (elastic), *U* (unit-elastic), or *I* (inelastic) in each space below, as appropriate to each demand situation:

a. Price falls from $6 to $5, and consumer expenditure falls from $60 to $55 .... (———)

b. When price falls from $6 to $5, consumer expenditure on this commodity remains the same .... (———)

c. Price rises from $5 to $6, and quantity purchased falls from 80 (@ $5) to 60 (@ $6) .... (———)

d. Price drops from $6 to $5, and there is no increase in quantity purchased at all .... (———)

e. Price rises from $5 to $6, and there is no decrease in quantity purchased at all .... (———)

f. As the result of a certain price increase, revenue received by suppliers goes up from $2000 weekly to $2010 .. (———)

g. Because of a price increase from $5 to $5.10, buyers stop buying the commodity entirely .... (———).

a. *I* b. *U* c. *E* d. *I* e. *I* f. *I* g. *E*

8. Instructors in economics always illustrate "inelastic demand" on the blackboard by means of a steeply sloping (near-vertical) line. We see, now, that this method can be quite deceptive. No straight-line demand curve has a uniform elasticity. It is here that the demand curve constructed in question 4 always reported the same "responsiveness" to each $1 price change: an increase (or decrease) of 4 in quantity demanded. But in percentage terms, the drop in price from $10 to $9 was *(far more / much less)* drastic than the drop from $2 to $1, for the latter reduction cut the price in half. That is why the elasticity of this demand curve is different in different regions. It is, in fact, different at every point.

This means that if you take any straight-line demand curve with some slope to it, no matter how steep, you can always find a section along that curve in which the quantity demanded is

elastic with respect to price (i.e., $E_D > 1$). All you need to do is move *(up / down)* the curve to a price that is sufficiently *(high / low)*. You can always find a region that is inelastic, too. Finally, there is always one point where the price elasticity of demand is unity. (Can you convince yourself that the point of unitary elasticity is always the midpoint of the line?)

———

much less; up; high

9. Whether or not demand is elastic, unit-elastic, or inelastic with respect to a price change depends on the response in quantity. But as the preceding questions indicate, a uniform quantity response to a series of price changes which are uniform in the sense of being the same in absolute amount does not mean a uniform (constant) elasticity. To repeat question 8, the $1 price cut from $10 to $9 is in percentage terms much smaller than the cut from $2 to $1. Similarly, if the various 4-unit quantity responses are expressed as percentages of total quantity demanded, they are no longer uniform.

This means we can develop a more precise measure of elasticity than the three-way division of question 4. We can get a quantitative demand-elasticity measure by (*a*) putting the quantity change in percentage terms, (*b*) putting the price change in percentage terms, and then (*c*) using these two percentage figures to form a fraction or ratio.

The result is the *elasticity coefficient*: percent change in quantity divided by percent change in price. (Note that we put quantity first; we make it the numerator in the fraction, because the bigger the percentage quantity response, the higher the elasticity coefficient should be.)

a. Using question 4 data, compute price-elasticity coefficients between the prices indicated below. [To figure the base for percentage change in quantity, use the average of the two *Q*'s. Thus for the price change from $7 to $6 (which raises *Q* from 12 to 16), use 14 as the base. The 4-unit *Q*-increase is about 28.6 percent of 14. Similarly, use the average of the two *P*'s. A fall of $1 in price is about 15.4 percent of $6.50 (the average of $7 and $6).]

(1) Between price $8 and price $7 _____

(2) Between price $5 and price $4 _____

(3) Between price $3 and price $2 _____

b. This elasticity-coefficient idea is just an extension of the three-way system of division outlined in the section preceding question 4. For example, in the unit-elastic case, the two percentage changes just cancel one another out—they are equal. This makes the elasticity-coefficient figure *(1 / greater than 1 / less than 1)*. In the price-elastic case, that figure must be *(1 / greater than 1 / less than 1)*. In the inelastic case, it must be *(1 / greater than 1 / less than 1)*.

———

a. (1) 40.0/13.3, or 3.0; (2) 18.2/22.2, or .82; (3) 13.3/40.0, or .33 **b.** 1; greater than 1; less than 1

10. **a.** A *perfectly elastic* demand curve is illustrated as a horizontal line. Such a line illustrates the ultimate in elasticity (i.e., "infinite elasticity") because it means (pick one):

(1) No matter what the change in price might be, within the range of prices indicated by length of this line, there would be no response in quantity purchased.
(2) The slightest increase in price above the level at which this horizontal line runs would cause purchases to respond—i.e., to decrease—to the point of falling to zero.

b. *Perfectly inelastic* demand signifies a vertical line, or zero elasticity. Which alternative above correctly indicates why such a demand curve would represent the ultimate in inelasticity? .... *(1 / 2 / neither)*

Notice that the two extreme cases of perfectly elastic and perfectly inelastic demand constitute exceptions to the point made in question 8. When a demand curve is illustrated as perfectly horizontal or perfectly vertical, the slope of that line does tell you what the elasticity of the demand curve is.

c. A demand curve with unitary elasticity everywhere along its length *(can / cannot)* be a straight line. It is characterized instead in terms of revenue linking price and quantity numbers such that total revenue must be *(always rising as the price climbs / always constant regardless of price / always falling as the price climbs)*.

---

a. (2)   **b.** (1)   **c.** cannot, always constant regardless of price

---

11. The idea of responsiveness to a price change applies just as easily to supply as it does to demand. In dealing with supply, however, we cannot use the association of elasticity to revenue. Why? Because the revenue asked by suppliers moving along a supply curve almost never has the "either-direction" character of the revenue paid by consumers moving along a demand curve. Along a conventional supply schedule, a higher price always means a higher quantity and thus more revenue.

Nevertheless, we can use for supply exactly the same elasticity-coefficient ("responsiveness') measure already developed for demand.

a. In this sense, "perfectly inelastic" supply would be represented by a *(vertical / horizontal)* line, and "perfectly elastic" supply by a *(vertical / horizontal)* line.

b. Perfectly elastic supply appears as a *(vertical / horizontal)* line because that indicates the "ultimate" in responsiveness. It indicates simply a particular price; it says that any desired quantity is available at that price; it says that if price were to drop even slightly below this level, quantity supplied would *(fall to zero / become infinitely large)*.

When you enter a supermarket and find you can buy as little or as much as you wish of any given item at its fixed price, in effect you are facing a perfectly elastic supply curve.

---

a. vertical; horizontal   **b.** horizontal; fall to zero

---

12. If there should be an increase in demand (a shift of the demand curve upward or to the right), price will rise. and suppliers will want to increase their supply offers. But the extent to which they can do so depends on the amount of time they are given in which to increase production. This is the basis for Alfred Marshall's *distinction between time periods*, on the supply side (see text).

a. If the demand increase is sudden and suppliers have no reserve inventories on hand, it may be that no greater quantity can be offered immediately, despite the price rise. If so, the supply curve must be shown as *(perfectly elastic / perfectly inelastic)*. This is what the text refers to as the new *(long-run / short-run / momentary)* equilibrium.

b. Given a little time, suppliers can adjust to the demand increase by working their plant and equipment more fully (e.g., by adding an extra shift of workers). The result of this increase in supply quantity is the new *(long-run / short-run / momentary)* equilibrium.

c. If this demand increase were sustained and existing and potential new suppliers were to have even more time to build new plant and install new equipment, then there would be a further increase in the quantity offered in supply. Finally, therefore, an equilibrium price that indicates *(long-run / momentary / short-run)* equilibrium may be reached.

d. Note carefully that all this is just a statement about price elasticity of supply. It says that the degree of responsiveness of supply to a price change will depend on the amount of adjustment time suppliers can have. The longer this time period, the *(higher / lower)* will be the price elasticity (or elasticity coefficient) of supply. The same kind of dependence of elasticity on time *(can / cannot)* be made for the demand side.

---

a. perfectly inelastic; momentary   **b.** short-run   **c.** long-run   **d.** higher, can

---

The concept of market equilibrium was introduced in Chapter 4. A price-quantity pair represents an equilibrium situation if the quantity supplied at the specified price exactly matches the quantity demanded at that price. Markets tend to move toward these equilibria all by themselves. Excess supplies caused by excessively high prices tend to lead suppliers to cut their prices in an effort to liquidate their surpluses; this tendency constitutes automatic pressure on the prices to move down toward an equilibrium when they are too high. Shortages caused by bargain prices tend to lead suppliers to hike their prices to take advantage of the high levels of demand; this tendency constitutes the opposite pressure on prices to move up toward equilibrium when they are too low.

Comparisons of market equilibria are therefore appropriate analytical tools with which to trace the effects of various changes in any given market. If markets tend toward equilibrium all by themselves, then we can get a fair idea of the impact of some change in, say, the demand schedule by tracing what happens to market equilibrium. If, to continue the example, higher demand means that the equilibrium price climbs, then we can conclude that higher demand will begin to push the price upward as soon as demand conditions change.

A methodology based on this type of reasoning has a name; it is called "comparative statics." It is the method through which many economic investigations are conducted; it is, in fact, the method employed in applications of supply-and-demand analysis that occupy the latter portion of Chapter 18.

When you are asked to trace the effect of some sort of demand or supply adjustment, you are being asked to do some comparative statics of your own. You should not, in this effort, hesitate to use the graphical tools that you know. First draw a typical supply-and-demand graph and identify the equilibrium intersection. Then ask yourself whether the adjustment to be studied affects the demand side or the supply side of the market. Few factors affect both sides simultaneously, so there should be one answer to this question. Decide whether or not the required adjustment is out (up) or in (down), and draw a new schedule in the appropriate position. Now you are finished. Comparing the new equilibrium with the old, you can read directly from the graph the direction of the effect you were asked to analyze. Playing around with the shapes of the supply and demand curves that you drew, you can even uncover the sensitivity of the result to supply-and-demand elasticities.

13.   a. Record the following supply schedule in the upper part of Figure 18-4 (question 4), using the Q_1 supply figures. (The Q_2 fill-in blanks are for part **b** of this question.)

P	$1.00	$2.00	$3.00	$4.00	$5.00
Q_1	0	12	20	24	26
Q_2	___	___	___	___	___
P	$6.00	$7.00	$8.00	$9.00	$10.00
Q_1	28	29	30	31	32
Q_2	___	___	___	___	___

With the demand curve previously drawn, the equilibrium price indicated is $(3 / 4 / 5 / 6).

b. A tax of $1 per unit sold is now levied on the suppliers of this commodity. (NOTE: Such a tax is an increase in cost per unit of $1; so the suppliers will now sell only at $5 the particular quantity they were formerly willing to sell at $4.) In the Q_2 line above, enter the new supply-schedule figures. Then record the new supply curve in Figure 18-4. Make it a broken or dotted line, to distinguish this supply schedule from the one previously drawn.

The new equilibrium price will be approximately $(3.00 / 3.10 / 3.60 / 4.00 / 4.50).

---

a. 4   **b.** 0, 0, 12, 20, 24, 26, 28, 29, 30, 31; 4.50

14. The text's discussion of the "incidence of a tax," a tax such as the one in question 13, is interesting because it shows how the greater part of a tax may be paid by buyers or by sellers. But the very first thing to recognize is that this case is simply a particular instance of a change in supply—in this instance, a decrease in supply. It is a reduction in the quantity that suppliers will offer for any given price, because of a change in a factor which affects suppliers—in this instance, a tax levied upon them for each unit sold.

Notice that the decrease in supply can be described either as a leftward or as an upward movement. In terms of the preceding paragraph, it is a leftward movement; in terms of question 13, an upward one.

a. In the case of such a per unit commodity tax, whether price to the consumer rises by approximately the full amount of the tax or by a much smaller amount depends on the shapes of the demand and supply curves. Which of the following (one or more) would make for a price rise very close to the amount of the tax (i.e., tax whose incidence falls mainly on buyers)?

(1) Highly elastic demand
(2) Highly inelastic demand
(3) Highly elastic supply
(4) Highly inelastic supply

b. Which alternatives in part **a** (one or more) would make for a very small price rise, i.e., a tax borne mainly by suppliers?
.... *(1 / 2 / 3 / 4)*

---

a. (2), (3)   **b.** (1), (4)

---

15. The various panels of Figure 18-5 illustrate some possible illustrations of comparative static exercises in the market for apartments. In each case, *DD* represents an initial demand curve, *SS* represents an initial supply curve, *E* represents an initial equilibrium, and *E'* represents a new equilibrium supported by either a new supply curve *S'S'* or a new demand curve *D'D'*. For each of the following, indicate in the blank provided which panel most accurately reflects the indicated change in the market for apartments.

a. A residence tax to be added to the rent .... (_____)

b. A fire that reduces the quantity of available apartment units
.... (_____)

c. A major transfer of residents to new jobs in another area
.... (_____)

d. Rent control that prevented rents from rising to their equilibrium levels .... (_____)

e. An increase in the incomes of the residents ..... (_____)

f. A technological advance that lowers the heat component of the rent computation .... (_____)

---

a. c   **b.** c   **c.** b   **d.** d   **e.** a   **f.** e

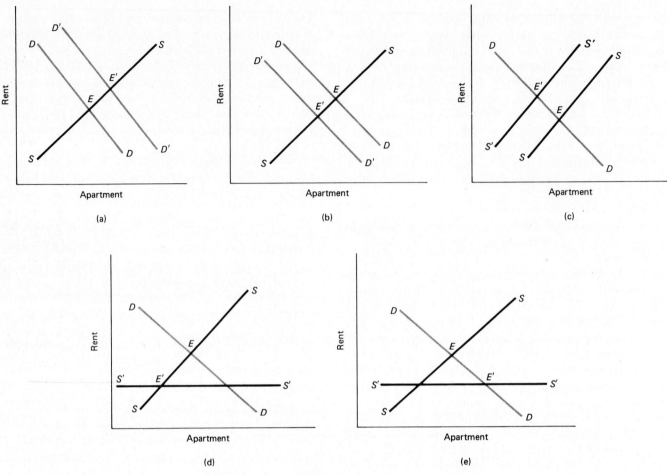

Figure 18-5

16. Necessities tend to be the types of goods that are inelastically demanded; they are needed regardless of the price (within reason), and so the quantity demanded *(is / is not)* terribly sensitive to changes in the price. The purchase of necessities also tends to exhaust a higher percentage of the income earned by families on the lower end of the income scale. Luxury goods tend to be the opposite; they can be forgone easily if the price climbs and are therefore usually *(elastically / inelastically)* demanded. Look at the two demand curves in Figure 18-6; the curve in panel *(a / b)* portrays a demand schedule that shows that good *(X / Y)* should be thought of as a necessity in the vicinity of a $10 price. Let supply be perfectly elastic at a price of $10. Draw the appropriate supply curve in both panels of Figure 18-6; it should be *(horizontal at P = $10 / sloped upward through point A / sloped downward through point A).* Now suppose that the government wants to raise as much money as possible by placing a $2 tax on one of the two goods.

The tax would raise $_____ in tax revenue if it were applied to good X and $_____ in revenue if it were applied to good Y. This is because *(X / Y)* is more inelastically demanded at *P* = $10 and the $2 increase in the price causes a *(smaller / larger)* reduction in the quantity demanded. Were the govern-

ment to pursue this program, would it be the more equitable policy? _____. Why or why not? _____

_____

_____ .

_____

is not; elastically; a; X; horizontal at *P* = $10; 96; 80; X; smaller; No; The efficiency of taxing the necessity causes low-income families to devote higher proportions of their incomes to the tax than would otherwise be the case

17. Consider Figure 18-7. The equilibrium price for X is

$_____ and the equilibrium quantity is _____ units. Were the government to want to restrict consumption to 500 units, it could exercise a number of policy options. It could, first of all, impose a price *(ceiling / floor)* of $_____; the quantity demanded would then be _____ units, but the quantity supplied would be _____ units. A *(shortage / surplus)* of _____ units would result in the short run, but suppliers would quickly catch on that production level was unsustainable. They would, therefore, lower their output to 500 units where the price they

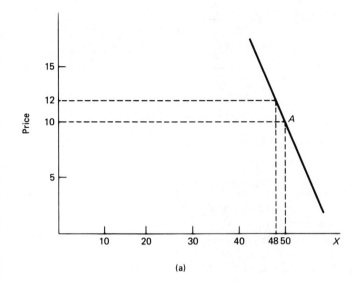

(a)

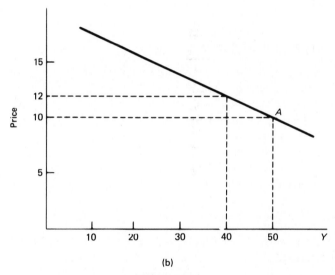

(b)

Figure 18-6

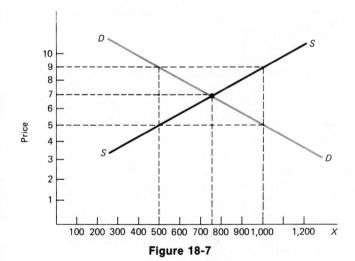

Figure 18-7

received would exceed the price required to get them to supply 500 units by $_____$. Alternatively, the government could set a production quota at 500 units, and suppliers would receive a price of $\$_____$ for every unit that they sold. Finally, the government could issue ration tickets and announce that one ticket and no more than $5 would be required to purchase one unit of X. If the tickets could be bought and sold, they would command a price of $\$_____$. Why? $_____$

$_____$

$_____$

$_____.$

7; 750; floor; 9; 500; 1000; surplus; 500; 4; 9; 4; They would assume a value equal to the difference between what people would be willing to pay for X and what they were allowed to pay

18. "The price of any commodity is determined by what it costs to produce that commodity." Circle all the following statements which seem to you correct observations with respect to this cost-of-production theory of price.

a. It is the most satisfactory explanation yet furnished as to how prices are determined.

b. It makes no allowance for the influence which demand— i.e., forces from the buying side—can exert on the level of price.

c. The level of production costs is one highly important factor influencing the position of the supply curve—i.e., quantity to be offered for sale at various prices—although not necessarily the only such factor at work.

d. As a theory of price determination, the cost-of-production view is unsatisfactory, since production costs are themselves prices—the prices of productive factors—and it fails to explain how prices are determined.

e. The existing supply of a commodity will sell at a price below its production cost if demand is insufficient to generate any better price, even though suppliers will not continue to produce the commodity if it cannot be sold at a price above costs.

b, c, d, e

19. The supply-and-demand analysis of this chapter does two things. First, it makes the critical separation between the influence upon price of buyer behavior and the influence of seller behavior. This is the all-essential beginning point, no matter what the commodity or service involved may be.

Second, this analysis discusses (as did Chapter 4) equilibrium price. This idea has narrower application. Strictly speaking, it applies only to a competitive market (although many economists argue that such a price is still approximated in less-than-perfectly-competitive markets).

The text sums up all such deviations from the competitive equilibrium price in one word (or phrase). What is it? _____

_____

_____

Monopoly (or monopolistic interference)

20. Examine Figure 18-8. It shows demand and supply curves for wheat for different years. Fill in the table accompanying Figure 18-9 with the required price and quantity data as well as the identification of the supporting supply and demand curves; row 1 is completed to illustrate the procedure. Plot the price

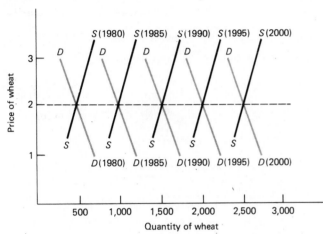

Figure 18-8

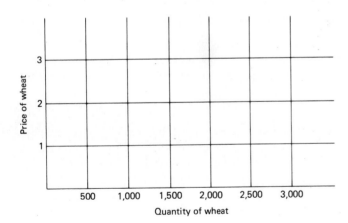

Quantity of wheat

Year	Price	Quantity	Demand curve	Supply curve
1980	$2	500	DD(1980)	SS(1980)
1985				
1990				
1995				
2000				

Figure 18-9

and quantity data that you recorded in the table on Figure 18-9, label the points by year, and connect them. You have plotted a line that *(slopes upward / is horizontal / slopes downward).* Is it a supply curve or a demand curve? _____. Why? _____

_____

_____

_____

_____.

Recording data by row: $2; 1000; SS(1985); DD(1985); $2; 1500; SS(1990); DD(1990); $2; 2000; SS(1995); DD(1995); $2; 2500; SS(2000); DD(2000); is horizontal; Neither; It collects the intersections of many different supply and demand curves, not points along any one supply or demand curve. The intersections would have represented a supply curve only if the supply schedule had remained fixed from 1980 through 2000; they would have represented a demand curve only if demand had been unchanged. They would have been one point if both had been constant

QUIZ: Multiple Choice

1. Consumers have budgeted a fixed money amount to buy a certain commodity. Within a certain range of prices, they will spend neither more nor less than this amount on it. Their demand in this price range would properly be designated as:
(1) in equilibrium.
(2) perfectly elastic.
(3) perfectly inelastic.
(4) highly inelastic but not perfectly so.
(5) unit-elastic.

2. The price-elasticity coefficient of demand equals:
(1) amount of price decrease divided by amount of quantity increase.
(2) percentage change in revenue divided by percentage decrease in price.
(3) percentage change in revenue divided by percentage increase in quantity demanded.
(4) percentage change in quantity demanded divided by percentage change in price.
(5) none of the above.

3. When the words "total revenue" are used in any discussion of demand curves, their meaning is:
(1) the profit, after deduction of costs, which the suppliers of the commodity involved earn from selling it to consumers.
(2) the total amount of money consumers will spend on the commodity at any particular price.
(3) the income suppliers will receive from sales if they sell the quantity they hope to sell.
(4) the quantity of the commodity that is associated with any particular price.
(5) no meaning at all—the words "total revenue" cannot have any meaning in relation to demand curves.

4. Alfred Marshall's concepts of "momentary," "short-run," and "long-run" supply curves were intended to bring out which fact?
(1) Over a long period of time, gradual increases in skill and improvements in the art of production tend to bring down the price of any commodity.
(2) Price increases as cost of transport to any given market increases.
(3) The extent to which quantity supplied will respond to a given price or demand change depends on the amount of time given producers to adjust their operations to this change.
(4) In order to make the supply-curve idea meaningful, it is necessary to speak of the quantity that will be supplied per period of time.
(5) Although demand may exert some short-run influence, ultimately the price of any commodity must be determined by the cost of its production.

5. The market price of a commodity and its costs of production are related in which way?
(1) If price is below cost of production, there will be a shift in the demand curve.
(2) Costs of production influence the quantity of goods that producers will offer for sale at each and any possible price.
(3) Price can never fall below costs of production.
(4) Price can never rise above costs of production.
(5) There is no significant relationship at all between price and production costs.

6. If a 10 percent reduction in price brings a 5 percent increase in the amount of money people spend to buy that commodity, then in this region of the demand curve, demand is (with respect to price):
(1) elastic.
(2) unit-elastic.
(3) inelastic, although not perfectly so.
(4) perfectly inelastic.
(5) perhaps any of these—information given is insufficient to determine elasticity.

7. Which alternative in question 6 would have been correct if the 10 percent reduction in price had caused a 5 percent increase in the quantity of the commodity that people buy?
(1).
(2).
(3).
(4).
(5).

8. If I can buy any quantity I please of a commodity at a fixed price, this means that the supply curve which confronts me is:
(1) perfectly inelastic.
(2) perfectly elastic.
(3) unit-elastic.
(4) elastic, but not necessarily perfectly elastic.
(5) none of these things, necessarily.

9. The government levies an excise tax of 5 cents per unit sold on the sellers in a competitive industry. Both supply and demand curves have some elasticity with respect to price. When this tax is represented on the supply-and-demand diagram:
(1) the entire supply curve shifts leftward by an amount indicating 5 cents, but (unless demand is perfectly elastic) price will not rise.
(2) the entire supply curve shifts upward by an amount indicating less than 5 cents, but (unless demand is highly elastic) price will rise by the full 5 cents.
(3) the entire supply curve shifts leftward by an amount indicating less than 5 cents.
(4) the entire supply curve shifts upward by an amount indicating 5 cents, but (unless supply is perfectly elastic) any price rise will be less than 5 cents.
(5) the entire demand curve shifts upward by an amount indicating 5 cents, and price will rise by 5 cents.

10. The change brought about by the tax levy described in question 9 would be designated as:
(1) a decrease in supply followed by a decrease in quantity demanded.
(2) a decrease in quantity supplied followed by a decrease in quantity demanded.
(3) a decrease in supply followed by a decrease in demand.
(4) a decrease in quantity supplied followed by a decrease in demand.
(5) none of the above.

11. A perfectly inelastic supply curve would be shown in the ordinary supply-and-demand graph as:
(1) a vertical line.
(2) a horizontal line.
(3) a straight line, but neither horizontal nor vertical.
(4) a curved line.
(5) perhaps any of the above.

12. Which alternative in question 11 would be correct for the graphical portrayal of a perfectly inelastic demand curve?
(1).
(2).
(3).
(4).
(5).

13. A change in quantity demanded, as distinct from a change in demand, means:
(1) that buyers have decided to buy more (or less) than they did before, at the existing price.
(2) that the elasticity of demand with respect to price has increased or decreased.
(3) simply that the quantity of purchases has changed, regardless of the factor which brought about this change in buying.
(4) that the market price has fallen or risen, and buyers have changed their total purchases accordingly.
(5) an increase in total purchases, but not a decrease.

14. Which alternative in question 13 would be correct for a change in demand, as distinct from a change in quantity demanded?
(1).
(2).
(3).
(4).
(5).

15. If a demand curve is described as being elastic with respect to price, the exact meaning of this is that any increase in price would bring about:
(1) an increase in quantity purchased by buyers.
(2) a decrease in quantity purchased by buyers.
(3) an increase in total expenditure by buyers.
(4) a decrease in total expenditure by buyers.
(5) a shift of the demand curve to a new position.

16. If a demand curve is unit-elastic throughout its entire length, this means, with respect to (*a*) graphical appearance of the demand curve and (*b*) total expenditure by buyers to purchase the commodity, that:
(1) the demand curve is a straight line, and total expenditure by buyers is the same at all prices.
(2) the demand curve is not a straight line, and total expenditure by buyers falls as price falls.
(3) the demand curve is a straight line, and as price falls total expenditure by buyers first increases and later decreases.
(4) the demand curve is not a straight line, and total expenditure by buyers rises as price falls.
(5) none of the above is correct.

17. An increase in demand for a certain product occurs. In Alfred Marshall's analysis, a new short-run and a new long-run equilibrium price will emerge. In the normal case, these would be related to the original price as follows: long-run equilibrium price would be:
(1) higher than both short-run and original prices.
(2) lower than short-run but higher than original price.
(3) lower than both short-run and original prices.
(4) related to short-run and original prices in a manner not indicated by any of the above.

18. Suppose that the demand curve for wheat is perfectly inelastic with respect to price. A tax of 50 cents per bushel sold is imposed on suppliers. Then:
(1) price will rise, but by less than 50 cents, and there will probably be some reduction in the quantity bought and sold.
(2) price will rise by the full 50 cents, but there will be no reduction in the quantity bought and sold.
(3) price will rise, but by less than 50 cents, and there will be no reduction in the quantity bought and sold.
(4) price will rise by the full 50 cents, and there will definitely be a reduction in the quantity bought and sold.
(5) none of the above is correct.

19. A crop failure reduces the amount of wheat available, and so the price rises. In precise terms, this is:

(1) a decrease in quantity supplied followed by a decrease in demand.
(2) a decrease in supply followed by a decrease in demand.
(3) a decrease in quantity supplied followed by a decrease in quantity demanded.
(4) a decrease in supply followed by a decrease in quantity demanded.
(5) none of these things.

20. One way to distinguish an increase in quantity demanded from an increase in demand is to say that the former:
(1) could result in an increase in price, whereas the latter could not.
(2) could not result in an increase in price, whereas the latter could.
(3) refers to the short-run increase in quantity purchased and the latter to the long-run increase.
(4) brings an increase in total expenditure by buyers, whereas the latter does not.
(5) is basically the same as the latter, except for a difference in price elasticity of demand.

21. Early in the 1970s, the Organization of Petroleum Exporting Countries (OPEC), by forming a cartel, raised oil prices very sharply. In elementary supply and demand curve terms, OPEC's action would be described as:
(1) a leftward shift of the supply curve.
(2) a leftward shift of the demand curve.
(3) a rightward shift of the supply curve.
(4) a rightward shift of the demand curve.
(5) an increase in equilibrium price, but with no change in either demand curve or supply curve.

22. Following the OPEC price rise, consumers of gasoline and oil products reduced their purchases—but not by very much. This means that their demand curve for such products:
(1) was price-elastic.
(2) shifted slightly to the right.
(3) was price-inelastic.
(4) shifted slightly to the left.
(5) was unit-elastic with respect to price.

23. Price control with rationing:
(1) is really an effort to restrain price rises by shifting the demand curve.
(2) is really an effort to restrain price rises by shifting the supply curve.
(3) means that supply and demand no longer have any influence in determining price.
(4) means that money incomes no longer have any influence upon demand.
(5) is not properly described by any of these.

24. As the result of an increase in family incomes in a certain community, purchases of butter rise from 1000 pounds daily to 1500 pounds daily. As a further result, the price of butter per pound rises from $1.25 to $1.50. This behavior:

(1) cannot be explained by the demand-curve-and-supply-curve analysis of price determination.

(2) represents a movement by consumers upward along their demand curve to a point of higher price and greater quantity.

(3) must be explained as a shift in the supply curve.

(4) represents a movement of price and quantity to a position above the equilibrium level.

(5) must be represented by a shift in the demand curve to a different position from that formerly occupied.

APPENDIX:
Cases on Supply and Demand

The material in the Appendix covers some of the topics that will appear in later chapters. It should be reviewed from time to time as the reader progresses through Chapters 21 and 22. Nonetheless, the Appendix is appropriate here because it serves to organize our thoughts about changes in supply and demand. It records a few propositions that efficiently summarize what happens in the usual cases. It also alerts the reader to the possibilities of particular note in which unusual results should be expected. By the time you have finished, you should both understand the propositions and recognize the potential for exception. In terms of academic progress, then, completing work on the Appendix should enable you to meet the following objectives.

LEARNING OBJECTIVES

1. Explain the statement about supply curves that is implicit in Proposition 1 of the text Appendix.

2. Explain the proposition about demand curves that is implicit in Proposition 2. Explain why Proposition 2 is a much firmer statement than Proposition 1.

Proposition 1(a) in this Appendix is, "As a general rule an increase in demand—supply being constant—will raise price." Be very clear on this: This is a proposition about movement along supply curves.

An "increase in demand" means a shift of the whole demand curve to the right, as in Figure 18A-1. If the supply curve does not shift (i.e., "supply being constant"), and if the outcome is that price is raised (e.g., from $C0$ to $F0$ in Figure 18A-1), then there is a strong likelihood that the supply curve must slope upward in the southwest-northeast direction illustrated by SS in Figure 18A-1.

Of course, price would increase if SS were vertical. But note part (b) of Proposition 1: "Probably also, but less certainly, it will increase the quantity bought and sold." If Q is to increase as well as P (in Figure 18A-1, it increases from $0A$ to $0B$), then SS must run in the southwest-northeast direction.

So Proposition 1 could be reworded: "In general, supply curves run in the southwest-northeast direction." The way to find out the nature of the supply curve is to change the position of the demand curve (i.e., allow demand to increase or to decrease), and then see where the new equilibrium point lies.

1.   a. The significance of a supply curve which runs generally in the southwest-northeast direction is that, in the event of an increase in demand, we would expect quantity bought and sold to (*increase / remain unchanged / decrease*) and price to (*increase / remain unchanged / decrease*).

b. There are numerous exceptions to this general rule. Supply curves can be flat or vertical, for example. There can also be falling supply curves (i.e., the supply line points downward rather than upward if you run your eye along it from left to right). Most of this Appendix is taken up with the reasons behind the general rule for supply curves and the reasons for the exceptions.

Figure 18A-2 shows three different supply-curve situations:

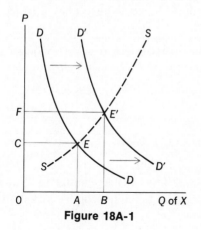

Figure 18A-1

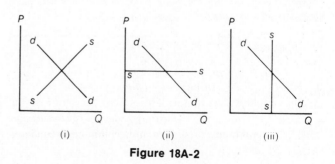

(i)   (ii)   (iii)

Figure 18A-2

i, ii, and iii. Its parts illustrate different "cases" discussed in the text.

(1) The *constant-cost* case is illustrated by *(i / ii / iii)*.

(2) The perfectly inelastic supply case is *(i / ii / iii)*.

(3) The *increasing-cost* case is *(i / ii / iii)*.

(4) The perfectly elastic supply case is *(i / ii / iii)*.

(5) The *economic rent* case is *(i / ii / iii)*.

(6) The case in which quantity supplied would respond neither to a price rise by increasing nor to a price fall by decreasing is *(i / ii / iii)*.

(7) The case in which suppliers are ready to sell, at the prevailing price, a greater quantity or a smaller quantity than they now sell is *(i / ii / iii)*.

c. Suppose an increase in buyer incomes pushes each of the demand curves of Figure 18A-2 to the right. The result will be a change in price and/or quantity bought and sold. Circle one or more letters, as appropriate. Letter *N* signifies that the outcome described fits none of the three cases of Figure 18A-2. Given this increase in demand:

(1) Price will rise in case(s) *(i / ii / iii / N)*.

(2) Quantity bought and sold will increase in case(s) *(i / ii/ iii / N)*.

(3) Both price and quantity will increase in case(s) *(i / ii / iii / /N)*.

(4) Price will not rise in case(s) *(i / ii / iii / N)*.

(5) Quantity will not increase in case(s) *(i / ii / iii / N)*.

(6) Neither price nor quantity will increase in case(s) *(i / ii / iii / N)*.

---

a. increase; increase   **b. (1)** ii; **(2)** iii; **(3)** i; **(4)** ii; **(5)** iii; **(6)** iii; **(7)** ii   **c. (1)** i, iii; **(2)** i, ii; **(3)** i; **(4)** ii; **(5)** iii; **(6)** N

2. The term "economic rent" was first used because it was thought the rental of undeveloped land illustrated the case involved. The owners of such land might receive a high rent if the demand were sufficiently high; but they would have been willing to rent the same amount of land for a low rent if necessary. The supply curve to illustrate this situation would be *(perfectly elastic / perfectly inelastic / neither perfectly elastic nor perfectly inelastic / backward-bending)*.

---

perfectly inelastic

3.   a. In one case, an increase in price might decrease the amount suppliers offer for sale. This is the *(backward-bending supply / economic-rent / increasing-costs / inelastic-supply)* case. The commodity or service most commonly associated

with this case is *(farm goods / labor service / manufactured goods / monopoly supply)*.

b. The explanation for this *backward-bending case* is that with a higher price (pick one):
(1) It will be impossible for the supplier to furnish the same amount of the service as before.
(2) Fewer people want to supply this service.
(3) The supplier can enjoy the same or more income and more leisure time.
(4) The supplier wants to reduce the amount of income obtained from supplying this service.

(Note that there is normally a limit on the degree of backward bend. Supply is unlikely to be cut back to such an extent that the supplier's money receipts are actually reduced.)

---

a. backward-bending supply; labor service   **b.** (3)

4.   Economists blithely recognize rising supply curves, horizontal supply curves, vertical supply curves, even some special backward-bending curves (as in the case of labor supply). But they suddenly become cautious if falling supply curves are suggested—i.e., any supply curve which goes beyond the perfectly horizontal into the northwest-to-southeast region.

Given such a supply curve, then an increase in demand would lower price, not raise it. Economists caution against accepting this case without explanation on the basis of the law of scarcity. If resources are scarce, then an increased pressure of demand on any part of those resources should, if anything, raise price, not lower it.

The thought that springs to mind to justify a falling supply curve involves "economies of scale" or mass-production opportunities. Opportunities for lower per unit costs at larger outputs arise from time to time, and firms will try to exploit them for as long as they exist. The firm that fails to seize such an opportunity could easily be driven out of business. Henry Ford, the founder of mass-production techniques, drove many small carriage builders into the ground when they did not follow his lead. To expand beyond the point where economies of scale disappear could, however, be equally disastrous. Quite frequently, though, expansion that exploits lower per unit costs can continue until one large firm covers the total quantity demanded in its market at almost any price. Such a firm is

called a _____. Putting this story into the supply-and-demand context, then, the text points out that many cases of economies of scale which look to the untrained eye like

falling-supply-curve cases are really cases of _____

---

monopoly; shifts of the supply curve to the right

Proposition 2 in this Appendix is, "An increase in supply—demand being constant—will almost certainly

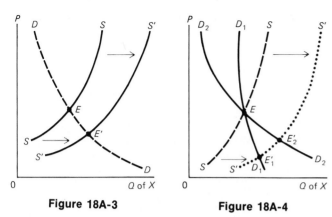

Figure 18A-3   **Figure 18A-4**

lower price and increase the quantity bought and sold."
This is an assertion about demand curves (just as Proposition 1 was an assertion about supply curves). It is illustrated by Figure 18A-3: an increase in supply (a shift of SS to position S'S') produces a lower price and a larger quantity bought and sold because the demand curve runs northwest-southeast.

Notice that Proposition 2 is much firmer about the probable consequences than was Proposition 1; hence the Appendix spends no time discussing any exceptions to this general characteristic of demand.

5. a. Proposition 2 is just a restatement of (pick one):
(1) The law of supply and demand
(2) The law of downward-sloping demand
(3) The principle of demand elasticity

b. The text does pause for a moment to note that the extent to which price will fall with any given supply increase (or rise with any given supply decrease) will be governed by demand elasticity with respect to price.

Figure 18A-4 illustrates the point. It shows two different demand curves: D_2 is more elastic than D_1. (Figure 18-3, Study Guide page 177, illustrates the same elasticity difference between two demand curves.) If supply were to increase in the manner indicated by the shift of SS to position S'S', the price fall would be greater if the demand curve were (D_1 / D_2) than if it were (D_1 / D_2). [Note: Remember that it is dangerous to associate price elasticity with the slope of the demand curve. It is, however, safe to say that if two demand curves are drawn on the same diagram (i.e., with the same scale used for both curves), then at the point where they intersect, the flatter curve is the more elastic of the two.]

In terms of a decrease in supply, the price rise associated with such a supply decrease will be greater, the more (*elastic / inelastic*) demand is with respect to price.

a. (2) **b.** D_1; D_2; inelastic

6. Throughout almost all of Chapters 4 and 18, it is taken pretty much for granted that market forces will push a competi-

tive price to its "equilibrium level" at the intersection of demand and supply curves. A change in demand or supply will, of course, produce a period of disequilibrium during which the market seeks out its new equilibrium, but that period will normally be short.

The *dynamic-cobweb theorem* argues that in particular circumstances these conclusions oversimplify matters. If equilibrium price is disturbed by a supply or demand change, the consequences may be a series of oscillations, with price swinging first above, then below, the equilibrium level.

The cobweb case really involves two supply curves. First, there is the "true" supply curve—i.e., the schedule of quantities producers would want to supply, given various possible prices. It is a conventional supply curve, running approximately from southwest to northeast—i.e., the higher the market price, the more they will wish to sell. In elasticity terms, this curve (*is perfectly price-elastic / has some price elasticity / is perfectly price-inelastic*).

What complicates matters is that producers are assumed to have to make their decision on quantity to be shipped to market before that market opens, and consequently before they know what market price is going to be. In the cobweb case, their forecasts generally prove to be wrong.

In the text's example, it is assumed that all suppliers estimate that the coming period's price will be the same as last period's price. So they produce the quantity they would like to sell at that price (according to their "true" supply curve) and ship that quantity to the market.

The assumption is that there is no holding back on any part of this supply quantity, once shipped. It must sell—all of it—for whatever price the market establishes. This means we have a second supply curve, one different from the "true" curve. This supply curve (*is perfectly price-elastic / has some price elasticity / is perfectly price-inelastic*).

When this supply reaches the market, things work out just as they are supposed to, in competitive conditions. Given a certain demand, an equilibrium price is quickly reached. But if demand conditions happen to have changed since the previous period, it will not be the same price as that earlier-period one, and consequently not the price that suppliers had anticipated. This is when they learn that their forecasts were wrong. For illustrative purposes, suppose this most recent price is (due to a decrease in demand) lower than the earlier-period price.

Next time around, suppliers must again guess what price is going to be. Again (in the simplest version of the cobweb theorem) they assume it will be what it was in the most recent period—the lower price. So (consulting their "true" supply curve) they ship a smaller quantity. Again the market works out an equilibrium: this time, smaller quantity, higher price. Another wrong forecast!

If suppliers stick rigidly to their belief that the next-period price will be the same as the previous-period price, the consequence will be a series of prices that swing from high to low to high. In extreme cases, these oscillations might even grow wider and wider. Of course, suppliers are unlikely to be so stupid as to cling to a forecasting method that proves to be consistently incorrect. Nevertheless, the cobweb theorem does help to explain cyclical price swings in markets for some farm products.

---

has some price elasticity; is perfectly price-inelastic

QUIZ: Multiple Choice

1. An increase in supply will lower price unless:
(1) supply is perfectly inelastic.
(2) demand is perfectly elastic.
(3) it is followed by an increase in quantity demanded.
(4) demand is highly inelastic.
(5) both demand and supply are highly inelastic.

2. An increase in demand will not raise price if:
(1) the case is that of "pure economic rent."
(2) demand is highly elastic.
(3) supply is perfectly elastic.
(4) it is followed by an increase in quantity supplied.
(5) demand is perfectly inelastic.

3. Which diagram in Figure 18A-5, if any, depicts the pure economic-rent case?
(1) a.
(2) b.
(3) c.
(4) d.
(5) None of them.

4. Which Figure 18A-5 diagram, if any, depicts the perfectly inelastic supply case?
(1) a.
(2) b.
(3) c.
(4) d.
(5) None of them.

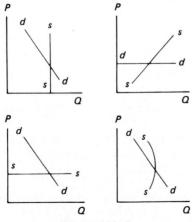

Figure 18A-5

5. Which Figure 18A-5 diagram, if any, depicts the constant-cost case?
(1) a.
(2) b.
(3) c.
(4) d.
(5) None of them.

6. If an industry is competitive (in the text's usage of this term), then the situation with respect to mass-production economies, or reduction in per unit cost for the individual firm due to larger-scale output, will be which of the following?
(1) There may be plenty of known economies which individual firms can still exploit, or there may not.
(2) Firms will have expanded their output sufficiently to have taken advantage of all known economies.
(3) Insofar as unexploited economies exist, the industry supply curve will be a falling one—i.e., will have some northwest-to-southeast inclination.
(4) Insofar as unexploited opportunities exist, the supply curve will be a rising one.
(5) None of the above.

7. The dynamic-cobweb supply-and-demand case refers to the following:
(1) A situation in which there is an interaction between supply and demand curves, so that a shift in one curve may set off a shift in the other, thus making it difficult for a stable equilibrium price to develop
(2) The tendency of price to be pulled toward the critical point at which supply and demand curves intersect
(3) A situation in which any disturbance of equilibrium price may set off a series of price oscillations, possibly with the swings growing wider as they continue
(4) The case in which consideration is given to the quantity that will be demanded and the supply offered per period of time, instead of the time factor being disregarded, as it is in ordinary supply-and-demand analysis
(5) A situation in which both demand curve and supply curve are highly elastic, so that any price fluctuations caused by a movement of either curve tend to be extremely wide

8. The results observed in the dynamic-cobweb supply-and-demand case depend in large part on the assumption that:
(1) the supply curve for the commodity is inelastic.
(2) the commodity involved can be stored and kept in inventory, so that sellers can withdraw part of their supply from the market if they do not like the price that prevails.
(3) the demand and supply curves intersect at a price that is satisfactory neither to suppliers nor to buyers.
(4) suppliers decide on the quantity they will send to market in this period on the basis of an earlier-period price.
(5) both demand curve and supply curve are highly inelastic, so that any shift in either curve results in a large change in price.

9. "Increasing costs" (as the term is used in the text) means:
(1) the same thing as perfectly inelastic supply.

(2) that at any higher price a larger quantity will be supplied.
(3) any upward shift in a supply curve due to an increase in input prices.
(4) any leftward shift of the supply curve following an increase in demand.
(5) none of the above, necessarily.

10. If the revenue received by a factor of production is classed as a "pure economic rent," and if the demand for this factor declines:
(1) the price of this factor will fall, but the quantity bought and sold will remain unchanged.
(2) the price of this factor will fall, and the quantity bought and sold will decline.
(3) the price of this factor will remain unchanged, but the quantity bought and sold will decline.
(4) both the price of this factor and the quantity bought and sold will remain unchanged.
(5) none of these is true.

11. "Perfectly elastic supply" indicates:
(1) constant cost.
(2) increasing cost.
(3) decreasing cost.
(4) that revenue received by suppliers is designated as economic rent.
(5) that a certain fixed supply will be offered no matter what price may be.

12. If a commodity's return is in the nature of a pure economic rent and a tax is imposed on the commodity, then:
(1) the incidence of the tax is borne wholly by the suppliers, and price to the buyers will not change.
(2) the incidence is borne wholly by the buyers.
(3) the incidence will be shared between the suppliers and the buyers.
(4) the output of the commodity will fall and its price will rise.
(5) the output of the commodity will not fall but its price will rise.

13. The law of diminishing returns plays the following background part in demand and/or supply curves:
(1) It explains, at least in part, the increasing-cost case.

(2) It explains why an increase in supply will almost certainly lower price.
(3) It accounts, in part, for the fact that price must be lowered if a greater quantity is to be sold.
(4) It explains, at least in part, the backward-bending supply curve case.
(5) Its part is not correctly indicated by any of these statements.

14. In the circumstances usually cited to explain the phenomenon of the backward-bending supply curve, it follows that:
(1) continual decreases in demand will continually increase the quantity of the service supplied.
(2) the supply curve will not bend back to such an extent that the total revenue received by the supplier or suppliers actually decreases with an increase in price.
(3) any increase in demand will tend to be followed by an increase in quantity supplied, but not by an increase in supply.
(4) the supply curve may ultimately climb to the point where it touches the vertical (price) axis.
(5) the return received by the supplier or suppliers will be known as pure economic rent.

15. If the land suited for growing wheat is fixed in quantity, the supply curve for wheat:
(1) should still have some price elasticity—i.e., indicate that as price rises, supply quantity offered would increase.
(2) must rise vertically, i.e., be perfectly inelastic.
(3) may in consequence be backward-bending.
(4) might be perfectly horizontal, since the supply of wheat and the supply of wheat-growing land are two different things.
(5) will not be influenced by the price offered for wheat.

16. If a good is produced under "constant-cost" conditions, the effect of a $1 tax on each unit sold would normally be:
(1) to raise price to consumers by $1.
(2) to raise price to consumers by less than $1, if demand is elastic.
(3) to require the entire tax to be paid by producers, unless demand is perfectly elastic.
(4) to raise price to consumers by less than $1, if demand is inelastic.
(5) none of these.

CHAPTER 19

THE THEORY OF DEMAND AND UTILITY

Demand theory constitutes the analysis of the economic factors that produce and affect demand curves. The power of demand curves as tools for economic investigation has already been noted. This chapter explores their sensitivity to changes in income, prices, and tastes. Having completed the chapter, you will have met the following objectives.

LEARNING OBJECTIVES

1. Explain the summation process that produces market demand curves from individual demand curves.

2. Define total utility. Distinguish it from marginal utility.

3. Explain the law of diminishing marginal utility.

4. State the rule to be satisfied if a consumer is to maximize utility.

5. Define substitution effect and income effect (terms which first appeared in Chapter 4). Explain the requirement necessary if there is to be a significant income effect.

6. Describe the paradox of value. Show how it can be resolved (or explained).

7. Describe the general idea behind the notion of consumer surplus.

The text notes that a market demand curve can be produced by the "horizontal" addition of individual demand curves—i.e., the summation, for every price, of the quantities demanded by all the individuals participating in the market.

1. Table 19-1 records the quantities of some good X that each of three people would demand for a variety of prices. Fill in the column indicated for the market demand schedule if these three people were the only people interested in X at any price. If individual A's income were to increase, (*higher* / *identical* / *lower*) quantities would be entered in the market demand col-

umn for (*the equilibrium price only* / *all prices* / *all prices below* $5). If X were considered a close substitute to Y by individual B only and the price of Y were to fall, then (*higher* / *identical* / *lower*) quantities would be entered in the market demand column for (*the equilibrium price only* / *all prices* / *all prices below* $5).

Reading down the column: 2, 4, 7, 10, 14, 20, 27; higher; all prices; lower; all prices below $5

Ordinarily, as a consumer, you have only a limited amount of money to spend in each period on the things you need and that please you. Each good has a market price; usually you cannot alter these prices. You must decide which goods to buy, and how much of each to buy, knowing that each purchase will take up part of your limited income or budget total.

If your budget were so large that you could buy all you wanted of all the goods that interested you, there would be no problem of choice. Ordinarily—alas!—that is not the case. You must decide—decide, for example, whether to buy 2 more units of good A (price $1), or instead to buy 1 more unit of good B (price $2). Each

Table 19-1

Price	Individual A	Individual B	Individual C	Market Demand
$8	2	0	0	_____
$7	3	0	1	_____
$6	4	0	3	_____
$5	5	0	5	_____
$4	6	1	7	_____
$3	7	3	10	_____
$2	8	5	14	_____

purchase would entail the same $2 outlay, and a limited budget says you can't have both. So you must carry inside your head some personal measuring scale which says that buying the 1 unit of B would yield you more satisfaction than would purchase of the 2 units of A (or vice versa). Tastes differ, of course. The individual next to you, with the same income, might well make the opposite choice.

This small A-or-B choice illustrates the more general problem of how to make the best use of a limited income. There are thousands of different assortments of goods, each one a little different from the next, which could be bought with a given income (and given prices). Which among them is the "best" choice?

It is easy to understand that decisions must be made in buying. Prices and incomes are objective, easily understood concepts, but tastes are more difficult. We have to devise some analytic concept—and it isn't easy!—to represent what we mean by personal "tastes," "preferences," or "needs."

Economists have developed the notion of utility to accomplish this representation. Each consumer is envisioned to evaluate commodities on the basis of his or her personal quantitative standard of satisfaction or utility. A certain buyer may reckon, for example, that buying 1 unit of A would yield 50 utility units ("utils"); 2 units would yield a total of 120 utils; and a third A unit would raise the satisfaction meter to 180 utils.

In real life, nobody is conscious of putting exact numerical values on each quantity of each good consumed. The utility notion represents consumers as being a lot more precise than buyers actually are. Don't be too impatient with the utility idea on this account. It says that consumers must do something at least approximating this, even if only intuitively, if they want to make the best possible use of a limited income.

This quantitative utility idea is employed because it is a way of showing how a consumer will go about "maximizing satisfaction"—i.e., making the best possible use of a limited income in the light of his or her own set of preferences.

The very first step is to distinguish carefully between *total utility* and *marginal utility*. In the example above, the buyer derived a total utility of 50 utils from consuming 1 unit of A, 120 utils from 2 units, and 180 utils from 3 units. Marginal utility is the extra utility contributed by the last unit consumed (the unit that is just at the edge or margin of consumption, so to speak). The marginal utility of the first unit of A must be 50 (because its consumption raised total utility from 0 to 50); that of the second unit, 70 (because total utils rose from 50 to 120); that of the third unit, 60 (from 120 to 180).

The second step is to note the *principle of diminishing marginal utility*. This principle says that as consumption of any single good increases, the total utility therefrom will increase up to a point at a decreasing rate; i.e.,

marginal utility gradually decreases. The third ice-cream cone (or the third martini) may add to your satisfaction, but not so much as the first one did; the fifth one may add still a little more satisfaction, but not so much as the third one did. In these circumstances, your total satisfaction is still rising, but the payoff from each additional (marginal) unit consumed is becoming less and less.

2. a. If the total utilities associated with the consumption of 1, 2, 3 units of B were to be, respectively, 100, 160, and 200, then the corresponding marginal utilities would be _____, _____, and _____.

b. Which of the following set of total utility figures (designated for 1, 2, 3, and 4 units consumed) illustrates the idea of diminishing marginal utility: *(200, 300, 400, 500 / 200, 450, 750, 1100 / 200, 400, 1600, 9600 / 200, 250, 270, 280)*.

c. Which of the following set of marginal utility figures (once again defined for 1, 2, 3, and 4 units consumed) would likewise illustrate the diminishing marginal utility principle: *(200, 150, 100, 50 / 200, 300, 400, 500 / 200, 200, 200, 200 / 200, 250, 270, 280)*.

d. Behind the notion of diminishing marginal utility is the simple idea that we can have too much of any good thing. Ultimately, enough of anything, no matter what, is enough. Diminishing marginal utility means that this point of satiation *(is being approached / has been reached)*.

If and when the satiation point is actually reached, the following utility situation will prevail (pick one):
(1) Total utility and marginal utility will be one and the same figure.
(2) Total utility will be zero, marginal utility will have reached its maximum.
(3) Total utility will have reached its maximum, marginal utility will be zero.
(4) Both total utility and marginal utility will be zero.
(5) Both total utility and marginal utility will have reached their maximum values.

---

a. 100, 60, 40 **b.** 200, 250, 270, 280 **c.** 200, 150, 100, 50 **d.** is being approached, (3)

Now we use the ideas of total and marginal utility to illustrate the idea of "maximizing satisfaction," or making the best possible use of a given income. Suppose that a fixed weekly budget will buy only three goods: A, B, and C. Table 19-2 shows your personal schedule of total utility for these three goods.

You want to spend your fixed income so as to obtain that particular ABC combination yielding the maximum number of utility units. The utility units for A are of the same kind as those for B and C. For example, if you buy 2 units each of A, B, and C, your total satisfaction would be 950 utility units (120 plus 700 plus 130).

In this table, the three sets of utility values are as-

Table 19-2
Total Satisfaction, Measured in Utility Units, Derived from Consumption of:

	1 Unit	2 Units	3 Units	4 Units	5 Units	6 Units	7 Units	8 Units	9 Units	10 Units	11 Units	12 Units
A	50	120	200	240	258	268	275	280	285	289	293	296
B	400	700	900	1,000	1,020	1,030	1,038	1,044	1,048	1,050	1,051	1,052
C	70	130	180	225	265	300	328	348	360	366	370	373

Table 19-3
Marginal Satisfaction or Utility, Measured in Utility Units, When Consumption Is:

	1 Unit	2 Units	3 Units	4 Units	5 Units	6 Units	7 Units	8 Units	9 Units	10 Units	11 Units	12 Units
A	50	70	80	40	18							
B	400	300	200	100								
C	70	60	50									

sumed to be independent of one another. That is, the amount of utility you get for any given quantity of A is not affected by the amount you happen to be consuming of B or of C. This is not necessarily true in real life; A and B might, for example, be close substitutes. The assumption of independence is made here only for the sake of simplicity and clarity.

3. In the selection of a "utility maximum," the idea of *marginal* utility proves to be crucial. First of all, then, use the information in Table 19-2 to record, in Table 19-3, marginal utilities of A, B, and C. To speed things up, a few of the marginal utility figures are already entered.

A: 10, 7, 5, 5, 4, 4, 3   B: 20, 10, 8, 6, 4, 2, 1, 1   C: 45, 40, 35, 28, 20, 12, 6, 4. 3

4. As the consumer of question 3, you have $52 per week to spend on commodities A, B, and C. (These are the only goods available, or the only ones that interest you.) A's price per unit is $1. B's is $2. C's is $4.

How much of A, B, and C should you buy, for maximum satisfaction?

There are plenty of ABC combinations that $52 would just buy. But which one buys the maximum total of utility units?

One possible combination is 12 of A, 10 of B, 5 of C (yielding a total of 1611 utility units). Does this "maximize utility"? No, for if you cut A purchases by 4 units, that allows purchase of 1 extra C unit, and the utility gain from increasing C will outweigh the utility loss from reducing A (by 19 utility units).

Marginal utility is the critical factor in measuring losses and gains, but it is not the only critical factor in evaluating utility-maximizing equilibrium. In the example above, the last units of A purchased were not the utility bargains when compared with C that they might have looked like if only price were

considered. But looking at marginal utility numbers alone would have been equally misleading. What must be asked to check to see if utility is maximized is really this: Are the three commodities offering equally good utility returns per dollar spent? Is, in other words, the marginal value of the dollar the same regardless of what good it is spent on? If it is—if the three goods are contributing equally to utility per dollar expended—then utility is maximized.

The method with which to check whether or not this is happening is simple. The ratios of marginal utility to price must be computed for each good. (An old physics trick can provide some insight here. The units of evaluation should be units of utility per dollar spent. If marginal utility is measured in units of utility per units of consumption and prices are measured in dollars per unit of consumption, then marginal utility divided by price must be in units of utility per dollar—the units of consumption cancel.) If the marginal-utility-to-price ratios are equal, then utility is maximized. If they are not, then there exists some adjustment in consumption that will increase utility—an increase in the consumption of the good with the high utility payoff per dollar and a reduction in the consumption of the good with the low utility payoff per dollar.

a. Use the data of Table 19-3 to compute the marginal-utility-to-price ratios indicated in Table 19-4 given A's price of $1, B's of $2, and C's of $4.

b. Table 19-4 has several such equal-utility combinations. Circle the *MU*-per-dollar figures in this table for three of them, namely:

(1) 6 of A, 5 of B, 5 of C. (Common *MU*/$: 10)
(2) 8 of A, 6 of B, 8 of C. (Common *MU*/$: 5)
(3) 12 of A, 8 of B, 9 of C. (Common *MU*/$: 3)

Among these three "shopping baskets," only one can just be bought for $52, namely, (_____).

Table 19-4
Marginal Utility Units per Dollar of Outlay (*MU* Divided by Price of the Commodity), When Consumption Is:

	1 Unit	2 Units	3 Units	4 Units	5 Units	6 Units	7 Units	8 Units	9 Units	10 Units	11 Units	12 Units
A	50	70	80	40	18							
B	200	150	100	50								
C	17.5	15	12.5									

c. Given your income constraint and the prices quoted by the market, the best possible expenditure of $52 is 8 of A, 6 of B, and 8 of C. Table 19-2 indicates that the total number of utility units attained from this ABC combination is *(1030 / 1658 / 3050)* units.

To check that this combination really "maximizes utility," experiment with a change. Reduce your C purchases from 8 units to 7. This saves you $4, which you use to buy 2 extra units of good B. Combining the reduction in total utility from lower C purchases with the increase from higher B purchases, the net change in total utility would be *(an increase / a decrease)* of *(8 / 7 / 6 / 5 / 4)* units.

a. A: same as Table 19-3; B: 10, 5, 4, 3, 2, 1, 0.5, 0.5; C: 11.25, 10, 8.75, 7, 5, 3, 1.5, 1, 0.75 **b.** (2) **c.** 1658; a decrease; 6

A summary of this procedure:

▶The problem is to find the maximum total of utility units which, given the stated prices, a specific income will buy.

▶The rule for solving the problem is to find that combination which makes marginal utility per dollar the same for all goods.

5.   a. Formally stated, the ABC maximum-utility consumer-satisfaction rule given in the text is:

_____ .

b. In the equilibrium of question 4, the ratio of *MU / p* would be for A _____ / _____, for B _____ / _____, and C _____ / _____. Disregarding any drop in marginal utility occurring within fractions of a commodity unit, the number of utility units bought by the very last dollar spent on each commodity would be the same for all, namely,

_____ units per dollar.

a. $\dfrac{MU_A}{p_A} = \dfrac{MU_B}{p_B} = \dfrac{MU_C}{p_C}$ **b.** 5; $1; 10; $2; 20; $4; 5

6.   a. Now suppose that your spendable income has just been cut from $52 to $36 per week. In the following table, show the details of your new "equilibrium (utility-maximizing) po-

sition." The heading "*MU / $*" in the right-hand column means "number of utility units bought with the marginal or last dollar of expenditure."

Quantity Purchased, Units	Price	Expenditure	Marginal Utility	*MU/$*
A _____	$1	_____	_____	_____
B _____	2	_____	_____	_____
C _____	4	_____	_____	_____

b. To compensate you for the pain suffered in part **a**, suppose finally that your budget is back to $52—and the price of commodity C has been reduced from $4 to $3. Again show the details of your resulting equilibrium position.

Quantity Purchased, Units	Price	Expenditure	Marginal Utility	*MU/$*
A _____	$1	_____	_____	_____
B _____	2	_____	_____	_____
C _____	3	_____	_____	_____

a. A: 6, $6, 10, 10; B: 5, $10, 20, 10; C: 5, $20, 40, 10   **b.** A: 11, $11, 4, 4; B: 7, $14, 8, 4; C: 9, $27, 12, 4

7.   a. Both Chapters 4 and 18 stressed the distinction between an *increase (or decrease) in demand* and an *increase (or decrease) in quantity demanded*. Question 6a illustrates this: There was a "leftward shift" of the consumer demand curve caused by an income drop. Formerly you bought

_____ units of A. After the income drop, even though A's price is unchanged, your purchases are only _____ units. In Chapter 18 language, this is a decrease in *(demand / quantity demanded)*.

b. The reduction in C's price in question 6b illustrates, with respect to C, an increase in *(demand / quantity demanded)*.

That is, out of the utility background, we can identify consumer demand curves. For example, with a budget of $52, and with A's and B's prices $1 and $2, respectively, you will

buy _____ units of C if its price is $4, and _____ units if its price is $3. Other points on the C demand curve would be derived by taking other C prices.

---

a. 8; 6; demand   **b.** quantity demanded; 8; 9

---

8. The relation between utilities of commodities B and C in Table 19-2 illustrates something of Adam Smith's *paradox of value*. Smith was puzzled by the fact that commodity prices often are poor indicators of the true relative usefulness of commodities. Water, which is essential for life, is cheap. Diamonds, which have no such status, are expensive.

In the equilibrium of question 4, you were buying

_____ units of B and _____ units of C. In this position,

the total utility of B is _____ units, and the total utility of

C is _____ units. Measured in terms of total utility furnished, B is the more useful or desirable of the two commodities. Yet the market sets a higher price per unit on C.

The explanation is that market prices are influenced by *(marginal / total)* utility. The *(marginal / total)* utility of extra units of a commodity such as B declines sharply after a certain total quantity is consumed. If the supply offered is sufficiently large, consumers will bid a price for extra units of B reckoned only in terms of its low *(marginal / total)* utility, and this price will hold for the entire supply. If B's supply were sufficiently reduced, its price *(would rise very sharply / would rise a little but not much / would fall)*. The "utility bargain" consumers get from purchasing a commodity with high total utility at a low price is termed:

_____.

When the price of C fell from $4 per unit to $3, total utility *(rose / fell / stayed the same)*. At the same time, consumer surplus *(rose / fell / stayed the same)*. If Figure 19-1 were to illustrate the demand curve for C in the $2 to $5 price range, then the change in consumer surplus caused by the price reduction from $4 to $3 would be *(area EDF / area KFIL / area EGIF / area FHI)*.

If the government were to stick a tax onto the $3 price of C so that $4 became the after-tax price, then the government would collect revenue equal to the *(area DGHK / area EGHF / area OGIL)*, and consumer surplus would fall by *(area EDF / area KFIL / area EGIF / area FHI)*. The amount of consumer surplus not extracted by the government in tax revenue—the deadweight loss of the tax—would be *(area EDF / area ILM / area FHI)*.

6; 8; 1030; 348; marginal; marginal; marginal; would rise very sharply; consumer surplus; rose; rose; area *EGIF*; area *EGHF*; area *EGIF*; area *FHI*

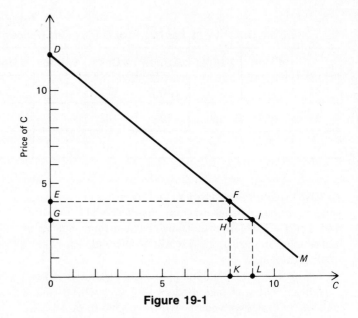

Figure 19-1

9. **a.** Back in Chapter 4, the text spoke of the two "effects" which explain why, if the price of a commodity falls, more of it is bought (or why less is bought if price rises). These "effects" are introduced once again in this chapter. Specifically, they are (1) the *(substitution / institutional)* effect, and (2) the *(envy / income)* effect.

In this question and the one following, we use the idea of marginal utility to examine in more detail the nature of these two effects. The table below is similar in general construction to Tables 19-2 and 19-3. It shows the levels of marginal utility *(MU)* and total utility *(TU)* associated with different quantities of commodities X and Y, measured in satisfaction units, as you, with your own personal tastes, measure satisfaction. (Commodities X and Y are the only ones you can buy, or the only ones in which you are interested.)

No. Units Consumed	MU of X	TU of X	MU of Y	TU of Y
3	32	348	20	130
4	28	376	18	148
5	24	400	16	164
6	20	420	14	178
7	16	436	12	190
8	12	448	10	200
9	8	456	8	208
10	5	461	5	213
11	3	464	3	216

b. Suppose that the prices of X and of Y are $2.40 and $1.00, respectively, and that you have just $20 per period to spend. What will be your equilibrium or maximum-satisfaction X-Y choice? (Look in the table for an X-Y combination with *MUs* which stand in the 24 to 10 or 12 to 5 ratio. When you find such a combination, see if it can be bought for just $20. If not, look for another one which can be so bought.) In this situation, you will buy _____ units of X and _____ units of Y. The total of satisfaction units you obtain, from X and Y combined, will be _____ .

c. Now let the price of X drop from $2.40 to $1. The price of Y is still $1, and you still have $20 to spend. What will be your new "equilibrium position"? (Since the prices of X and Y are now equal, look for an X-Y combination with equal *MUs*, purchasable for just $20.) You will now buy _____ units of X, as compared with 5 previously, and will now buy _____ units of Y, as compared with 8 previously.

In the new situation, the X quantity has (*increased / decreased*). This is not surprising, since X's price has fallen. The Y quantity has (*increased / decreased*). Why this should happen is not so immediately obvious. Y's price has not fallen; indeed in relative terms—relative to the price of X—that price has risen.

d. What has happened is that you were spending considerably more than half your income on X. Thus a reduction in X's price had an effect similar to a substantial rise in your income—as witness the rise in your total satisfaction level, from the original total of 600 units to (*620 / 664 / 670 / 674*) units. With what is equivalent to a larger income, you buy more of X—and more of Y.

When X's price falls, there are thus two resulting effects which operate upon Y purchases. Insofar as X and Y are substitutes, you will be disposed to buy (*more / less*) of Y. But countering this is the "income effect" just discussed, which inclined you to buy (*more / less*). In this case, the "income effect" won out over the "substitution effect." Had X and Y been to a greater extent substitutes, the Y quantity would have fallen instead of rising.

---

a. substitution; income **b.** 5; 8; 600 **c.** 10; 10; increased; increased **d.** 674; less; more

10. Question 9 was based upon the notion that X and Y were substitutes. We should therefore have expected that any reduction in the price of X would reduce purchases of Y. This "substitution effect" can, as in question 9, be blurred or concealed by an "income effect"—the effect of the increase in real income caused by the price reduction that inspires the typical consumer to buy more of everything, including Y. To get a measure of the "pure substitution effect," which is uncluttered by the income effect, some type of economic benchmark was needed to establish a constant basis of comparison. Economists have found such a benchmark—the level of utility or satisfaction. This question is designed to show you how this helps us isolate the substitution effect. It asks you to consider how you

would respond to the lower price of X if your money income were simultaneously reduced just enough to permit you to achieve at best only your original level of satisfaction.

a. Let the price of X fall from $2.40 to $1.00 while your budget income simultaneously falls from $20 to $12. Assume that the price of Y is $1 throughout.

The top and bottom lines in the table below summarize the two situations discussed in question 9. In the blank spaces in the middle line, fill in the details of the "equilibrium situation" required by the conditions just outlined.

Budget	X Price	Y Price	X Quantity	Y Quantity	Satisfaction Units
$20	$2.40	$1.00	5	8	600
12	1.00	1.00	_____	_____	_____
20	1.00	1.00	10	10	674

Compare the top line with the one you have just completed. X's price has fallen, but so has income. You adjust your purchases as best you can to the new conditions. When you have done so, your satisfaction level (*has risen / is unchanged / has fallen*). There is no "income effect" arising from the lower X price, because your money income is deliberately (if temporarily) squeezed by just enough to keep your satisfaction constant.

Compare purchases in these two situations. Purchases of X (*rise / fall*) from 5 to (*3 / 7 / 10*). This is the "pure substitution effect" (of the reduction in X's price) upon X purchases. Purchases of Y (*rise / fall*) from 8 to (*5 / 7 / 10*). This is the "pure substitution effect" on Y purchases. We get what we would expect if X and Y were substitutes and X's price fell: (*an increase / a reduction*) in Y purchases.

b. Now we return you to your $20 income (with the reduced price of X still in effect). This means we compare the middle line in the table with the third line. Purchases of X rise further from 7 to 10; those of Y, from 5 to 10. These are the "income effects" of the reduction in X's price. All we have done is to "break apart" the price reduction of question 9. First we observe the results of the "pure substitution effect" (comparing top line with middle one); then the results of the "income effect" alone (comparing the middle line with the bottom one). In question 9, we went straight from the top to the bottom line (the two effects combined) without any intermediate pause.

To summarize, with matters still put in terms of a reduction in the price of X: given such an X-price reduction, the "substitution effect" tends to (*increase / leave unchanged / decrease*) X purchases, and to (*increase / leave unchanged / decrease*) Y purchases. The "income effect" of such a price reduction (with a small qualification noted below) tends to (*increase / leave unchanged / decrease*) X purchases, and to (*increase / leave unchanged / decrease*) Y purchases.

The qualification mentioned concerns "inferior goods." By

definition, a "normal good" is one of which the consumer wants to buy more as his or her income increases; an "inferior good," to buy less. Thus, within the small category of inferior goods, the "income effect" works in the opposite direction. The implications of all this are discussed more fully in intermediate price-theory texts.

a. 7; 5; 600; is unchanged; rise; 7; fall; 5; a reduction   **b.** increase; decrease; increase; increase

11.   A consumer has $50 per week to exhaust on either commodity X (price $5) or commodity Y (price $4).

For each of the four cases below, indicate, if you can, whether or not this consumer is "at equilibrium," i.e., deriving the maximum-attainable satisfaction. If you lack sufficient information to answer, explain why. If you know the consumer is not at equilibrium, indicate the required direction of movement, e.g., buy more of X and less of Y, less of X and more of Y, more of both, etc. (Any increase in purchases of either commodity would increase total utility but would decrease *MU*—i.e., the utility schedules follow the same general pattern indicated in Tables 19-2 and 19-3.)

a.   Purchases are now 2 of X and 10 of Y. Total utility of X at this level is considered to be 500 utility units; total utility of Y, 400 units.

_____ .

b.   Purchases are now 6 of X and 5 of Y. Total utility of X at this level is considered to be 400 utility units; marginal utility (*MU*) of X, 60 units; total utility of Y, 800 units; *MU* of Y, 30 units.

_____ .

c.   Purchases are now 6 of X and 5 of Y. *MU* of X at this level is considered to be 25 units; *MU* of Y, 20 units.

_____ .

d.   Purchases are now 6 of X and 4 of Y. *MU* of X at this level is considered to be 25 units; *MU* of Y, 20 units.

_____ .

a. Impossible to tell; *MU*s are not given   **b.** Buy more of X, less of Y   **c.** Now at equilibrium   **d.** Buy more of both. *MU*s are balanced with prices, but not all income is spent.

QUIZ: Multiple Choice

1.   By the "marginal utility" of a commodity is meant:
(1) an indication of the last use to which the commodity has been put, or the use to which it would next be put if more were available.
(2) the same thing as the price of that commodity.
(3) the relationship which the total utility of that commodity bears to the total utility of all other commodities that are consumed.

(4) the extra utility yielded by each successive last unit consumed of that commodity.
(5) the same thing as total utility.

2.   The "paradox of value," with respect to prices and consumer purchases, refers to which of the following?
(1) Prices of commodities are not always proportional to the total satisfaction they give us, as witness the fact that some absolute necessities of life are cheap.
(2) It is impossible to explain the price of a commodity either in terms of demand factors alone or supply factors alone.
(3) It is impossible to explain why people's tastes are what they are, or why they vary from one person to the next.
(4) Some consumers tend to value commodities according to their price, even to the point of buying more if price goes up.
(5) None of the above.

3.   The "income effect," as used in explaining the law of downward-sloping demand, means that:
(1) if people's money incomes fall, they will normally purchase less of any given commodity.
(2) any fall in price of a major purchase has an effect similar to a small rise in people's incomes, and this may prompt them to buy a little more of that good.
(3) the amount purchased of certain goods known as "inferior goods" may actually decrease as people's incomes rise.
(4) as people's incomes rise, they save proportionately more out of income; hence they actually spend a smaller fraction of their income.
(5) if the price of a good drops, it is as though the prices of all other goods had risen, in relative terms; hence slightly less of those other goods will tend to be bought.

4.   An "inferior good," by definition, is one:
(1) which consumers will not buy, except at a very low price.
(2) whose quantity purchased would decrease if its price should fall.
(3) whose marginal utility is either zero or negative.
(4) whose quantity purchased would decrease if the consumer's income should rise.
(5) not properly described by any of the preceding.

5.   The meaning of "equilibrium position" in consumer behavior may properly be described as follows:
(1) that position at which, given existing prices, the consumer would need a larger income in order to reach a higher satisfaction level.
(2) always that position which the consumer is actually occupying.
(3) the position to which the consumer would wish to move if only he or she had sufficient extra income.
(4) that position at which the consumer has no desire to have any more of any commodity.
(5) that position at which the consumer has no desire to have any more of any of the commodities now purchased.

6. When the consumer "equilibrium position" discussed in question 5 is attained, then (with "satisfaction" measured in the consumer's own personal measure of satisfaction units):
(1) the total satisfaction derived from each commodity must equal the total satisfaction derived from every other commodity.
(2) the ratio between total satisfaction derived from any commodity and the price of that commodity must be equal for all commodities.
(3) the satisfaction derived from the last tiny unit of each commodity bought must be equal as among all commodities.
(4) the ratio between total satisfaction derived from any commodity and the total expenditure on that commodity must be equal for all commodities.
(5) none of the preceding descriptions is necessarily correct.

7. A consumer's demand curve for any given commodity is most likely to shift to the right (or upward) with:
(1) a rise in the price of substitutes, or a fall in the price of complements.
(2) a rise in the price of either substitutes or complements.
(3) a fall in the price of substitutes, or a rise in the price of complements.
(4) a fall in the price of either substitutes or complements.
(5) none of these cases.

8. You have $20 per week available to spend as you wish on commodities A and B. The prices of these commodities, the quantities you now buy, and your evaluation of the utility provided by these quantities, are as follows:

	Price	Units Bought	Total Utility	Marginal Utility
A	70¢	20	500	30
B	50¢	12	1,000	20

For maximum satisfaction, you should:
(1) buy less of A, more of B.
(2) buy same quantity of A, more of B.
(3) buy more of A, less of B.
(4) buy more of A, same quantity of B.
(5) remain in your present position, since that position is the best-attainable one.

9. You regard goods X and Y as substitutes. If the price of X rises and there is some income effect from this price rise, then this income effect should induce you to (barring the special case of an inferior good):
(1) purchase more of good Y.
(2) purchase less of good Y.
(3) purchase the same amount of Y.
(4) purchase more Y only if the price of X exceeds that of Y.
(5) purchase some new, but indeterminable amount of good Y.

10. Which alternative in question 9 would have been correct if it had referred to the substitution effect and not the income effect?
(1).
(2).
(3).
(4).
(5).

11. Three of the following four statements are reasonably accurate in the sense of conforming to what the text says regarding "utility," "total utility," and "marginal utility." One is false—i.e., it runs counter to the text's ideas. Which one?
(1) Two different consumers may place quite different utility measures upon the same commodity.
(2) When total utility reaches its maximum, marginal utility must be zero.
(3) The "utility" idea is an attempt to indicate how the consumer evaluates the satisfaction derived from commodities purchasable.
(4) Total utilities may differ from one consumer to the next, but marginal utilities must be the same for both.

12. A consumer gradually increases the quantity of good X consumed until finally the level of "satiation" is reached with respect to X. Through this sequence of increases:
(1) total utility from X always remains constant, whereas marginal utility gradually falls.
(2) both total and marginal utility remain constant, up to the satiation level.
(3) total utility always rises, whereas marginal utility gradually falls.
(4) total utility may fall, but if so, marginal utility rises.
(5) both total and marginal utility may fall.

13. The price of good X is $1.50 and that of good Y $1. If a consumer considers the marginal utility of Y to be 30 units, and is in equilibrium with respect to purchases of X and Y, then he or she must consider the marginal utility of X to be:
(1) 15 units.
(2) 20 units.
(3) 30 units.
(4) 45 units.
(5) none of the above necessarily—information given is insufficient to tell.

14. If, in question 13, the figure of 30 units had been the total (rather than marginal) utility of Y, which alternative would be correct with respect to the total utility of X?
(1).
(2).
(3).
(4).
(5).

15. The price of good X falls. The "income effect" (if any) of this price change:
(1) will normally cause X purchases to be increased.

(2) will normally cause X purchases to be decreased.

(3) may cause X purchases either to increase or to decrease, there being no "normal" consequence.

(4) by definition, neither increases nor decreases X purchases.

(5) will not apply, since "income effects" refer to changes in spendable income, not to price changes.

16. If the marginal utility of a commodity is zero, then:

(1) total utility for this commodity has reached a maximum.

(2) the commodity in question has no utility, i.e., it is not one that consumers want to use.

(3) the paradox of value must be involved.

(4) the consumer has reached his or her equilibrium position with respect to purchase of this commodity.

(5) total utility for this commodity must be zero also.

17. A consumer moves to a new equilibrium position as a result of some change either in market price or in income. In this new equilibrium situation, marginal utilities are all lower than they were in the old equilibrium situation. Tastes or preferences are unchanged. This means that (in utility terms) this consumer:

(1) is definitely worse off in the new situation.

(2) is definitely better off in the new situation.

(3) is definitely worse off in the new situation if income has changed, but not otherwise.

(4) is definitely better off in the new situation if price has changed, but not otherwise.

(5) may be better off or worse off in the new situation, since the information given does not necessarily indicate one or the other.

18. The idea of "consumer surplus" reflects the fact that:

(1) in some purchases, the gain consumers obtain from buying exceeds the gain suppliers obtain from selling.

(2) the purchase of many goods is an immense bargain to consumers, for, if necessary, they would pay far more than they actually do in order to get them.

(3) the marginal utility of the first units of a product consumed may considerably exceed the total utility which this product supplies.

(4) total utility increases either when consumer incomes rise or when the prices they must pay for goods fall.

(5) when demand is inelastic with respect to price, buyers can obtain a larger quantity for the expenditure of less money.

APPENDIX:
Geometrical Analysis of Consumer Equilibrium

This Appendix deals with the same central problem discussed in the chapter: how to use a given budget or income to the best advantage, if one has particular tastes, and faces a given set of consumer-goods prices.

Only the illustrative method is different. Here, it is the *indifference-curve* approach. By this method, the whole problem of "maximizing satisfaction" (given individual tastes and subject to a budgetary constraint on possible levels of consumption defined by income and prices) can be illustrated on a single graph. To be sure, the graph deals with a very simple case: only two goods are involved. Despite this simplicity, however, the method still reveals with some increased clarity the nature of the general problem where choices are made over a large number of goods and services. The indifference curve approach is not, in other words, limited to the simple two-good case in its most general form. It is simply the only case that we can graph on a page of paper.

Indifference-curve analysis has a further advantage. It avoids the assumption that consumers put numerical "utility values" onto each quantity of each commodity, an assumption which many economists (not unreasonably) dislike. It assumes, instead, that people can simply display their preferences by ranking various possible combinations of goods. Given any two bundles of goods, to be more specific, indifference-curve theory assumes only that people can tell the economist which they prefer, if either. Having worked through this Appendix, you should have mastered the following objectives.

LEARNING OBJECTIVES

1. Define (*a*) indifference curve; (*b*) indifference map.

2. Explain whether indifference curves (maps) are identical for all consumers, or whether they vary from one individual to the next.

3. Show that it would be impossible (save for a most unusual individual) for an indifference curve to run in the southwest-to-northeast direction.

4. Draw a line at any angle across an indifference map graph, starting at the origin. Move northeast along that line, crossing indifference curves as you do so. Explain whether, in this movement, you are reaching lower levels of utility, higher levels, or are not changing the utility level at all.

5. Describe what is meant by a budget (or consumption-possibility) line.

6. Explain how the budget line shifts (if it does) with a price increase for one of the two goods involved. Explain how it would move (if it does) for an income increase.

1. **a.** "Indifference curves" are intended to depict a consumer's tastes. Any single indifference-curve line, such as that in text Figure 19A-1, is made up of a series of points. Each point on such a line stands for a different *(amount of money / level of satisfaction / combination of two commodities)*. What these points—all the points on any one line—have in common is that they all represent the same *(amount of money / level of satisfaction / combination of two commodities)*, in the eyes of this consumer.

b. We can represent a consumer's indifference map by drawing any one or two of *(several / an infinite number of)* indifference lines or curves. Given any two such indifference curves, the one lying farther from the graph's origin—i.e., farther to the northeast—must stand for the *(higher / same / lower)* level of satisfaction. On text Figure 19-2A, draw lightly a 45° line from the origin (bottom left-hand corner) of the graph. The four points at which this line crosses the four indifference curves mark four different clothing-food combinations. The farther out the indifference curve from the origin, the larger is the indicated level of consumption of both food and clothing and thus the higher the level of utility (recall that marginal utility is always positive, so supplements in the consumption of any good without some sacrifice of another must improve utility).

c. If two different clothing-food combinations lie on the same indifference curve—i.e., if they indicate the same satisfaction level for you as a consumer—the second must represent more food and less clothing (or vice versa) than the first. (You cannot be at the same level of satisfaction as before if you have more food and more clothing, or if you have less food and less clothing.) This is indicated by the fact that any single indifference curve runs in a generally *(northeast-to-southwest / northwest-to-southeast)* direction.

---

a. combination of two commodities; level of satisfaction **b.** an infinite number of; higher **c.** northwest-to-southeast

2. **a.** Now set aside for a moment the indifference-curve idea—i.e., the representation of a particular consumer's tastes. Turn instead to what you could buy (regardless of your tastes), if blessed with a given income and faced with a particular set of prices.

In the simple two-good case here discussed, all the possible combinations purchasable can be represented by a straight line on a graph—the *budget line* or *consumption-possibility line* in the text's Figure 19A-3.

Be sure you understand the information which this budget or consumption-possibility line is intended to convey. Each and any point on this line stands for a different *(amount of money income / level of satisfaction / combination of the two commodities)*. The combinations are all different, but they all have one thing in common, namely that, given the prices specified, they all *(are purchasable for the same money income amount / stand for the same level of satisfaction)*.

b. So you can move up or down this budget line as you wish; all points thereon are equal so far as the expenditure of money income is concerned. Which point should you choose? That is a matter of your tastes. In the matter of the satisfaction they yield, the various food-clothing combinations on the budget line are not equal. You should pick the combination which you like most—or in more elegant terms, which "maximizes your satisfaction."

The mention of tastes pulls us back to indifference curves again. The task of moving back and forth along the budget line, seeking the maximum-satisfaction food-clothing combination, is just a matter of finding the point on this budget line which reaches the *(highest- / lowest-)* attainable indifference curve. This is illustrated in text Figure 19A-4. The highest-attainable indifference curve is always the one which lies farthest to the *(northeast / southwest)* on an ordinary graph.

---

a. combination of the two commodities; are purchasable for the same money income amount **b.** highest-; northeast

---

It is important to note that the division of tastes and budget concerns that is apparent in the organization of questions 1 and 2 is more than an accident. It is a division that is, in economic terms, equally clear and well-defined. Factors that influence preferences are reflected in only indifference curves; factors that influence what you can afford are reflected only in the budget line.

3. Studying text Figure 19A-4, you will see that point *B*, the equilibrium or maximum-satisfaction point, is one at which the indifference curve is just tangent to the budget or consumption-possibility line. That is, equilibrium is a situation where the slope of the one line matches the slope of the other.

It happens that the slope of the budget line is a matter of the prices of the two commodities involved. This question explores the matter more fully.

The slope of the line in text Figure 19A-4 (neglecting its negative sign) is $6/4$, or $1\frac{1}{2}$. At the two extreme positions, you could have either 6 of *C* and zero *F* (point *N*), or 4 of *F* and zero *C* (point *M*). If you move any distance down the line from point *N*, you find that this $6/4$ (or $3/2$) swapping ratio applies. If you move from *N* to the middle dot on *NM*, you must give up 3 units of *C*, but you gain 2 units of *F*.

The prices of *F* and *C* govern this swapping ratio. Giving up 3 units of *C* (price \$1) recovers \$3 of your budget. This you can use to buy 2 units of *F* (price \$1.50). So, whether measured at 6/4, 3/2, or \$1.50/\$1, the slope measures market swapping terms. (But note that when we switch from quantities to prices, *C* and *F* change places. You can buy the commodity with the lower price in greater quantity.)

To exercise your understanding of this part, suppose that a budget limits combined expenditure on clothing (*C*) and food (*F*) to \$40. With the prices for *C* and *F* as indicated below, compute the slope of the consumption-possibility line (the budget line) first as a ratio of C/F and then compare that slope to the ratio p_F/p_C. F is the commodity measured along the horizontal axis, as it is in the text. Assume that all slope values are preceded by an unrecorded minus sign.

	Ratio C/F		Ratio p_F/p_C	
A $p_c = \$1, p_F = \$4$	_____ / _____		_____ / _____	
B $p_C = \$5, p_F = \$2$	_____ / _____		_____ / _____	
C $p_C = \$2, p_F = \$10$	_____ / _____		_____ / _____	

A: 40, 10; \$4, \$1   B: 8, 20; \$2, \$5   C: 20, 4; \$10, \$2

4. The text chapter Appendix concludes with a brief survey of the effects of a change in income or in price upon the equilibrium position.

a. Consider income changes first. If your income is halved (as in the text example), then you must cut down on your purchases. The income cut means—look at text Figure 19A-5—a shift of the budget line to the *(northeast / southwest)*. The new half-the-income budget line *(is / is not)* parallel to the old one because the prices that define the slope *(have / have not)* changed (see question 3 again if you do not know what prices have to do with anything).

In this new and painful income situation, you will not necessarily buy food and clothing in the same proportions as before. You must cut your purchases, and may indeed cut each of them by 50 percent. (This is what happens in the text's illustration.) But the point you pick on your new budget line will be governed, as before, by your tastes. You may wind up buying relatively more food and less clothing, or vice versa.

b. An increase in the price of food or of clothing works somewhat like an income reduction: it pulls you down to a lower satisfaction level. But compare text Figure 19A-6 (illustrating an increase in food price) with text Figure 19A-5 (income reduction). In both instances, the budget line shifts in position. In Figure 19A-6, the new budget line *(is / is not)* parallel with the old one. The point is that if you wanted to spend all your income on clothing, a food-price increase would not affect you. Point N (text Figure 19A-6) is still attainable. At the other extreme, if you spent all your income on food, a doubling of its price would *(leave you unaffected / require you to halve your purchases)*.

That is why the budget line shifts as it does. And as before, you pick the best-attainable position on your new budget line, as your personal tastes dictate.

There is more to be said on these topics, but it must be left for more advanced texts.

a. southwest; is; have not   **b.** is not; require you to halve your purchases

5. In the upper part of Figure 19A-1, the line AB_0 is a consumer's initial *"budget line,"* and E_0 is his or her equilibrium

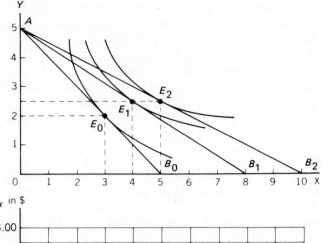

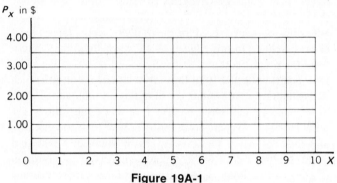

Figure 19A-1

point thereon. The curved line is an indifference curve for this consumer, and it is tangent to the budget line at this E_0 point. (The two other curved lines are also indifference curves.) The price of good X is \$4.

a. The consumer's income or budget must be:
(1) \$50.
(2) \$20.
(3) \$10.
(4) \$5.
(5) \$2.
(6) impossible to tell.

b. The price of good Y must be:
(1) \$1.
(2) \$2.
(3) \$3.
(4) \$4.
(5) \$5.
(6) impossible to tell from diagram.

c. The budget or consumption-possibility line shifts from position AB_0 to position AB_1. Such a shift could be caused only by:
(1) a fall in the price of X.
(2) a rise in the price of X.
(3) a rise in the price of Y.
(4) a fall in the price of Y.
(5) an increase in income.

d. Quantitatively, what change is indicated by the shift from AB_0 to AB_1? That is, whether it is price of X, price of Y, or income that has changed, what is its new value?

(1) $50.
(2) $20.
(3) $10.
(4) $5.
(5) $2.50.
(6) $2.
(7) $1.

e. If a further shift in the *AB* line occurs, from AB_1 to AB_2, which alternative in part **c** explains it? . . . . *(1 / 2 / 3 / 4 / 5)*

f. Which alternative in part **d** indicates the new value of the magnitude which has changed? . . . . *(1 / 2 / 3 / 4 / 5 / 6 / 7)*

g. Use the lower part of Figure 19A-1 to show the demand curve of the consumer in the preceding questions for commodity X. This demand curve is to be drawn given the particular level of income and price of good Y indicated by the preceding questions. Plot three points on this curve, correctly indicating the consumer's demand for X in these circumstances. (HINT: What price or prices of X must go with the three consumption-possibility lines illustrated? What quantity or quantities of X will be bought? Join these three points with a smooth curve.)

---

a. $20   **b.** $4   **c.** a fall in the price of X   **d.** $2.50   **e.** (1)   **f.** (6)   **g.** There are three combinations of price and quantity that can be gleaned from the top of Figure 19A-1: ($P = \$4$; $X = 3$), ($P = \$2.50$; $X = 4$), and ($P = \$2$; $X = 5$)

QUIZ: Multiple Choice

1. The position and shape of any indifference curve for any particular consumer are governed:
(1) by his or her tastes and by the amount of the income or budget.
(2) solely by the prices of the goods bought.
(3) by tastes, by the amount of income, and by the prices of the goods bought.
(4) by the prices of the goods bought and by the amount of income, not by tastes.
(5) solely by his or her tastes.

2. Which alternative in question 1 correctly names the factor or factors governing the budget line?
(1).

(2).
(3).
(4).
(5).

3. On an indifference-curve map, a consumer's approach to the equilibrium position is properly described as follows. The consumer:
(1) moves to that point on the budget line representing the combination of goods having the highest money value.
(2) moves to that point on the budget line whose slope equals the ratio of the two prices.
(3) moves along the budget line until the extra utility supplied by one good is just equal to the extra utility supplied by the other.
(4) picks the highest-valued indifference curve which the budget line makes attainable.
(5) picks the highest-valued budget line which the indifference curve makes attainable.

4. Among the following five statements describing indifference-curve analysis, one is incorrect. Which one?
(1) Each point on an indifference curve stands for a different combination of two goods.
(2) Each point on a budget line stands for a different combination of two goods.
(3) All points on an indifference curve stand for the same level of real income in the sense of satisfaction.
(4) All points on a budget line stand for the same level of money income.
(5) All points on an indifference curve stand for the same level of money income.

5. You are told that an indifference curve involving goods X and Y runs from southwest to northeast. Your response to this statement is that this:
(1) must indicate an increase in the consumer's income.
(2) is impossible, because it would indicate that the consumer gets no satisfaction at all from X, or else none from Y.
(3) must indicate a change in the consumer's tastes.
(4) must indicate a change in the price of either X or Y.
(5) is impossible because larger quantities of both X and Y cannot indicate the same satisfaction level as lesser quantities thereof, unless the consumer wants no more of either of these two goods.

CHAPTER 20

BUSINESS ORGANIZATION AND INCOME

There were, early in the 1980s, more than 16 billion businesses in the United States. The largest preponderance of these businesses were, and still are, independent proprietorships (76 percent by actual count), but these forms of business are hardly ever very large. For average annual sales of less than $40,000, proprietors work long and hard (50 to 60 hours per week). They typically face chronic cash flow problems, but they find bankers reluctant to lend them money without assessing high-risk premiums. Help in these matters is sometimes available from the Small Business Administration and/or small business investment companies, but not always. Proprietors own their own businesses and are thus their own bosses, of course, but they face the progressive personal tax rate if they are unusually successful and unlimited liability even if they are not. It is not life on Easy Street.

The least popular form of business organization is the partnership; there were only about 1 million of these in the United States during the early 1980s. Partnerships are typically larger than an individual proprietorship, with average annual sales in the neighborhood of $200,000, but the good news might stop there. Partners face the progressive personal tax schedule, risk, unlimited liability, and experience cash flow problems just like the proprietor. In addition, partners share decision-making authority with other people. Partnerships may, therefore, appear to some to capture all the bad characteristics of proprietorships without garnering any of the advantages.

Corporations represent the third and last major form of business organization. They tend to be large and powerful. Their average annual sales hover around $2 million, but over 250 corporations sell more than $1 billion in goods and services annually. Owners typically forfeit decision-making authority to professional managers, but they are rewarded for this sacrifice with liability limited to the amount of their investment. Corporations can last forever, too, so that a voluntary or involuntary decision of one owner to leave the corporation is hardly ever noticed—his or her stock is simply sold in the market or

bequested in a will to someone else. Corporate income is subject to the corporate income (profits) tax, and dividends are awarded out of the remaining after-tax income to individual stockholders. These dividends are, of course, subject themselves to the personal income tax. The system therefore effectively sets up a sort of double taxation that has made the corporate income tax one of this country's most controversial.

Having worked through the story of the computer software company in the text and the problems recorded here, the reader should have met the following objectives.

LEARNING OBJECTIVES

1. Explain the differences between the three major forms of business organization: proprietorship, partnership, and corporation.

2. Explain the meaning of "unlimited liability" as it applies to each of the three forms.

3. Explain why any growing business is likely to find itself in potentially acute need of more capital financing.

4. Explain the propensity of large businesses to be incorporated.

5. List the advantages and/or disadvantages to any individual with money to invest across the three business forms.

6. Distinguish between (a) bonds, (b) common stock, (c) bank loans, and (d) retained earnings as mechanisms for raising new capital. Note the advantages and disadvantages of each in the context of the corporate income tax.

7. Outline what is meant by the "divorce of ownership and control" in large corporations. List social problems that this divorce might create.

8. Define and explain the following sources of growth: (a) knowledge, (b) sales personnel, (c) economies of scale, (d) vertical integration, (e) horizontal integration, and (f) diversification.

9. Understand the basic objectives for and defenses against takeovers.

Much of this chapter concentrates on a single theme:

▶The form a particular business takes—individual proprietorship, partnership, or corporation—is almost always dictated by the amount of money needed to operate in that line of business.

In many industries there is no room for choice, and only a single business form is found: the corporation. If large quantities of money are needed for successful operation in a given line of business, then no individual proprietorships or partnerships will be found.

Two principal reasons explain why any business demands that money be "tied up" in it. First, it may be necessary to buy expensive, long-lasting machinery, tools, and equipment; perhaps also a building to house them.

But a need for money capital arises quite apart from the necessary investment in such "fixed assets." It arises out of the inevitable lag between money expenditure and money receipts. Money must be spent to buy materials and hire labor. Money is collectible only after the materials have been processed and the resulting finished goods sold. So a growing business needs more *working capital* even when it is not buying more machinery or equipment.

Above all, the corporation is a device for raising money in large volume. This is the key to understanding its characteristics. Ownership shares can be sold to a small number of people or to a large number. The properties of shares of stock are attractive to most holders of money. You can buy 5 shares of stock, or 5000. You need not "follow your money"; professional managers will tend to the running of the business. "Limited liability" assures you that, at worst, you can lose only the money you spent to buy the stock. You are free to sell the stock at any time without asking the corporation's consent. All such features tend to attract those with money available to put into business enterprise.

1. Five people own equal shares in a partnership. For any one of the five, the meaning of "unlimited liability" is this: that person is responsible for *(20 percent of the partnership's debts, up to the amount he or she has invested in the business / 20 percent of the partnership debts, no matter how large the amount / 100 percent of the partnership debts, if necessary, in the event the other partners cannot pay their shares, no matter how large the amount).*

---

100 percent of the partnership debts, if necessary, in the event the other partners cannot pay their shares, no matter how large the amount

2. Note that in this chapter the word "capital" has a meaning quite different from that given it in Chapter 3. "Capital" in that earlier chapter meant *(money used to finance a business / money loaned with a strong element of risk involved / manufactured productive inputs, not money).*

"Capital" in this present chapter means money. (To complicate life still further for you, the word has a still different meaning in the chapter Appendix, which deals with accounting records.)

The terms "venture capital" and "equity capital" are not precisely defined, but their meanings overlap. Risk is the common element. Venture capital (the more loosely used term) means money furnished to a business, with risk of loss involved, without specification as to the manner in which it is furnished. Equity capital means, in contrast (pick one):
(1) The excess of assets over liabilities.
(2) Money which typically buys a share of ownership in the business and the chances of gain or loss going with it.
(3) Money loaned to a business involving any form of risk whatever.

---

manufactured productive inputs, not money; (2)

3. **a.** A corporation *(must / may or may not)* have common stock. The law which created the corporate form says that a corporation must have owners—and the stockholders are its owners.

This stock *(must / may or may not)* be listed on an exchange, such as the New York Stock Exchange. (Actually, only a relatively small number of giant corporations have their stock so listed. Most corporations are "private," in the sense that their stock is not publicly listed for trading. Often this stock is held entirely or almost entirely by members of a single family, only rarely changing hands.)
b. A corporation *(must / may or may not)* have bonds outstanding. The vital difference between stocks and bonds is that bonds are *(certificates of ownership / IOUs)*. The corporation is free to borrow (i.e., issue such IOUs) or not to borrow, as it sees fit.

---

a. must; may or may not   **b.** may or may not; IOUs

4. Put a check in the spaces below if the description properly applies to a bond (*B*), a common stock (*S*) and/or a stock option (*O*):

	B	O	S
a. Income generated is called interest.			
b. Income generated is called a dividend. ..			
c. Does not pay more than a fixed and stated amount of income to owner.			
d. No specified dollar amount of income implied in ownership.			
e. Represents a share of ownership in corporation.			

	B	O	S

f. Represents corporation's IOU, not a share of ownership. . . . .

g. Offers complete assurance of steady annual income for owner. . . . .

h. Annual payment to purchaser is a fixed obligation of corporation. . . . .

i. Offers a chance for "capital gain." . . . . . .

j. May be sold or canceled at any time by purchaser without consulting corporation. . . . . .

k. Among these three types, offers greatest assurance of steady annual income. . . . .

l. Corporation will buy it back for stated amount at specified future date. . . . .

m. Must be issued by every business corporation. . . . .

n. Has "limited liability" feature for owner. .

o. Income anticipated is essentially a capital gain if executed. . . . .

p. Income must be paid to owner in all circumstances short of bankruptcy. . . . .

q. Represents a purchase agreement contracted on a contingency basis. . . . .

r. Income paid to owner only when board of directors decides it should be paid. . . . .

s. Income received therefrom is subject to personal income tax. . . . .

t. Is "equity capital" for corporation. . . . . . .

u. Is a "fixed charge" for corporation. . . . . .

Bond: a, c, f, h, i, j, k, l, n, p, s, u
Option: d, i, j, n, o, p, q, r, s, t
Common: b, d, e, i, j, m, n, r, s, t

5. **a.** Two businesses are identical with one another with respect to size, machinery, competence of working force, cash on hand, etc. They differ only in that No. 1 is a newly organized concern and No. 2 has established a good reputation over 20 years. If you could buy either of these for the same price, the better buy would be *(No. 1 / No. 2)*. In fact, the worth of *(No. 1 / No. 2)* would exceed that of the other company. The best possible estimate of the extra worth of this company in dollars is called its *(fixed assets / net worth / monopoly power / goodwill / equity capital)*.

b. Suppose promoters buy such an established company. They then sell stock to the public, and in the process they deliberately exaggerate the money worth of such *(fixed assets / net worth / monopoly power / goodwill)*, or the worth of other assets, in order to sell the stock at a higher price. This process is called *(watering the stock / incurring fixed charges / obtaining inequity capital / making a capital gain)*.

An established and well-regarded company does have "goodwill," and it is a most valuable asset. But its exact money worth is exceedingly difficult—impossible, in fact—to establish. For this reason (and perhaps also because, in the past, grossly exaggerated valuations were sometimes used), today you are unlikely to find "goodwill" listed among the assets on a corporation's balance sheet.

Usually it is only when a business is being sold that the goodwill issue arises. The seller quite naturally wants to be paid for it. The figure that buyer and seller agree upon may or may not be a good estimate of the worth of goodwill. All that can be said of it is that this is the bargain they have struck.

a. No. 2; No. 2; goodwill **b.** goodwill; watering the stock

6. Put an (*H*) in the space below if the act in question represents *horizontal integration*; put a (*V*) if *vertical integration*; put an (*N*) if neither.

a. An aluminum-manufacturing company buys a bauxite mine. (Bauxite is the ore from which aluminum is made.). . . . . (_____)

b. The same company buys a competing aluminum-manufacturing concern. . . . . (_____)

c. It builds a fabricating plant to process aluminum sheeting into finished aluminum consumer goods. . . . . . . (_____)

d. It buys a chain of retail hardware stores in order to market its aluminum products more effectively. . . . . (_____)

e. It buys a second chain of retail stores to expand its market still further. . . . . (_____)

a. *V* **b.** *H* **c.** *V* **d.** *V* **e.** *H*

7. **a.** The function of an investment banking firm is to (pick one):
(1) accept money deposits from its customers or clientele and to lend out this money to corporations.
(2) act as intermediary between corporations wishing to raise money by a bond or stock issue and people with money available to purchase such securities.
b. When an investment banking firm underwrites a stock or bond issue, this means it gives its assurance to (pick one):
(1) the buyers of the issue that it is of good quality, at the risk of incurring liability to those buyers should trouble later develop.
(2) the sellers of the issue that they will receive a specified price, the bank taking the risk that it may itself have to buy some part of the issue at that price, then sell it later at a lower price.

a. (2) **b.** (2)

8. Corporations must pay a federal income (profits) tax. Unlike the personal tax, though, the tax rate does not keep climbing as income climbs; it is assessed at a constant rate for all corporations with (taxable) incomes above $100,000. This does not mean, however, that the tax is inconsequential. Even within a constant tax rate tax, the deductibility of interest payments against income before the tax rate is applied makes borrowing more attractive than it might otherwise be. Accelerated depreciation and investment tax credits can, meanwhile, encourage investment activity that might otherwise be forgone. Some people argue that the corporate income tax should be abolished and the revenue lost generated by an adjustment in the personal income tax. Others argue that depreciation allowances and investment credits have already abolished the tax. This question will explore why there might be an issue here.

a. When a shareholder receives a dividend, the amount *(is / is not)* subject to personal income tax. The personal income tax *(also applies / does not apply)* to profit undistributed by the corporation.

b. Suppose you are considering incorporation of your business. If the income from that business is high, and you do not incorporate, you are subject to a high personal-income-tax rate (say, 50 percent). Incorporation means a maximum tax rate of about 25 percent. Viewed in isolation from other facts, this is an argument *(for / against)* incorporation.

c. But incorporation means that in addition to the corporate tax, personal income tax applies to all income paid out as dividends ("double taxation"). This is an argument *(for / against)* incorporation.

d. However, zero personal income tax is applied to whatever corporation income is not paid out in dividends. This is an argument *(for / against)* incorporation.

---

a. is; does not apply **b.** for **c.** against **d.** for

QUIZ: Multiple Choice

1. The term "limited liability" is frequently used in enumerating the characteristics of a corporation. It means the following:
(1) any officer of the corporation is strictly limited in his or her ability to speak for the corporation and commit it to any liability.
(2) once shareholders have paid for their stock, they have no further financial obligation, regardless of how much trouble the corporation gets into.
(3) the corporation's liability to pay dividends to its stockholders is a limited one, since it need pay them only if it has earned a profit.
(4) there are certain obligations which a corporation can legally refuse to pay.
(5) the corporation has only a limited obligation to meet claims made by any single person or firm against it (provided it has acted within the scope of its charter), so that there is some protection for its assets and financial position.

2. A corporation's obligation to pay interest on bonds it has issued is properly described as follows:
(1) interest must be paid regardless of whether a profit has been earned or not.
(2) interest must be paid whenever a profit has been earned.
(3) interest need not be paid even if a profit has been earned, but it must be paid before any dividend is paid.
(4) normally, interest ranks ahead of dividends, but there are some circumstances in which a dividend can be paid without payment of bond interest.
(5) interest ranks behind dividends, and is paid only after dividends have been paid in full.

3. In considering the order or ranking in which a corporation is obligated to pay out various sums of money, payment of dividends on common stock takes precedence over (ranks ahead of):
(1) corporation income taxes.
(2) local property taxes.
(3) salaries of the board of directors.
(4) bond interest.
(5) none of these obligations.

4. The primary business of an investment banking firm is to:
(1) make loans to small business.
(2) sell corporation securities.
(3) accept money deposits from its customers.
(4) own the shares of a number of corporations—i.e., act as a "holding company".
(5) sell its own securities, using the proceeds to buy stock in other corporations.

5. A preferred stock is like a:
(1) bond, because the dividend must always be paid by the corporation.
(2) bond, because the holder of such stock is legally a creditor of the corporation rather than a part owner.
(3) bond, since both bond interest and preferred-stock dividend payments are considered operating costs rather than distributions of profit.
(4) common stock, because dividends on both stock types ordinarily increase when company profits increase.
(5) common stock, since no dividend need be paid on either stock if the board of directors decides it is inappropriate to pay one.

6. The term "goodwill" refers to:
(1) a valuation placed on the personal integrity of those who own or operate the business.
(2) a fictitious increase in the company's net worth position, created by inflating the value of one or more assets to an exaggerated figure.
(3) the earning power of the business.
(4) the extra earning power of the business resulting from its established position.
(5) providing working capital for established customers by allowing them extra time for settlement of their accounts.

7. A corporation that is considering "debt financing" (financing via a bond issue) must recognize the fact that:
(1) it always involves a fixed annual charge to be paid to debt holders whether the corporation has earned profits or not.
(2) issue of debt gives the debt holders a voice in the management of the corporation's affairs, so that they may usurp some part of management's authority.
(3) the new debt holders are not necessarily the same group as the original stockholders, so that the ownership shares of those stockholders are diluted by debt financing.
(4) it does not actually bring in any additional cash to the corporation.
(5) this method of financing first requires an amendment to the corporation's charter.

8. If a steel-producing company merges with two other companies, one a producer of iron ore, the other a company which fabricates steel into finished or semifinished steel products, this would be an example of:
(1) vertical integration.
(2) establishing a holding company.
(3) the acquisition of venture capital.
(4) the development of goodwill.
(5) none of the preceding.

9. Today's most common ownership and control arrangement for large American corporations (according to the text) is best described as follows:
(1) The professional managers are also the group owning a majority or near-majority of stock, so that they can make all major decisions without real consideration of the wishes of minority stockholders.
(2) The professional managers make all major decisions, and the board of directors does not intervene unless it is losing confidence in those managers.
(3) The professional managers control the company on all matters of importance except for basic decisions on such matters as production, new plants and new products, these being left to the board of directors as stockholder representatives.
(4) The board of directors makes the decisions on all matters of real importance, the role of the professional managers being confined to routine matters.
(5) The stockholders rather than the board of directors are increasingly making major decisions, through voting-power control exercised at stockholder meetings.

10. The application of the federal personal income tax to the shareholders of a corporation, with respect to the income (i.e., profit) of that corporation, applies:
(1) in full to the corporation's entire income whether distributed as dividends or not.
(2) only to that part actually distributed as dividends.
(3) only to that part of income not paid out as dividends— i.e., only to undistributed profit.
(4) neither to dividends nor to undistributed profit.
(5) both to dividends and to undistributed profit, but with a heavier rate applicable to undistributed profit.

11. Had question 10 referred to the corporation income tax, not the personal income tax, which alternative in that question would be correct?
(1).
(2).
(3).
(4).
(5).

12. If an investment banking house "underwrites" a stock or a bond issue for some corporation, it:
(1) gives its personal guarantee that the interest or dividend promised in this issue will be paid as specified.
(2) lends the corporation an amount of money equal to the value of that issue, to be repaid when the issue in question has been fully sold to the public.
(3) sells the issue to its customers, with the assurance that, upon request and within a specified time period, it will buy back any part thereof, at a specified minimum price.
(4) acts as agent for the corporation, but without any firm guarantee as to the amount of the issue it will sell, or the price it can obtain.
(5) guarantees the corporation full sale of that issue at a fixed price, even if the bank has to buy part of the issue itself.

13. A corporation's obligation with respect to payment of interest on loans (B) and dividends on common stock (CS) is correctly described as follows. It:
(1) must pay its bond interest if it has earned sufficient profit to do so, but pays a CS dividend only if the board of directors so decides.
(2) must pay both if profits are sufficient to do so.
(3) must pay its interest regardless of profit earned or loss incurred, but pays its CS dividend only if the board of directors so decides.
(4) must pay both regardless of profit earned or loss incurred, unless so doing would force it into bankruptcy.
(5) need pay neither regardless of the amount of profit earned, unless the board of directors decides on such dividend payment, although the bond interest must have priority.

14. The usual progression through business forms is:
(1) partnership, proprietorship, corporation.
(2) proprietorship, partnership, corporation.
(3) partnership, corporation, proprietorship.
(4) nonexistent because there does not exist a typical evolution.

15. Which of the following is not a potential source of growth for an individual business of any form?
(1) Vertical integration.
(2) Diversification.
(3) Extended sales force.
(4) Investment tax credits.
(5) None of the above.

16. Which of the following sources of investment capital comes from internal sources?
(1) Stock sales.
(2) Bank loans.
(3) Depreciation.
(4) Bond sales.
(5) None of the above.

APPENDIX:
Elements of Accounting

Accounting concepts are cornerstones of life in the economic age. This Appendix provides an introduction to two of the basics: the balance sheet and the income statement. The balance sheet is a snapshot of financial health; it reflects the economic condition of an economic entity at some prescribed point in time. The income statement is, by way of contrast, a motion picture—it reflects growth or problems over a given period of time; it clarifies the blur between two different snapshots. Having completed work on this Appendix, you will have met the following objectives.

LEARNING OBJECTIVES

1. Explain carefully the information which a balance sheet is intended to convey. List the major categories appearing on the two sides of a balance sheet, and indicate the meaning (or definition) of each of those categories.

2. List the major items appearing on an income statement, in order of their appearance, so as to indicate the information which that statement is intended to convey. (Include the beginning inventory and closing inventory items in your listing, and explain the need for their appearance.)

3. Explain why some cash expenditures by a firm do not appear on its income statement, and why some items that are not cash expenditures do appear.

4. Distinguish between (*a*) "straight-line" depreciation, "declining-balance" depreciation, and "accelerated" depreciation; (*b*) depreciation charges on the income statement and allowance for depreciation on the balance sheet; (*c*) addition to earnings retained on the income statement and earnings retained on the balance sheet.

The principal lesson of this Appendix concerns the kinds of information that two accounting forms are intended to convey: the balance sheet and the income (or profit-and-loss) statement.

▶The balance sheet is a point-in-time statement. Its primary function is to record what the company is "worth," as closely as can be estimated, at some point in time.

The balance sheet begins by listing the firm's assets: everything it owns—cash, buildings, equipment, inventory, and so on. Each item is given a money value, the best possible estimate of its money worth at that point in time. Sometimes the estimating job isn't easy. There is no problem in figuring the worth of a given amount of cash. But reckoning the true present worth of a factory building or of an elderly machine may be a tough job.

Among these assets, the company can and should include legitimate money claims on others (e.g., money owed by its customers). Sometimes, "intangible" assets are included; but you should disregard these for now. (Goodwill, for example, is such an intangible asset; on this, see question 5, page 206.)

The firm's "worth" is not likely to be the same figure as the total of its assets. Any debts owed to others—its liabilities—must be deducted. The resulting figure is its net worth. Note carefully:

▶Net worth, by definition, is assets minus liabilities.

Accordingly, it must also be true that

▶Total assets = total liabilities + net worth.

Balance sheets are ordinarily drawn up in precisely this manner: assets in one column; liabilities in an adjoining column; net worth below liabilities.

To say that "the balance sheet always balances" is just to say that the assets column total must be the same as the liabilities plus net worth column total. This must be true, because net worth is defined to be whatever figure is needed to make things come out even; that's how it is computed.

Turning now to the income (or profit-and-loss) statement:

▶The income statement is a period-of-time statement. Its primary function is to record how much profit the company earned from its sales during that period (e.g., 1 year).

The income statement begins by listing the total of goods sold during the period in question, at their sale price. From this sales total are deducted all the expenses that ought properly to be charged as part of the cost of making and selling the goods in question, but only the expenses that ought to be so charged. What's left after deduction of these expenses is the company's profit for the period in question.

Watch out for the most common of income-statement mistakes: do not assume that income statements record only cash transactions. It is true that the sales total is likely to be matched by a cash inflow of approximately the same amount, but some of the "expenses" listed on an income statement need not entail any cash outpayment during the period involved. And some cash outpayments that were made during the period will not show up on the income statement at all. (The review questions take you through this set of complications.)

If some items shown on an income statement do not stand for cash transactions, and if some cash transactions during the period aren't shown on that statement, then net profit (at the bottom of the income statement) is certainly not going to be an accurate record of the change in the company's cash position. It isn't intended to be. Every item on an income statement, or on a balance

Table 20A-1

Assets	Liabilities and Net Worth
Cash .... $ _____	Liabilities ..... $ _____
	Net worth:
	Capital ..... $ _____

sheet, has a money figure appended. But in almost all instances, this is using "money" in its abstract, "estimate-of-value" sense, and not in the sense of "cash on hand." If you want to know how much cash a company has, its balance sheet is a very good place to look. But don't look for it under esoteric categories like net worth or retained earnings. Just look under cash on hand.

1. In December 1979, the Utter Confusion Manufacturing Company was formed, with sale for cash of 5000 shares of common stock at $10 apiece.

On Table 20A-1, show this firm's balance sheet as of December 31, 1979. Assume that the proceeds from the entire $50,000 stock sale are still held in cash and that no other transactions have yet taken place. Note that Table 20A-1 is set up in the conventional way: a column headed "assets" at the left, a column headed "liabilities and net worth" on the right.

Assets	Liabilities and Net Worth
Cash $50,000	Liabilities .... $ 0
	Net worth:
	Capital 50,000

2. During 1980 the firm's operations were as follows:
1. Money received (all in cash):
   A. Sales of merchandise manufactured .. $115,000
   B. Bonds sold (100 bonds @ $1,000) 100,000

2. Money paid out (all in cash):
   A. Machinery purchased $170,000
   B. Raw materials purchased for use 50,000
   C. Wages paid to labor 24,000
   D. Interest paid on bond issue 10,000

3. Other facts (not involving cash received or paid):

All raw materials purchased were fully used up in manufacturing before the year-end (i.e., closing inventory of raw materials was zero).

All finished goods manufactured were sold (i.e., zero finished-goods closing inventory).

Depreciation on machinery was estimated at $17,000. (Note that this is just a way of saying that while the machinery was worth $170,000 when bought—say, on January 1—it was estimated as being worth only $153,000 on December 31, having been partly "used up" or worn out by use during the year. It does not mean a cash outlay of $17,000.)

a. How much cash did Utter Confusion have on December

Table 20A-2

Assets (in thousands)	Liabilities and Net Worth (in thousands)
Current: Cash .... $ _____	Current liabilities ...... $ _____
Fixed:	Long-term liabilities:
Machinery $ _____	Bonds .... $ _____
Less dep'n allow-	Net worth:
ance $ _____ $ _____	Capital $ _____
$ _____	Ret'd. earnings $ _____ $ _____
	$ _____

31, 1980? (Start with the cash it had when the year began; you have this figure from question 1. Add the money received from sales of merchandise and bonds, listed above; then deduct the various cash outlays also listed.) $ _____ .

b. On Table 20A-2, draw up the firm's balance sheet as of December 31, 1980, in three steps:

▶First, run through the information above for assets held at the year-end, to be listed at their proper value on that date. (HINT: You have already dealt with cash; you should find only one other asset.)

▶Second, do the same for liabilities. (HINT: You should find only one.)

▶Third, repeat for net worth. Remember that net worth must be whatever figure is needed to prop the balance sheet into balance. But follow the convention of dividing net worth between capital and retained earnings. Leave capital at $50,000 (because no more stock was sold during the year). Let retained earnings be the line within net worth to perform the balancing act.

a. 11,000

b. (To save space, the final three zeros have been dropped—e.g., $11,000 is written $11)

Assets	Liabilities and Net Worth
Current: Cash .... $ 11	Current liabilities ..... $ 0
	Long-term liabilities:
Fixed:	Bonds 100
Machinery $170	Net worth:
Less dep'n	Capital $50
allowance 17 153	Ret'd. earnings .. 14 64
$164	$164

[Note that assets have been divided between current and fixed, and liabilities between current and long-term. The original value of machinery ($170) is shown; then accumulated depreciation is deducted, in order to reach its proper current value of $153. These are simply accounting conventions; at this stage, it is not important if your answer did not recognize them. But you may as well acquire the habit of following such conventions.]

3. In this and the three questions following, we develop the firm's income (or profit-and-loss) statement for 1980, using the information already furnished in question 2.

Remember that this income statement (1) records revenue earned from sales in 1980, (2) deducts from this revenue the costs of making and selling the goods in question, and (3) shows the income (or profit) remaining after that deduction. It indicates also the disposition of that profit (paid out as a dividend, or retained within the business).

The sales figure is obviously $115,000. Raw materials purchases and wages are clearly expense items to be subtracted from sales revenue. But the other items? Ought the machinery expenditure of $170,000 be included as a cost to be deducted on the income statement? . . . . *(Yes / No)*

No (Deduct only costs that should be applied against the goods sold. The $170,000 did not go into the making of those goods, as witness the fact that at the close of the period, the firm still has something worth $153,000 left out of its initial $170,000 outlay)

---

4. a. Is there, however, any "machinery cost" associated with 1980 production? _____ . .

b. This depreciation *(was / was not)* a cash outlay. It *(should / should not)* be recorded as an expense on the 1980 income statement *(despite / because of)* this fact.

---

a. Yes, depreciation, $17,000 (This is an estimate, in money terms, of the extent to which the machinery was "used up" or worn out as a result of its work in 1980) **b.** was not; should; despite (For comment on this point, see the introductory discussion immediately preceding question 1)

---

5. The 1980 bond sale of $100,000 *(ought / ought not)* to appear on the income statement. What must be recorded on that statement, however, is _____ .

---

ought not; bond interest (The fact that the company borrowed $100,000 to buy machinery and the like has nothing to do with the income statement. But the interest it must pay on borrowed money is a cost of doing business, and as such must be recorded as an expense)

---

6. On Table 20A-3, draw up the income statement.

Table 20A-3

Sales		$ _____
Less manufacturing cost of goods sold:		
Raw materials bought:	$ _____	
Labor cost (wages)	$ _____	
Dep'n. on machinery	$ _____	$ _____
Gross profit		$ _____
Deduct bond interest		$ _____
Net profit and addition to retained earnings		$ _____

Sales		$115
Less manufacturing cost of goods sold:		
Raw materials bought	$50	
Labor cost (wages)	24	
Dep'n. on machinery	17	91
Gross profit		$ 24
Deduct bond interest		10
Net profit and addition to retained earnings		$ 14

(Note the convention of deducting bond interest after manufacturing costs)

7. The addition to retained earnings figure on this income statement is *(the same as / different from)* the retained earnings figure on the year-end balance sheet. This *(is / is not)* a coincidence. The earnings retained in the business figure on the balance sheet is the total of all income (profit) earned, for all years since incorporation, minus all dividends paid out throughout that period.

For example, if Utter Confusion's income statement for the following year (1981) ended with an addition to retained earnings of $18,000, the retained earnings on the end-of-1981 balance sheet would be $*(14,000 / 18,000 / 28,000 / 32,000)*.

---

the same as; is not; 32,000

Before continuing, be sure that the points in questions 1 through 7 are reasonably clear. Review them if necessary to make sure you have (at least in terms of the simple example used) a fair perspective on what a balance sheet is—what kinds of items go into it, and what do not. Do the same for an income statement.

8. Now we tackle a tricky but important income-statement point. Look at the sample income statement in the text Appendix. In general, it resembles that of question 6 with the one exception: the text statement continues with two additional lines labeled "Add: Beginning inventory" and "Deduct: Closing inventory." The inventories in question are, in general, either raw materials, goods in process of being manufactured, or unsold finished items.

Why these two lines? Because without them, the total of costs incurred in manufacturing the goods sold would be incorrect, for two principal reasons. The second reason is outlined in question 9; the first we'll tackle immediately. It is this:

▶The physical quantity of goods a firm sells during the year is unlikely to be exactly the same in total as the physical quantity it manufactures.

In general, of course, a firm must keep its manufactures in rough correspondence with its sales. It can't provide customers with goods that it hasn't manufactured; it mustn't keep on piling up an inventory of finished goods that it can't sell. Nevertheless (unless the firm produces only custom-made items, with nothing "standard" or "stock"), the total volume of goods manufactured in any period will usually be somewhat different from the total volume the firm manages to sell.

This difference (along with the differences in raw-materials inventories, which we'll tackle later) must be recognized on the income statement. This is so because:

▶The income statement is expected to report net revenue from goods sold during the year. And it is expected to list as expenses to be deducted from such revenue the cost of the goods sold—not the cost of the goods manufactured, which is usually a somewhat different figure.

a. We now work through a few simple examples to illustrate the point involved. Suppose, first of all, that, in addition to everything listed in questions 1 through 7, Utter Confusion had ended 1980 with an inventory of unsold finished goods of $6000. (Its sales were $115,000, as before.) Note carefully that this $6000 is an "at-cost" valuation, based on the raw materials, labor, and depreciation that went into those unsold goods. Utter Confusion expects to sell them next year, and for more than $6000. But until finished goods are sold, they are always valued "at cost."[1]

Thus in 1980, Utter Confusion *(sold more goods than it made / made more goods than it sold)*. Its total manufacturing expenses for materials, labor, and depreciation were (as before) $91,000. A small part of these expenses went into the making of these unsold goods. In fact, since the $6000 is an "at-cost" figure, the cost amount attributable to these unsold goods is *(less than $6000 / $6000 / more than $6000)*.

The general rule that we have been following bears repeating: do not load costs onto merchandise if those costs are really attributable to the manufacture of other goods. With total manufacturing costs of $91,000, and with $6000 of that total attributable to the unsold goods, the manufacturing cost of goods sold in 1980 ought to be $*(80,000 / 85,000 / 90,000 / 91,000 / 97,000)*. This *(is / is not)* the correct manufacturing cost of goods sold.

The introduction of this $6000 closing inventory *(will / will not)* change Utter Confusion's 1980 net profit. Specifically, this profit will *(remain at / be changed to)* $*(6000 / 12,000 / 14,000 / 20,000)*. This is true only because prices have been assumed to be stable. As will become clear in subsequent questions, this invariance in profit will typically disappear during periods of inflation (or deflation for that matter).

b. Everything is now as it was in questions 1 through 7 (including a zero end-of-1980 finished-goods inventory) except that Utter Confusion began 1980 with a $2000 inventory of unsold finished goods. It had bought them for $2000 from a company overloaded with inventory. For convenience, let's say it was a bargain purchase, in that this $2000 was an "at-cost" figure, in the same sense of representing only the labor, materials, and depreciation that went into these goods.

[1]More precisely, the valuation rule is "at the lower of cost or market price." Its purpose is to cover the unhappy situation in which market price has fallen so much (or the goods are so unattractive to customers) that the merchandise cannot be sold even for the basic costs of its manufacture. This complication can be disregarded in an introductory survey.

Since the year-end finished-goods inventory was zero, these goods must have gone into Utter Confusion's sales of $115,000. So the $2000 cost of these goods—see the income statement rule as to expenses set out above—must go into the income statement. (The $91,000 total for labor, materials, and depreciation incurred during 1980 pertains only to the goods manufactured in 1980. It had nothing to do with the stocks in the opening inventory.) Thus the 1980 manufacturing cost of goods sold total should be $*(87,000 / 89,000 / 91,000 / 93,000 / 95,000)*.

Suppose you list manufacturing costs just as in question 6, total them—and then continue with a line "Add: Beginning inventory, $2000." The figure so produced will be $*(89,000 / 91,000 / 93,000)*—which is the *(correct / incorrect)* manufacturing cost of goods sold figure.

The introduction of this $2000 beginning inventory *(would / would not)* change the 1980 net profit figure. Specifically, this profit will *(remain at / be changed to)* $*(8000 / 10,000 / 12,000 / 14,000 / 16,000)*.

---

a. made more goods than it sold; $6000; 85,000; is; will; be changed to; 20,000   **b.** 93,000; 93,000; correct; would; be changed to; 12,000

9. These "Add: Beginning inventory" and "Deduct: Closing inventory" lines can be needed for a second reason:

▶A firm's inventory of raw materials (and of goods in process of manufacture) is unlikely to be the same in physical quantity or in value at the end of a year as it was at the beginning of that year.

a. Suppose Utter Confusion ended 1980 with a raw-materials inventory of $7000; i.e., it didn't use up in manufacture all the $50,000 in materials it had bought during that year. (Everything else is as before: sales of $115,000; zero year-beginning raw-materials inventory; zero year-beginning and year-end finished-goods inventories.)

The value of raw materials that went into the goods sold was therefore $*(43,000 / 50,000 / 57,000)*, and that is the amount that should be charged against the goods sold.

Look again at the income statement in question 6. After listing and totaling the various manufacturing cost items as before, bring in a new line, "Deduct: Closing inventory, $7000." This makes the manufacturing cost of goods sold total $*(84,000 / 91,000 / 98,000)*, which *(is / is not)* the correct figure.

Allowing for such a $7000 closing raw-materials inventory, Utter Confusion's net profit for 1980 would become $*(7000 / 12,000 / 14,000 / 21,000 / 28,000)*.

b. Finally, suppose that just after incorporation near the end of 1979 but before commencing operations in 1980, Utter Confusion bought raw materials for $3000. At the end of 1980, it had a closing raw-materials inventory of $4000. Everything else is as before: sales of $115,000; raw materials purchased during 1980 of $50,000; zero beginning and closing inventories of finished goods.

In this case, the quantity of raw materials that went into

the goods sold must have been (in value) $(47,000 / 48,000 / 49,000 / 50,000 / 51,000 / 52,000 / 53,000 / 54,000)$. So try the usual add-and-deduct technique—that is, total the manufacturing cost on the income statement as usual, and then follow with "Add: Beginning inventory, $3000," and "Deduct: Closing inventory, $4000." As before, this *(will / will not)* yield the correct manufacturing cost of goods sold total.

In this case, Utter Confusion's net profit for 1980 would be $(10,000 / 11,000 / 12,000 / 13,000 / 14,000 / 15,000 / 16,000)$.

In ordinary and real situations, these beginning and closing inventories usually involve a mixture of raw materials, goods-in-process (of manufacture), and unsold finished goods. That doesn't matter. To get the inventory total, just add up their values—remembering that unsold finished goods are to be valued "at cost."

Note in passing that a different—and more puzzling—inventory problem is discussed briefly in question 18.

---

a. 43,000; 84,000; is; 21,000 **b.** 49,000; will; 15,000

10. Questions 8 and 9 lead you systematically through the problems introduced by correctly treating the differences between beginning and closing inventories. The recognition of such inventory differences affects not only the income statement but also the balance sheet.

The balance sheet is affected in three ways: (1) Any net profit change means a matching change in net worth (and within net worth, in retained earnings). (No net worth change would be needed if the net profit change were just matched by an equivalent change in dividends paid out. But Utter Confusion hasn't paid any dividends as yet.) (2) Any closing inventory must be recorded as a current asset. (3) If the change described involved an expenditure of money (as it did in two of the four preceding examples), then the cash asset must be changed accordingly.

What changes are needed in the end-of-1980 balance sheet of question 2, if allowance is made (taking each case one at a time) for the various amendments brought into questions 8 and 9? Specifically, these were (with everything else unchanged):

8a: A closing finished-goods inventory of $6000.
8b: An opening finished-goods inventory of $2000.
9a: A closing raw-materials inventory of $7000.
9b: An opening raw-materials inventory of $3000, and a closing raw-materials inventory of $4000.

Write your answers in the four columns of Table 20A-4; notice that the "assets" and "liabilities and net worth" columns are simply stacked vertically instead of horizontally. Remember, too, that the changes will (or may) involve the current asset items of cash and of inventory, and the net worth item of retained earnings.

8a. Add current asset (CA): Inventory, $6; change ret'd. earnings from $14 to $20 **8b.** Change CA cash from $11 to $9; change ret'd. earnings from $14 to $12 **9a.** Add CA inventory, $7; change ret'd. earnings from $14 to $21 **9b.** Change CA cash from $11 to $8; add CA inventory $4; change ret'd. earnings from $14 to $15

Table 20A-4

		(8a)	(8b)	(9a)	(9b)
Assets					
Current assets:					
Cash	$ 11	___	___	___	___
Inventory	0	___	___	___	___
Fixed assets					
Machinery	$170				
Depreciation	17 153	___	___	___	___
Total	164	___	___	___	___
Liabilities and net worth					
Current liabilities					
Accounts payable	0	___	___	___	___
Notes payable	0	___	___	___	___
Taxes payable	0	___	___	___	___
Long-term liabilities					
Bank notes	0	___	___	___	___
Bonds	100	___	___	___	___
Net Worth					
Common stock	50	___	___	___	___
Retained earnings	14	___	___	___	___
Total	164	___	___	___	___

11. Notice from questions 8 and 9 the difference between manufacturing cost (manufacturing expenses incurred during the year) and manufacturing cost of goods sold (manufacturing cost after adjustment for year-beginning and year-ending inventories).

For example, if manufacturing cost exceeds manufacturing cost of goods sold, this must mean that beginning inventory *(exceeds / is less than)* closing inventory.

A different case: If the closing inventory should turn out to be smaller than the beginning inventory, then manufacturing cost must *(exceed / be less than)* manufacturing cost of goods sold.

---

is less than; be less than [You may well have found this a tricky question. These problems of differences between year-beginning and year-end inventories (and consequent differences between manufacturing cost and manufacturing cost of goods sold) are easy once you get the hang of them—but not until then. If necessary, work out or check your answer by assuming some arbitrary manufacturing cost figure. Then use the add-and-subtract procedure with respect to beginning and closing inventories, so as to obtain manufacturing cost of goods sold]

Table 20A-5

	(a)	(b)	(c)	(d)
Balance Sheet				

Assets (in thousands)

Current (cash) .... $ _____ $ _____ $ _____ $ _____

Fixed:

    Machinery .... $ _____ $ _____ $ _____ $ _____

    Less depreciation .... $ _____ $ _____ $ _____ $ _____ $ _____ $ _____ $ _____ $ _____

    Total .... $ _____ $ _____ $ _____ $ _____

Liabilities & net worth (in thousands)

Current .... $ _____ $ _____ $ _____ $ _____

Long-term (bonds) ...... $ _____ $ _____ $ _____ $ _____

Net worth:

    Capital .... $ _____ $ _____ $ _____ $ _____

    Retained earnings .... $ _____ $ _____ $ _____ $ _____ $ _____ $ _____ $ _____ $ _____

Total .... $ _____ $ _____ $ _____ $ _____

| **Income Statement** | | | | |

Sales .... $ _____ $ _____ $ _____ $ _____

Less Manufacturing costs of goods sold

    Raw materials .... $ _____ $ _____ $ _____ $ _____

    Labor costs .... $ _____ $ _____ $ _____ $ _____

    Depreciation on machinery ... $ _____ $ _____ $ _____ $ _____ $ _____ $ _____ $ _____ $ _____

Gross profit .... $ _____ $ _____ $ _____ $ _____

Less bond interest .... $ _____ $ _____ $ _____ $ _____

Net profit .... $ _____ $ _____ $ _____ $ _____

12. Suppose question 2's operations were amended as described below. What change (if any) would each of these require in the question 2 balance sheet and the question 6 income statement? Write your answers on the separate columns of Table 20A-5.

a. The firm also paid (in 1980) a cash dividend of $2000 to stockholders.

b. The firm's 1980 operations required it to pay corporation income taxes of $3000 in cash during the year.

c. The firm incurred this $3000 tax obligation on account of its 1980 operations, but it had not made the payment by the close of the year.

d. Raw materials bought were $50,000 as before, but a $5000 bill for part of this was unpaid at year-end.

a. *Balance sheet:* Cash down from $11 to $9; ret'd. earnings down from $14 to $12; *income statement:* record dividend payment at bottom, making addn. to ret'd. earnings $12, not $14   **b.** *Balance sheet:* Cash down from $11 to $8; ret'd. earnings down from $14 to $11; *income statement:* deduct taxes after bond interest, making addn. to ret'd. earnings $11, not $14   **c.** *Balance sheet:* Cash unchanged at $11 but include taxes unpaid current liability of $3; answer otherwise same as **b   d.** *Balance sheet:* Cash up from $11 to $16; include accts. payable current liability of $5; *income statement:* unchanged (The income statement records raw materials bought and used; it doesn't care whether or not they have yet been paid for)

13. Now redo Utter Confusion's end-of-1980 balance sheet and its 1980 income statement on Table 20A-6 with a fuller set of transactions. Specifically, the initial balance sheet was as in question 1, and 1980 operations were in full as below.

[Developing the cash figure requires some work. For example, the sales figure is $115,000, but only $105,000 represents cash incoming; there are year-end accounts receivable (sales for which the customers have not yet made payment) of $10,000. A similar adjustment is needed with respect to raw-materials purchases; some are not yet paid for.]

For convenience, the final 000s are omitted—e.g., the bond issue figure of $100 stands for $100,000.

Bond issue (100 @ $1,000)	$100
Sales of finished goods	115
Purchases: Machinery	170
Raw materials	50
Labor cost (wages)	24
Taxes paid	3
Bond interest paid	10
Dividends paid	2
Accounts payable (raw materials) at year-end	5
Accounts receivable (from customers) at year-end	10
Depreciation on machinery for 1980	17
Opening inventories: Raw materials	zero
Finished goods	zero
Closing inventories: Raw materials	5
Finished goods	6

Table 20A-6

Balance Sheet

Assets			Liabilities and Net Worth		
Current:			Current liabilities:		
Cash	$ —		Accts. payable$	$ —	
Accts.			Long-term		
receivable	$ —	$ —	liabilities:		
Inventories	$ —		Bonds	$ —	$ —
Fixed:			Net worth:		
Machinery	. . . . $ —		Capital	$ —	
Less dep'n.			Ret'd earnings	$ —	$ —
allowance	. . . $ —	$ —			$ —
		$ —			

Income Statement

Sales		$ —
Less manufacturing cost of goods sold:		
Manufacturing cost:		
Raw materials bought	$ —	
Dep'n. on machinery	$ —	
Labor cost (wages)	$ —	$ —
Add beginning inventory	$ —	$ —
Deduct closing inventory	$ —	$ —
Gross profit		$ —
Bond interest paid		$ —
Taxes paid		$ —

Table 20A-6 (Cont.)
Income Statement (Cont.)

Net profit	$ —	
Dividends paid	$ —	
Addition to retained earnings	$ —	

Balance Sheet

Assets			Liabilities and Net Worth		
Current:			Current liabilities:		
Cash	$ 1		Accts. payable	$ 5	
Accts.			Long-term		
receivable	10		liabilities:		
Inventories	11	$ 22	Bonds	100	$105
Fixed:			Net worth:		
Machinery	$170		Capital	$50	
Less dep'n.			Ret'd earnings . . .	20	70
allowance	17	153			
		$175			$175

Income Statement

Sales		$115
Less manufacturing cost of goods sold:		
Manufacturing cost:		
Raw materials bought	$50	
Dep'n. on machinery	17	
Labor cost (wages)	24	
	91	
Add beginning inventory	0	
	91	
Deduct closing inventory	11	80
Gross profit		35
Bond interest paid		10
		25
Taxes paid		3
Net profit		22
Dividends paid		2
Addition to retained earnings		$ 20

14. **a.** If, in the following year (1981), depreciation on machinery were again $17,000, that would of course be the depreciation expense to record on the 1981 income statement. On the firm's end-of-1981 balance sheet, the total of allowance for depreciation would be $(*zero / 17,000 / 34,000 / 51,000*). That is, the depreciation figure on this end-of-1981 balance sheet would be (*different from / the same as*) the figure on the 1981 income statement. This is so because the balance sheet depreciation figure represents depreciation for the (*year just ended / total for all years since purchase*).

b. The machinery value cited in previous questions has been $170,000 (original purchase value). Each year, a depreciation expense is recorded for that machinery on the income statement. If we were to add up all such depreciation entries on all the income statements over the whole life of this machinery, the resulting total would be—assuming a scrap value of zero—(*less than $170,000 / $170,000 / more than $170,000*).

a. 34,000; different from; total for all years since purchase **b.** $170,000

15. The balance sheet always balances, no matter what, for the reason already indicated in the introductory comments: net worth must go up or down, if necessary, by whatever amount is needed to keep things in balance. To use the text's example, if a thief steals all the firm's cash—$5000, let's say—then cash (within assets) drops by $5000, and retained earnings (within net worth) drops by the same amount.

Ordinarily, a firm draws up its balance sheet only at intervals—once each year, or once each quarter. But it always has a balance sheet, as of any point in time, always in balance.

Below are six transactions. Show how each would affect the firm's balance sheet. Write your answers on a separate sheet of paper, and use the abbreviations CA and FA, CL and LTL, and NW for current and fixed assets, current and long-term liabilities, and net worth, respectively. (Some of these transactions may involve more than two balance sheet accounts.)

a. Utter Confusion buys a new factory building for $50,000, using money provided by a local bank on a 15-year mortgage loan.

b. The firm's principal stockholders contribute $25,000 extra cash to the business, for which they receive new shares of common stock of equivalent value.

c. The Internal Revenue Service rules that the company owes an extra $2000 in corporation taxes for the preceding year. The company pays at once by check.

d. Accounts payable of $6000 fall due. The firm is temporarily short of cash, and creditors agree to accept interest-bearing 90-day notes for this amount.

e. The company sells goods for $20,000. Of these sales, $15,000 is paid in cash, and $5000 still stands as accounts receivable. These goods had been valued in the finished-goods inventory ("at cost") at $12,000.

f. A customer owing $2000 goes bankrupt. Cash of $1000 is received in full settlement of the amount he had owed.

a.	(FA) Buildings	+ $50	(LTL) Mortgage	+$50
b.	(CA) Cash	+ 25	(NW) Capital	+ 25
c.	(CA) Cash	− 2	(NW) Ret'd earnings	− 2
d.			(CL) Accts. payable	− 6
			(CL) Notes payable	+ 6
e.	(CA) Cash	+ 15	(NW) Ret'd earnings	+ 8
	(CA) Accts. rec.	+ 5		
	(CA) Inventory	− 12		
f.	(CA) Cash	+ 1	(NW) Ret'd earnings	− 1
	(CA) Accts. rec.	− 2		

16. If a corporation has issued bonds (or debentures), they must always be recorded on its balance sheet within the *(net worth / liabilities)* section. When it issues stock—either common or preferred—the issue must always be recorded on its balance sheet within the *(net worth / liabilities)* section.

---

liabilities; net worth [Bonds or debentures are debts owed to outsiders, and so must be recorded as liabilities. The issue of shares of stock is an issue made to the corporation's owners (or part owners); so it must be recorded within the net worth section]

17. Inflation poses a new set of business accounting problems. Consider depreciation on equipment. The accounting rule has always been that depreciation expense should be based on the original cost of that equipment. On the income statement, this expense is not a cash outlay (see question 4 preceding). Thus—in noninflationary times—the company has an opportunity, over the life of that equipment, to accumulate enough cash to replace it when worn out.

a. If price inflation means that replacement costs twice or three times as much, however, that cash buildup will be insufficient. On the income statement, the depreciation expense entry does not reflect the true cost of current equipment use. In this sense, net income (or profit) is *(understated / overstated)*. It is thus understandable if firms try to "accelerate" depreciation expenses on the income statements to the extent that the law allows—and the law allows a lot in many cases. That is to say, businesses would prefer to list higher expense figures than rules built for noninflationary times would allow, and they would like to list them early. The use of such accelerated depreciation *(increases / decreases)* net income (profit) for the year. So it *(increases / decreases)* the amount of income (profit) tax payable for that year. Depreciation expense (as you were reminded above) *(is not / is)* a cash outlay. Hence, although accelerated depreciation causes recorded profit to go *(up / down)*, the fact of a reduced cash outpayment for taxes means that cash held by the firm will be *(decreased / increased)*.

(Notice that although price inflation intensifies the desire of business firms for accelerated depreciation, this cash-increase feature provides a strong incentive therefore, even in noninflationary times.)

b. The accounting rule still holds: you must stop charging depreciation expense once its total, over all years and income statements involved, reaches the original cost of the equipment (minus scrap value). Thus in later years there *(will / will not)* be a corresponding *(decrease / increase)* in taxes due, because *(accelerated depreciation can be carried on indefinitely / depreciation expense must stop once its total reaches original cost)*.

Don't think that since accelerated depreciation only postpones the evil day, no real gain is involved. Suppose you save $100,000 in taxes this year, but must pay it 5 years hence. If you put the money in a savings bank for 5 years at 10 percent interest per year, do you gain? Or if you plow it back into your own firm to earn 15 percent per year, do you gain?

---

a. overstated; decreases; decreases; is not; down; increased   **b.** will; increase; depreciation expense must stop once its total reaches original cost

18. Price inflation presents a comparable problem for materials cost and inventory valuation. Suppose you buy—early in the year—your raw material for $1. Near the end of the year, a second and equal purchase of the same material costs $3. For simplicity, let's assume that the physical volume of material you have left at year-end is just equal to either of these two during-the-year purchases. What raw material cost do you show on your income statement? What value do you put on your closing inventory?

One's first inclination is probably to say that you used first (in manufacture) what you bought first: first into the warehouse, first out of it (FIFO). So your raw material cost was $1; your closing inventory was $3.

The alternative would be LIFO (last in, first out). That would make raw material cost $3, closing inventory $1.

Now compare FIFO and LIFO in terms of their effects upon net income (on the income statement) and net worth (on the balance sheet). As compared with LIFO, FIFO (lower materials cost) will record a *(higher / lower)* profit. On the balance sheet, FIFO (which lists the inventory asset at a higher value) will record a *(higher / lower)* net worth.

So the issues are much the same as those involving depreciation (question 17). On the income statement, FIFO's higher profit (and higher taxes) incline the company toward use of *(FIFO / LIFO)*. Moreover, FIFO's use of a $1 figure for materials used in goods sold *(overstates / understates)* what the replacement cost of those materials would be.

In consequence, there has in recent years been a strong trend among corporations toward the LIFO valuation method. One of the great mysteries of corporate finance is why this trend has not been complete and immediate.

---

higher; higher; LIFO; understates

---

19. Two small established corporations, A and B, are bought by a group of promoters, who intend to merge them into one new concern. The combined balance sheet of these two firms at time of purchase is:

Assets		Liabilities and Net Worth	
Plant, equipment, etc...........	$100,000	Liabilities........	none
Goodwill.........	50,000	Net worth	$150,000
	$150,000		$150,000

The $50,000 is a fair estimate of the true worth of goodwill—i.e., the "extra earning power" of the two concerns due to their established position. (See Review question 5, page 206, on goodwill, if necessary.)

The promoters now organize a new firm, corporation C, with 60,000 shares of common stock. Half this stock is to be sold to the public at $10 per share (thus bringing in cash of $300,000). The promoters take the remaining 30,000 shares themselves. In exchange, they give corporation C the assets of the two original concerns. The true worth of these assets is only $150,000, but the promoters inflate this to $300,000 by writing up the value of goodwill from $50,000 to $200,000.

There being no Securities and Exchange Commission to reveal such action, the public innocently buys its 30,000 shares at $10 each, for cash.

a. On a separate sheet, draw up the balance sheet of the new concern after all stock has been sold and cash paid in by the public. Use the inflated goodwill figure.

b. The real worth of a share of stock is $ _____

c. This process of exaggerating stock values is called:

_____ .

d. How are stockholders most likely to discover they have paid too high a price for their stock?

_____

_____

_____ .

a. Assets		Liabilities and Net Worth	
Cash...............	$300		
Plant and equipment......	100		
Goodwill	200	Net worth............	$600

b. $7.50 [($150,000 + $300,000)/60,000) = (true net worth + cash from stock)/ (# of shares) = $7.50 **c.** watering the stock **d.** Earnings and dividends below their expectations

QUIZ: Multiple Choice

1. In the preparation of an income statement for a certain period (in particular, the manufacturing cost section):
(1) all expenses listed therein must represent cash actually paid out during that period, and all such cash outpayments (pertaining to manufacturing) must be listed.
(2) every cash outlay (pertaining to manufacturing) during the period must be listed, and in addition some expenses which did not involve an outlay of cash may appear.
(3) some expenses listed may not represent cash outlays during the period, and some cash outlays during the period (pertaining to manufacturing) may not be listed.
(4) all expenses listed must represent cash actually paid out during the period, but not all such cash outpayments (pertaining to manufacturing) need be listed.
(5) none of the preceding statements is a correct description.

2. If a manufacturing corporation sells an issue of long-term bonds, then on its income (profit-and-loss) statement for the period in which the bonds were sold:
(1) both the bond sale and any interest paid thereon during the period will be recorded.
(2) the bond sale will be recorded, but not any interest paid thereon.
(3) the bond sale will not be recorded, but any interest paid thereon will be.
(4) neither the bond sale nor any interest paid thereon will be recorded.
(5) only that fraction of the bond sale chargeable to that period will be recorded.

3. If an income statement records no depreciation expense for particular machinery, even though that machinery was used for production during the year, a reasonable explanation from the accounting viewpoint would be that:
(1) the company did not find it necessary to spend money on maintenance or repair of the machines during the year.
(2) depreciation entries equal in total to the original cost of

the machines had already been made on earlier income statements.

(3) because sales for the year have been below normal, the company has decided not to charge any depreciation cost for this year.

(4) because of an increase in market prices, it is estimated that the money worth of the machinery is unchanged even though it has undergone some depreciation through use during the year.

(5) no explanation is needed, since depreciation entries are properly made on the balance sheet, not the income statement.

4. When an allowance for depreciation figure is entered in the fixed-asset section of a company's balance sheet, its purpose is:

(1) to prevent an overstatement of net profit.

(2) to reduce the original cost of some asset to an estimate of its true present worth, as closely as can be estimated.

(3) to assure that there will be sufficient cash on hand to replace assets when they are worn out.

(4) to record the money actually spent in keeping some asset or group of assets in working condition.

(5) to record the total amount of money spent on purchase of new assets during the period in question.

5. Which alternative in question 4 would be correct as to the purpose of listing depreciation as an expense on a company's income statement?

(1).

(2).

(3).

(4).

(5).

6. "A balance sheet must always balance" specifically because:

(1) total assets, properly specified, equal total liabilities, properly specified.

(2) net profit is defined as total revenue earned minus total expenses incurred.

(3) the definition of net worth is total assets minus total liabilities.

(4) current assets plus fixed assets must equal current liabilities plus long-term liabilities.

(5) the definition of net worth is capital stock plus retained earnings.

7. A company's total assets at the end of 1980 were $100,000, and its total liabilities, $70,000. At the end of 1981, its total assets were $115,000, and its total liabilities, $75,000. It paid dividends totaling $15,000 in 1981. Assuming no change in its capital stock, its net profit after taxes for 1981 must have been:

(1) $10,000.

(2) $15,000.

(3) $20,000.

(4) $25,000.

(5) $30,000.

8. A "sinking fund" is:

(1) another name for the depreciation account.

(2) a liability reserve set up to cover future commitments of fairly certain amount.

(3) a special type of surplus reserve.

(4) a "pool of liquid assets" found on the assets side of some firms' balance sheets.

(5) the special account used to value a firm's goodwill.

9. A money figure which would appear both on a company's income statement for a given year and on its balance sheet for the end of that year would be:

(1) labor cost.

(2) cash on hand at year-end.

(3) dividends paid.

(4) beginning inventory.

(5) closing inventory.

10. A company's 1980 income statement shows a net profit earned (after taxes) of $200,000. This means that on its end-of-1980 balance sheet, as compared with its end-of-1979 balance sheet:

(1) the total of assets will be up by $200,000, and so will the total of liabilities plus net worth.

(2) retained earnings will be up by $200,000 minus the total of dividends paid.

(3) current assets minus current liabilities will be up by $200,000.

(4) cash on hand minus expenditures for new fixed assets will be up by $200,000.

(5) net worth will be up by $200,000 minus the total of any bond interest paid.

11. An income statement will not ordinarily record the following transaction:

(1) sale of goods which must be sold at a price below their manufacturing cost.

(2) amount of expenditure on an advertising campaign.

(3) amount of salary payments to administrative or "overhead" personnel.

(4) any quantity of goods which, although sold during the year in question, were not manufactured during that year.

(5) amount of expenditure to purchase new machinery.

12. If the term "retained earnings" appears on a firm's balance sheet, it means:

(1) the name of an account on the assets side, having no connection with cash on hand.

(2) the name of an account on the assets side, indicating cash on hand.

(3) the name of an account on the liabilities and net worth side, having no connection with cash on hand.

(4) the name of an account on the liabilities and net worth side, indicating cash on hand.

(5) that something is wrong, since "retained earnings" is not ordinarily a term used in connection with balance sheets.

13. The use of "accelerated depreciation," or "fast write-off," has, during the period of write-off, the effect of:

(1) increasing stated profits but decreasing taxes paid.

(2) decreasing stated profits but increasing taxes paid.

(3) increasing both stated profits and taxes paid.

(4) decreasing both stated profits and taxes paid.

(5) none of these.

14. If, on a company's income statement, its manufacturing cost is less than its manufacturing cost of goods sold, its:

(1) beginning inventory for that period must be higher than its closing inventory.

(2) profit for that period must be lower than its profit for the immediately preceding period.

(3) profit for that period must be higher than its profit for the immediately preceding period.

(4) dividends paid for that period must exceed its addition to retained earnings.

(5) beginning inventory for that period must be lower than its closing inventory.

15. A company's total assets were $600,000, and its total liabilities, $400,000, at the end of 1980. At the end of 1981, its total assets were $550,000, and its total liabilities, $200,000. During 1981, it (*a*) paid a dividend of $50,000, and (*b*) sold additional shares of its own stock for $100,000. With these figures, its net profit after taxes for 1981 must have been:

(1) zero.

(2) $50,000.

(3) $100,000:

(4) $150,000.

(5) $200,000.

FURTHER EXERCISES

1. A company's balance sheet as of December 31, 1980, in condensed form (the figures showing thousands of dollars) was as follows:

Assets			Liabilities and Net Worth		
Cash		$14	Liabilities:		
Inventory		20	Bonds issued		$30
Bldgs. and equipment	$76		Net worth:		
Less dep'n allowance	22	54	Capital stock	$40	
			Ret'd earnings	18	58
Total		$88	Total		$88

During 1981, its entire transactions were as follows:

1. It sold goods, all for cash, for a total of $80.

2. Manufacturing expenses during the year for wages, raw materials, and miscellaneous costs (excluding depreciation) were $37. Of this, $35 was paid in cash; the other $2 stood as accounts payable at end of 1981.

3. Depreciation on buildings and equipment during 1981 was estimated at $5.

4. Total selling and administrative costs, interest, and taxes were $22, all paid in cash during the year.

5. Dividends of $15 were paid in cash during the year.

6. New equipment costing $18 was bought for cash.

7. The closing inventory was $24.

Prepare this company's income statement for year 1981, and its balance sheet as of December 31, 1981.

Income Statement—1980

Sales		$80
Less: Manufacturing cost of goods sold:		
Manufacturing cost:		
Depreciation	$ 5	
Other manufacturing cost	37	
	42	
Add: Beginning inventory	20	
	62	
Deduct: Closing inventory	24	38
Gross profit		42
Deduct selling and admin. costs, interest, taxes		22
Net profit		20
Dividends paid		15
Addition to retained earnings		$ 5

Balance Sheet—December 31, 1980

Assets			Liabilities and Net Worth		
Current:			Current liabilities:		
Cash	$ 4		Accounts payable	$ 2	
Inventory	24		Long-term liabilities:		
Fixed:			Bonds	30	$32
Buildings, equipment	$94				
Less depreciation	27	67	Net worth:		
			Capital stock	40	
			Earned surplus	23	63
		$95			$95

2. You are presiding over a stockholders' meeting to review the financial statements of the year for your company. Answer the following questions fired at you by an irate shareholder.

a. "I happen to know that you spent $20,000 on equipment just before the year's end, and yet you haven't shown that cost on your income statement. Why not?"

b. "Are you going to show that $20,000 expenditure on next year's income statement?"

c. "You show a depreciation expense of $15,000 on your buildings and equipment during the year, yet I happen to know that you didn't spend a cent all year on maintenance and repair. What do you mean by showing $15,000 worth of money which you didn't spend at all?"

d. "You have retained earnings of $30,000 on hand, the balance sheet says so, right there under the net worth section. Why didn't you pay out that money in dividends?"

a,b,c. Expenditures for purchase of capital equipment are not recorded on an income statement. The income statement does record the depreciation on such equipment, each year that it is used—until, at the end of the equipment's life, the total of such year-after-year recorded depreciation equals the original expenditure amount (minus any scrap value the equipment may have.) See Review questions 3 through 5.

Any expenses incurred each year for maintenance and routine repair of equipment are recorded on the income statement, in addition to the depreciation expense entry.

d. The "retained earnings" total (sometimes called "earned surplus"), as recorded within the net worth section of a balance sheet, does not stand for cash. This retained earnings figure is simply whatever figure is needed to make the two sides of the balance sheet balance. Whatever cash the company may have is recorded as cash on hand, on the asset side of the balance sheet.

3. A new manager for a hitherto unsuccessful business reports at the end of his first year: "We have finally begun to get this firm out of the red. Profit was $8000.

"Total sales for the year were $100,000, all for cash. Our cash expenses during the year for materials, wages and salaries, advertising, and so on, totaled $82,000. We also allowed depreciation expense of $5000. We paid property and similar taxes of $5000.

"One of the firm's troubles has been that it had too much money tied up in inventories. We managed to work inventories down to a much better level: we got raw materials down from $5000 to $3000 by the end of the year, and finished goods down from $12,000 to $2000."

No relevant information has been omitted. Comment.

If the report is set out as an income statement, making allowance for beginning and closing inventories, it develops that the firm in question lost $4000 for the year

---

4. The figures (thousands of dollars) in the two columns below, A and B, pertain to two different corporations. Prepare, for company A and for company B, its income (or profit-and-loss) statement for 1980, and its balance sheet as of December 31, 1980. Note that in neither instance is the retained earnings figure for December 31, 1980, supplied you; this you must compute. Otherwise, the figures are assumed to be complete.

	A	B
Bonds (or debentures) issued:		
Principal amount owed, Dec. 31, 1980	$ 4,000	$1,000
Interest paid, 1980.	300	90
Buildings owned (original cost)	10,000	2,000
Cash on hand, Dec. 31, 1980	800	600
Common stock (original issue price).	3,000	1,500
Depreciation:		
Buildings, all years up to end of 1979	1,000	540
Buildings, 1980 only	200	60
Equipment, all years up to end of 1979	1,000	950
Equipment, 1980 only	200	50
Dividends: Already paid for 1980	225	180
Declared for 1980, not yet paid.	75	70
Equipment owned, original cost	4,000	2,500

	A	B
Finished and semifinished goods:		
1980 net finished-good sales for cash	6,500	3,750
1980 sales, payment not yet received	600	250
Inventory, Dec. 31, 1979	750	550
Inventory, Dec. 31, 1980	500	600
Labor cost: Wages paid in cash, 1980	1,950	900
Maintenance and repair expense paid, 1980. . .	500	390
Mortgage:		
Principal outstanding, Dec. 31, 1980.	2,500	500
Interest paid, 1980.	200	50
Note payable to bank:		
Principal outstanding, Dec. 31, 1980.	1,000	0
Interest paid, 1980.	100	0
Patents owned and goodwill, Dec. 31, 1980 . . .	600	0
Raw materials:		
Inventory, Dec. 31, 1979	500	450
Bought for cash, 1980	1,600	800
Bought 1980, not yet paid for	200	250
Inventory, Dec. 31, 1980	800	300
Retained earnings, Dec. 31, 1979	2,925	620
Selling and administrative costs, 1980:		
Already paid	400	350
Incurred, but not yet paid.	50	0
Taxes on profit, 1980, not yet paid	700	450

A.   **Income Statement—1980**

Sales		$7,100
Less: Manufacturing cost of goods sold:		
Raw materials bought	$1,800	
Labor cost	1,950	
Depreciation	400	
Maintenance and repair expense	500	
	4,650	
Add: Beginning inventory	1,250	
	5,900	
Deduct: Closing inventory	1,300	4,600
		2,500
Less: Selling and administrative cost		450
		2,050
Less: Interest paid.		600
Net profit before taxes		1,450
Federal income taxes.		700
Net profit after taxes		750
Dividends paid		300
Addition to retained earnings		$ 450

Balance Sheet

Assets				Liabilities and Net Worth			
Current:				**Current liabilities:**			
Cash on hand.		$ 800		Accounts payable		$ 250	
Accounts receivable.		600		Dividend payable.		75	
Inventory.		1,300	$ 2,700	Note payable		1,000	
Fixed:				Taxes payable		700	$2,025
Buildings.	$10,000			**Long-term liabilities:**			
Less depreciation	1,200	8,800		Bonds		4,000	
Equipment.	4,000			Mortgage		2,500	6,500	$ 8,525
Less depreciation	1,200	2,800	11,600	**Net worth:**			
Patents and goodwill			600	Capital		3,000	
				Retained earnings		3,375	6,375
			$14,900				$14,900

B.

Income Statement—1980

Sales		$4,000	$1,450
Less: Manufacturing cost of goods sold:			Less: Selling and administrative cost	350
Raw materials bought	$1,050		1,100
Labor cost	900		Less: Interest paid.	140
Depreciation	110		Net profit before taxes	960
Maintenance and repair expense	390		Federal income taxes.	450
	2,450		Net profit after taxes	510
Add: Beginning inventory	1,000		Dividends paid.	250
	3,450		Addition to retained earnings	$ 260
Deduct: Closing inventory	900	2,550	

Balance Sheet

Assets				Liabilities and Net Worth			
Current:				**Current liabilities:**			
Cash on hand.		$ 600		Accounts payable		$ 250	
Accounts receivable.		250		Dividend payable.		70	
Inventory.		900	$1,750	Taxes payable		450	$ 770
Fixed:				**Long-term liabilities:**			
Buildings.	$2,000			Bonds		1,000	
Less depreciation	600	1,400		Mortgage		500	1,500	$2,270
Equipment.	2,500			**Net worth:**			
Less depreciation	1,000	1,500	2,900	Capital		1,500	
				Retained earnings		880	2,380
			$4,650				$4,650

CHAPTER 21

ANALYSIS OF COSTS

This chapter explores the nature of costs. Minimum production costs of a firm are represented along a total cost schedule that depends on the level of output. Two different cost components are, however, identified: fixed costs (start-up costs incurred before production begins) and variable costs (operating costs that change with output). Other concepts, notably average and marginal costs, are derived from the total cost schedule; they are explored in both short- and long-term time horizons. Opportunity cost is covered, too; it is related both to the decisions that firms must make and to the decisions that individuals must make as they trade various opportunities off against one another in a world of scarcity. By the end of the chapter, the reader should have mastered the following objectives.

LEARNING OBJECTIVES

1. Define and describe total cost, fixed cost, variable cost, marginal cost, and average cost.

2. Understand the relationships that exist between the various measures of cost. Be able, in particular, to derive average and marginal cost from total, fixed, and variable cost.

3. Understand why marginal cost equals average cost is the minimum of a U-shaped average cost curve.

4. Develop and explain the long-run cost envelope from short-run cost schedules.

5. Understand opportunity cost and apply it to individual and firm management decisions.

Total cost means all costs incurred in producing and selling that output. In the markets of everyday experience, supplying firms incur selling costs—i.e., they advertise their goods and employ salespeople. Production costs are incurred by every firm; they are like taxes and

death—unavoidable. Selling costs are, however, different. They may or may not be important components of a firm's cost picture depending upon the structure of the market in which the firm operates. Individual wheat farmers, for example, do not advertise their products; they take the price of wheat as given and sell as much as they can. Toothpaste manufacturers, on the other hand, spend enormous amounts of money on advertising. To avoid confusing the two sources of cost, the present chapter concentrates exclusively on production costs. Selling costs will be introduced later in the context of market structures in which they are important.

Total cost has two parts and one important derivative:

1. *Variable costs*—meaning those costs whose total amount varies with the amount of output produced. For example, direct labor cost is a cost whose total amount will rise as the amount of output rises; this is a variable cost.

2. *Fixed costs*—meaning those costs which are fixed in amount regardless of the level of output and which would accordingly have to be paid by the firm even if its output were zero. Interest on a bond issue is a cost the firm must pay whether it is operating at zero output or at maximum capacity; this is a fixed cost.

3. *Marginal costs*—meaning the increase in total cost resulting from a 1-unit increase in output.

The distinction between fixed and variable costs turns out to be important and interesting. Sometimes you cannot understand a firm's situation and problems until you have grasped the distinction between these two kinds of costs. Marginal cost, though, depends only upon variable costs. Why? Because fixed costs do not, by their very definition, change as output is increased or reduced.

1. In each space below, put (*V*) if you think the item would be a variable cost; put (*F*) if a fixed cost.

a. Cost of raw materials. .... (_____)

b. Depreciation on machinery, when quantity of output produced is considered to be the factor responsible for the amount of this cost. .... (_____)

c. Annual fire insurance premium on buildings. . (_____)

d. A sales tax levied on the firm on each unit of output sold. .... (_____)

e. Depreciation on machinery, when time rather than quantity of output produced is considered to be the factor principally responsible for the amount of this cost. .... (_____)

f. Salaries paid to supervisors on an annual basis. (_____)

g. Local property taxes on buildings. .... (_____)

h. Cost of electric power for machines. .... (_____)

i. Cost of maintaining the research department. . (_____)

j. A royalty paid for the use of certain machines, paid according to number of units produced. .... (_____)

k. Extra pay for overtime work by labor. ..... (_____)

a. *V* b. *V* c. *F* d. *V* e. *F* f. *F* g. *F* h. *V* i. *F* j. *V* k. *V*

2. In Table 21-1, the figures in columns (1) and (2) indicate the estimated total cost incurred in producing quantities of output from 0 to 20 units weekly for a particular firm. Fixed cost is $50 per week.

Table 21-1

(1) Output	(2) Total Cost	(3) Average Cost	(4) Increase in Total Cost	(5) Marginal Cost
0	$ 50.00			
			$10.00	$ 5.00
2	60.00	$_____		
			10.00	5.00
4	70.00	17.50		
			10.00	5.00
6	80.00	13.33		
8	90.00	_____		
			10.50	5.25
10	100.50	10.05		
			11.00	
12	111.50	_____		
			13.00	6.50
14	124.50	8.89		
16	140.50	8.78		
				11.00
18	162.50	_____		
			40.00	
20	202.50	10.13		

a. In column (3), complete the missing figures for *average cost*—i.e., cost per unit of output, or total cost divided by number of units produced.

b. Table 21-1 indicates that, for this firm and this product, average cost reaches its minimum level at an output in the vicinity of (10 / 12 / 14 / 16 / 18 / 20) units.

c. In column (4), complete the missing figures for increase in total cost—i.e., the rise in cost resulting from an increase from 0 to 2 units, from 2 to 4, etc. Notice that these figures are not lined up opposite 0, 2, 4 units, etc. Instead, they are set between 0 and 2, between 2 and 4, etc., to indicate that each figure marks the cost of moving from one output figure to the adjacent one. If output is increased from 2 units to 4, total cost rises by $10; if it is reduced from 4 units to 2, total cost falls by $10.

The text emphasizes the importance of the concept of *marginal cost.* Column (4) is leading up to marginal cost for this product. But this column dealt with 2-unit changes in output and cost—whereas marginal cost is a per unit cost figure.

d. To obtain marginal cost, the figures in column (4) must be divided by 2. Marginal cost is, more precisely, the ratio of a change in total cost divided by a change in output. If that output change equals 1, then the change in total cost is marginal cost. If it is some number other than 1, however, then the change in total cost must be adjusted to a "per unit" level by dividing by that number. Complete, then, the missing marginal cost figures in column (5).

Note carefully that marginal cost, even though it is also a per unit cost measure, is not the same thing at all as average cost. Marginal cost measures only the change in total cost resulting from the last unit produced, or that would result if 1 more unit were produced.

Because this table deals with 2-unit output changes, column (5) is not precisely accurate as a measure of marginal cost. If the table were enlarged to show unit-by-unit (rather than 2-unit) changes, then, for example, the 8-to-9 marginal cost figure in column (5) would be a little below $5.25, and the 9-to-10 figure a little above. But $5.25 is a reasonably close estimate for both.

a. $30; $11.25; $9.29; $9.03 b. 16 c. $10; $16; $22 d. $5; $5.50; $8; $20

3. a. In Figure 21-1, plot the total cost curve, using columns (1) and (2) of Table 21-1 (i.e., plot the several points indicated by these columns; then join them with a smooth curve).

b. In Figure 21-2 use columns (1) and (3) of Table 21-1 to plot the average cost (*AC*) curve. Also in Figure 21-2, use columns (1) and (5) to plot the marginal cost (*MC*) curve. (Because the *MC* values are in-between points, record them opposite odd-numbered quantities of output—1, 3, 5, 7, etc.) Mark your two curves on Figure 21-2 as *AC* and *MC*, respectively.

Total cost in $

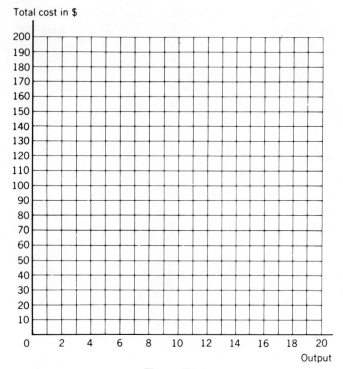

Figure 21-1

AC, MC in $

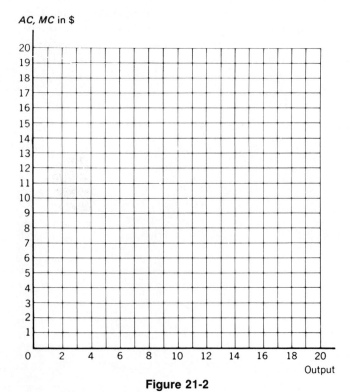

Figure 21-2

c. Figure 21-2 indicates that (pick one or more):
(1) The *AC* curve, as it moves to the right, cuts through the bottom point of the *MC* curve.
(2) The *MC* curve, as it moves to the right, cuts through the bottom point of the *AC* curve.

(3) The *MC* curve, as it moves to the right, cuts through the *AC* curve, but not at its bottom point.
(4) The *AC* curve, as it moves to the right, cuts through the *MC* curve, but not at the *MC* curve's bottom point.

---

c. (2) and (4) (Note that this property of the *MC* curve—that it always cuts through the bottom point of the *AC* curve—is discussed more fully later on)

---

4. Recall once again that the total cost of production can be separated into two parts: fixed cost and variable cost. Fixed cost is the cost that would be incurred even at zero output.

Divide each of these three aggregate cost measures (total, fixed, and variable) by the quantity of output being produced, and you get three corresponding per unit figures: *average cost* (*AC*), *average fixed cost* (*AFC*), and *average variable cost* (*AVC*).

Note one point: Because total cost is made up of fixed cost and variable cost, it must be true that ($AC = AFC - AVC$ / $AC = AFC + AVC$ / $AFC = AC + AVC$).

$AC = AFC + AVC$

---

5. a. Table 21-2 extends Table 21-1. From it, compute a few *AFC* figures. When output is 4, *AFC* would be $_____; when output is 8, *AFC* would be $_____; when output is 12, *AFC* would be $_____.

Notice that the mathematical computation involved is not overwhelmingly complicated. As we move to higher outputs, we are just dividing $50 by successively larger figures. On a graph such as the text's Figure 21-1(b), which shows what

Table 21-2

Output	Total Cost	Average Cost	Marginal Cost	Average Variable Cost
0	$50.00			
			$5.00	
2	60.00	$30.00		$5.00
			5.00	
4	70.00	17.50		____
			5.00	
6	80.00	13.33		5.00
			5.00	
8	90.00	11.25		____
			5.25	
10	100.50	10.05		5.05
			5.50	
12	111.50	9.29		____
			6.50	
14	124.50	8.89		5.32
			8.00	
16	140.50	8.78		5.66
			11.00	
18	162.50	9.03		6.25
			20.00	
20	202.50	10.13		7.63

happens to per unit costs as output is increased, *AFC* would *(fall / rise)* continuously. *AFC* simply keeps dropping all the time because a fixed money cost is being spread over more and more units of output, and that's all there is to *that*.

b. To compute *AVC* for any output, you must first establish (total) variable cost, by subtracting *(marginal / fixed / variable)* cost from total cost—i.e., in the case of Table 21-2 subtracting $_____ from total cost.

Complete Table 21-2 by writing in the three missing *AVC* figures, those for outputs of 4, 8, and 12.

c. Using the *AFC* and *AVC* figures you have already worked out in this question for outputs 4, 8, and 12, check to make sure the rule is satisfied: *AFC* + *AVC* = *AC*.

---

a. 12.50; 6.25; 4.17; fall   **b.** fixed; 50; $5; $5; $5.12

6. **a.** In Table 21-2, for outputs from 0 to 9, *AVC* is a *(rising / constant / falling)* figure. On a per unit cost graph, it would be illustrated as a *(rising / flat / falling)* line.

Often *AVC* is described as *falling* (rather than constant) for outputs that are small relative to plant capacity. It is not altogether clear which of these two behaviors (flat or falling) is typical of actual cost performance. But the point is of minor importance here. What *is* important is that as output is increased, *AVC* in due course begins to *(rise / fall)*.

b. In Table 21-2, for outputs up to 10, *AVC* is *(the same as / different from)* *MC*. (This is because *AVC* is assumed constant up to that output level.) At output 12—and indeed at all outputs including and beyond 10—*AVC* and *MC* are *(the same / different)*. Specifically for any output such as 12 or higher, *MC* is *(greater / less)* than *AVC*.

It is not difficult to see the relation between *MC* and *AVC*. Marginal cost is nothing but the variable cost of the last unit produced; it is the extra cost occasioned by producing that last unit. Average variable cost is the average of all these separate *MC* figures, from the first unit of output right up to the particular quantity of output in question. So if *MC* starts to rise, *AVC* will in due course rise also. But because *AVC* is an average of all per unit variable (or marginal) costs, it cannot change as rapidly as *MC*. Being held back by all the other figures of which it is the average, *AVC* will rise more *(rapidly / slowly)* than *MC*.

---

a. constant; flat; rise   **b.** the same as; different; greater; slowly

7. **a.** Suppose we had used a case in which (unlike Table 21-2) *AVC* initially falls. If *AVC* is an average of all the previous *MC*s, and if *AVC* falls as we move from output 2 to output 3, from 3 to 4, and from 4 to 5, this must mean that the *MC* for outputs 3, 4, and 5 is *(greater than / the same as / less than)* the corresponding *AVC* figure. It is the inclusion of that extra figure *(MC)* which pulls down the average. In sum, if *AVC* is falling, *MC* must be *(less / greater)* than *AVC*.

b. This point can be illustrated by an example involving classroom grades. In a given class of students, the average examination grade is always 70. Now we add a few new students (some extra or "marginal" students) to this class. They are weaker students; they always score between 50 and 55 on examinations. So, when added to the class, they *(increase / pull down)* the class average from 70 to, say, 65. (When marginal value is below average value, the marginal pulls down the average.)

c. We add a few more students. They are a little better; they score from 60 to 63. But they are likewise below the new class average of 65. So that average is *(pulled down / increased)* just a little more—say, from 65 to *(64 / 66.)*

d. We add one more student, who always scores 64. This addition does not change the class average. (When marginal equals average, average does not change.)

Finally we add a few students who always score above 64. Their addition will accordingly *(increase / decrease)* the class average. (When marginal exceeds average, marginal pulls up average.)

---

a. less than; less   **b.** pull down   **c.** pulled down; 64   **d.** increase

8. The implications of the preceding question need to be considered carefully. To grasp them, look at Figure 21-3, showing the per unit cost curves for a firm with a plant of some given size. The average cost (*AC*) curve is approximately U-shaped. If output is gradually expanded from a zero level, *AC* will initially *(rise / fall)*, because fixed cost is being spread over increasingly *(larger / smaller)* outputs. However, as plant capacity is approached, *AC* must ultimately *(rise / fall)* because of the influence of *(fixed cost / the law of diminishing returns)*.

In these circumstances, the marginal cost (*MC*) curve must always cut through the exact bottom point of the *AC* curve. (It may take you a little time to think this through, but it follows from the reasoning of question 7. If *AC* is falling, it must mean that *MC* is below *AC*. If *AC* turns around and begins to rise, it must be because *MC* has risen above *AC*.)

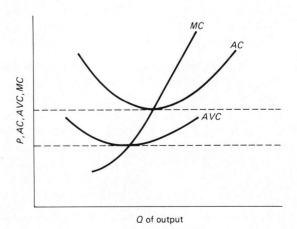

Q of output

Figure 21-3

Exactly the same conclusion applies with respect to the AVC curve; the MC curve must cut through its bottom point. AVC is exactly the same kind of average as AC. The only difference between them is that AC includes the unchanging figure of fixed cost, whereas AVC does not.

So Figure 21-3 illustrates the general relationship that must exist between the three most important per unit cost measures. AC must be, at least approximately, U-shaped, and MC must cut through its bottom point. AVC may or may not be U-shaped, but it most certainly will rise as plant capacity is approached. If it *is* U-shaped, and if it has a unique bottom point, then MC will cut through that point.

---

fall; larger; rise; the law of diminishing returns

---

9. The text notes a distinction between short-run and long-run cost schedules. This question will explore that distinction.

Short-run cost curves of the type illustrated in Figure 21-3 answer one type of question: Given the plant that we now own and assuming fixed input prices, what would be the average and marginal cost of producing any particular level of output?

That is not, however, the only question in town. The firm can ask a different question with a different time frame: What would be the lowest cost of producing any given level of output, no matter how small, if we had complete freedom over the size of the plant? Put another way: For any output, what size plant would produce that output at the lowest possible cost, given the current state of technology and the current level of input prices?

When a firm asks this second question, it is thinking in a maximum-profit mode—moving beyond the limitation of its present fixed plant size. It is thinking in terms of freedom in the matter of plant size, and looking for the output that (with such freedom) would yield maximum profit. For this purpose, it needs a *long-run average cost curve (LRAC, or LAC)*. Such a curve is unlike the AC curve of Figure 21-3, which refers to a plant of given size. In building the $LRAC$ curve, you ask: For each and every output, what is the lowest-attainable AC (given present input prices and technology), no matter what the plant size needed to obtain that AC? (The firm is assumed to have complete and reliable information as to the AC curve that goes with each and every plant that could possibly be built.)

The graph illustrating $LRAC$ for a firm is structurally the same as that for the short-run situation: AC is measured on the vertical axis; quantity of output is measured horizontally. But on the long-run diagram, Figure 21-4, we show all possible short-run AC curves. There is one such short-run AC curve for each possible plant size. (We exclude, of course, any plants that would not be efficient for producing some output quantity.) The "bottom edge" resulting from this accumulation of short-run curves is the long-run curve.

This long-run curve is sometimes called (borrowing a mathematicians' term) the "lower envelope curve," or the "planning curve."

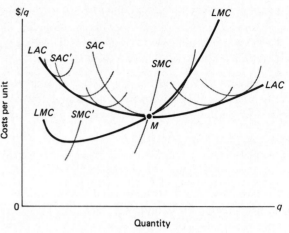

Figure 21-4

So the firm's long-run AC curve for commodity X could be used to indicate (pick one or more):
(1) The lowest possible AC at which any quantity of X could be produced, and the particular size of plant needed in order to obtain that AC.
(2) The level of output at which it would be most profitable to produce X.
(3) The particular quantity (or quantities) of X at which the very lowest per unit cost (AC) of all would be possible, and the plant size (or range of plant sizes) required for that minimum AC.
(4) The price the firm ought to charge in order to obtain the maximum profit from the sale of X.

---

(1) and (3)

---

10. a. The long-run AC is usually depicted as a saucer-shaped, U-shaped curve—first falling, then flat, and finally rising. Sometimes the bottom is flat over a region; sometimes the bottom is simply a single point.

The falling region is that of *increasing returns to scale*, where, as the size of plant is increased and the scale of operations expanded, the result is a *(higher / lower)* short-run AC. The flat region (or the bottom point) represents minimum-attainable AC (given present technology and input prices).

At some level of output (perhaps very large), presumably some inefficiencies of too-large size set in, so that the $LRAC$ curve will ultimately begin to turn up, even if only slightly. (Particularly as a consequence of recent developments in communication and record-keeping methods, such as computers, it is clear that a firm can often become very large indeed without incurring inefficiencies of large size that are of sufficient importance to offset the economies of large-scale operation.)

b. The theory of perfect competition envisions new firms entering and old firms leaving an industry at will. Notice now that this type of long-run adjustment may also involve some change in the size of plant for existing firms. If there are economies of scale to be obtained from increasing plant size, then business firms—given sufficient time—will gravitate toward those larger plants.

This fact uncovers one of the paradoxes of pure (or perfect) competition in its relation to contemporary economic life. The argument for such competition is its presumed *efficiency* (in the sense of using a given resource stock to the best advantage). Each firm is too *(small / large)* to be able to exert any "monopolistic" control over price. And there is the presumed tendency for price to gravitate in the long run toward minimum possible *AC*.

Yet if the *LRAC* curve is such that minimum-level *AC* requires a large output and plant size, the firm needed to operate that plant may be too *(small / large)* for the requirements of pure competition. Pure competition then becomes inefficient.

---

a. lower **b.** small; large

11. Economists who work on the theory of pure or perfect competition are aware that, in actual experience, the per unit cost of various firms in an industry sometimes goes down and not up as that industry develops and expands. We have just noted one reason that that might happen. An industry might be composed of a group of firms that can move down their long-run average cost curves so that, as demand climbs, the price can fall. We now turn to a second reason why this counterintuitive price response might occur—external economies.

Economies are designated external if they are caused by effects that lie outside the decision range of a single firm. Consider beekeeping. You raise bees for the honey that they produce. The enterprise is, without any other factors being considered, profitable. Your bees might, however, also benefit your neighbors if those neighbors should own an orchard. Your bees would then pollinate their trees, free of charge, and their operation would be more profitable than it would otherwise be simply because their orchard happens to be located close to your bees. Your bees, in other words, would provide your neighbors with an external economy. This question will explore the difference between these two explanations.

a. If your current output is not pressing hard against your capacity constraint, then you might therefore note that your average costs would decline if you could only raise your output. On your short-run per unit cost diagram, this would be a *(movement down an existing AC curve / shift of the entire AC curve to a new and lower position)*. Or you may recognize that building a larger plant equipped for mass production would reduce your per unit costs. On your long-run per unit cost diagram, this would be a *(movement down an existing AC curve / shift of the entire AC curve to a new and lower position)*. These are *internal* economies, not external.

History can furnish many illustrations in which, as new products were introduced successfully, per unit cost and price went down as demand went up (e.g., television sets, ballpoint pens, pocket calculators). Unfortunately, few of these (possibly none) furnish valid examples of an "external economy." They came about because the supplying firms gradually found out how to make their product more efficiently (or in more technical terminology, crept down their "learning curves"), developing better production methods. A genuine, money-back-guarantee external economy must be reversible. When the industry expands its output, each member firm's per unit cost curves shift downward. If a decrease in demand were subsequently to force a reduction in output, then, for a proper external economy, those per unit cost curves would have to shift back upward again.

We cannot, therefore, count as an "external economy" any technological breakthrough reducing per unit costs, even if it were prompted by increased demand. Such a change in the technique of production presumably would still exist even if industry output had to be reduced. It would count as an external economy only if that economy became unusable (even with a smaller number of supplying firms) when industry output fell.

b. Which of the following suggests an external economy (in the first of the two senses outlined above)? (Pick one or more.)
(1) A mine in northern Canada must rely on diesel engines for power. More mines spring up in the area, and as a result, a dam is built to generate hydroelectric power for all mines.
(2) General Motors introduces a new mass-production automobile plant which significantly reduces the per unit cost of automobile assembly.
(3) Expansion of the electronics industry in a particular area brings more engineers to that area, thus somewhat reducing the acute shortage of (and exceedingly high salaries paid to) engineers in that area.
(4) Sears Roebuck opens a new store in a shopping plaza. Smaller shops in the plaza benefit from the increased number of buyers attracted to the area by Sears's arrival.

c. In sum, for any single firm, an external economy means (pick one):
(1) An average or marginal cost curve that falls as it moves toward higher outputs—i.e., runs southeasterly.
(2) A reduction in an input's per unit cost when the firm buys that input in sufficiently large quantities.
(3) A reduction in per unit cost occurring when the size of the firm's plant is expanded.
(4) A downward shift or displacement in the position of the industry supply curve.
(5) None of the above.

---

a. movement down an existing *AC* curve; movement down an existing *AC* curve **b.** (1), (3), (4) [Neither (1) nor (3) would be a valid example unless it is agreed that this economy would reverse itself if the industry subsequently had to contract in size: the dam would not be maintained; most of the engineers would leave] **c.** (5)

13. The text mentions that "opportunity cost" elements should be included in a firm's costs. You run your own firm—and so, in reckoning costs, should include that of your own labor. You do include your own labor cost—at $5 per hour. Now you learn that you could get a job down the street at $10 per hour. The fact of this opportunity means that you should include in costs your labor at *(zero / $5 / $7.50 / $10)* per hour.

(Of course, you may prefer to run your own business. If so, you may be happy to continue to run it, even though conceivably it might seem to be running at a slight loss when this full opportunity cost is counted.)

$10

---

13. Suppose that you are considering whether to fly from Boston to Washington or to take the bus. The airfare is $100 and the flight takes 1 hour. The bus fare is only $50, but the drive takes 6 hours. How much would the two options cost

a. if you are a businessperson whose time costs $40 per hour?

_____ .

b. if you are a student whose time is worth $4 per hour? _____

_____ .

c. to you? _____

_____ .

a. including the cost of time, airfare is $100 + $40 = $140 and bus fare is $50 + 6 ($40) = $290   **b.** airfare is $100 + $4 = $104 and bus fare is $50 + 6 ($4) = $74   **c.** I do not know the cost of your time, but if it exceeds $10 per hour, then the plane is the better deal

---

14. Given the production-possibility frontier shown on Figure 21-5, the opportunity cost of increasing the production of wheat by 1000 units would be _____units of corn if the economy were originally at point *A* and _____units of corn if the economy were originally at point *B*. Why?

_____

_____

_____ .

1000; 0; opportunity cost involves transferring utilized resources from one activity to another, and movement from *B* to *C* simply employs resources that were otherwise unemployed

---

QUIZ: Multiple Choice

1. Fixed cost for a firm's operating plant means:
(1) any cost whose amount is established at the time the input is purchased.
(2) the minimum cost of producing any given quantity of output under the most favorable operating conditions.
(3) any cost whose per unit amount has been settled for some considerable future period, such as a long-term wage contract with a labor union.

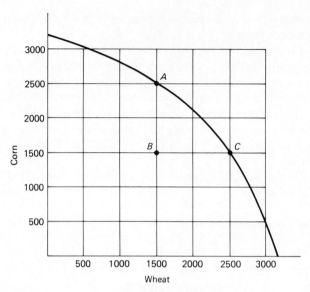

Figure 21-5

(4) the amount of cost that must be incurred even if zero output is produced.
(5) none of these things.

2. Marginal cost for a firm's operating plant means:
(1) the increase over normal cost that must sometimes be paid to obtain output, such as the extra amount of overtime pay
(2) the cost incurred even if the firm produces zero output.
(3) the difference between the amount of total cost actually incurred to produce any given output and what is considered to be the minimum possible total cost of producing that output.
(4) the increase in total cost that accrues from an increase in quantity produced of 1 unit.
(5) the increase in total cost that accrues from any increase in quantity produced, whether 1 unit or more.

3. The property taxes a firm must pay on its plant are increased—i.e., its fixed cost is increased. On a graph illustrating this firm's cost curves, the marginal cost curve would be affected by this fixed cost increase as follows. It would:
(1) move to the right.
(2) move to the left.
(3) move upward.
(4) move downward.
(5) not move at all.

4. Total cost in a certain plant, at an output level of 1000 units daily, is $4900. If production were to be reduced by 1 unit (to a total of 999 units), total cost would become $4890. Within the output range thus indicated:
(1) average cost (*AC*) would exceed marginal cost (*MC*).
(2) *AC* and *MC* would be approximately equal.
(3) *MC* would exceed *AC*.
(4) no comparison between *MC* and *AC* is possible, since the information given is not sufficient to determine *MC*.
(5) no comparison between *MC* and *AC* is possible, since the information given is not sufficient to determine *AC*.

5. If the term "opportunity cost" is used with respect to any of a firm's costs, it means:

(1) including as the cost of any input the market price or return that input is offered in any other occupation.

(2) certain nonrecurring or once-and-for-all costs involved in getting production under way.

(3) costs which would be incurred even at zero output but which do not increase in amount as output is increased.

(4) any cost incurred which does not involve an actual outlay of cash.

(5) nothing at all, since the term would not be used with respect to production costs.

6. At the quantity of output where average cost has reached its minimum level:

(1) average variable cost will equal fixed cost.

(2) profit must be at its maximum level for the firm.

(3) marginal cost will equal average variable cost.

(4) marginal cost will equal average cost.

(5) none of the above is necessarily true.

7. If marginal cost exceeds average cost (*AC*) within a certain range of plant outputs, then, with respect to any increase in output within that range:

(1) *AC* must rise.

(2) *AC* must fall.

(3) *AC* must either rise or fall.

(4) *AC* must remain constant.

(5) *AC* may rise, fall, or remain constant.

8. In a certain plant, marginal cost is $2 at 400 units of output weekly, and it is $2.50 at 500 units of output. Referring to output increases within this 400-to-500 range, average cost:

(1) must rise.

(2) must fall.

(3) must remain constant.

(4) may rise, may fall, or both, but cannot remain constant throughout this output range.

(5) may rise, may fall, or may remain constant throughout this output range.

9. The text chapter discusses the firm's "long-run average cost curve" (also described as the "long-run planning envelope curve"). This curve is intended to show (referring to given conditions of technology):

(1) the minimum cost of producing any given output quantity, if the firm can select, for each such output, the plant most economical for producing that quantity.

(2) the minimum cost for the profit-maximizing output, using the particular plant best suited for that particular output.

(3) the minimum cost of producing any given output quantity, using a plant of one given size only for all such outputs, but the plant which yields the lowest-attainable average cost figure.

(4) the minimum cost of producing any given output quantity, using a plant of one given size only for all such outputs, but the plant which yields the lowest-attainable marginal cost figure.

(5) the future increase or decrease in average cost that can be expected as the number of firms entering the industry increases or decreases.

10. If the short-run marginal cost curve of a typical firm in a competitive industry should fall continuously over a substantial range of increasing outputs, the consequence indicated by the text chapter is that:

(1) new firms must enter that industry.

(2) the profit earned by that typical firm can be expected to rise.

(3) the marginal cost of that firm will exceed its average cost through the output range in question.

(4) the total amount of fixed cost which this firm must pay will fall.

(5) pure (or perfect) competition is likely to give way to imperfect competition.

CHAPTER 22
COMPETITIVE SUPPLY

Chapter 21 presented the litany of cost concepts that occupy the economist's mind. We are now ready to apply those concepts to an analysis of how a competitive firm decides how much it wants to produce when confronted by the market with some arbitrary price over which it has no control. The link between cost and the output decision will be based upon an assumption that firms are motivated primarily by a desire to maximize their profits. It will, in particular, be assumed that every firm chooses its desired level of output for any price by maximizing the difference between the revenue that it can earn by selling the targeted output at the given price and the *minimum* cost required to produce that output. The result of our study will be the development of insight into not only the firms' individual and market supply curves, but also the structural and efficiency properties of competitive markets.

Having completed your work in this chapter, you should have accomplished the following objectives.

LEARNING OBJECTIVES

1. Describe the notion of perfect competition in terms of structure and in terms of what it does to the sphere of economic variables over which a competitive firm has influence.

2. Identify the profit-maximizing goal of each firm and indicate decision rules through which each firm can achieve that goal.

3. Review clearly the notions of total cost, fixed cost, variable cost, average cost, and marginal cost.

4. Develop the supply curve of a competitive firm in terms of marginal cost.

5. Explain breakeven and shutdown conditions and their relevance to the competitive marketplace.

6. Explain the long-run and short-run equilibrium conditions for the competitive firm and the competitive market.

7. Understand more fully why decreasing costs lead to monopolistic and oligopolistic market structures.

8. Explain the efficiency of perfect competition in terms of (*a*) marginal cost and marginal utility, (*b*) consumer surplus and net social welfare, and (*c*) a utility-possibility frontier.

This is, to be sure, a longer than usual list of learning objectives, but this is a chapter of unusual importance. There are not very many purely competitive markets in the world, but an understanding of the implications and workings of their purity is essential in the understanding of the imperfections that we find throughout the rest of reality. Perfect competition is, in short, another one of those benchmark notions against which a wide variety of other concepts can be cast and thereby be more easily understood.

Perfect competition can be characterized in terms of three simple conditions. In a perfectly competitive market, the firm (1) is faced with a market price for its output over which it has no control; it is too small relative to the market to be able to affect the price; (2) can sell as much or as little as it wants to at the given price without incurring selling costs of any kind; and (3) selects its desired level of output and sales for any given price by maximizing profits.

1. a. The text refers to both *the firm* and *the industry;* the difference between these terms is important. The individual unit producing and selling output in the hope of making a profit is the (firm / industry), and its supply curve shows what this unit would offer for sale at each possible price. The total of all individual units together is the (firm / industry), and the supply curve of this aggregate shows total quantity that will be offered for sale by all these units combined at each possible price.

b. A "competitive firm," as the term is used in this chapter, means one operating under the special conditions of pure (or perfect) competition. Remember carefully what was said above: *In these conditions, the firm can choose the quantity of output it is going to produce and sell, and it is assumed to choose the quantity which (given the market price offered) yields it the highest-attainable profit.*

"Profit" here means (pick one):

(1) Total cost incurred in producing output minus total revenue or income from selling that output.

(2) Total revenue or income from selling output, without regard to costs incurred.

(3) Total revenue or income from selling output, minus total cost incurred in producing that output.

"Profit" means, then, the revenue that you take in from sales of your product, minus the costs incurred in producing that product.

c. Under conditions of perfect competition, the short-run industry supply curve can be derived from the supply curves of the individual firms *(by adding the price received by each firm for a given output to determine a market price / by adding the quantity produced by each firm for a given price to determine a market quantity supplied / only by a trained statistician).* The short-run market supply curve therefore depends critically upon *(the number of firms in the market / the output of each firm at each price / the number of consumers in the market).*

---

a. firm; industry **b.** (3) **c.** by adding the quantity produced by each firm; the number of firms in the marketplace *and* the output of each firm at each price

---

2. The terms "revenue" and "cost" are used extensively in the next few chapters. They need careful review.

Revenue, or *total revenue,* means total number of units sold, multiplied by market price at which they sold.

Total cost means all costs incurred in producing and selling that output. This chapter deals with the special situation of pure (or perfect) competition, however, where there are no such selling costs. So far as this chapter is concerned, there are only production costs.

Recall, as well, that total cost can be divided into two distinct parts:

1. *Variable costs*—meaning those costs whose total amount varies with the amount of output produced.

2. *Fixed costs*—meaning those costs which are fixed in amount regardless of the level of output and which would accordingly have to be paid by the firm even if its output were zero.

In addition, two other derivative cost notions are important:

3. *Marginal costs*—meaning the extra cost that would be incurred if the firm were to produce 1 more unit of output.

4. *Average costs*—meaning the ratio of total cost to total output.

3. Table 22-1 records a wide variety of cost and revenue information for various levels of output and two possible price specifications. It shows the total revenue obtained for each price for various quantities of output from 10 to 20 as well as the profit to be earned for each of these outputs. Complete the blanks in this table.

a. From Table 22-1, it is clear that the profit-maximizing output for a price of $11.20 would be *(12 / 14 / 16 / 18 / 20)* units. At this output, average cost would be $_____ and marginal cost would approximate $_____ .

b. At a price of $8.80, profit-maximizing output would be *(12 / 14 / 16 / 18 / 20)*, with average cost equalling $_____ and marginal cost approximating $_____ .

Reading down the columns: *AC:* $10.05; $9.29; $8.89; $8.78; $9.02; $10.13 *MC:* ?; $5.50; $6.50; $8.00; $11.00; $20.00 Revenue: $112.00; $201.60; $224.00 Profit: $22.90; $38.70; $39.10; $21.50 Revenue: $88.00; $105.60; $123.20; $140.80; $158.40; $176.00 Profit: −$12.50; −$5.90; −$1.30; $.30; −$4.10; −$26.50 **a.** $18; 9.02; $11 **b.** 16; 8.78; 8

Table 22-1

Quantity	Cost Data			Revenue Data			
	Total Cost	Average Cost	Marginal Cost	Price = $11.20		Price = $8.80	
				Revenue	Profit	Revenue	Profit
10	$100.50	___	___	___	$11.50	___	___
12	111.50	___	___	$134.40	___	___	___
14	124.50	___	___	$156.80	32.30	___	___
16	140.50	___	___	$179.20	___	___	___
18	162.50	___	___	___	___	___	___
20	202.50	___	___	___	___	___	___

4. a. At maximum-profit output, price *(P)* and *(average / marginal)* cost are equal. Think of the firm as expanding weekly output from 10 units to 11, from 11 to 12, and so on. As output quantity changes, the *AC* figure changes, and so does the *MC* figure. For maximum profit, the firm should halt output expansion when *(MC has fallen / AC has fallen / MC has risen / AC has risen)* to a level equal to price.

b. At price $8.80, it does not pay to produce and sell the 17th and 18th units that could be sold profitably at price $11.20. This is so because the firm has a plant of fixed size, and when its capacity output is approached, per unit costs begin to rise. Specifically, total cost will rise by *$(6.50 / 8 / 11 / 20)* for each of the 17th and 18th units. The simple but basic point involved is this: in profit terms, it pays to produce and sell an extra unit of output only if the extra revenue that unit brings in (here, the price of that unit) exceeds the extra cost (marginal cost, the rise in total cost) which was incurred in producing and selling that extra output unit.

---

a. marginal; *MC has risen*   **b.** 11

---

5. The relation between revenue, costs, and profit can be directly illustrated by a diagram on Figure 22-1. Draw the total revenue line for a price of $11.20. (Just show the point that would indicate revenue from 2 units sold at $11.20 each, from 4 units so sold, etc. Then join your points.) Now plot total cost.

Total profit for any output is the distance vertically down-

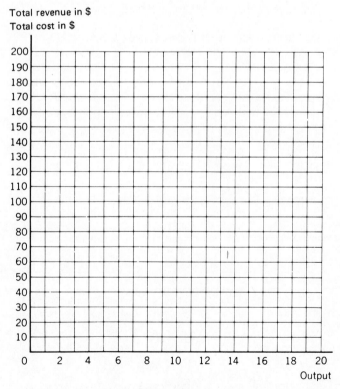

Total revenue in $
Total cost in $

Figure 22-1

ward from the total revenue line *(TR)* to the total cost line *(TC)*. The search for maximum-profit output is the search for the output level at which this distance is greatest.

Draw a similar *TR* line for price $8.80 in a different color and note that at most outputs, *TC* is higher than *TR*; at any such output, a loss would be incurred. For identification, mark your first line $11.20 and your second $8.80.

Finally, draw two more lines for prices of $7 and $4 in still different colors if possible.

Your four *TR* lines should be four straight lines radiating out from the origin, with $11.20 highest, $4 lowest, neither the $7 nor the $4 line should intersect *TC*

---

6. Clearly, if price falls much below $8.80, there will be no output at which the firm can do as much as to break even. In such circumstances, ought the firm to shut down (supply zero output) rather than incur a loss?

As preliminary to exploring this question, complete the missing figures in Table 22-2, showing *TR*, *TC*, and "negative profit" for various outputs at prices $7 and $4.

At $7: −$27.50; −$28.50   At $4: −$63.50; −$76.50

---

7. The point now to be stressed is this: our firm cannot escape loss just by shutting down its operations. It has fixed cost of $50 (e.g., the interest which must be paid on a debenture issue), and it is stuck with this cost even when shut down (until or unless it goes bankrupt).

The all-encompassing profit-maximizing rule is this: do the best you can. Pick the output that maximizes your profit. If market price is so low that there is no output yielding a positive profit, then minimize your loss. The worst that can happen is that you will incur a loss equal to your fixed cost by shutting down. If you can find an output level which, even though it incurs a loss, means a loss less than that fixed cost, then operate at that output.

a. Specifically, if market price were $7, application of this rule means that the firm should (pick one):

Table 22-2

Quantity	Price: $7			Price: $4		
	Revenue	Total Cost	Profit	Revenue	Total Cost	Profit
10	$ 70.00	$100.50	−$30.50	$40.00	$100.50	−$ 60.50
12	84.00	111.50	——	48.00	111.50	——
14	98.00	124.50	−26.50	56.00	124.50	−68.50
16	112.00	140.50	——	64.00	140.50	——
18	126.00	162.50	−36.50	72.00	162.50	−90.50
20	140.00	202.50	−62.50	80.00	202.50	−122.50

(1) Shut down.

(2) Operate at output 10, since a loss of $30.50 is preferable to a loss of $50.

(3) Operate at output 14, since loss at that output ($26.50) is lowest among the figures listed in Table 22-1, and is preferable to a $50 loss.

b. If market price were to be $4, the firm should (*operate at output 10 / operate at output 14 / shut down*).

c. The general rule which emerges out of these considerations is the following (pick one):

(1) If there is some output at which loss would be less than the amount of fixed cost, produce and sell that output; shut down operations if loss exceeds fixed cost at all (nonzero) outputs.

(2) Shut down whenever there is no output at which it is possible to earn a profit or at least to break even.

(3) If there is some output at which loss would be greater than the amount of fixed cost, produce and sell that output; shut down operations if loss is less than fixed cost at all (nonzero) outputs.

---

a. (3) **b.** shut down **c.** (1)

In summary, then, the preceding questions have illustrated a two-part rule for profit-maximizing output decisions:

▶Pick the output at which $MC = P$. This is the best possible (nonzero) operating output.

▶If this best possible (nonzero) output yields a loss, compare this loss with fixed cost. If loss is less than fixed cost, operate at that output. If loss exceeds fixed cost, disregard the $MC = P$ rule, and shut down.

Warning: The first of the two rules stated above applies only in the special case of pure (or perfect) competition treated in this chapter. It is a special instance of a more general rule. When we turn to nonperfect competition, in Chapters 23 and 24, the same general reasoning applies; but the profit-maximizing rule is restated in a different and more general form.

8. An example may illustrate more fully the nature of the *shutdown rule*—the second of the two rules recorded above. Figure 22-2 depicts two different situations. The height of

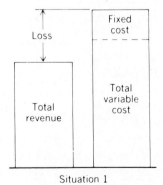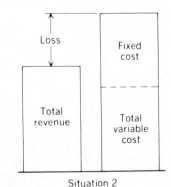

Situation 1   Situation 2
Figure 22-2

each block indicates the dollar value of revenue or of cost, when the firm is at its best possible operating position. The two situations are exactly alike in respect to total revenue, total cost, and operating loss incurred. They differ only in the distribution of costs as between fixed and variable. The amount of fixed cost is larger, and that of variable cost is smaller, in situation (*1 / 2*).

The shutdown rule says the firm should cease production in situation (*1 / 2*), and continue to operate despite loss in situation (*1 / 2*). The reasoning behind this rule is just that set out at the beginning of question 7. You are stuck with a loss no matter what you do. The worst that can happen is that you incur a loss equal to fixed cost. If you can find an operating level at which the revenue earned from sales more than covers your variable cost, then some part of that revenue remains to be applied against fixed cost—so that your loss is then less than fixed cost. The $P = MC$ rule is then (*still / not*) useful, because it (*will / will not*) indicate the minimum-loss operating level.

2; 1; 2; still; will

9. Figure 22-2, along with the discussion which ended the preceding question, suggests an alternative statement of the shutdown rule. It is this: shut down when total revenue (at the best possible operating position) is (*less / greater*) than total variable cost.

There would be no great point in developing a second version of the shutdown rule, were it not that this leads to a third version, and one that is often very useful. The blocks in Figure 22-2 stand for TR and TC at some particular quantity of output (the one indicated by the $P = MC$ rule). Divide TR by that quantity of output, and we get price (since TR = price × quantity). Divide total variable cost by quantity, and we get average variable cost, or variable cost per unit of output.

We could, therefore, frame the shutdown rule in a still different way: shut down when market price (*exceeds / is less than*) average variable cost.

The special significance of this alternative is that it is framed in price terms. It indicates the particular price which is just sufficiently low that the firm then decides to stop supplying anything to the market. A price which is just equal to average variable cost is the razor's edge. The firm's supply curve "breaks" at this price. Below it, the firm shuts down.

---

less; is less than

10. Now consider Figure 22-3. The three horizontal lines recorded there indicate the demand curves corresponding to three possible levels of market price. [Remember that the firm in pure (or perfect) competition has no selling problems. It can sell as much or as little as it pleases at the prevailing market price, without advertising or other sales cost.]

a. For example, if price were HO, then the firm could move anywhere along d_1d_1. The point at which MC has risen to

P, AC, AVC, MC

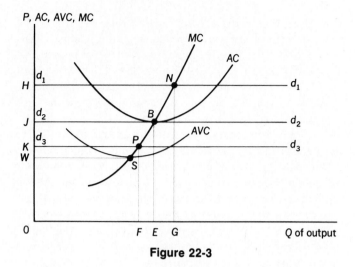

Figure 22-3

equality with *that* market price is N; i.e., if *HO* were the market price, the firm would produce and sell quantity *(OF / OE / OG).* Note carefully that in this position, price is above *AC,* so that the firm would be *(earning a profit / just breaking even / incurring a loss).*

b. If price happened to be *JO,* then the firm's demand curve would be *(d₁d₁ / d₂d₂ / d₃d₃),* and its maximum-profit output would be *(OF / OE / OG).* It would then be *(earning a profit / just breaking even / incurring a loss).*

c. If price were *KO,* the firm's best possible position would be to produce *(nothing / output OF / output OE).* In this position, its loss would be *(less than / equal to / greater than)* the amount of its fixed cost.

d. If price fell so low that it did not even cover average variable cost, then the firm would do better to cease operations entirely. (REMEMBER: If price does not cover average variable cost, then operating loss exceeds fixed cost.) On Figure 22-3, the boundary of this shutdown price zone is marked by price *(HO / JO / KO / WO).* This price is *(greater than / just equal to / less than)* the minimum level of *(average variable / average fixed)* cost.

***

a. *OG;* earning a profit   **b.** *d₂d₂; OE;* just breaking even   **c.** output *OF;* less than   **d.** *WO;* just equal to; average variable

Most of the preceding work has concentrated on the short-run notion of equilibrium from the firms' perspective. We now turn to consider the long run.

11. The market price which each firm in pure (or perfect) competition must accept is the price resulting from the intersection of industry demand and supply curves. At any moment of time, it could be any of Figure 22-3's prices—*HO, JO, KO,* or even *WO.* However, it is argued that there is a long-run tendency for price to gravitate toward level *JO,* the *(breakeven / shutdown)* price.

The reasoning behind this argument is not difficult to grasp.

Suppose price were below *JO.* This would mean that all supplying firms would be losing money. (For convenience, think of every firm as having the set of cost curves indicated by Figure 22-3, because they all produce the same product with the same technology, all paying the same prices for their inputs.) If price persisted below the *JO* level, some firms would eventually drop out. Either they leave voluntarily as some of their fixed-cost obligations come up for renewal and give them an exit opportunity, or else bankruptcy would force them out.

When they leave, industry supply will be *(increased / decreased),* and market price will thereupon *(rise / fall).*

Suppose, on the other hand, that price happened to be *above JO.* This would mean that the firms presently in the industry are earning profits. These profits will attract new firms to the industry. Even at breakeven price *JO,* the typical firm is earning a "normal" return on its invested capital. If new firms enter, this will mean *(an increase / a decrease)* in industry supply. So price will thereupon *(rise / fall).*

In sum, whenever price happens to be below *JO,* the tendency is for price to rise. If it is above *JO,* the tendency is for price to fall. This is strictly a long-run tendency: enough time must be allowed for new firms to enter, or for old firms to depart.

The *JO* price is a goal toward which things are gradually tending. That *JO* level would be reached if enough time were allowed for conditions to work themselves out. In actual experience, this is unlikely to happen, because other factors typically change before this long-run equilibrium goal is reached. Thus suppose that price is gradually moving toward *JO,* but is still above that level because new firms have not had sufficient time to enter. Then a change in input costs, or in technology, causes the Figure 22-3 cost curves to shift to new positions. The long-run *JO* goal toward which things were gravitating is destroyed. A new long-run goal is set up—which in turn may be destroyed before it is realized.

***

breakeven; decreased; rise; an increase; fall

***

12. Notice that a firm bent on profit maximization has no special incentive to try to produce that output at which its *AC* is lowest. With its given plant, the lowest *AC* it can attain is indicated in Figure 22-3 by *BE.* This is obtained only when output is *(OF / OE / OG).* But the firm will want to produce that output if and only if market price happens to be *(HO / JO / KO / WO).*

There is nonetheless, a long-run tendency outlined in question 11 for price (*P*) to gravitate to the *JO* level, where market price, *AC,* and *MC* all are equal, and *AC* is at its minimum level; hence the "long-run equilibrium condition" stated in the text for the firm:

$$P = MC = \text{minimum-level } AC$$

Note carefully that in this phrase "long-run equilibrium condition," the word "equilibrium" is being used in a somewhat different and fuller sense.

The firm's basic profit-maximizing rule is: pick the output at which $P = MC$. But now we also have $P = AC$ in the "equilibrium requirement," and $P = AC$ is not ordinarily a profit-maximizing rule. Any firm which hopes to make a lot of money by picking a level of output at which price and AC are one and the same is going to be terribly disappointed. In this position, the firm by definition is *(earning a profit / just breaking even / losing money)*.

The firm with profit maximizing as its goal will deliberately pick the $P = MC$ position. But there is a long-run tendency for it to be pushed to a position where $P = AC$. (Thus, if P exceeds AC, the chance of profit attracts new firms, and the increase in supply resulting from their entry pushes down P. Through the mechanism of changes in market price, each firm is pushed toward the $P = AC$ position.) The $P = MC$ part of the long-run equilibrium condition refers to the firm's profit-maximizing goal. The $P = AC$ part refers to the fact that things will not have completely "settled down" for the industry or for any firm therein until this $P = AC$ condition has been pretty well satisfied. (Remember the point made at the close of question 11: this long-run position may never be reached, but it is still a goal toward which things are trending.)

OE; JO; just breaking even

13. One of the foundations of the theory of perfect competition is that we *(must /need not)* know the market demand curve to determine the market clearing long-run equilibrium price. That price is, more specifically, always given by *(the minimum of the average cost curve of the typical firm / the intersection of demand and a short-run supply curve / the intersection of the marginal cost curve of the typical firm and its average variable cost curve).*

---

need not; the minimum of the average cost curve of the typical firm (Equilibrium always occurs at the breakeven point because of adjustments in the number of firms of the type just noted)

14. To see why the individual firm has no power over the price of its output, consider the following mental exercise. Suppose that one firm were to try to increase its price above an established equilibrium. The result would be *(a collapse / an explosion)* of its market share and the *(entry / exit)* of a competitor to take its place. No help there! Now suppose that the wary firm were to try the opposite strategy—a lower price. The result would be *(an increase / a decrease)* in the number of consumers wanting to buy its output, *(an increase / a decrease)* in its desired level of output, and *(a reduction / an increase)* in its pure economic profit. Another bad idea!

The analytical implication of this exercise is that even though market demand curves for competitive markets are usually *(upward-sloping / horizontal / downward-sloping)*, the effective demand curve facing an individual competitive firm is *(upward- / horizontally / downward-)* sloped *(through /*

at) the established price. Any attempt to move from that curve will be disastrous.

---

a collapse; entry; an increase; a decrease (because the lower price would move the firm down and in along its positively sloped MC curve); a reduction; downward-sloping; horizontally; through

15. We are now ready for a more thorough exploration of the long run. The long run allows, to review one more time, enough time for firms to exit or enter the industry at will and enough time for firms to pick a different plant size if necessary. It allows, in other words, the maximum possible supply response, in terms of quantity change, to any change in industry demand. Suppose there *is* a big change in supply output. What will this do to input prices?

Let us start with a competitive industry in full long-run equilibrium. For each and every firm, $P = MC = $ minimum long-run AC. Suddenly there is a big increase in industry demand for the product. The upper left-hand diagram in Figure 22-4 shows this shift of dd to a new position $d'd'$ (broken line). Price consequently rises from JO to KO.

The ss supply curve in this diagram is short-run supply. The rise in industry output from OA to OB is consequently the extra supply that the given total of firms can produce by employing their given plant and equipment more intensively.

Because price has risen, all firms are now making profits. This will attract new firms, and the ss curve will begin to shift to the right as this new supply is added to industry supply. (In the top left-hand diagram of Figure 22-4, sketch in lightly, in pencil, a new ss curve to the right of the present one.)

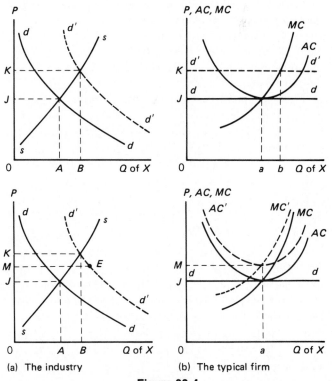

(a) The industry   (b) The typical firm

Figure 22-4

Industry output has now risen for two reasons: the already-existing firms are producing more, and new firms have entered. This calls for greater employment of inputs. And this may raise input prices.

a. For the moment, we deliberately assume that this input price rise does not happen. The firms in the industry can get all the extra labor, materials, power, and so on, without raising the price of any such input. If such is the case, then the industry's long-run supply curve will be a horizontal line. In the upper left part of Figure 22-4, draw a horizontal line to the right from the intersection of *dd* and *ss*. Carry it far enough to intersect *d'd'*.

This is the *constant-cost* situation. New firms enter and add to supply until price has (in the long run) returned to its old level of *JO*.

The situation of the typical firm in this constant-cost situation is indicated by the upper right diagram. When market price rose from *JO* to *KO*, the firm expanded its output from *Oa* to *Ob*. But as new firms enter, market price reverses itself and begins to *(fall / rise)*. Finally, the firm is back at its original position, with output *Oa*, at price *JO*.

b. Suppose, however, that input prices *are* affected as the demand for inputs increases. The normal expectation would be that input prices will *(rise / fall)*. And it is to be expected that this rise in production costs will work its way into the price of the finished product.

We now have two effects working on the price of this finished good. Entry of new firms, by increasing industry supply, is pushing price *(down / up)* from its new short-run level *KO*. But higher input cost is tending to push price *(down / up)*.

The long-run outcome must be one in which price has *(fallen / risen)* somewhat from its *KO* level, but has *(fallen / risen)* somewhat from its original *JO* level. In the bottom left part of Figure 22-4, illustrate this by drawing a long-run supply curve from the intersection of *dd* and *ss* upward through the point *E* on *d'd'*.

This is the *increasing-cost* case. What it really says is that if people want more of a particular good in the face of a limited stock of resources, they may have to pay a higher price to get it, even in the long run, when supplying firms have had all possible opportunity to adjust to the demand increase.

c. The situation of the typical firm, in the increasing-cost case, is shown in the bottom right diagram. In general, the sequence of events will begin as it did in the constant-cost case: the increase in industry demand will push up market price, and the firm will therefore expand its output (just as the constant-cost firm expanded its output from *Oa* to *Ob*). However, the rise in input prices complicates matters. This rise is brought about because (1) existing firms want to produce more output, and (2) new firms are entering.

The individual-firm *AC* and *MC* curves, such as shown in the two right-hand diagrams, are drawn on the assumption of given input prices, because the quantity of input bought by any one firm will not be sufficiently large to affect that input's

market price. But when all firms together demand more inputs, those input prices do rise. This is depicted as an upward shift of the entire *AC* and *MC* curves for the individual firm, as indicated by the broken lines in the bottom right diagram.

The process of adjustment to a new long-run equilibrium is considerably more complicated when input prices change. We can, however, state the most basic characteristics of this new equilibrium. The individual firm's cost curves must rise. And market price will be as suggested by *MO* (bottom left diagram). It must be *(higher / lower)* than the original *JO* level.

---

a. fall **b.** rise; down; up; fallen; risen **c.** higher

---

16. Figure 22-5 shows marginal cost, average cost, and average revenue (per unit revenue) for a particular firm operating in circumstances of pure (or perfect) competition. The firm wishes to operate so as to maximize its profit.

a. At what level of output will the firm operate?
(1) *OG*.
(2) *OH*.
(3) *OJ*.
(4) *OK*.
(5) *BO*.

b. Which of the following correctly indicates the price at which it will sell its product?
(1) *OG*.
(2) *DO*.
(3) *BF*.
(4) *OK*.
(5) *OB*.

c. Which correctly indicates the level of average cost at this maximum-profit output?
(1) *PH*.
(2) *VJ*.

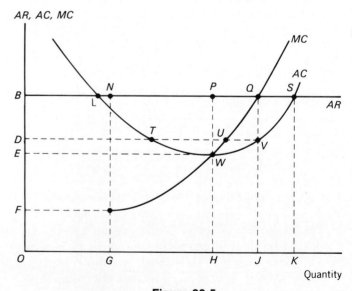

Figure 22-5

(3) *SK.*
(4) *DV.*
(5) *EW.*

d. Which correctly indicates the level of marginal cost at the maximum-profit output?
(1) *OG.*
(2) *DO.*
(3) *BF.*
(4) *OK.*
(5) *OB.*

e. Which rectangle correctly indicates the amount of total cost of producing the maximum-profit output?
(1) *DVJO.*
(2) *BQJO.*
(3) *BPHO.*
(4) *BSKO.*
(5) *EWHO.*

f. Which rectangle in part **e** correctly indicates the firm's total revenue at maximum-profit output?
(1).
(2).
(3).
(4).
(5).

g. Which rectangle correctly indicates total profit earned at this output?
(1) *BQJO.*
(2) *DVJO.*
(3) *BQVD.*
(4) *BPHO.*
(5) None of the preceding four.

---

a. (3) **b.** (5) **c.** (2) **d.** (5) **e.** (1) **f.** (2) **g.** (3)

---

17. You are a consultant on profit maximization. What do you recommend in each of the 10 cases listed in Table 22-3? Each firm operates in circumstances of pure (or perfect) competition, and wants to maximize its profit (or minimize its loss).

Answer for each case by putting *one* of the numbers 1 through 7 from the code below into the extreme right-hand column of the table. (The same number may of course be used for more than one question.)
(1) Firm is now at correct position.
(2) Firm should increase price.
(3) Firm should decrease price.
(4) Firm should increase quantity of output and sales.
(5) Firm should decrease quantity of output and sales.
(6) Firm should shut down operations.
(7) A nonsense case—figures supplied are inconsistent and could not all be correct.

Table 22-3

Case	Price	Q of Output	Total Revenue	Total Cost	Total Fixed Cost	Total Variable Cost	Average Cost	Average Variable Cost	Marginal Cost	With Increase in Output, MC Would	Answer
a.	$2.00	10,000		$16,000			At minimum level			rise	
b.			$10,000		$2,000		$4.00	$3.00	$6.00	rise	
c.	2.00	2,000			2,000	$5,000			2.00	fall	
d.			6,000	6,000			4,500	At minimum level	0.75	rise	
e.	5.00	2,000						5.25	5.00	rise	
f.			20,000	18,000			3.60		4.00	rise	
g.		4,000	16,000	16,000			At minimum level	5.00	3.00	fall	
h.	4.50				9,000	12,000	5.25	At minimum level		rise	
i.		3,000	9,000						3.25	3.00	rise	
j.		2,000	16,000		3,000				7.00	8.00	rise	

Enough information is supplied in each case, despite the blanks, to provide an answer. But note that there is at least one "nonsense" case among the 10, in which the figures are inconsistent and could not all be correct.

NOTE: These problems are not easy. They require you to know the profit-maximizing rules for the firm in pure (or perfect) competition (price to equal marginal cost; marginal cost to be rising with any increase in output; production to be shut down in the event of a loss exceeding the fixed-cost amount), and to know the relationship among the various cost curves.

Listed here are lines of reasoning that produce answers to the 10 cases of Table 22-3.

a. **(1)** Get AC from Q and TC:AC = $1.60.
(2) Get MC from fact that AC is at minimum: MC = $1.60.
(3) P > MC, therefore increase output.
Answer: 4

b. **(1)** Get AFC from AC and AVC:AFC = $1.
(2) Get Q from AFC and TFC:Q = 2000.
(3) Get P from Q and TR:P = $5.
(4) P < MC, therefore decrease output.
Answer: 5

c. P = MC, but MC is falling. Therefore output should be increased.
Answer: 4

d. **(1)** Get Q from TVC and AVC:Q = 6000.
(2) Get P from Q and TR:P = $1.
(3) Get AC from Q and TC:AC = $1.
(4) Get MC from fact that AC is at minimum: MC = $1.
(5) P = MC, and there is no loss, therefore position okay.
Answer: 1

e. **(1)** P = MC, but check for possible loss.
(2) P < AVC, therefore loss exceeds TFC; shut down.
Answer: 6

f. **(1)** Get Q from TC and AC:Q = 5000.
(2) Get P from Q and TR:P = $4.
(3) P = MC, and there is no loss, therefore position okay.
Answer: 1

g. MC is said to be falling, therefore output should be increased. But AC is said to be at its minimum level—at which MC should be rising. This alone indicates an impossible case. Moreover, at that minimum AC level, AC = MC. This must mean that AC = $3. But AVC alone is specified as $5—which further makes this an impossible case.
Answer: 7

h. **(1)** Get TC from TFC and TVC:TC = $21,000.
(2) Get Q from TC and AC:Q = 4000.
(3) Get AVC from Q and TVC:AVC = $3.
(4) Get MC from fact that AVC is at minimum: MC = $3.
(5) P > MC, therefore increase output.
Answer: 4

i. **(1)** Get P from Q and TR:P = $3.
(2) P = MC, and MC is rising, but check for possible loss.
(3) Compare P and AVC. The fact that P < AVC indicates not only that there is a loss, but one of such magnitude that the firm should shut down.
Answer: 6

j. **(1)** Get P from Q and TR:P = $8.
(2) P = MC, and MC is rising, but check for possible loss.
(3) Get TVC from Q and AVC:TVC = $14,000.
(4) Get TC from TVC and TFC:TC = $17,000.
(5) Since TR is $16,000, loss is $1000. This is less than TFC of $3000, so firm should continue to operate.
Answer: 1

18. Perfect competition, it was argued in the text, breaks down under circumstances of decreasing costs. When marginal cost is falling as output climbs, average cost must be *(rising / falling / constant)*, and higher outputs must be associated with *(higher / lower / identical)* profits for any price. The first few firms to achieve this type of decreasing-cost situation will therefore be able to *(increase / decrease)* output and *(raise / cut)* prices at the same time to *(drive out / complement / minimally compete with)* slower firms with higher costs. The result of this process can be *(monopoly / stable oligopoly / price warfare among large suppliers)*.

falling; higher; increase; cut; drive out; any of the choices is a possible outcome

19. Figure 22-6 shows a production-possibility frontier for an economy that can produce only two goods: X and Y. Point *(A / B / C)* represents a point of allocational efficiency in the "Pareto" sense outlined in the text if all people value X and Y equally. Point A *(is / is not)* efficient because _____

_____

_____ .

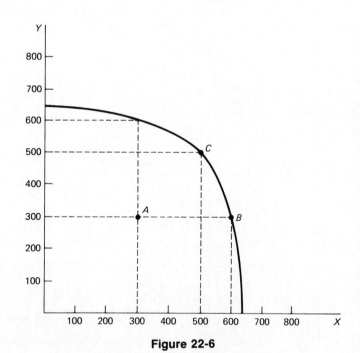

Figure 22-6

Point B *(is / is not)* efficient because _____

_____

_____ .

Point C *(is / is not)* efficient because _____

_____

_____ .

In particular, social welfare can be improved by moving from point B to C because the 100 fewer units of X can release sufficient resources to produce _____ more units of Y, of which _____ units can be used to compensate those who sacrificed their units of X and _____ units represents a surplus.

C; is not; A reflects unemployed resources so that increases in the supplies of both X and Y can increase the welfare of anyone without sacrifice; is not; B is on the frontier, but does not reflect the equal value preferences of the people (too much X and too little Y is produced); is; C is on the frontier and reflects prices accurately; 200; 100; 100

---

20. Figure 22-7 depicts demand / marginal (cardinal) utility curves for some good X for two different people (A and B) on its left side and supply/marginal cost curves for X for two different firms (I and II) on the right. Assume that these two people and two firms represent the entire market for X and that the market is competitive. Carefully draw the market supply and demand curves for X on the middle graph and fill in the blanks on Table 22-4 for the resulting equilibrium. Notice in Table 22-4 that the efficiency conditions that $MU = MC = P$ *(is / is not)* satisfied for both firms and both individuals. Total consumer surplus at equilibrium is $_____.

Now suppose that the two firms are, in fact, the two individuals (A = I and B = II) who produce X entirely from their own labor. In that case, the individual marginal cost curves would reflect *(input costs other than labor / the marginal disutility of work / the wage rate)*. If the two people

Table 22-4

	Price	Quantity Demanded, Units	Quantity Supplied, Units	Marginal Utility/ Marginal Cost
Market	$ _____	_____	_____	MU = MC =
				$ _____
Individual A		_____		MU = _____
		_____		MU = _____
Individual B			_____	MC = _____
Firm I			_____	MC = _____
Firm II				

were to cooperate in a way that would maximize their joint consumer surplus, A would make _____ units of X and consume _____ units; B would make _____ units and consume _____ units. This allocation would be achieved by the payment of $_____ per unit of X for each of the _____ units that A would *(sell to / buy from)* B.

Finally suppose that an economic planner wanted to call out a single price for X that would generate an allocation of consumption and work effort that would maximize total consumer surplus in the X market. What price would be specified?

$_____

The demand curve should be a straight line connecting (X = 0; price = $9) and (X = 16; price = $0); the supply curve should be a straight line from (X = 0; price = $2) and continuing through (X = 8; price = $5); reading across table rows: $5; 8; 8; $5; 3; $5; 5; $5; 5; $5; 3; $5; is; 28; the marginal disutility of work; 5; 3; 3; 5; 5; 2; sell to; 5

---

21. Figure 22-8 shows three utility-possibility loci (allocations of utility between two people that could be achieved by distributing a specific production mix of two goods between

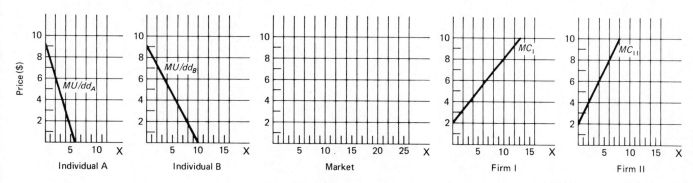

Figure 22-7

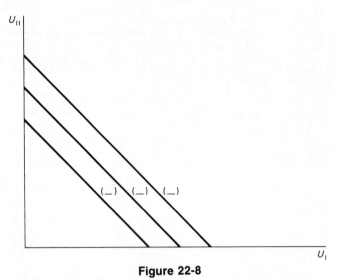

Figure 22-8

the two people in different ways) drawn under the following assumptions:

1.   There are only two goods.
2.   Both goods are equally valued by two people (I and II).
3.   The marginal utility of both goods is positive and constant for both people.

Label the three loci A, B, or C corresponding to the points indicated in Figure 22-6. Label the point, given the outer frontier, corresponding to I having everything and II having nothing. Is that point Pareto efficient? _____. Socially acceptable? _____.

The inner locus is point A, the middle locus is B, and the outer locus corresponds with C; the latter is the actual utility frontier (Each utility locus traces possible allocations between I and II of the output combinations indicated by the points in Figure 22-6. Going from A to B can be accomplished by increasing the consumption of both X and Y, so that everyone's utility can improve simultaneously.

Thus the move out from the inner locus to the middle one. The further jump to the outer frontier is accomplished by movement from B to C in Figure 22-6; i.e., it is accomplished by the realignment of resources outlined in the answer to question 19); point on frontier C on the I axis; Yes; No

22.   Consult Figure 22-9. Panel **(a)** shows the marginal cost schedule for a power generator; marginal cost is constant at $2 up to 100,000 units, but 100,000 units is an absolute capacity constraint. Panel **(b)** shows a similar schedule for an older generator. Draw, in panel **(c)**, the marginal cost schedule for the firm owning these two generators. What price should, from a social perspective, be charged in off-peak times when dd_1 represents the market demand curve? $_____. What price should be charged during the peak period when dd_2 is the demand curve? $_____. Is the old generator ever used during an off-peak time? _____. What price should be charged during the peak time if dd_3 were the demand curve?

$_____.

2; 5; No; 6

QUIZ: Multiple Choice

1.   The profit-maximizing rule for a firm in pure (or perfect) competition is: price to equal marginal cost. The meaning of this rule is:

(1) keep increasing output quantity (Q) until price (P) has risen to equality with marginal cost (MC).
(2) keep increasing Q until P has fallen to equality with MC.
(3) keep increasing Q until MC has fallen to equality with P.
(4) keep increasing Q until MC has risen to equality with P.
(5) keep decreasing P until P reaches equality with MC.

2.   The supply curve of a firm in pure (or perfect) competition is the same thing as:

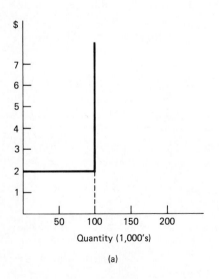

(a)

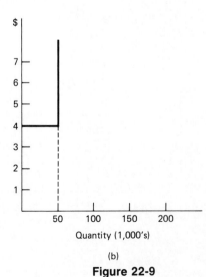

(b)

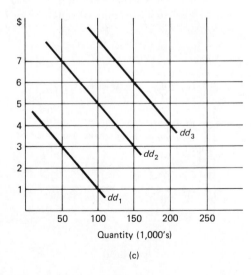

(c)

Figure 22-9

(1) its entire marginal cost curve.

(2) a part of its marginal cost curve.

(3) its average cost curve.

(4) that entire part of its average cost curve in which *AC* rises or remains constant as output increases.

(5) none of these.

3. A firm operating in circumstances of pure (or perfect) competition faces a market price of $10. It is producing 2000 units of output daily, at a total cost of $19,000. This firm:

(1) to improve its profit position, should increase the amount of its output.

(2) to improve its profit position, should reduce the amount of its output.

(3) to minimize its loss, should shut down.

(4) although making some profit, may or may not be at the output level yielding maximum profit—the information furnished is not sufficient to cover this point.

(5) from the information given, is apparently now at its maximum-profit position.

4. If the firm described in question 3 were to increase its output to 2001 units, total cost would thereupon become $19,010. Would this additional information change your answer to that question? The correct alternative would then (or still) be:

(1).

(2).

(3).

(4).

(5).

5. A firm operating in circumstances of pure (or perfect) competition finds that, at its best possible operating position (for any nonzero output), its total revenue does not cover its total cost, although this revenue is more than sufficient to cover fixed cost. This firm:

(1) is incurring a loss, and would improve its position by shutting down.

(2) is incurring a loss, but minimizes that loss by continuing to operate at its present position.

(3) is incurring a loss, but could reduce or perhaps remove it by increasing its production and sales.

(4) is incurring a loss, but the information given is not sufficient to indicate whether it would minimize that loss by continuing to operate or by shutting down.

(5) may be incurring a loss or earning a profit—the information furnished is insufficient to tell.

6. Which alternative in question 5 would be correct had that question specified that the firm's total revenue (although still insufficient to cover total cost) was more than sufficient to cover its total variable cost?

(1).

(2).

(3).

(4).

(5).

7. A firm which operates in short-run conditions of pure (or perfect) competition, and wants to earn as much profit as the situation will allow, must:

(1) try to set a price equal to average cost.

(2) try to produce an output at which its average cost is at the lowest-attainable level.

(3) try to produce an output at which average cost is just equal to market price.

(4) try to make its total revenue just equal to its fixed cost.

(5) take none of these actions, necessarily.

8. One among the following five statements is false, by reference to the material in this chapter. Which one?

(1) If market price is less than average variable cost, the firm would do better to shut down operations.

(2) As plant capacity is approached or reached, marginal cost will increase.

(3) The firm's objective or goal is to "maximize" its total revenue.

(4) If the firm finds that (at its current output level) marginal cost is a higher figure than market price obtainable, it should reduce its output.

(5) Fixed cost is a cost whose money total does not increase if the firm should increase its output.

9. The "long-run" equilibrium condition, "price equal to minimum per unit (average) cost," used in pure (or perfect) competition theory:

(1) is a rule which the firm need not consider in the short run, but must obey in the long run if it wants to choose the output level that will maximize its profit.

(2) is a rule the firm must obey in the short run only if it wants to choose the output level that will maximize its profit.

(3) is not a rule any profit-maximizing firm need consider either in the short or the long run, but indicates a situation toward which it is said all firms will be pushed in the long run.

(4) is a rule any profit-maximizing firm must respect in both the short and the long run.

(5) has no status either as a profit-maximizing rule or as a situation toward which firms will tend to be pushed, whether in the short or the long run.

10. A firm is operating in circumstances of pure (or perfect) competition. It is producing that quantity of output at which average cost is at its minimum level. This firm:

(1) must be at its maximum-profit output level, but may or may not be charging the best price it could get for that output.

(2) must be at its maximum-profit output level and need not reconsider its price, since this is a market price over which it has no control.

(3) is not at its maximum-profit position, and should increase its output.

(4) is not at its maximum-profit position and should decrease output.

(5) may or may not be at its maximum-profit position—information furnished is insufficient to tell.

11. A firm operates under conditions of pure (or perfect) competition. At its present level of output, all the following have a value of $1: price it is charging, marginal cost, average cost. Marginal cost would rise with any increase in output. This firm:

(1) definitely is at its maximum-profit position.

(2) definitely is not at its maximum-profit position.

(3) may or may not be at maximum-profit position; average variable cost would have to be known before answering.

(4) may or may not be at maximum-profit position; total cost and total revenue would have to be known before answering.

(5) may or may not be at maximum-profit position; total fixed cost would have to be known before answering.

12. A firm operating in conditions of pure (or perfect) competition is producing a daily output such that its total revenue is $5000. That output is its profit-maximizing output. The firm's average cost is $8, its marginal cost is $10, and its average variable cost is $5. Its daily output is:

(1) 200 units.

(2) 500 units.

(3) 625 units.

(4) 1000 units.

(5) impossible to tell from the information furnished.

13. The fixed cost for the firm described in question 12 is:

(1) $10.

(2) $100.

(3) $500.

(4) $1500.

(5) impossible to tell from the information furnished.

14. The daily profit earned, or loss incurred, by the firm in question 12 (profit being the excess of total revenue over total cost, and loss the excess of total cost over total revenue) must be:

(1) a loss of $500.

(2) neither profit nor loss, for the firm just "breaks even."

(3) a profit of $500.

(4) a profit of $1000.

(5) impossible to tell from the information furnished.

15. The text refers to the "breakeven point" for a firm in pure (or perfect) competition. This breakeven point occurs at the output level where two cost magnitudes are just equal, namely:

(1) marginal cost (MC) and average cost (AC).

(2) average variable cost (AVC) and average fixed cost (AFC).

(3) MC and AVC.

(4) AC and AVC.

(5) MC and AFC.

16. The text refers also to the "shutdown point" for a firm in pure (or perfect) competition. Which alternative in question 15 would be correct had that question referred to the shutdown point?

(1).

(2).

(3).

(4).

(5).

17. A firm operating in circumstances of pure (or perfect) competition produces and sells 200 units of output daily at a price of $7. Its average cost is $4.99. If it were to increase output and sales to 201 units daily, average cost would rise to $5. To maximize its profit, and from the information supplied, this firm should:

(1) increase its output, since marginal cost (MC) is approximately $6.

(2) reduce its output, since MC is approximately $6.

(3) remain at its present output, since MC is approximately $7.

(4) certainly not reduce its output, and probably increase it, since average cost is approximately $5.

(5) increase its output, since MC is approximately $5.01.

18. A firm must sell its product at a market price of $1.90. Its present operating figures are as follows: average cost, $2; marginal cost, $1.50; average variable cost, $1.50; total fixed cost, $500 per period. By the rules of maximum profit (or minimum loss) for a competitive firm, this firm should:

(1) definitely increase its present output level.

(2) definitely reduce its present output level.

(3) remain at its present output position.

(4) shut down.

(5) perhaps increase, perhaps decrease its output—the one critical figure needed to make this decision is lacking.

19. In this chapter the text presents a basic "maximum-profit" rule for firms in pure (or perfect) competition. The essence of that rule is the following:

(1) look for the output at which average cost of production is at its minimum level, in given conditions of technology.

(2) produce and sell until the extra cost which more output would entail begins to exceed market price.

(3) move to the minimum-cost point on your long-run average cost curve.

(4) set a price at which the excess of price over average cost is at its highest-attainable level.

(5) none of the above.

20. If the short-run marginal cost curve of a typical firm in a competitive industry should fall continuously over a substantial range of increasing outputs, the consequence indicated by the text chapter is that:

(1) new firms must enter that industry.

(2) the profit earned by that typical firm can be expected to rise.

(3) the marginal cost of that firm will exceed its average cost through the output range in question.

(4) the total amount of fixed cost which this firm must pay will fall.

(5) pure (or perfect) competition is likely to give way to imperfect competition.

21. Because of a city tax reduction, the total fixed cost a firm must pay is reduced by $500 monthly. The firm operates in conditions of pure (or perfect) competition. Variable cost is not affected by this fixed cost change. If the firm seeks to maximize its profit, this cost reduction should (at least in the short run) result in:
(1) a reduction in price.
(2) an increase in output.
(3) an increase in price.
(4) a reduction in output.
(5) no change in output or in price.

22. A firm operates in circumstances of pure (or perfect) competition. The market price at which it can sell its product is $5. At its present level of output and sales, average cost (total cost per unit of output) is $4. This firm:
(1) could increase its profit by increasing its output.
(2) could increase its profit by reducing its output.
(3) is making a profit, but the information furnished is insufficient to indicate whether that profit would be increased by any increase or decrease in output.
(4) is not making any profit, and should shut down operations.
(5) is not making any profit, but is nevertheless doing better than it would do if it were to shut down.

23. Which alternative in question 22 would be correct, had the figure of $4 referred to marginal cost, not average cost?
(1).
(2).
(3).
(4).
(5).

24. Given the situation of question 22, if both AC and MC were $4, then we would expect (in the long run with the usual downward-sloping demand assumption):
(1) the market price to fall and the quantity to fall.
(2) the market price to rise and the quantity to fall.
(3) the market price to fall and the quantity to rise.
(4) the market price to rise and the quantity to rise.
(5) nothing because we haven't sufficient information.

25. Monopoly is most likely to emerge when:
(1) average cost is declining over some range of initial levels of production.
(2) average cost is declining until it equals marginal cost.
(3) average cost is constant over all levels of output.
(4) average cost is declining over the range of output that might be demanded by the entire market.
(5) none of the above.

26. Which of the following is a characteristic of allocational efficiency of the Pareto sort?
(1) There exist no trades between two people that would make both better off.

(2) The combination of goods produced by the economy cannot be rearranged so that those hurt by the adjustment can be more than compensated for their losses by those helped by the adjustment.
(3) The combination of goods produced by the economy cannot be increased by putting unemployed resources to work.
(4) The distribution of final goods could be achieved by a set of competitive markets.
(5) All of the above.

27. Which of the following is a characteristic of allocational efficiency of the Pareto sort?
(1) The allocation can be represented by a point on the economy's utility frontier.
(2) The allocation can be supported by a point on the economy's production-possibility frontier.
(3) The allocation maximizes the economy's total consumer surplus.
(4) The allocation achieves the equality of marginal utility, price, and marginal cost for every good produced.
(5) All of the above.

28. Consider a competitive industry composed of firms employing only the labor of their owners as inputs. Let this industry face a downward-sloping demand curve, and assume that price exceeds the marginal disutility of the labor involved in producing the good. What should be the expected movement of price and market output in the long run?
(1) Price up and quantity down.
(2) Price up and quantity up.
(3) Price down and quantity down
(4) Price down and quantity up.
(5) Cannot tell from the information given.

29. Given the usual downward-sloping shape of a market demand curve, what should the effect of a tax on inputs that increases the marginal cost schedule (at every output) of each firm in a competitive industry be on the market price and output?
(1) Price up and quantity up.
(2) Price up and quantity down.
(3) Price down and quantity up.
(4) Price down and quantity down.
(5) Cannot tell from the information given.

30. Given the usual downward-sloping shape of a market demand curve, what should be the effect of a tax that affects only the fixed cost of every firm in a competitive market on the price received by and the quantity supplied by each competitive firm?
(1) Price up and quantity up.
(2) Price up and quantity down.
(3) Price down and quantity up.
(4) Price down and quantity down.
(5) Cannot tell from the information provided.

CHAPTER 23
IMPERFECT COMPETITION: MONOPOLY AND REGULATION

Perfect competition was defined in Chapter 22 to be the market structure that incorporates many small firms selling identical products. It has been studied extensively, as was noted there, not because of its wide application to reality, but because of its analytical properties. Perfect competition, for example, was seen to support allocational efficiency characterized by the inability to adjust a competitive equilibrium to make one person better off without hurting someone else. Perfect competition is, as a result, a standard against which the efficiencies of other market forms can be measured. Additionally, the workings of perfect competition are easy to understand and easy to work with; there is a certain methodological convenience in examining certain economic issues first in the context of competitive markets. The list of reasons for concentrating on perfect competition can, of course, be extended, but that is not the point of Chapter 23. It is, instead, to turn to different types of market organization spawned by the failures of the competitive model—the rampant forms of imperfect competition.

This chapter presents the sources, patterns, and costs of imperfect competition, a theoretical discussion of monopoly (the exact opposite of perfect competition) based upon the notions of marginal cost and marginal revenue, and a review of the regulatory alternatives open to a society that would like either to curb or to control the deficiencies that monopolies can generate. The germ of the content of the entire chapter is found in the quotation from Adam Smith's *Wealth of Nations* that precedes the text chapter: "The monopolists, by keeping the market constantly understocked, . . . sell their commodities much above the natural price, and raise their emoluments, whether they consist of wages or profit. . . ." Having worked through the chapter, you will have achieved not only an understanding of precisely where the truth in that statement lies, but also the following objectives.

LEARNING OBJECTIVES

1. A general overview of the patterns of imperfect competition in the United States and the sources of that imperfection (cost conditions and barriers to competition).

2. An understanding of the distinctions among the various market structures that emerge from imperfect competition.

3. An insight into the notion of marginal revenue and its role in determining the profit-maximizing level of output where marginal revenue equals marginal cost.

4. Recognition that the price-equals-marginal-cost profit-maximizing-rule of perfect competition is really a special case of the more general marginal-revenue-equals-marginal-cost rule.

5. Understanding the inefficiencies caused by monopolies that produce too little and charge too much, and the measurement of the cost of those inefficiencies through deadweight loss.

6. General familiarity with the various tools available to economies to curb monopoly distortions.

7. A more thorough familiarity with the economic regulation of imperfect competitors and the circumstances in which regulations can either improve or reduce general welfare.

The notion behind the evolution of imperfect competition is quite easy to explain. Imperfect competition arises whenever firms face demand curves with some measure of negative slope; the negative slope gives these firms some degree of power over not only the quantity that they will produce, but also the price at which they will market their output.

1. One measure of the control (or potential control) over the price is the "concentration ratio" discussed in the text. The four-firm concentration ratio is, for example, the percentage of the total industry output produced by the largest four firms in an industry. In perfectly competitive markets, we should expect that this ratio would be nearly equal to *(0 / 50 / 75)* percent. From 1947 through 1972, the average four-firm ratio *(rose / remained constant / fell)* from 37 percent to *(38 / 37 / 26)* percent. Based on the data provided in Figure 23-2 of the text, it is apparent that the cigarette, U.S. auto, breakfast food, aluminum, and light bulb industries all display four-firm concentration ratios in excess of *(75 / 85 / 95)* percent. Were the ratios to include worldwide competition, though, we should expect that these ratios would *(rise / remain unchanged / fall)*.

0; rose; 38; 75; fall

2. The text identifies two major sources of market imperfection. One, listed under the general rubric of "cost conditions," can be represented graphically. Which of the panels of Figure 23-1 illustrate relative cost circumstances that might lead to imperfectly competitive market structures? _____ . The existence of "natural monopoly" *(does / does not)* fall under this classification; if so, which panel illustrates "natural monopoly?" _____ . What name should be attached to the structure suggested by panel **(b)**? _____ .

The second rubric is entitled "barriers to entry," and incorporates a variety of situations. Indicate with a *(B)* in the spaces provided those items in the following list that can reasonably be included in this second category.

a. 17-year patents for new products ....(_____)

b. Regulated entry into an industry ....(_____)

c. Tariff protection from foreign competitors ..(_____)

d. Artificial product differentiation ....(_____)

e. Deliberate overinvestment in capacity to threaten new entrants with impossibly low price competition ...(_____)

In the case of product differentiation, the distinction between products (whether real or perceived), generates market power by moving the demand curve that the firm faces *(in / nowhere / out)* relative to the market demand curve for the general class of product. The result is that panel *(a / b / c)* of Figure 23-1 can become an appropriate representation of the firm's individual market situation.

(a) and **(b)**; does; **(a)**; oligopoly; all items qualify as a "barrier"; in; **(a)** and/or **(b)**

3. Figure 23-2 starts on the left-hand side with monopoly and proceeds to the right along two branches. Along the top branch, the number of firms selling the same product increases from 1 (the monopoly box) to a few (in box A) to an arbitrarily large number (in box B). Along the bottom branch, the number of firms producing differentiated but nearly identical products increases from 1 to a few (in box C) to an arbitrarily large number (in box D). Label each box by the market structure suggested by the process just noted (box C is already labelled "differentiated oligopoly"), and record an example of each type of structure from your knowledge of the American economy and the information recorded in Table 23-2 in the text. Along which branch would you expect advertising total expenditure to grow with the number of firms? _____ . Along which branch would you expect to see persistent market power over price? _____ . Provide a list of industries that display monopoly structures.

_____

_____ .

Upper branch: A: oligopoly; steel and/or aluminum; B: perfect competition; wheat and/or corn   Lower branch: C: differentiated oligopoly; autos and/or machinery D: monopolistic competition; gasoline and/or food products; lower; lower;   Local telephone, electric utilities; gas utilities; TV cable, etc.

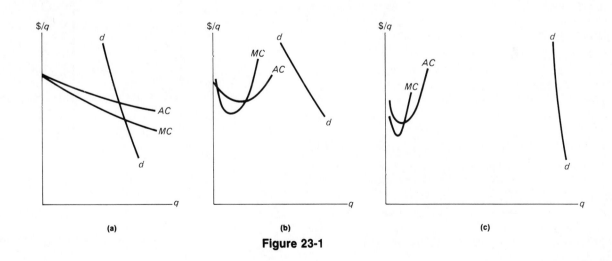

Figure 23-1

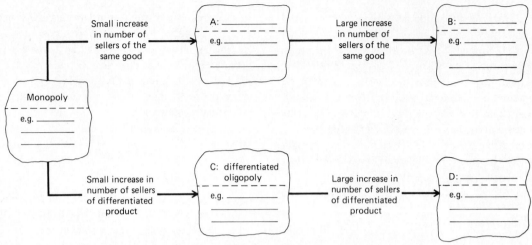

Figure 23-2

We turn now to an examination of the profit-maximizing behavior of a monopoly firm. Analytically, this monopoly case is decidedly easier than the so-called intermediate cases—those not perfectly competitive, and yet not completely monopolistic. It would be unwise to tackle these more intricate cases before having mastered the elementary ideas of monopoly pricing.

The terms and diagrams involved in a description of monopoly pricing may seem complicated at first. Yet the basic idea involved is simple. The monopoly firm is assumed to be motivated by profit in exactly the same way that the perfect competitor was motivated in Chapter 22. The results will be different only because the monopolist has power over price as well as quantity.

To review the basic ideas of "profit maximization":

1. "Maximizing profit" means earning as much revenue net of costs as market and production conditions will permit.
2. To "maximize profit," there must be something the firm can do that will influence its profit. There must be some variable which the firm can control and which changes profit.
3. This chapter assumes that the monopoly firm can control the quantity it sells, just as the firm in pure (or perfect) competition can do. (In real life, this control is at best indirect and incomplete. There are other and more complex decisions to be made, but this chapter tackles a simple case.) It looks, quite simply, for the particular quantity that will maximize its profit. In this respect, the monopoly firm is exactly like the firm in pure (or perfect) competition. That firm also looked for its profit-maximizing output quantity.
4. The monopoly firm is assumed to know the price which that profit-maximizing quantity will fetch. More generally, it knows the demand schedule for its product; it knows the price which goes with each possible quantity sold.
5. From this demand schedule, it is easy to develop a revenue schedule (total revenue being quantity sold multiplied by price per unit)—a schedule showing revenue associated with each possible quantity sold.

6. The firm must know also the total cost of each and every level of output. By bringing together the revenue and cost schedules, it can identify that output quantity at which the excess of revenue over cost (profit) is greatest. It can tell, as well, the price to charge for this maximum-profit output just by going back to its demand schedule. Again, this is just what the firm in pure (or perfect) competition did. The only difference is that that firm faced different demand conditions. The perfect competitor faced a perfectly elastic demand curve. The monopoly firm we are now considering faces a "tilted" demand curve.

4. Columns (1) and (2) of Study Guide Table 23-1 represent a demand schedule. We assume that a firm has done its market

Table 23-1

(1) Price	(2) Quantity	(3) Total Revenue	(4) Extra: Quantity	(5) Revenue	(6) Marginal Revenue
$14.00	10	$140			
			7	$64	$9.14
12.00	17	204			
			8	46	5.75
10.00	25	___			
				29	___
9.00	31	279			
			8	33	4.13
8.00	39	312			
			11	___	3.45
7.00	50	___			
				14	___
6.50	56	364			
			7	14	2.00
6.00	63	378			
			8	13	1.63
5.50	71	391			
5.00	80	___			
			10	5	0.50
4.50	90	405			
			11	___	−0.09
4.00	101	___			
				−5	−0.38
3.50	114	399			

research homework accurately and has developed this schedule to indicate the quantities it can sell at various prices.

This firm must operate under conditions of *(perfect / imperfect)* competition, since as the output to be sold increases, price *(remains constant / must be reduced)*.

---

imperfect; must be reduced

5. We now turn to the determination of profit-maximizing output and price.

a. Column (3) of Table 23-1 shows total revenue—price times quantity. As a small exercise, complete the four blanks in this column.

Use the figures in columns (2) and (3) to illustrate total revenue on the upper panel of Figure 23-3; i.e., show the total revenue associated with various output quantities. Join the points with a smooth curve.

b. Notice, incidentally, that this demand schedule becomes price-inelastic when price is sufficiently low—specifically, when price falls below $*(8 / 7 / 6 / 5 / 4)*.

---

a. $250; $350; $400; $404 **b.** 4

6. a. Table 23-2 shows the firm's total cost and marginal cost for production of the commodity whose demand curve is

Table 23-2

(1) Output	(2) Total Cost	(3) Extra Cost	(4) MC per Unit
0	$90		
		$60	$12.00
5	150		
		35	7.00
10	185		
		30	6.00
15	215		
20	235	———	———
		15	3.00
25	250		
		12	2.40
30	262		
		10	2.00
35	272		
		8	1.60
40	280		
		6	1.20
45	286		
		5	1.00
50	291		
		4	0.80
55	295		
		5	1.00
60	300		
65	308	———	———
		10	2.00
70	318		
		12	2.40
75	330		
		15	3.00
80	345		
		20	4.00
85	365		
		35	7.00
90	400		

detailed in Table 23-1. Table 23-2 is similar in construction to tables presented in previous chapters, but just to refresh your memory on the process of computing extra cost, complete the four blanks in columns (3) and (4) of Table 23-2 with the proper figures.

The graph of columns (1) and (2) of Table 23-2 is already drawn on the top panel of Figure 23-3 as a total cost curve (*TC*). Mark the curve that you drew earlier with *TR* to distinguish it from the cost curve. Now plot the marginal cost curve (denote it *MC*) in the bottom panel of Figure 23-3.

b. It is now possible to see at once why the profit-maximizing process outlined here is a simple one. The firm is doing nothing more than searching for the output at which the vertical distance between *TR* and *TC* is greatest. This distance, for any output, is *(fixed cost / price / profit or loss)*. (If *TR* is above *TC*, it is profit; if *TC* is above, it is loss. It is thus preferable to look for "greatest vertical distance" with *TR* above *TC*. The greatest distance with *TC* on top marks the maximum possible loss—somewhat less desirable as an operating position.)

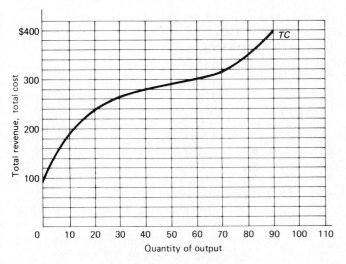

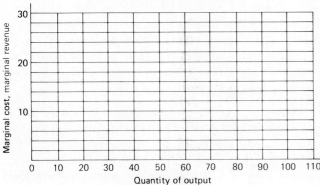

Figure 23-3

---

a. $20; $4; $8; $1.60 **b.** profit or loss

7. a. Figure 23-3 is too small to indicate quickly the precise maximum-profit position. But even a glance is sufficient to indicate that this best possible position is approximately *(45 / 65 / 85)* units of output.

The firm can be thought of as gradually increasing its output and sales, pausing at each increase to see if its profit position is improved. Each extra unit of output brings in a little more revenue (unless demand has reached its price-inelastic range); each extra unit incurs a little more cost. The profit position is improved if this small amount of extra revenue *(exceeds / is equal to / is less than)* the small amount of extra cost.

b. In more precise terms, the extra revenue brought in from the sale of *1* extra unit of output is *marginal revenue* (MR). It is the increase in total revenue resulting from the sale of that 1 further unit. For maximum profit, the firm should increase its output and sales if this MR exceeds marginal cost (MC)—the increase in total cost occasioned by that 1 extra unit (a concept discussed in Chapters 21 and 22). Total profit increases, with each unit increase in output, by an amount equal to the difference between MR and MC.

If the firm finds its operating level is such that MR is less than MC, it should *(increase / decrease)* the quantity it produces and sells. The "in balance" position is where MR is *(less than / equal to / greater than)* MC.

c. Column (4) in Table 23-1 shows the extra number of units sold if price is reduced. Column (5) shows the extra revenue (positive or negative) accruing from that price reduction. Complete the blanks in these two columns.

---

a. 65; exceeds   **b.** decrease; equal to   **c.** Col. (4): 6, 6, 9, 13; col. (5): $38, $9, −$1

---

8. Although column (5) in Table 23-1 carries "extra revenue" figures, these are not *marginal* revenue figures, since MR is a per unit concept. The top figure in column (5) is $64—but it came from an increase of 7 units sold. The $64 must be divided by 7 to get the MR figure of $9.14 in column (6). [For a reason to be discussed in a moment, even the column (6) figures are not precisely accurate MR figures; but they are reasonable approximations.]

Complete the missing MR figures in column (6). Plot the marginal revenue curve (denote it MR) on the lower panel of Figure 23-3.

Marginal revenue is a concept of sufficient importance that you should pause for a moment, to make sure you have it straight. Note three things (which in part repeat what has already been said about MR):

a. Marginal revenue is precisely analogous to the marginal cost of Chapters 21 and 22. Marginal cost in those two chapters was the extra cost resulting from the last unit of output produced. Similarly, marginal revenue is the extra revenue yielded by the last unit of output produced and sold.

b. MR falls as quantity of sales is increased. It can even become a negative figure (and will, if demand becomes price-inelastic).

c. The MRs of column (6) in Table 23-1 are not precisely accurate, since that table records only price changes of $1 or 50 cents. A true MR table would show extra revenue from each separate extra unit, not from an average of anywhere from 6 to 11 extra units. Table 23-1 would have to be greatly enlarged to show MR's precise unit-by-unit performance.

$4.83; $2.33; $1

---

9. The general profit-maximizing rule is: expand your output until you reach the output level at which $MR = MC$—and stop at that point.

Chapter 22 gave a profit-maximizing rule for the firm in pure (or perfect) competition: $P = MC$. This is nothing but a particular instance of the $MR = MC$ rule. It is assumed in pure (or perfect) competition that the demand curve facing the individual firm is perfectly horizontal, or perfectly price-*(elastic / inelastic)*. That is, if market price is $2, the firm receives *(less than $2 / exactly $2 / more than $2)* for each extra unit that it sells. In this special case, MR (extra revenue per unit) is *(greater than / the same thing as / less than)* price per unit (which could be called average revenue, or revenue per unit). So in pure (or perfect) competition, $P = MC$ and $MR = MC$ are two ways of saying the same thing.

---

elastic; exactly $2; the same thing as

---

10. a. In imperfect competition, the firm's demand curve is *(tilted / flat)*—and things are different. From inspection of the figures in Table 23-1 [compare columns (1) and (6)], it is evident that with such a demand curve, MR at any particular output is *(greater than / the same thing as / less than)* price for that output.

b. Why is this so? Suppose, at price $7, you can sell 4 units; at price $6, 5 units. Revenues associated with these two prices are, respectively, $28 and $30. Marginal revenue from selling the 5th unit is accordingly $*(2 / 5 / 6 / 7 / 28 / 30)*. It is the difference in revenue obtained as a result of selling the 1 extra unit. Why only $2—when the price at which that 5th unit sold was $6? Because to sell that 5th unit, price had to be reduced. And that lowered price applies to all 5 units. The first 4, which formerly sold at $7, now bring only $6. On this account, revenue takes a beating of $4. You must subtract this $4 from the $6 which the 5th unit brings in. This leaves a net gain in revenue of $2—marginal revenue.

c. Notice also that MR and price elasticity are related. Recall that demand is price-inelastic if, when price is reduced, revenue goes *(down / up)*. This means that when demand is inelastic with respect to price, MR is *(negative / zero / positive)*. At elasticity of unity, MR is *(negative / zero / positive)*. When demand is price-elastic, *MR* is *(negative / zero / positive)*. Check to make sure that the *MR* and *TR* curves that you drew in Figure 23-3 conform to the results of this question.

---

a. tilted; less than **b.** 2 **c.** down; negative; zero; positive

---

11. Now return to the fortunes of the firm in Tables 23-1 and 23-2. The tables do not provide sufficient unit-by-unit detail to show the exact maximum-profit output level. But Table 23-1 does indicate that between sales outputs of 63 and 71, *MR* is $1.63. The *MR* figures fall as sales are expanded, so that the $1.63 would apply near the midpoint of this range, say, at output 67. *MR* would be somewhat higher between 63 and 66; somewhat lower between 68 and 71.

Similarly, *MC* (Table 23-2) would be about $1.65 at output of 67 units. So the maximum-profit position would fall very close to 67 units produced and sold per period. Check to make sure that the *MR* and *MC* curves that you drew on the bottom panel of Figure 23-3 intersect at roughly 67 units.

To sell this output, the firm would charge a price (see Table 23-1) of about $(7 / 5.75 / 4 / 1.60)*. Its total revenue [look for nearby figures in column (3)] would be roughly $(380 / 580 / 780)*. Total cost (Table 23-2) would be roughly $(310 / 510 / 710)*, leaving profit per period of about $70.

5.75; 380; 310

---

12. In the section of the text labelled "Let Bygones Be Bygones," it is emphasized that a firm, in setting output and price according to *MR = MC*, will disregard fixed cost. This does not mean that fixed cost can be ignored completely; maximum profits might be negative, for example, if fixed costs were too large. Nonetheless, in the determination of the profit-maximizing production/sales point, marginal revenue and marginal costs are the critical parameters.

a. Suppose a firm's fixed cost were to increase (e.g., by a flat tax levied on a monopolist). Would the effect of this tax be to raise the firm's *AC* curve? . . . . *(Yes / No)*

b. Would the tax affect the monopolist's variable cost, or the *AVC* curve? . . . . *(Yes / No)*

c. Would the tax affect the monopolist's marginal cost curve? (Remember: *AVC* is the average of all *MCs*, from zero up to the output in question.) . . . . *(Yes / No)*

d. If the *MC* curve were unaffected, would such a flat tax change the maximum-profit output? (Presumably the tax will not affect demand for the product, so it will not affect marginal revenue.) . . . . *(Yes / No)*

e. If the tax did not affect *MC*, *MR*, or maximum-profit output, would the price be changed? . . . . *(Yes / No)*

---

a. Yes **b.** No (because the tax affects only fixed cost and the *AFC* curve) **c.** No **d.** No **e.** No

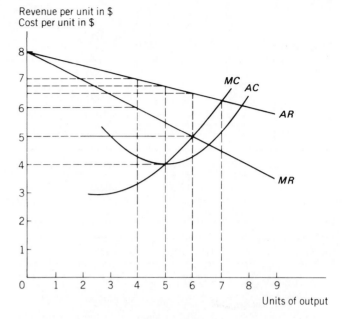

Revenue per unit in $
Cost per unit in $

Figure 23-4

13. Figure 23-4 shows the per unit cost and revenue measures confronting a firm which operates under conditions of monopoly or imperfect competition. The *AR* line is average revenue—price obtainable per unit. *MR* is marginal revenue; *MC* is marginal cost; *AC*, average cost.

a. Which line indicates the demand curve? . . . . . . _____

b. If output is 4, what must price be? . . . . _____

c. What is marginal revenue with output 4? . . . _____

d. At what level of output does average cost fall

to its minimum level? . . . . _____

e. What would price be with output at this

minimum *AC* level? . . . . _____

f. What would total cost be (at this level)? . . . . . _____

g. What would total revenue be? . . . . _____

h. What would profit be? . . . . _____

i. At what output would profit be maximized? . . _____

j. What is marginal revenue at this output? . . . . _____

k. What is marginal cost at this output? . . . . _____

l. What is average cost at this output? (Assume

it is 20 cents above minimum level.) . . . . _____

m. What is price at this output? . . . . _____

n. What is total profit at this output? . . . . _____

---

a. *AR* **b.** $7 **c.** $6 **d.** 5 **e.** $6.75 **f.** $20 **g.** $33.75 **h.** $13.75 **i.** 6 **j.** $5 **k.** $5 **l.** $4.20 **m.** $6.50 **n.** $13.80

Table 23-3

Case	Price	Marginal Revenue	Quantity of Output	Total Revenue	Total Cost	Fixed Cost	Average Cost	Marginal Cost	Answer
a.	$8.00	$4.00	2,000			$2,000	$4.00	$3.00	
b.	5.00	4.00	1,000		$4,000	1,000	At minimum level		
c.			4,000	$ 8,000			1.80	2.00	
d.	8.00	zero		32,000		5,000		4.00	
e.	1.00	2.00	10,000			2,000	2.00	2.00	
f.	3.00		2,000		6,000		At minimum level		
g.	2.50	2.00	10,000			4,000	3.00	2.00	

14. You are a consultant on profit maximization. What do you recommend in each of the seven cases listed in Table 23-3? Each firm is a monopoly, or operates in circumstances of imperfect competition, and wants to maximize its profit (or minimize its loss).

Enough information is supplied in each case, despite the blanks, to provide an answer. Note that there is, among the seven, at least one "nonsense" case in which the figures are inconsistent and cannot all be correct.

Answer for each case by putting one of the numbers 1 through 5 from the code below into the extreme right-hand column of the table. (The same number may of course be used for more than one question.)

(1) Firm is now at correct position.
(2) Firm should increase price and reduce quantity produced and sold.
(3) Firm should reduce price and increase quantity produced and sold.
(4) Firm should shut down operations because loss at best possible operating position exceeds fixed cost.
(5) A nonsense case—figures supplied are inconsistent and could not all be correct.

---

a. 3   **b.** 1 (When *AC* is at minimum level, *AC* = *MC*)   **c.** 2 (Get *P* from *Q* and *TR*:*P* = $2. If *P* = $2, *MR* < $2)   **d.** 2   **e.** 5 (*MR* cannot exceed *P*) **f.** 2. [As in part **(b)**, *AC* at minimum level implies *AC* = *MC*. Get *AC* from *Q* and *TC*: *AC* = $3. Since *P* = $3, *MR* < *MC*]   **g.** 4

15.   a. The text says that imperfect competition (of which monopoly is the extreme example) is mainly undesirable from an economic standpoint because (*of the profits obtained by monopolists* / *it distorts the allocation of resources*).

Chapter 22 noted that in pure (or perfect) competition, the firm operates with marginal cost (*less than* / *equal to* / *greater than*) market price. In the matter of "ideal" resource allocation, the underlying idea is that it is only when prices do reflect (*average* / *marginal*) costs that we can get the right balance with respect to quantities of goods produced. The resource supply out of which they are produced is limited; if these resources are fully employed, then more of good A means less of B, or of C, or of D. An overall price-equals-marginal-cost situation means that we have just the right quantity of good A, just the right quantity of B, and so on. The quantities are "just right" in the sense that any rearrangement would worsen rather than improve the community's welfare.

b. The monopoly profit-maximizing rule is: *MR* = *MC*. Now in monopoly, marginal revenue is (*less than* / *equal to* / *greater than*) price. This means that (in monopoly), price is (*less than* / *equal to* / *greater than*) marginal cost.

Suppose, for example, that the monopoly firm sets its price at $2, with marginal revenue at $1. This means (by the profit-maximizing rule) that marginal cost must be $(*1* / *2*). The consumer pays $2 for each unit bought, including the last unit. Yet that last unit added only $1 to total production cost. It would cost only another $1 (or just over $1) to produce one further unit. Why shouldn't consumers be able to buy that unit for what it would cost to produce it? A resource is not being used to its best advantage if consumers, reckoning in terms of the price they must pay for an additional unit, halt their purchases at a point where the extra cost of using the resource to produce that additional unit is significantly less than price. Overall, resources are not being "allocated properly."

---

a. it distorts the allocation of resources; equal to; marginal   **b.** less than; greater than; 1

---

16. It follows from *P* > *MR* = *MC* that the price which a monopolist charges is (*too high* / *too low* / *just right*) relative to the competitive price. Since monopoly firms face downward-sloping demand curves (otherwise they would have no monopoly power, right?), the monopolist must therefore produce (*less output than* / *more output than* / *the same output as*) the competitive firm. On the basis of the efficiency properties of the perfectly competitive market, it is thus clear that

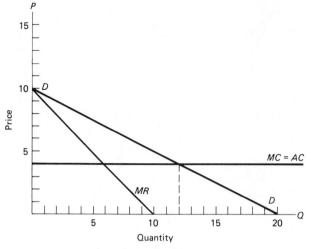

Figure 23-5

the marginal utility derived from consuming the monopolist's product is *(greater than / less than / equal to)* the marginal cost of producing the good in question.

Consult Figure 23-5. The competitive output and price for a market with the indicated cost structure must equal _____ units and $_____ , respectively. A profit-maximizing monopolist would, meanwhile, sell _____units at a price of $_____ . The result would be a reduction in consumer surplus from $_____ to $_____ . Of that reduction, $_____ would go to the monopolist in the form of excess economic profit and $_____ would represent lost welfare that would disappear (deadweight loss).

The text notes that the dimension of the actual deadweight loss caused by imperfect competition across the United States appears to be *(less than / about equal to / more than)* what might be expected. The loss has been estimated to be in the neighborhood of *(0.1 to 2.0 percent / 5.0 to 7.0 percent / over 10.0 percent)* of GNP. To conclude, in light of these numbers, that monopoly power should not be a major concern would, however, be to ignore the distortion in the distribution of income that excessive monopoly profits can create. More study is required to conclude that imperfect competition is a "non-problem."

---

too high; less output than; greater than; 12; 4; 6, 7; 36; 9; 18; 9; less than; 0.1 to 2.0 percent

The text mentions at least five mechanisms that come to mind when society considers trying to curtail the abuses of monopoly power: taxation, price control, government ownership, antitrust policy, and regulation. Regulation is the subject of section C of the text, and we will turn to that topic shortly. Antitrust policy will be covered in Chapter 24. The first three possibilities are, however, more problematical and less popular in

the United States. They are therefore reviewed only briefly before a more detailed consideration of regulation is presented. The next two questions cover the points raised in that review.

17. Suppose that the monopolist depicted in Figure 23-5 were to face a lump-sum tax on profits of $18. The profit-maximizing monopolist would then *(increase / decrease / maintain)* the quoted price to support a *(larger / smaller / constant)* level of production and sales.

Suppose, instead, that government were to tax the monopolist's implicit return to capital so that the effective (constant) marginal cost of production were increased from $4 to $6 per unit. Output would *(fall to / rise to / continue to remain fixed at)* _____units; price would *(climb to / fall to / stay put at)* $_____ , representing an increase in price *(equal to / less than / greater than)* the $_____ increase in unit costs.

---

maintain; constant; fall to; 6; climb to; 8; less than; 2

18. Price controls are mentioned in the text as a second possible means of controlling the potential abuses of monopoly power. It is argued there that pervasive use of price controls to control the occasional monopolist can be expected to cause a plethora of economic problems. In the spaces provided, note with (Y) those effects that might be expected to appear in a list of these possible difficulties.

a. Alienation of business and government   ..... (_____)

b. International trade problems   .... (_____)

c. Shortages and surpluses   .... (_____)

d. Absence of necessary flexibility in relative prices
.... (_____)

e. Increased unemployment   .... (_____)

Government ownership is also an option, but it is seldom exercised in the United States. It is, though, a bit more popular in Japan and Western Europe. It would appear, then, that the choice between regulation and government ownership is

more a matter of _____ and _____ than it is a matter of economic advantage.

---

all Y (enforced price specifications are likely to cause problems in every economic sphere where adjustment to unpredictable events is required); history; institutions

19. Regulation is, in the United States, the most popular mechanism with which governments at all levels protect their citizens from potential abuses of market power, particularly when a natural monopoly is under scrutiny. Regulation, in its broadest context, includes all rules and laws designed to change or control the operation of an economic enterprise. There are, in fact, two major categories within that context: social and economic. Place (*E*) or (*S*) in the blanks provided to indicate the general category into which each of the following regulatory activities falls.

a. Restraints on price setting practices among

firms .... (———)

b. Clean air policy .... (———)

c. Limits on the rates of return earned by utilities ....

.... (———)

d. Drug testing by the FDA .... (———)

e. Requirement to provide electricity to everyone

who asks for it .... (———)

f. Constraints on entry into and exit from given

markets .... (———)

E; S; E; S; E or S; E

20. It should not be concluded, on the basis of your work in this chapter, that all economic regulation in the United States is directed at controlling monopolies. In the spaces provided below, indicate on the basis of Figure 23-8 in the text whether or not cited industry (*a*) is subject to significant government regulation of price and/or quantity and (*b*) displays a high, medium, or low degree of natural monopoly. Yes (*Y*) or no (*N*) in the first column will answer the regulation question; high (*H*), medium (*M*) or low (*L*) in the second column will answer the monopoly question.

Steel .... (———)   (———)

Agriculture .... (———)   (———)

Banking .... (———)   (———)

Local telephone .... (———)   (———)

Airlines .... (———)   (———)

Electricity .... (———)   (———)

Trucking .... (———)   (———)

Automobiles .... (———)   (———)

Oil drilling .... (———)   (———)

Railroads .... (———)   (———)

Reading down columns: N; Y; Y; Y; N; Y; Y; N; N; Y   M; L; M; H; M; H; L/ M; M; L; H

21. Consult Figure 23-6. For the indicated demand and cost curves, it is clear that the unregulated monopolist would produce ———— units of output for sale at a price of $————. Excess pure economic profits of $———— would

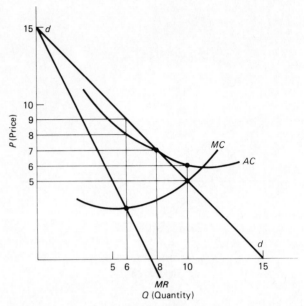

Figure 23-6

then be earned. Regulation to the point of zero profits would require a price specification of $———— at which ———— units of output would be expected. Consumer surplus would, in that case, increase from the unregulated monopoly level of $18 to $————. Regulation to the point where the efficiency conditions of *MR = MC* were satisfied would, meanwhile, require a price specification of $————, with ————units of output expected only if the monopolist's losses in the amount of $———— were covered. Consumer surplus would rise further to $————, but would actually equal $———— if the subsidy to cover the losses just noted were deducted. This (*would / would not*) represent an improvement over the average cost pricing alternative.

6; 9; 6; 7; 8; 32; 5; 10; 10; 50; 40; would

QUIZ: Multiple Choice

1. Which of the following are possible sources of imperfectly competitive markets?
(1) Declining average costs over the range of possible quantities demanded.
(2) Legal barriers to entry.
(3) Perceived product differentiation.
(4) Tariff protection from foreign competition.
(5) All of the above.

2. The average percentage of domestic manufacturing output contributed by the largest four firms across all industries in the United States is about:
(1) 50 percent.
(2) 12 percent.
(3) 38 percent.

(4) 5 percent.

(5) over 60 percent.

3. If a firm's marginal revenue exceeds its marginal cost, maximum-profit rules require that firm to:

(1) increase its output in both perfect and imperfect competition.

(2) increase its output in perfect but not necessarily in imperfect competition.

(3) increase its output in imperfect but not necessarily in perfect competition.

(4) decrease its output in both perfect and imperfect competition.

(5) increase price, not output, in both perfect and imperfect competition.

4. Whenever a firm's demand curve is horizontal or "perfectly elastic":

(1) the firm cannot be operating under conditions of perfect competition.

(2) the profit-maximizing rule of *MR*-equal-to-*MC* does not apply.

(3) price and marginal revenue must be one and the same.

(4) price and marginal cost must be one and the same.

(5) none of these conclusions is necessarily correct.

5. A basic difference between the firm in pure (or perfect) competition (the PC-firm) and the monopoly firm (the M-firm), according to economic analysis, is that:

(1) the PC-firm can sell as much as it wishes at some given price, whereas the M-firm must lower its price if it wishes to increase the volume of its sales by any significant amount.

(2) the M-firm can always charge a price yielding a significant profit, whereas the PC-firm can never earn such a profit.

(3) the price elasticity of demand facing the M-firm is a higher figure than that facing the PC-firm.

(4) the M-firm seeks to maximize profit, whereas the PC-firm's rule is to equate price and average cost.

(5) the M-firm deliberately seeks to operate at the minimum level of average cost, whereas the PC-firm does not.

6. "Oligopoly" means:

(1) the same thing as imperfect competition.

(2) a situation in which the number of competing firms is large but the products differ slightly.

(3) a situation in which the number of competing firms is small.

(4) that particular condition of imperfect competition which is just removed from monopoly, regardless of the number of firms or type of product.

(5) none of these.

7. When a monopoly firm seeking to maximize its profits has reached its "equilibrium position," then:

(1) price must be less than marginal cost.

(2) price must be equal to marginal cost.

(3) price must be greater than marginal cost.

(4) price may be equal to or below marginal cost, but not above it.

(5) none of the above is necessarily correct since equilibrium does not require any particular relation between price and marginal cost.

8. The text, in this chapter, sets out a general rule which a firm supposedly should follow with respect to maximizing its profit. The essence of this rule can be stated as follows. Its purpose is to identify:

(1) that output at which total revenue is at its maximum.

(2) that output at which the excess of price over average cost is greatest.

(3) that output at which the excess of total revenue over total cost is greatest.

(4) the highest-obtainable price.

(5) that output at which average cost is at its minimum.

9. "Marginal revenue" means:

(1) the price that can be obtained for the very last unit sold.

(2) total revenue divided by quantity of units sold.

(3) total revenue minus the price received for the very last unit sold.

(4) the amount of increase in total revenue brought in by the very last unit sold minus the increase in total cost which that unit occasioned.

(5) the amount of increase in total revenue brought in by the very last unit sold.

10. "Monopoly" exists, according to the economist's definition of this term:

(1) whenever there is only one seller of a particular product.

(2) whenever the seller has at least some degree of control over the price she or he can charge.

(3) whenever profit earned by the seller exceeds the amount that should properly be earned as interest on money invested, plus an allowance for risk undertaken.

(4) whenever a seller manages to maintain his or her position through successful advertising.

(5) in none of these situations, necessarily.

11. A firm operating in a situation of imperfect competition finds that at its present output level, marginal revenue is $2 and average cost is $1.75, this being the minimum or lowest-attainable value of average cost. For maximum profit, this firm should:

(1) increase price.

(2) decrease price.

(3) decrease output and sales.

(4) leave price and output unchanged.

(5) perhaps do any of these things—information given is insufficient to tell.

12. Which alternative in question 11 would be correct had it specified that price rather than marginal revenue is $2?

(1).

(2).

(3).

(4).

(5).

13. The essential characteristic of (or "acid test" for) all cases of imperfect competition, according to the text, is that the single firm's:
(1) demand curve has a downward tilt.
(2) marginal revenue exceeds the price it charges.
(3) average cost curve falls over a substantial or large range of outputs.
(4) product is "differentiated" from one firm to the next.
(5) average cost curve rises over a substantial or large range of outputs.

14. If the price a firm obtains for its output exceeds the marginal cost associated with that particular output, maximum-profit rules would require that firm to:
(1) increase its output in both perfect and imperfect competition.
(2) increase its output in perfect but not necessarily in imperfect competition.
(3) increase its output in imperfect but not necessarily in perfect competition.
(4) decrease its output in both perfect and imperfect competition.
(5) increase price, not output, in both perfect and imperfect competition.

15. Which alternative in question 14 would be correct had that question said that price is less than marginal cost?
(1).
(2).
(3).
(4).
(5).

16. To explain why imperfect competition is far more prevalent than perfect competition, the text lays considerable emphasis upon the fact that, for the firms in many industries:
(1) advertising has now become more powerful than price as a sales weapon.
(2) marginal revenue tends to equal or even to exceed price.
(3) average cost continues to fall until a large output has been reached.
(4) a high price charged to consumers has become the most effective method of maximizing profits.
(5) marginal revenue tends to fall significantly below price.

17. A correct statement of the relationship between marginal revenue (*MR*) and elasticity of demand (with respect to price) is this. When *MR* is:
(1) negative, demand must be inelastic.
(2) zero, demand must be inelastic.
(3) positive, demand must be inelastic.
(4) negative, demand must be unit-elastic.
(5) positive, demand must be perfectly elastic.

18. Among the five statements below, one must be false with respect to any firm operating under conditions of imperfect competition. Which one?
(1) The number of competing sellers offering similar (although differentiated) products can be large.
(2) Other firms may sell products which are identical or almost identical with this firm's product.
(3) The number of competing sellers offering similar (although differentiated) products can be small.
(4) The firm's marginal revenue will be less than the price it obtains.
(5) The demand curve facing the firm can be perfectly horizontal.

19. If a firm discovers that demand for its product is inelastic with respect to price, in the price-and-output range in which it is selling, and if it seeks to maximize its profit, it should:
(1) remain at its present position.
(2) always lower its price and seek to increase its sales.
(3) always raise its price, even at the cost of a sales reduction.
(4) raise its price, but only if that price reduction will not reduce its sales.
(5) perhaps do any of the above—the information given is not sufficient for any change in decision.

20. Which alternative in question 19 would be correct had it specified "elastic with respect to price," not "inelastic"?
(1).
(2).
(3).
(4).
(5).

21. Marginal revenue could exceed price:
(1) in circumstances of oligopoly.
(2) and does, in all genuine monopoly situations.
(3) if, somehow, increased sales would bring about a higher price.
(4) in the circumstances of "differentiated" products.
(5) in no conceivable circumstances whatsoever.

22. Which of the following industries is an example of an industry with strong tendencies toward natural monopoly with little or no regulation into either the prices that it charges or the quantities that it produces?
(1) Trucking.
(2) Banking.
(3) Aircraft manufacturing.
(4) Airlines.
(5) Agriculture.

CHAPTER 24
IMPERFECT COMPETITION AND ANTITRUST POLICY

Chapter 23 explored the various sources of monopoly power as well as the potential consequences of exploiting that power in a mixed economy. Based upon the results of that chapter, it is perhaps surprising that the profitability of supplying a market in the United States appears to increase only slightly as the concentration of market power in the hands of a few suppliers climbs. Perhaps even more surprising is the observed high advertising budgets for firms servicing concentrated American industries. If these firms were exploiting a truly strong market position of the type considered in the previous chapter, one might expect just the opposite—high profits and little advertising. If you have that kind of power, why not use it? And why advertise if you have no competition? In addition, empirical studies have found that concentrated industries have typically produced large research and development budgets. This is perhaps reassuring (suggesting that large firms are not necessarily lazy firms), but it is a third observation that is not explained very well by our models of monopoly behavior. Concentrated industries have, finally, displayed little in the way of flexibility in the pricing of their products. This is a troublesome reminder that size itself can breed potential for laziness—concentrated industries might be the homes of firms too big to bother constructing procedures with which to maintain efficient prices.

The theoretical basis for understanding why these observations make sense cannot, quite clearly, rest entirely on the monopoly modeling of Chapter 23. It will rest, instead, on modelings of intermediate forms of imperfect competition—market structures that lie somewhere between the efficiencies of perfect competition and the potential perversities of monopoly. Chapter 24 begins with an overview of a few of these models. Subsequent sections provide a little more insight into not only what actually goes on in the boardrooms of large American corporations that enjoy some market power, but also how the U.S. judicial system responds to that behavior.

Upon completion of your work in this area, you will have accomplished the following objectives.

LEARNING OBJECTIVES

1. A review of the determinants of market power.

2. An understanding of the potential risks and gains involved in collusion between firms concerning price and/or quantity.

3. An ability to reproduce and to manipulate some simple models of noncollusive behavior in imperfectly competitive markets: the dominant firm model, the price leadership model, the limit pricing model, and monopolistic competition.

4. A conceptualization of how the profit-maximizing behavior postulated by economists can be extracted from the actual behavior displayed by professional managers in the boardrooms of American corporations.

5. An evaluation of the Schumpeterian hypothesis that significant market power leads to extensive, socially desirable research and development programs that would otherwise not be forthcoming.

6. A cursory knowledge of the history of antitrust activity in the United States.

Antitrust policy is, of course, written with full knowledge that imperfect competition has both a good and a bad side. Unbridled exploitation of market power can, on the one hand, depress output and generate excessive prices and profits. But, on the other hand, there do exist economies of scale that should not be sacrificed simply for the sake of having many firms instead of a few. There is, moreover, a demonstrable correlation between market concentration and research into discovery and development of new products and new processes. In light of this dichotomy of properties, it is the primary lesson of this chapter that antitrust activity should (1) keep the barriers to competition low, (2) tolerate bigness when size is determined by technology, and (3) be vigilant against anticompetitive practices whenever they occur.

Oligopoly, the circumstance when there exist only a few sellers of the same good, is conceptually the simplest intermediate case of imperfect competition. It can emerge as the prevailing market structure for many reasons. Oligopoly can, first of all, appear whenever average costs decline through levels of output equaling 20 percent to 40 percent of market demand. These situations are, to some degree, "natural oligopolies" in the same sense that "natural monopolies" display declining costs across the demand of the entire market. They reflect economies of scale that should be exploited. Other, more artificial and sometimes less desirable conditions can, however, also produce oligopolistic markets. These include both legal and illegal barriers to entry; for example, tariffs, patents, and tacit or overt price collusion to threaten potential entrants all fall under the general rubric of artificial constraints on competition. The first few questions will examine your understanding of the oligopoly models presented in the text.

1. The case of *pure oligopoly* illustrates with special clarity the problems confronting the firm in imperfect competition. In this situation, the number of firms engaged in close competition is *(large / small, or comparatively small)*, while the products they sell are *(uniform / differentiated)*.

The important consequence of this uniformity or "homogeneity" of product is that all firms must charge the same price. If any one company tries to raise its price and the others do not follow suit, that company will most probably *(gain / lose some of its / lose all or practically all of its)* customers. On the other hand, if this company reduces price, it is most likely that all rivals will be forced to follow suit. Thus, each firm has some influence over the price buyers must pay, particularly because of its ability to reduce price.

The knowledge that "we're all in the same boat" may produce a tacit agreement among the firms to abide by some given price. (Economic theory still has a long way to go in describing how oligopoly members reach agreement as to the level of that price.) With price established by the industry price leader, and accepted by other industry members, the participants then use competitive weapons other than price (notably advertising or, more generally, selling effort) to secure business. There is rivalry among the member firms; there is a struggle for business; there is competition; but there is rarely any price competition. (Powerful customers sometimes receive under-the-counter price concessions. In the event of serious recession when business is scarce, however, the convention against using price as a competitive weapon may weaken.)

One interesting consequence of this method of competition is that even though the competing products can be essentially uniform (i.e., no one firm's product is really worth much more than any other firm's product), each supplier may try hard in its advertising to persuade the buying public that its product is "different" as part of the attempt to retain and to expand its "share of the market." Thus on the surface the competing products may seem to be "differentiated." Yet if you examine the advertised differences carefully, you may find that they are trivial, and that for analytic purposes the products are really homogeneous or uniform.

small, or comparatively small; uniform; lose all or practically all of its

2. In each space below, put (*I*) if the description suggests a firm operating in one of the categories of imperfect competition. Put (*P*) if it is typical of a firm in perfect competition. Put (*B*) if it applies to firms in both situations; put (*N*) if it applies to neither situation. (Only short-run effects are considered here.)

a. Any decline in industry demand normally causes price charged by this firm and by its competitors to fall. .... (_____)

b. In some circumstances, the firm is willing to sell at price below *AC*. .... (_____)

c. Any excess of price over *AC* is temporary; entry of new firms will push price down to equality with *AC*. .... (_____)

d. The firm seeks an output level at which $MR = MC$. .... (_____)

e. Industry of which it is a member consists of only six or seven firms, which, however, compete vigorously with one another for business .... (_____)

f. It operates at an output where price = *MC*. .... (_____)

g. It finds it necessary to reduce price if it wants to increase the quantity of its output and sales. .... (_____)

h. It may reach price-fixing agreements or understandings with other firms out of a fear that price competition will result in excessive losses .... (_____)

i. When demand declines, it does not change price .... (_____)

j. The product it sells is somewhat differentiated from that sold by its competitors. .... (_____)

k. In the long run, it can be expected to operate at an output where *AC* is at its minimum level. .... (_____)

l. It operates at an output where *MC* is well above price. .... (_____)

m. It has some degree of choice, some alternatives, as to the price it may charge for its product.

.... (_____)

n. It operates at an output where MC is well below price. .... (_____)

---

a. P **b.** B **c.** P **d.** B **e.** I **f.** P **g.** I **h.** I **i.** I **j.** I **k.** P **l.** N **m.** I **n.** I

To review the material of question 1, recall that oligopolistic firms in the same industry must recognize that they are mutually interdependent. The actions of one firm always affect the circumstances facing the others. This point is most clearly illustrated in a careful consideration of the profitability of collusion and the temptation to cheat. Cheating, it can be shown, can pay dividends, but it can also produce significant losses.

3. To see why all this is true, consider Figure 24-1. On that graph, DD represents the effective demand curve facing some oligopolist who abides by a colluding agreement with a few competitors. It could, for example, be the result of a consistent 30 percent share of total sales for any price along a market demand curve. Notice that every reduction of $1 in the price produces, for the firm when all other firms conform, an increase in sales of 10 units. Marginal revenue is given by MR. Average cost and marginal cost are assumed, for simplicity only, to be constant at $4 per unit regardless of output level.

Based on the assumption of perfect collusion, the firm will maximize profits along DD by agreeing to a price of $_____, therefore selling _____ units and earning excess profits of _____.

Now suppose that the firm could, by lowering its price relative to its colluding partners (i.e., by cheating on its colluding agreement), pick up an extra 20 units of sales for every $1

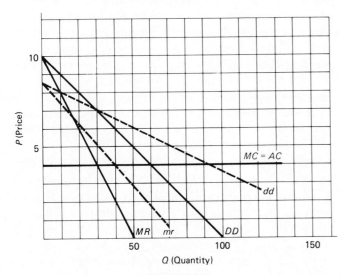

Figure 24-1

---

reduction in price. It could, in other words, increase its market share at the expense of other firms by lowering its price alone. The resulting demand and marginal revenue curves are represented in Figure 24-1 by dd and mr, respectively. The firm could, in this case, move to a new profit-maximizing position by *(reducing / maintaining / increasing)* its price to $_____ and selling _____ units. The result would be $_____ in excess profits.

It is, of course, highly unlikely that the other firms would not catch on. Suppose, in response to the cheating of the first firm, that all of the other firms changed their prices to the cheater's new price. DD would again be relevant, and the cheating firm's profits would fall to $_____ as sales declined to _____ units.

It is clear, therefore, that successful cheating is better than successful collusion, but runs the risk of reducing profitability if everyone catches on and follows to protect themselves. Were the process to continue, in fact, the firms would, collectively, end up producing the *(competitive / monopoly / duopoly)* output and selling it at the *(competitive / monopoly / duopoly)* price. In terms of Figure 24-1, price would converge to $_____, output would converge to _____ units, and profits would converge to $_____.

7; 30; $90; reducing; 6,50; 40; 100; 87.50; 35; competitive; competitive; 4; 60; 0

---

4. Now consult Figure 24-2. Panel **(a)** there represents the MC schedule of one of two oligopolistic firms facing the demand curve of panel **(b)**. Remember the text's argument that colluding firms tend to share the monopoly output between themselves, draw the combined MC curve of the two firms in panel **(b)**. Acting as a monopolist, profit-maximizing colluders equipped with knowledge of this joint MC curve would agree to charge a price of $_____ for an expected _____ units of sales. Each firm would, under the agreement, expect to sell _____ units.

The joint MC curve is a straight line from ($Q = 10$; $P = 2) with half the slope of the MC curve of panel **(a)**; 7; 30; 15

---

5. Figure 24-3 illustrates a situation that might face a typical dominant firm. Curve DD represents the market demand curve for the industry in question, and MR traces the "market marginal revenue curve" corresponding to DD. Curve dd, meanwhile, represents the dominant firm's effective demand curve after the competitive fringe has been factored out of its market; the corresponding effective marginal revenue is indicated by curve mr. For simplicity, once again, it is assumed that $MC = AC = 5; i.e., that variable costs are proportional to output.

Given dd, the dominant firm would produce _____ units of output with the expectation of supporting a price of $_____. In that circumstance, the competitive fringe would

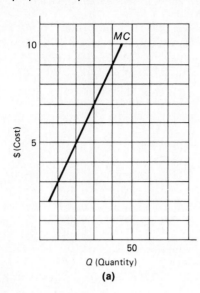
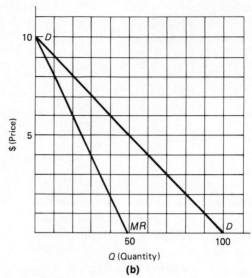

Figure 24-2

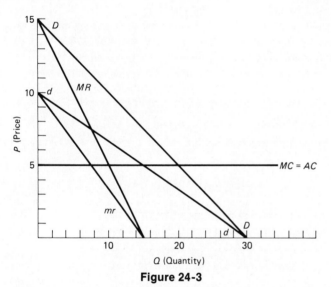

Figure 24-3

produce _____ units, and the total quantity demanded and actually produced by either the dominant firm or the competitive fringe, would equal _____ units.

Now contrast this equilibrium with one in which the dominant firm were, in fact, a firm exploiting monopoly power derived from facing *DD* alone. Total output would then be *(higher / the same / lower)* than the dominant firm case, equaling _____ units and supporting a profit-maximizing price of $_____. The competitive solution would, meanwhile, include total production of _____ units for a price of $_____.

It is clear, from this example, that the dominant firm market structure outlined in the text allows the same types of inefficiencies as the monopoly: price *(greater than / equal to / less than)* marginal cost, output therefore suboptimally *(low / high)*, and supportable economic profit *(in excess of / exactly equal to / substantially less than)* zero. The only difference

appears to be in degree; the distortions permitted under a dominant firm structure are *(smaller / larger)* than those created by a profit-motivated monopolist.

7.5; 7.50; 7.5; 15; lower; 10; 10; 20; 5; greater than; low; in excess of; smaller

---

6. A second form of imperfect competition has been identified in the literature. It applies to many sellers of products that are, to some degree, "differentiated" from those of other firms—a situation which is said to give each firm some degree of "monopoly power"—i.e., power to set its own price.

The fact that there are many sellers suggests that it is fairly easy for new firms to enter the industry in question. New firms will be tempted to enter, in fact, whenever existing firms are earning profits. This entry may of course take time; by the convention mentioned previously, entry (or exit) of firms is a "long-run" consideration.

a. Insofar as new firms *do* enter, they take over some part of the market of already-operating firms. This means that, for any one of such older firms, its demand curve tends to be pushed *(to the right or upward / to the left or downward)*. This *(reduces / increases)* the profit of the older firm. If the entry tendency persists, the firm's demand curve will wind up just touching, or tangent to, the average cost curve. Such a tangency situation means that the firm in question can *(still earn a profit / just break even / operate only at a loss)*.

When this tangency point is reached for the typical firm—i.e., for most, if not all, firms—the profit feature which attracted new entrants *(still / no longer)* exists.

b. Each firm's demand curve, in this "differentiated seller" situation, is assumed to be a *(tilted / flat)* one, because the fact of product differentiation supposedly *(gives some / does not give any)* degree of monopoly power to the firm. But if the demand curve is tilted, and if things wind up with this demand curve just touching the average cost curve, the tangency point *(must / cannot)* occur at the very bottom of the *AC* curve. (A tangency point is one at which the two curves involved have the same slope. If the demand curve is tilted at the point in question, so must be the *AC* curve.)

c. Thus our hypothetical firm winds up earning no profit, yet operating at an output level which is *(less than / equal to / greater than)* its minimum-*AC* output. In the sense that a larger output would reduce its *AC*, this firm has "excess capacity." Economists were much taken with these ideas when Edward H. Chamberlin introduced them. They suggested that "competition" might not work quite as pure (or perfect) competition theory had suggested it would. In squeezing out profits, it might not work toward minimum average cost. The argument of pure competition theory had been that—if only in the long run—we would get the best of all the worlds: minimum average cost of production, and zero profits.

(Chamberlin would have insisted that any such comparison between the supposed "long-run" results of pure and of monopolistic competition must not be used to condemn monopolistic competition. He was convinced that monopolistic competition was the near-universal and inevitable situation. Pure competition theory might point to an "ideal" situation; but it was an unattainable ideal in real-life circumstances.)

a. to the left or downward; reduces; just break even; no longer   **b.** tilted; gives some; cannot   **c.** less than

7. For an industry structure that satisfies the characterization of monopolistic competition presented in the text, long-run equilibrium is represented by a tangency between a firm's average cost curve and the effective demand curve for its differentiated product. It is, as a result, necessary that *(P > MC / P = MC / P < MC)* in equilibrium because the effective demand curve is *(negatively sloped / positively sloped / horizontal)*. Furthermore, the properties of cost curves therefore require that *(MC > AC / MC = AC / MC < AC)* at the equilibrium level of output. Compared with the perfectly competitive equilibrium, the monopolistic competitor produces *(too much / too little / just the correct amount)*.

Now consider the plight of a monopolistic competitor in an industry whose production costs have suddenly increased. In the short run, economic profits for this firm would be *(less than zero / equal to zero / still slightly positive)*. In the long run, though, firms would *(enter / exit / proceed as before)* so that the effective demand curve facing our firm would *(shift in for every price / shift out for every price / do nothing)*. The result, ultimately, would be *(lower / higher / identical)* prices and *(negative / zero / positive)* economic profits.

It was observed in Chapter 23 that a lump-sum tax would affect neither the price decision nor the output decision of a profit-maximizing monopolist. We now know that this conclusion *(applies equally well / does not apply at all)* to the monopolistic competitor.

P > MC; negatively sloped; *MC < AC*; too little; less than zero; exit; shift out for every price; higher; zero; does not apply at all

8. The text notes that, compared with perfect competitors, imperfect competitors pay, in practice, *(more / the same / less)* attention to maximizing profits. This is true, in part, because most earn *(positive / zero / negative)* economic profits and *(are / are not)* on the same knife-edge of economic viability as their perfect competitor colleagues. "Bounded rationality" is given as one reason for this behavior; it is a notion that focuses attention on the expense and difficulty involved in collecting and processing the information required to set marginal cost precisely equal to marginal revenue. Instead of making the effort to accomplish that task, it is argued, "rules of thumb" emerge in boardrooms all across the country to help guide executives in making their pricing and output decisions without detailed knowledge of the underlying marginal schedules.

Markup pricing is the most popular of these rules, but the dimension of that markup is not a number that executives agree upon without some market analysis. It is, of course, this analysis that, in the long run, can make the search for a pricing rule look like a procedure that implicitly tries to maximize profits. Executives may not compute marginal cost and marginal revenue schedules, but they might still behave as if they did. This question is designed to illustrate how this "deception" might be achieved.

For a monopoly firm facing demand curve *DD* in Figure 24-3, we already know that profits would be maximized by setting a price equal to $_____ and expecting to sell _____ units. Relative to average cost, that price amounts to a _____ percent markup over cost. Complete, now, Table 24-1 to convince yourself that a sequence of trial markup percentages could lead a careful manager to the profit-maximizing intersection of *MR* and *MC* without computing either schedule.

less; positive; are not; 10; 10; 100; (reading across rows) 60%: $8; 14; $42   80%: $9; 12; $48   100%: $10; 10; $50   120%: $12; 8; $48   110%: $10.50; 9; $49.50   105%: $10.25; 9.5; $49.88 (The manager might, after noting that markup increases generated higher profits until 120 percent, begin to back up until the peak at 100 percent was discovered)

9. The Schupeterian hypothesis, about the large firms that dominate imperfectly competitive markets, postulates that

Table 24-1

Markup Percentage	Price	Output, Units	Profit
60%	_____	_____	_____
80%	_____	_____	_____
100%	_____	_____	_____
120%	_____	_____	_____
110%	_____	_____	_____
105%	_____	_____	_____

"big business may have had more to do with creating our (high) standard of life than (with) keeping it down." This hypothesis is based, at least in part, upon the notion that *(research and development expenditure / purchasing power / real competition)* seems to be concentrated most heavily in the largest firms on the American scene. Since Mansfield has argued that the social return to invention is *(3 / .5 / 5)* times the private gain, it can certainly be argued that research and development is *(overfunded / properly funded / underfunded)*. Moreover, the private gain to invention is *(larger / smaller)* for large firms than it is for small firms. A case can be made, therefore, that if big business conducts a large proportion of this country's research into new products and new production processes, then we should tolerate their bigness. Corporate giants in the United States currently account for *(10 / just under 50 percent / over 75 percent)* of our funding of pure research and development, so the Mansfield argument has some empirical basis of support. The effect on our total expenditure on research and development of any policy or circumstance that reduces industrial concentration, like the breakup of AT&T, may thus be a source of major concern. Nonetheless, small success stories, like Apple Computers, sometimes turn into big success stories. Policy designed to foster research should therefore be the product of a balanced approach; it should not, in particular, concentrate its efforts exclusively on fostering big business research at the expense of other sources of ingenuity and invention.

research and development expenditure; 3; underfunded; larger; just under 50 percent

10. One of the most significant changes in the way that the legal system of the United States deals with the potential problems of imperfect competition is the recent focusing of judicial attention on how business is actually conducted. It is, according to this new view of how the law should be enforced, far more important to attack types of behavior that signify the abuse of market power than it is to concentrate simply on markets that display offensive types of industrial organization. These abusive methods of conducting business, including (*a*) price fixing, (*b*) output restraint, (*c*) market division, (*d*) predatory pricing, (*e*) resale agreements, and (*f*) price discrimination, *(are / are not)* necessarily confined to the concentrated industries with extreme and potentially profitable market power. They can appear in competitive markets just as easily.

The following list of behaviors contains examples of the six types of conduct just noted. Identify each with the conduct that it represents, and record your answer in the space provided.

a. Agreement between retailers and the manufacturer not to sell a certain doll for less than $25.00 ....

_____

b. The pricing of computers below production costs to prevent entry by potential competitors ....

_____

c. An agreement among suppliers of oil not to sell more than 1 million barrels per day ....

_____

d. One firm selling hammers to hardware stores for $8.99 and to the Defense Department for $410.22 ....

_____

e. An agreement among sugar retailers to sell only in specified geographic regions of the United States ....

_____

f. An agreement among airlines to increase fares 20 percent over the weekend ....

_____

g. The destruction of thousands of pounds of coffee beans before they get to market ....

_____

The notion behind this concentration on conduct is that research and development into new products and into new cost-reducing technologies will continue in any market with any structure as long as collusion, tacit or overt, does not undermine competitive pressures (actual or potential). Based upon this notion, concern about mergers should proceed on a case-by-case basis. General prescriptions should therefore be difficult to come by, but one is apparent: of the three types of

merger activity—_____, _____,

and _____—the one most likely to be trou-

blesome is the _____ type which may lower competitive pressures by increasing the market concentration of the largest firms.

are not: **a.** resale agreements **b.** predatory pricing **c.** output restraint **d.** price discrimination **e.** market division **f.** price fixing **g.** output restraint; vertical; horizontal; conglomerate; horizontal

QUIZ: Multiple Choice

1. Which of the following characteristics tends to prevail in concentrated markets?
(1) Slightly higher than normal profits.
(2) Higher than normal advertising expenditures.
(3) Higher than usual research and development expenditure.
(4) Less price flexibility than normal.
(5) All of the above.

2. Which of the following represents a legal barrier to entry that might support an oligopolistic market structure?
(1) Price setting below the lowest price a new entrant could afford to charge.
(2) A tariff that kept all but a trickle of foreign products off the domestic market.
(3) Product differentiation among a few producers.

(4) Average cost curves that reach their minima at roughly 30 percent of market demand.

(5) All of the above.

3. Which alternative to question 2 would have been correct if the barrier to entry were a cost barrier?

(1).

(2).

(3).

(4).

(5).

4. Which alternative to question 2 would have been correct if the barrier to entry were collusion?

(1).

(2).

(3).

(4).

(5).

5. OPEC presents to the world a market structure most accurately represented by:

(1) the price leader model.

(2) the dominant firm model.

(3) the monopolistic competition model.

(4) the collusive oligopoly acting like a monopolist model.

(5) perfect competition.

6. Which alternative to question 5 would have been correct if the market in question had been the cigarette market in the United States?

(1).

(2).

(3).

(4).

(5).

7. Which alternative to question 5 would have been correct if the market in question had been the aluminum industry, in which one company sets the price that prevails in the market?

(1).

(2).

(3).

(4).

(5).

8. To earn positive economic profits over the long run, the dominant firm must have captured, by virtue of its size, a cost advantage over the competitive fringe. Otherwise:

(1) the fringe would be profitable enough to attract new firms.

(2) the fringe would be able to maintain short-run positive profits even as it undercut the dominant firm's price.

(3) the positive profits would continue until sufficient new suppliers drove them to zero.

(4) the ultimate long-run equilibrium would be the perfectly competitive solution, with the dominant firm either closing down or making zero economic profit along with everyone else at the market-determined price.

(5) all of the above.

9. According to the text, if we have an industry of many sellers of differentiated products, and if entry into this industry is free, the long-run equilibrium position of the typical firm will have these properties:

(1) Average cost (*AC*) will be at its minimum possible level, and price charged (*P*) will be equal to that *AC*.

(2) *AC* will be at its minimum level, and *P* will be above that *AC*.

(3) *AC* will be above its minimum level, and *P* will be above that *AC*.

(4) *AC* will be above its minimum level, and *P* will be equal to that *AC*.

(5) None of the above, necessarily.

10. One reason why a firm operating under conditions of imperfect competition is likely to want to use an administered or markup price is:

(1) lack of sufficient knowledge of marginal revenue at various levels of output

(2) lack of sufficient knowledge of marginal cost at various levels of output

(3) desire to have a breakeven point occurring at a high level of output

(4) that it fears the charging of any higher price would attract new competition into the field.

(5) that this price indicates the most efficient plant output level.

11. Aside from the "bounded rationality" problems of managing a large corporation, which of the following accurately describes a potential problem with the management/owner dichotomy so common in American business?

(1) Managers all graduate from the same business schools, so that they always know what the competition is doing.

(2) Collusion is illegal but managers cannot be thrown in jail for violating the antitrust laws.

(3) Managers are profit-motivated and thus tend not to take risks on new projects that might help America grow more quickly.

(4) None of the managers have been trained to deal with foreign markets.

(5) All of the above.

12. The Schumpeter hypothesis is that:

(1) big business is not necessarily bad business.

(2) firms never really have the power over price and output that economists attribute to them.

(3) research and development is more than sufficiently supported by a consortium of government, small business, and big business.

(4) innovation would be accelerated if managers of large firms were required to be owners of large firms.

(5) all of the above.

13. In light of the pros and cons of imperfect competition, policy should probably be directed at:

(1) keeping the barriers to competition low.

(2) attacking anticompetitive business conduct.

(3) tolerating bigness if it is founded in technology.

(4) encouraging the research and development efforts of large and small firms.

(5) all of the above.

14. The merger of United Technologies, a high-tech company, and Otis Elevator is an example of:

(1) a vertical merger.

(2) a horizontal merger.

(3) a conglomerate merger.

(4) a tax bailout.

(5) none of the above.

15. Which alternative to question 14 would have been correct if the merger in question had been the union of Standard Oil of Indiana and the Gulf Oil Corporation?

(1).

(2).

(3).

(4).

(5).

16. Which of the alternatives listed in question 14 is most likely to be the source of concern for those who worry about the conduct of antitrust policy in the United States?

(1).

(2).

(3).

(4).

(5).

17. Which of the following major contributions to the antitrust laws of the United States includes, in its amended state, a provision preventing the acquisition of one company by another if it will substantially lessen competition?

(1) The Sherman Antitrust Act.

(2) The Clayton Antitrust Act.

(3) The Humphrey-Hawkins Bill.

(4) The Federal Trade Commission Act.

(5) The General Agreement on Trade and Tariffs.

18. Which alternative in question 17 would have been correct if the provision in question had prohibited unfair and deceptive methods of competition?

(1).

(2).

(3).

(4).

(5).

19. Which alternative in question 17 would have been correct if the provision in question had prohibited conspiracy to monopolize trade with foreign nations?

(1).

(2).

(3).

(4).

(5).

20. To which of the alternatives in question 17 would one appeal to fight the proposed friendly (and hypothetical) purchase of the stock of Braniff Airlines by American Airlines?

(1).

(2).

(3).

(4).

(5).

PART FIVE

WAGES, RENT, AND PROFITS: THE DISTRIBUTION OF INCOME

INCOMES AND LIVING STANDARDS

Chapter 25 is the first in a series of chapters that focus our attention on the distribution of income. Together, these chapters will bring the fundamentals of supply-and-demand analysis to bear on questions of how individual incomes are determined. Critical in this determination must be, of course, the ownership of the factors of production and the prices that they command, but there is more to it than that. Chapter 25 defines what economists mean when they speak of income, wealth, and equality (or inequality, as the case may be). Chapter 25 also explores the sources of wealth in a modern economy. Subsequent chapters will build on these concepts to develop a theory of income distribution and to apply that theory to an understanding of the employment of land, labor, other natural resources, and capital in a productive enterprise.

Having completed your work in this initial chapter of Part Five, you will have accomplished the following objectives.

LEARNING OBJECTIVES

1. Outline, in brief and summary form, the differences in real income per capita between the "developed" nations of North America and Western Europe and the "less developed" nations in other parts of the world.

2. Review, in the light of the experience of various parts of the world over the past half-century, the expectation expressed by Marx and Engels that the rich will get richer and the poor will get poorer.

3. Come to grips with the position of the United States in terms of both its wealth vis à vis the rest of the world and its own internal distribution of wealth among its citizens.

4. Understand the difference between wealth as a stock measure and income as a flow measure.

5. Outline, as to a Lorenz curve, (*a*) the information such a curve is intended to convey, (*b*) how it is constructed, and (*c*) how the degree of "bulge" in the curve is to be interpreted.

6. Review the difference, as indicated by statistics, between the typical distribution of abilities and the typical distribution of income.

7. Identify and explain seven potential sources of inequality in the distribution of income in the United States and elsewhere.

1. **a.** Suppose the group consists of 10 individuals. The first receives an income of $1 weekly, the second $2, and so on, the tenth receiving $10. The first individual is low man on the income totem pole, representing the bottom 10 percent (ranked in terms of income) of this particular population. The $1 received by this poverty-stricken person is about 2 percent of the total weekly income received by all, which totals $55. Complete the remaining figures below. For example, the lowest 20 percent of the population consists of the $1 individual plus the $2 individual. Their combined income total of $3 is about 5½ percent of the combined incomes of all 10; i.e., $3 is about 5½ percent of $55. So 5½ should go in the first blank below.

Percent of Income Received by Lowest

10%	20%	30%	40%	50%	60%	70%	80%	90%	100%
2%									100%

b. In Figure 25-1 (shown at the top of the next page), draw the Lorenz curve illustrating this distribution of income. (Note that the Lorenz curve chart is by nature a square. Most diagrams found in the text are not bounded on all four sides in this way.) Begin by labelling the axes of Figure 25-1, consult the text for correct labelling of a Lorenz curve.

c. If the distribution of income were more unequal than that indicated at the beginning of this question, then the Lorenz curve would (*bulge closer to the lower right-hand corner / draw nearer to the diagonal*); if it were less unequal, the curve

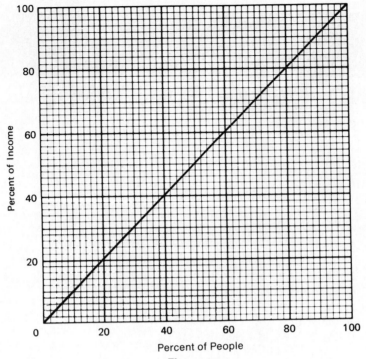

Figure 25-1

would *(bulge closer to the lower right-hand corner / draw nearer to the diagonal)*.

---

a. 5½%; 11%; 18%; 27¼%; 38%; 51%; 65½%; 81¾%   **c.** bulge closer to the right-hand corner; draw nearer to the diagonal

2. Suppose, using the data provided in question 1, that a 20 percent income tax were imposed by the government. That tax would collect, assuming no disincentive effects, $11 in revenue. Assume that the administration of the tax cost $1 that is not returned to the people, but that the remaining $10 is distributed to everyone as equal $1 "social" payments. Fill in the table at the bottom of this page and draw a new Lorenz curve to illustrate the resulting after-tax and payment distribution of income on Figure 25-1.

Reading across rows: Taxes paid: $.40; $.60; $.80; $1.00; $1.20; $1.40; $1.60; $1.80; $2.00   Income after taxes: $1.60; $2.40; $3.20; $4.00; $4.80; $5.60; $6.40; $7.20; $8.00   Income after payment: $2.60; $3.40; $4.20; $5.00; $5.80; $6.60; $7.40; $8.20; $9.00   Percentage: 8.1%, 14.4%, 22.2%, 31.5%, 42.2%, 54.4%, 68.1%, 83.3%; the Lorenze curve should be closer to the 45° line

3. The following list records changes in a Lorenz curve that might be expected in response to some change in economic circumstance:

(1) Movement up toward the 45° line

(2) Movement away from the 45° line

(3) No movement at all

(4) Movement of the lower portion closer to the 45° line and the upper portion away from the 45° line

In the spaces provided, indicate the likely effect of the following changes in economic condition on a Lorenz curve illustrating a distribution of income.

a. A 5 percent proportional income tax whose revenues are not redistributed .... (_____)

b. A 5 percent proportional income tax whose revenues are redistributed equally to everyone .... (_____)

Person	10%	20%	30%	40%	50%	60%	70%	80%	90%	100%
Income	$1	$2	$3	$4	$5	$6	$7	$8	$9	$10
Taxes paid	$ .20	____	____	____	____	____	____	____	____	____
Income after taxes	$ .80	____	____	____	____	____	____	____	____	____
Income after taxes and payment	$1.80	____	____	____	____	____	____	____	____	____
Percent of total income after the program received by the lowest indicated %	3.3%	____	____	____	____	____	____	____	____	100%

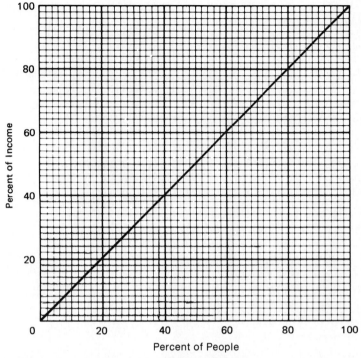

Percent of Income

0   20   40   60   80   100
Percent of People

Figure 25-2

c. A progressive income tax whose revenues are not redistributed .... (_____)

d. A progressive income tax whose revenues are redistributed equally to everyone .... (_____)

e. A 5 percent sales tax whose revenues are not redistributed .... (_____)

f. A deep recession that cuts employment for the working class .... (_____)

---

a. (3) **b.** (1) **c.** (1) **d.** (1) (more strongly) **e.** (2) (because lower-income classes spend a higher proportion of their incomes and thus sacrifice a higher proportion of their incomes to a sales tax) **f.** (2)

4. Consider the two distributions of income indicated in the table below.

Distribution A:			
% Population	40%	60%	100%
% Income earned	10%	40%	100%
Distribution B:			
% Population	60%	90%	100%
% Income earned	40%	60%	100%

Plot Lorenz curves (connecting points with straight lines) for the two distributions on Figure 25-2, carefully labelling each.

Which distribution is more equal? _____.
Under which distribution are the poor better off in terms of the

relative incomes that they earn? _____. Now look at the area

between the Lorenz curves that you have drawn and the 45° line; this area is the "Gini coefficient." The area, i.e., the Gini coefficient measure of income equality, is larger for *(A / B / neither)*. In general, you should expect that the larger the Gini coefficient, the *(more / less)* equal is the indicated distribution of income.

Cannot judge; B; neither; less

5. Question 4 uses a simple example to illustrate that it is extremely difficult to measure the degree to which income is distributed equitably. Perhaps more significantly, though, the very concept of equality is at best a slippery and controversial issue. Most people would agree that equal opportunity, equal access to adequate education, and equal access to the electoral process are essential elements of the American experiment in democracy. But what about a (more) equal distribution of income? Should, more specifically, a progressive income tax system be used to redistribute income? The text does not offer an answer to this question. There is, in fact, no definitive response to which everyone would agree. The text, instead, identifies seven potential sources of inequity in the distribution of income that would exist regardless of the tax structure of the United States. List them in the space provided below.

a. _____

b. _____

c. _____

d. _____

e. _____

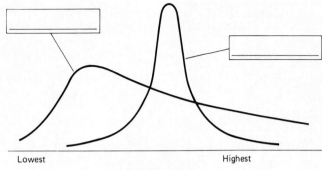

Figure 25-3

f. _____

g. _____

a. ability **b.** occupation **c.** education **d.** work effort **e.** property **f.** risk taking **g.** inheritance

6. Figure 25-3 plots the distributions of ability and income in the United States. Label the two curves correctly. The importance of the discrepancy between the two distributions is that differences in ability cannot entirely explain observed difference in earnings across the American population.

the curve that peaks first is income (the left box)

QUIZ: Multiple Choice

1. Karl Marx and Friedrich Engels expected that capitalism would make the rich richer and the poor poorer. That did not happen, at least not everywhere as predicted. Which of the following statements is an accurate statement of the actual experience of the past few years?
(1) Average working hours in the United States have declined steadily since the turn of the century.
(2) Per capital real incomes have risen steadily since the turn of the century.
(3) The distribution of wealth in the United Kingdom and the United States is less equitable than the corresponding distributions of income.
(4) The top 1 percent of the population in the United States currently holds title to 19 percent of the wealth.
(5) All of the above.

2. A "Lorenz curve chart" is a graph on whose axes the following things are measured:
(1) Amount of income in dollars on one axis, total number of individuals or families receiving that income or a lower one on the other.
(2) Percent of people (10 percent, 20 percent, etc.) on one axis, percentage of total income received by the lowest 10 percent, the lowest 20 percent, etc., on the other.
(3) Number of individuals or families receiving a certain income on one axis, percentage of total population represented by that number on the other.

(4) Number of individuals or families in different occupations on one axis, mean or median amount of income received in that occupation on the other.
(5) Income classes (e.g., $0 to $1999, $2000 to $3999, etc.) on one axis, number or percentage of individuals or families in each such income class on the other.

3. On a Lorenz curve chart, absolute or total equality in income distribution would appear as:
(1) a curved line well bowed out from the diagonal.
(2) a curved line close to the diagonal.
(3) a right-angled line.
(4) a diagonal line.
(5) none of the preceding.

4. Which alternative in question 3 would be correct, had that question referred to absolute inequality in income—i.e., a situation in which one individual or family gets all the income, the others receive no income at all?
(1).
(2).
(3).
(4).
(5).

5. The trend in the United States over the past decade or so has been for the:
(1) lowest 20 percent of the income distribution to become poorer and the highest 20 percent of the income distribution to also become poorer relative to the middle 60 percent.
(2) the upper 20 percent to become relatively poorer and the lowest 20 percent to become relatively richer.
(3) the upper 20 percent to become relatively richer and the lowest 20 percent to become relatively poorer.
(4) both the upper and the lowest 20 percent of the income distribution to become richer at the expense of the middle class.
(5) none of the above.

6. The net wealth of the average American family in 1984 was:
(1) $32,000.
(2) $42,000.
(3) $72,000.
(4) $92,000.
(5) over $100,000.

7. The present (middle 1980s) level of per capita weekly income in the United States, according to the text, is:
(1) over $100 but less than $130.
(2) between $130 and $160.
(3) about $205.
(4) about $255.
(5) over $300.

8. As a measure of poverty, the percentage of families below a given benchmark measured only in terms of income:
(1) is insignificant.
(2) is smaller than the percentage under the benchmark when welfare transfer payments are included.

(3) is larger than the percentage under the benchmark when welfare transfer payments are included.

(4) cannot be trusted because the data cannot be measured.

(5) is a waste of time because there are no poor people in America that are not simply lazy.

9. In terms of per capita GNP, which of the following countries ranks below the United Kingdom?

(1) Japan.

(2) Italy.

(3) France.

(4) West Germany.

(5) France and Italy.

10. With respect to the distribution of incomes in the United States and the relationship between the median and the mean of such income:

(1) the mean is higher than the median, due to the presence of a large number of relatively low incomes.

(2) the median is higher than the mean, due to the presence of a small number of exceptionally high incomes.

(3) the mean is higher than the median, due to the presence of a small number of exceptionally high incomes.

(4) the median is higher than the mean, due to the presence of a large number of relatively low incomes.

(5) the median, which used to be lower than the mean, has recently become somewhat higher, due to the influence of progressive income taxation.

11. By the "median" family income is meant:

(1) the figure obtained by listing all incomes from lowest to highest and taking the one exactly in the middle of the ranking.

(2) the income figure that would result if the total incomes received by all families were divided equally among those families.

(3) the income it is estimated a family must have in order to reach the "minimum comfort" level of consumption.

(4) the level of income found at the exact midpoint of a Lorenz curve.

(5) none of the preceding.

12. Which alternative in question 11 would be correct had that question referred to the "mean" rather than to the "median" family income?

(1).

(2).

(3).

(4).

(5).

13. If there is any inequality at all in the distribution of income, then the following will be true of the group making up the lowest 20 percent in the income ranking:

(1) It is just as likely as not that it will receive more than 20 percent of this total income.

(2) It must receive exactly 20 percent of this total income.

(3) It will usually, but not always, receive less than 20 percent of this total income.

(4) It must have received less than 20 percent of the total income of all groups together.

(5) None of the above is necessarily true.

14. If the distribution within any large population of a physical or a mental trait such as the intelligence quotient is illustrated by means of a frequency-distribution (FD) chart or a Lorenz curve chart, it will most commonly appear as follows:

(1) On an FD chart as a curve with a long tail at one end only, and on a Lorenz chart as a right-angled line.

(2) On an FD chart as a symmetrical or bell-shaped curve, and on a Lorenz chart as a right-angled line.

(3) On an FD chart as a symmetrical or bell-shaped curve and on a Lorenz chart as a straight line.

(4) On an FD chart as a symmetrical or bell-shaped curve and on a Lorenz chart as a curved line.

(5) On an FD chart as a curve with a long tail at one end only and on a Lorenz chart as a straight line.

15. Differences in ability are commonly cited to explain differences in income. In the text's view, this explanation:

(1) is only partial because there are so many more instances of skewness in ability than in income distribution.

(2) is only partial because the shape of the income frequency-distribution curve is significantly different from that of the ability-distribution curve.

(3) is only partial because the measured range of individual ability differences is much wider than the range of income distribution.

(4) gives a reasonably accurate interpretation of income differences.

(5) is almost meaningless because there is no suitable way of comparing ability differences against income differences.

16. If inequalities of income and of wealth in the United Kingdom (U.K.) and the United States (U.S.) are compared, the following statement emerges (according to the text) as true:

(1) The U.K. has much greater inequality as to both incomes and wealth.

(2) The U.S. has much greater inequality as to both incomes and wealth.

(3) Wealth inequalities are both the same in both, but the U.K. has much greater inequality of income.

(4) The U.K. has much greater inequality of wealth, but income inequalities are both the same in both.

(5) There is no significant difference between the two countries as to either income equality or wealth inequality.

CHAPTER 26
THEORY OF PRODUCTION AND MARGINAL PRODUCTS

Having studied pricing/production decisions in products markets, it is now time to consider pricing/employment decisions in input markets. Scarcity and need were seen to determine why it costs more to purchase some goods than it does others, but what makes the wages and salaries offered to those engaged in some occupations higher than those offered to others? Scarcity, need, or something else? Secondarily, if all inputs work interdependently to produce any given product, how are their respective contributions assessed to compute the appropriate compensation for those contributions? How, more specifically, are wage rates determined? And interest rates? And land rents? And so on. Finally, why is it the case that wages have, over the last century, consistently accounted for approximately 75 percent of the GNP of the United States?

The answers to all these questions will be found in a familiar arena—the workings of supply and demand. The only fundamental differences between product markets and input markets will be found in the sources of supply and demand. In a goods market, for example, demand emerges because the good being sold generates some utility for the consumer. In an input market, though, factors of production are demanded only because they can be employed to produce something valuable—some good or service that can be sold in a goods market. The demand for inputs is therefore a "derived demand" based not upon the immediate, innate value of an input to the firm, but upon the value of some other good that the input can be employed to produce.

This chapter concentrates on the demand for inputs. Because a producing firm must hire labor and buy raw materials and machinery, it is a demander of productive inputs. We must expect it to try to keep its costs of production for any given output at a minimum. The inputs it buys, and the quantity of each it buys, will therefore be strongly influenced by this rule of cost minimization. (Its purchases also will be influenced by the price it can get for the commodity it produces.)

In working through the chapter, then, you will accomplish the following learning objectives.

LEARNING OBJECTIVES

1. Explain what is meant, in economics, by the theory of distribution.

2. Define the production function. Explain what further information (if any) is needed, in addition to the production function, in order to derive a firm's total cost curve.

3. Define (a) marginal product (for an input) and (b) marginal revenue product (for an input).

4. State the algebraic rule that must be satisfied (with respect to overall input employment) if a firm is to be producing any given output at minimum total cost.

5. State the algebraic rule that must be satisfied (for each and every input employed) if a firm is to be operating at its maximum-profit position, and understand what happens to that position if an input price changes.

6. Explain what is meant by "the marginal-productivity theory of distribution" (as first outlined by John B. Clark). Explain also what is meant by "exhaustion of the product" in connection with this thoery.

7. Understand the connection between the firm specific model of profit-maximizing employment decisions and the derivative insights into aggregate behavior uncovered by Solow, Kendrick, and Denison.

8. Explain why cost-minimizing–profit-maximizing behavior in input markets produces an efficient outcome that can be located on the production-possibility frontier of an economy.

The first concept to grasp is that of the production function. We deal, in this chapter of the Study Guide, with some given product X whose production requires inputs to be denoted A, B, and C. When you read A, B, and C, think of, for example, capital, labor, and material.

▶ The production function is a statement of the quantitative relation between inputs A, B, and C and output X, in given conditions of technology.

As such, the production function provides some information that is absolutely critical to the firm that wants to make the most efficient use of its inputs.

▶ The production function identifies, for any combination of inputs A, B, and C, the maximum quantity of X that can be produced.

▶ The production function also identifies, for any given quantity of output X, the various combinations of inputs A, B, and C that could produce that quantity.

The second of these two points needs consideration. The production function may specify *fixed* proportions between inputs. It takes just one person to drive a truck; a second driver is no help at all. This is a *fixed-proportions* case: there is one and only one ABC combination appropriate for any given X quantity.

In the more general case, you can (within limits) substitute one input for another. (If the truck driver is given a larger vehicle, the labor-capital proportions will have been changed.) This means there will be more than one ABC combination possible for any given X quantity. A production function sums up all the possible ABC combinations, for each and any X quantity.

In this more general case—assuming that each of inputs A, B, and C have a market price per unit—different ABC combinations, all alike in that they are just capable of producing some given X quantity, will involve different total costs. ("Total cost" means total A quantity multiplied by its price per unit, plus the same for B, plus the same for C.)

▶ When the text speaks of "minimizing cost," it means choosing that particular combination of inputs that would cost least (given the prevailing prices of inputs) for the particular quantity of X involved.

In the special fixed-proportions case mentioned above, there is no problem of "minimizing costs" because there is only one ABC combination possible and thus one total dollar cost figure for producing any given X quantity (given in ABC prices). The "cost-minimizing rule" developed in the text chapter is applicable only when there is a choice between alternatives to be made. It is simply a rule used to make sure that the particular ABC alternative selected is—given the prevailing ABC prices—the minimum-cost one.

1. a. Note that the production function itself will not tell you the minimum-cost ABC combination; it is just a summing up of all the physical relationships between inputs and output. You also need input prices to answer a question about cost. Still, you must begin with the production function, which indicates (pick one):
(1) What it will cost to produce any given quantity of X by using A, B, and C.
(2) What the prices of A, B, and C are.
(3) For each and any X quantity, the various combinations of A, B, and C which could produce that X quantity.

b. Suppose it is true that 10 units of A, 30 units of B, and 20 of C, used in the best-known way, could just produce 200 units of X. This is (pick one):
(1) An example of a production function
(2) Not an example of a full production function, but rather of the kind of information a production function is expected to supply

---

a. (3) **b.** (2)

There are two reasons why a producing firm might incur an excessive production cost for the output it is turning out. One has already been mentioned: it might not be using the cheapest available ABC combinations.

The second reason is that the firm might use its inputs foolishly, or without adequate supervision, so that the ABC combination employed produces less output than it could turn out in the given conditions of technology.

▶ The production function will link with any given ABC combination the highest output figure attainable; that is, it assumes the inputs are used to the best advantage.

2. For example, suppose 10-30-20 is a workable ABC combination for 200 X (when these inputs are used to the best advantage). If these input quantities were to be doubled to 20-60-40, then this higher combination could certainly produce more than 200 X—perhaps 400 X. (The figure 400 would signify "constant returns to scale": double all input quantities and you just double output quantity; halve all input quantities, and you just halve output quantity. The constant-returns case gets some consideration later in this chapter. But for the moment we need not give it special attention.)

a. Excluding the fixed-proportions case, the production function will indicate ABC combinations other than 10-30-20 for an output of 200 X. The combination 20-60-40 *(could / could not possibly)* be among them. If 10-30-20 is sufficient for 200 X, then use of 20-60-40 would be wasteful, and the production function rules out wasteful combinations. The 20-60-40 combination will show up within the production function associated with a *(lower / higher)* X quantity, perhaps *(150 / 200 / 400)* of X.

b. Given that 10-30-20 is one possible ABC combination reported by the production function for 200 X, pick the one alternative among the four below that could be another such combination:
(1) 20 A, 40 B, 30 C
(2) 10 A, 35 B, 20 C

(3) 8 A, 25 B, 19 C
(4) 10 A, 28 B, 21 C

c. From the information in part **b**, it follows that if 200 X is being produced with the 10-30-20 ABC combination, this output level could be maintained by (pick one):
(1) Replacing 1 A unit by 2 extra B units.
(2) Replacing 2 B units by 1 extra C unit.
(3) Replacing 1 B unit by 2 extra C units.
(4) Replacing 2 A units by 2 extra C units.

---

a. could not possibly; higher; 400   **b.** (4) [This is the only combination in which one input is reduced in quantity, and compensated for by a larger quantity of another. If 10-30-20 is a legitimate report from the production function, then each of the other three alternatives is either wasteful or impossible. Alternative (3) would make 10-30-20 wasteful]   **c.** (2)

3.   a. The text stresses *marginal product (MP)* as the critical measure in cost-minimizing decisions. The marginal product of factor A is defined as (pick one):
(1) Change in quantity of X resulting from increasing or decreasing A by 1 (small) unit, with inputs B and C held constant.
(2) Change in quantity of X resulting from increasing or decreasing A by 1 (small) unit, with inputs B and C increased or decreased in proportion.
(3) Change in quantity of X resulting from increasing or decreasing B and C by 1 (small) unit each, with quantity of input A held constant.
(4) Total quantity of X produced, divided by total quantity of A used.

b. Suppose that the production function says this: X output is 200 units with a 10-30-20 ABC combination, and X output is 203 units with a 10-31-20 ABC combination.

This means that at this point in the production function *(the MP of X is 3 units / the MP of B is 3 units / the MP of A is 3 units)*.

c. If the employment of some input such as B were gradually increased, with the employment of all other inputs, such as A and C, held constant, we would expect the *MP* of B gradually to *(increase / decline)* because of the *(law of diminishing returns / relative scarcity of B that would develop)*. Similarly, if the B quantity were reduced (with A and C quantities held constant), we would expect the *MP* of B gradually to *(increase / decline)* because of the *(law of diminishing returns / relative scarcity of B that would develop)*.

---

a. (1)   **b.** the *MP* of B is 3 units   **c.** decline; law of diminishing returns; increase; relative scarcity of B that would develop [The *MP* of any input such as B is not a constant, it depends on the quantity of B that is being used; it depends on the quantities of the other inputs (here A and C) being used]

4.   a. Suppose that 200 units of X could be produced, as in question 2, by either of two ABC combinations: 10-30-20, or 10-28-21.
Suppose further that the prices of A, B, and C are, respec-

tively, $2, $1, and $3. In terms of minimizing cost, the preferable combination would be the *(10-30-20 / 10-28-21)* one.
Change the ABC prices to $2, $2, and $1. The minimum-cost combination would then be *(10-30-20 / 10-28-21)*.

b. The text provides a rule with which the firm can look at any possible combination of A, B, and C and determine, without any reference to the costs of other possible combinations, whether or not that combination is a least-cost combination. Write down this least-cost rule expressed in terms of marginal products and input prices:

---

a. 10-30-20; 10-28-21   **b.** $MP_A/P_A = MP_B/P_B = MP_C/P_C$

5.   a. Suppose that the quantity of X produced is 200 units. The quantities employed, prices, and *MP*s of inputs A, B, and C are as shown in Table 26-1.

Table 26-1

	A	B	C
Quantity employed	10	30	20
Price	$2	$1	$3
MP	2	3	1

Total cost incurred for the 200-unit output is $*(90 / 100 / 110 / 120 / 130)*. The least-cost rule of question 4 *(is / is not)* being satisfied.

Leave input A to one side in order to compare B and C. The last unit of B employed added *(1 / 2 / 3 / 4)* unit(s) of X to output. Since B's price is $1, each of these units costs approximately *(10 / 25 / 33 / 39 / 75)* cents. In contrast, the last unit of C employed added *(1 / 2 / 3 / 4)* unit(s) of X. Since C's price is $3, that unit cost $*(1 / 2 / 3 / 4)*.

b. The conditions of part **a** mean that total cost could be reduced by increasing the employment of *(B / C)* and decreasing that of *(B / C)*. What would output be if the employment of C were reduced by 3 units and the employment of B were increased by 1 unit? Assuming that C's marginal product remains constant over the 3-unit change, it would be *(196 / 197 / 200 / 201 / 203)* units of X. Total cost would, as a result of this change, *(rise / fall)* from $110 to $*(100 / 102 / 106 / 108 / 112)*.

c. As the employment of B rose, we should expect B's marginal product to *(rise / fall)*; as the employment of C fell, we would expect C's *MP* to *(rise / fall)*. Thus, as the changes indicated are made, we would be *(approaching / moving away from)* the least-cost position.

d. Now reverse the marginal product numbers for B and C given at the beginning of this question; make them 1 and 3, respectively. This revised situation *(would / would not)* then be a least-cost position, assuming that A employment did not change.

Suppose, for one final example in this question, that the *MP*s of A, B, and C were 4, 2, and 6, respectively. Let their prices remain as before. This *(would / would not)* be a least-cost position.

---

a. 110; is not; 3; 33; 1; 3 **b.** B; C; 200; fall; 102 **c.** fall; rise; approaching **d.** would; would

---

6. The ideas set out in this chapter need to be related to those discussed earlier. Chapters 22 through 24 dealt at length with the firm's choice of its profit-maximizing output, the basic rule being $MR = MC$. In this chapter—thus far, at any rate—we have not considered the profit-maximizing output. Our concern has been with the rule which tells the firm, for any output, whether or not that output is being produced at minimum-attainable cost.

Why go to the trouble of establishing the total cost of each and all outputs if the firm's real interest is finding that one particular level of output and sales that maximizes its profit? Because the total cost curve (from which marginal cost is obtained) is an essential ingredient in the $MR = MC$ profit-maximizing choice. This total cost curve indicates minimum-attainable cost for all possible outputs. The least-cost rule is needed in order to develop the total cost curve; the total cost curve is needed in order to identify the $MR = MC$ profit-maximizing output position.

a. In summary: When the firm establishes a least-cost output position, it has established (pick one):
(1) the total cost curve.
(2) one point on the total cost curve,
(3) one point on the total cost curve, given the existing production function and the existing ABC prices.

b. If the firm wants to maximize its profits, it will follow a process suggested above. Steps in that process are listed below, but they are out of order. Indicate their proper order by writing their numbers in the proper sequence in the space provided.
(1) Pick the output where marginal cost equals marginal revenue.
(2) Compute the least-cost combination of inputs for output levels in the anticipated range.
(3) Compute marginal revenue for various levels of sales in the anticipated range from information about the demand side of the market.
(4) Compute marginal cost for various levels of sales in the anticipated range from the least-cost data.
(5) Collect information about input prices and the technology that defines how inputs can be utilized to produce various levels of output.

Order: _____

---

a. (3) **b.** Order: (5), (2), (4), (1) [with (3) falling anywhere before (1)]

---

7. With this link between the least-cost rule and the total cost curve established, we can now draw the idea of the least-cost rule closer to the $MR = MC$ idea discussed earlier.

a. If we say that A is an input, X is the product produced, and the *MP* of input A is 2, then the 2 refers to *(units of A / units of X / dollars)*. This *MP* is, so to speak, the "payoff" in X output resulting from employment of the last unit of A. But payoff is more commonly thought of in money terms. To know what this *MP* payoff is worth in dollars, we must know what revenue the sale of the additional X units will bring in—i.e., we need to know the *(price of A / marginal revenue accruing from sale of X)*.

b. If the marginal revenue accruing from sale of 1 additional X unit is \$3 (the *MP* of input A being 2), then the dollar payoff resulting from hiring the last unit of A is \$*(2 / 3 / 5 / 6 / 10 / 12)*. (We disregard the slight drop in *MR* that might come from selling the second of these 2 X units.)

c. The technical name for this dollar payoff is the *marginal revenue product (MRP)*. That is, the *MRP* of, say, factor input A is specifically (pick one):
(1) *MP* of A multiplied by marginal revenue accruing from sale of X, or *MP* of A multiplied by *MR*.
(2) *MP* of A multiplied by price of A.
(3) *MP* of A not multiplied by anything.

d. In the special case of pure (or perfect) competition—but only in that case—this *MRP* of A could be defined as the *MP* of A multiplied by the price of X. But "marginal revenue from X" is more general. It takes in all the cases, pure competition included.

Barring the special case of pure (or perfect) competition, as the firm increases its output and sales, the marginal revenue from sale of X will *(rise / remain constant / fall)*. As a result, the marginal revenue product of each and every input will, as employment increases, *(rise / remain constant / fall)* for two reasons:

1. _____
2. _____

---

a. units of X; marginal revenue accruing from sale of X **b.** 6 **c.** (1) **d.** fall; fall; diminishing marginal revenue; diminishing marginal product

---

8. Suppose our firm is in a "balanced" position with respect to input employment; i.e., it is satisfying the least-cost rule with respect to inputs A, B, and C. Now it wants to find out if it is at its maximum-profit output level.

To do this, it can look at any one of its inputs—say, input A. A's price is, say, \$4 per unit. A's *MP* is 3. The marginal revenue from sale of X is \$1.

a. This means that A's *MRP*—the dollar payoff from employing the last unit of A—is \$*(1 / 2 / 3 / 4 / 7 / 12)*.

It cost \$*(1 / 2 / 3 / 4 / 7 / 12)* to buy that last unit of A services. So its employment *(added \$1 to / subtracted \$1 from / did not change)* total profit.

Our firm, remember, is in a "balanced" position in reference to its input employment; the same conclusion would have been reached had we looked at input B or input C. Hence, in the given circumstances, the firm *(definitely is / definitely is not / may or may not be)* earning maximum possible profit. For that maximum, it should *(reduce / increase)* its output—i.e., *(reduce / increase)* its employment of inputs.

b. Try, now, a different example, to illustrate the point more fully. Suppose that the *MP*s of A, B, and C are, respectively, 12, 8, and 2. Their prices are, respectively, $6, $4, and $1. The firm *(is / is not),* therefore, producing its current output at minimum cost.

The marginal revenue from sale of X is $1. Thus input A's *MRP* is $(12 / 10 / 8 / 6 / 4 / 2). Input B's *MRP* is $(12 / 10 / 8 / 6 / 4 / 2). Input C's *MRP* is $(12 / 10 / 8 / 6 / 4 / 2).

This firm *(is / is not)* operating at maximum-profit output. For such a maximum, it should *(increase / decrease)* its output, by *(increasing / decreasing)* the employment of *(input A only / B only / C only / all inputs).*

c. As employment is so changed, input *MRP*s will *(fall / rise).* The increase in input employment should be halted when each *MRP* has *(fallen below / reached equality with / risen above)* the price of the *(input / finished product).*

---

a. 3; 4; subtracted $1 from; definitely is not; reduce; reduce   **b.** is; 12; 8; 2; is not; increase; increasing; all inputs   **c.** fall; reached equality with; input

9. The process just described is nothing more than an elaboration of the *MR = MC* maximum-profit rule set out in earlier chapters. Think of the firm (as we did in those earlier chapters) as gradually approaching this *MR = MC* output level, starting from an output where *MR* exceeds *MC.* As output is expanded, *MR* gradually falls [unless the situation is one of pure (or perfect) competition], and *MC* gradually rises.

The output increases needed to reach this *MR = MC* equality are obtained by increasing the employment of A, B, and C. However, as this increase is undertaken, things mut be kept "in balance"; i.e., the minimum-cost rule of question 4 must be satisfied. If it is not, the output in question could be produced at lower cost, and the firm would be "above" its true total cost curve rather than "on" it.

With employment "balance" maintained, expanding output moves toward the *MR = MC* maximum-profit position. That position can be described in *MRP* terms, as well as *MR = MC* terms. As output is increased, *MRP*s fall (see question 7d). When they have fallen to equality with input prices, for all inputs employed, *(a)* the "in-balance" rule is automatically satisfied, and *(b)* so is the *MR = MC* maximum-profit rule.

a. Take the *MP*s for inputs A, B, and C of question 8b (12, 8, and 2, respectively). If you knew that ABC prices were $6, $4, and $1, respectively, and that the firm had reached its maximum-profit output, what must have been the *MR* from the sale of the last X units? *($8 / $6 / $2 / $1 / 50 cents)*

b. Change to different figures. If *MR* were $2, if ABC prices were $8, $4, and $10, and if the firm were at maximum-profit output, A's *MP* must have been *(1 / 2 / 3 / 4 / 5)* units of X,

that of B must have been *(1 / 2 / 3 / 4 / 5)* units, and C's *(1 / 2 / 3 / 4 / 5).*

---

a. 50 cents   **b.** 4; 2; 5

10. In everyday terms, the explanation of the maximum-profit rule for input employment (namely, equate the *MRP* of that input with its price) is this (pick one):
(1) The price of the factor input should equal the price of the output X.
(2) The marginal product of each and all inputs should be the same amount.
(3) Any extra unit of an input is worth hiring or buying so long as the extra revenue it brings in (via extra production and extra sales) exceeds what it costs to hire or buy it; the buying process should be halted only when the extra revenue has fallen to equality with the extra cost.
(4) The price of each factor input should be equal to marginal revenue from the last unit of X sold.

---

(3)

11. The preceding questions have tried to indicate the considerations that are most important to a firm in deciding how much of any input it will want to buy, given some set of prices. If A's price were, for example, to rise or to fall, the calculations would have to be redone. In sum, we are trying to isolate the considerations that lie behind a firm's demand for any input, at various possible prices of that input.

The demand for any input is sometimes called a *derived demand.* People want a finished good, such as X, for the satisfaction it provides them. Nobody wants an input such as A for *that* reason. Nevertheless, A is wanted because it is useful in the production of X. The demand for A is "derived from" the demand for X.

A highly important factor in this derived demand for A is its "productivity" in producing X—more specifically, its *MP.* The value of this *MP* is strongly influenced by the quantity of A employed. It *(depends as well / does not depend)* on the quantities of inputs B and C employed. We cannot speak of the "productivity" of A, or of the demand for A, without assuming something about the extent to which B and C are available to work cooperatively with A.

Moreover, demand for A will be affected by the price of X, the finished good which A helps to produce. The higher X's price, the greater will be the demand for A.

So the demand for A must assume given quantities of B and C employed. It must likewise assume given prices of X and of inputs B and C. A change in any of these prices would require all least-cost and best-profit positions to be recomputed.

In sum, the demand for an input is very much an "other things equal" demand. Alternatively, and in the language of the text, it is a "_____ demand."

---

depends as well; jointly interdependent

12. Finally, we return to the puzzling and difficult question with which the chapter began: that of income distribution. What are the forces which settle the manner of division of a cooperatively produced output? How much can any one contributing input expect to receive?

Clearly, the demand for the input (as discussed in the preceding question) is important in settling this question. Demand (together with available supply) determines the price per unit of input services. And if you know relative input prices, you know something about how those inputs are likely to share in the total value of goods produced.

The "marginal productivity" analysis outlined in this chapter first began to emerge late in the nineteenth century. Economist John B. Clark, who did much to develop it, felt that this analysis pointed strongly toward the underlying laws which governed the distribution of real income (goods and services) among the inputs which had cooperated in the production of those goods and services.

Clark pointed out that if each input is paid a price just equal to the market value of its *MP*, there will—in the right circumstances (this we'll get to in a moment)—be just enough to pay off all the inputs, with no deficit, and nothing left over.

Suppose that total output is 200 units of X, produced with a 10-30-20 ABC combination. Suppose the *MP*s of A, B, and C are 9 of X, 3 of X, and 1 of X, respectively. Suppose further that X is the product to be sold in a competitive market at a price of $1. Complete the following table in light of this information.

Quantity of Input	MRP of Input	Total Payment of Input
_____ units of A × $_____		= $_____
_____ units of B × $_____		= $_____
_____ units of C × $_____		= $_____
	Total payment =	$_____

It is assumed that A, B, and C are the *only* inputs contributing to X's production. When each is paid according to its *MRP*, the total payments *(are less than / just equal / exceed)* the total value of the total amount of X produced; i.e., $1 × 200 units = $200.

This approach had two seemingly attractive features. Payment according to *MRP*s just "exhausts the product"; i.e., there is just enough to go around. Moreover, payment according to (marginal) productivities carries with it some suggestion that the distribution is "fair" or "just."

Today it is conceded that income distribution is too complicated a business to be handled in such simple terms. Opinions differ sharply as to the meaningful content of the "marginal productivity" approach. Moreover, Clark's treatment works as outlined above only with a *constant returns to scale* production function; i.e., when doubling or tripling all input quantities just doubles or triples output quantity and halving all input quantities just halves output quantity. There is no necessary reason why production function should display this property; many clearly do not. If they do not, payment by marginal productivities will not "just exhaust the product." (The explanation of why a constant-returns production function has the product-exhaustion property is mathematical and is not explored either in the text or here.)

Reading across rows: 10, 9, 90; 30, 3, 90; 20, 1, 20; 200; just equal

13. Economists like Robert Solow, John Kendrick, and Edward Denison have spent a good deal of time exploring the aggregate distribution of income of the United States. They have explained the consistent 75 percent of GNP devoted to paying labor over the last century by demonstrating that a 1 percent increase in labor seems to increase GNP *(2 / 3 / 4 / 5)* times faster than a 1 percent increase in capital. They have also noted that technological innovation has been responsible for an increase in American productivity of *(1 to 2 percent / 3 to 4 percent / 0 to .5 percent)* per year over most of the twentieth century. The American capital stock has increased *(faster than / at the same rate as / slower than)* labor, moreover, accounting for another *(0 to .5 percent / 1 to 2 percent / 3 to 4 percent)* annual increase in wages. Nonetheless, the share of GNP paid to capital has remained stable mostly because of *(foreign marketing / technological change / addition of women to the work force)*.

3; 1 to 2 percent; faster than; 1 to 2 percent; technological change

---

14. Consult Table 26-2, in which the outputs of identical fields of corn are recorded for a variety of levels of employment of labor. Let there be 10 workers in an economy defined by the two corn fields, and let the world determine the price of corn at

Table 26-2

Labor Employed	Corn Output (bushels)	Marginal Product of Labor	Marginal Revenue Product of Labor
0	0	na	na
1	10	_____	_____
2	19	_____	_____
3	27	_____	_____
4	34	_____	_____
5	40	_____	_____
6	45	_____	_____
7	49	_____	_____
8	52	_____	_____
9	54	_____	_____
10	55	_____	_____

$2. Fill in the marginal product and marginal revenue product columns of the table. The numbers that you record there will be used to demonstrate that paying labor (the input, here) its marginal revenue product will result in a level of output that maximizes the value of the corn crop, i.e., an output that represents a point on the production-possibility frontier of this ridiculously simple economy.

Suppose, initially, that 7 workers toiled on the first field (field A) and 3 toiled on the second (field B). Output on field A would be _____ bushels worth $_____; each worker, if paid his or her marginal revenue product, would receive $_____. Output on field B would meanwhile be _____ bushels worth $_____; each worker there would receive $_____. In response to the wages that you computed, you should expect that workers would want to move *(from A to B / from B to A)*.

Suppose that happened, and 4 workers remained to work field A and 6 worked field B. Output in field A would fall to _____ bushels with a value of $_____, and output in field B would climb to _____ units worth $_____ on the world market. The total value of output would, in fact, have climbed from $_____ to $_____.

To equalize the wages paid to workers on both fields so that there would be no incentive for workers to want to switch from one to the other, however, _____ workers would have to work each field. Were that the case, total output would climb to _____ bushels worth $_____ and each worker would earn $_____. There *(exists / does not exist)* any other distribution of workers that would increase the output of corn and thus increase the value of the economy's production on the world market.

The marginal product column; 10, 9, 8, 7, 6, 5, 4, 3, 2, 1; marginal revenue product column: $20, $18, $16, $14, $12, $10, $8, $6, $4, $2; 49; 98; 8; 27; 54; 16; from A to B; 34; 68; 45; 90; 152; 158; 5; 80; 160; 12; does not exist

---

15. You are a consultant on cost minimization and profit maximization. What do you recommend with respect to each of the six cases listed in Table 26-3?

In all of them, product X is made through the employment of inputs A and B (and there are no other inputs involved). In all of them—note carefully—A's marginal product is 3 units of X, and B's marginal product is 9 units of X.

"*MR* from X Sale" in the table means marginal revenue at the current output and sales level. "*P* of A" and "*P* of B" indicate the prices the firm must pay for these two inputs.

a. As to each case, is the firm at its maximum-profit position? Write Yes or No in the column indicated.

b. What, if anything, is wrong with the firm's present position?

Answer by putting *one* of the numbers 1 through 5 in the right-hand column, according to the following code:

1. Present position is the correct one.
2. For present output, A-employment is too high, B-employment too low.
3. For present output, A-employment is too low, B-employment too high.
4. Reduce output by employing less of both A and B.
5. Increase output by employing more of both A and B.

Table 26-3

Case	MR from X Sale	P of A	P of B	At Maximum Profit?	Answer
1	$1	$2	$10	_____	_____
2	2	6	18	_____	_____
3	3	12	18	_____	_____
4	4	9	18	_____	_____
5	5	21	54	_____	_____
6	6	12	63	_____	_____

Case 1: No, 3; Case 2: Yes, 1; Case 3: No, 2; Case 4: No, 5; Case 5: No, 4; Case 6: No, 3

QUIZ: Multiple Choice

1. If inputs A, B, and C together produce product X, the marginal product of input A is defined as:
(1) the extra output of X resulting from the employment of 1 extra unit of A, inputs B and C being increased proportionately.
(2) the amount of input A required to produce 1 extra unit of X, amounts of inputs B and C being held constant.
(3) the extra output of X resulting from the employment of 1 extra unit of A, amounts of inputs B and C being held constant.
(4) the amount of input A required to produce 1 extra unit of X, amounts of inputs B and C being increased proportionately.
(5) none of the above.

2. When a firm has employed all its inputs in such quantities that the ratio of input price to input *MP* is the same for all inputs, this means that the firm:
(1) is operating in such a way that it has made the marginal revenue product of each input equal to its price.
(2) is operating at maximum-profit output and is producing that output at minimum cost.
(3) is operating at maximum-profit output, buy may or may not be producing that output at minimum cost.
(4) may or may not be operating at maximum-profit output, but is producing its present output at minimum cost.
(5) may or may not be at maximum-profit output and may or may not be producing its present output at minimum cost.

3. The production function will tell a firm:
(1) what it will cost to produce any given quantity of output.
(2) the maximum-profit level of output.
(3) the various combinations of inputs that should be used in order to produce any given quantity of output most efficiently, i.e., at least money cost.
(4) the various combinations of inputs that could be used in order to produce any given quantity of output.
(5) none of these.

4. According to John B. Clark's theory of income distribution, if 10 units of a particular input are employed, the price paid to each of those units should be equal to the value of:
(1) the average of the *MP*s of each of the 10 units.
(2) its own *MP*.
(3) the *MP* of the tenth unit.
(4) the *AP* (average product) of the 10 units.
(5) none of the above.

5. The text chapter cites some findings as to changes in the productivity of labor and capital in the American economy, and as to the payments made these two inputs. One statement among the following five is false as to those findings. Which one?
(1) The share of national income going to labor is approximately 3 times the share going to property.
(2) The productivity of both labor and capital has increased because of new technologies and skills.
(3) The growth in the capital stock has exceeded the growth in the labor force.
(4) The total return to capital has increased because of growth in its size, but the return per unit of capital has fallen.
(5) A small percentage increase in the labor input seems to increase output more than a corresponding increase in capital.

6. The marginal revenue product of input A, used to produce product X, is defined as:
(1) the marginal product *(MP)* of A multiplied by price of A.
(2) the average product *(AP)* of A multiplied by price of X.
(3) the *MP* of A multiplied by quantity of X.
(4) the *AP* of A multiplied by marginal revenue of X.
(5) none of the above.

7. A, B, and C are inputs employed to produce good X. If the quantity of A used is increased, we would ordinarily expect A's marginal product to:
(1) increase, in all circumstances.
(2) increase if the quantities of B and C are left unchanged, but not necessarily to increase if B and C quantities are increased in the same proportion.
(3) decrease, in all circumstances.
(4) decrease if the quantities of B and C are left unchanged, but not necessarily to decrease if B and C quantities are increased in the same proportion.
(5) decrease if B and C quantities are increased in the same proportion, increase if B and C quantities are left unchanged.

8. A firm operates in conditions of imperfect competition. The price of one of its inputs, A, is $10, and the marginal product of A is 5 units of finished product X. If this firm is at its maximum-profit output position, then the marginal revenue from sale of X must be:
(1) $1.
(2) $1.50.
(3) $2.
(4) $5.
(5) $10.

9. Input A's marginal revenue product, in question 8 circumstances, must be:
(1) $1.
(2) $1.50.
(3) $2.
(4) $5.
(5) $10.

10. A firm operates in conditions of *imperfect competition*. The price of one of its inputs, A, is $10, and the marginal product of A is 5 units of finished product X. The price of X is $2. The firm has satisfied the least-cost rule for input employment. This firm:
(1) cannot be at its maximum-profit position, and to reach that position should decrease its output.
(2) cannot be at its maximum-profit position, and to reach that position should increase its output.
(3) is at its profit-maximizing position.
(4) is at its maximum-profit position but should employ less of input A and more of other inputs.
(5) may or may not be at maximum-profit position—one essential item of information is lacking.

11. Given the data of question 10, if the marginal revenue product of input A must be one of the five following dollar amounts, that marginal revenue product is:
(1) $1.
(2) $2.
(3) $3.
(4) $4.
(5) $5.

12. Change the information of question 10 in one respect only: The firm operates in conditions of pure (or perfect) competition. Which alternative in question 10 would then be correct?
(1).
(2).
(3).
(4).
(5).

13. When a firm has satisfied the least-cost rule for input employment, then it:
(1) cannot be at its maximum-profit position.
(2) may or may not be at its maximum-profit position, but must

be operating at the particular output level which yields lowest-attainable average cost.

(3) must be at its maximum-profit position.

(4) may or may not be at its maximum-profit position, but will have equated the marginal product of each input with marginal revenue.

(5) may or may not be at its maximum-profit position—the information furnished is insufficient to be able to tell.

14. One of the following is not a correct statement of the relationship between the total product of an input or factor and the marginal product *(MP)* of that factor. Which one?

(1) Total product at any output level equals the sum of all *MPs* up to that level.

(2) *MP* at any output level multiplied by that output quantity equals total product.

(3) Graphically, the slope of the total product curve at any output level equals *MP* at that level.

(4) Graphically, the area under the *MP* curve for any quantity of the input equals the total product associated with that input quantity.

(5) *MP* is defined as the increment in total product resulting from a 1-unit increase in the factor (other factor quantities being held constant).

15. A firm employs such quantities of inputs A and B that the marginal product of A is 60 units, and that of B is 40 units. Prices of A and B are $4 and $2, respectively. Assuming A and B to be the only inputs involved, this firm is:

(1) producing its present output at minimum cost, but definitely is not earning maximum possible profit.

(2) not producing its present output at minimum cost, and is not earning maximum possible profit.

(3) producing its present output at minimum cost, but may or may not be earning maximum possible profit.

(4) not producing its present output at minimum cost, but nevertheless is earning maximum possible profit.

(5) possibly in any of the positions just described—information furnished is insufficient to tell.

16. In question 15, change the price of input A from $4 to $3, all other information remaining as before. Which alternative in that question is then correct?

(1).

(2).

(3).

(4).

(5).

17. In a simple one-product economy, such as the example used in the text chapter, the demand curve for labor is really:

(1) labor's total revenue curve.

(2) the residual left after payment of rent.

(3) labor's total product curve.

(4) labor's marginal physical product curve.

(5) none of the preceding.

18. In the one-product economy mentioned in question 17, with two factors or inputs, one fixed in supply and the other variable, it is correct to say that:

(1) each factor earns a return based on its average productivity.

(2) the return to the factor in variable supply is a "pure economic rent."

(3) the sum of the two factor shares equals total product.

(4) the area under the total product curve of the variable factor equals national product.

(5) none of the statements above is correct.

19. Which of the following statements accurately states a part of the economic experience of the United States since the turn of the last century?

(1) Wages have consistently accounted for 75 percent of GNP.

(2) A 1 percent increase in labor tends to increase GNP 3 times faster than a 1 percent increase in capital.

(3) Productivity has grown, on the average, at a rate between 1 percent and 2 percent per year.

(4) Capital accumulation has proceeded more rapidly than the labor force has expanded so that wages have increased another 1 percent to 2 percent per year on top of the productivity increase.

(5) All of the above.

APPENDIX:
Production Theory and Firm Decisions

This Appendix deals with the same topic which the chapter discusses: how to choose among input combinations so as to obtain that particular alternative which costs the least. If we limit the number of inputs to two (e.g., labor and land), the idea of the "production function" can be illustrated by a series of *equal-product lines*. On the same diagram, we may easily draw any number of *equal-cost lines*. Taken in combination, equal-product and equal-cost lines readily outline the whole business of cost minimization.

After studying the text Appendix to Chapter 26 and the preceding review material, you should be able to meet the following objectives.

LEARNING OBJECTIVES

1. Define (in terms of the graphical illustration of the production function) (*a*) an equal-cost line, (*b*) an equal-product line.

2. Explain why the minimum-cost point for any given output

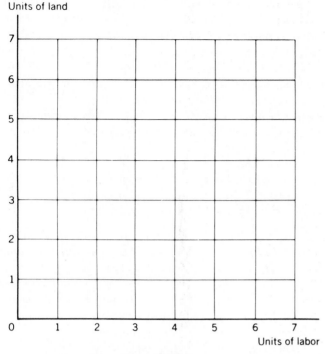

Units of land

Figure 26A-1

is found at the point of tangency between an equal-cost line and the equal-product line for that particular output.

3. Show how it is possible to develop a firm's total cost curve by reference to a series of these tangency points.

1. From Table 26A-1 in the text, show on Figure 26A-1 here the various land-labor combinations that will produce an output of 346 units. Join these points with a smooth curve. Repeat (also on Figure 26A-1) for outputs of 490 and 282. For identification, label the three curves $q = 282$, $q = 346$, and $q = 490$.

Each of the three resulting curves in Figure 26A-1 is an equal-product line. It is correctly described as follows (pick one):

(1) Each and every point on the curve stands for a different combination of labor and land quantities; these combinations all have the common property that they can be bought for the same total dollar outlay.

(2) Each and every point on the curve stands for a different quantity of output; these quantities all have the common property that they can be bought for the same dollar outlay on labor and land.

(3) Each and every point on the curve stands for a different combination of labor and land quantities; these combinations all have the common property that they can produce some given quantity of output.

2. a. Equal-cost lines may also be drawn on Figure 26A-1. Suppose labor costs $2 per unit, and the rental of a unit of land costs $3. Pick, at random, any dollar amount that would be sufficient to buy a few units of land and labor at these prices—say, $12. Now you must draw a line which shows all the possible combinations of land units and labor units which (given these prices) $12 would just buy.

If, for example, the entire $12 were spent on land, it would buy *(1 / 2 / 3 / 4 / 5 / 6)* units. So one point on the $12 equal-cost line would, on Figure 26A-1, be on the *(vertical / horizontal)* axis—the one measuring land units.

Another possibility would be to spend all the $12 on labor units. If so, it would buy *(1 / 2 / 3 / 4 / 5 / 6)* units; and another point on the $12 equal-cost line would be on the *(vertical / horizontal)* axis.

The full $12 equal-cost line is a straight line joining these two end points. (Draw this line on Figure 26A-1). Take *any* land-labor combination that $12 will just buy (given the two prices specified)—for example, 2 land units and 3 labor units. The point on the diagram corresponding to these two values falls on the line just drawn. That is, this line sums up all the possible land-labor combinations which $12 will just buy.

b. Which of the equal-product curves drawn earlier does this $12 equal-cost line barely touch at a point of tangency? *(the 282 line / the 346 line / the 490 line / none of them)*

---

a. 4; vertical; 6; horizontal   **b.** The 346 line

---

3. One point on this equal-cost line is 1½ labor and 3 land. The output which this combination would produce, according to Figure 26A-1 would be *(less than 282—probably about 250 / between 282 and 346—probably about 300 / between 346 and 490—probably about 420 / more than 490—probably about 530)*. In the given circumstances, and with the goal of minimizing cost, it *(would / would not)* be sensible to spend $12 to buy this particular combination of inputs.

---

between 282 and 346—probably about 300; would not

---

4. a. Which alternative in question 1 correctly describes the equal-cost line you have drawn? . . . . *(1 / 2 / 3)*

b. Remember that the cost figure of $12 was picked at random. There is nothing to indicate that it is the amount of cost the firm would actually incur, or should incur; it is just some figure convenient for illustration. (There are plenty of other cost figures that could be used, and plenty of other equal-cost lines that could be drawn; we'll come to this in a moment.) But suppose we assume arbitrarily that the firm did have just $12 to spend, and wanted to spend it to the best advantage. Expressing this $12 as an equal-cost line, what would the firm seek to do? (Pick one.)

(1) Move up or down that line seeking the highest-attainable equal-product curve the line encounters.

(2) Find the point on the equal-cost line which represents the lowest dollar outlay for the labor and land inputs.

(3) Move up or down that line seeking the lowest-attainable equal-product curve the line encounters.

c. Still assuming land and labor prices of $3 and $2, respectively, draw on Figure 26A-1 the equal-cost line signifying total expenditure of $6—another cost figure picked at random. Now note the properties of the two equal-cost lines They are *(parallel / not parallel)*. The line for $12 cost lies *(below and to the left / above and to the right)* of the $6 cost line.

Thus, given a fixed pair of input prices, the higher the cost figure selected, the *(higher and farther to the right / lower and farther to the left)* the corresponding equal-cost line will be. If the input prices are the same for any two or more such lines, then they will be parallel; i.e., they will have the same slope. Given such fixed input prices, the swapping terms between land and labor (the rate at which you could exchange a little less of one for a little more of the other) are fixed, regardless of the amount available to be spent.

---

a. (1)   **b.** (1)   **c.** parallel; above and to the right; higher and farther to the right

5.   Draw a third equal-cost line parallel to the previous two, but this time draw it so that it just touches your 282 equal-product curve. Drawing this line parallel to the other two implies that (pick one):
(1) The dollar expenditure on each of the inputs is the same.
(2) It touches the same equal-product curve as did the other two.
(3) The prices of land and labor are again $3 and $2.

The equal-cost line you have just drawn stands for a dollar outlay of approximately $*(5 / 10 / 12 / 15 / 18)*. (HINT: Use the same device employed in question **2a**. Go to either one of the line's two end points, where all the money is spent on one of the two inputs. How much does it cost to buy that particular quantity?)

---

(3); 10

6.   a. As you study these equal-product and equal-cost curves, it becomes evident that the points of tangency between them—the points where an equal-cost curve just touches an equal-product curve—are important. Why is that so? (More than one of the alternatives may be correct.)
(1) Because for any given level of output it indicates the lowest possible equal-cost line that can be reached—i.e., it indicates minimum cost for that output.
(2) Because for any given level of outlay on factors it indicates the highest possible equal-product line that can be reached—i.e., it indicates the maximum output that can be obtained for that dollar outlay.
(3) Because it indicates maximum-profit output level.
(4) Because it indicates the minimum possible level of output that can be attained for any given dollar outlay.

b. You now have drawn three equal-cost curves, and two of them are tangent to equal-product curves. (An equal-product curve indicating somewhere around 140 units of output, had you drawn it, would be tangent to the third equal-cost curve, that was identified with cost $6.)

Studying carefully these tangency points, you will notice that each such point defines a pair of numbers. For the two tangency points involved here, therefore, there are two pairs of numbers corresponding to cost and output. Which of the following accurately describes these pairs?
(1) Output 282, cost $12; output 346, cost about $10
(2) Output 282, cost about $10, output 346, cost $12
(3) Output 346, cost $12; output 490, cost $15
(4) Output 282, cost $12; output 490, cost $15

c. You must think through the significance of these pairs of figures. Given the specified prices of land and labor, an output of 282 units cannot be produced for less than $*(6 / 10 / 12 / 15 / 20)*, and an output of 346 units cannot be produced for less than $*(6 / 10 / 12 / 15 / 20)*. The significance of these two pairs of figures, then, is that (pick one):
(1) One of them is maximum-profit output.
(2) They are two points on the total cost curve.
(3) They discourage anyone from studying economics.

d. Thus, given the production function and input prices, the firm can develop its total cost curve—that is, the minimum cost of production, in the given circumstances of technology and input prices, for each and any level of output. (We have here developed the minimum cost for two levels of output. The cost for the many other possible levels would be obtained by consulting other tangency points between equal-cost and equal-product curves.)

Students often make the mistake of assuming that the firm first settles on its maximum-profit output level, and then finds the cost of producing that output. Not so: cost is one of the elements in profit computation, and you can't pick your maximum-profit output until you know the total cost of each and all possible outputs. So the sequence is to (pick one):
(1) First pick maximum-profit output, then find the minimum cost of producing that output.
(2) First establish the minimum cost of producing any and all outputs, then combine cost and revenue data to pick maximum-profit output.

---

a. (1) and (2)   **b.** (2)   **c.** 10; 12; (2)   **d.** (2)

---

7.   Any point where equal-cost and equal-product lines are tangent to one another (i.e., just touch, do not cross) is a minimum-cost point. At this point, they have the same slope. Using E (earth) and L as symbols for land and labor, respectively, then the slope of the equal-*(cost / product)* line is always—P_L/P_E. Slope of the equal-*(cost / product)* line is always—MP_L/MP_E. A point at which the two slope values are equal is always a minimum-cost point.

Do not be too disturbed if these matters of slope cause you difficulty. The essential point, which is not too hard to grasp, is that a least-cost point must be one where an equal-product line is just tangent to an equal-cost line. When we go on to express this tangency point in terms of the slopes of these two lines, we are just trying to state the nature of this least-cost position in more precise (and mathematical) form.

In particular, you may have trouble understanding why the slope of any equal-product line must be $-MP_L/MP_E$. Here is a rough explanation: slope is always the ratio of the two changes needed to move from one point on the line to another point very close by. Suppose land is reduced by 1 tiny unit and that labor must be increased by 2 tiny units to compensate (stay on the equal-product line). That would make the slope of the equal-product line $-\frac{1}{2}$.

When land was reduced, output fell—by an amount dictated by MP_E. The amount of labor needed to make up that output loss was dictated by MP_L. Since it took the addition of $2\,L$ units to compensate for the removal of $1\,E$ unit, labor's MP must be only one-half that of land. So slope can be measured by the ratio of MPs as well as by the ratio of input quantity changes.

---

cost; product

8.   a. If the conditions of production are such that for any given output level there is only one possible input combination, then (pick one):

(1) There is no production function.

(2) There are no equal-product curves.

(3) This is a case of fixed proportions.

Figure 26A-2 contrasts this case, the "fixed-coefficients case," with that assumed up to this point. Both curved and right-angled lines illustrate equal-product curves for some given output quantity. (You can of course draw as many of these equal-product curves as you wish, one for each possible output level. Figure 26A-2 shows only one illustrative curve for

each situation.) A curved line implies that *(different input combinations are / only one input combination is)* possible for the output in question. A right-angled line implies that substitution of one input for another (thus producing a different input combination) *(is / is not)* possible.

b. In Figure 26A-2, the inputs are A and B, and in the fixed-proportions case, the required "mix" has (arbitrarily) been made 3 to 2. If B inputs were to be increased from 2 to 3 (with A inputs at 3), this would mean *(a rightward / an upward)* movement away from the "corner" on the right-angled equal-product line. With B inputs increased to 3, total output would be *(increased / unchanged / decreased)*, for we would still be on the same equal-product line.

This means that in the fixed-proportions case, the marginal product *(MP)* of each input must be *(positive / zero / negative)*. The least-cost marginal product rule set out in the chapter cannot be applied in this case, but then there is no need for it, either; there is no longer any problem of choice. Given any set of positive input prices, there is only one possible cost figure associated with each possible output level, assuming the inputs are used to the best advantage.

There is considerable dispute over the extent to which the fixed-proportions case is found in reality. (In part, it may be a question of what you mean by "input" or "factor." If you speak in general terms of "labor" or "capital," substitution is certainly possible. The more specific you become about the *type* of labor or capital, though, the more likely fixed proportions seem to become.)

---

a. (3); different input combinations are; is not   **b.** an upward; unchanged; zero

---

9. Figure 26A-3 illustrates a production function involving the employment of inputs X and Y. The two curved lines are equal-product lines for outputs of 300 and 420 units. *AB* and *CD* are equal-cost lines. *AB* marks a cost outlay of $36.

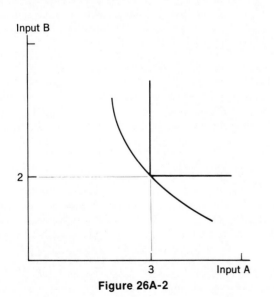

Figure 26A-2

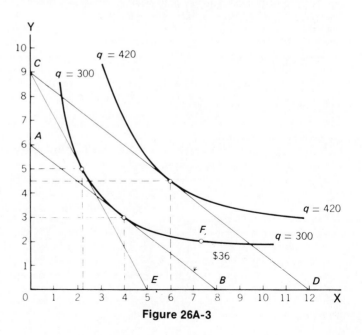

Figure 26A-3

a. From examination of *AB*, the price of X must be $(2.50 / 4.50 / 5.50 / 6.00 / 8.00), and the price of Y must be $(2.50 / 4.50 / 5.50 / 6.00 / 8.00). The minimum total cost of producing 300 units of output is $(36 / 45 / 54 / 100 / 160). Average cost is (5 / 10 / 12 / 15 / 60) cents.

The quantities of X and Y used to produce 300 units of output at minimum cost would be (2¼ of X, 5 of Y / 4 of X, 3 of Y / 5 of X, 9 of Y / 8 of X, 6 of Y).

Given the above prices of X and Y, equal-cost line *CD* must indicate a total outlay of $(36 / 45 / 54 / 100 / 160).

b. Suppose the firm is operating at point *F*. This (is / is not) a minimum-cost point. Operating at *F*, the quantity of output produced would be (100 / 300 / 360 / 400 / 420). Total cost of that output would be (approximately) $(36 / 45 / 54 / 100 / 160). Average cost would be (approximately) (5 / 10 / 12 / 15 / 60) cents. For this expenditure amount, the maximum output quantity that *could* be produced would be (approximately) (100 / 300 / 360 / 420 / 500).

c. Suppose equal-cost line *CD* (still signifying the same total cost amount as before) were to shift to position *CE*. This would indicate (a decrease / an increase) in the (price of X / price of Y / quantity of output produced).

Specifically, the price of (X / Y) would have (risen / fallen) to $(3.50 / 4.00 / 6.00 / 7.80 / 10.80).

This shift in *CD* (would / would not) require a comparable shift in line *AB*.

d. Given part **c**'s price change, the minumum cost of producing 300 units of output would become $(36 / 45 / 54 / 100 / 160). The X and Y quantities needed to produce that 300-unit output would be (2¼ of X, 5 of Y / 4 of X, 3 of Y / 5 of X, 9 of Y / 8 of X, 6 of Y).

The total (minimum) cost of producing 420 units would then be (approximately) $(36 / 45 / 54 / 86 / 150).

---

a. 4.50; 6.00; 36; 12; 4 of X, 3 of Y; 54   **b.** is not; 300; 45; 15; 360   **c.** an increase; price of X, X; risen; 10.80; would   **d.** 54; 2¼ of X, 5 of Y; 86

QUIZ: Multiple Choice

1. On an equal-product-curve diagram involving product X and inputs A and B, any equal-cost line indicates:
(1) different quantities of X, showing the increase in X that would entail an equal increase in cost.
(2) the various quantities of A and B that would be equally costly at various prices of either A or B.
(3) all the various combinations of A and B (in physical quantities of each) that could just be bought for some given money outlay.
(4) different combinations of A and B (in physical quantities of each), all having the common property that they could just produce some given quantity of X.
(5) none of the above, there being no such line on an equal-product-curve diagram.

2. Which alternative in question 1 correctly describes any equal-product line?
(1).
(2).
(3).
(4).
(5).

3. The equal-product-curve diagram illustrates:
(1) the total cost curve.
(2) the separate marginal products of the inputs involved.
(3) the point of maximum profit.
(4) the production function.
(5) different quantities of the product involved that would be equally profitable to produce.

4. The slope of an equal-cost line is a measure of:
(1) the ratio of the price of the factor on the vertical axis to the price of the factor on the horizontal axis.
(2) the ratio of the price of the factor on the horizontal axis to the price of the factor on the vertical axis.
(3) the various outputs which may be produced at a given cost.
(4) the total cost of producing a given output.
(5) the marginal productivity of one of the factors.

5. If factor or input proportions are fixed, this affects the value of the marginal product (*MP*) of these inputs as follows:
(1) *MP*s must be zero.
(2) *MP*s will be higher than if proportions were not fixed.
(3) It makes no difference—*MP*s will be the same as if proportions were not fixed.
(4) *MP*s of all inputs must be equal, but they will not be zero.
(5) None of the above is correct.

6. In Figure 26A-4, the line *GH* is an equal-cost line, with respect to employment of inputs of factors A and B. A shift of *GH* to a position such as *GJ* would be caused by:
(1) a fall in the price of input A.

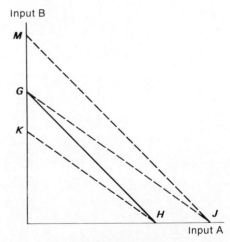

Figure 26A-4

(2) a rise in the price of both inputs.

(3) a fall in the price of input B.

(4) a rise in the price of input B.

(5) a fall in the price of both inputs.

7. Suppose, in Figure 26A-4, that the equal-cost line *GH* had instead shifted to position *MJ* (there being no change in the total cost figure assumed). Which alternative in question 6 would correctly explain this shift?

(1).

(2).

(3).

(4).

(5).

8. Suppose, in Figure 26A-4, that the equal-cost line *GH* had instead shifted to position *KH*. Which alternative in question 6 would correctly explain this shift?

(1).

(2).

(3).

(4).

(5).

9. When an equal-cost line such as *GH* in Figure 26A-4 is drawn, it is assumed with respect to that line that the following is given or held constant. The:

(1) total expenditure on input A.

(2) total expenditure on input B.

(3) quantity of the product produced.

(4) total expenditure on either A or B, but not both.

(5) total expenditure on the two inputs combined.

10. Had question 9 referred to an equal-product rather than an equal-cost line, which alternative in that question would then be correct?

(1).

(2).

(3).

(4).

(5).

11. Equal-product lines and equal-cost lines have this property in common: any point on either of these two lines is intended to mark some:

(1) quantity of finished-product output.

(2) figure of total revenue in dollars.

(3) combination of physical quantities of inputs.

(4) pair of input prices.

(5) figure of total cost in dollars.

12. When the difference between the "fixed-proportions" *(FP)* and "variable-proportions" *(VP)* cases (with respect to the use of inputs in production) is illustrated by means of equal-product curves or lines, it shows up as follows. The:

(1) *FP* case is a straight line, the *VP* case is a right angle.

(2) *FP* case is a right angle, the *VP* case is a curved line.

(3) *FP* case is a curved line, the *VP* case is a right angle.

(4) *FP* case is a right angle, the *VP* case is a straight line.

(5) *FP* case is a curved line, the *VP* case is a straight line.

CHAPTER 27

PRICING OF FACTOR INPUTS: RENTS ON LAND AND OTHER RESOURCES

Chapter 26 provided some insight into the demand side of an arbitrary input market; it is a derived demand based upon cost minimization by a profit-maximizing firm and the marginal-productivity theory of income distribution. With that "mouthful" behind us, it is now time to consider the supply side of the same type of market. Chapter 27 begins that consideration, with particular emphasis on the rents earned by land and other natural resources of fixed supply. The concepts developed in this application are especially important when one considers what happens when these rents are not charged: for example, the indiscriminate pollution of our air and water, the exploitation of forests and fisheries to the point of exhaustion, the congestion that develops on certain highways on weekends or around rush hour, etc.

Having completed your work in this chapter, you should have accomplished the following learning objectives.

LEARNING OBJECTIVES

1. Define (*a*) derived demand, (*b*) derived market demand, and (*c*) economic rent.

2. Explain the special result obtained in the economic-rent case, when there is a decrease or increase in demand for the input or factor in question. Show the application of this result with respect to taxation policy.

3. Show how from one perspective the payment made to an economic-rent input must be considered as a legitimate cost of production, whereas from another perspective it need not be so considered.

4. Discuss the general reasoning behind Henry George's single-tax movement.

5. Understand and explain both the generalization of the "George" taxing idea into the "Ramsey" efficiency taxes, and the equity-efficiency tradeoff incumbent in their definition.

1. The market demand for any input is the (*vertical / geometric / horizontal*) sum across all firms interested in employing that input of their individual demand schedules. More specifically, suppose that there were only three firms interested in employing some input X, and let their demands be 3, 4, and 5 units, respectively, given a price of \$3 per unit. Market demand for \$3 would, in this case, be _____ units. At a price of \$4, though, we would expect, in general, that the quantity demanded by the market would (*increase / fall*) because the individual demands of the three firms would probably (*rise / fall*).

---

horizontal; 12; fall; fall

---

2. a. Consider Figures 27-1 and 27-2. The one which illustrates the perfectly price-inelastic situation is (*27-1 / 27-2*). A supply curve such as Figure 27-1 implies that if price should drop, say, from p_1 to p_0, the quantity offered for sale would (*increase / decrease / remain the same as before*). Sketch on Figure 27-1 a demand curve passing through the point on SS corresponding to p_1. Then sketch another to indicate a leftward shift of demand reducing the equilibrium price to p_0.

b. The significance of economic rent is best understood by considering an input supply curve having the more customary shape, as in Figure 27-2. Here, if price drops from p_1 to p_0, quantity offered for sale will (*increase / decrease / remain the same as before*). Sketch two corresponding demand curves on Figure 27-2.

c. Implicit in Figure 27-2 is an essential question: Why does a price drop cause part (or all, if the drop is large enough) of supply to be withdrawn? What happens to the quantity of input services AB if they disappear from supply offered?

To answer this question, we need to spell out more carefully the nature of the supply curve we are discussing. Suppose it is specifically the land supply offered for rental to farmers who want it for growing corn.

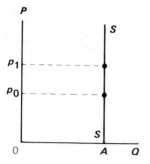

Figure 27-1

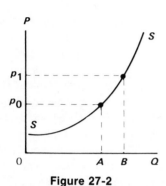

Figure 27-2

In these circumstances, a fall in price from p_1 to p_0 will persuade the landowners to rent part (or all) of their land to other demanders (for example, farmers who want land for barley growing). This would explain why, in the corn market, there is the reduction in supply quantity AB, in Figure 27-2. If the demand of corn growers for land decreases, thereby reducing the land-rental price from p_1 to p_0, the AB quantity is transferred to farmers who want more land for barley production. Note carefully that this assumes the land in question has at least one alternative use; i.e., it can be used for barley production as well as for corn production.

If, however, the land has no alternative use, so that it is literally useful only in corn production, then any decrease in demand for land by corn growers will reduce only its price. The quantity of land supplied will *(increase / decrease / remain the same as before)*, so that Figure 27-1 is the relevant illustration. The landowners would be not happy over the price reduction but they could not do anything about it.

---

a. 27-1; remain the same as before   **b.** decrease   **c.** remain the same as before

---

It is now possible to present a precise definition of "economic rent":

▶Economic rent, strictly interpreted, is the return paid to an input which has just one single occupation; it is useful in production of one single commodity only. Because its employment is so limited, the input's supply curve with respect to that occupation is perfectly price-inelastic.

The problem here is, of course, the precise meaning of "one single occupation." Land suited for corn production could almost certainly be used for other grain crops. The idea of "economic rent" was developed by British economists in the nineteenth century. (One of them was David Ricardo, and the reason for his interest in this question is more clearly indicated in question **3c** below.) When these economists spoke of "corn production," they really meant "grain production," or "food production"; i.e., they interpreted the words "occupation" and "commodity" rather broadly. And we can speak of Iowa farmland in the same broad sense: if we say it has only a single occupation, we mean that its effective usefulness is pretty much limited to grain or food production, so that the only effective demand of significance is that of farmers who want to use it for this purpose.

Nevertheless, this land is not a "single-commodity" input unless the word "commodity" is used loosely. Thus the term "rent" is often used with reference to any input whose total supply is perfectly inelastic with respect to price even though it may have several occupations. You will notice that this is how the text chapter uses the term, even though it also discusses "single-occupation" rent cases.

3. a. When an input has only a single employment, the supply curve facing demanders who want to use it in that employment will be perfectly inelastic with respect to price because the suppliers have no alternative to which to turn should price be low. They must supply the same quantity, if necessary, even at a very low price. If the market for this input is competitive, *will* the price be low? (Pick one):
(1) Yes, if competitive forces are operating.
(2) It is impossible to tell. Price will be set where the demand curve crosses this perfectly inelastic supply curve; this may be a very high price, if the demand for this limited supply is sufficiently great.

b. The single-occupation case illustrates how fallacious a "cost of production" theory of price can be. Suppose that the input is cows, and that cows are useful only for giving milk. Demand for milk has driven up its price to a high level. The resulting "derived demand" for cows has driven up *their* price to a high level. Here, it is incorrect to say that (pick one):
(1) The price of cows is high because the price of milk is high.
(2) The price of milk is high because the price of cows is high.

In short, you *(can / cannot)* in this case give a meaningful explanation of the price of milk in terms of the costs involved in producing milk.

c. The cows-and-milk example illustrates the more general issue which produced the term "economic rent." It arose from David Ricardo's exploration of changes in the prices of food and of land in early-nineteenth-century England. As in the cows-and-milk instance, a higher demand for food had driven up the rental price of land. Analytically, the proper conclusion was simple: the increased price of food cannot be blamed on the higher rental price of land. Land's price has risen because the demand for food has increased.

Remember that this conclusion holds only for a single-occupation, perfectly inelastic supply input. Suppose that land has many uses other than food production. Demand in some of those other uses has driven up the rental price of land. Food producers must now pay a higher price for that part of the total land supply which they use, even though this price rise has nothing to do with the demand for food. Here, the higher price of food *(could / could not)* legitimately be blamed on the higher cost of inputs required to produce food.

***

a. (2) **b.** (2); cannot **c.** could

4. Economists' interest in the case of the single-occupation, perfectly inelastic supply input led them to ask another question: Does the payment made to such an input constitute a cost of production?

At first, this may seem an odd question. Each separate user of that input must pay the money price, high or low, for the quantity of that input which he or she buys, and to that buyer his or her outlay most certainly *is* a cost of production.

Money cost is supposed to be only the surface manifestation of real cost to society. The text's Chapter 2 pointed out that you can look at real cost in this way: the cost of getting more guns is the sacrifice of butter which (when resources are fully employed) is necessary if more guns are to be produced. The way to get more guns is to switch some of those inputs which are useful in either occupation from butter production to gun production. This is the notion of "opportunity cost."

Economic-rent inputs, by definition, are those which have only one occupation and so cannot be switched. By the real-cost definition just outlined, their employment *(still entails / does not entail)* a cost to society. When such inputs are put to work, their employment does not entail any sacrifice of an alternative commodity.

From the perspective of a single farmer, one among many such farmers, the supply curve of single-occupation land will not appear perfectly inelastic. If the rental market for land is a competitive one, each farmer sees only the market price of land, at which price he or she can rent as much or as little as he or she wishes. To the farmer, land supply appears *(perfectly elastic / somewhat elastic / perfectly inelastic)* with respect to price.

Consider now the case of an input which happens to have several widely differing possible occupations, and whose total supply curve (the supply quantity offered to all buyers taken together) is perfectly price-inelastic. To any one class of buyers, the supply curve of this input will not be perfectly inelastic.

To illustrate: suppose the input in question can be used for making any of goods X, Y, or Z, so that there are three classes of buyers. For some reason, the demand for this input on the part of those who use it for making X declines sharply. Because this demand is part of total demand, the input's price should *(fall / rise)*. Consequently, the producers who use it for making Y and Z will be disposed to buy *(more / less)*. That is, the input's total fixed supply will be redistributed: more goes toward Y and Z,

and less toward X. Thus, to X producers, supply *(will / will not)* be perfectly inelastic, for when their demand decreases (and the input's price consequently falls), the quantity supplied to them decreases.

***

does not entail; perfectly elastic; fall; more; will not

5. Henry George's *single-tax* movement drew on the idea of perfectly inelastic supply. In his book *Progress and Poverty*, George argued that the main explanation for continuing poverty in the midst of economic progress was high land rent. Landlords were exacting large incomes from land which they (or their ancestors) had been shrewd (or lucky) enough to acquire before the present need for such land had evolved. Land's price was high because (a) the demand for it was now exceedingly high, and (b) supply, being fixed, had not expanded to match the increase in demand. Hence the single-tax movement—the single tax proposed being, of course, a tax on land. (Remember that this is not strictly a "pure economic rent" case. George was talking about land and land rental; but the land he discussed was not necessarily single-occupation land.)

Regardless of the merits or demerits of Henry George's single-tax movement, instances of perfectly inelastic input supply—if they can be found—have interesting implications for taxation policy.

As illustration, consider the case in which supply is not perfectly price-inelastic. Figure 27-2 for example, might illustrate the fact that labor will work longer hours only if it is offered a higher price (for all hours supplied) for so doing. If an increased demand for labor were to push the price up from p_0 to p_1, that higher price would accomplish two things: (a) It would coax out the additional quantity supplied AB, which would not have been forthcoming at price p_0; and (b) it would ration out the total available supply OB to those willing to pay the higher price.

Suppose now, with price at p_1, a tax were levied on the sale of this input. Its effect would be to reduce the after-tax return received by labor to, say p_0. As a consequence, market quantity supplied would be reduced from OB to OA. The tax would have the unfortunate effect of "distorting production incentives"; i.e., people would decide to supply somewhat less labor in order to escape paying part of the tax.

By contrast, consider the case of perfectly inelastic supply—Figure 27-1. Here, a price rise from p_0 to p_1 (brought about by an increase in demand) would accomplish *(neither / only one / both)* of the results in the Figure 27-2 case. It *(would / would not)* coax out an additional supply quantity. It *(would / would not)* ration the available supply.

Moreover, if a tax were to be levied on the sale of this input, results would be different in the inelastic-supply case. The important thing is that if such a tax were to reduce the after-tax return of suppliers from p_1 to p_0, this would produce *(a large / a small / no)* reduction in supply quantity. Imposition of this tax *(would / would not)* cause any reduction in total real output, since there would be no reduction in quantity of work hours supplied.

only one; would not; would; no; would not

6. Even if you favor taxing economic-rent inelastic-supply cases because taxation does not reduce supply quantity, you still must find them. They are not so widely available as might be thought; and mistakes can be made in picking them out.

a. This is true even of land. Ricardo spoke of land as "the original and inexhaustible gift of nature." But there are initial costs of clearing nature's gift for cultivation; there are continuing costs of keeping it drained and fertilized. The greater the derived demand for land, the greater the incentive to bring into cultivation land with higher maintenance costs. To the extent that this is true, there will be for each piece of land a critical rent below which it will ultimately disappear from cultivation. This makes the supply curve for land *(completely / less than completely)* inelastic in the long run.

b. Some highly specialized machinery has been built for rental to manufacturers. The costs of servicing this machinery and keeping it in good running order for rental are negligible. Will the supply curve (short-run) for this machinery be perfectly inelastic, and ought the return received by its owners to be termed "economic rent," from the information thus far supplied? .... (Yes / No)

Suppose, however, that the equilibrium price established is below the level needed to cover replacement costs plus interest on the money tied up in this machinery. This indicates that the long-run supply curve *(will / will not)* be perfectly price-inelastic. Consequently, we *(ought not / should still)* designate

the income received by suppliers of this input as "economic rent."

a. less than completely   **b.** Yes; will not; ought not

7. Modern tax theory has generalized the notion of taxing inputs whose supply is perfectly inelastic into what are called "Ramsey taxes." The observation behind this generalization is that taxes are more efficient in (a) raising revenue and (b) minimizing the loss in consumer surplus if they are imposed on goods with either (relatively) inelastic demand or inelastic supply. Figure 27-3 will help you explore the rationale behind this result.

In panel (a), a demand curve *DD* is drawn though point *E* to indicate, given supply curve *SS*, an equilibrium price and quantity pair of (price = $5; quantity = 9). Demand curve *D'D'* had also been drawn to reflect the effect of a $2 per unit tax on the sale of good X. Since $5 is required by suppliers to produce X, the new, after-tax equilibrium quantity would be _____ units for which people would spend $_____ per unit and suppliers would receive $_____ per unit. Before the tax, consumer surplus was $_____; after the tax it will have *(risen / fallen)* to $_____, a reduction of _____ percent. Tax revenue would, moreover, equal $_____.

Panel (b) repeats the process for a demand curve *DD* that, through the (price = $5; quantity = 9) equilibrium, is *(more elastic / more inelastic)*. *D'D'* again represents effective demand after a $2 per unit tax has been imposed. The after-tax equilibrium would, in this second case, be _____ units selling at a price of $_____ of which $_____ per unit would

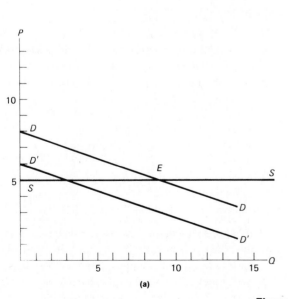

(a)

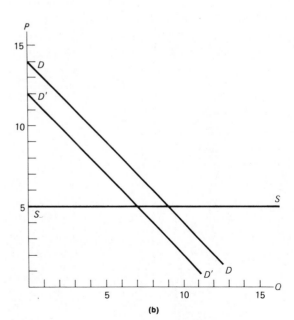

(b)

Figure 27-3

show up in the hands of the supplier. Consumer surplus would, in this case, (*rise / fall*) from $_____ before the tax to $_____ after the tax—a reduction of _____ percent; total revenue generated by the tax would, meanwhile, equal $_____ .

3; 7; 5; 13.5; fallen; 1.5; 89; 6; more inelastic; 7; 7; 5; fall; 40.50; 24.50; 40; 14

8. The inability of an economy to charge rents for the utilization of resources of fixed supply produces an (*over / under*) utilization of those resources. Three reasons were advanced by the text to explain this inability. They were:

a. _____

b. _____

c. _____

Now give an example from reality that illustrates each reason:

(1) _____

(2) _____

(3) _____

---

over; **a.** no ownership   **b.** owner does not charge for use   **c.** monitoring costs excessive   (1) grazing on common land   (2) hazardous dumping   (3) carbon emissions

9. Consult Figure 27-4; *DD* there represents a demand curve for rental housing; *SS* represents a supply curve. The equilibrium rent for housing would, in this case, be $_____ . Suppose that the rent control authorities have determined that rents should be lowered and have imposed a ceiling equal to 80

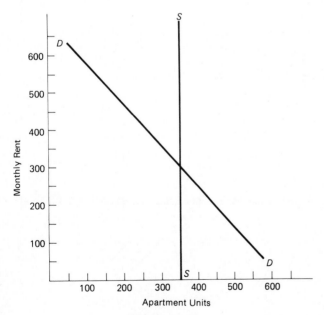

Figure 27-4

percent of the equilibrium price. The quantity of rental housing provided would, in the short run illustrated in Figure 27-4, (*increase / remain the same / decline*) while the quantity demanded would (*increase / remain the same / decline*). Additionally, the ceiling would (*provide incentives for / remove all incentives for*) landlords to increase the supply.

Now consider a 20 percent tax on rents collected by landlords. This policy would produce (*the same / a different*) equilibrium in the rental market in terms of quantity supplied in the short run. The rent paid would, meanwhile, (*climb / remain the same / fall*), and a shortage of rental housing (*would / would not*) materialize.

300; remain the same; increase; remove all incentives for; the same; remain the same; would not

QUIZ: Multiple Choice

1. One characteristic of an economic-rent situation is that:
(1) price will increase with an increase in demand but will not decrease with a decrease in demand.
(2) total quantity supplied will increase with an increase in demand but will not decrease with a decrease in demand.
(3) total quantity supplied will not change if price falls.
(4) price will not change with an increase in supply.
(5) none of the above.

2. If land is fixed in total supply but has many alternative uses (one of which is tobacco production), then normally a 50 percent tax on rental price of any land used for tobacco production will result in:
(1) a 50 percent increase in the rent which tobacco producers must pay.
(2) a 50 percent decrease in the rent paid by users of such land.
(3) a 50 percent decrease in the rent received (net) by owners of such land.
(4) no change in amount of rent paid or received.
(5) none of these consequences.

3. If supply is perfectly inelastic with respect to price, and if there should be a decrease in total demand (a leftward demand curve shift), then:
(1) quantity supplied will not be reduced, thus causing price to fall more than it otherwise would.
(2) quantity supplied will not be reduced, thus causing price to fall less than it otherwise would.
(3) quantity supplied will fall, thus causing price to fall more than it would otherwise.
(4) quantity supplied will fall, thus causing price to fall less than it otherwise would.
(5) none of these results will occur.

4. If a productive input has just one single employment (i.e., there is only one commodity it can help to produce), then (according to the text chapter), the price paid to it:
(1) will tend to fall below the normal competitive level, because of the absence of competitive bidding.

(2) will be a cost to each of its separate users, but not a cost to the whole community or society.

(3) should not be counted as a cost by each of its separate users, although it will still be a cost to the whole community or society.

(4) will be a cost both ot its separate users and to the whole community or society.

(5) will not be a cost either to its separate users or to the whole community.

5.   It would be correct to say that economic rent is not a cost of production, in the following sense:

(1) It is not a payment to a factor of production that actually makes a contribution to the output of finished goods.

(2) The suppliers of the input in question can receive the same price for employment in occupation A as they can in occupation B.

(3) The rent payment in question is really a payment for buildings or improvements to the land, not for the use of the land itself.

(4) If, when this factor is used for the production of good A, this employment does not entail any sacrifice of any other good B.

(5) Competition among the suppliers will continually tend to push the price of this factor toward zero.

6.   Henry George's "single-tax" explanation of the prevalence of proverty:

(1) assumes that the land-supply curve is perfectly or almost perfectly inelastic with respect to price.

(2) finds the explanation of poverty in the multiplicity of taxes imposed on the poor by the capitalist class through the agency of government.

(3) is essentially the same as the Marxist analysis of the exploitation of workers by capitalist manufacturers.

(4) is based on the assumption that supply curves for many scarce inputs are "backward-bending," so that increased quantities of these inputs will be supplied if prices are lowered, not raised.

(5) is not correctly described by any of these statements.

7.   A tax levied on a factor of production:

(1) must always be borne entirely by the suppliers of that factor.

(2) will be shifted forward to buyers if the factor supply is perfectly inelastic.

(3) will be partly shifted forward to buyers if supply is perfectly elastic.

(4) must always be borne by the buyers of that factor.

(5) will be shifted forward to buyers the more any price fall reduces quantity supplied.

8.   If the return to a productive input is classed as one of economic rent, this means that the supply curve of that input which confronts any one of its demanders must be:

(1) perfectly inelastic.

(2) perfectly elastic.

(3) nonexistent.

(4) highly inelastic.

(5) not necessarily any one of the above.

9.   The verdict of the text chapter on rent payments is (in part) that:

(1) unless competitive rent payments are made, society's resources cannot be allocated into employment properly.

(2) the more elastic with respect to price an input's supply is, the more its rental payments should be taxed.

(3) it still is correct, broadly speaking, to say that rent does not enter into the cost of production.

(4) the allocation of resources tends to be distorted by the fact that certain input supplies are inelastic with respect to price.

(5) the more inelastic with respect to price an input's supply is, the more its rental payments should be taxed.

10.   If we say that "the supply curve of input A is perfectly inelastic with respect to price," we are most likely to mean, if speaking correctly, that its supply curve will be perfectly inelastic when set against the demand curve of:

(1) any single user only.

(2) any single class of users (i.e., any single industry) only.

(3) all its users combined only.

(4) any single user or any single class of users, but not when set against the demand curve of all users combined.

(5) any of the above—i.e., it will be perfectly price-inelastic no matter what demand curve it is set against.

11.   Ramsey taxes:

(1) are higher the more inelastic demand happens to be.

(2) frequently run into the notion of equity because necessities tend to be inelastically demanded.

(3) are lower the more elastic supply happens to be.

(4) are computed to minimize the loss in consumer surplus and maximize tax revenue.

(5) all of the above.

12.   The "tragedy of the commons" is, among the following list of examples, best illustrated by:

(1) the proliferation of fast-food hamburger joints.

(2) the overfishing of the Georges banks.

(3) the development of a shopping center on the town commons.

(4) the poisoning of Harvard students on the "Commons."

(5) none of the above.

CHAPTER 28
WAGES, SALARIES, AND THE LABOR MARKET

Wages are, perhaps, the most important prices determined by the operation of a mixed economy. Total payments for wages and salaries account for nearly 80 percent of the national income of the United States, and that percentage is typical of developed, Western economies. Despite their importance, though, wages are just prices—prices determined by the interaction of supply-and-demand schedules in very special markets, to be sure, but simple prices nonetheless. It is the variation in economic structure across these markets that piques an economist's interest.

Chapter 28 introduces you to the scope of this variability. Why? To explain why real wages are so much higher in the United States and Western Europe than they are elsewhere around the world. To explain why wages and salaries differ so much across the populations of individual countries. And to explain the contribution of discrimination to that intracountry variation.

Completing your work on this chapter, therefore, you will have not only gained some insight into these fundamental issues of wage determination, but also achieved the following more specific objectives.

LEARNING OBJECTIVES

1. Use the simple, homogeneous labor model to explain why wages can differ so dramatically from one country to another.

2. Explain the determinants of both the supply of labor and the demand for labor, noting in particular the possibility that the supply-of-labor curve might actually bend backward toward lower supplies as the real wage climbs.

3. Understand the various economic reasons why wages can differ so dramatically from one type of occupation to another: compensating wage differentials, quality differences, elements of economic rent, the existence of noncompeting groups, and discrimination.

4. Relate the scope of discrimination in the United States and the empirical evidence of its manifestation in wage differentials.

5. Relate and evaluate the "Iron Law of Wages" advanced by Malthus and Marx and the "lump-of-labor" fallacy frequently embraced by labor unions.

Although wages vary across the populations of most countries, the general wage level in the United States has risen markedly over the past century. This growth in real purchasing power has been supported by increases in the real wages paid to virtually every category of labor. Question 1 refreshes your memory about the meaning of the difference between the real wage and the nominal wage.

1. a. Real wages are (pick one):
(1) the same thing as money wages
(2) money wages after allowing for tax and other witholdings deducted from such wages
(3) money wages in relation to the consumer price level—i.e., what money wages can buy in real goods

b. Between 1960 and 1980 in a certain country, (1) money wages tripled and (2) the consumer-good price index rose from 400 to 600. It follows that real wages (*did not rise at all / rose by a factor of 1½ / doubled / tripled / more than tripled*).

c. We say that, other things equal, an increase in population would lower wage rates because of the diminishing-returns law. We mean by this that an increase in the labor force would lower wage rates (pick one):
(1) Even if there were a corresponding increase in the available supply of other inputs such as raw materials and capital goods
(2) With the supply of other inputs held constant

---

a. (3) **b.** doubled **c.** (2)

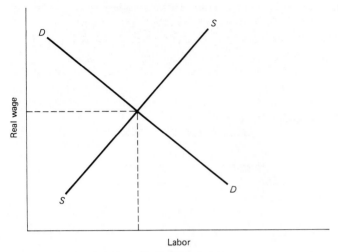

Figure 28-1

2. Figure 28-1 in the text provides some insight into why real wages in North America are so much higher than they are in South America. From the units on the graph, in fact, it would appear that the real wage in North America is *(2 / 2½ / 3)* times larger. One key to this difference is that *(the supply-of-labor curve is so much higher in the South America panel / the demand-for-labor curve is so much higher in the North America panel / the demand-for-labor curve is so much higher in the South America panel)*. Inasmuch as the demand-for-labor curve is a *(potential / derived / product)* demand curve, the text gives three reasons why it should be so positioned in panel **(a)** relative to panel **(b)**. List them below:

a. _____

b. _____

c. _____

Each of these has the effect of raising the productivity of North American labor and thus the wage that employers are willing to pay. The demand curve is, nonetheless, downward-sloping because *(the marginal product of labor declines as employment increases / the price of output declines as output and thus employment increases)*.

2½; the demand-for-labor curve is so much higher in the North American panel; derived **a.** More resources **b.** More advanced technology **c.** More skilled labor force (both of the answers given contribute to the downward slope of the derived demand curve)

3. The supply of labor has four general dimensions. List them below:

a. _____

b. _____

c. _____

d. _____

Based upon the supply and demand curves depicted in Figure 28-1, indicate in the spaces provided the likely effect on the real wage of each of the following economic adjustments. Denote an increase by (+), a reduction by (−), and no chnage by (0).

(1) An increase in the working population ...... (_____)

(2) A move toward shorter workweeks .... (_____)

(3) An increase in labor-force participation by women ......

.... (_____)

(4) Passage of stronger child labor laws .... (_____)

(5) Restriction of certain types of people from

employment .... (_____)

(6) A large wave of immigrants who all want to

work .... (_____)

Buried in your answers to these wage questions are the answers to questions like: *(a)* Why do labor unions push for shorter workweeks? *(b)* Why does labor fear opening U.S. borders to anyone who wants to come? *(c)* Why do some drag their feet in the fight against discrimination on personal economic grounds?

---

a. population **b.** labor-force participation **c.** hours worked per week **d.** quality of work force (1) (−); (2) (+); (3) (−); (4) (+); (5) (+); (6) (−)

4. a. The hourly wage offered to you rises. You have some freedom of choice as to the number of hours you may work per day or week. In these circumstances, you could, if you wished, work (pick one or more):

(1) the same number of hours and earn more daily or weekly income

(2) more hours and earn more income

(3) fewer hours and earn the same income

(4) fewer hours and earn more income

b. The fact that you may choose any one of the four alternatives of part **a** indicates the opposite and conflicting pulls of *substitution effect* and *income effect*.

When you are offered a higher wage for each hour worked, you are then sacrificing more money income than before for each hour you do *not* work. The higher hourly wage is an inducement to work *(more / fewer)* hours per day or week because "leisure (not working) has become more expensive." This by itself is the substitution effect. It inclines a worker to give up some *(working hours in favor of leisure / leisure hours in favor of work)*.

c. However, leisure time is (for most people) a desirable thing: as real incomes rise, they want more of it. The offer of a higher hourly wage makes possible more leisure *(with / without)* the sacrifice of any of the commodities the worker is now buying. The pull of the income effect is toward *fewer* working hours and *more* leisure.

d. For example, suppose that at $4 hourly, you decide to work 40 hours weekly and to earn $160. At $6 hourly, you would choose to earn $210—that is, work *(35 / 40 / 45)* hours weekly. Here, the *(substitution / income)* effect has dominated.

---

a. All four are possible   **b.** more; leisure hours in favor of work   **c.** without   **d.** 35; income

---

5.   The term "economic rent" is not usually applied with respect to labor. But in instances like Babe Ruth in the good old days of baseball and "Dr. J" in the good old days of the Philadelphia 76ers, it applies. Babe Ruth was paid the fantastic sum (for the 1920s) of $80,000 annually for playing baseball. Had diminished competition among baseball-club owners forced him to do so, he would probably have played for $10,000 annually. His unique skill seems to have been in baseball alone, so it is unlikely that any alternative employment open to him would have paid anything like $80,000. (If the Babe played today, he could earn substantial supplementary income by extolling the joys of shaving cream or hair tonic on TV commercials, but that fact does not alter the reasoning. He would be paid this *only because of* his status as a baseball player earning a king's ransom every year.)

This means that Babe Ruth's labor supply curve to baseball clubs would be perfectly inelastic with respect to wage or salary prices (pick one):

(1) From $80,000 annually to zero annually.

(2) From $80,000 annually to some figure such as $8000 annually.

(3) Only at $80,000 annually; it would be less than perfectly elastic at *any* lower figure.

---

(2)

---

6.   There are four panels in Figure 28-2; one each for the four parts to this question listed below. In each part, draw a new supply and/or demand curve on the corresponding panel to represent the effect of the change indicated, and predict the direction that the change will push the real wage and employment. For example, if one of the parts asked you to consider an increase in the supply of labor, then you would draw a new supply curve to the right of the existing one and predict that wages would fall (−) and employment would climb (+). Record your predictions on the table provided below.

(1) The job in question is more onerous than usual, and people demand compensation for its additional burdens.

(2) The job is really very specialized, and only one person can accomplish the task that it requires.

(3) Education and training have improved the quality of the labor employed.

(4) The job market is suddenly cut in half because of noncompeting discrimination.

Part	Effect on Employment	Effect of Wages
A	_____	_____
B	_____	_____
C	_____	_____
D	_____	_____

A: draw new supply curve above and left of SS; (−); (+)   B: draw new supply curve vertical at L = 1; (−); (+)   C: draw new demand curve above and right of DD; (+); (+)   D: same answer, though probably exaggerated, as part A

---

7.   The *iron law of wages* idea evolved in the arguments of both Thomas Robert Malthus and Karl Marx (although for quite different reasons). The essence of the iron-law idea is that wages tend to be pushed to the *(competitive / minimum-subsistence / marginal-product)* level. (Malthus' argument rested on the belief that population would increase until this level was reached; Marx's, on the belief that this outcome was part of capitalist exploitation of the labor force.)

The text expresses *(agreement / qualified agreement / disagreement)* with the idea. Figure 28-3 shows why. With the wage set at $w°$, unemployment *(would / would not)* exist, and the operation of the labor market might eventually push the wage *(up / down)* to equilibrium at $(w° / w_E / w_M)$. There would, however, be no way for the market to push the wage down to the subsistence level because, while employers would love to see that happen, there would be *(excess supply / excess demand)* for labor at w_M that would push the wage back up.

---

minimum-subsistence; disagreement; would; down; w_E; excess demand

---

8.   Consult Figure 28-4. It shows two labor markets separated by discrimination. Demand curves in both are indicated with *DD* notation, and supply curves are vertical at 10 and 5, respec-

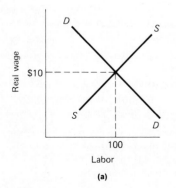

(a)

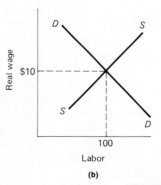

(b)

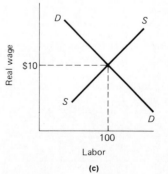

(c)

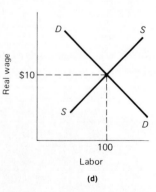

(d)

Figure 28-2

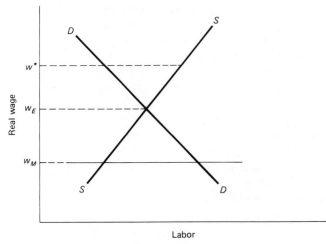

Figure 28-3

tively. If that discrimination were to lapse, then the demand curve in panel **(a)** would apply to everyone. The result would be *(an increase / a reduction)* in the wage paid to those initially

alone in market A from \$_____ to \$_____. This change would be caused by *(diminishing marginal productivity / diminishing labor utility / increasing productivity)*. At the same time, those who were initially confined to market B would see

their wage *(climb / fall)* from \$_____ to \$_____, a change that can be attributed to *(diminishing marginal productivity / increased productivity / increased labor utility)*.

If the derived demand curve in market A were extremely inelastic, how would your answers to the qualitative parts of the above paragraph change?

_____

_____

_____.

a reduction; 10; 8; diminishing marginal productivity; climb; 5; 8; increased productivity; If the curve $D_H D_H$ were sufficiently inelastic [sufficiently vertical through (10, \$10)], then the addition of 5 workers from market B could lower the wage below \$5. All 5 would not move, if that were the case, and the equilibrium wage in both markets would still exceed \$5

Notice, in passing, that the analysis of question 8 applies to all types of discrimination—discrimination caused by geography (wage differentials across countries), discrimination by sex or race, discrimination caused by noncompeting groupings within the larger labor market.

9. Referring finally to Table 28-4 in the text, record the earnings ratios of the groups indicated below to whites and/or males:

a. Cuban-American .... _____

b. Chinese-American .... _____

c. Black .... _____

d. Women .... _____

The point of this question is not that you remember these numbers, but that you are aware of the dimension of discrimination that still exists despite the progress that Richard Freeman has documented.

a. 95% **b.** 82% **c.** 76% **d.** 58%

QUIZ: Multiple Choice

1. The concept of "noncompeting groups in the labor market" is considered useful in seeking to explain:
(1) structural unemployment.
(2) wage differentials among different categories of labor.

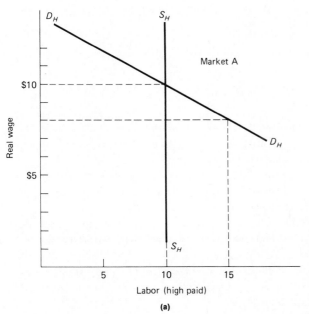

(a)

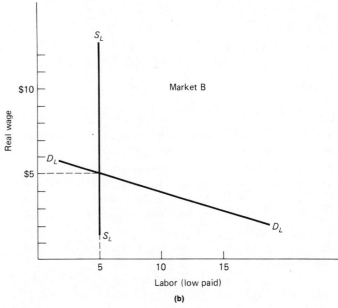

(b)

Figure 28-4

(3) the lack of mobility among older workers.

(4) the impact of wage increases in unionized sectors of the economy upon nonunionized sectors.

(5) why wage rates in certain industries have risen faster than the average.

2. A situation which indicates an imperfect labor market would be one in which:

(1) certain firms must make a decision on the wage policy they are going to adopt.

(2) different wages are paid for different jobs in order to compensate for differences in risk.

(3) different wages are paid for different jobs because the jobs have different requirements.

(4) the wages paid for certain jobs fall into the category of economic-rent payments.

(5) the excess of one wage rate over another is a "compensating differential."

3. The dimensions that help define the supply of labor of a given economy include:

(1) the size of its population.

(2) the rate of participation of its population in the labor force.

(3) the standard or legislated length of the workweek.

(4) the quality and level of skill embodied in the work force.

(5) all of the above.

4. If, from a situation of discrimination that depressed the wage in one labor market relative to a second market of otherwise identical workers, an economy were to move to a situation in which no discrimination in wages were allowed:

(1) the wage paid to those initially in the low-wage market would necessarily rise, and employment in that market would fall.

(2) everyone's wage would fall regardless of where he or she was initially employed.

(3) the wage paid to those initially in the low-wage market would necessarily rise, and employment in that market would therefore rise.

(4) the wage in both markets would necessarily rise in response to the increase in productivity caused by the elimination of discrimination.

(5) none of the above.

5. According to Malthus' analysis of wage determination:

(1) it is impossible for either employers or unions to fix wage rates at anything but the competitive level.

(2) employers will be able to force wages down to the equilibrium level by maintaining a high degree of unemployment.

(3) the long-run supply-of-labor curve is a horizontal line at the wage level where workers will just be able to maintain and reproduce themselves.

(4) the money wage received by workers must always equal the real wage.

(5) employers will be able to force wages down to the subsistence level by maintaining a high degree of unemployment.

6. Four of the following five statements more or less repeat ideas discussed in the text chapter. One of the five runs counter to what is said therein. Which one?

(1) A wage increase in a single industry may have particular effects upon labor's real income and employment, but it is dangerous to apply the same conclusions when reasoning as to a wage increase applicable to the whole economy.

(2) The facts make it clear that unions have managed to raise real incomes for their members.

(3) The average wage in unionized industries is decidedly higher than that in nonunionized industries.

(4) The percentage differential between wages in unionized and nonunionized occupations has been narrowing over the past half-century.

(5) Unionized industries, as compared with nonunionized ones, tend to be made up of large-scale firms and of firms using labor of higher-than-average skills.

7. The so-called substitution effect, as applied to a worker's decision to change or not change the number of hours worked daily when offered a different price per hour of labor, refers specifically to the following fact:

(1) If the price offered labor rises, the worker's disposition is to buy better but more costly goods, hence to work longer hours.

(2) A general increase in wages tends to produce a general rise in consumer prices, which cancels out the worker's real-income gain.

(3) Because leisure (nonwork) time is desirable, a worker's normal inclination is to choose more leisure as part of any rise in real income.

(4) The cost of working is leisure (nonwork) time sacrificed, hence if the wage offered labor falls, leisure becomes relatively less expensive.

(5) Any labor cost increase prompts employers to try to substitute capital for labor in production.

8. Which alternative in question 7 would be correct had that question referred to the "income effect," not to the "substitution effect"?

(1).

(2).

(3).

(4).

(5).

9. The "lump of labor" viewpoint is essentially a belief that:

(1) the quality of a hand-crafted product is inherently superior to that of a machine-made product.

(2) the supply of labor will not vary significantly with the price that is offered for it; i.e., the labor supply curve is almost perfectly inelastic.

(3) labor effort is the ultimate measure of value, and the prices of goods should reflect the amount of labor effort that went into making those goods.

(4) any commodity embodies a fixed quantity of labor (direct or indirect) in its manufacture, regardless of the production technique used.

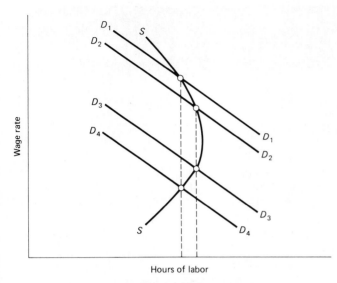

Figure 28-5

(5) there is only a finite and fixed amount of useful work to be done.

10. The viewpoint referred to in question 9 arose principally out of:
(1) the experience of workers in the depression periods.
(2) the clash between income effects and substitution effects.
(3) the experience of workers in inflationary periods.
(4) the fact that the total labor supply curve is highly inelastic with respect to price.
(5) the belief that the total fund of money out of which wages must be paid is essentially fixed in amount.

11. Figure 28-5 illustrates a backward-bending or backward-rising labor supply curve and four possible demand curves. If the demand curve were to change from position 1 to position 2:
(1) the substitution effect would dominate over the income effect.
(2) the substitution effect and income effect would cancel one another out.
(3) the income effect would dominate over the substitution effect.
(4) the income effect and the substitution effect would work in the same direction.
(5) none of these statements would be correct.

12. Referring to the same figure, if the demand curve were to move from position 2 to position 3, which alternative in question 11 would be correct?
(1).
(2).
(3).
(4).
(5).

13. Again referring to this figure, if the demand curve were to move from position 3 to position 4, which alternative would be correct?
(1).

(2).
(3).
(4).
(5).

14. Still referring to this figure, if the demand curve were to move from position 4 to position 3, which alternative would be correct?
(1).
(2).
(3).
(4).
(5).

15. To say that there is an "economic-rent" element in a person's income means that:
(1) this income comes at least in part from property ownership rather than the labor supply.
(2) this income exceeds what it would be were the labor market perfectly competitive.
(3) if the price offered for this person's labor were increased, he or she would want to reduce the number of daily hours worked.
(4) this income is much above average, but is the result of some relatively unique natural talent.
(5) this person's labor supply curve is perfectly inelastic with respect to price, at least within some range of prices.

16. Between two periods, the index of money wages fell from 600 to 540. The index of consumer prices fell from 400 to 300. This means that, between the two periods, real wages:
(1) rose by 50 percent.
(2) rose by 20 percent.
(3) rose by 10 percent.
(4) did not change.
(5) fell by 20 percent.

17. A trade union which wants to raise wages for its members and at the same time to maintain as much employment as possible for them will be helped by:
(1) an elastic derived demand for labor.
(2) an elastic supply of labor.
(3) an inelastic demand for the finished product.
(4) a perfectly competitive labor market.
(5) an imperfectly competitive market for labor.

18. If everyone in the labor force were exactly alike (i.e., no difference in skills or competence), and if the labor market were perfectly competitive:
(1) any wage-rate differences would have to be explained as "qualitative differentials."
(2) there would still be a considerable range of different wage rates, with several different reasons to explain them.
(3) any wage-rate differences would have to be explained as equalizing differences.
(4) any wage-rate differences would have to be explained in terms of the differing wage policies adopted by different firms.
(5) there would be only one wage rate.

LABOR UNIONS AND COLLECTIVE BARGAINING

Labor is not owned; it is "rented." This was one of the implications of the Civil War in the United States, and it is an implication that has had far-reaching effects on the labor markets of this country. Because labor is "rented," there must exist, between management and labor, some sort of contract outlining compensation schedules, work rules, procedures, and avenues for voicing grievances in both directions. The first part of Chapter 29 conducts a review of the role of labor unions in the process of forming these contracts. Their history is briefly chronicled, as is the role of government in shaping that history. So is their overall organization. The result is a thorough introduction into the issues surrounding unions before a cursory analysis of how unions try to increase wages is conducted in the later sections.

Having completed your work in this chapter, then, you will have accomplished the following objectives.

LEARNING OBJECTIVES

1. List the three layers of structure within the structure of American unionism, and discuss their evolution.

2. Review the circumstances that led to the growth of industrial unions at the expense of craft unions.

3. Outline the changing mood of the federal government in its treatment of unions as portrayed in the legislation that impacted directly on union power.

4. Discuss the issues of strikes, deregulation, and foreign competition with reference both to the actions of unions and to the ultimate effect on their power.

5. Analyze the ways in which unions try to increase wages.

Twenty-three million Americans belong to unions— about one-quarter of the adult labor force. At least 20 percent of the workers employed by each and every manufacturing industry in the United States work under a contract negotiated by a union, even if they do not personally belong to a union. Even though the growth in union membership has leveled off in recent years, labor is still a powerful economic force in America that must be recognized.

1. Indicate by a (D) or an (A) which of the following industries are currently experiencing declines or accelerations in union activity and power.

(1) Steel workers .... (————)

(2) Police .... (————)

(3) Postal workers .... (————)

(4) Auto workers .... (————)

(5) Miners .... (————)

(6) Teachers .... (————)

(7) Garment workers .... (————)

(8) Government employees .... (————)

(1) D   (2) A   (3) A   (4) D   (5) D   (6) A   (7) D   (8) A

2. If all or most workers within a large plant belong to the same union, this would most probably be classified as *(a craft / an industrial)* union. If all or most union members have the same occupation, or closely allied occupations, this would most probably be classed as *(a craft / an industrial)* union.

an industrial; a craft

3. Note in the blanks provided whether the indicated efforts should cause union power to increase (I), decrease (D), or remain unchanged (U). When a particular industry is identified, presume that the question pertains to the union employed in that industry.

(1) Deregulation in the airline industry .... (_____)

(2) The imposition of quotas to limit the importing

of Japanese automobiles .... (_____)

(3) The breakup of AT&T .... (_____)

(4) The elimination of import quotas .... (_____)

(5) An increase in unemployment as part of the

business cycle .... (_____)

(6) Election of conservatives to the National La-

bor Relations Board .... (_____)

(7) Repeal of the National Labor Relations Act (_____)

(8) A doubling of OPEC oil prices .... (_____)

(9) The eradication of the air-traffic controller's

union by the President .... (_____)

(10) Widespread adoption of robot technology (_____)

---

(1) *D*;   (2) *I*;   (3) *D*;   the rest are *D*'s, as well

Several points can be made in light of the answers to question 3. First of all, much of recent history has worked against the power of unions, at least at the source of its traditional power. From the intervention of the President of the United States in the PATCO strike to the composition of the NLRB, the lot of the traditional labor union has declined. Second, general equilibrium effects are rampant in the labor market so that "no change" was the answer to none of the parts of question 3. You are hereby challenged to come up with one significant change in economic circumstances that will not influence the power of some labor union to some degree.

4. In 1890, a federal act was passed which, for the next 20 years, was used as a weapon against union formation and activity, although this had not been the principal intent of the framers of this legislation. In 1914, another bill was passed, specifically excluding labor unions from application of the first act.

The first of these laws was the _____ Act, and

the second was the _____ Act.

Sherman; Clayton

5. Are the following statements concerning the National Labor Relations Board true or false?

a. On petition from a union claiming to represent a majority of workers, the NLRB can take a secret ballot of the workers to determine if this claim is valid .... *(T / F)*

b. If a majority vote upholds the union claim in **a**, then the NLRB can require that the employer recognize the union as a collective bargaining agent and deal with it ...... *(T / F)*

c. The NLRB can enter a union-management dispute and seek to mediate the differences .... *(T / F)*

d. If the dispute persists, the NLRB can, on petition to the courts, act as an arbitrator to settle it .... *(T / F)*

e. The NLRB can designate an "unfair labor practice" and, if necessary, take the employer to court to enforce a "cease and desist" order against such practice .... *(T / F)*

---

a. *T*   **b.** *T*   **c.** *F*   **d.** *F*   **e.** *T*

6. Insert the appropriate number to indicate the federal act which contains the provision or prohibition described. The same number may be used more than once.
(1) Clayton Antitrust Act (1914).
(2) Fair Labor Standards Act (1938).
(3) Landrum-Griffin Act (1959).
(4) Norris-La Guardia Act (1932).
(5) Sherman Antitrust Act (1890).
(6) Taft-Hartley (Labor-Management Relations) Act (1947).
(7) Wagner (National Labor Relations) Act (1935).
(8) No federal act contains this provision.

a. Explicitly stated that workers have the right to form unions, to bargain collectively, and to engage in concerted activities for purposes of collective bargaining; set up machinery to protect exercise of

these rights by workers .... (_____)

b. Included safeguards against misuse of union funds (e.g., prohibited excessive loans to union

officers) .... (_____)

c. Required unions to file regular financial reports,

with stated penalty for noncompliance .... (_____)

d. Prohibited the union shop .... (_____)

e. Provided that the attorney general may secure a court injunction to suspend strikes in "essential

industries" .... (_____)

f. Established the National Labor Relations Board to act as watchdog against "unfair labor practices"

on the part of employers .... (_____)

g. Vastly reduced the employer power to obtain federal court injunctions to break strikes or harass

unions .... (_____)

h. Included a union member "Bill of Rights" (e.g., limiting power of unions to discipline their

members) .... (_____)

i. Stated that union activities were *not* to be considered a "conspiracy in restraint of trade" such as would violate the Sherman Antitrust Act .... (_____)

j. Sharply restricted the closed shop .... (_____)

k. Established an hourly minimum wage for most workers in occupations involving interstate commerce .... (_____)

l. Defined "unfair labor practices" on the part of unions .... (_____)

m. Prohibited unions from making loans to union officials .... (_____)

---

a. (7) **b.** (3) **c.** (3) **d.** (8) **e.** (6) **f.** (7) **g.** (4) **h.** (3) **i.** (1) **j.** (6) **k.** (2) **l.** (6) **m.** (8)

---

7. Deregulation and foreign competition can diminish the ability of unions to maintain high wages because both *(increase / decrease)* the market power of employers. As long as employers have market power, they can price their products *(above / at / below)* average cost, i.e., *(above / at / below)* the competitive price. And since the wage offered to labor in the competitive labor market model is the multiplicative product of *(the price of output and the marginal utility of labor / the price of output and the marginal product of labor / the price of capital and the marginal product of labor)*, labor can receive a wage that is *(higher than / equal to / lower than)* the competitive wage. If deregulation and foreign competition make the output market more competitive, therefore, they *(increase / reduce)* the ability of labor to derive a higher wage.

---

decrease; above; above; the price of output and the marginal product of labor; higher than; reduce

---

8. One of the four methods by which a trade union can try to raise wages involves a direct attempt to increase the wage rate. If this path is followed, the most desirable situation from the union's standpoint (to minimize any unemployment arising out of the wage increase) would be to have the derived demand for labor *(elastic / inelastic)* with respect to the wage, and the supply of labor *(elastic / inelastic)*.

---

inelastic; inelastic

---

9. Which of the following union practices operates primarily by shifting the labor supply curve to the left, and which by moving the derived demand curve for labor to the right? After each, put (S) for supply curve or (D) for demand curve.

a. Putting featherbedding rules in local building codes .... (_____)

b. Setting long apprenticeship periods for entrants into the occupation .... (_____)

c. Asking consumers to buy only union-made goods .... (_____)

d. Imposing high initiation fees upon entrants into the occupation .... (_____)

e. Limiting use of labor-saving tools and equipment .... (_____)

f. Agitating for tarriff protection .... (_____)

g. Agitating for limitations on immigration ... (_____)

---

a. *D* **b.** *S* **c.** *D* **d.** *S* **e.** *D* **f.** *D* **g.** *S*

---

10. When the text speaks of the possible "shock effect" of trade-union activity for higher wages, it is referring to (pick one):
(1) The discovery by unions that higher wages may mean unemployment for some of their members.
(2) The fact that a firm or industry may be galvanized out of complacency and forced to look to new methods for using labor more efficiently.
(3) The fact that higher wages in a unionized industry tend to raise wages in nearby nonunionized industries.
(4) The inclination of a firm to shut down completely under the excessive wage demands.

---

(2)

---

11. The four panels of Figure 29-1 illustrate the four ways that unions can try to increase the wage paid to their members. List the four ways below and identify which of the four panels is the most appropriate representation of each. The original demand and supply curves in each panel are designated *DD* and *SS*; the modified curves created by the union activity are designated *D'D'* and *S'S'* where appropriate.

a. _____; Panel (_____)

b. _____; Panel (_____)

c. _____; Panel (_____)

d. _____; Panel (_____)

Notice that employment falls in two of the cases and that employment increases in the other two cases.

---

a. Restrict supply; panel (**d**) **b.** Raise the standard wage; panel (a) **c.** Increase productivity; panel (**c**) **d.** Remove exploitation panel (**c**)

QUIZ: Multiple Choice

1. Which of the following statements is accurate?
(1) The membership roles of unions totaled across the United States include approximately 23 million names.
(2) At least 20 percent of the people employed in each and every manufacturing industry in the United States work under an arrangement negotiated by a union, whether or not they are union members.
(3) Union membership has leveled off recently, after growing for over 50 years.
(4) Union wages tend to be about 15 percent higher than non-

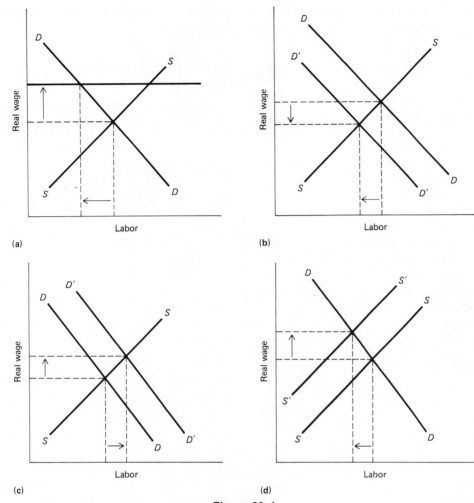

Figure 29-1

union wages, but the share of GNP devoted to labor has remained remarkably constant over the past 60 years.
(5) All of the above.

2. The term "industrial union" means:
(1) the same thing as a trade union.
(2) a trade union in manufacturing, as opposed to the service trades or agriculture.
(3) a union with members in the same craft throughout industry.
(4) a union whose membership is drawn from all or nearly all the workers in a given industry.
(5) an organization of employers in an industry.

3. Collective bargaining agreements are usually negotiated by:
(1) the federation of national unions.
(2) the local union, but increasingly with the assistance of the federation.
(3) the local union, but incrasingly with the assistance of the national union.
(4) the national union, but increasingly with the assistance of the federation.
(5) the national union, but increasingly with the assistance of the local union.

4. In the United States by 1910, according to federal law:
(1) labor organizations were considered legal, provided their purpose or activity could not be construed as an attempt to raise wages.
(2) all efforts on the part of labor to organize collectively (i.e., form unions) were still illegal.
(3) labor organizations were considered legal, provided their activity did not involve a conspiracy in restraint of trade or a monopolistic restraint of trade.
(4) all efforts on the part of labor to increase wages, whether they involved union organization or not, were still illegal.
(5) all nonviolent collective bargaining activity was already entirely legal.

5. "Exclusive bargaining agent" refers to:
(1) the craft union principle early adopted by the AFL, whereby each union had complete jurisdiction over workers in its class, and two unions could not conflict in attempting to organize the same workers.
(2) the union recognized by the National Labor Relations Board as exclusively entitled to represent all workers within the group concerned, in bargaining with management.
(3) a provision in the Taft-Hartley Act which restrains the union from attempting to bargain on behalf of nonmembers.

(4) the official who is designated by the union to negotiate with management on behalf of its members.

(5) none of these.

6. One of the important principles by which Samuel Gompers ran the AFL was that:

(1) labor must learn to live within a capitalistic system and realize that it was unrealistic to expect "more and still more."

(2) wherever possible, member national unions should be organized by industry rather than by craft.

(3) although greater emphasis should be placed on business unionism, pro-union government intervention in collective bargaining was to be sought through political action.

(4) the autonomy of each member union with respect to its craft specialty must be clearly recognized.

(5) although labor must learn to live with capitalism, in the long run effective business unionism would lay the basis for a philosophy of political action.

7. The act generally considered the most important piece of legislation in American labor history, in the sense of marking a real turning point in that history, is:

(1) the Landrum-Griffin Act (1959).

(2) the Wagner Act (1935).

(3) the Sherman Act (1890).

(4) the Fair Labor Standards Act (1938).

(5) the Walsh-Healey Act (1935).

8. One of the duties of the National Labor Relations Board is to:

(1) issue injunctions where needed to prevent strikes in "essential" industries.

(2) prevent unions from engaging in "unfair union labor practices."

(3) see that the provision of the Taft-Hartley Act prohibiting the union shop is enforced.

(4) enforce the federal minimum-wage law with respect to interstate commerce.

(5) hold elections to see which union is entitled to act as collective bargaining agent for workers in a plant.

9. If the President feels that a strike would endanger the nation's welfare, to suspend the strike he or she may:

(1) apply the "essential industry" provision of the Wagner Act.

(2) apply the "restraint of trade" provision of the Clayton Act.

(3) apply the court injunction provision of the Taft-Hartley Act.

(4) apply the "national emergency" provision of the Landrum-Griffin Act.

(5) simply use the prestige of his office to prevent it, since there is no provision in any federal act which gives him any explicit power toward suspension.

10. The AFL's opposition to the "industrial union" movement was due to:

(1) conflict with the AFL business unionism principle.

(2) the disapproval of John L. Lewis.

(3) a belief that the rise of mass-production industries would make this movement obsolete.

(4) conflict with the AFL exclusive-jurisdiction principle.

(5) the rise of the Knights of Labor.

11. The Taft-Hartley Act (1947), among other things:

(1) prohibited nonwage payments to union representatives by employers.

(2) required unions to give 60 days' notice before any strike.

(3) was for many years used by the courts to curb union formation and activity.

(4) removed labor unions from the charge of being a "conspiracy in restraint of trade."

(5) established a Labor Relations Board charged with the duty of making sure that employers did not engage in "unfair labor practices."

12. Had question 11 referred to the Clayton Act (1914), which alternative would have been correct?

(1).

(2).

(3).

(4).

(5).

13. Had question 11 referred to the Wagner Act (1935), which alternative would have been correct?

(1).

(2).

(3).

(4).

(5).

14. Had question 11 referred to the Sherman Act (1890), which alternative would be correct?

(1).

(2).

(3).

(4).

(5).

15. Had question 11 referred to the Landrum-Griffin Act (1959), which alternative would be correct?

(1).

(2).

(3).

(4).

(5).

16. Which of the following is evidence of imperfection in the general labor market?

(1) Wage stickiness.

(2) Wage policies in major corporations and small businesses alike.

(3) Periods of prolonged unemployment.

(4) All of the above.

(5) Numbers (1) and (2) only.

17. Given the initial conditions in a labor market characterized by the demand and supply curves shown in Figure 29-2,

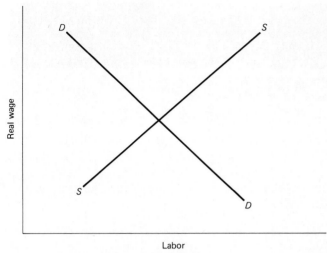

Figure 29-2

which of the following is the likely effect of union action that restricts the supply of qualified labor?

(1) Wages up and employment down.

(2) Wages down and employment up.

(3) Wages down and employment down.

(4) Wages up and employment up.

(5) Cannot tell.

18. Which answer to question 17 would have been correct if it had referred to an action that would increase the productivity of labor?

(1).

(2).

(3).

(4).

(5).

19. Which answer to question 17 would have been correct if it had referred to an action that would increase the standard wage paid by management?

(1).

(2).

(3).

(4).

(5).

20. Over the past 60 years, the share of GNP devoted to paying labor has:

(1) grown slightly.

(2) more than doubled.

(3) fallen.

(4) been halved.

(5) remained roughly constant.

CHAPTER 30

INTEREST, PROFITS, AND CAPITAL

Preceding chapters have outlined how the rents earned by resources and the wages earned by labor are determined. It is now time to study the determination of the return to capital. Of the three major categories of inputs, this determination is the most complicated. The return to capital depends upon many factors, economic and psychological, that lie well beyond the straightforward intersection of a derived demand curve and a simple supply curve. The return to capital depends upon the willingness of people to forgo present consumption to finance increased consumption in the future. It depends upon the uncertainties inherent in forecasting the future, and the aversion of people to the risks that those uncertainties create. It depends, in a more fundamental way, upon the macroeconomic policies of the federal government and the central bank. The list goes on. For our purposes here, though, only the simplest of theories will be explored. Brief mention of these and other complications will be made, but the focus of the chapter is the naive, simple view of the workings of the capital market.

This rather extreme caveat notwithstanding, your work in Chapter 30 will produce substantial insight into one of the most critical topics of contemporary research. Having completed the chapter, in fact, you will have accomplished the following objectives.

LEARNING OBJECTIVES

1. Define or explain (*a*) the net productivity of capital, (*b*) capitalized present value, and (*c*) discounting.

2. Explain the major factors that produce (*a*) the derived demand curve for capital and (*b*) the supply curve for capital in the traditional theory.

3. Cite the two types of thrift involved in investment in capital goods.

4. Explain why, according to the traditional theory, it might be expected that net investment in real capital might fall to zero and why net investment has, in fact, not achieved that limit.

5. Explore qualifications to the theory that are required to handle (*a*) technological change, (*b*) uncertainty and risk aversion, (*c*) inflation and the distinction between real and nominal interest rates, and (*d*) intrusions of macroeconomic policies.

6. Define "profit" in a statistical sense, and explain the roles of (*a*) implicit rents, interest payments and wages, (*b*) rewards for risk taking, and (*c*) monopoly rents in determining the level of profit.

7. Explain the three types of risk involved in profit.

8. Explain the distinctions between monopoly rents derived from (*a*) natural scarcities, (*b*) contrived scarcities, and (*c*) innovation.

The text makes an implicit distinction between money capital and real capital. They are different, to some degree, but they are linked by the concept of the rate of interest. This chapter of the Study Guide begins by making the distinction a little more explicit.

Money capital means simply borrowable and lendable money. When you borrow, you are ordinarily expected to return, at some later date, not just the amount borrowed, but a somewhat larger amount. Suppose you borrow $100 today and agree to return $110 to the lender 1 year later. That excess of $10 is interest. You are paying 10 percent per annum for your loan.

That interest rate is a *price*, the price paid for the use of money for a specified time period. There is a market for loanable funds, with demanders (those wanting to borrow, and prepared to pay for the use of money) and suppliers (those with funds available, at a price). Whether you pay 5 percent per annum to borrow, or 10 percent, or 15 percent, depends on the strength of the forces on the two sides of the market. (The interest rate struck depends also, of course, upon the degree of risk associated with the loan—the risk, as viewed by the lender, that the borrower may default. Moreover, if inflation is at work, the purchasing power of money returned at a later date is expected to be less than its present-day purchasing power, and *that* factor will increase the interest rate demanded by the suppliers of loanable funds.)

Real capital means any "capital good" which is "productive" in the sense that it can contribute to production of finished goods. A house is a real capital good: it can provide consumer services in the form of shelter. A machine tool is a real capital good, just so long as the output it can yield is a step toward the production of one or more consumer goods.

Just as with money capital, time is a critical element with respect to real capital. If we could somehow press a button on any real capital item, with the result that it instantaneously yielded its entire outflow of services in one enormous heap, then it would be a consumer good, not a capital good. The essence of a capital good is that it "pays off" slowly. You must wait until tomorrow for at least part of the output that it can produce. (Inventories of semifinished goods, and of any wholly finished but unsold goods, also count as capital goods. These items do not "pay off" slowly, in the machine-tool sense, but they are not available for immediate consumption, either. They must await tomorrow's consumption, and so they are included in the total reckoning of capital goods.)

Whenever time is involved, the idea of an interest rate is also involved. Suppose a given capital good would cost you some given money amount to build. If built, it would yield a stream of output (some commodity or some service) stretching into the future. Each item of that output would have some money value. (Because it is a future item, you have to estimate what that value would be. If you are thinking of building this capital good, though, you must make this estimate, just as you must estimate how far into the future this output stream will extend.) This expected stream of future revenue is the "money payoff" of real capital.

Two points should be emphasized in summary:

▶There is always an interest rate that will just equate the capital good's money cost with its total stream of expected future money revenues.

▶This interest rate—the interest rate which investment in this capital good would yield—is called the capital good's "net productivity."

1. Consider an asset that will cost you $100, right now, to construct. If you construct it, there will be no payoff for 2 years. But 2 years from now, this asset will pay you $121—nothing before that, and nothing after. This $121 is free of any incidental costs or expenses; it is the net return on your $100 outlay. The $121 return is safe; there is no uncertainty about its arrival.

This capital asset has an annual *net productivity* of 10 percent. Ten percent is the annual interest rate at which a loan of $100 will just "grow," with annual compounding of interest, into $121 in 2 years. At the end of year 1, the principal amount of $100 will earn $10 interest. This interest is left to become extra principal for year 2, so that in the second year the loan is $110,

not $100. At the end of year 2, the interest for that year is $11. So the total repayment at the end of year 2 will be $121—$110 principal, plus $11 interest.

a. Two dollar figures are involved: in the example, a cost figure of $100 today, a revenue figure of $121 just 2 years from today. An interest rate (10 percent annually in the example) "matches up" the two differing dollar figures. So the "net productivity" of a capital asset is expressed as *(a dollar figure / an interest rate)*.

b. If you had to borrow $100 to construct the asset of part **a**, and could borrow this money in the money capital market at 5 percent annually, would you do so? *(Yes / No)*.

c. Would you borrow the money at 9 percent annually? *(Yes / No)*. At 11 percent annually? *(Yes / No)*.

---

a. an interest rate **b.** Yes (for you would be ahead of the game financially even after paying your interest) **c.** Yes [for the same reason (remember that there is no uncertainty about your $121 return)]; No (you would be out of pocket after paying interest)

More typically, a capital good promises a *series* of future revenue figures, strung out over time, rather than the single $121 payoff of the example above; it may entail a series of cost figures (an initial cost, then some later outlays). This complicates the algebra, but it does not upset the principle that there is always an interest rate which matches a cost (or set of costs, at specified dates) with a set of revenues (also at specified dates, coming somewhat later in time than the first of the cost dates). Don't worry about the detail of the algebra (there is more on this in the chapter Appendix). Just note that there is always an interest rate which is the "net productivity" of an asset with given cost and revenue figures.

2. Suppose you have money available to lend, or to use in the purchase of some revenue-yielding asset. The market interest rate is 10 percent annually. The borrowers in this market are of such good credit standing that the risk of any borrower defaulting on his or her loan is virtually nonexistent.

The owner of an asset such as that described in question 1 (i.e., guaranteeing a single return of $121 at the end of 2 years) offers to sell it to you.

a. If this asset could be bought for $90, would you buy it? *(Yes / No)*. If you did, the interest rate you would be getting on your outlay would be *(less than 10 percent / 10 percent / more than 10 percent)*.

b. If the asset could be bought for $100, then it would be *(an unusually good buy / an unusually poor buy / as good as, but no better than, other available alternatives)*.

c. Would you pay $102 for this asset? *(Yes / No)*. If you did, the interest rate you would be getting on your outlay would be *(less than 10 percent / 10 percent / more than 10 percent)*.

---

a. Yes; more than 10 percent **b.** as good as, but no better than, other available alternatives **c.** No; less than 10 percent

3.   a. Suppose the market rate of interest is 4 percent annually, not 10 percent. Would you now buy the asset of question 1 for $102, if you had the opportunity? *(Yes / No)*. If you did, the interest rate you would be getting would be *(less than 4 percent / 4 percent / more than 4 percent)*.

b. Actually, with a market interest rate of 4 percent annually (i.e., if the return generally available for "investing" money capital is 4 percent per year), the market price of this asset would stand at about $112 (more precisely, $111.85). Why? (Pick one.)
(1) Because $112 is the amount which, if lent out for 2 years at 4 percent annually, would "grow" to $121.
(2) Because the interest return or net productivity of this asset is 10 percent regardless of the amount of money laid out to build or buy it.

---

a. Yes; more than 4 percent   **b.** (1) (This asset's net productivity is 10 percent *only* if it can be bought or built for $100)

To repeat: An asset's "net productivity" is an interest rate. If, concerning an asset, you are asked, "What is its net productivity?" then you need two pieces of information.

1. The amount it would cost to build or buy this asset now.

2. The amounts of future net revenue it is expected to bring in, and the expected dates of their arrival. (*Net* revenue means revenue after allowing for any costs incurred in using the asset or collecting the revenue.)

Given this information, there is always one interest rate that indicates the "rate of return" on (net productivity of) the asset in question.

Question 3 took you to a different, but closely related, question: What is the maximum amount you should pay for a given asset? What is its present value?
To reply, again you need two pieces of information:

1.   As before, amounts and dates of the future revenue the asset is expected to bring in

2.   The *market* interest rate

From this information, you can compute the asset's present market value—more precisely, its *capitalized present value*. Thus, in question 3, the asset yielding $121 just 2 years from now has a capitalized present value of $100 if the market interest rate is 10 percent. Its capitalized present value is about $112 if the market rate is 4 percent.
To "capitalize" an asset is to value it as it should be valued: in terms of the present value of the future net revenues it is expected to bring in. This stream of future revenues is reduced to a single present value by means of the market interest rate.

4.   After you have computed an asset's capitalized value, suppose you find this figure is different from the asset's actual construction cost. If so, then this asset's net productivity (which is an interest rate, remember) is different from the market interest rate.

Suppose actual cost is less than capitalized value. Then it *(would / would not)* be profitable to borrow money to construct it. This asset's net productivity is *(less than / equal to / greater than)* the market interest rate.

If capitalized value is less than construction cost, the asset *(would / would not)* be worth building. The market value of such an asset already constructed would be *(less than / equal to / greater than)* its construction cost.

---

would; greater than; would not; less than

To capitalize an asset's future revenues is to *discount* them. (The chapter Appendix has a fuller discussion of discounting.) To discount is to determine the present value of some future sum using the market interest rate. If that rate is 10 percent annually, then $121 due 2 years from now discounts down to a present value of $100. If the market rate is 4 percent annually, that $121 would discount down to a present value of approximately $112.

Suppose an asset promises income at the ends of years 1, 2, and 3. Then we discount each of these revenue items separately to obtain their present values. The sum of all such discounted figures is the asset's present value.

Note the sequence: first discount each item of future income separately, then add the resulting discounted values to obtain capitalized (or discounted) value. Do not try to add together revenue figures accruing at different points in future time, before discounting them. The further away in future time any money amount lies, the lower will be its present discounted value.
Summarizing:

▶Discounting is the process of cutting any expected future money figure down to its present value (a lower dollar amount) by means of the market interest rate.

▶The further away in future time this money amount lies, the deeper the discounting knife cuts.

For example, if a revenue amount of $121 is expected 2 years from now, its present value, given a market interest rate of 10 percent, is $100; if expected 4 years from now, its present value is about $83.
Note, as well, that:

▶The higher the market interest rate, the sharper the discounting knife.

If the market interest rate should rise from 10 percent to 12 percent, the present discounted value of $121 due 2 years from now would fall from $100 to about $96.

5. This means, then, that if market interest rates rise, the present discounted value of any sum expected at some date in the future will *(rise / remain unchanged / fall)*. And if the market interest rate should fall, an asset's capitalized value (assuming no change in its expected future receipts) must *(rise / remain unchanged / fall)*.

---

fall; rise

---

6. **a.** You own a piece of land which brings you net rental income (after allowing for maintenance cost, etc.) of $500 yearly. You expect annual rental to continue at this figure. The capitalized value of this land would be (pick one):
(1) $500.
(2) the sum of all expected future receipts of $500.
(3) the sum of all expected future annual receipts, each "discounted" down to a present-value figure by means of the market interest rate.

b. Suppose the asset in part **a** is expected to yield $500 yearly and keep on doing so throughout the future; i.e., it represents a "perpetual-income stream." Each $500 can then be thought of as the interest yield on a loan which has no maturity date (date for repayment of principal). Or it can be thought of as the yield on a loan which has a finite maturity date but which is automatically renewed once again at each such date.

What is the amount of principal that would have to be involved if its interest yield is $500 annually and the interest rate is 4 percent annually? .... $_____.

c. The text gives a simple formula for computing the capitalized value of such perpetual-income assets. Write it down, and make sure the formula works for the case of part **b**.

_____ .

d. Is this formula consistent with the rule that capitalized values are reckoned as the sum of the discounted values of all expected future revenues? (Pick one.)

(1) No—the perpetuity case has to be handled by means of a different formula, because of the infinite number of expected future revenue items.
(2) Yes—in this special case.

---

a. (3) **b.** 12,500 **c.** $V = \$N/i$, *or* $\$12,500 = \$500/0.04$ **d.** (2)

All this discussion of capitalized values and discounting is a lead into the problem of the determination of the level of interest rates. ("Interest," remember, is the income received by those who supply money capital to borrowers.)

We must begin by thinking of the interest rate as a rate determined by the demand for loanable money and the supply of such money. But talk of "supply and demand" is empty unless we probe for the factors lying *behind* the demand curve and *behind* the supply curve. Prominent among the demanders of money capital are business firms with investment projects (the building of capital goods) to undertake. Their decisions to borrow will be influenced by the level of the interest rate because some projects will be worth undertaking at low interest rates, and not worth undertaking at high ones. Why? Because the "net productivity" of such projects (and remember that this productivity is expressed as an interest rate) will be below a high market interest rate, and above a low market interest rate.

In sum, computations of net productivity must lie behind the demand curve for loanable money. The suppliers of such money are largely those who have saved (or who are handling the money which other people have saved and entrusted to them). From here, we work our way into the traditional, and simplified, version of capital and interest theory outlined in the chapter.

Figures 30-1 through 30-3 illustrate this theory. On all three diagrams, the interest rate (a percentage figure per annum) is measured vertically, with zero interest at bottom.

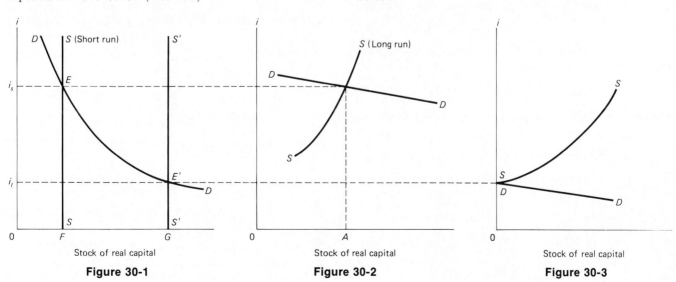

Figure 30-1   **Figure 30-2**   **Figure 30-3**

Figure 30-1 corresponds to the text's Figure 30-1. It is assumed in this case that all capital goods are exactly alike, so that we can add them together in physical units and get a meaningful total, just as we can add dollar figures together. The SS line in Figure 30-1 indicates the economy's *total* stock of capital at some particular period of time. It stands for some figure such as 400 units of capital. SS is vertical because the present capital stock is 400 units no matter whether the interest rate is 2 percent, 10 percent, or any other figure.

The *DD* curve is the "demand" of business firms for such capital goods. It intersects SS at point E, indicating an interest rate of i_s. To grasp the meaning of the *DD* curve, suppose that i_s indicates an interest rate of 8 percent. Then *DD* intersects SS at the 8 percent level, because the firms estimate that the last (or marginal) units of that 400-unit capital stock have a net productivity of 8 percent. This estimate is based on the cost of producing more capital goods and on the estimated net revenues that those capital goods will bring in.

7. To further grasp what *DD* means and why it intersects SS where it does, suppose that the situation is a little different. With the capital stock at 400, business firms are optimistic about the payoff of capital goods. Specifically, they think that the last units of a 400-unit stock have a net productivity of 10 percent. Then, if the interest rate is not 10 percent but 8 percent, they will want to have *(more than 400 / just 400 / less than 400)* units of capital. The interest rate must be 10 percent before their disposition to use capital goods is limited to 400. That is to say, *if* business firms were more optimistic about the net productivity of capital, then the *DD* curve in Figure 30-1 would lie (pick one):
(1) farther to the right than is now indicated.
(2) just where it is now.
(3) farther to the left than is now indicated.
It would intersect the SS curve at a point indicating *(less than 8 percent / 8 percent / more than 8 percent)*.

---

more than 400; (1); more than 8 percent

---

8. Given the existing stock of capital and its net productivity, the interest rate in this economy, at this period of time in its history, is i_s.

The people in this economy are, however, still saving money. Moreover, in the traditional account, people save *because of* the interest rate, and they are willing to lend this saved money to business-firm borrowers.

The SS curve in Figure 30-2 illustrates this situation. Its southwest-to-northeast direction illustrates the assumption that people would save and lend more if the interest rate were increased.

There is also a *demand* for this money, or money capital. Business firms are willing to pay 8 percent on borrowed money because there are still some projects on which new capital goods (additions to the present total stock) would have a net

productivity of 8 percent. Of course, large additions to the capital stock would lower its net productivity because of diminishing returns, but that comes later. For the time being, business firms are willing to borrow (in each period of time) the amount of money indicated by *OA* in Figure 30-2 at 8 percent because they think there is still useful employment for this amount of money at this rate. *DD* in Figure 30-2 is close to being flat at rates even a little above 8 percent, because it is assumed that there are few would-be borrowers who see projects with a payoff in excess of 8 percent. But if the rate were to drop a bit below 8 percent, that might produce a substantial increase in the quantity of money capital demanded (i.e., demand might be highly elastic with respect to interest-rate changes, if there are plenty of unexploited projects with net productivity a little below 8 percent).

a. 0A in Figure 30-2 indicates, per period of time (pick one):
(1) the number of units of capital to be added to the capital stock.
(2) nothing whatever with respect to the capital stock.
(3) money that will be spent on construction of new units to be added to the capital stock.

b. Accordingly, as time goes by (in this traditional account), if the situation is not disturbed by technological change or the like, the stock of capital goods will *(fall / remain constant / increase)*. In terms of Figure 30-1, the vertical SS curve will *(move to the left / remain unchanged / move to the right, from F toward G)*. The interest rate will *(fall / remain constant / increase)*.

This rightward movement of SS means that more and more homogeneous capital units are being built. The diminishing returns law accordingly causes capital's net productivity to fall. Business firms will no longer bid 8 percent for money, since there are no projects left with an 8 percent net productivity. In Figure 30-2, the *DD* curve *(falls / rises)*.

This shift in *DD* (Figure 30-2) lowers the interest rate. And by the traditional account here outlined, as the interest rate falls, the public's disposition to save decreases. At rates below i_s (see the SS curve in Figure 30-2), the amount saved (and loaned) decreases. And at a sufficiently low rate, nothing will be saved; all of income will go to consumption. This is shown in Figure 30-3 by the fact that SS is zero at i_l.

c. That is to say, after a sufficiently long period of time and a sufficient increase in the capital stock, the process of capital accumulation comes to an end. In terms of Figure 30-1, the economy's capital stock has then increased to the level indicated by _____, and the interest rate is _____.

In terms of Figure 30-3, the *DD* curve begins at interest rate i_l because (pick one):
(1) there are no more projects worth undertaking at i_l, only those at rates below that level.
(2) people will supply money only at rates below i_l.

---

a. (3)   **b.** increase; move to the right, from *F* toward *G*; falls   **c.** *OG*; i_l; (1)

9. Questions 7 and 8 have reviewed the traditional theory of capital and interest in terms of demand and supply curves. But (to repeat) a proper grasp of the theory requires that we look *behind* these curves. According to the text, the fundamental element behind the demand-for-money-capital curve is the

_____ .

The corresponding element behind the supply curve is the

_____

_____ .

technical net productivity of real capital; willingness of public to save rather than consume part of its income

10. The text notes a number of qualifications that must be made in the traditional theory of capital and interest if that theory is to accord with reality.

a. For example, it is doubtful that people's consumption-saving decisions are greatly influenced by the level of the interest rate. At least, those decisions do not seem to be altered by moderate changes therein.

Suppose (1) that the decision to save out of income were quite unresponsive to any change in the interest rate, and (2) that whatever amount people did save, they were willing to lend it out at any positive interest rate. In Figure 30-2, this would affect the *(DD / SS)* curve; it would, in fact, become *(vertical / horizontal / a diagonal line)*.

However, the second of the assumptions above is probably unsound. While the amount people save may be unresponsive to interest-rate changes, the amount they lend probably is responsive. (This draws us back to the demand for money discussed in Chapter 16.) That is, at lower interest rates, they will lend *(more / less)*. The SS curve now shown in Figure 30-2 *(indicates / does not indicate)* such an attitude.

b. If real and money incomes gradually rise over time, people can and do save more money out of incomes. This affects the *(DD / SS)* curve in Figure 30-2. Such income increases shift that curve to the *(right / left)*.

c. If you try to compute the income accruing from any proposed capital project, you must look into the future, and that future is always uncertain. You must, nonetheless, make your best guess about the future when you are thinking about borrowing money to finance a project. In the process of deciding whether or not to undertake the project, therefore, you must recognize that your best guess might turn out to be overly optimistic. As a result, the net productivity factor used in the decision should be *(reduced below / hiked above)* your best guess to reflect a hedge against the uncertainty. It is a conservative measure to *(cut down / increase)* your revenue estimates to allow for uncertainty, and this makes it *(more / less)* likely that you will decide to undertake the project.

This factor of uncertainty surrounding the future is so important that it is unwise to think of business firms typically

changing their investment plans in response to small changes in market interest rates. Uncertainty makes their estimates of net productivity rough even at best.

d. Estimates of probable net productivity are influenced also by a quite different factor: the climate of optimism or pessimism. If business firms, looking into the uncertain future with respect to projected capital plans, suddenly become more pessimistic, this will shift the *(DD / SS)* curve in Figure 30-2 to the *(right / left)*.

Similarly, if lenders, trying to decide whether or not borrowers will really make good on their borrowing obligations, suddenly become more pessimistic on this score, this will shift the *(DD / SS)* curve in Figure 30-2 to the *(right / left)*.

e. The net productivity of capital may be altered by technological change. We would ordinarily expect such changes to *(increase / decrease)* capital's net productivity. In Figure 30-2, such technological change would shift the *(DD / SS)* curve to the *(right / left)*.

Continuing this line of reasoning in the context of Figure 30-4, suppose that short-run equilibrium were initially at point E with S_1S_1 representing the initial short-run supply of capital, S_LS_L representing the long-run supply of capital, and DD representing the initial demand for capital. Suppose, for the sake of argument, that every increase in the supply of capital over time were accompanied by a technological advance that preserved the rate of interest. The long-run equilibrium rate of interest would then be _____ percent instead of _____ percent, and the steady state stock of capital would be *(higher / lower)* than it would have been otherwise. Point *(E_1 / $E°$ / $E°°$)* would then represent long-run equilibrium. Draw a demand curve on Figure 30-4 that supports this equilibrium. With the technological change, then, capital *(deepening / widening)* would continue further despite the higher long-run rate of interest.

It is interesting to note that this is apparently what has been

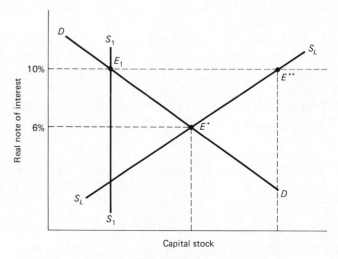

Figure 30-4

happening in the United States. Despite the tendency illustrated in Figure 30-2 for interest rates to *(rise / remain constant / fall)* over time, interest rates in the United States have tended to *(rise / remain constant / fall)* over much of our recent history (at least through 1979, but that is another story left for parts **f** and **g** of this question).

f. Inflation plays an important role in the determination of interest rates. Investment and lending decisions depend, in particular, upon the *(natural / real / nominal)* rate of interest. The equation that relates nominal and real rates is

[Nominal rate] = [real rate] + [_____].

This equation explains why, in the face of 18 percent nominal interest rates and 16 percent inflation, investors can behave as if the interest rate were really 2 percent.

g. Macroeconomic policy also plays a critical role in the investment decision. If, for example, tight monetary policy were to cause a recession, saving would *(rise / fall)* with GNP and the short-run supply curve in Figure 30-1 would *(shift to the right / rotate to a line with a positive slope / shift to the left)*. Meanwhile, business conditions would dampen the optimism of investors that capital projects would earn high returns and therefore *(shift the demand curve to the right / rotate the demand curve toward the vertical / shift the demand curve to the left)*. The net effect on investment would then be *(a reduction / an increase)* and the interest rate would *(fall / remain constant / rise)*.

h. Lenders also face uncertainties when they lend money. The result is their requiring risk premiums in the interest rates that they charge derived from:

(1) _____

(2) _____

a. SS; vertical; less; indicates   **b.** SS; right   **c.** reduced below; cut down; less   **d.** *DD*; left; *SS*; left   **e.** increase; *DD*; right; 10; 6; higher; $E^{\circ\circ}$; (draw a downward-sloping demand curve through $E^{\circ\circ}$); deepening; fall; remain constant   **f.** real; rate of inflation   **g.** fall; shift to the left; shift the demand curve to the left; a reduction; any of the three, depending upon the relative sizes of the shifts   **h.** the risk of default; their own risk aversion

We now turn our attention to the concept of profit. Classical economic theory identified three general types of inputs: land (resources), labor, and capital. If that is all there is to it, where does profit fit into the picture? The remaining questions will focus on this query.

11.   a. Suppose that you run a roadside fruit and vegetable stand, situated on your own land. Typically, you will describe your net income as "profit." But part of that income should properly be considered as *(rent / interest)* earned by your land, and another part as *(wages / profit)* for the labor you have supplied.

Similarly, it is possible to think of at least part of a corporation's earnings as interest on money which the shareholders put up.

If you are self-employed, those parts of your income which you call "profit" but which can be fitted into one of the other three categories may also be called *("implicit" / "unearned" / "surplus")* wages, interest, or *(income / rent / surplus)*.

b. However, economists are usually persuaded that it is impossible to translate *all* profit into factor earnings of the other three types, except in the very special situation of *(monopoly / perfect competition / imperfect competition)*, where everything has worked itself out to a full equilibrium level. In that situation, which in consequence is characterized by *(extremely settled and stable conditions / changing conditions / self-employment of all factors / no obligation to learn economics)*, there can be implicit wages, interest, or rent, but there will be no "pure economic profit."

a. rent; wages; "implicit"; rent   **b.** perfect competition; extremely settled and stable conditions .

If, in situations other than perfect competition, there is some part of profit which cannot be converted into implicit wages, implicit rent, or implicit interest, then it is necessary to answer the question: What useful function is performed or undertaken by the individual who receives a profit? Profit is the reward for doing what? There are, in response to this rather fundamental question, many different viewpoints.

12.   a. One, associated at its inception with economist Frank Knight, views profit as the return for dealing with unavoidable *(scarcity / competition among self-employed factors / entrepreneurship / uncertainty)*. Profit, or at least part of profit, is the reward society gives to those who shoulder the burden of *uncertainty* successfully. The only circumstances in which this profit-or-loss uncertainty would not exist would be those of perfect competition. The conditions of perfect competition are *(a goal we should strive for / unlikely to be attained / quite unattainable)*.

Three types of risk caused by this uncertainty were identified in the text. List them below:

(1) _____

(2) _____

(3) _____

b. The positive side to the risk of trying to exploit a new technology or other innovation is the monopoly power that success can bring. The power to control the price and the size of the market might be fleeting, but it is nonetheless real. In his work, Joseph Schumpeter argued that innovation lay at the very heart of productive capitalism, and that it was the real justification for a "profits system." He felt that most of the gains in real income that have accrued under capitalism have come, not from more careful allocation of a given stock of resources, but from the creation of new goods and new productive techniques.

Innovation, in the Schumpeterian view, is a risky and uncertain business, and the majority of would-be innovators *(fail / succeed)*.

In this Schumpeterian view, situations of "monopoly" and of "innovation" are *(inextricably mixed / completely separate)*. A firm may be in a monopolistic position, but that position may have resulted entirely from successful innovation. Schumpeter thought we should be cautious in our monopoly-opposing public policies; he was afraid that too-harsh policies might destroy the very incentive to innovate on which truly significant gains in real income depend. Schumpeter thought that most monopoly situations acquired through innovation are in due course toppled by other successful innovations originating elsewhere—producing what he called "the process of creative destruction."

---

a. uncertainty; quite unattainable; pure risk; risk of bankruptcy or default; risk of innovation and/or enterprise **b.** fail; inextricably mixed

---

13. a. In a second major view, profit is considered unnecessary and undesirable; it is a _____ return resulting from a "_____ scarcity."

b. The point is that when a good is offered for sale by a monopoly firm, price will be *(higher / lower)* and output will be *(higher than / lower than / the same as)* it would be under conditions of *(pure, or perfect, competition / no competition)*.

---

a. monopoly; contrived **b.** higher; lower than; pure, or perfect, competition

---

14. The monopoly view of profits is complicated by the fact that a genuine "monopoly return" may at the same time be a legitimate rent or interest return. Suppose that the original monopolist has an asset which for some reason is protected against competitive inroads and so is earning a large monopoly return. This monopolist sells this asset at its full capitalized value (i.e., the value established by its total discounted future earnings). The purchaser must charge *(the same price as / a higher price than / a lower price than)* the original monopolist did in order to receive *(the normal competitive return / a monopoly return)* on the money thus invested.

---

the same price as; the normal competitive return

To summarize, then, many sources of profits have been identified in the preceding questions. One source embraces the implicit rents, wages, and interest payments collected by an entrepreneur or a major corporation in the course of doing business. The second source identifies profits as reward for bearing risk—risk associated with falling flat on your face (default), risk associated with the business cycle as you see it, and risk associated with undertaking an innovative project. Finally, profit can be the return to monopoly power, derived from natural scarcities, temporary scarcities produced by innovation, or contrived scarcities. Some of

these sources are laudable, but others are the cause for some concern.

QUIZ: Multiple Choice

1. The "net productivity of capital" is:
(1) an amount of time.
(2) a dollar figure.
(3) a figure in dollars per unit of time.
(4) an interest rate or percentage.
(5) a figure in units of output per period of time.

2. An asset's "capitalized value" is:
(1) its original cost plus an estimate of maintenance expense throughout its lifetime.
(2) the same thing as its original cost.
(3) the sum of all its discounted net earnings.
(4) the sum of all its net earnings, without discounting.
(5) the rate of interest at which the asset would just become worth buying or building.

3. If the "net productivity" of any capital asset were to be computed, several items of information would be needed. Which among the following would not be required for proper computation of net productivity? The:
(1) original cost of purchasing or constructing the asset.
(2) rate of interest that must be paid if money is borrowed to finance the original cost.
(3) estimated maintenance or operating cost that must be incurred in order to keep the asset in satisfactory operating (revenue-earning) condition throughout its life.
(4) estimated revenue that the asset will produce throughout its lifetime.
(5) degree of "riskiness" surrounding estimated revenue, i.e., the degree of uncertainty as to whether revenues in the estimated amounts will really appear or not.

4. The law of diminishing returns plays the following part in interest-rate determination, according to traditional theory:
(1) as capital goods accumulate relative to supplies of land and labor, the net productivity of increments to the capital stock must fall.
(2) the cost of producing additional capital goods must necessarily increase (in the absence of innovation).
(3) a steady increase in the output of whatever consumer good a particular capital good produces must lower the price of that consumer good and thus lower the net productivity of the capital good.
(4) it explains why innovation cannot continually check the long-run tendency of the interest rate to fall.
(5) it must be used if the net productivity of any capital good is to be computed.

5. In traditional interest-rate theory, the rate of interest is determined by:
(1) the estimated net productivity of capital.
(2) the extent to which the public wishes to use the income it receives for consumption.

(3) both the estimated net productivity of capital and the extent to which the public wishes to use the income it receives for consumption.

(4) the estimated net productivity of capital and the size of the capital stock.

(5) the estimated net productivity of capital and the rate of technological development.

6.   Traditional interest-rate and capital theory held a particular view regarding a "long-run equilibrium" position for the economy; namely, that there is:

(1) a tendency toward such an equilibrium in which the market interest rate would be zero.

(2) a tendency toward such an equilibrium in which gross investment would be zero.

(3) a tendency toward such an equilibrium in which net investment would be maintained at a steady and nonzero rate.

(4) a tendency toward such an equilibrium in which saving out of income would be zero.

(5) no tendency toward any such long-run equilibrium.

7. The traditional theory described in question 6, the text points out, neglected the fact that:

(1) the amount saved out of income might be influenced by the interest rate.

(2) it is necessary to discount future items of income in order to establish their present value.

(3) while the iterest rate may approach zero, it cannot actually reach zero.

(4) technological change might continually increase the net productivity of capital.

(5) people are typically impatient to consume now, rather than accumulate for future consumption.

8. In a centrally planned socialist state, the rate of interest would (or should) play a role as follows (according to the text). It would:

(1) reflect the public's decision as to the allocation of the national product between consumption and investment.

(2) govern the state's decision regarding the allocation of the national product between consumption and investment.

(3) rank proposed capital-goods projects according to their net productivity.

(4) serve to indicate the attainable increase in national product to be expected over future years.

(5) do none of these things, interest being essentially a capitalist phenomenon.

9. A certain asset is expected to yield a steady net income (i.e., after allowing for all costs or expenses) of $100 annually, from now until eternity. If the market rate of interest is 8 percent per annum, the market value of this asset ought to be:

(1) $800.

(2) $1250.

(3) $8000.

(4) $10,000.

(5) infinity.

10. Should market interest rates generally fall, this would affect the "present discounted value" of any given capital-goods asset as follows. That value would:

(1) fall, since lower interest rates indicate that revenue amounts accruing at any future date are now given a higher present value.

(2) fall, since lower interest rates indicate that revenue amounts accruing at any future date are now given a lower present value.

(3) remain unchanged, unless relevant cost or revenue factors thereby changed.

(4) rise, because lower interest rates indicate that revenue amounts accruing at any future date are now given a lower present value.

(5) rise, because lower interest rates indicate that revenue amounts accruing at any future date are now given a higher present value.

11. Which alternative in question 10 would be correct, had the question referred to the asset's "net productivity," not to its "present discounted value" (still referring to a fall in market interest rates)?

(1).

(2).

(3).

(4).

(5).

12. In a period of deflation (i.e., of generally falling prices), the "real" rate of interest obtained by any lender on money lent:

(1) will exceed the nominal rate.

(2) will become a negative figure.

(3) will fall below the stated rate, although not to the extent of becoming a negative figure.

(4) will become a meaningless or incalculable figure.

(5) is not correctly described by any of the preceding.

13. If a nation deliberately introduces a "tight" fiscal policy and an "easy" monetary policy, then its purpose in choosing these alternatives (in addition to the maintenance of full employment) would presumably be to:

(1) attain the highest-possible level of consumption.

(2) keep the government's budget balanced.

(3) avoid inflationary price increases.

(4) produce a high level of growth in the capital stock.

(5) restrict investment to projects with high net productivity.

14. With respect to the market rate of interest and the net productivity of capital, which of the following is true?

(1) Although both are expressed as percentages per annum, they are never the same thing.

(2) Since both are expressed as percentages per annum, they are always the same thing.

(3) Given any rate of interest, society should undertake all investment projects whose net productivity exceeds that rate of interest.

(4) Given any rate of interest, society should undertake all investment projects whose net productivity is less than the rate of interest.

(5) An economy must be in long-run equilibrium whenever the net productivity of capital equals the market rate of interest.

15. The "net productivity" of any capital good could reasonably be described as:
(1) that particular rate of interest at which the capital good would just be worth buying or building, i.e., revenues would just be matched by costs (including interest).
(2) the dollar amount of profit that would accrue if that capital good were bought or built.
(3) the same thing as the market rate of interest.
(4) the physical increase in output (as distinct from the money value) that would accrue if that capital good were bought or built.
(5) the percentage figure obtained by adding up all net revenues that would accrue from the capital good and dividing this total by its cost.

16. In the traditional interest-rate theory described in the text, there is a long-run tendency for the interest rate to:
(1) rise, because of the law of diminishing returns, unless checked by technological change.
(2) rise, because of an increasing amount being saved out of higher real incomes.
(3) fall, because of an increasing amount being saved out of higher real incomes.
(4) fall, because of the law of diminishing returns, unless checked by technological change.
(5) reach an equilibrium level from which there would be only short-run departures, even though the stock of capital goods may steadily increase.

17. If business firms generally become more optimistic regarding the revenues that would accrue from the investment projects that they are planning, then the net productivity of capital:
(1) will increase, since revenues enter into the computation of net productivity.
(2) will decrease, since the net productivity is an interest rate, and the interest rate goes inversely to the value of the investment project.
(3) will not change, since the net productivity is governed by technical considerations, not by expected revenues.
(4) will probably fall, although there is a special case in which it would rise.
(5) may do any of the above, since the effect of a change in expected revenues upon net productivity is unpredictable.

18. In the view of Frank H. Knight, "profit" should be regarded primarily as:
(1) the return received by an entrepreneur who faces a downward-sloping demand curve for the product in question, and who seeks maximum profit in pricing that product.
(2) essentially a random distribution of profit among business firms—i.e., a distribution settled by chance, over which no firm has any control.
(3) the return received for activity in which some element of

uncertainty is involved, so that loss is a possible outcome of this activity.
(4) only the return received by someone who engages in a particular form of uncertainty-involving activity, namely, "innovation."
(5) none of the preceding descriptions.

19. If the economist named in question 18 had been Joseph Schumpeter, which of the alternatives listed would have been correct?
(1).
(2).
(3).
(4).
(5).

20. If profit is regarded as the return earned by successful innovators, it would be correct to say that in equilibrium under perfect competition, there would be no profit (other than the implicit returns to labor or property) because:
(1) all profit, properly seen, is always an implicit return to labor or property.
(2) all demand curves, those of industry as well as those of individual firms, would be infinitely elastic.
(3) earnings on invested capital would be too low to encourage innovation.
(4) in such a situation, losses would have to balance gains exactly.
(5) if innovations were occurring, the situation would no longer be one of equilibrium in perfect competition.

21. If profit is regarded as a monopoly return, it would be correct to say that in equilibrium under perfect competition, there would be no profit (other than the implicit returns to labor or property) because:
(1) all profit, properly seen, is always an implicit return to labor or property.
(2) if profit existed, it would immediately be competed away by entry into the industry involved.
(3) owners of labor and property would hire their services out to other employers in preference to being in business for themselves.
(4) such an equilibrium would involve the removal of all scarcities.
(5) the rate of interest would have dropped to zero.

22. If our concern is for the best possible employment of a given stock of productive resources, we would want to see "profit" eliminated:
(1) as Knight defines profit, as Schumpeter defines it, and as it is defined in both contrived-scarcity and implicit-return views.
(2) as Knight and Schumpeter define it, but not as it is defined in the contrived-scarcity and implicit-return views.
(3) not as Knight and Schumpeter define it, but as it is defined in both the contrived-scarcity and implicit-return views.
(4) only as it is defined in the contrived-scarcity view, not in any of the others mentioned above.

(5) only as Knight defines it, not in any of the other views mentioned.

23. In the view of Joseph Schumpeter, an "entrepreneur" is:
(1) any individual engaging in activity in which any risk, uncertainty, or speculation is involved.
(2) the individual (or group of individuals) furnishing the risk-taking money capital by which any enterprise is financed.
(3) one who invents a new product or process.
(4) that individual (or group of individuals) responsible for making the major operating decisions within any business.
(5) none of the above.

24. One of the following would be a poor example of profit earned by the "uncertainty" definition of profit, namely, income earned by:
(1) a firm which gambles successfully on the introduction of a new product.
(2) a speculator in wheat.
(3) a firm now operating at a profit after a long investment of time and money in developing new cost-saving machinery for its production line.
(4) an insurance company which protects its policyholders against the risk of property damage by fire.
(5) a farmer who successfully grows a crop on land hitherto considered impossible or unsatisfactory for that crop.

25. A "contrived scarcity" is to be expected whenever:
(1) the seller of a product faces a horizontal demand curve.
(2) the seller of a product faces a downward-sloping demand curve.
(3) the entrepreneur undertaking the activity in question faces more than a usual degree of risk or uncertainty.
(4) profit can be considered an "implicit" factor return.
(5) heavy taxes are imposed in such a way as to discourage the undertaking of risky projects.

26. Joseph Schumpeter felt that the status of profits in a capitalist economy ought to be evaluated primarily as follows. They:
(1) arise mainly out of monopolistic distortion of prices, and

should be eliminated insofar as elimination is possible without undue disruption of the economy.
(2) are largely illusory, since the reported figures are in the main disguised wages, interest, or rents.
(3) have a positive contribution to make, since continuing profit opportunities are the true driving force behind further expansion of real output.
(4) would continue to exist even under conditions of static perfect competition.
(5) are essentially what is elsewhere described as "economic rent."

27. With respect to the profits referred to in question 26, Schumpeter's further view was that:
(1) in a full reckoning, they will be exactly balanced by the losses of other participants in the economy.
(2) in most instances, they can and should be eliminated by taxation.
(3) they have equal status in a socialist economy.
(4) usually, they will in due course be competed away as further innovations appear in the economy.
(5) the distortions in income which they produce may ultimately destroy the capitalist system.

28. Four of the following five statements more or less concur with Frank Knight's theory of profits. One statement runs counter to Knight's views. Infer from your reading of the text which one.
(1) Successful innovation cannot be regarded as a valid instance of profit arising out of the acceptance of uncertainty.
(2) The operation of an insurance company cannot be regarded as a valid instance of the acceptance of risk.
(3) If profit is considered the reward for assuming risk, then the net total of profit in any given year might be a negative figure.
(4) Profit is a necessary component in national income if people by and large dislike risk and are prepared to pay in order to avoid risk.
(5) Profit, or a large part of it, is society's reward to those who shoulder the burden of uncertainty.

APPENDIX:
Theoretical Aspects of Interest and the Return to Capital

The text chapter has covered the simple, traditional model of interest-rate determination; the Appendix tends to some of the qualifications to that model in a little more detail. In working through the Appendix, more specifically, you should accomplish the following objectives.

LEARNING OBJECTIVES

1. Note explicitly that the interest rate is determined by the interaction of two forces: productivity on the demand side of

the capital market and impatience (or the lack thereof) on the supply side.

2. Conceptualize the rate of interest as the rate at which present consumption can be turned into future consumption.

3. Note the possibility that the real rate of interest could be negative (if people were sufficiently impatient and/or technology did not offer much of a tradeoff into future consumption), but that the nominal rate of interest must always be greater than or equal to zero—the nominal return to holding currency.

4. Understand that the ordering of capital projects on the basis of their net productivity is a general result that depends neither on the assumption of homogeneous capital goods nor on the assumption of a capitalistic society.

1. Draw a demand curve for capital on a separate piece of paper; it is *(downward- / upward-)* sloping because it is a derived demand curve and the marginal revenue product of capital *(declines / increases)* with the quantity of capital employed. It is this type of curve, of course, that reflects the net productivity of capital. Can you, on the basis of this curve alone, determine the equilibrium rate of interest? _____ . If you can, what is it? _____ percent.

Now draw on a separate graph either a long-run or a short-run supply curve for capital. It is this curve that reflects the willingness of people to save for the future—the inverse of their impatience for present consumption. Can you, on the basis of this curve alone, determine the equilibrium rate of interest? _____ . If you can, what is it? _____ percent.

You could not, of course, pick out an equilibrium rate of

interest in either of these two exercises in futility. Only when the two components interact so that supply plays off against demand can an equilibrium be achieved.

---

downward-; declines; No; undetermined; No; again undetermined

2. The three panels of Figure 30A-1 display three alternative Fisher diagrams. Panel *(a / b / c)* depicts the production-possibility frontier in which technology offers society the most advantageous transfer of present consumption into future consumption. Conversely, panel *(a / b / c)* indicates a frontier in which deferring consumption into the future earns the least in terms of future consumption.

Now consider the indifference curves that also appear in the three panels of Figure 30A-1; they are identical across the three graphs. Panel *(a / b / c)* illustrates the situation in which additions to future consumption are the largest. It also illustrates the situation in which the rate of interest, represented by the slope of line *(0A / DEF / 0B)*, is the highest. Recalling your answers in the first paragraph of this question, therefore, it is clear that the case in which technology provides the best trade-

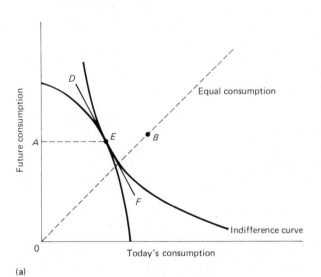

(a)

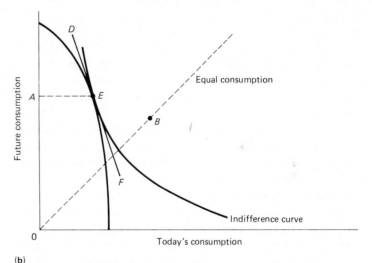

(b)

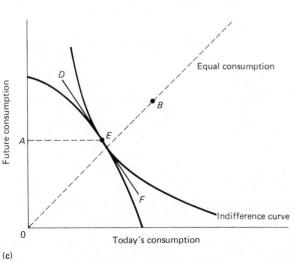

(c)

Figure 30A-1

off into future consumption inspires the *(largest / smallest)* quantity of saving for future consumption supported by the *(lowest / highest)* rate of interest.

Conversely, when the tradeoff into future consumption is worst, in panel _____, the indifference curve that maximizes welfare indicates the *(smallest / largest)* deferment into future consumption and the *(smallest / largest)* rate of interest.

The rate of interest, therefore, is an accurate reflection of *(society's aversion to risk / the tradeoff rate between present consumption and future consumption / society's inherent rate of return).*

(b); (c); (b); *DEF;* largest; highest; (c); smallest; smallest; the tradeoff rate between present consumption and future consumption

3. The assumption of homogeneity is convenient but false. Capital goods are in fact heterogeneous in the extreme. In the text Appendix, it is asserted that when this fact of nonhomogeneity is recognized, the tendency of capital's net productivity to fall *(still / no longer)* applies.

To put it briefly and nonrigorously, the best projects are usually undertaken first, leaving the lower-productivity items for later. Of course, technological change can shake things up, producing a new ordering of productivities. Projects which benefit from new technology will become more attractive. That is to say, their net productivity will be *(raised / lowered).*

still; raised

4. Classical economists often regarded the interest rate as the device by which people choose between present and future consumption. If the rate is 5 percent per annum, and you have $100, you may choose between $100 consumption today or $105 consumption a year from now. Or you may pick $50 today and $52.50 next year, or any such intermediate combination. The point is that you save or you lend to transfer consumption from year to year or from one year to the next. It follows from this reasoning that a different interest rate would produce a different consumption-saving distribution.

In the classical view, there is a long-run interest-rate "floor," established when the rate falls sufficiently that people feel the extra return is not worth waiting for. But if saving persists regardless of the interest-rate level, will that rate drift down toward zero?

For two reasons, any such tendency seems unlikely. First, technological innovation should persistently *(increase / decrease)* the net productivity of new capital projects. Second, the lending process is always haunted by some uncertainty or risk that the money loaned will not come back, or will not come back in full. So if there is an interest-rate floor, it will be set by refusal to *(save / lend)* anything at rates at or below this floor.

increase; lend

5. a. You must decide whether asset A or asset B has the higher market value. Asset A promises to make four income payments of $1225 each at the end of years 1, 2, 3, and 4. Asset B promises to make five payments of $1000 each at the end of years 1, 2, 3, 4, and 5. The confidence with which payments can be expected is the same in both. The valuation rule to follow is to choose the asset which (pick one):
(1) has higher total income payments, regardless of the date on which these accrue.
(2) pays income for the longer period of time.
(3) pays off more quickly.
(4) yields the higher capitalized value—determined by discounting all income items by means of the market interest rate and summing all such discounted values.

b. Thus (to repeat something already said in the chapter), do not try to value assets by what they would cost, or did cost, to construct. Value them instead in terms of the future revenues they are expected to bring in. But *discount* these revenues.

The basic discounting formula is simple. Take any one item of expected future revenue, $N. It is due to arrive t years from now. The market interest rate, expressed as a fraction (e.g., 5 percent = 5/100) is i. The discounted value (the present value) of that expected future revenue item is $N / (1 - i)^t$.

The capitalized values of assets A and B accordingly depend on the market interest rate. The higher this rate, the sharper the discounting knife. The further away in time any revenue item is, the more deeply it cuts. So the higher the interest rate, the more probable that asset *(A / B)* will have the higher capitalized (discounted) value.

a. (4) **b.** A (A and B have equal capitalized values when the interest rate is approximately 4½ percent annually. At any lower rate, B has the higher value; at any higher rate, A has)

6. "Traditional" capital and interest theory suggests that as an economy grows and matures, interest rates will (over the long run) gradually fall. As they do, the economy will gradually take up more "roundabout" methods of production. (If you are hungry, you want things in a hurry; if you are rich, you can afford to wait.) One example of a "roundabout" method would be a process involving a capital good which costs a lot to build, and lasts for 50 to 100 years. You must wait a long time before you get the full payoff from your real capital investment.

Now consider the primitive example of roundaboutness outlined in the text. Two alternative methods of producing 1 unit of some finished product exist. Both require the input of some labor *now*; then you must wait until the finished product arrives or matures. Specifically (assuming 1 year as the "waiting-period" unit):

Method A: 7 labor units now, then wait 2 years.
Method B: 5 labor units now, then wait 3 years.

Here, method B is the more "roundabout": the waiting period is longer.

Which method would be more attractive to producers? That depends on the interest rate. In this example, you can say unequivocally that A would be preferable at any rate above 40 percent annually; at 40 percent there would be no difference; below 40 percent, B would be preferable.

Start with the case where the market interest rate is 40 percent per year. Let the finished product be worth $10. Since this product accrues in the future (either 2 years or 3 years away), you must discount this $10 to get its *present* value. Discounted from 2 years ahead (see the formula in question **5b**) at the 40 percent rate, $10 is reduced to $5.11; discounted for 3 years, to $3.65.

Suppose labor costs 73 cents per unit. It makes no difference whether you use method A (hire 7 units of labor now at 73 cents each, total cost $5.11, then wait 2 years) or method B (5 units of labor now, total cost $3.65, then wait 3 years). Either way, your payoff will be $10, and the return on your investment will be 40 percent—just the market rate.

Now suppose the market rate is only 20 percent annually. Given the same input and output prices as before, both method A and method B would now be highly attractive. In both instances, their net productivity would still be 40 percent—twice the new market rate of return.

But now raise the cost of the investment, which in our example means increasing the price of labor. Method A, which requires more labor than method B, will cease to be profitable (cease to earn the market rate of return) while method B is still profitable. At 20 percent interest, $10 discounts down to $6.95 for 2 years, $5.79 for 3 years. Let labor's price be $1 rather than 73 cents. It *(would still / would not)* pay to spend $7 (method A) to get a return with a present value of $6.95. It *(would still / would not)* pay to spend $5 (method B) to get a return with a present value of $5.79.

This illustrates the traditional argument: a gradual fall in interest rates will prompt society to move from the less roundabout method (A) to the more roundabout one (B).

---

would not; would still

QUIZ: Multiple Choice

1. Equilibrium interest rates are determined:
(1) by the interaction of the net productivity of capital and the risk aversion of individual lenders.
(2) by the interaction of the (lack of) impatience of society to consume and the risk aversion of potential investors.
(3) primarily by the federal government in its role in stabilizing macroeconomic variables.
(4) by the interaction of the net productivity of capital and the (lack of) impatience of society to consume.
(5) none of the above.

2. The Fisher diagram can be used to illustrate:
(1) how an increase in the impatience of society to consume can raise the interest rate.

(2) how an increase in the technological tradeoff that turns forgone present consumption into future consumption can increase the rate of interest.
(3) that a negative real interest rate is possible.
(4) that the construction of the production-possibility frontier can be used to explore the market for capital.
(5) all of the above.

3. If the market rate of interest rises, other things equal, the present discounted value of any given capital asset should:
(1) rise, and the more the asset's expected revenues extend far into the future, the more it will rise.
(2) rise, and the more the asset's expected revenues accrue in the immediate rather than the remote future, the more it will rise.
(3) fall, and the more the asset's expected revenues extend far into the future, the more it will fall.
(4) fall, and the more the asset's expected revenues accrue in the immediate rather than the remote future, the more it will fall.
(5) not be changed at all.

4. Which alternative in question 3 would be correct, had that question referred to the capital asset's net productivity rather than its discounted value (other factors remaining unchanged)?
(1).
(2).
(3).
(4).
(5).

5. Those who invest in any new capital good always face some degree of uncertainty as to the future revenues which that good will bring in. In interest-rate theory, the effect of this uncertainty factor is:
(1) fully recognized in the traditional account of capital and interest.
(2) to set an effective ceiling or maximum level for the market interest rate.
(3) to make the task of establishing an "easy" monetary policy an easier one.
(4) to make the task of establishing a "tight" monetary policy a more difficult one.
(5) to set an above-zero floor or minimum level for the market interest rate.

6. The present discounted value of $500 payable 1 year from now, at a market interest rate of 9 percent annually, is:
(1) $545.
(2) $500.
(3) a little more than $455, but less than $500.
(4) $455.
(5) a little less than $455.

7. Implicit in the text's discussion of capital and interest is a rule for the proper method of deciding what the "worth" or "value" of any asset is, and how this value should be determined. This rule is to:
(1) value assets according to original cost of construction or

purchase, deducting from this cost figure an appropriate depreciation figure to arrive at present value.

(2) value assets according to the net revenue they are expected to yield in the future, capitalized value being the sum of all such expected future revenues.

(3) value assets according to the net revenue they are expected to yield in the future, capitalized value being the sum of all such expected future revenues after each has been discounted to present value by means of the interest rate.

(4) determine the dollar figure which represents the net productivity of the asset and then discount that net productivity figure by means of the interest rate, should such a procedure be necessary.

(5) do none of the preceding.

PART SIX

EQUITY, EFFICIENCY, AND GOVERNMENT

CHAPTER 31
GENERAL EQUILIBRIUM OF MARKETS

Part Six of the text will lead you through some of the thorniest topics of economic analysis. It begins in Chapter 31 with a discussion of the efficiency properties of an economic system that determines all prices and wages simultaneously. Previous chapters have shown that individual competitive markets lead to efficient solutions of the production question when they are allowed to operate in isolation; i.e., under the partial equilibrium assumption that all other prices and quantities in the surrounding economy are fixed and unchanging. But what about a general-equilibrium system in which the effects of production decisions in one market on the pricing and production decisions in another market are explicitly considered and allowed to feed back into the original decision? Can anything be said about efficiency, or lack thereof, in such a general-equilibrium setting?

In addition to gleaning some understanding of the qualifications that must be placed upon an economy to ensure that the answer to the last question is "Yes, efficiency is achieved," your work in this chapter will allow you to accomplish the following objectives.

LEARNING OBJECTIVES

1. Review the seven micro-based steps, covered in preceding chapters, with which the competitive system solves the questions of *What, How,* and *For Whom*.

2. Describe the circular pattern of interactions, in product and input markets, between households and businesses.

3. List the qualifications that must be applied before the existence of a competitive general equilibrium can be demonstrated, and illustrate the resulting efficiency in terms of a utility-possibility frontier.

4. Show how each of the qualifications listed in objective 3 leads to concern about the ability of Adam Smith's *invisible hand* to promote efficiency under a laissez-faire economic policy.

5. Describe the distributional-equity possibilities of a perfectly competitive general equilibrium.

Microeconomics, in its purest form, is analysis focusing upon individual consumers seeking to maximize satisfaction (given a pattern of tastes, a limited income, and a set of consumer-goods prices) and single business firms seeking to maximize profit.

Analysis of the price of a single commodity is likewise termed microeconomics. But in this instance we make the first step toward *macro* analysis, since we lump together all individual buyers on the demand side and all individual sellers on the supply side. Macroeconomics in its purest form, though, is more than a market-by-market aggregation. Macroeconomics deals explicitly with aggregates defined across all markets taken together across an entire economy. It is not, however, the purpose of this chapter to explore that "mega-aggregation." It is, instead, to try to understand how markets relate to one another across an entire economy, but underneath the aggregation of macro theory.

1. a. List the seven steps identified in the text with which an economy solves its *What, How,* and *For Whom* questions in the spaces provided. Indicate, as well, what is held constant in the usual partial equilibrium analysis of each step.

(1) _____

_____

(2) _____

_____

(3) _____

_____

(4) _____

_____

(5) _____

_____

_____

(6) _____

_____

(7) _____

_____

These issues, all involving the behavior of single markets, households, or firms, are all subjects of partial equilibrium analysis. They have, thus far, been explored under the assumption that (*all other people are equal / all other things are equal / all government policies are equal*).

b. There is a gap between "micro" and "macro." You cannot take ordinary "micro" analysis and use each bit of it as a building block toward a "macro" whole. Suppose there are only three goods in the economy—X, Y, Z. You cannot first develop supply-and-demand analysis for X, then turn to Y, and then to Z—finally lumping them into an "aggregative" or "macro" supply-and-demand whole.

The reason for this difficulty is that micro analysis uses an "other things equal" approach. The demand curve for X is drawn on the assumption that all factors other than the price of X which might affect the demand for X (the level of buyer incomes, the level of the price of Y, and so on) are held given and fixed. To some extent, we can handle changes in these "other variables." If Y's price changes, or if the level of buyer incomes changes, we say that the demand curve for X must be shifted to a new position in order to reflect this change.

For some problems, this method is useful and appropriate. For others, it breaks down. Suppose, for example, that we deal with just two commodities, butter and margarine. Initially, prices of both are in equilibrium. Now a technical development sharply reduces the cost of margarine production. In supply-and-demand terms, we say the margarine supply curve shifts downward (or to the right), establishing a new and (*higher / lower*) "equilibrium" price.

But the butter demand curve is drawn on the basis of the *former* margarine price. The two goods being substitutes, the fall in margarine's price causes the butter demand curve to shift (*leftward / rightward*)—producing a new "equilibrium" butter price.

The margarine demand curve, unaffected up to this point, is drawn on the basis of the original butter price. So *it* shifts, producing a new margarine price—which throws the disturbance back to the butter market.

Ultimately the two prices will settle down at mutually compatible levels once again. But the point is that the levels of butter and margarine prices are (*mutually interdependent / independent*).

Using the ordinary supply-and-demand diagram to illustrate a price change means deliberately ignoring the impact which that change will have on other prices—and the possible "feedback" effect which *those* price changes may have on the price first altered.

Until (and unless) prices establish a "general-equilibrium" relationship with one another, some prices will continually change and so will provoke changes in other prices. This idea of the mutual interdependence of prices is not too difficult to grasp intuitively (it was mentioned as early as Chapter 3; see review question 3 and 4, page 57). But there is no simple device for illustrating it comparable to the ordinary supply-and-demand diagram.

Notice that the GNP equilibrium cases of Chapters 12 and 13 are simple "general-equilibrium" models. They do not deal with prices, but they do deal with *mutually compatible* levels of GNP, consumption spending, and investment spending.

---

a. (1) Competitive supply-and-demand schedules determine equilibrium in individual markets given other prices and incomes   (2) Marginal utility analysis determines individual demand curves given other prices and income   (3) Marginal cost curves determine competitive supply curves   (4) Production functions determine cost curves given input prices   (5) Marginal revenue products determine derived demand curves for inputs given other input employment levels and output prices   (6) Supply schedules for inputs interact with derived demand curves to determine input prices, holding everything else fixed   (7) Net productivity and societal impatience for present consumption determine the capital stock and the interest rate, given all other prices; all other things are equal.
b. lower; leftward; mutually interdependent

2. a. The text has emphasized the special case of "perfect competition" because (more than one may be correct):
(1) It has special significance with respect to the "best" use of a given but limited stock of resources or inputs.
(2) With only a few monopoly exceptions, the structure of the real-life American economy corresponds reasonably well to the requirements of perfect competition.
(3) Although structurally the American economy does not satisfy the requirements of perfect competition, it is still highly "competitive" in many other senses. This prompts some economists to think that analysis built as though perfect competition applied can still give useful results (in some cases) when applied to the American economy.

b. Perfect competition has special significance from a "welfare" standpoint. If we take as given the stock of resources, the conditions of their ownership, and the state of technology, then the set of prices which would emerge under perfect competition would yield (pick one):
(1) The most efficient allocation of all such resources among their various possible allocations.
(2) The most desirable distribution of income among the people who make up the population in question.

c. The table below is intended to illustrate the meaning of "efficient resource allocation." It assumes that the economy produces only three goods, X, Y, and Z. A general equilibrium has been reached; as part of this, XYZ quantities produced are as in line 1 and XYZ prices as in line 3.

	X	Y	Z
1. Total quantities of goods produced and bought	3,000	4,000	5,000
2. Marginal utilities of goods for a typical consumer	100	50	200
3. Price of good	$2	$1	$4
4. Marginal cost of good	$2	$1	$4

Given the XYZ prices of line 3, the "typical consumer" *(has / has not / may or may not have)* reached his or her maximum-satisfaction position.

If supplying firms operate under conditions of perfect competition, then, with prices as in line 3 and marginal costs as in line 4, they *(have / have not)* reached maximum-profit positions.

(Note the general-equilibrium quality of this. Consumers reach maximum-satisfaction positions by juggling their XYZ purchases. Producers adjust the level of their marginal cost by varying the quantity of X, Y, or Z that they produce and sell. The quantities in line 1 and the prices in line 3 must be such as to satisfy *both* consumers and producers. The situation must be one in which neither consumers nor producers can see any advantage in any change of position.)

The significant property of this situation is indicated by comparing line 2 with line 4. Here, prices are an accurate indication of marginal costs. And marginal cost is a money indicator of the real cost of getting another unit of X, Y, or Z.

d. Now suppose all figures—save one—in the table above are unchanged. But the case is now a different one. Good X in this new case is produced under conditions of imperfect competition. This means that each producer of X will equate marginal cost with the *(price of X / marginal revenue from X)*. In imperfect competition, marginal revenue is *(the same as / greater than / less than)* price. The price of X is still $2; but its marginal revenue to producers is, say $1.20. The *MC* figure for X in line 4 above must then be $1.20. All other figures are unchanged, and general equilibrium prevails. Note that the producers of X, by equating *MR* and *MC*, produce and sell a quantity of X which is *(the same as / less than / more than)* the quantity they would have produced by equating *MC* with price.

In this new case, consumers are still at equilibrium. But the prices they must pay are no longer a true indicator of real underlying marginal cost—since X's *MC* is $1.20, not $2.

Here there is a contrived scarcity of X which buyers must accept as though it were a real scarcity—i.e., as though it would really cost $2 in real resources to produce 1 more unit of X. It is evident that if the price of X were to fall to $1.20, a new general equilibrium would have to be worked out, with new XYZ prices and quantities. And it can be shown—although it is not

easy to show—that the new XYZ quantities would represent a slight gain in the community's real income.

a. (1); (3)   **b.** (1)   **c.** has; have   **d.** marginal revenue from X; less than; less than

3. Kenneth Arrow and Gerard Debreu, both of whom have won Nobel Prizes, were among the first to prove the existence of competitive general equilibrium. Their proof depended upon a long list of qualifications. List at least five in the spaces provided, and state *in parentheses* which competitive condition would have been violated if this qualification had been ignored.

(1) _____

_____

_____

(2) _____

_____

_____

(3) _____

_____

_____

(4) _____

_____

_____

(5) _____

_____

_____

(1) No increasing returns to scale (otherwise, positive profits and prices in excess of marginal cost would emerge)   (2) No externalities (otherwise, the prices of some goods would not match their true social costs)   (3) Flexible wages and prices (otherwise unemployed resources would be possible)   (4) No uninsurable risk (otherwise inefficient losses might occur)   (5) No monopolies or other types of imperfect competition (otherwise prices in excess of marginal cost would be forthcoming)

4. The previous question began a list of qualifications that undermine the application of the efficiency virtues of the competitive general equilibrium to support a laissez-faire policy recommendation. This question will build on that list. Indicate in the spaces provided below the inefficiencies caused by each of the following qualifications.

a. Monopoly or monopolistic competition: _____

_____

b. Unrestrained water and/or air pollution: _____

_____

c. Discrimination against blacks in labor markets: _____

_____

d. Settlements that prevent wage responses to slack demand:

_____

_____

e. Monopoly power in a labor union: _____

_____

f. Government regulation that prevents competition: _____

_____

a. prices too high, output too low, wages and input prices distorted **b.** output too high because marginal cost too low, price too low, input prices distorted **c.** unequal pay for equal work, prices distorted, income distribution distorted **d.** unemployed resources during recession, prices stay too high **e.** wages too high, prices too high, output too low, other input prices distorted **f.** government-created monopolies—see part **a.**

5. Figure 31-1 displays several points relative to a utility-possibility frontier. Record in the spaces below which point(s) illustrate the effects of the following circumstances relative to a Pareto-efficient allocation indicated by point *E*.

a. An unethical distribution of income .... (_____)

b. Unemployed resources .... (_____)

c. Wage discrimination against individual A .. (_____)

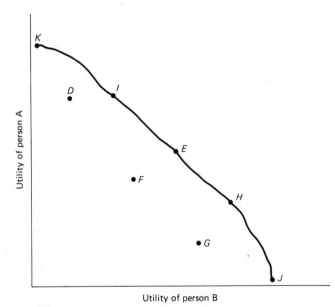

Figure 31-1

d. Unrestrained pollution in the production of a good consumed exclusively by B that hurts only

A .... (_____)

a. *J, K* (though some may object to *H* and *I*, as well) **b.** *D, F, G* **c.** *G* **d.** *G* (The answers to the last two are not *H* or *J* because both involve inefficiencies that allow the possibility of improving the utilities of both *A* and *B*; the answers cannot, therefore, be on the frontier)

6. *Welfare economics* has nothing necessarily to do with improving the status of the poor. It means only that branch of economics in which the words "better" and "worse" are used—i.e., in which it is said that some situation A is more desirable than some alternative situation B.

The statement that A is preferable to B demands some value scale. Since individual preference scales differ, this makes welfare economics a difficult and dangerous area. However, the following statement seems fairly safe: situation A is preferable to B if, in the course of a change from B to A, some people would be made better off while nobody would be made worse off.

Unfortunately, there are probably not too many of these convenient nobody-worse-off changes. The next step in welfare economics is to a situation in which there are losers as well as gainers—but the predicted gain of the gainers exceeds the predicted loss of the losers. So the gainers could "bribe" the losers to make the change. Or the gainers could be taxed by a sufficient amount to compensate the losers and still have some part of their gains left.

It is in this sense that the equilibrium of perfect competition is declared to be "efficient." When this equilibrium is reached, it is impossible to find any alternative attainable combination of goods and services in which those who gain by the change could *(fully / less than fully)* compensate the losers and still be better off.

Note particularly that this is ultimately a matter of the "efficient" allocation of a given and limited resource stock—limited in the particular sense that it cannot yield enough output to satisfy everybody's demands for everything he or she would like to have. Perfect competition (so it is argued) allocates this resource stock into employment in the best possible way—allocates it, that is, so that the combination of goods and services produced meets the requirement set out in the preceding paragraph.

This "efficiency" definition is acceptable only insofar as the assumptions underlying perfect-competition theory are acceptable. The theory assumes that there *(are / are no)* significant economies of large-scale operations. There *(are / are no)* "external diseconomies." (There is an external diseconomy if a plant pollutes the air or water and is not required to bear the cost which this pollution imposes.) The distribution of income, equal or unequal, is *(declared to be the most appropriate / accepted without comment on its desirability)*. The stock of resources is assumed to be *(fixed / increasing)*. The state of technology is assumed to be *(given / improving)*. (Schumpeter, for example, insisted that assumptions such as the last two miss the whole point of the "efficiency" of competitive capitalism—see review question 12, pages 308–309.)

---

fully; are no; are no; accepted without comment on its desirability; fixed; given

QUIZ: Multiple Choice

1. In general equilibrium and in a situation of perfect competition:
(1) for each consumer, the marginal utility of each good consumed is equal to the price of that good.
(2) for each consumer, marginal utilities of all goods consumed are proportional to the marginal costs of those goods.
(3) the marginal physical product of each input is equal to the price of that input.
(4) the marginal revenue product of each input is equal to the price of the finished good it produces.
(5) none of these statements is necessarily correct.

2. The profit-maximizing motive in perfect competition differs from the profit-maximizing motive in imperfect competition in this respect:
(1) The perfect competitor tries to equate price and average cost, which does not lead to maximum profit.
(2) The perfect competitor tries to equate price and marginal cost, which does not lead to maximum profit.
(3) The perfect competitor tries to equate marginal revenue and marginal cost, which does not lead to maximum profit.
(4) The imperfect competitor tries to equate price and marginal cost, which leads to a larger profit than the equating of marginal revenue and marginal cost.
(5) In none of these ways, the firms in both situations being equally interested in earning as much profit as possible.

3. The theory of perfect competition, according to most economists:
(1) gives a reasonably accurate description of real performance, even though it cannot be used to evaluate the efficiency of that performance.
(2) describes real performance in rough outline despite competitive imperfections, and is most important for appraising the efficiency of that performance.
(3) is most important for appraising the efficiency of real performance, even though it is not even approximately correct in describing that performance.
(4) bears almost no resemblance to real performance, and cannot be used to evaluate its efficiency, but is most important because its material is a lead into the theory of imperfect competition.
(5) with relatively minor monopoly exceptions, gives a closely accurate outline of real performance, and can be used to identify the monopoly exceptions.

4. Four of the following five alternatives state conditions which must be satisfied if the equilibrium conditions of all-around perfect competition are to be satisfied. One alternative states a condition not so required; i.e., one which perfect competition would not necessarily produce. Which one?
(1) Price is equal to average cost.
(2) For each individual, and for each good he or she consumes, the ratio between marginal utility and price is the same for all such goods.
(3) Price is equal to marginal cost.
(4) There is no significant inequality in the distribution of income among individuals.
(5) Price is equal to minimum average cost.

5. Four of the following five alternatives state conditions which indicate that the conditions of all-around perfect competition are not satisfied. One alternative states a condition which must be satisfied, to meet the requirements of perfect competition. Which one?
(1) Market prices are steady in the sense of being unresponsive to short-run changes in demand or in supply.
(2) Price is equal to average cost but not to marginal cost.
(3) Different wage rates are paid in different geographic locations for work whose requirements are exactly the same in both locations.
(4) Product differentiation yields a price that equals average cost, but not minimum-attainable average cost.
(5) Marginal cost is equal to average cost.

6. The theory of perfect competition began by recognizing two facts, namely, that resources are scarce and that the price system is a mechanism for allocating the use or employment of those resources. From here, the theory gradually developed a set of rules which, if satisfied (it was believed), would indicate that the scarce resources were being utilized "optimally"—i.e., to the best possible advantage, in terms of the output they produced. These rules were stated with special regard for one kind of influence that might drive results away from the perfectly competitive equilibrium. That disrupting influence was:
(1) laissez-faire pricing activity.
(2) activity over time.
(3) interdependence among the inputs employed.
(4) the presence of monopoly or of monopoly elements.
(5) space, or geographic, differences.

7. Perfect competition theory's equilibrium requirements, as indicated in question 6, set out rules for the "optimum" allocation of scarce resources. Yet the result, even with these rules fully satisfied, may not be "optimal," to the extent that:
(1) price is equal to marginal cost.
(2) external economies or diseconomies are present.
(3) monopoly or monopoly elements are present.
(4) price is equal to average cost.
(5) it is possible to substitute one input or resource in place of another.

APPENDIX:
Review of Commodity and Factor Pricing: General Equilibrium and Ideal Pricing

The example of a fully collectivized society can be employed to accomplish two rather general objectives: (1) a review of the workings of the perfectly competitive general-equilibrium price system and (2) a more thorough introduction of the notions behind "welfare economics." The Appendix to Chapter 31 speaks to both of these general goals as well as to the following list of more objectives.

LEARNING OBJECTIVES

1. Explain why the example of a collectivized or planned society is a useful device for illustrating the nature of the basic economic problems confronting all societies.

2. Cite the basic requirements that should be satisfied in the pricing of consumer goods, in such a planned society.

3. Discuss the problems involved in the distribution of income, in such a society.

4. Review the problems of pricing productive inputs (other than labor) and intermediate goods, in such a society.

5. Explain the special significance of marginal cost, in such a society.

6. Explain similarly the role of the interest rate (or explain why in such a society the interest rate would be unnecessary or meaningless).

1. Chapter 2 said that any economy's stock of resources is always "scarce" in the sense that there are not sufficient inputs to meet everybody's wants fully. Even with inputs fully employed to the best advantage, there are always some unsatisfied wishes. Chapter 3 said that the pricing system is important in making the best of this problem of scarcity.

After a lengthy survey of price and price making in Parts Three and Four, we can now look more carefully at the tasks which a properly functioning price system is expected to perform.

This matter is illustrated conveniently by considering an authoritarian, centrally directed society, since the people in control of such a society must consciously think about the role prices are to perform.

In that situation, there might be a completely arbitrary decision as to how inputs are to be used to produce particular goods in particular quantities, and a comparable decision as to how they are to be distributed. But it may alternatively be decided, in order to avoid resentment and unrest against such arbitrary decisions, to give the population some opportunity to exercise *choice*. This entails a resort to money—whether the word "money" is used, or some other name. Money is a device whereby people *vote* for the goods they want to be produced and supplied to them.

Suppose we deal only with goods X, Y, and Z. The state has produced some quantities of X, Y, and Z, and has given the people money to buy them. It has made a guess as to proper XYZ prices and will use these "guess prices." Clearly, the money supply *(M)* distributed must bear some relation to these prices. If *all* the M distributed is to be used in buying the available XYZ quantities, then the following relation must hold:

If this relation is not satisfied, then either the state winds up with unsold goods or else the people wind up holding M, which (at least for the time being) can buy *(goods / nothing)*.

$X \times p_x + Y \times p_y + Z \times p_z = M$; nothing

2. a. The next problem the state will face is that, unless the planners were very farseeing indeed in their guesses, the relation between the three prices will need adjustment. People will decide that, at the prices asked, say, X and Y are the most desirable goods. So they buy X first, then Y, and turn to Z only when the shelves are empty of X and Y. All Z will ultimately be sold—if there is no other way to spend the money. But the fact that X and Y vanish so quickly should be a signal to the state to (pick one):

(1) Raise X and Y prices; leave Z price unchanged.
(2) Increase the supply of money.
(3) Raise X and Y prices; lower Z price.
(4) Lower X and Y prices; raise Z price.

b. Suppose the state continues, period after period, to produce the same XYZ quantities. But it experiments with prices until all three goods seem to disappear totally into consumer hands at about the same time. This is at least a rough indication that for consumers the marginal utilities of X, Y, and Z are *(equal / proportional to XYZ prices)*.

a. (3) **b.** proportional to XYZ prices (see Chapter 19)

3. a. The state has now developed a set of XYZ prices which are most appropriate to consumer tastes for X, Y, and Z—given the *fixed* XYZ quantities produced each period. But the state should now examine those quantities; specifically, it should compare XYZ prices with XYZ marginal costs. Suppose the prices of X and Y are $2 and $1, respectively. Their *MC*s are just reversed; they are $1 and $2. This means that the state is *(overcharging / undercharging)* the public in its price for X. To produce 1 more unit of X would involve an additional cost of only $1; yet the public pays $2 for each unit. By the same reasoning, the public was *(overcharged / undercharged)* for the last unit of Y sold.

b. The point of this is that the XY prices are not true indicators to the public of XY costs of production. Money marginal cost is the surface indicator of real input cost. Here, the quantity of X produced should be *(increased / decreased)* and the quantity of Y *(increased / decreased)* by a transfer of resource employment. This will *(raise / lower)* X's *MC* and *(raise / lower)* that of Y. As a result of these changes in quantities offered for sale, X's price will *(fall / rise)* and Y's will *(fall / rise)*. This in turn will move price and *MC* *(closer together / farther apart)*.

a. overcharging; undercharged   **b.** increased; decreased; raise; lower; fall; rise; closer together (Notice especially that *marginal* cost, not average cost, is the true cost criterion which prices ought to reflect)

4. A farmer owns two equal-sized plots of land, A and B. His sons have a total of 800 worker-hours in the crop season to work them. Results of five different allocations of this labor power are shown below. (In each instance, the worker-hour total over A and B combined is 800.) "Marginal product" means the extra yield from the very last hour worked.

Situation	Plot A				Plot B			
	Worker-Hours	Total Bushels	Marginal Product	Product per Worker-Hour	Worker-Hours	Total Bushels	Marginal Product	Product per Worker-Hour
1.	400	3,900	8.5	9.8	400	2,300	2.0	5.8
2.	500	4,700	7.5	9.4	300	2,000	4.0	6.7
3.	600	5,400	6.0	9.0	200	1,500	6.0	7.5
4.	700	5,900	4.0	8.4	100	840	7.5	8.4
5.	800	6,100	1.0	7.6	0	0	—	—

a. In situation 1, labor power is equally divided between A and B. The resulting crop is *(2300 / 3900)* bushels from A and *(2300 / 3900)* from B. Since the plots are of equal size, *(A / B)* is consequently the more fertile of the two.

The object is to get the maximum total crop from A and B. This occurs in situation *(1 / 2 / 3 / 4 / 5)*, where the total of bushels from A and B combined is *(3900 / 6000 / 6900 / 10,000)*.

b. Suppose, however, that the sons are actually in situation 4: 700 worker-hours on A, 100 on B. They have not bothered to look at the increase in crop that would come from switching to situation 3. They simply justify 4 by pointing out that the "payoff per worker-hour" (product per worker-hour) is exactly the same on both plots, namely, *(6.0 / 7.5 / 8.4 / 9.2)*.

If the objective is a maximum quantity of bushels, this rule of thumb of equal product per worker-hour is *(correct / incorrect)*. The proper maximum-product rule is to distribute the labor so as to equate *(marginal / average)* products on the two plots. In this instance, correct labor-power allocation would yield a marginal product of *(4.0 / 6.0 / 7.5 / 8.0)* on each plot.

c. Suppose the labor is correctly distributed (situation 3). But the sons assigned to plot B feel humiliated because their product per worker-hour is lower than that of the sons working plot A. They complain that they could raise their productivity if only Papa would let them join their brothers on A. The father could equate the returns to labor on the two plots by imposing a "rent" of *(1 / 1½ / 3 / 5 / 6)* bushels for each worker-hour spent on more fertile plot A. This would underscore the fact that the higher worker-hour return on A is attributable to A's greater fertility, not to better-quality labor. This illustrates the *(phenomenon of general equilibrium / necessity of setting a price, if only an "accounting price," on any scarce resource)*.

a. 3900; 2300; A; 3; 6900   **b.** 8.4; incorrect; marginal; 6.0   **c.** 1½; necessity of setting a price, if only an "accounting price," on any scarce resource

QUIZ: Multiple Choice

1. Which of the following would not be determined by the forces of supply and demand under an "ideal" socialist system?
(1) The accounting prices of intermediate goods.
(2) The amount of the social dividend each individual receives.
(3) The price of labor (wage rates).
(4) The prices of consumer goods.
(5) None of these.

2. A socialist state wants to use its scarce resources to the best advantage. It uses a pricing system for distribution and sale of consumer goods. The state should instruct the manager of each consumer-good plant to try to set price at a level equal to:
(1) marginal cost of production *(MC)*, provided *MC* is rising.
(2) *MC*, provided *MC* is falling.
(3) *MC*, whether *MC* rises or falls.
(4) average cost of production *(AC)*, provided *AC* is rising.
(5) *AC*, whether *AC* is rising or not.

3. In terms of "efficient resource allocation," if grain is to be grown on two adjacent plots of land, A and B, A being naturally more fertile or productive than B (and both owned by the same landlord), then, quite apart from the landlord's desire to get maximum rent for the land:
(1) the same (nonzero) rent should be charged for both plots.
(2) no rent should be charged for either plot.
(3) a higher rent should be charged for B than for A.
(4) a higher rent should be charged for A than for B.
(5) plot A should be used intensively, plot B not at all.

4. The use (if any) of an interest rate in a fully socialist state would be:
(1) to regulate or at least influence the amount of money saved by its people.
(2) to regulate the total amount of investment undertaken.
(3) to regulate the amount of the social dividend available for distribution.
(4) to establish or at least influence the priority order in which investment projects were undertaken.
(5) not applicable at all.

CHAPTER 32

ECONOMIC ROLE OF GOVERNMENT: PUBLIC CHOICE AND EXTERNALITIES

Government has, in most advanced industrial countries, been growing in dramatic fashion over the past few decades. Government spending has climbed, both in absolute terms and in terms of a proportion of GNP. Taxation has been growing, as well. So have income-supported programs and regulatory intervention into both the marketplace in specific and society in general. The size of government has, in fact, turned into one of *the* political issues of the 1980s in the United States, the United Kingdom, and elsewhere around the democratic world.

Chapter 32 begins a two-chapter introduction to the economic issues that surround this growth. Section A of this chapter provides, to begin the process, a brief chronicle of its recent trends. A second section introduces you to an avenue of theoretical analysis, bearing the suggestive name of "public choice," that brings the old study of "political economy" up to date. Finally, the analysis developed in this second section is applied to the problem of economic externality in section C. The general notion of public goods (and bads) is reviewed there before a specific pollution example crystallizes the role of government in that type of market failure.

It must be emphasized from the beginning, though, that the possibility of "government failure" is not precluded. There can, and do, exist governmental policies that do more harm than good; and care needs to be taken in developing a line of analysis into the functioning of government to make certain that that potential is recognized and that specific cases are easily identified.

Proceeding through this first of two chapters, then, you will be able to accomplish the following objectives on the route to a preliminary understanding of how contemporary economic analysis deals with government activity.

LEARNING OBJECTIVES

1. Chronicle the growth in government spending, taxation, and regulatory activity over the past few decades, particularly in the United States.

2. List, explain, and give examples of the four major functions of government.

3. Understand the basic motivation behind the study of "public choice": the need to determine whether or not governments are organized in a manner that allows them to reach the objectives that they themselves set forth.

4. Identify a few of the various voting rules with which public, collective decisions can be made under the Constitution of the United States, and use the utility-possibility frontier first introduced in Chapter 31 to explore their similarities and their differences. Identify, as well, any difficulties that might arise with each of these rules.

5. Note the possibility that a majority voting rule can generate a stream of results that cycles with no unambiguous outcome, the consequential importance of agenda and decision-making rules in those circumstances, and the potential of logrolling to accommodate the intensity of preference and thereby reduce the severity of the potential cycling.

6. State and illustrate the Arrow theorem, which holds that there exists no majority voting scheme whose outcome (*a*) guarantees efficiency, (*b*) respects individual preferences, and (*c*) is independent of the agenda ordering.

7. Define externalities in general, and public goods in specific. Pay careful attention to the categorization of goods according to (*a*) whether they are public or private (or somewhere in between) and (*b*) whether they are allocated by collective, social decisions or individual, market decisions.

8. Analyze the inefficiency of, say, a pollution externality and the various mechanisms with which a society can try to bring it under control.

You are already familiar with a wide range of decisions through which government influences the everyday lives of people, businesses, and other economic agents across the nation and around the world. Parts Two and Three of the text concentrated on the macro policies of government, for example. These are stabilization policies that are typically directed at macro variables like unemployment and inflation; nonetheless they make it more or less difficult to buy a house, sell a car, or send kids to college. Parts Four and Five reviewed the myriad of roles that government can play on a micro level, and found no less significant activity. Regulation and antitrust action are but two items of a long list of micro-based roles that government has assumed. The point of the next two chapters is not to reiterate; it is, instead, to investigate the norms against which these activities are measured and how decisions about their directions are made in a democratic society.

1. Since World War I, the size of government, measured in terms of expenditures, taxation, and/or regulation has *(remained remarkably stable / fallen slightly since World War II after growing rapidly between wars / grown dramatically).* Compared with spending about $3 billion in 1913, government budgets across the United States had, by 1984, reached the *($1.4 trillion / $1.6 trillion / $2000 billion)* mark.

Over the same period of time, tax revenues collected by all levels of government have *(kept pace with / grown at a slightly slower pace than / grown at a slightly faster pace than)* expenditures, with enormous shortfalls coming during *(the Great Depression / World War II / and the Reagan years).* Nonetheless, tax revenues are still perhaps *(5 / 50 / 500)* percent larger now than they were at the turn of the century.

Regulatory activity, started perhaps in *(1913 / 1887 / 1778)* with the formation of the *(Federal Reserve System / Department of Agriculture / Interstate Commerce Commission),* reached its high point during the *(Nixon / Carter / Reagan)* administration. The entire range of activity was initiated not because the founding fathers thought that it was a good idea, but because they included in the Constitution a phrase about *(taxation without representation / equal protection under the law / securing the public interest),* whose interpretation lead quite naturally to economic and social regulation. Since the mid-1970s, though, "deregulation" has been the popular trend; name two industries that have been deregulated recently:

_____ and _____ .

---

grown dramatically; $1.4 trillion; grown at a slightly slower pace than; all three; 500; 1887; Interstate Commerce Commission; Carter; securing the public interest; banking; airlines

2. It is extremely interesting to note that the size of the government in a nation's economy seems to depend upon the size of that economy; measured as a proportion of GNP, poor, less developed countries show a tendency to tax and spend *(less than / more than / about the same as)* advanced countries. On the basis of your reading of Figure 32-2 of the text, circle the country in each of the following pairs whose government spends more as a fraction of GNP.

a. United States / Nicaragua

b. United States / United Kingdom

c. United States / France

d. United States / Japan

e. United States / West Germany

f. United States / Sweden

g. India / Switzerland

h. Sri Lanka / Netherlands

Notice that the United States, despite all the political furor about the size of the American government, ranks far from the top among developed countries in this ordering. In absolute terms, the size of the American government is enormous, of course; but relative to GNP, its size is considerably more modest.

---

less than **a.** United States **b.** United Kingdom **c.** France **d.** United States **e.** West Germany **f.** Sweden **g.** Switzerland **h.** Netherlands

3. The text identifies four major functions of government in a mixed economy. List them in the spaces provided:

a. _____

b. _____

c. _____

d. _____

Each of the following activities falls into at least one of the four categories that you just identified; indicate which ones in the spaces provided.

(1) A tax cut to reduce unemployment .... (_____)

(2) Specifying that the manufacturer is liable for any harm caused by his product .... (_____)

(3) Placing a tax on a steel producer's pollution .... (_____)

(4) Legislating that it is illegal to discriminate on the basis of sex .... (_____)

(5) Enacting an incomes policy that penalizes larger than specified wage increases .... (_____)

(6) Enacting a program of aid to families with dependent children .... (_____)

(7) Enacting daycare help to allow women to work .... (_____)

(8) Writing laws that allow triple damages to be awarded in cases of gross and wanton negligence .... (_____)

---

a. Prescribe legal framework **b.** Work toward macroeconomic stability **c.** Allocate resources efficiently **d.** Allocate resources equitably (1) macro (2) legal (3) efficiency (4) legal, efficiency, and equity (5) macro (6) equity (7) equity and efficiency (8) legal

Much of the material that has been presented thus far indicates in general, and sometimes in specific terms, what governments that want to do certain things "ought to do" to accomplish their goals. Public choice analyzes whether or not they, in fact, do what they ought to. Do they work to promote efficiency and equity, for example, or do they do the opposite even when their truly espoused goals are efficiency and equity? Are there barriers preventing governments from achieving their goals built into the way they operate—the rules of their games? If so, are there any general principles to be discovered to help break down those barriers?

Voting procedures define the rules of the decision-making game in the United States. We elect representatives who make decisions on our behalf and who want to continue to do so. These representatives therefore have an incentive to behave in a manner that will maximize their chances of (re)election. This behavior generates a supply of government activity, if you will, that is matched in the political arena against a demand for government activity generated by the voters. Two of the primary purposes of public choice theory applied to the United States are therefore (1) to analyze the workings of this "political marketplace" and (2) to evaluate the properties of its likely set of outcomes. The next few questions will review your brief introduction to that endeavor.

4. Figure 32-1 provides three reproductions of the same utility-possibility frontier. Movement from point *E* in a specific direction can be used to illustrate the result of a Pareto-improving government activity; shade in the area that captures all possible Pareto-improving points relative to point *E* in panel (a). A second area captures all points that would signify a redistribution of resources from individual A to individual B; shade in the area capturing all such points in panel (b). A third area signifies government failure so that government activity would leave both A and B worse off. Shade in the area that captures all these points in panel (c).

Of the three panels that you now have before you, panel *(a / b / c)* indicates with its shaded area all the possible outcomes that might arise from a unanimous voting rule. That is, because both A and B would have to approve the activity, and that would happen only if both A and B were helped by the activity—i.e., only if the utilities of both were increased. To illustrate the area of potential outcomes under majority rule (under the additional assumption that there are more type B people than there are type A people), you would need to

combine the shaded areas of panels _____ and _____.

Unanimity, as a voting rule, has its drawbacks. For one thing, any one individual can block a decision that can enhance the welfare of everyone else. That means that unanimity can produce only *(a Pareto-improving / an income-transferring / an expansionary)* government policy. In addition to being enormously cumbersome, therefore, unanimity would lead to the potential extortion of most of the gains of any policy by a clever skeptic from the population at large. Because anyone could play that game, unanimity would, more probably, lead to *(a flurry of small actions / no action / the abandonment of government of any kind)*—a *(maintenance / shattering)* of the status quo.

Majority rule, on the other hand, is not necessarily more efficient, but it is certainly more manageable. To avoid the potential tyranny of the majority, though, some important issues require majorities of *(greater than 50 percent / less than 50 percent)* to pass. Although it is subject to the pressures of special-interest groups in its most pragmatic form, majority rule seems to work fairly well in most circumstances.

---

shade in area I; shade in area II; shade in area III; (a); (a); (b); a Pareto-improving; no action; maintenance; greater than 50 percent

Public choice theory has extensively investigated the workings of majority rule, and its conclusions are not as reassuring as those gained from casual observation. For one thing, the result of a process involving majority rule

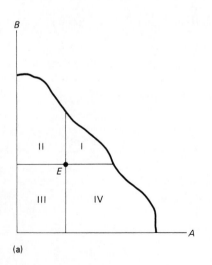

(a)

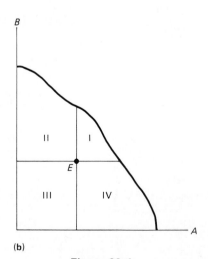

(b)

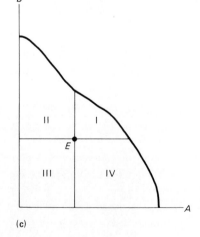

(c)

Figure 32-1

Table 32-1
Individual Rankings of Three Options

Individual Option	I	II	III
A	First	Second	Third
B	Second	Third	First
C	Third	First	Second

Table 32-2
Net Benefits to Individuals

Individual Project	Railroad (RR)	Farm Program (FP)	Earthquake Insurance (EI)	Status Quo (SQ)
A	100	−15	−10	0
B	−20	100	−25	0
C	−20	−10	40	0

Table 32-3
Combined Benefits to Individuals

Individual Project	RR & FP	RR & EI	FP & EI	All Three
A	_____	_____	_____	_____
B	_____	_____	_____	_____
C	_____	_____	_____	_____

need not be efficient. For another, there exists the possibility that a sequence of majority-rule referenda will cycle endlessly. That is the import of the Arrow impossibility theorem: there exists no majority-rule scheme that guarantees (1) efficiency, (2) respect of individual preferences, and (3) the independence of the result from the order of the agenda. Cycling, in particular, means that whoever controls the agenda controls the outcome. The next question explores this theorem.

5. a. Consider, first of all, the preferences of three people indicated in Table 32-1. Assume that, in voting between two options, that each person votes for the option that ranks higher in his or her preference ordering. Record, in the blanks, the outcomes of majority-rule decisions in the following contests:

(1) Option I against option II . . . . _____

(2) Option II against option III . . . _____

(3) Option I against option III . . . . _____

Now suppose that the Rules Committee of the process decides that option II will run off against the winner of an initial vote between I and III. The eventual winner will be option *(I / II / III)*. If option I were to run off against the winner of a vote-off between II and III, then the winner would be option *(I / II / III)*. And finally, allowing option III to run off against the winner of a I to II contest would produce option *(I / II / III)* as a winner. There would, in fact, be *(no / a single)* unambiguous winner until the agenda—the order of the voting decisions—were specified. This is an example of the impossibility theorem that contributed to Arrow's winning a Nobel Prize in Economics.

b. Suppose, now, that preferences according to individual were formed on the basis of net benefits indicated by Table

32-2. Regardless of the order of the vote, *(RR / FP / EI / SQ)* would win in pairwise contests of one project against another despite the fact that social welfare would be maximized by passage of *(all three programs / only FP and EI / only FP and RR / only RR and EI / only EI / only RR / only FP).*

c. Consider the possibility of logrolling to accommodate the intensity of the preferences reflected in Table 32-2. Record, in Table 32-3, the net benefits of the indicated combined packages for the three geographical regions. Record, in columns (1) through (3) of Table 32-4, the preferences of the three geographical regions in each of the three indicated pairwise elections. Note, in column (4), the winner and, in column (5), the combined net benefit of the winning package. Any of these packages *(would / would not)* beat the status quo in a majority-wins election; and *(would / would not)* beat a combination of all three.

On the basis of your entries to Table 32-4, it is clear that *(there exists / there does not exist)* an unambiguous winner to a sequence of pairwise elections. This is true despite the fact that *(the status quo / passage of all three proposals / passage of any two of three proposals)* maximizes the increase in net welfare. In fact, among the three two-project logrolling alterna-

Table 32-4
Pairwise Preferences

Election	Individual A (1)	Individual B (2)	Individual C (3)	Winner (4)	Net Benefit (5)
(RR & FP) vs. (RR & EI)	_____	_____	_____	_____	_____
(RR & FP) vs. (FP & EI)	_____	_____	_____	_____	_____
(RR & EI) vs. (FP & EI)	_____	_____	_____	_____	_____

tives, *(FP & EI / RR & FP / RR & EI)* generates the largest increase in net welfare.

---

a. (1) option I; (2) option II; (3) option III; II; I; III; no   **b.** SQ; all three programs
c. (reading down the columns of Table 32-3) RR & FP: 85; 80; −30; RR & EI: 90; −45; 20; FP & EI: −25; 75; 30; All three: 75; 55; 10; (reading down the columns of Table 32-4) (1): RR & EI; RR & FP; RR & EI; (2) RR & FP; RR & FP; FP & EI; (3) RR & EI; FP & EI; FP & EI; (4): RR & EI; RR & FP; FP & EI; (5): 65; 135; 80; would; would not; there does not exist; passage of all three proposals; *RR & FP*

---

6. Within the political system of the United States, there can be found a variety of problems that inhibit the workings of the pure majority-rule system envisioned by the public choice theorists. For one thing, while there is a one-person, one-vote rule, money *(does / does not)* matter. It can cost $1 million to run for Congress, and that money can come from across the country if the district is targeted by a large Political Action Committee (PAC). Jesse Helms spent over $17 million to run for reelection to the Senate in 1984—almost $400 per registered voter. For another, the activities of special-interest group lobbying can produce unrepresentative government. Government "by the people and for the people" or the "best government that money can buy"?—that is the question. The U.S government tends, in addition, to be *(shortsighted / longsighted)* because the longest term is *(2 / 4 / 6)* years for a U.S. *(Congressmember / President / Senator)*. This time limitation has a tendency to produce a *(high- / medium- / low-)* consumption economy aimed at making sure that the *(short / medium / long)* term is prosperous. It is little wonder, therefore, that fiscal policy is directed at employment and monetary policy is directed at unemployment (to see why, refer to Chapter 17).

---

does; shortsighted; 6; Senator; high-; short

---

7. Figure 32-2 plots two dimensions along which goods can be differentiated: (*a*) public vs. private and (*b*) market vs. collec-

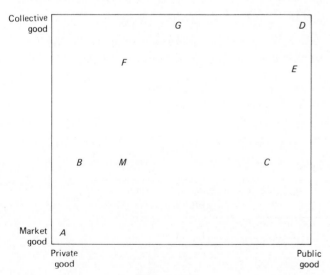

Figure 32-2

tive. Match each of the following goods with its most appropriate position in the figure. Indicate that position by recording the identifying letter in the spaces provided.

a. Hamburgers .... _____

b. National defense .... _____

c. A lighthouse .... _____

d. Medical care .... _____

e. An automobile .... _____

f. An ambulance .... _____

g. Pure research in economics .... _____

h. Interstate highways .... _____

i. Space research .... _____

j. College education .... _____

---

a. A **b.** D **c.** D **d.** B **e.** A **f.** E **g.** C **h.** G **i.** E **j.** H

---

8. Near the close of the text chapter, the term *external diseconomies* is used. Behind it lies a relatively new area for governmental activity, backed by the demands of environmentalists for a better society.

First, the term itself: from the economist's standpoint, a "diseconomy" is (roughly) something undesirable. More precisely, it is a cost that ought to be paid by the individual or firm responsible for that cost. It is "external" (rather than internal) if the individual or firm can escape paying it.

One classic example: heavy smoke from a factory chimney. No matter how disagreeable it might have been to those who worked or lived nearby, the factory's owners typically felt no obligation to clean up their act until public pressure, usually in the form of legislation, forced them to do so. A more recent version is "acid rain." Many plants, especially those involved in metal processing, emit sulfur dioxide and nitrogen oxide from their chimneys. These chemicals combine with moisture in the atmosphere to form sulfuric and nitric acid. The acidity of falling rain and snow is thereby increased creating more acidic lakes and rivers in which fish cannot reproduce. Moreover, there may be long-term impacts on human health from these and other chemical emissions.

Presence of such external diseconomies *(weakens / strengthens)* the case for laissez-faire. That case has assumed that the private market system, if fully competitive, would yield (in the form of market prices) an exact balance of costs and benefits. Insofar as external diseconomies exist (and insofar as they are growing more widespread), the market system *(will still / cannot)* furnish an accurate or adequate measure of costs.

Note that further discussion of "external diseconomies" (and of "external economies") shows up later in the text.

---

weakens; cannot

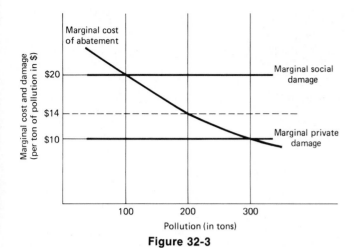

Figure 32-3

9. Figure 32-3 represents a simplification of Figure 32.7 in the text; the marginal social and private damages of pollution are assumed to be constant. The numbers recorded in Figure 32-3 can be used to explore the four mechanisms with which a pollution externality of the type illustrated can be handled. Two involve indirect influence by the government; they are

(1) _____

(2) _____

Two more would result from direct collective action; they are:

(3) _____

(4) _____

Given the curves defined in Figure 32-3, one of these actions is required because the privately determined level of pollution

would be _____ tons, at which the marginal cost of abatement equals *(the marginal social damage caused by the pollution / zero / the marginal private damage caused by the pollution).* That quantity *(exceeds / equals / is smaller than)* the

efficient level of pollution—_____ tons defined by the equality of the marginal cost of abatement and *(the marginal social damage caused by the pollution / zero / the marginal private damage caused by the pollution).*

Suppose, first of all, that those hurt by the pollution offered to pay the polluter $4 for every unit of pollution not emitted. In that case, the marginal private damage caused by the pollution would *(climb by $4 / remain the same / fall by $4)* because each unit emitted would mean a loss of $4 in potential compensation. The result would be, on the basis of the private decision

of the polluter, _____ tons of pollution. It would cost those

paying the "bribe" $_____, but that would *(exceed / fall*

short of) the reduction in extra social cost of $_____ that they would otherwise incur. The end result *(would / would not)* be optimal, but it *(would / would not)* represent an improvement.

Second, the possibility exists that government would hold

the polluter liable for the full extent of the social damage that his or her pollution produced. If it were 100 percent certain that these damages would be imposed, then the marginal social damage curve *(would / would not)* become the marginal private damage curve, and the optimal level of pollution *(would / would not)* be achieved. If the probability of assessing damages were not 100 percent, then there *(would / would not)* be some improvement as long as the chances of the polluter's being held liable were 0 percent.

Direct control is, of course, an option. Were the government interested in setting a standard above which the polluter could not stray, then it would set a maximum level of pollution at

_____ tons. Alternatively, a tax of $_____ per ton could achieve the same result. The polluter, if it were left to him or her, would prefer the *(standard / tax)*, because that would

allow the free emission of _____ tons of pollution.

_____

(1) Promoting negotiation given property rights; (2) Setting liability rules; (3) Setting standards; (4) Setting pollution taxes; 300; the marginal private damage caused by the pollution; exceeds; 100; the marginal social damage caused by the pollution; climb by $4; 200; 400; fall short of; 1000; would not; would; would; would; 100; 10; standard; 100

_____

10. Recalling that public goods are enjoyed by everyone, consider the two demand curves for some public good G represented in the two panels of Figure 32-4. If 10 units of G were offered, then the two people represented here would be

willing to pay $_____, $_____ from individual A and

$_____ from individual B. This suggests that a community's demand for a public good should be the *(vertical / horizontal)* addition of the individual demand curves of its citizens. Moreover, it suggests that, if the cost of the public good were efficiently distributed, then each person should *(necessarily pay an equal proportion / pay according to the marginal benefit that he or she would receive as indicated by the individual demand curves / pay according to how much they earn in income and how much property they own).*

_____

15; 10; 5; vertical; pay according to the marginal benefit that he or she would receive as indicated by the individual demand curves

_____

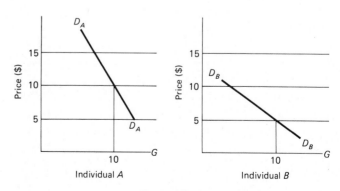

Figure 32-4

QUIZ: Multiple Choice

1. Which of the following statements is an accurate description of the history of government spending in the United States?
(1) The cost of government at all levels climbed from $3 billion in 1913 to slightly less than $1 trillion in 1984.
(2) The cost of government at all levels climbed from $100 billion in 1913 to $1.4 trillion in 1984.
(3) The cost of government at all levels climbed from $3 billion in 1913 to $1.4 trillion in 1984.
(4) The cost of the federal government in the United States climbed from only $3 billion in 1913 to $1.4 trillion in 1984.
(5) None of the above.

2. Taxation in the United States:
(1) has grown at a rate that far exceeds the rate of growth of government spending.
(2) has grown at a rate that, until 1981, roughly matched the rate of growth of government spending.
(3) has fallen in size in terms of a fraction of GNP since 1939, but has climbed in absolute terms.
(4) has risen dramatically in the 1980s in an effort to balance the federal budget.
(5) none of the above.

3. The initial source of regulatory activity in the United States was a clause in the Constitution that made a point of
(1) no taxation without representation.
(2) securing the public interest.
(3) guaranteeing equal pay for equal work.
(4) guaranteeing the freedom of speech against inferior products.
(5) anticipating the Equal Rights Amendment.

4. Regulatory activity in the United States
(1) began with the formation of the Interstate Commerce Commission in 1913 and reached a peak during the Reagan administration.
(2) began with the formation of the Interstate Commerce Commission in 1887 and reached a peak during the Carter administration.
(3) began with the advent of the Federal Reserve System to regulate banks and peaked with the deregulation of trucking during the Reagan administration.
(4) began with the formation of the Interstate Commerce Commission in 1887 and died with the deregulation of airlines during the Reagan administration.
(5) none of the above.

5. Regulation grew in the United States as it became clear that a laissez-faire policy was vulnerable to:
(1) pockets of poverty that are exploited by the more fortunate.
(2) the business cycle that buffeted the economic lives of nearly every citizen.

(3) widespread, inefficient discrimination on the basis of sex, race, and other factors.
(4) the flagrant abuse of the environment.
(5) all of the above.

6. Government can play a number of roles in a mixed economy. These potential roles include:
(1) prescribing a legal framework that defines "the rules of the game."
(2) reallocating resources to accomplish greater efficiency in the face of, say, monopoly or pollution.
(3) effecting macrostabilization by prudent exercise of fiscal, monetary, and other policies.
(4) reallocating resources to accomplish greater equity.
(5) all of the above.

7. Referring to the utility-possibility frontier depicted in Figure 32-5, a move that would illustrate a government failure might move an economy from a point like *A* to:
(1) a point like *B*.
(2) a point like *C*.
(3) a point like *D*.
(4) a point like *E*.
(5) none of the above.

8. If question 7 had referred to a transfer of resources from individual I to individual II, then the appropriate answer would have been:
(1).
(2).
(3).
(4).
(5).

9. If question 7 had referred to a move that would have been approved by a unanimous voting rule, then the appropriate answer would have been:

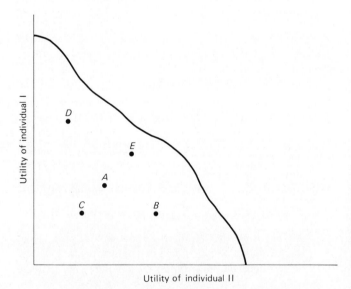

Utility of individual II

Figure 32-5

(1).
(2).
(3).
(4).
(5).

10. If question 7 had referred to a move that would have been approved by a majority voting rule given more people of type I than type II, then the appropriate answer would have been:
(1).
(2).
(3).
(4).
(5).

11. The Arrow impossibility theorem stated that
(1) it is impossible for people to agree so that a unanimous voting rule is necessarily a prescription for paralysis.
(2) it is impossible for a majority-rule system to last because of the tyranny that would necessarily be imposed by the majority.
(3) it is impossible for any voting rule to be analyzed because of the imponderables of the human mind.
(4) it is impossible for public choice theorists to glean any insight from voting behavior because majority voting rules always produce ambiguous results.
(5) none of the above.

12. Whenever majority rule produces a potential for cycling:
(1) the power falls to those who set the agenda.
(2) the possibility of logrolling to accommodate the intensity of preferences might help reduce that potential.
(3) there exists no other voting rule that would preserve efficiency, respect individual preferences, and guarantee that cycling would not occur.
(4) the need for rules beyond those that prescribe voting procedures is paramount.
(5) all of the above.

13. In the United States:
(1) there is a one-person, one-vote rule, but money and special interests are nonetheless powerful.
(2) the inherent democracy of one person, one vote overpowers all other factors in determining the outcome of any decision.
(3) the bureaucratic imperative is diminished by the watchdog arm of the U.S. Congress.
(4) the long time horizon of most politicians causes problems in maintaining short-term prosperity.
(5) all of the above.

14. A public good is one in which:
(1) the cost of exclusion is low and the marginal cost of one more consumer is low.
(2) the cost of exclusion is high and the marginal cost of one more consumer is low.
(3) the cost of exclusion is low and the marginal cost of one more consumer is high.

(4) the cost of exclusion is high and the marginal cost of one more consumer is high.
(5) the cost of exclusion and the marginal cost of consumption are irrelevant.

15. Public goods and public bads:
(1) are just mirror images of themselves, with the effect of their provision extending beyond the producer.
(2) can both be analyzed as externalities—one positive and one negative.
(3) are subject to the same types of governmental intervention because a market for neither exists.
(4) are hard to evaluate because their utility and/or harm extends beyond the confines of one individual.
(5) are all of the above.

16. Referring now to Figure 32-6, the efficient level of emissions is indicated by:
(1) point *A*.
(2) point *B*.
(3) point *C*.
(4) point *D*.
(5) none of the above.

17. If question 16 had referred to the level of emissions that would emerge in response to a $2 per unit emissions tax, then the most appropriate level would have been:
(1).
(2).
(3).
(4).
(5).

18. If question 16 had referred to the level of emissions that would emerge in response to an offer of $1 for every unit of pollution not emitted, then the most appropriate answer would have been:
(1).
(2).
(3).
(4).
(5).

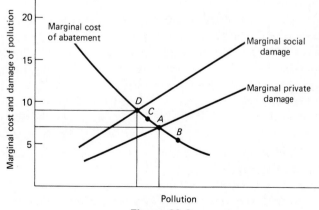

Figure 32-6

19. If half of the population of 10,000 were willing to pay $10 for the provision of a park and the rest were not willing to contribute a dime, then an expenditure of:

(1) $50,000 would match the town's demand price for parkland.

(2) a price less that $25,000 would reflect the town's collective demand for parkland.

(3) some amount of money for parkland would be appropriate only if one more person wanted to contribute to guarantee a more than 50 percent majority.

(4) a price in excess of $50,000 would certainly reflect the town's true demand for parkland.

(5) none of the above.

20. The Coase result states that:

(1) negotiation would always solve an externality problem if only government would get out of the way.

(2) the potential exists for negotiation to diminish the magnitude of an externality if property rights are well defined and negotiation costs are not too severe.

(3) negotiation must be forgone in lieu of direct governmental intervention whenever an externality problem becomes too severe.

(4) negotiation will always generate an efficient solution as long as costs are not too high and property rights are clearly defined.

(5) none of the above.

ECONOMIC ROLE OF GOVERNMENT: EXPENDITURE AND TAXATION

Chapter 32 provided some insight into theory behind the analysis of the role of government in a mixed economy; Chapter 33 now turns to the actual roles assumed by governments at all levels in the American economy. The first part reviews the major expenditure patterns of federal, state, and local government in the United States. The second accomplishes the same task with respect to taxation, with some discussion provided about the general principles upon which our tax policy is constructed. Toward the end of the chapter, some more theory is provided to introduce the notion of tax incidence—the attempt to answer the complicated question: "Who pays this here tax?" The theory will, however, lead to an application of this incidence theory to the distribution of the overall burden of our tax and transfer system.

Having completed your work on this chapter, you will have accomplished the following objectives.

LEARNING OBJECTIVES

1. Describe the nature of the patterns of expenditure by local, state, and federal government in the United States, and outline the recent evolution of those patterns into what we see today.

2. Relate, on the basis of these patterns, the construction of an efficient system of "fiscal federalism" and the blurring that necessarily occurs along the boundaries of the different levels of government.

3. Describe the conflicting principles of taxation—a benefit approach and an ability-to-pay approach—and the compromise between the two that has been accomplished in the United States.

4. Note specifically the difference between progressive and regressive taxation, and apply this distinction to differentiate the characters of various taxes employed in the United States.

5. Describe the character and importance of (a) individual income taxes, (b) sales taxes, (c) excise taxes, (d) payroll taxes,

(e) corporate income taxes, and (f) property taxes in the United States.

6. List briefly the sources of erosion in the base of the federal income tax.

7. Discuss efficiency as an issue in the design of a tax system and relate it to (a) the Laffer curve, (b) the integration of the corporate income tax into the individual income tax, and (3) the flat tax proposal.

8. Define the term "tax incidence" and explain why and how a tax might not fall on the economic agent identified in the tax codes.

9. Describe the procedure and the results of the Brookings study that concluded that the pattern of expenditure in the United States turns a mildly progressive tax structure into a fairly progressive fiscal structure.

The United States has evolved a pattern of fiscal federalism that assigns various types of expenditure programs to the lowest level of government that spans most of the potential spillover effects of each program. As a result, we see the federal government taking care of national defense, space exploration, and foreign affairs. We see local governments taking care of police protection, fire protection, public education, and other "local public goods." Finally, we see state governments administering highway, port, and welfare programs. Frequently the money required to support these programs at state and local levels flows down from the federal government, but the administration of the programs is conducted at the lowest possible level.

It should, of course, be noted that this structure is in a constant state of flux. The boundaries between governments and the spillover effects of programs are typically hard to define, and programs are forever being transferred from one level of government to another. Moreover, the growth in federal support for state and local administration of various programs was brought to an abrupt halt in the first months of the Reagan administration. The description recorded in this chapter will, therefore, probably become quickly dated as the United States moves into the next decade.

1. For the fiscal year 1985, annual expenditure by the United States federal government was estimated to be $*(600 / 735 / 925 / 1050)* billion. This is a total that exceeded the 1980 level of expenditure by nearly $400 billion.

The largest single item within this total for 1985, as indicated in Table 33-1 in the text, was *(interest on the public debt / national defense and international affairs / education, labor, and development / income security including social security).*

The expenditure for this item amounted to $_____ billion. It should be noted that income security was, in 1980, the largest component; a change in federal priorities toward defense expenditure *(is / is not)* therefore suggested by a cursory glance at expenditure patterns.

925; national defense and international affairs; 316; is

Some idea of the enormous increase in the size and importance of the federal government within the past few generations is to be gleaned by noting that in 1939, just before World War II, (1) total expenditure for national security was around $1 billion annually; (2) the federal Social Security program did not exist at all; and (3) other federal expenditures for health and welfare were of trivial importance. In sum, the federal government and its operations meant almost nothing in the everyday life of most people prior to the second world war.

World War II changed all that. Ordinary citizens were then required to pay income taxes, to complete income-tax forms (a privilege hitherto reserved for the rich), and to meet a host of federal restrictions. Wartime rationing was temporary, but widespread federal taxation was not.

2. Development of the Social Security system has proven far and away the most important factor accounting for growth in federal government outlays and collections since World War II. The demand for wider coverage has grown. Social security benefits, and deductions from wages and salaries to cover those benefits, have increased steadily. Social security is not only the second biggest item in the federal budget today; it is but one item in a collection of "welfare security" programs that has increased most spectacularly over the middle term. In 1970, total expenditure for "health, labor, welfare, and education" (i.e., expenditure for income security plus outlays for some of the other items listed in Table 33-1 of the text) came to $62.9 billion. In 1973; $99.1 billion. In 1976: $161.4 billion. For income security *alone,* the fiscal 1985 figure was $114 billion. That is down from 1980, but expenditure for income security has nonetheless *(almost doubled / doubled / just about tripled)* since 1970.

This postwar rise in welfare expenditures might have been offset (at least in part) by a sufficient decline in money spent on national security after World War II. But this spending category did not fall, as most people expected and hoped it would. Instead, "the cold war" began—and it was fought through the preparation of newly developed and horrendously expensive nuclear weapons. Beginning in the 1950s, and continuing thereafter, the total of spending on national defense persisted at levels that would have been literally incredible by the standards of 1939.

In recent years, this national-defense spending has, by comparison with items like income security and health, accelerated again after being relatively stable during the 1970s. The Vietnam war pushed it upward (although not by any spectacular amount). The expenditure total has risen since then, but the increases through 1981 probably reflected as much the impact of inflation as they did a larger fraction of real national product being directed toward weapons of war. Since 1981, though, the growth has been explosive, both in absolute terms and in terms of a fraction of GNP.

---

almost doubled

3. Questions 1 and 2 dealt with expenditure, and with increases in expenditure, by the federal government on income security and on national defense. They are both "government spending" items. Nevertheless, a critical distinction must be made between them. It is the same distinction whether the level of government is federal, state, or municipal. But the two items discussed—income security and national defense—illustrate it.

a. Chapter 2 in the text stressed the *law of scarcity:* the basic scarcity of *(productive inputs / money / consumer goods).* One of the two types of government spending is that which buys goods and services. Here, the law of scarcity is directly involved. In its purchases, the government *(competes / does not compete)* with private consumers. It is claiming the use of some part of the limited resource supply. Automobile manufacturers can and do make tanks. When the government places an order for tanks, labor and machines must work on that order, whereas they might otherwise have worked to produce privately bought automobiles.

The example just cited—the manufacture and purchase of tanks—is clearly an example of governmental expenditure on *(national security / health and welfare).* Some people regard much (or even all) of the money spent on national defense as money wasted. Others think altogether differently. But this difference of opinion is not the issue here involved. In principle, *all* goods and services bought by governments are bought for the public's benefit. Nevertheless, when the government buys any good—no matter whether a tank, or a typewriter for use in a national-park office—it is competing with private consumers by claiming the use of some part of the limited resource supply. Under full-employment conditions, private (nongovernmental) expenditures (for goods and services) and "public" or "social" (governmental) expenditures (also for goods and services) are competing alternatives for the use of the limited resource supply. So the choice between them can be illustrated by a diagram used extensively in text Chapter 2, and again in this chapter, namely, the _____ diagram.

b. Much of the federal government's expenditure on income security and health falls into an altogether different category— and here we reach the distinction between the two kinds of government expenditure mentioned at the beginning of this question. Outlays for income security and health are largely *transfer expenditures* (or transfer payments). They are outlays in which the government pays money, because it is considered in the national interest to do so, without exacting the supply of any commodity or service in return. An example would be *(purchase of a typewriter / payment of an unemployment benefit)*. People within the societies of the Western world have increasingly demanded that government assume at least part of the responsibility for (1) sickness and accident, (2) unemployment, (3) old age, and (4) poverty. The postwar rise in living standards has evidently prompted a belief that no individual or family should fall below some minimum level of income.

The term "transfer payment" applies because these outlays *(do not increase / increase)* the total of claims on the nation's limited productive-resource supply. Instead, they transfer some part of such claims from one person or family to another. If you pay taxes you must pay taxes to finance some veterans benefit, and part of the claim you would otherwise have had on goods and services is transferred to someone else. There are administrative costs so that the transfer is never dollar for dollar, but the size of the transfer seriously overestimates the cost in terms of real resources (Okun's leaky bucket).

Some of these payments might be designated as charity payments. Most are not. One person may be admitted to a veteran's hospital, not because he or she is destitute, but because of war service in Korea or in Vietnam. Others may receive social security benefits because for years their paychecks were subject to social security deductions. However, these people give no *concurrent* service in return for the benefit claimed. That is the definition of a government transfer payment (or transfer expenditure)—a payment for which the recipient gives no concurrent service in return.

---

a. productive inputs; competes; national security; production-possibility **b.** payment of an unemployment benefit; do not increase

4. Pick the transfer payments (one or more) from among the following. Payment from the government made to:
(1) An older citizen in the form of a social security check.
(2) A schoolteacher employed by a local school district.
(3) An unemployed worker laid off because of the effects of a deep recession.
(4) A government engineer, for a report deemed unacceptable by his superiors.

---

(1), (3)

The next two questions relate the expenditure and taxation behavior of government back to preceding chapters; one on macro policy and the other on the role of government.

5. a. A government's *fiscal policy* means its policy as to the nature and money total of its *(expenditures / tax collections / expenditures and tax collections)*.

b. Circle each of the following that would be regarded as a decision or action involving fiscal policy:
(1) An increase in the income-tax rate.
(2) A decision to finance an expenditure increase by issuing new government bonds.
(3) A decision to enter the nuclear-energy field by building plants to process uranium ore.
(4) An increase in transfer payments—specifically payments to the aged to cover medical expenses.
(5) A reduction in expenditures on armaments.

---

a. expenditures and tax collections **b.** all: (1) through (5)

6. a. The choice between social consumption (i.e., commodities and services provided through the agency of government) and private consumption can be illustrated by means of a production-possibility curve, because (pick one):
(1) Both kinds of consumption draw on the same scarce and limited supply of productive inputs.
(2) The kinds of inputs needed for social consumption are basically different from those needed for private consumption.

b. Most items within "social consumption" (government-supplied services) are things it would not be feasible to supply by charging each person a price and letting him or her buy the quantity chosen. The factor which the text cites to explain this, and which it regards as common to most social consumption items, is this (pick one):
(1) The service is too big to be handled by private business, or if it were so handled, the result would be a monopoly, and the price charged would be too high.
(2) If this service is provided for any single person, it thereby accrues to others as well; the benefit cannot be restricted so as to be available to that person alone.

---

a. (1) **b.** (2)

One question dominates all discussion of taxation: *From whom shall taxes be collected?*

If the benefit from some government project accrued entirely to some identifiable group within the population, then it might be fair to argue that taxes collected to finance that project should come from the group that benefits; e.g., taxes for road building should come from those who use the road.

Results of most expenditures are, however, too diffused to allow application of this "benefit principle." In that case, what is a fair or equitable basis for distributing the burden of taxation? In particular, how is it to be distributed between rich and poor? The debate on this question is a never-ending one. One side argues that the rich should carry most or all of the burden, simply because they are rich, and can afford it as the poor cannot. The opposition insists that "making money" is at least one of the incentives for personal initiative and effort. Hence, when you have accepted the soak-the-rich argument, you may carry your tax system to the point where it discourages incentive and encourages the most talented and inventive members of the population to move to another region where the tax laws are less severe.

In purely technical terms, the issues are summed up in the terms *progressive taxes* and *regressive taxes*. A progressive tax thrusts most of its burden on people of above-average income. A regressive tax bears more heavily on poorer people. A tax is not, however, progressive simply because it collects more money from a rich individual than from a poor one. To establish whether a tax is regressive or progressive, you must (1) find the amount of tax typically paid at various income levels within the population, and then (2) express this tax paid as a percentage of income. If these percentage figures rise as income rises—that is, if as income rises, the percentage of income paid in tax rises also—then the tax is progressive. If the percentage figures go down as you move to higher income levels, then the tax is regressive. If the percentage figure is pretty much the same at all income levels, then the tax is neither progressive nor regressive; it is "proportional."

7. In order to know whether a tax is progressive or regressive, it is (*essential* / *not strictly essential*) to know how much money it typically collects from individuals at different levels of income.

One existing United States tax is easily classified within this

progressive-regressive distinction; namely, the _____

_____ tax. This tax is (*progressive* / *regressive*).

_____

essential; personal income; progressive

8. a. A tax levied as 1 percent on the first $5000 of income, 2 percent on the next $5000, 3 percent on the next $5000, and so on would be (*progressive* / *proportional* / *regressive*).

b. A tax of 10 percent on all income except the first $1000—that $1000 being exempt from tax—would be (*progressive* / *proportional* / *regressive*).

c. If it is true that (among cigarette smokers) people with a yearly income of $8000 typically buy four packs of cigarettes per week, whereas with an income of $16,000 typically buy six packs per week, then an excise tax of 10 cents per pack would be a (*progressive* / *proportional* / *regressive*) tax.

_____

a. progressive   **b.** progressive (This one is sneaky. The tax is *almost* proportional; but the tax, expressed as a percentage of income, goes up as income goes up. See the definition of "progressive" in the preceding introduction)   **c.** regressive (The tax of 40 cents weekly is a higher fraction of $8000 than 60 cents is of $16,000)

9. Frequently it is not an easy matter to conclude whether a tax is progressive or regressive in nature. The tax on corporations' net income (profit) is a case in point. It takes a little thought to evaluate this tax.

Currently, this tax takes nothing of the first $50,000 of corporate profit. Above $100,000 of profit, the rate is 46 percent; and it stays at that figure, no matter how high the profit. Between $50,000 and $100,000, it takes 23 percent. Looking at these percentage increases, your first inclination may be to say this is a mildly progressive tax; the higher the income (profit), the higher the tax rate. However, for a big corporation, $100,000 is a rather minor amount. It is only a fairly minor simplification to say that the tax rate is a flat 46 percent of net income. So you may say: it's a progressive tax, but very moderately so; it's close to being a proportional tax.

This is the wrong way to evaluate the corporate income tax. If corporations were living people, things would be different; but they are *not* living people. Not being human, they do not feel the tax. Those who do feel it are its owners: the (*bondholders* / *shareholders*). The tax is levied on earnings which belong to them.

It is important here to grasp just how our reasoning is going. A corporation doesn't usually pay out all of its profit in dividends to stockholders. Part of that profit is typically "ploughed back" to expand its operations. Nevertheless, in principle, all profit belongs to the shareholder-owners. Hence a tax on that profit is a tax levied on those shareholders. There is one important reason why things may work differently; it is discussed in the next question. Here, we assume that the tax is really what it seems to be: a tax on income earned by the company's shareholders (even though they typically do not receive all of that profit as cash income).

Now (disregarding the lower percentages applicable below profit of $100,000) the tax is "proportional" in the sense that it is 46 percent of profit whether you own 1 share or 10,000 shares. But remember that in taxation, the term "proportional" is intended to mean a tax which takes the same percent of income at every income level, right across the entire population.

The critical point is that only a fraction of the population owns corporation stock. So the tax is a tax on a particular segment of the population.

Suppose all corporation stock is owned by poor people. (Never mind the fact that if they owned all that stock, they wouldn't be poor!) As a tax on the incomes of the poor, the corporate tax would be a (*progressive* / *regressive*) one. Alternatively, suppose all the stock is owned by rich people. That would make the tax (*progressive* / *regressive*).

The facts are that some people in the lower income brackets own a little stock; many in the middle brackets do; but the great bulk of corporate stock is owned by people with above-average incomes. So the corporate tax is (subject to the one vital qualification discussed in the next question, on balance, (*progressive* / *regressive*).

_____

shareholders; regressive; progressive; progressive

10. Suppose that the maximum corporation income tax rate were raised from 46 to, say, 55 percent; but let corporations respond to this tax by raising their prices just enough that their after-tax profit is unchanged. If so, this is an instance of *tax shifting,* and the *incidence* of the extra tax falls on the *(corporations / corporation's customers).* This possibility raises the interesting potential that most of the corporate tax, possibly even all of it, is not paid out of shareholders' incomes at all. It is passed on to other people via higher prices. If a corporation's customers happened to consist almost entirely of people in the lower half of the income range, and if it did manage to shift the tax via higher prices, this would make the tax (with respect to this particular corporation, anyhow) *(progressive / regressive).*

Conceivably, the tax might be shifted in another way. Corporations, when this tax is loaded upon them, might just possibly manage to *(lower / raise)* the prices they pay for their inputs, such as labor. There is a fair amount of evidence to suggest that at least part of the corporate tax is shifted via higher prices for the goods corporations sell, but the evidence is not all in. The issue is still being debated and explored.

The words "shifting" and "incidence" are important with respect to taxes; study their meaning. The government may require you to pay a certain tax; but you do not really pay it if, through the device of charging a higher price or paying a lower price, you make the tax come out of someone else's pocket. You have shifted the tax; and the true incidence of the tax is on the person out of whose pocket the money really comes.

Problems of tax incidence can become extremely complicated; it may be difficult to establish what the facts really are. Business firm or individual A may manage to shift part or all of a tax on to B; B in turn may shift some part of it to C—and so on. The one tax as to which there is almost no incidence problem is the _____ tax.

corporations' customers; regressive; lower; personal income

11. Some people complain that the corporate income tax entails "double taxation." They mean that after this income has been taxed, and part or all of the remainder is paid out in dividends, the dividends *(are / are not)* subject to personal income tax. This complaint assumes, of course, that the corporate tax *(is / is not)* shifted.

Insofar as the "double taxation" argument is valid, it applies *(to all of profit / only to that part of profit paid out as dividends / only to that part of profit which is retained undistributed).*

are; is not; only to that part of profit paid out as dividends

12. A tax imposed directly on an individual—i.e., whose amount payable is calculated by some factor such as size of income or value of certain of that person's assets—is designated as *(a direct / an indirect)* tax. A tax levied on a transaction, most commonly on the purchase and sale of a commodity, is *(a direct / an indirect)* tax. Some taxes, such as the corporate income tax, do not fall neatly into either the direct or indirect category.

Problems of determining real incidence are usually more difficult with *(direct / indirect)* taxes.

a direct; an indirect; indirect

13. **a.** The *benefit received* taxation principle argues that the distribution of tax levies between citizen A and citizen B should be in proportion to the benefit each receives from the expenditures of government—a "pay for what you get" principle. Which of the following (one or both) may be considered a valid criticism of this principle?
(1) It assumes the particular tax in question can be linked to a particular type of expenditure. If a government's expenditures are large and varied, this is often difficult to determine.
(2) Even if a particular tax can somehow be linked to a particular type of spending (e.g., federal government spending on national defense), it is difficult to decide, in quantity terms, how much benefit rich citizen A derives from it in comparison with poor citizen B.

b. An alternative principle is that tax payments constitute a sacrifice by citizens, and that the distribution of sacrifices should match their "ability to pay." It isn't altogether easy to establish what "ability to pay" really means, but an interpretation outlined in the text is that (pick one):
(1) Every citizen should pay an equal amount of money in taxes, thus equalizing sacrifices.
(2) Taxes should be levied and collected in strict proportion to the amount of income received by citizens.
(3) The tax system should be used to change the distribution of incomes, if needed, so that the after-tax distribution more closely approximates what is considered a socially desirable income distribution.

a. both (1) and (2)   **b.** (3)

14. The ability-to-pay approach raises two distinct issues of equity. The first, simply put, asserts that equals should pay equal taxes. This is identified in the literature as *(horizontal / vertical / reasonable)* equity. As simple as that assertion appears, it buries a fundamental question of how to determine when two people are equals. Are, for example, two people earning $20,000 per year equal if one of them has incurred $5000 in medical expenses? The tax codes say no. Medical expenses above 3 percent of adjusted gross income were deductible in 1984 (unless the taxpayer takes the "standard deduction"), so the person who faced the medical problem could be taxed on the basis of an income of $16,500 rather than $20,000 if he or she would have otherwise itemized his or her deductions.

The second equity issue involves the taxation of unequals; it is captured under the general rubric of *(horizontal / vertical / redistributive)* equity. This is the more controversial issue because of the (dis)incentive effects of income taxation.

---

horizontal; vertical

15.   a. Both of the following are tasks accomplished by taxation. Which is the more fundamental task—(1) or (2)?
(1) Taxes raise the money needed to finance government expenditures.
(2) Taxes reduce private purchasing power and thereby free for government use the real resources needed to carry out government projects.

b. Taxation may also accomplish the following purpose(s) (choose either or both):
(1) Taxes may be used to change the pattern of income distribution.
(2) Taxes spread the costs of providing government service as equitably as possible among the people.

---

a. (2)   **b.** both (1) and (2)

16.   a. Disregarding social security taxes, the two taxes which yield the most revenue for the federal government, ranked in order of their revenue importance, are:

(1) _____

(2) _____

b. The most important tax at the level of state government is the _____ tax; the most important tax at the level of local government is the _____ tax.

c. The single most important expenditure item at the state and local government level is _____ .

---

a. (1) Personal income tax   (2) Corporation income tax   **b.** sales; property
c. education

17. The difference between a *sales tax* and an *excise tax* is this: if the tax applies to all items sold, omitting only items specifically named in the law as exempt, it is *(a sales / an excise)* tax. If, on the other hand, the tax applies *only* to commodities or services named in the law (e.g., liquor, cigarettes), it is *(a sales / an excise)* tax.

---

a sales; an excise

18. A *value-added* tax is a tax imposed on each producing firm, on the value added to goods at that stage of production. If a textile firm buys $4000 of yarn and other raw materials, and employs labor to weave these materials into cloth which it sells

for $10,000, then the value which it added to its beginning materials was $(*4000 / 6000 / 10,000 / 14,000*), and that is the amount on which the tax is levied.

Suppose another firm—a garment manufacturing firm—bought all of this cloth and paid the full $10,000 for it. It paid a further $2000 for all its other raw materials, such as thread. It sold the resulting output of garments for $20,000. Then the value added by this firm would be $(*2000 / 4000 / 6000 / 8000 / 10,000 / 20,000*).

6000; 8000

19. The *marginal* tax rate on income means the fraction or percent *(of the last dollar of income that must be paid in tax / obtained by comparing total tax against total income)*. Alternatively, it is the extra amount of tax you would have to pay if you received an extra $1 in income (expressed as a percentage). If the personal income tax system is progressive (as it is in the United States and most other countries), this percentage figure will be higher than the *average* tax rate, which is the percent *(of the last dollar of income that must be paid in tax / obtained by comparing total tax against total income)*. That is, as the income level goes up, the marginal tax rate *(goes up / goes down / remains the same)*.

---

of the last dollar of income that must be paid in tax; obtained by comparing total tax against total income; goes up

20. The Laffer curve, as a theoretical construction, simply notes the potential for high income-tax rates to eventually *(encourage people to work more / encourage people to invest less / encourage people to work less)*. Figure 33-1 provides an illustration of such a curve. The 25 percent tax cut instituted by the Reagan administration in 1981 was based on the belief that

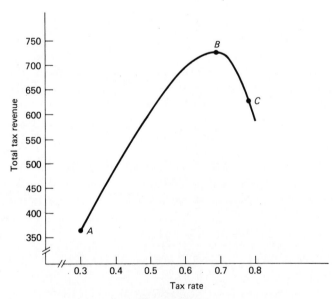

Figure 33-1

the economy was being taxed to a point like *(A / B / C)* so that revenues would actually climb with the reduction. That theory *(did / did not)* seem to work. On the basis of empirical work by Don Fullerton, in fact, it is most likely that the economy is being taxed to a point like *(A / B / C)*.

A second type of reform of the individual income tax, known as the flat tax proposal, has been advanced in both liberal and conservative quarters. It is estimated that the entire system as it now stands could be replaced by a proportional tax that takes *(10 / 20 / 30)* cents of every dollar earned by every American worker. Concern has been raised, however, that this would amount to *(an even larger transfer of the burden of the tax from the poor to the rich / a transfer of the burden from the rich to the poor / no transfer of the burden at all)*. Since a strict flat tax would allow no deductions, in its purest form, there might also be an enormous *(increase / decrease)* in the value of property in the United States because mortgage interest payments would no longer be deductible.

---

encourage people to work less; *C*; did not; *A*; 20; a transfer of the burden from the rich to the poor; decrease

---

21. The base of the individual income tax is eroded by a number of factors. First of all, personal exemptions amounting to $*(500 / 1090 / 2190)* per person were allowed in 1985. In addition, many sources of income receive preferential treatment. List five such sources in the spaces provided below.

a. _____

b. _____

c. _____

d. _____

e. _____

The net effect of these tax expenditures is to *(increase / leave unaffected / decrease)* the effective progressivity of the individual income tax of the United States.

1090; **a.** tax-exempt interest; **b.** Social Security benefits; **c.** Capital gains; **d.** Implicit homeowner rents; **e.** Retirement account contributions; decrease

---

22. Suppose that there were 100 people in an economy, and suppose that they could be ordered according to their incomes so that each earned $1000 more per year than the next lowest person. That is to say, suppose that person 1 earned $1000, person 2 earned $2000, and so on up to person 100, who earned $100,000 per year. Let each pay 10 percent of that income in taxes, and suppose that the revenue collected by the tax were divided equally among the first 50 people.

Figure 33-2 illustrates this structure. Line _____ illustrates the tax program, line _____ illustrates the transfer program, and line _____ illustrates the overall program in the same way that the curves on Figure 33-6 of the text portray the actual distribution of the net burden of the present U.S. structure. Is the overall program progressive? _____. Is the tax structure progressive? _____. Is the transfer program progressive? _____.

Now let the 10 percent tax rate apply only to incomes above $10,000 so that people 1 through 10 paid no taxes but shared in the transfer program. New lines are now required to portray this new structure; they are recorded in Figure 33-3. Line _____ now portrays the tax structure, line _____ portrays the new transfer schedule, and line _____ portrays the overall program. Is the transfer program now more progres-

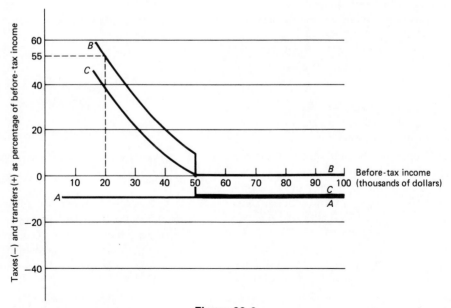

Figure 33-2

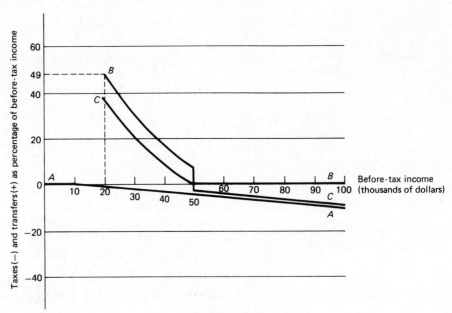

Figure 33-3

sive? _____. Is the tax system now more progressive? _____. Is the overall program now more progressive? _____.

AA; BB; CC; Yes; No; Yes; AA; BB; CC; No; Yes; Yes

QUIZ: Multiple Choice

1. A government's "fiscal policy" would properly be defined as its policy with respect to:
(1) the relation between the total of its purchases of goods and services and the total of its welfare payments.
(2) the regulation and control of banking and credit.
(3) the total and types of its expenditures, and the manner of financing these expenditures.
(4) that part of government operation whose services are sold to the public at a price per unit (e.g., the post office).
(5) none of the above.

2. Government transfer expenditures (transfer payments made to individuals) are basically different from all other types of government expenditure in this respect:
(1) Being fully financed by taxation, they merely transfer money from one person to another.
(2) They are always payments for which the recipient gives no concurrent service in return.
(3) Receipt of this payment does not increase the recipient's total purchasing power.
(4) They involve a "means test" (a check to ensure that without this payment the individual could not survive, or at least would suffer hardship).
(5) They have no effect either on private production or on private consumption.

3. A "production-possibility frontier" diagram can be used with respect to governmental activity to illustrate:
(1) the impact on production that will result if a given increase in taxes is levied to finance a given spending program.
(2) the choice between quantities of socially consumed goods and privately consumed goods, both of which must be produced out of the same stock of resources.
(3) the various means that a government can employ to finance its expenditures, such as the choice between taxation and the issue of bonds.
(4) the choice that government must make between its transfer payments and its purchases of commodities and services.
(5) none of the preceding.

4. One branch of federal government activity, considered highly important today but virtually nonexistent in 1930, is that of:
(1) the deliberate use of fiscal policy to keep unemployment at low levels.
(2) control over the purity of food and drugs.
(3) control over the money supply and the commercial banking system.
(4) construction (or assistance in construction) of highways and other transportation aids.
(5) the use of federal power to restrain the growth of monopoly and conspiracies directed toward monopoly.

5. There is a critical distinction to be made between two kinds of government expenditure. The distinction involves:
(1) welfare expenditures versus transfer payments.
(2) federal expenditures versus state or local expenditures.
(3) items with a monetary value versus items that cannot be so valued.
(4) transfer expenditures (transfer payments) versus purchases of goods and services.

(5) national-security outlays versus expenditures for peacetime activity.

6. The following payment made by a government would be classified as a "transfer payment": Payment:
(1) of a rental to the owner of a building used for government purposes.
(2) made to a consultant for a report where the recommendations made therein were not adopted.
(3) made to a former member of the armed forces to finance university education.
(4) made to a doctor for work in treating charity patients.
(5) for shoveling snow made to a worker who has lost his job and would otherwise receive unemployment benefits.

7. The largest single money item in the U.S. federal government budget is currently:
(1) energy, science, and environment.
(2) national defense and international affairs.
(3) interest on the public debt.
(4) general government (including justice).
(5) income security.

8. Any highway that is built by the government and made available toll-free to the public furnishes an example of:
(1) private consumption.
(2) a transfer expenditure.
(3) a welfare expenditure.
(4) monetary policy.
(5) none of the above.

9. A "welfare expenditure" means:
(1) any purchase by government of a commodity or service.
(2) a transfer payment.
(3) an expenditure by government that results in a useful service being made available to the public.
(4) an expenditure by government not financed by tax collections.
(5) any payment made by the public to government to cover the costs of social consumption.

10. A government may reasonably introduce a widespread program of transfer payments in order to:
(1) create a surplus in its budget.
(2) effect some change in the social decision on the question *For Whom* goods are to be produced.
(3) provide more social consumption.
(4) move the economy's production-possibility curve outward and to the right.
(5) reduce inflation.

11. The corporation income (profits) tax is defined as a tax levied on:
(1) all dividends paid to stockholders.
(2) the value added to production by each corporation.
(3) the corporation's total net sales.
(4) additions to corporate retained earnings.
(5) dividends paid plus undistributed profits.

12. One type of income not subject to taxation at all under U.S. income-tax law is this:
(1) Income in the form of dividends from stock owned.
(2) Income in the form of interest on corporation bonds owned.
(3) Real income in the form of housing services from a house occupied by its owner.
(4) Real income (i.e., any income not in the form of money) of any and all kinds.
(5) Income in the form of capital gains.

13. An argument made in favor of the corporation income tax is that:
(1) it taxes only earnings above the normal return on invested capital.
(2) without it, some fraction of corporation income may not be currently taxed at all.
(3) on balance, it is a regressive tax.
(4) it taxes te income received by bondholders.
(5) it means double taxation (at least in part) of corporation earnings.

14. Which alternative in question 13 would be correct had it referred to an argument against the corporation income tax?
(1).
(2).
(3).
(4).
(5).

15. The tax yielding the largest annual revenue for the federal government (disregarding social security withholdings from wages and salaries) is the:
(1) personal income tax.
(2) corporation income tax.
(3) value-added tax.
(4) excise tax on liquor and tobacco.
(5) property tax.

16. The tax on an income of $20,000 is $4000. If this income were to rise to $22,000, the tax would rise to $4800. The marginal rate of tax implicit in these figures is:
(1) 20 percent.
(2) about (but not more than) 21 percent.
(3) more than 21 percent, just under 22 percent.
(4) 40 percent.
(5) none of the preceding.

17. A government introduces a new and very regressive tax. If a Lorenz curve is used to show the distribution of after-tax income, the effect of this new tax upon the Lorenz curve will be to:
(1) push the curve up to a new and higher level.
(2) cause it to bulge farther away from the diagonal line.
(3) cause it to move closer to the diagonal line.
(4) leave the curve unchanged.
(5) perhaps do any of the above—impossible to tell from the information given.

18. A relatively unqualified advantage of the property tax, from the standpoint of the local government imposing it, is this. It:

(1) is steady in yield through prosperous and recession periods.

(2) is very similar in effect to an income tax, property and income being so closely related.

(3) inflicts little hardship upon property owners in a recession.

(4) involves few problems of "equity" in taxing different property owners.

(5) is not correctly described by any of these statements.

19. A correct statement with respect to "capital gains" (e.g., profits made in stock market transactions) in the United States would be that such gains are:

(1) not taxed at all under present law.

(2) taxed just as though they were any other form of income received.

(3) taxed at a heavier percentage rate than other forms of income.

(4) taxed as though they were regular income, but with an additional $600 exemption allowed.

(5) not properly described by any of the preceding.

20. A general sales tax, without any exempted commodities, is considered to be:

(1) a progressive tax because it applies to luxuries as well as necessities.

(2) a regressive tax because wealthy people spend a smaller percentage of their total income on taxed commodities, and hence the proportion of tax payments to income is greater for poor people.

(3) a progressive tax because wealthy people spend more than poor people.

(4) a regressive tax because more money is collected from a poor person than from a rich one.

(5) a proportional tax because everybody pays the same tax percentage on each purchase.

21. A "proportional" tax is correctly defined as one such that (taking the taxpaying population overall, or in terms of the typical taxpayer):

(1) the ratio of money tax amount collected to money income received is about the same at all income levels.

(2) about the same amount of tax money is collected per taxpayer, regardless of taxpayer incomes.

(3) as one turns to higher incomes, one finds that the percentage of income taken in tax falls.

(4) at higher incomes, the amount of money taken in tax rises.

(5) does not fit any of the preceding descriptions (i.e., none of them is correct).

22. Which alternative in question 21 would be correct had that question referred to the correct definition of a "progressive" tax?

(1).

(2).

(3).

(4).

(5).

23. Which alternative in question 21 would be correct had that question referred to the correct definition of a "regressive" tax?

(1).

(2).

(3).

(4).

(5).

24. By the "incidence" of a tax is meant:

(1) its tendency to fluctuate in total amount collected, as between boom and recession periods.

(2) its relative importance in the budget of the government involved.

(3) the extent to which payment can be avoided through one or more "loopholes."

(4) its burden, in the sense of identifying the people whose real income is actually reduced by reason of that tax.

(5) the effect to which its imposition is likely to induce those who must pay it to work less, in an effort to avoid part of such payment.

25. The tax systems of state and local governments in the United States compare with the federal system as follows:

(1) They are both more progressive.

(2) They are both more regressive.

(3) The state system is more progressive than the federal, the local system less so.

(4) The local system is more progressive than the federal, the state system less so.

(5) None of the preceding statements is correct.

26. According to the text, the largest single tax expenditure in the existing federal personal income tax law concerns:

(1) the provision on capital gains.

(2) illegal tax evasion by the self-employed.

(3) depletion allowances for crude oil holdings.

(4) nontaxation of income in the form of services from owner-occupied homes.

(5) income from securities that by law are tax-exempt.

CHAPTER 34
POVERTY, EQUALITY, AND EFFICIENCY

Americans seem to be driven by two distinct motives as they work to shape their society. Americans want, on the one hand, to have a chance to live the "American dream"—to work hard, to work honest, perhaps to be lucky, but somehow to wind up a success in life. They want the opportunity to become wealthy, or at least to get ahead, and they do not think it fair or appropriate for economic or social policy to get in the way.

Americans also want to provide some measure of equity across the land. They are bound by the very wording of the Constitution to try to provide equal opportunity for all people. They have not always been very successful in that effort, though, and they have tried to compensate. The social fabric of the United States is filled with programs that try to help those individuals and families who have not been fortunate enough to ride opportunity to a position of economic security.

As noble as these two goals are, it is one of the major lessons of economics that they frequently get in each other's way. The very programs that provide some measure of protection for the disadvantaged cost money to run; they therefore require tax revenues to operate, and taxation makes the American dream more difficult. The programs, themselves, are often accused of generating disincentives among the disadvantaged against attempting to get head. The whole business is summarized in what Arthur Okun called "the big tradeoff." It is the classic tradeoff between equity and efficiency.

Chapter 34 reviews this tradeoff in theoretical as well as practical terms. It begins with a section that defines poverty and identifies its sources in contemporary America. A seond section proceeds to explore the Okun thought experiment of the leaky bucket—the conceptual construction that allows the equity-efficiency tradeoff to be clearly delineated. Antipoverty programs currently in place in the United States are finally reviewed in the last section, and are compared with at least one theoretical alternative—the negative income tax.

Having completed your work in this chapter, you will have accomplished the following objectives. You should not, however, be misled by the tone of this list into thinking that all Americans think that antipoverty programs are worth the expense. The recent trend of government during the Reagan administration has been to reduce the size of these programs. The purported rationale for these reductions was a tightening of qualifying requirements to make certain that only the truly needy get the welfare benefits. The reductions are, however, perhaps more consistent with the purported objectives of the supply-side tax cuts of the same administration; a more honest rationale might be a belief that the country had strayed too far toward equity in the practical tradeoff between equity and efficiency. In the context of Okun's bucket, the Reagan people seem to have determined that the leaks were too large.

LEARNING OBJECTIVES

1. Define poverty in the United States and discuss its various sources.

2. Describe the incidence of poverty in the United States in the mid-1980s, and explain the recent trend toward larger numbers.

3. State the Rawlsian view of social welfare, and explain why maximizing the utility of the least advantaged citizen need not prescribe an absolutely equal distribution of income.

4. Explain Arthur Okun's leaky bucket, graph it, and delineate the costs that cause the leaks.

5. Record a list of major welfare programs still in place in the mid-1980s to fight poverty, and explain why their structures can lead one to conclude that the poor face the highest effective marginal tax rates in the country.

6. Describe the negative income tax proposal, and outline both sides of the debate over its adoption.

345

Classical economists believed that the distribution of income was determined by economic law, and that nothing could change it. Wages, rents, and profits were all determined in the marketplace, they thought, and any attempt to alter the distribution that emerged from that determination would be futile. A majority of Americans in the 1960s would, however, have nothing to do with that conclusion. Before he died, President John Kennedy announced a "war on poverty" as part of the New Frontier; his dreams were embodied in the Great Society programs of the Johnson presidency. To what end? The percentage of American families living below the poverty line fell from 22 percent in 1960 to 11 percent in 1970. The percentage was still roughly 11 percent in 1980, but it has climbed steadily since then to something in excess of 15 percent. Poverty is still a problem in the United States, and it is growing.

1. The poverty line is determined by computing *(a maximum poverty index / a minimum-subsistence income / an average American's food budget)*. Social workers provide some information for the computation, and their numbers are corroborated by multiplying a subsistence food budget by *(2 / 3 / 4)*. Why? Because families at the lower end of the income scale typically spend *(one-quarter / one-third / one-half)* of their incomes on food. In 1962, the poverty line income for a family of 4 was $*(2500 / 3100 / 4400)*; in 1984, the same benchmark income was $*(7800 / 9600 / 10,600)*.

a minimum-subsistence income; 3; one-third; 3100; 10,600

2. The text cites five causes of income inequality. Name at least three, listing first the factor specified as responsible for the greatest disparities in income.

a. _____ .

b. _____ .

c. _____ .

d. _____ .

e. _____ .

There are limits to the income which superior talent or energy can earn. A popular television personality may earn huge sums annually. But income is limited by the number of performances he or she is physically capable of giving. Moreover, earnings may dwindle if popularity fades, or old age begins to set in.

Property income is not subject to equivalent restraints. Ownership of stocks and bonds may demand comparatively little supervisory effort. If you have somehow made a good start in security ownership, you may reinvest your earnings and watch them grow. Moreover, unless checked by death or inher-

itance taxes, property and its income can be passed on to your children, as talent and energy cannot.

a. Differences in property wealth   **b.** Differences in personal ability   **c.** Differences in education and opportunity   **d.** Class barriers to opportunity   **e.** Differences in age and health.

3. Table 34-1 in the text records the incidence of poverty in some of the major demographic groups of the United States in 1982. Families headed by women *(rank first on / rank second on / rank third on)* the list, with _____ percent of their numbers falling below the poverty line. Blacks rank *(second / first / fourth)*, with _____ percent. Perhaps most tragically, children under the age of 6 rank *(above / the same as / below)* the overall average with _____ percent—almost one kid in every four in the richest country in the world!

Referring now to Figure 34-1, note that the average income of the bottom one-fifth of the population (ranked by income) has climbed _____ percent since 1930 from $_____ (real 1984 dollars) to $_____. As a percentage of national income, however, the income earned by the lowest 20 percent of the population *(fell / remained the same / rose)*, to stand at *(2 percent / 5 percent / 10 percent)* in 1984. Through the lowest 20 percent, therefore, 60 years of history has *(shifted the Lorenz curve in toward the 45° line / done nothing to the Lorenz curve / shifted the Lorenz curve away from the 45° line)*, indicating *(a trend toward greater equality / no trend toward greater equality / a trend toward less equality)*, in the lower incomes. Put another way, the average income of the lowest 20 percent of the population has climbed only because *(total income has fallen / total income has remained the same / total income has risen)*.

rank first on; 40.6; second; 35.6; above; 23.8; 130; 3000; 7000; remained the same; 5 percent; done nothing to the Lorenz curve; no trend toward greater equality; total income has risen.

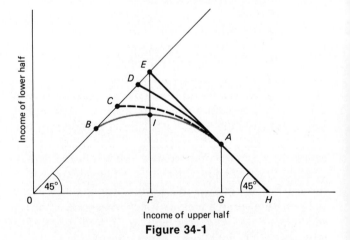

Figure 34-1

4. Figure 34-1, which is similar in general construction to text Figure 34-2, can illustrate the "disincentive" or "leaky bucket" consequence of income redistribution. The horizontal and vertical axes measure, respectively (to the same scale), the incomes of the upper half and the lower half of the population.

This diagram has a 45° line emerging from the origin. If there were complete equality in income distribution (if each individual received exactly the same income as every other individual) then the words "upper half" and "lower half" would be meaningless. Alternatively, the so-called upper half (*any half*) of the population would receive exactly the same total income as the so-called lower half. The distribution between them would have to be represented by some point (such as *E*) on this 45° line. (Remember, the scales on the two axes are the same.)

a. In fact, incomes are not equally distributed. On this diagram, then, the point indicating the distribution between the two halves must lie (*to the right of and below / to the left of and above*) the 45° line. (Somehow, it always seems to work out that the upper half gets more income than the lower half.)

Suppose that total income received by both halves is 0*H*, divided between an upper-half total of 0*G*, and a lower-half total of *GH*. Let us (temporarily) record this total and its division on the horizontal axis. However, this axis is reserved for upper-half income receivers, and they will probably object to this trespass by those lower-half people on their territory. So draw a 45° line from point *H*, extending up to the other 45° line. Point *E* is where the two lines meet. On *EH*, pick point *A* such that *AG* is equal to *GH*.

Now we have things sorted out as they should be. 0*G* (measured horizontally) is the upper-half income total. *AG* (measured vertically) is the lower-half total. Point *A* indicates the distribution of income between the two halves.

Any movement toward greater equality of income distribution would mean a move away from *A* (*toward / and also away from*) *E*. Suppose there is such a movement, with absolutely no "disincentive" or "leaky bucket" effect. That is, the population's entire income total is (*reduced / not reduced at all*). On the diagram, this redistribution movement will follow the straight line[1] *EH*, from *A* toward *E*.

b. It is usually argued that any movement directed toward greater equality of income distribution would have at least some "disincentive" consequences; i.e., there would be at least

a small leak in the bucket. Suppose this redistribution is tackled by means of heavier progressive income taxation. The extra taxes thus collected from higher-income people would be passed on to lower-income groups via a "negative income tax," or some other such transfer-payment device. Insofar as people try to avoid heavier taxation by working shorter hours, or in other ways earning less money income, the total of real GNP will (*fall / rise*). The path of redistribution will no longer run along the straight line *EH*. Starting at *A*, it will drift (*above / below*) *EH*. The total of real income will become (*less / more*) than it was at point *A*. The more sweeping the intended income redistribution—i.e., the farther the planned movement from *A* toward *E*—the (*less / more*) pronounced this disincentive effect is likely to be.

c. The three curved lines in Figure 34-1, *DA*, *CA*, and *BA*, show three possible sets of discentive consequences. Among them, the smallest disincentive effect is indicated by (*DA / CA / BA*).

Notice that line *CA* is approximately flat in the region close to point *C*. This means that if redistribution toward complete equality were pressed hard enough, there would be a sufficient drop in total GNP that the real income of the lower half, in absolute terms, would (*increase only slightly / not increase at all / decrease*). In *relative* terms—that is, relative to income received by the upper half—the share of the lower half would (*still increase / remain constant / decrease*).

d. The most drastic disincentive effect is illustrated by line *BA*. If redistribution effects are such that total income follows this path, the lower-income half of the population will at first (as the movement from *A* toward *B* commences) experience a moderate (*increase / decrease*) in real income. But thereafter the real income of this lower half of the population will (*increase / decline*), in absolute terms.

If the likely redistribution path is as indicated by *DA*, society may well decide that some movement from *A* toward *D* is worthwhile: the sacrifice of total real income is justified by the resulting greater equality. But if the probable path of redistribution is indicated by *BA*, or even by *CA*, the cost in terms of total real income sacrificed is greater, and society must put a higher priority on income equality if either of these two paths is to be followed, even for a short distance away from *A*.

---

a. to the right of and below; toward; not reduced at all **b.** fall; below; less; more **c.** *DA*; not increase at all; still increase **d.** increase; decline

[1] In a more advanced analysis, we would have to recognize that *EH* might not be a straight line. We put matters in terms of a transfer of *money* income between the two groups. But of course it is the resulting transfer of *real* income that matters: one group gains more purchasing power, the other group loses it. Of necessity, we measure real income in money terms; but it is still the transfer of real income we want to indicate by any move along *EH*. Suppose that money dollars are transferred from the upper-income half to the lower-income half. If the result is to change any of the money prices at which the items of real income are valued—and it probably will, if the tastes of the two groups are at all different—then things become more complicated. The dollar-for-dollar transfer can still be depicted as a movement along a straight 45° line, but the real income transfer will no longer be a straight line, even if there is no disincentive effect. This complication is best left completely to one side in an introductory survey.

5. John Rawls, an economic philosopher of considerable reputation, suggested a welfare objective that would mandate society's attempt to maximize the utility of its (*least well-off / average / most well-off*) citizen. A mapping of the indifference curves associated with this objective in the geometry of Figure 34-1 is provided in Figure 34-2. Notice that as you move along line *JK* from point *J* to point *K*, society's welfare is unaffected even though the income of the upper half climbs.

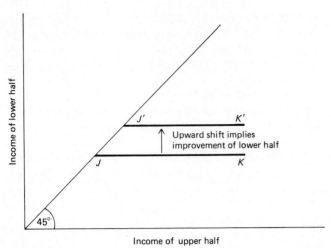

Figure 34-2

Why? Because the least well-off people—the lower half of the income distribution—receive nothing. To maximize society's welfare, therefore, the Rawls criteria would require that you simply push horizontal welfare lines as high as possible given some sort of feasibility constraint.

Now use the leaky-bucket lines of Figure 34-1 as constraints. For each of the following tradeoff curves, indicate in the spaces provided which point would be chosen according to the Rawls criteria.

a. *AE* .... (_____)

b. *AD* .... (_____)

c. *AC* .... (_____)

d. *AB* .... (_____)

It is apparent, from this exercise, that the Rawls prescription mandates complete equity only when the leaks are *(not too big / are enormous)* and the tradeoff schedules are not *(too curved / too straight)*. It is an objective function that, for at least one example, qualifies precisely what might be meant by "equity, but not at any cost."

___

least well-off; **a.** *E*; **b.** *D*; **c.** *C* (barely); **d.** *I*; not too big; too curved

How big are the leaks? What are their sources? First, there are the administrative costs of running welfare and tax-redistribution programs. Although these costs might be enormous in absolute terms in an economy as large as America's, they do not mount up very quickly relative to the magnitudes of the programs actually administered.

Second, there is the potential for welfare programs to create disincentives to work. Jerry Hausman has determined that these effects are potentially significant, but his work is disputed by many others who find that, for example, the elasticity of the supply of labor to changes in the wage rate is quite small.

Third, there is the potential for progressive taxation to retard saving and investment and thus growth. Okun, himself, discounted this worry by noting that saving and investment accounted for 16 percent of GNP in 1929 and 16 percent of GNP in 1973. 1929 was before the imposition of the full force of the progressive income tax, and 1973 was at the height of the American welfare state. In response to the tax incentives with which the Reagan program tried to stimulate investment and saving, incidently, the combined total of saving and investment actually fell to 13 percent of GNP.

Finally, there are potentially harmful changes in attitude and behavior that might be fostered by a progressive tax and welfare state. More people might cheat on their taxes, or lay around and not work, and so on. These costs are hard to measure, and their jury is still out.

6. **a.** Circle the numbers of those among the following statements which repeat, at least approximately, the text's views on welfare programs—other than the "negative income tax" (discussed in part **b** of this question).

(1) The *discentive* effect within many welfare programs means a loss of billions of dollars in potential national product.

(2) These programs are very costly; many are unnecessary and should be done away with as soon as reasonably possible.

(3) A welfare recipient who takes a minimum-wage job often finds that with the consequent reduction or termination of welfare payments, he or she is worse off economically than when not working.

(4) Many, or most, programs are shot through with gross abuses. Most recipients could work, but avoid doing so because of the opportunity to remain on welfare.

(5) The cost of welfare programs has become a tremendous financial burden to many large metropolitan areas.

(6) Most of the programs are necessary, but they are costly, often inefficient, often degrading to the recipients.

b. The proposal for a "negative income tax" is a comparatively recent one. The text chapter's overall verdict upon it is *(favorable / unfavorable)*.

Conservatives and liberals often join in support of this proposal. The difference is that the conservative frequently wants the negative income tax to *replace* most or all of the other welfare programs. The liberal often regards continuation of at least some of these other programs as still necessary; in this sense, the negative tax is wanted as a supplement.

One feature of the negative-tax proposal is important and gives it a resemblance to the ordinary tax system. Suppose you receive $3000 annually from the government as a negative income tax. Through personal effort, you then manage to increase your own earnings by $3000. The consequence will be that your negative-tax payment *(ceases entirely / remains at $3000 / is reduced by some intermediate figure such as $1500)*. That is, your total receipts (negative tax plus earnings) *(go up / go down / are unchanged)*. Hence, there *(is an / is not* *any)* incentive to increase total receipts built into the system. In this, it *(differs from / is the same as)* most other welfare programs.

---

a. (1); (3); (5); (6) **b.** favorable; is reduced by some intermediate figure such as $1500; go up; is an; differs from

---

7. Consider a welfare system that operates according to the following rules:

1. Basic welfare payments are $4000 less 25 percent of any earnings.

2. $3000 in food stamps are available at 40 cents for each dollar earned up to a limit of $7000.

3. $2500 in medical care is provided to families with incomes less than $6000.

Fill in the blanks of the following table to record the benefits received by three different families according to these rules. Family A has no outside income, family B has an outside income of $2000, and family C has an outside income of $9000. The net total income of each family is the sum of the total benefits received, recorded in row D, and the outside income earned.

	Family (A)	Family (B)	Family (C)
(A) Basic welfare	_____	_____	_____
(B) Food stamps	_____	_____	_____
(C) Medical care	_____	_____	_____
(D) Total welfare	_____	_____	_____
(E) Outside income	$0	$2,000	$9,000
(F) Net total	_____	_____	_____

It is clear that the effective average tax rate faced by family B is

_____ percent; the effective average tax rate

faced by family C is _____ percent.

Now assume that the government would pay the full value of the welfare program if the income earner were no longer living at home. Leaving would generate $_____ in extra income for family B and $_____ in extra income for family C. This provision would clearly generate a strong incentive for poor families to dissolve.

(reading down the columns) family A: $4,000, $3,000, $2,500, $9,500, $9,500; family B: $3,500, $2,200, $2,500, $8,200, $10,200; family C: $1,750, $0, $0, $1,750, $10,750; (11,500 − 10,200)/2000 = 65; (18,500 − 10,750)/9000 = 86; 1,300; 7,750

---

8. Based on the figures provided by Table 34-3 in the text,

place the following welfare-transfer programs in the order of their importance in the federal budget of 1984: Medicare; Medicaid; Social Security; unemployment compensation; food stamps and child nutrition; housing; aid to families with dependent children; aid to aged, blind, and disabled.

(1) _____

(2) _____

(3) _____

(4) _____

(5) _____

(6) _____

(7) _____

The total amound budgeted for these programs was, in 1984,

$_____ billion. This is a large amount of money, but it is a smaller total than that of 1980 (and lower in each and every category of the specific programs designed to aid the poor).

Social Security; Medicare; unemployment compensation; Medicaid; aid to aged, blind and disabled; aid to families with dependent children; food stamps; 319.7

QUIZ: Multiple Choice

1. The poverty line, computed to reflect a minimum-subsistence income:

(1) has grown from $3100 in 1962 to over $10,500 by the mid-1980s.

(2) has been nearly stable in real terms over the 20-year interval between 1962 and 1982.

(3) is roughly 3 times the minimum-subsistence food budget.

(4) has seen its food component climb to more than $3500 by 1984.

(5) all of the above.

2. The War on Poverty, initiated by President John Kennedy and embodied in the Great Society of Lyndon Johnson

(1) managed to reduce the percentage of American people below the poverty line from 22 percent in 1962 to 15 percent in 1971, where it remains today.

(2) managed to cut the percentage of Americans below the poverty line from 22 percent in 1962 to 11 percent by 1970, where it remained until 1981 when it started a climb back above 15 percent.

(3) had little or no effect on the percentage of Americans below the poverty line and thus warranted cancellation by the Reagan administration.

(4) had a small effect on lowering the percentage of people below the poverty line until participation requirements were tightened by the Reagan administration in 1982.

(5) none of the above.

3. Differences in education and training are considered to be major factors in determining the likelihood that an individual will find himself or herself in poverty. This link is reflected in the correlation of statistics about American blacks in the 1980s. While twice as many blacks as whites found themselves below the poverty line in 1982:
(1) the percentage of whites having completed high school was 10 points higher for whites than for blacks.
(2) the percentage of blacks having completed college was one-half the percentage of whites who completed college.
(3) the median income of white families with which a college or professional education could be financed for white children was nearly twice the median income of black families.
(4) the median formal schooling experience of white men over 25 years of age was almost a full year longer than it was for black men of the same generation.
(5) all of the above are accurate statements with which to support the correlation of education and training to poverty.

4. Which of the following is not a reason that might explain the incidence of poverty in contemporary America?
(1) Differences in education and training.
(2) The existence of noncompeting groups.
(3) Differences in economic environment, including the distribution of wealth.
(4) The asymmetric effect of recession on demographic groups.
(5) Differences in ability among all people.

5. The average income of the lowest 20 percent of the population has increased by more than 130 percent since 1929:
(1) so the need for antipoverty programs is a myth.
(2) but the percentage of total income that represents has held steady at 5 percent.
(3) but almost all that growth is explained by growth in total GNP.
(4) choices (2) and (3) only.
(5) none of the above.

6. Of all children living in the United States in 1984, less than:
(1) 1 in 10 were living below the poverty line.
(2) 1 in 20 were living below the poverty line.
(3) 1 in 4 were living below the poverty line.
(4) 1 percent were living below the poverty line.
(5) 1 million were living below the poverty line.

7. The Rawls notion of social welfare:
(1) necessarily mandates that the best distribution of income is an equal distribution of income.
(2) focuses attention on bringing the welfare of the least well-off citizen up to the level of everyone else regardless of the efficiency losses.
(3) simply asks that society attempt to improve the welfare of the least well-off citizen as much as possible.
(4) is irrelevant in a practical discussion of poverty because it leads to no concrete suggestions of policy or direction.
(5) none of the above.

8. Referring to Figure 34-3, let point *A* represent some initial

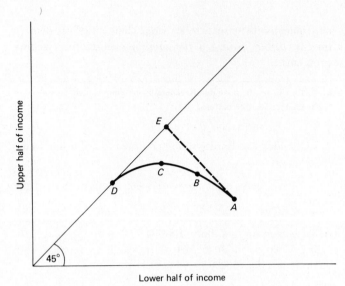

Figure 34-3

distribution of income between the indicated upper half and the lower half. Which point represents the equal distribution of income if there were no leaks in the bucket?
(1) *A*.
(2) *B*.
(3) *C*.
(4) *D*.
(5) *E*.

9. Which answer to question 8 would have been correct if it had asked for the point that would represent equality given the leaks that produce curve *ABCD*?
(1).
(2).
(3).
(4).
(5).

10. Which answer to question 8 would have been correct if it had asked for the point that would be selected if society chose on the basis of Rawlsian objective criteria?
(1).
(2).
(3).
(4).
(5).

11. Which of the following is not likely to be a significant source of "leaks" in the equity-efficiency tradeoff?
(1) The administrative costs of running a welfare–income redistribution program.
(2) The work disincentives of the progressive income tax.
(3) The disincentives against saving and investment produced by the progressive income tax.
(4) A change in attitude that makes cheating on taxes more acceptable.
(5) All of the above could be significant, though there is little evidence to support choice (3).

12. Which of the following was the largest item in the 1984 budget targeted directly at helping the poor?
(1) Medicaid.
(2) Aid to families with dependent children.
(3) Food stamps and child nutrition.
(4) Aid to aged, blind, and disabled.
(5) Housing assistance.

13. Despite its importance in explaining the incidence of poverty, spending on programs that support the education and training of the poor fell from 1981 to 1984, as did most of the spending targeted directly at helping the poor:
(1) by less than 1 percent.
(2) by about 5 percent.
(3) by nearly 8 percent.
(4) by almost 15 percent.
(5) by more than 25 percent.

14. One serious problem with the current structure of the U.S. welfare state is:
(1) the inability of government to get all those eligible for a program to apply.
(2) the inability to make absolutely sure that anybody who is not eligible does not enter a program.
(3) the workings of the eligibility requirement that give the poor the country's highest effective marginal income tax rates.
(4) the migration of the poor to states with high benefits.
(5) all of the above are serious problems with the current state of affairs.

15. By the "inefficiency" of income redistribution is meant:
(1) the reduction in total output caused by those unfavorably affected by redistribution, and by their decision to pay less in income tax by working less.
(2) the administrative costs of redistribution.
(3) the lesser skills of the gainers from redistribution.
(4) the total amount of income transferred from upper-income to lower-income groups.
(5) the resulting reduction in total taxes collected by the government.

16. A poor family's employment earnings are supplemented by a "negative income tax"—in the amount, say, of $1500. Under this tax proposal, if family employment earnings were to rise by $1000, the income received from the "negative tax" would typically:
(1) fall by $1000.
(2) fall by more than $1000.
(3) fall by some amount such as $500.
(4) not fall at all.
(5) rise by some amount such as $500.

17. The text evaluates the negative-income-tax proposal as being:
(1) undesirable because of its "disincentive" effect, even though in other respects it would be superior to existing welfare programs.
(2) superior to existing welfare programs in its "incentive" effect, although some existing programs would probably have to be retained.
(3) undesirable in that it would be inferior in most effects to existing welfare programs.
(4) not much better and not much worse than existing programs, hence hardly worth introduction because of the costs of such introduction.
(5) superior to existing welfare programs to such an extent that it would substitute for virtually all of them.

18. Some social scientists have been convinced that the matter of income distribution is dictated by natural or social laws, beyond the power of any elected government to alter (except in the very short run). The text's verdict on this view is, in general, as follows:
(1) It is valid in that there is a reasonably close match between distribution of income and distribution of energy or talent, but in other respects the evidence fails to support it.
(2) There is no supporting evidence, and it should be dismissed outright.
(3) Elected governments *can* alter income distribution, and could easily have done much more than they have done were it not for pressure brought by special-interest groups.
(4) It is almost completely valid, because the great bulk of the evidence supports it.
(5) Elected governments *can* alter income distribution, although the redistribution process is more complex and difficult than some reformers are prepared to admit.

19. During some periods in U.S. history, income disparities appear to have widened; during other periods, to have narrowed. A period within which (the text suggests) the lower-income groups probably lost ground was that of:
(1) World War II.
(2) the Great Depression of the 1930s.
(3) World War I.
(4) the late 1970s.
(5) the prosperity of the 1920s.

20. Among question 19's five time periods, there was one within which—again, the text suggests—the lower-income groups probably gained ground. Which one was it?
(1).
(2).
(3).
(4).
(5).

CHAPTER 35
WINDS OF CHANGE: ECONOMIC ALTERNATIVES

The text thus far has concentrated on the modern mainstream view of how a mixed economy like that of the United States works to solve the fundamental economic questions of *How*, *What*, and *For Whom*. Your introduction to this type of structure is almost complete. Chapter 35 focuses on economic alternatives to mixed capitalism, and has been included at this point for two important reasons.

First of all, the profession did not arrive at its current state overnight. The mainstream view espoused by many economists in mixed economies is the product of an evolutionary process that has proceeded slowly over the course of more than two centuries. You should be aware of at least the broad outline of that evolution. Second, not all the world's economies operate in a fashion that is best described by the mixed structure envisioned by mainstream economic thought in the United States. Over 1½ billion people across the world live in societies whose economic structures are based on the principles of Marxism or socialism. You should also be aware of the major differences that these structures impose on the workings of those economic structures.

The general objectives of this chapter are thusly defined; simply put, they prescribe your being exposed to different ways of looking for answers to the same fundamental questions. With your horizons thus broadened, you should have accomplished the following more specific objectives.

LEARNING OBJECTIVES

1. Distinguish between normative economics," or "what ought to be," on the one hand, and "positive economics," or "what is," on the other.

2. Explain briefly Adam Smith's argument of laissez-faire. Explain also why Smith's *The Wealth of Nations* received such widespread acceptance so rapidly after its publication.

3. Outline briefly David Ricardo's forecast about the future distribution of income among the major economic classes within society.

4. Summarize the major contributions which the neoclassical school made to classical economic theory. Include a list of the major objections to unrestricted laissez-faire raised by this neoclassical school.

5. Place the Keynesian revolution into its historical context, and describe the modern mainstream view of the world in terms of its historical antecedents.

6. Explain the modern critiques of the mainstream ranging from the libertarian view of the Chicago School through the Galbraithian ruminations about modern capitalism and into the New Left prescriptions of the radical economists.

7. Explain what Marx meant by "the exploitation of labor by capital," and by "surplus value."

8. Describe what the rule of the labor theory of value, fully applied, would mean in terms of (*a*) the prices of finished goods, and (*b*) the distribution of income.

9. Outline what (in Marx's view) sets the rate of surplus value imposed by capitalists upon workers.

10. Outline why, in Marx's view, capitalism was inevitably headed for a crisis generated by the failure of purchasing power to match the total value of goods produced.

11. List the major developments that have taken place since Marx wrote and have (thus far, at any rate) proven Marx's forecasts to be incorrect.

12. Describe the Soviet economic structure and compare its performance with the major developed, mixed economies of the West.

Adam Smith's *The Wealth of Nations* occupies a unique place in the esteem of economists, less because it argued in favor of laissez-faire and more because it was the first coherent account of the working of a market system. Much of what is found in Chapters 2 and 3 of the text derives from Adam Smith: the law of scarcity; the role of prices; the need for competition and the consequences of monopoly. Smith's argument is sometimes incomplete, sometimes confused, sometimes contradictory. Yet these are the inevitable shortcomings of a pioneer work of immense scope.

Two further points about the classical economists deserve mention. First, their work developed out of a lively and perceptive interest in contemporary issues. *The Wealth of Nations* is a frontal attack on the then-influential mercantilist philosophy of governmental interference in trade matters. Malthus and Ricardo dealt at length with issues arising from the Napoleonic Wars, notably war-induced price inflation and tariff protection. When Napoleon's power play ended and normal shipping was resumed, the British food-growing aristocracy found itself exposed to new competition from America and elsewhere. The English landowners contrived an increase in the grain tariff—the famous Corn Laws. Subsequently, and largely in consequence of the influential writings of the classical economists, the Corn Law rates were reduced and, in 1846, abolished.

Second, there is just enough unanimity of viewpoint among the English classical economists to warrant grouping them together as a school, and no more. Malthus and Ricardo conducted a lengthy correspondence on innumerable issues. Almost always, they disagreed. (These disagreements did nothing to destroy a touchingly warm and enduring friendship which terminated only with Ricardo's death at the age of 51.) For example, most of the classical economists accepted, at least in rough outline, Say's Law of full-employment purchasing power. Malthus did not, although he could not build an alternative theory. It was more than 100 years later that Keynes did construct such a theory.

It is this inner diversity of views, as well as its uniformity of views, that explains why the classical school provided inspiration for both Marxist and "bourgeois" economists.

1. The most prominent members of the early English "classical school" of economists were:

Adam Smith (1723–1790)
Thomas Robert Malthus (1766–1834)
David Ricardo (1772–1823)

Match these names with the following descriptions:

a. Sought, as a major part of his work, to discover the "laws of distribution"—i.e., the economic laws by means of which the national product was divided between three classes: laborers, landowners, and entrepreneurs (manufacturers and merchants): _____.

b. Enunciated the doctrine of lassez-faire—i.e., government should not interfere with human activity, save in such restricted areas as the maintenance of law, police duties, and national defense: _____.

c. Best known today for his theory of population growth, but in fact dealt with a wide range of contemporary economic problems: _____.

d. Developed the hypothesis that, in the long run, land was the crucially scarce economic factor, so that economic growth would result in a continuing increase in the rental price per acre received by owners of land. (Note that although one of the three economists cited is particularly associated with this hypothesis, it is implicit also in the reasoning of another of the three.) _____.

e. Set out the doctrine of self-regulating "natural order" of human affairs, and used the *invisible hand* concept to illustrate this doctrine: each individual, pursuing his own self-interest within a market system, is "led by an invisible hand to promote an end which was no part of his intention": _____.

f. Relied heavily on the law of diminishing returns in his analysis. (NOTE: *Two* of the three economists did so.)

_____ and _____.

---

a. Ricardo **b.** Smith **c.** Malthus **d.** Ricardo; Malthus **e.** Smith **f.** Malthus; Ricardo

2. The English classical economists had, so to speak, roughed out the general shape of economic analysis. Thereafter, one group—the neoclassical economists, still predominantly English until the early twentieth century—undertook to correct, to refine, and to enlarge classical ideas. Another group—Marx and his followers—attempted a more fundamental revision.

The classical account, perhaps because it felt impelled to emphasize the basic scarcity of productive factors (Chapter 2), had stressed *supply* factors as the principal ingredient within commodity prices. Demand elements were not given much consideration. As the text puts it, it is almost as though all classical supply curves were (*horizontal / vertical*), so that any shift in the demand curve (*would / could not*) change the level of price.

This classical supply-side account vacillated between a labor theory of value and a cost-of-production theory. (The latter asserts that the price of a commodity must be explained in terms of the quantities of labor, land, and capital required for its production.) Both labor and cost-of-production theories may seem plausible at first. But on closer inspection, they prove to be after-the-event explanations.

Marx handled this problem by accepting the labor theory of value, but adding to it his concept of *surplus* value (discussed in the Appendix). Prices, Marx said, are *not* equal to labor values in capitalist society; but they *would* be, in a properly functioning society. The labor theory of value, thus made over into "what ought to be" as much as "what is," became a banner in the crusade. Marxists sometimes called for acceptance of the labor theory somewhat as a fundamentalist Christian faith may demand unquestioning acceptance of the literal truth of everything in the Bible.

The neoclassical school, in contrast, stuck (or tried to stick, at any rate) to "what is." They recognized labor cost, and costs of production generally—i.e., the supply side of the matter—as having a major part to play in price determination. But they added the element which earlier had been neglected, namely:

_____. The outcome—and here the work of Alfred Marshall (1842-1924) was most important—was the demand-curve and supply-curve approach of Chapters 4 and 18.

Demand and supply curves are graphs; therefore they have a mathematical background, whether that background is recognized or not. Economics was becoming more mathematical. The neoclassical introduction of "marginalist" concepts (marginal utility in Chapter 22, marginal cost and revenue in Chapters 23 through 25, marginal product in Chapter 27) illustrates the point. If you have had training in calculus, you will know that "marginal" is a way of explaining the differential calculus.

It was as part of this more mathematical trend that the theory of general equilibrium (Chapter 31) was developed.

The major figures here were: _____, _____

_____, and _____.

---

horizontal; could not; demand; Leon Walras; Stanley Jevons; Wilfred Pareto

3. In the twentieth century, the major development in economics has been the development of Keynesian analysis, already discussed at length earlier in the text. Bitterly resented upon its introduction because it seemed to upset so many traditional beliefs, this analysis warns that in developed societies relying heavily on investment spending, the market system cannot be left to its own devices with assurance that a full-employment equilibrium will result. In brief, Keynesian analysis banished any belief in (*the law of scarcity / the law of supply and demand / Say's Law / the law of diminishing returns*).

Say's Law

4.   a. The Chicago School of economists, including _____

_____, _____, _____, and Milton Friedman, generally feels that markets (*work / don't work*) and that government intervention is (*necessary and beneficial / unnecessary and detrimental*). The rational-expectations macroeconomics of the Chicago and Minnesota schools, covered in the Appendix to Chapter 16, is in fact simply a

logical extension of this line of reasoning—a line of reasoning that traces its origins directly back to the (*invisible hand of Adam Smith / the lament of diminishing productivity of Malthus and Ricardo / the spending multipliers of Keynes*). Lest anyone think that it is a line of reasoning that abides only in the halls of academia, it should be emphasized that the Economic Report of the President prepared for President (*Nixon / Carter / Reagan*) by the Council of Economic Advisers in (*1972 / 1978 / 1982*) endorsed almost the entire philosophical picture of the Chicago School.

b. A second critique, made popular by John Kenneth Galbraith, also holds that mainstream theory is out of touch with reality. Circle each of the following statements if it accurately reiterates either one of the contentions of the Galbraithian view or a commonly held opinion of his work.

(1) His theory is basically Marxist both in its origins and its conclusions.

(2) His work is more a criticism of existing theory than an outline of an identifiable and testable alternative theory.

(3) His argument presents a serious challenge to Keynesian economics.

(4) His reasoning is in large part a synthesis of other people's ideas; his role has been to merge these ideas, and to present them in unusually persuasive fashion.

(5) Big business is not necessarily bad, though not necessarily good, either.

(6) Consumers are not the masters of their own fates; they are manipulated by advertising and salespeople to the point of not always knowing precisely what is in their best interest.

(7) The public sector seems to be starved for resources, while the private sector squanders enormous wealth that could otherwise be used to improve the welfare of all.

c. Radical economists come at the world from the New Left. They espouse many types of government intervention; list at least four in the spaces provided.

(1) _____.

(2) _____.

(3) _____.

(4) _____.

---

a. Frank Knight, Henry Simons, Friedrich Hayek; work; unnecessary and detrimental; *invisible hand* of Adam Smith; Reagan; 1982   **b.** (2), (4), (5), (6), (7)   **c. (1)** Markets need democratic planning; **(2)** Price controls are needed to free resources; **(3)** Industrial policies are necessary; **(4)** Greater equity is essential

The term *socialism* has been applied to a variety of political and economic movements. It is generally agreed that the characteristic common to most of these movements is a belief that the privilege of unlimited ownership of private property is not an inalienable right. In particular, socialists challenge the right of private ownership of productive resources in the form of land and capital goods.

While the origins of socialist thought can be traced back to the Greeks, the socialist movement developed its real momentum in the eighteenth and nineteenth centuries. The Industrial Revolution profoundly altered European economic and social conditions. It brought immense wealth to some members of the new entrepreneur class. It brought degradation and misery to many workers employed in the new industries. To people of conscience, it seemed that in the new economy, the cards were stacked against anyone unlucky enough to be forced to try and earn his or her living from labor alone. Members of this "proletariat" class would inevitably be exploited by a small group of employers exercising power acquired through ownership of productive inputs other than labor.

However unanimous socialists may have been on the indignities of the new industrial society, they were far from agreement on the proper method of return. The anarchists believed in total abolition of the state; later, anarchism came to be associated with the view that capitalism (and the state) could be overthrown only by violent means. The "utopian" socialists hoped to reform society by establishing as seeds within that society small communal groups whose behavior would be governed by "high-minded" rules.

Karl Marx regarded these utopian projects as fatuous diversions of the reform effort. He insisted on a socialism that would be "practical" in the essential sense of being based on a *scientific* analysis of human society. In 1848, to express these views, he and Friedrich Engels published the *Communist Manifesto.*

Marxism's intellectual foundation is "dialectical materialism," an adaptation of Hegel's "dialectical idealism." This Marxian system describes human history in terms of movement and change. Each stage of development within that history contains some inner contradiction which is the seed of its own destruction. Change is the process by which one contradiction is removed, only to produce another. The fundamental assumption in Marxism, as stated in the *Communist Manifesto*, is that "the history of all hitherto-existing society is the history of class struggles." In this history, the ruling class exploits one or more other classes. Feudalism was one stage in human history, in which the ruling class consisted of land-owning nobility. The inner contradiction within this system led to its overthrow by capitalism. According to Marx, the bourgeois ruling class of capitalists would in due course be overthrown by the proletarian laboring class. Marx thought this would be the final stage of the class struggle, since the overthrow of capitalism would result in a classless society.

To enlarge his argument that capitalism carries within it an inner contradiction leading to its own destruction, Marx developed his theory of surplus value.

5. **a.** Karl Marx's principal work was his three-volume *Das Kapital.* In the text's evaluation, referring particularly to opinion among rebels and dissenters, *Das Kapital* is *(no longer / still)* considered Marx's major contribution to reform.

b. Marx's forecasts in this work included the following: the real wage of laborers would *(rise / fall)*; the "reverse army of the unemployed" would *(increase / decrease)* in number; the rate of capitalist profit would *(rise / fall)*; business cycles would *(grow / diminish)* in intensity; the capitalist system would collapse by reason of *(an excess / a deficiency)* of purchasing power.

Thus far, these forecasts *(have / have not)* been vindicated.

c. Interest in Marx is today turning toward other aspects of his thought. Two ideas in particular are mentioned, namely:

(1) _____ .

(2) _____

_____ .

a. no longer **b.** fall; increase; fall; grow; a deficiency; have not **c. (1)** alienation; **(2)** the economic interpretation of history (the view that behavior is shaped by material interests, or in more Marxian terms, by the conditions of production)

6. Circle as many of the following as correctly indicate characteristics of the Soviet Union:

a. The state owns all land.

b. The state owns almost all capital equipment.

c. Consumer goods are given money prices, and workers choose among these consumer goods according to these prices; the wages of workers are paid in money.

d. Central planners once were plagued with the problem of a widespread piling up of consumer goods which could not be sold; now this problem is much less acute.

e. Workers have, in general, no choice as to the geographic area in which they may work.

f. Workers have very little choice as to the occupation they would like to enter.

g. Planners use prices to support and achieve their planning goals.

h. There are no important differences in wages or salaries; i.e., there are no significant departures from equality of income distribution.

i. Such inequalities of income distribution as do exist tend to reflect political influence rather than special competence or skill in some occupation.

j. In the decision on *What* goods to produce, top priority is given to investment projects and defense production, consumer goods being produced to the extent possible after these requirements have been satisfied.

k. Industrial workers are now given a fair degree of freedom to bargain collectively with plant managers on wages and other terms of employment.

l. Industrial plants operate by being given a quota of output which they are expected to meet or exceed.

m. The quota system is presently used only to allocate productive resources, while consumer goods sell at competitive prices because markets are allowed to function.

n. Enterprise managers are rewarded for achieving quantity targets, and this system breeds poor quality, hoarding, and reluctance to take risks and pursue innovations.

o. Prices change frequently without warning because planning is an imprecise science.

p. Political control of economic planning has moved gradually, but steadily, away from centralization and toward decentralization.

q. Material balances help planners keep track of thousands of different goods and factors of production.

r. The state levies a tax on the sale of goods at each production stage, so that consumer-goods prices considerably exceed wages paid to produce those goods.

s. Marxist concepts with respect to value are still employed with respect to relative prices set on consumer goods and on investment goods.

---

a; b; c; g; j; l; n; q; r

7. Westerners who think that "criticism of the system" is discouraged (and dangerous) in the Soviet Union are correct in reference to *political* criticism. However, complaints over shoddy consumer goods or poor production techniques, via gripe letters to the newspapers, are *encouraged*. Such criticism evidently performs a corrective function. Russian production is still governed, in part, by authoritarian direction from above, rather than by consumer demand. Consumers still must resort to this clumsy letter-to-the-editor device to try to get things changed. In Western societies, the equivalent corrective device is one of

---
_____ .

a system of markets, prices, and profit incentives

8. Circle as many of the following as correctly described comparisons between the United States, the Soviet Union, and other economies (according to the text).

a. The Soviet Union's rate of growth in GNP since World War II has exceeded that of all Western countries.

b. As the Soviet Union's output grows and in consequence turns more toward services, it is estimated that her rate of growth will increase, since services do not involve the same heavy investment in capital equipment.

c. GNP in the Soviet Union is a little more than one-half of the United States GNP, according to the presently available statistics.

d. The Soviet Union has been able to imitate technologies already developed elsewhere. This fact has made it somewhat easier for her to maintain a high GNP growth rate.

e. The long-term rate of growth in GNP in the United States is fractionally above 5 percent annually.

f. The Soviet Union devotes a larger fraction of her GNP to military expenditure than the United States does.

g. Experience with GNP figures since World War II furnishes no clear answer to the question of whether collectivist societies or decentralized societies are better adapted to rapid rates of growth.

---

c; d; f; g

QUIZ: Multiple Choice

1. The concept of a "natural order" is associated in economics particularly with the name of:
(1) John Maynard Keynes.
(2) Leon Walras.
(3) Adam Smith.
(4) Karl Marx.
(5) Alfred Marshall.

2. Which of the five economists cited in question 1 was the author of the statement, "People of the same trade seldom meet together, even for merriment and diversion, but the conversation ends in a conspiracy against the public or in some contrivance to raise prices"?
(1).
(2).
(3).
(4).
(5).

3. An important part of David Ricardo's argument was that:
(1) the income or payment received by each productive factor or input would be governed by that factor's marginal productivity.
(2) economists relied to excess on the deductive process, and neglected the requirement of verifying their conclusions empirically.
(3) supply and cost factors alone could not explain price or value, since demand was a factor of equal importance.
(4) the rate of business profit was bound to fall.
(5) land's rental price would gradually increase, and labor's price would gradually fall.

4. Which alternative in question 3 would be correct, had that question referred to Karl Marx (and to capitalist society) rather than to David Ricardo?
(1).
(2).
(3).
(4).
(5).

5. The contemporary economist whose name is most prominently associated with the principle of laissez-faire earlier advocated by Adam Smith is:
(1) Milton Friedman.
(2) Thomas Kuhn.
(3) Robert Solow.
(4) John G. Gurley.
(5) John Kenneth Galbraith.

6. The law of diminishing returns played a prominent part in:
(1) Leon Walras's theory of general equilibrium.
(2) the mercantilist theory of tariff protection.
(3) Adam Smith's principle of the *invisible hand*.
(4) David Ricardo's theory of income distribution.
(5) Karl Marx's theory of the business cycle.

7. Neoclassical theory contributed to the development of economic analysis in that it:
(1) developed a mathematical theory of general equilibrium and in the process brought marginalist concepts into use.
(2) developed the theory of econometric measurement of economic variables.
(3) in large part reversed the classical emphasis on deduction, insisting that economists verify empirically the hypotheses on which they relied.
(4) set out a non-Marxist account of how the economy might reach an equilibrium which was substantially below the level of full resource employment.
(5) gave the first clear account of the significance of the law of scarcity as applied to both demand and supply sides of the market.

8. The "economic interpretation of history" doctrine set out by Marx and Engels says that:
(1) the distribution of income by class is governed by the iron law of marginal productivity.
(2) the driving force behind entrepreneurial behavior is the maximization of money profit.
(3) each class has its own economic interest and beliefs and behavior are dictated by such economic interest.
(4) an authoritarian leader, thrown up by world revolution, is an imperative before any change in the conditions of production can be accomplished.
(5) the inescapable scarcity of land must lead to the progressive impoverishment of the growing body of laborers who must work on that land.

9. In Marxian terminology, "constant capital" signifies:
(1) equipment or materials which represent the fruit of past labor.

(2) the value of total output in a capitalist society.
(3) the money cost that would be incurred even if production were zero.
(4) the value of total output in a socialist society.
(5) the markup of price over the actual value of labor incurred in production.

10. In a socialist regime, according to Marx, the price per unit of each commodity would (or should) equal:
(1) the value of direct labor required for that commodity's production.
(2) variable capital per unit plus constant capital per unit.
(3) the value of 1 hour of socially necessary labor.
(4) the costs of that commodity's production, including all necessary services of land, labor, and capital, but excluding profit.
(5) none of the above.

11. Marx's argument was that the output which requires labor effort is given a price which exceeds the money wage paid that labor. The verdict of neoclassical economic theory on this argument is that it:
(1) may have some validity as to labor-intensive production, but not as to capital-intensive production.
(2) is entirely false.
(3) is correct, since inputs other than labor contribute to production.
(4) may have some validity as to capital-intensive production, but not as to labor-intensive production.
(5) is meaningless, since demand is a more powerful factor in price determination than is labor cost.

12. Marx's approach to the economic problem of values was that:
(1) the emphasis of the classical economists upon values was a distraction, the important thing being the exploitation of labor.
(2) the important thing is relative values, the valuation of one commodity as against another.
(3) surplus value has to be measured altogether differently from labor value.
(4) there has to be an absolute measure of value, the measure being labor value.
(5) in capitalist societies, prices bear no consistent relationship to values whatsoever.

13. British socialism and Russian communism differ in which respect?
(1) Since World War II, the emphasis on public ownership of industry has been somewhat moderated in communism but not in socialism.
(2) Significant inequalities of income are accepted as necessary in socialist thinking but not in communist.
(3) Socialism accepts and encourages the trade-union movement; communism does not.
(4) Significant inequalities of income are accepted as necessary in communist thinking but not in socialist.
(5) None of the above.

14. In the Soviet Union, the problem of *What* to produce is settled as follows. The decision is made:
(1) first on total consumer-goods production, then defense, the residual in total output being capital goods.
(2) principally through a pricing system, except for defense and defense-related production.
(3) according to a system of national priorities, among which any of consumer goods, capital goods, or defense may rank highest at any particular time.
(4) by the central authority, but there is no clear evidence as to the priority system.
(5) on defense and capital-goods production first, consumer goods being the residual in total output.

15. The distribution of income and privilege within the Soviet Union today is best described by which of the following?
(1) There are no significant class distinctions nor differences of privilege, and the only significant differences in income take the form of merit bonuses for exceeding production quotas.
(2) There are significant class distinctions, but these are based almost entirely on occupation, not on income, since differences in income and in privilege are minor.
(3) The income distribution is "polarized," with a few party members enjoying high income and privilege, and the remainder of the population receiving low and approximately equal incomes.
(4) There are marked social classes and differences of privilege, and there is considerable inequality in income, mainly because party members may receive substantial incomes derived from property ownership.
(5) There are marked social classes and differences of privilege, and there is considerable inequality in income distribution, although no significant amount of income is attributable to ownesrhip of capital goods or other such property.

16. The Soviet government acquires much of the revenues needed for its operation through:
(1) levying of an income tax, although not a progressive income tax.
(2) levying of a turnover tax applied on goods at each stage of production.
(3) payments made by each industrial plant in proportion to cost of plant construction, much as a Western company might pay interest on a bond issue.
(4) levying of taxes on privately owned property.
(5) levying of a progressive income tax.

17. The best available estimates suggest that total and per capita real GNPs in the United States and in Soviet Russia compare about as follows. The U.S.S.R.'s total GNP (compared with that of the United States):
(1) is slightly over one-half, but its per capita GNP is less than one-half.
(2) is approximately equal, and its per capita GNP is slightly higher.
(3) is about one-third, and its per capita GNP is even less, perhaps about one-quarter.
(4) has by now risen slightly above that of the United States, although its per capita GNP is still only about five-sixths.
(5) simply cannot be compared with that of the United States, because commodities consumed in the two countries are so different as to make comparisons meaningless.

18. In Soviet Russia, which of the following items has been eliminated or virtually eliminated:
(1) Significant differences in wage payments.
(2) Taxation on the sale of finished goods.
(3) Piece rates and "incentive payments" to workers.
(4) Private ownership of personal property.
(5) None of the above.

PART SEVEN

ECONOMIC GROWTH
AND INTERNATIONAL
TRADE

CHAPTER 36

ECONOMIC GROWTH: THEORY AND EVIDENCE

Most of the text, particularly in the macro sections, has focused on the short- to medium-term changes in economic conditions associated with the business cycle. These fluctuations are important, to be sure, for anyone whose job is in jeopardy during a recession or whose variable rate mortgage payments are out of control during an inflationary boom. Viewed in the context of long-term patterns of growth, however, they are dwarfed by trends that have persisted for centuries.

Chapter 36 looks at the American economy from a different perspective. It introduces the long-term view of economic development by tracing the history of the American economy in broad terms over the past 80 years; it also ponders the processes by which the American standard of living has improved so dramatically and by which the stock of American capital has grown so large. These are not merely topics of academic curiosity. They are the topics that are important when policymakers and economic theorists question, for example, the sources of the recent slowdown in American productivity and search for remedies that can revitalize our economic growth. They are also the topics that need to be understood if we are to be able to assist developing economies in their attempts to improve the lots of their citizens. That is the message of Chapter 37.

Having completed your work in this chapter, you will have prepared for that application by accomplishing the following objectives.

LEARNING OBJECTIVES

1. Define or explain briefly (*a*) the labor theory of value; (*b*) the law of diminishing returns; (*c*) the capital-output ratio; (*d*) the "deepening" of capital.

2. Outline the major problem (or problems) opened up for economic analysis once that analysis moves beyond the simple "labor theory of value" to recognize that there are two (or more) types of inputs involved in production.

3. Describe briefly the sequence of events predicted from application of the Malthus-Ricardo interpretation of the law of diminishing returns.

4. Describe the sequence predicted when capital is considered to be the variable and increasing factor in the absence of technological change and with labor being the fixed factor. Explain how the conclusions so reached are altered (if at all) when allowance is made for technological change.

5. Briefly summarize the trends in the United States since 1900 in (*a*) total real output; (*b*) real wages; (*c*) the real rate of interest or profit; (*d*) growth in the capital stock; (*e*) growth in population or the labor force; (*f*) the capital-output ratio; (*g*) the effect (if any) of diminishing returns.

6. Record the equations of growth accounting, and use that accounting to indicate the major sources of growth in per capita output in the United States.

7. Note the recent decline in American productivity, and record the potential of changes in investment, research support, higher employment, and arms control to stimulate growth in potential GNP.

The perspective of Chapter 36 is admittedly long-term, and the analysis might appear at first blush to be a bit more complex than usual. You should, nonetheless, quickly become comfortable with the approach once you realize that it is based firmly in the fundamentals of modern microeconomics presented in previous chapters. Long-term growth is, in fact, explained almost exclusively in terms of the interplay between diminishing marginal productivity and technological change.

Each new stage in this interplay affects the distribution of income between labor and capital. The point of this chapter, therefore, is to outline how, as a result of the interaction between diminishing returns and technological progress, (1) the economy's output grows, and

(2) the income distribution between labor and capital is affected.

The diminishing-returns law was introduced back in Chapter 2. It describes what happens when there are two productive inputs, one fixed in available supply and the other capable of being increased. As the quantity of the variable input increases, total output increases, but the "marginal product" of this variable input diminishes. Finally, total output hits its maximum when no extra output is added by further increases in the variable input (i.e., when the variable input's marginal product has fallen to zero).

What matters most in growth analysis, of course, is that input proportions change. Why? Because diminishing-returns reasoning can be applied even when supplies of both inputs are increasing, as long as they are not increasing at the same rate. The input with the slower rate of increase can be considered to be "the fixed input," while the other is viewed as "the variable (and increasing) input."

The most important aspect of all this is that the payment made per unit to the variable input is equal to its marginal product so that diminishing returns works against the well-being of this input. For example, *if* diminishing returns were to reach the point where the marginal product of the variable input is zero, then the competitive payment made to every unit of that input would be zero. (It is of course most unlikely that diminishing returns would push as far as that limit. For example, if labor is the variable input, its supply is bound to stop increasing when the minimum-subsistence wage level is reached.)

Early discussions of economic growth were conducted mainly in terms of land (the fixed input) and labor (the variable input). With the emphasis on diminishing returns, it was inevitable that economists like Malthus should conclude that labor's future looked gloomy. In more recent discussions, labor has been the fixed input and capital the variable one (because the stock of capital is growing faster than population). Now the shoe is on the other foot: capital, it would seem, is the input that is vulnerable to the ravages of diminishing returns. But capital has another card to play: technological progress. The diminishing-returns effect which continually works against the return to the owners of capital is more or less continually being offset (or more than offset) by technological advance. The first few questions explore this offset potential.

1.   In Figure 36-1, the solid line 0P is the ordinary diminishing-returns diagram. (Disregard for the present the two broken lines 0Q and 0R.) 0P shows how output of good Q increases as more and more of variable input A is added to a *fixed* quantity of another input, B. The line is straight from 0 to H. This means that until the A quantity reaches 0D, the marginal product of A

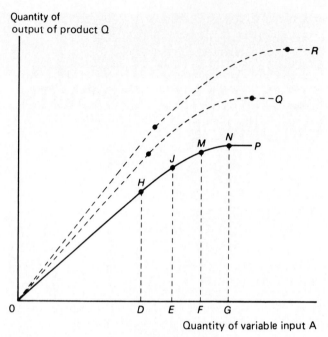

Quantity of output of product Q

Quantity of variable input A

Figure 36-1

is *(increasing / constant / decreasing)*. Thereafter it is *(increasing / constant / decreasing)*. This marginal product is measured by the slope of the line; so marginal product reaches zero when the line is *(flat / vertical)*; i.e., when A's quantity reaches *(0D / 0E / 0F / 0G)*.

---

constant; decreasing; flat; 0G

---

2.   In very early attempts to construct economic theory (e.g., in Adam Smith), the discussion was often carried on as though production were exclusively a matter of labor cost (thus, the *labor* cost of hunting animals for food). So long as only one type of input was considered, there could not be any conflict between two or more input classes over division of the output that they cooperatively produced.

Soon, however, it became evident (and this drew major emphasis in the works of Malthus and Ricardo) that land was likewise a productive input, and one scarce or limited in supply; moreover, there was no comparable limit to the size of population that might ultimately appear. Hence "the law of diminishing returns" evolved—and with it, consideration of the clash between interests of the two input categories.

a.   In the Malthus-Ricardo approach to diminishing returns, *(land / labor / capital)* is the fixed input, and *(land / labor / capital)* is the variable one. Malthus felt that a final "equilibrium" would be reached when labor had *(increased / decreased)* sufficiently to make the wage per worker just equal to the minimum-subsistence level.

b.   This wage per worker would be labor's *(marginal / total)* product. The remainder of total product, after these wages were paid, would go to landowners. In Figure 36-1 terms, the Malthusian equilibrium would be reached with labor at a total *(of OG / necessarily less than OG, say, OE or OF)*, and with total output *(NG / JE or MF)*.

---

a. land; labor; increased   **b.** marginal; necessarily less than *OG*, say *OE* or *OF*; *JE* or *MF*

---

3. **a.** The two ingredients in Malthus-Ricardo diminishing-returns analysis were land and labor, with labor the variable and increasing element. In modern development theory, the participants change. The fixed input is considered to be *(land / labor / capital)*. The variable input is *(land / labor / capital)*. When *this* variable input is increased relative to the fixed input, the condition is described by economists as a *(widening / deepening / maintenance)* of capital.

b. If the stock of capital (i.e., machinery, tools, and other such equipment) is gradually increased over time, we would expect that increase to be accompanied by at least some technological improvement; i.e., the appearance of different and more efficient capital goods. But suppose that we assume that this type of technological change were absent. An increase in capital with labor or population fixed—or more generally, an increase in the ratio of total capital to total labor—would lead to *(an increase / a decrease)* in the return to each unit of capital (the profit rate or interest rate), and *(an increase / a decrease)* in the wage paid to labor.

---

a. labor; capital; deepening   **b.** a decrease; an increase

---

4. Consider the process indicated in question 3 in more detail. Designate the variable input capital as *K*, the fixed input labor as *L*, and quantity of total output as *Q*. Then, with no technological progress, the following results are to be expected as *K* is increased relative to *L*:

a. The *capital-labor ratio K/L (increases / decreases)*.

b. The *capital-output ratio K/Q* will *(increase / decrease)*. When the law of diminishing returns is operating, any increase in the variable input yields an increase in output *Q* that is *(less than / exactly / more than)* proportionate to the *K* increase.

c. As the *K/L* ratio increases, the interest or profit rate (price of *K* per unit) *(increases / decreases)* and the wage rate (price of *L*) *(increases / decreases)*.

d. The fractional or percentage share of total output going to *K* owners *(must increase / might increase / must decrease)*.

---

a. increases   **b.** increase; less than   **c.** decreases; increases   **d.** might increase

---

5. The text presented some different geometry to portray each of the trends noted in question 4. Figure 36-2 reproduces that geometry. Deepening of the capital stock, in the absence of technological progress, would move an economy from a point like *A* in panel (a) to a point like *(B / C / D)*. Looking then at panel (b), the resulting *(higher / lower)* wage must be associated with a move from point *a* to a point like *(b / c / d)* indicating *(a reduction / an increase / no change)* in the rate of interest. The effect on the share of GNP going to capital is therefore *(necessarily positive / necessarily negative / ambiguous)* because the increase in the capital stock *(is / might be)* canceled by the *(increase / reduction)* in the rate of profit. Because of diminishing returns, though, the ratio of capital to GNP must *(rise / fall)*.

D; higher; *d*; a reduction; ambiguous; might be; reduction; fall

---

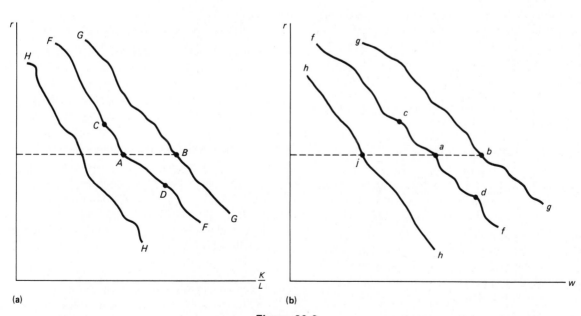

(a)   (b)

Figure 36-2

6. **a.** In the United States, over the past century, the stock of capital has grown more or less steadily, and grown more rapidly than population or the labor force. To this extent, then, it is appropriate to apply the reasoning of questions 3 through 5.

But what about technological progress, which improves the performance of K (capital), and which was specifically ruled out in those questions? In terms of Study Guide Figure 36-1 (where the variable input is now K), technical progress lifts the output curve from OP to OQ, and from OQ to OR. [The black dots on the OQ and OR lines mark the points at which curvature begins (the line begins to "bend over")—i.e., the point at which the influence of diminishing returns first begins to set in.] Thus even though K is increasing, the shift in position of the total product curve means that the marginal product of K will *(increase / decrease)*. The rate of interest or profit (per unit of capital) will thus *(fall / rise)* relative to labor's wage rate.

b. Combining the two effects (diminishing returns and technological progress), we see that the increase in the capital stock *(raises / lowers)* total output. Technical progress *(raises / lowers)* total output. The increase in the capital stock (disregarding technical progress) *(raises / lowers)* the demand for labor. Hence we would expect labor's wage or price to *(increase / decrease)*. The exception to this is the case of technical progress which greatly *(increases / decreases)* the interest or profit rate and *(increases / decreases)* the demand for labor.

c. The same general effect can be noted in Figure 36-2. Curve *(FF / GG / HH)* shows what happens when progress increases the performance of capital in panel (a). The net effect on the ratio of wages to interest rates *(can / cannot)* therefore be in either direction. Experience in the United States has, in fact, displayed *(climbing / falling / steady)* real wages and *(climbing / falling / steady)* real interest rates; a move from point *a* on curve *ff* in panel (b) to a point like *(j / b / d)* therefore most accurately portrays that experience.

---

a. increase; rise **b.** raises; raises; raises; increase; increases; decreases **c.** GG; can; climbing; steady; *b*

7. The facts of U.S. growth since 1900, as indicated in the text, are these:

a. The labor force has approximately *(remained constant / doubled / increased threefold / increased sixfold)*. The stock of capital has approximately *(remained constant / doubled / increased fourfold / increased eightfold / increased elevenfold)*.

That is, the capital stock, in proportion to the labor force, has *(increased / decreased)* by a factor of approximately *(2 / 4 / 6)*. There *(has / has not)* been a deepening of capital.

If both capital and labor had increased elevenfold, we would expect output (disregarding technical progress) also to have increased by a factor of 11. But with labor only tripled, we would expect the output increase to be *(more / less)* than eleven times its value in 1900.

b. In fact, output has increased by a factor of about *(4 / 8 /*

11). This means that the ratio of capital stock to annual output has *(increased / remained about constant / decreased)*. Things *(have / have not)* worked out as the simple law of diminishing returns would indicate, the reason evidently being *(that the law has been incorrectly set out / technological change / the higher real wage paid to labor)*.

c. The actual capital-output (K / Q) ratio in the United States is at present about *(1 year / 3 times K / 3 years / 5 times L)*.

d. Real wages *(have risen / have fallen / show no clear trend either up or down)*. The interest or profit rate—the "price of capital"—*(has risen / has fallen / shows no clear trend either up or down)*.

e. Output per work hour, or Q/L, has *(risen / remained constant / fallen)*. The increase in the wage rate *(has significantly exceeded / has been approximately equal to / has fallen behind)* the *(increase / decrease)* in output per worker-hour.

---

a. increased threefold; increased elevenfold; increased; 4; has; less **b.** 11; remained about constant; have not; technological change **c.** 3 years (i.e., value of the capital stock is reckoned as approximately equal to value of 3 years' output) **d.** have risen; shows no clear trend either up or down **e.** risen; has been approximately equal to (though slightly higher); increase

8. Seven basic trends in major economic variables have been typical of growth in the United States as well as most developed countries. Indicate the direction of each in the spaces provided below.

(1) The capital-labor ratio has _____.

(2) The real wage has _____.

(3) The share paid to labor has _____.

(4) The real rate of interest has _____.

(5) The capital-output ratio has _____ since 1950 after _____ for five decades.

(6) The savings-output ratio has _____.

(7) Output has _____.

Trend (6), combined with a small level of net foreign investment, implies that the investment-output ratio has *(risen / remained steady / fallen)*. Trends (1) and (2) are consistent with the neoclassical model of growth *(only when technological change is introduced / even without technological change)*. Trend (3) is a coincidence of nature and is not the theoretical implication of any part of the model. Trends (4) and (5) *(do / do not)* depend on technological change because no progress would always combine with a deepening capital stock to predict *(higher / lower)* real interest rates and *(higher / lower)* capital-output ratios.

---

(1) risen; (2) risen; (3) risen (slightly); (4) been trendless; (5) been constant; falling slowly; (6) been stable; (7) increased (dramatically); remained steady; even without technological change; do; lower; higher

9. The terms "labor-saving" and "capital-saving" innovations lack precise, universally accepted meanings. The text suggests that an "X-saving" innovation is one which has the effect of reducing (*X's price / X's relative share in total product / amount of X employed per unit of output*).

X's relative share in total product

10. Complete the following table on the basis of the growth accounting procedures presented in the text.

	Case I	Case II	Case III
Rate of growth of labor	1%	0%	1%
Rate of growth of capital	4%	4%	5%
Rate of technological change	2%	2%	2%
Rate of growth of output	_____	_____	_____
Rate of growth of output per worker	_____	_____	_____

Rate of growth of output: I: 3¾%; II: 3%; III 4%   Rate of growth of output per worker; I: 2¾%; II: 3%; III: 3% [*Note:* Percent change in (*K/L*) equals percent change in *K* minus percent change in *L*.]

11. Labor productivity in the United States fell from an average of _____ percent per year from 1948 through 1973 (and

_____ percent per year from 1948 through 1965) to _____ percent per year from 1973 through 1983. According to text Table 36-2, the combined effect of (*a*) a 20 percent increase in net investment and saving, (*b*) a 20 percent increase in support for research as a fraction of GNP, (*c*) a reduction in the natural rate in unemployment by almost 20 percent, and (*d*) an arms-control agreement that released government resources to

investment would cause potential GNP to grow _____ percentage points faster per year. This is, of course, (*an easy / a difficult*) prescription to reverse the recent decline.

2; 2.5; 0; .64; a difficult

QUIZ: Multiple Choice

1. Suppose agricultural output requires only two inputs, labor and land. The quantity of land available is fixed; the quantity of labor is variable. Then, as labor quantity is increased in order to increase output quantity, the law of diminishing returns will begin to operate, and:
(1) the ratio of labor to land will increase; the ratio of land to output will fall.
(2) both the labor-land ratio and the land-output ratio will fall.
(3) both the labor-land ratio and the land-output ratio will increase.

(4) the labor-land ratio will fall, and the land-output ratio will increase.
(5) the labor-land ratio will increase, but the land-output ratio will not change.

2. In the simple theory of value, demand for goods plays the following role. It:
(1) interacts with supply to determine price, as in any other case.
(2) dominates over supply in the determination of price, but does not influence quantities produced and consumed.
(3) settles quantities produced and consumed, but has no influence on price.
(4) has no influence either on quantities produced and consumed or on price.
(5) dominates over supply both as to price and as to quantities produced and consumed.

3. The most important single factor accounting for increased productivity and growth in the American economy thus far appears to have been:
(1) a deepening of the capital stock.
(2) technological change.
(3) a widening of the capital stock.
(4) the use of growth-encouraging monetary and fiscal policy.
(5) the increase in skills of the labor force.

4. Since 1900, the stock of capital in the United States (according to the text) has increased:
(1) eightfold, and operation of the diminishing-returns law has significantly reduced the capital-output ratio.
(2) tenfold, and operation of the diminishing-returns law has significantly increased the caapital-output ratio.
(3) only by an amount proportionate to the increase in the labor force, so that the diminishing-returns law has had no application.
(4) threefold, and operation of the diminishing-returns law has significantly reduced the capital-output ratio.
(5) elevenfold, but the capital-output ratio has not increased significantly despite the diminishing-returns law.

5. In the United States the share of wages and salaries in national product since 1900:
(1) has significantly increased.
(2) has remained about constant, or shown a very slight upward trend.
(3) has significantly fallen, except for a period during and immediately after World War II.
(4) rose fairly steadily until about 1930 and remained constant until 1945 (excluding World War II), but has fallen perceptibly since then.
(5) is not correctly described by any of the above.

6. If the amount of capital employed is increased, if the amount of labor and other inputs stays approximately fixed, and if the capital-output ratio remains constant, then:
(1) the capital-labor ratio must have fallen.
(2) the price of capital must have fallen.
(3) the law of diminishing returns has been in operation.

(4) technological improvements would explain this result.

(5) total output must have fallen.

7. If the capital-output ratio increases, then it should follow that:

(1) the real wage of labor must fall if there has been no technological change, but not otherwise.

(2) the real wage of labor must fall, regardless of the extent of technological change.

(3) the total stock of capital must have decreased, or at best remained constant.

(4) the real rate of interest or profit must fall if there has been no technological change, but not otherwise.

(5) the real rate of interest or profit must fall, regardless of the extent of technological change.

8. A deepening of capital must, in the absence of technological change:

(1) increase the capital-output ratio.

(2) decrease the capital-output ratio.

(3) increase output more than proportionately to the increase in capital.

(4) increase output in proportion to the increase in capital.

(5) increase the share of capital owners in the total of output.

9. According to the law of diminishing returns, if land is the fixed input and labor the variable input, then as the quantity of output is increased:

(1) the relative share of labor in total product must fall.

(2) the price of land must fall.

(3) the share of labor in total product or output must rise.

(4) land's percentage share in total product or output must rise.

(5) none of the above is necessarily correct.

10. By "deepening of capital" is meant:

(1) an increase in the stock of capital relative to the size of the labor force.

(2) the introduction of new capital goods which embody technological change.

(3) a change in either productivity or amount of capital which increases the share of capital-owners in total product.

(4) an increase in the productivity of capital which reduces, or at least does not increase, the total of the capital stock.

(5) none of the above.

11. If capital is considered the variable input, then in the operation of the law of diminishing returns (without technological change), as output is increased:

(1) the share of capital-owners in total output must increase.

(2) the capital-output ratio must decrease.

(3) the share of capital-owners in total output must decrease.

(4) the capital-output ratio must increase.

(5) the capital-output ratio must, by definition, remain constant.

12. If a nation's capital-output ratio gradually increases over time, this indicates that:

(1) the share of capital-owners in total output is increasing.

(2) the diminishing-returns stage has not yet been reached with respect to capital.

(3) the marginal physical product of capital must have reached zero.

(4) technological progress must be improving the productivity of capital.

(5) the law of diminishing returns is operating with respect to capital's productivity.

APPENDIX:
Modern Economic-Growth Theories

Chapter 36 introduced the analysis of economic growth in its simplest form. Growth is, however, not a simple phenomenon, and models of its properties can quickly become extremely complex. The point of this Appendix is not to record the differential equations that reflect some of the advance modeling of economic growth. It is, instead, included to give the interested reader some flavor of the difficulty involved in conceptualizing what we mean, in precise terms, by economic growth and how we can use modeling to discover what drives it and what can shut it down.

Having completed your work in both the text and the extended treatment in the Study Guide, you will have accomplished the following objectives.

LEARNING OBJECTIVES

1. Explain what is meant by "the stationary state." Outline the views which prompted some classical economists to argue that there was a long-run tendency for any economy to gravitate toward this stationary state, and set out two counter arguments.

2. Describe what is meant by a "balanced rate of growth," indicating the two independent "rates" which are in need of balance. Explain the "Keynesian" possibility which is set aside in the development of such balanced-rate analysis.

3. Describe what is meant by a "warranted rate of growth." Distinguish it from the balanced-rate analysis mentioned above, and cite the two magnitudes that are needed to establish an economy's warranted-rate growth path.

4. Explain how a Leontief input-output table is constructed, and outline the type of problem with respect to which such a table is intended to be useful.

1. Economic growth analysis often begins by drawing on the Ricardo-Mill idea of *the stationary state*. Many classical economists thought that nations would grow until they reached a final "stationary-state" condition. Thereafter, there would be no further growth—not, at any rate, in the capital stock. When this final state was reached, the economy's stock of capital goods might be very large, but there would be no net investment.

Joseph Schumpeter was prominent among the critics of this stationary-state idea. He argued that any such tendency is repeatedly offset by the work of crazy and not-so-crazy inventors who want to do things *differently* and better.

There is an important distinction to be made here. The inventor is one who thinks up a new idea. But there is a huge gap between that new idea and the new (or improved) and commercially successful product in which the idea finds its expression. Schumpeter called the individual who bridges (or tries to bridge) that gap *(a speculator / an economist / an innovator)*.

In Schumpeter's view, if you want to understand what "capitalism" has meant, and how it has really behaved over the past 100 or 150 years, you must look at the process of technological change—at the two stages of that change. Inventors invent. Innovators seek to profit from invention. (Inventor and innovator may or may not be the same individual.) Some innovators have succeeded; very few have succeeded spectacularly. Most of them have (with less publicity) gone broke. But the lure of winning the grand prize in the innovation lottery remains undiminished.

Normally, innovators go to the money capital markets, seeking the finance they need. They have thus bid *(up / down)* the interest rate, thus *(encouraging / discouraging)* saving out of income as financing for the new projects. Repeated innovations thus keep pushing the economy into bursts of capital accumulation and growth.

an innovator (or entrepreneur); up; encouraging

2. Stationary-state reasoning has also been attacked for its view that the amount people save out of income is governed primarily by the level of interest rates. In the Keynesian view, people save against life's uncertainties, and they go on saving no matter how low the interest rate may be.

The interest rate may instead dictate what people do with income saved. People may save when interest rates are low, but they do not necessarily lend. Instead, they may display "liquidity preference." In periods when profit opportunities look bleak, investment will be *(high / low)*, and the reduced demand for investment money will make the interest rate *(high / low)*. However, this *(high / low)* interest rate will not of itself reduce saving. Thus, the disparity between saving and investment must be ironed out by a *(rise / fall)* in incomes and production, and by an *(increase / decrease)* in unemployment.

This is, of course, "short-run analysis" (as Schumpeter pointed out with respect to Keynes). These periods of unemployment may in time be overcome by further technological change, and consequently a surge of new investment. If we combine Schumpeter's views with those of Keynes, the conclusion is that capitalist economies are more likely to continue to grow rather than to drift toward a stationary-state equilibrium. Technological change will persistently create new investment opportunities, and the public's continued disposition to save will (except, just possibly, in certain low-interest-rate periods) provide financing for investment.

low; low; low; fall; increase

3. Much of this Appendix deals with the concepts of *the natural rate of growth* and *the warranted rate of growth*, used in Harrod-Domar growth models.

"Growth" means here year-to-year increases in total output. These models tackle the question: Can a capitalist economy maintain reasonably steady growth without drifting off its growth path into unemployment and depression on the one side, or inflation on the other? The answer: "Yes," provided several independent forces mesh together properly; otherwise, no.

The major forces involved are: (*a*) the rate of increase in the capital stock (i.e., rate of net investment); (*b*) the rate of saving out of income by the public (saving being the means by which investment is financed); (*c*) the rate of increase in population, and consequent increase in the labor force;[1] (*d*) the law of diminishing returns; and (*e*) technological change.

To approach the Harrod-Domar models in detail, begin with the chapter's discussion of diminishing returns. If the capital stock K is increased, then total input will increase also. But if K grows more rapidly than the labor force L, then the percentage output increase will be less than the percentage K increase because K will feel the impact of diminishing returns. However, K's "marginal productivity" can be restored or even improved if new and more efficient capital goods are developed—if, in other words, there is technological innovation. This would have to be "labor-saving" innovation: less L needed in production per unit of K.

Now let's tackle the "natural rate of growth." We begin by assuming there is *no* technological change. Thus as K increases, it is under a continuing diminishing-returns threat. However, we here use the diminishing-returns law in simplified form.

The usual diminishing-returns outline says that as the amount of the variable input is increased (relative to the fixed-amount input), its marginal product will gradually fall, ultimately reaching zero. It is often argued that this outline exag-

[1] Strictly speaking, population and the labor force need not correlate exactly. If more married women enter the labor force, as has happened in recent years, that labor force can increase even with a fixed population. If working hours are reduced, the total labor force may remain constant even with an increasing population.

gerates the extent to which variability of input proportions is typically possible in actual production. By and large, in this view, a given capital stock needs a given labor force to operate it. If there are insufficient capital goods, some part of that labor force will be unemployable. If the capital stock is too large, some part of that K will be unusable until and unless L is increased. Note carefully that this is not a denial of the diminishing-returns effect. It says that this effect, instead of occurring gradually, will occur all at once, at the point where the fixed K/L ratio is reached, suddenly and completely.[2]

In Harrod-Domar models, the relationship in production (dictated by technology) between the total capital stock K and total labor force L is assumed to be sufficiently close to fixed that it is no great distortion to treat this K/L ratio as being exactly fixed. If this fixed-proportions requirement is not satisfied, the factor in excess, whether K or L, will be unemployable.

Now consider the fact that population and the labor force ordinarily grow year by year. Let this growth rate, expressed as a fraction, be designated g. For example, if the growth in L is 3 percent annually, then $g = {}^3/_{100}$.

We have assumed that technology dictates a fixed K/L ratio. Assume further that the current and actual K/L ratio is "just right" (i.e., there is no excess of either input). But L is increasing. This necessitates a matching increase in K to maintain the proper K/L ratio. *Will it occur?* That is the question underlying the "natural-rate-of-growth" idea. The forces that govern increases in population and the labor force are markedly different from those that govern increases in K.

Using our example of a 3 percent annual increase in L, we want K's annual increase to be ${}^3/_{100}$ of K to maintain the proper K/L ratio. More generally, we want the annual increase in K to be gK. However, any increase in K (whether the desired gK or some other figure) is what we more usually call net investment I. There must be just enough of each year's total output Q channeled into investment rather than consumption, to provide the required K increase.

(In growth analysis, the symbol Q is conventional for "total annual output"—the same thing more commonly called GNP. We shall use Q for the balance of this question.)

This means that just the right amount of Q must be saved, since net investment spending is financed out of saving S. (In natural-rate-of-growth analysis, it is assumed that there is no "Keynesian" problem in which saving fails to flow smoothly into investment.)

So the problem is: How much must be saved out of Q (what fraction of Q must be saved) in order to produce the needed I (the K addition desired so as to match the L addition)?

Let s = the fraction of Q saved annually. Thus total annual saving will be sQ.

Now we can fit things together. By the assumption that all saving flows into investment, we have $sQ = I$, and the desired $I = gK$. Hence, if things are to go as desired, we must have $sQ = gK$. Or to put that equation in another form:

$$s = g \times \frac{K}{Q}$$

The expression K/Q, on the right-hand side of this equation, is the capital-output ratio, a measure already introduced in the chapter immediately preceding this Appendix, and one which crops up in all these growth models: the ratio between the value of the total capital stock and the value of total annual output. If total K is valued at \$10, and annual Q is \$3, then the capital-output ratio is 10/3, or $3^1/_3$ (years). Assuming that the same ratio applies to additional K and additional Q, as is done in these models, this means that if \$10 is spent on net investment in some new capital goods, then that investment can yield, for each year of the life of those capital goods, an additional output of \$3.

Now consider the common-sense meaning of the equation above. In our example, L grows at 3 percent per year, so we want both K and Q to grow at 3 percent to stay on the natural-rate-of-growth patch. This calls for net investment and thus an equal amount of saving to finance that investment. How much saving and investment? One may be at first tempted to say: 3 percent of Q. Not so. The capital-output ratio says that *that* amount of new capital goods would fall short of producing an additional 3 percent of Q. It tells us that 10 units of I are needed for 3 additional units of Q. Putting 10 percent of Q into investment will yield just a 3 percent increase in Q annually. (It will also increase K by just 3 percent. The value of total K is $3^1/_3$ times Q. So 10 percent of Q equals 3 percent of K.)

a. In brief, given any labor-force growth rate g, we must multiply g by the capital-output ratio K/Q in order to determine the required rate of saving s out of income. With a K/Q ratio of $3^1/_3$ and a labor-force growth rate of 3 percent annually, 10 percent of income must be saved and invested to keep this economy on its natural-rate-of-growth path.

If, instead, L's annual growth rate were 4 percent (with the same K/Q ratio), then the required s-value would be approximately *(8.5 / 10.0 / 13.3 / 15.0 / 16.7)* percent. If the L growth rate were 5 percent, then the required s-value would become *(8.5 / 10.0 / 13.3 / 15.0 / 16.7)* percent.

b. If saving *does* take place at the percentage rate required, we have "balanced growth": the saving rate is balanced against the labor-force growth rate. Using the 3 percent L growth figure, if saving *is* 10 percent of Q, then output will grow annually at

---

[2]The essence of diminishing returns, expressed in terms of Study Guide Figure 36-1 is that when you have too much of input A relative to input B, you cannot get further increases in output by adding more of A. But you are warned of this because the marginal product of A *gradually* falls to zero. In the fixed-proportions case, there is no such warning. In Figure 36-1 terms, when proportions are fixed, the output line OP no longer gradually "bends over." It is a straight line all the way from O to N. At point N, there is a kink. To the right of N, the output line is perfectly flat.

Suppose the available quantity of variable input A is only, say, OD. Then the A/B proportions are wrong; part of the given stock of input B is redundant, and that part cannot be employed in production. As the quantity of input A is increased beyond OD, more of B becomes employable. When the A quantity is OG, things are "just right" with respect to the specified fixed A/B proportions. Beyond OG, input A would become the redundant factor. Any such quantity of A in excess of OG would be unemployable for lack of available B with which it could work.

(3 / 10) percent. Allowing for population increase, output and income per capita will increase *(by 3 percent / by 10 percent / not at all)*. (Hence this is "growth" only in a qualified sense; we return to this point in question 7.) The capital-labor proportion K/L will *(rise / remain constant / fall)*.

c. If saving falls short of that required by population growth, then the ratio K/L will *(rise / remain constant / fall)*, and the result will be *(unemployment / inflation)* by reason of an *(excess / insufficiency)* of capital goods.

---

a. 13.3; 16.7 **b.** 3; not at all; remain constant **c.** fall; unemployment; insufficiency

---

4. a. In actual fact, as was pointed out earlier in the chapter, in the United States the ratio K/L has *(risen / fallen / remained constant)*. This suggests that the path followed has not been that of "balanced growth." But in the illustration of question 3, technological change was specifically excluded. When consideration is given this element, U.S. growth may still have been "balanced."

Technological innovation may take many forms. Typically, it appears in the form of new and different capital goods, which human labor is trained to operate. One way of handling technological change analytically is to think of it as a development increasing the productivity of labor.

By this approach, the increase in L (the labor force) does not fully indicate the increase in the "effective" labor supply—if L is increasing not only in numbers but in productive efficiency. The text uses the symbol L° to measure the effective labor force. That is, if L grows, and this growth is accompanied by greater training and skill, L° grows *(even faster / more slowly)*.

If the ratio K/L rises, as it has done in the United States, it is *(impossible / still possible)* for the ratio K/L° to remain constant.

b. In the United States since 1900, the division of GNP between K owners and L owners has *(shifted in favor of K owners / shifted in favor of L owners / remained approximately constant)*. Further, the capital-output ratio K/Q (i.e., K / GNP) has *(increased significantly / decreased significantly / remained approximately constant)*, particularly since 1950. These two facts *(correspond / do not correspond)* to "balanced growth."

c. In the United States, the real wage per unit of L has *(risen / remained constant)*. In "balanced growth," the wage per unit of L° *(rises / falls / remains constant)*. The actual rise in U.S. wage per unit of L *(can be / cannot be)* consistent with "balanced growth." (Remember that L is smaller than L°. So an unchanged per capita income for each L° unit will mean a higher per capita income for each L unit.)

---

a. risen; even faster; still possible **b.** remained approximately constant; remained approximately constant; correspond **c.** risen; remains constant; can be

---

"Balanced-growth" analysis, in summary, notes that we must reckon with two basic and largely independent elements: growth in population (or the labor force), and the propensity of the population to save. These two elements must harmonize in the sense that saving finances investment, and that investment take the form of the new capital goods with which the increase in population must work. Growth is "balanced," and it occurs at "the natural rate," when these two basic elements are in reasonable harmony.

The elements are not in harmony when saving fails to provide the required amount of new capital goods. But they are not necessarily out of harmony when saving appears "too great," so that its tendency is to increase the K/L ratio. This is an incentive toward "labor-saving innovation"—i.e., technological change designed to change the fixed K/L ratio, to increase it to a higher "workable" level.

The economists who argue that factor proportions are fixed (or nearly so) consequently do not regard the observed rise in K/L as a contradiction of their view. They consider input proportions to be fixed only in a particular state of technology—i.e., with given equipment. A more "automated" technology defines a new and higher (but again fixed) K/L relationship.

If the rate of saving is high in relation to the growth in the labor force, it is far from safe to assume that technological change will always save the day. Even if such output-increasing changes are directed toward an increase in the K/L ratio (i.e., toward "automation"), their effects typically appear rather slowly in actual production.

If we assume, as natural-growth analysis does, that whatever is saved will be invested, then getting just enough in new capital goods to match the population increase reduces to getting just the right proportion of income saved (not used for consumption). That reasoning ducks the Keynesian problem. *Will* the amount of scheduled investment equal the amount saved? Chapters 7 and 8 stressed the point that investment plans are made independently of saving plans. If the total of scheduled investment is less than the total amount the public plans to save, GNP will fall. (With incomes lowered, saving will be lowered as well.)

There is a further complication, not taken up in Chapters 7 and 8. Because net investment creates new plant and equipment, it adds to productive capacity. That capacity is gradually increased, and so is the "full-employment" level of GNP. If the public wants to save some given fraction of its income (a rising income), we need not steady investment spending, but gradually rising investment spending.

This brings us to *warranted-rate-of-growth* analysis. It tackles a question different from the natural-growth one: Will enough new capital goods be produced, through investment, to match all the saving the public wants to undertake?

The four beginning ingredients in Harrod's warranted-rate analysis are as follows:

1. Just as in the natural-rate case, it is assumed that in production, input proportions are fixed; i.e., K/L is fixed. We also have a given capital-output ratio, K/Q, or K/GNP.

2. We start with more than enough L for the existing K. Part of the labor force is unemployed for lack of capital goods with which to work. An increase in K is needed if even part of this unemployment is to be removed. (For this notion, it makes no difference whether total L is increasing annually, as in question 3, or is fixed in amount.)

3. Business firms are assured that there will be some extra L available to work with any extra K created. But they still must ask this question: If we build this extra K, will there be sufficient demand for the extra output thereby producible to have made that investment worth undertaking? In sum: Will there be a sufficient rise in GNP to justify building the extra K? So the underlying question is: What will be the rate of rise in GNP?

4. The public plans to save some fixed fraction of GNP.

The public does the saving, but a different group—business firms—does the investment (I) spending. The amount of S imposes an upper limit on the amount of I spending possible, but there is no guarantee that business firms plan to spend on I as much as the public plans to save.

Assuming the existing capital stock K to be fully employed, the amount of I spending planned by business firms will be governed by their expectations as to the future level of GNP (or Q). (As in question 3, hereafter we use only the term Q, not GNP.)

Suppose that business firms are pretty confident that Q will rise by 10 percent—say, from \$100 to \$110 billion. Since their present K is fully occupied, they will want to have built just enough extra K to meet that \$10 billion increase in demand for output.

How do we convert that anticipated \$10 billion Q rise into a dollar total for extra K? The "rate of exchange" is provided by the capital-output ratio, K/Q. If this ratio is 3, business will want to use saving of \$30 billion (and not more), since that amount of investment (addition to K) is just capable of producing an extra \$10 billion of Q annually. Thus the combination of business expectations and the K/Q ratio will determine the amount of I spending.

5.   a. If business firms instead anticipate a Q rise from \$100 to \$120 billion, with the same K/Q ratio of 3; their desired I spending will be \$*(zero / 20 / 40 / 60 / 80 / 100)* billion. If they expect *no* rise in Q, then their planned I spending will be \$*(zero / 20 / 40 / 60 / 80 / 100)* billion. The planned I spending total equals the expected Q rise multiplied by the capital-output ratio.

Let W stand for the expected Q rise, stated as a fraction. (If a rise from \$100 to \$110 billion is anticipated, $W = 1/10$; if from \$100 to \$120 billion, $W = 1/5$.) What is the general expression for I, stated in terms of W, Q, and K/Q? _____

b. At long last, we reach the "warranted rate of growth." It is that rate of annual growth in Q, expressed by the symbol W (a fraction of Q) that, once started, would just keep the economy progressing in a smooth, continuing rate of growth. Remember, the fraction of Q that people want to save is assumed to be fixed. That fixed fraction of Q saved would be just enough to equal the amount that business firms would want to invest, given their expectations as to future Q.

The essential requirement, then, is just $S = I$. And finding W, the warranted rate of growth, is just a matter of (1) putting S in place of I in the equation worked out in part **a** above, and then (2) rearranging that equation so that W sits alone on the left-hand side thereof. Use a separate scrap of paper for the detail, then show the resulting equation below.

_____ .

c. In the equation you just wrote down, S stands for total saving. The text equation uses the symbol s_a to indicate that fixed fraction of Q which the public insists on saving. Thus, $S = s_a Q$. Make this substitution in the equation above, and you get the text's equation, namely:

$$W = \frac{s_a}{K/Q}$$

If the fraction of Q that people wish to save is always 12 percent, and the capital-output ratio is 4, the warranted rate of growth would be *(zero / 1 / 2 / 3 / 4 / 5)* percent per annum. If K/Q is 5, and saving is always 10 percent of income, the warranted rate would be *(zero / 1 / 2 / 3 / 4 / 5)* percent growth per annum.

a. 60; zero; $I = W \times Q \times K / Q$ (or simply, $I = WK$)   **b.** $W = S/Q \times K / Q$
c. 3; 2

6. The "warranted-rate-of-growth" idea is pretty clearly related to the "acceleration-principle" view discussed in Chapter 10; i.e., investment spending is largely governed by the rate of growth in GNP (or Q). In the warranted-rate outline, such spending is much more dependent upon business firms' expectations about the likely rate of GNP increase than it is in the acceleration-principle argument.

Notice that the "warranted rate of growth" is not envisaged as a growth rate that will necessarily remove all unemployment of L, even though creation of new plant and equipment will add to employment. (Unlike the "balance-growth" model of question 3, warranted-rate analysis pays relatively little attention to L's size. There must be enough L on hand to operate the additional K created, but that's about the extent to which warranted-rate analysis considers the L matter.)

The essential point to grasp about the warranted-rate argument is this: if the economy manages to get started along its warranted-rate growth track, it will (so the argument goes, anyhow) continue on that steady growth track (assuming the fixed capital-output and saving percentage figures persist) until and unless some disturbance bumps it off.

One possible source of disturbance is the limit on the labor force *L*. If *K* grows so rapidly as to overtake *L* (even though *L* may be rising), then, with employed *L* removed, *K* runs into the fixed *K*/*L* ratio, and investment meets a bottleneck. The amount of *I* spending will (*increase / decline*), saving will (*exceed / fall short of*) investment, and GNP will be thrown off its warranted-rate path. While in due course technology may change things by increasing the *K*/*L* ratio, the shorter-run adjustment may be the Keynesian one: a fall in incomes and in saving.

---

deline; exceed

---

7. If an economy gets aboard its (positive) warranted-rate growth track, and manages to stay aboard, presumably one result to be expected is something we normally associate with "growth," namely, an increase in per capita incomes. But now turn back to the "natural-rate-of-growth" model examined in question 3. This is growth only in a limited sense. The capital stock *K* will be increasing—but only in proportion to *Q* and to *L*. Everything continues just as it was before, except that it is being done on a somewhat larger scale. Output *Q* grows, to be sure. But *L* grows at the same rate. There is no increase in per capita income.

Such a growth in *K*—just enough to maintain the existing *K*/*L* ratio—is sometimes called a *widening of capital*—in contrast to a *deepening of capital* which means an increase in the *K*/*L* ratio. The results of capital deepening (without technological change) are those described in diminishing-returns analysis. To review part of question 3 and some of the questions used in the chapter preceding this Appendix, when capital is so deepened, *Q* will grow (*more than / exactly / less than*) in proportion to the *K* increase. The capital-output ratio *K*/*Q* must (*increase / remain constant / decrease*), since *K* is increasing (*faster than / at the same rate as / less than*) *Q*. The rate of return to *K* (the interest rate, or rate of profit) will gradually (*increase / decrease*). The wage rate, or rate of return to *L*, will (*rise / remain constant / fall*).

These results rely crucially upon the assumption of no technological change. In the actual history of recent times, there most certainly has been such change. Hence the results discussed in the text, and in question 4 on page 369.

---

less than; increase; faster than; decrease; rise

---

8. The *Leontief input-output system* is not at all concerned, as Harrod-Domar models are, with "aggregate growth." Although it involves some interest in the matter of growth, the Leontief construction is "microeconomic" in the particular sense that it deals with the individual products which collectively make up

GNP, and with the individual inputs required for manufacture of these finished products.

Suppose that GNP is composed of just three types of finished goods: X, Y, and Z. Suppose further that (for whatever reason) this problem is posed: we need a 5 percent increase in X output, a 15 percent increase in Y output, and we can afford to reduce Z output by 10 percent. Overall, what would these output changes call for in the way of extra productive inputs needed?

This is the type of question the Leontief system is constructed to answer. As its base, it uses statistical material covering production in past years.

It is appropriate to illustrate the nature of the Leontief system through the example of a three-good GNP. But in real life, things are rather more complicated. Within any actual GNP, there are thousands upon thousands of different items. Even a computer-aided system cannot take full account of them all. The most appropriate simplification is to lump products together by industry, thus making *the industry* the microeconomic unit. Even a quite modest plan of division yields several hundred industries for a Leontief system to digest.

Typically, the output of any one industry goes in two directions. Part of that output may be a finished consumer good for households. But part (or all) may go to other industries as inputs. Fuel oil is an output used by families for home heating. It is also an input used by firms for their manufacturing needs.

A Leontief table is built to record this fact. Each industry gets a line (technically a *row*), showing where its output went. On the X-industry line, so much of X output went to the Y industry as a raw-material input, so much to the Z industry for similar use—and finally, so much of X to households for consumption purposes.

This arrangement of rows, one for each industry, means that each industry also gets a *column* (a vertical listing), showing the inputs it got from other industries—that is, the raw materials it needed to produce its own finished product. At the bottom of each column is a figure showing that particular industry's total *labor* input.

This is the information at the surface of a Leontief system. Suppose the table indicates that 6 labor units, *L*, were used per unit of X produced. This is only the *direct* requirement. X's *total L* requirements were greater, for X's production also called on inputs from Y and Z, and *they* used labor too. (Of necessity, a Leontief system must work in money terms, but these money figures are intended as equivalents of *real* input-output relationships.)

The Leontief system probes for total input-output needs: the total *L* per unit of X, total Y per unit of X, total Z/X relation, and so on. Each such input-output figure (e.g., 10 *L* units per X unit) is assumed to be fixed; this is really the same "fixed-factor-proportions" assumption used in Harrod-Domar models.

If the Leontief system has developed these "input-output coefficients" correctly, it can then indicate the requirements for any given increase in output. Suppose (to use a simplified version of the illustrative problem with which this question began) the question is: What would be needed in order to obtain a 10 percent increase in net final output of X—with no increase in net final outputs of Y and Z?

Insofar as Y and Z are needed as inputs in X production, more of these commodities will have to be turned out even though there is to be no increase in their final output. And the required increase in X output may have to be more than 10 percent if X is needed as an input in Y production or in Z production.

The Leontief system will accordingly report that such a 10 percent increase in net final X output would require so many extra units of X, so many of Y, so many of Z, and so much extra *L*. We would expect the *L* requirement to be *(less than / the same as / greater than)* the extra *L* needed directly in the X industry. The rise in Y production will *(increase "final consumption" of Y / be fully absorbed as inputs for other industries)*. The same is true of Z production. Of the increase in Y production, *(all will go directly to the X industry / some may go, for example, to the Z industry, hence only indirectly to the X industry)*.

---

greater than; be fully absorbed as inputs for other industries; some may go, for example, to the Z industry, hence only indirectly to the X industry

QUIZ: Multiple Choice

1. A "deepening of capital" can be expected to reduce the rate of interest or profit unless:
(1) the capital-output ratio remains constant.
(2) the capital-output ratio increases.
(3) the capital-labor ratio increases.
(4) the capital-labor ratio decreases.
(5) output remains constant.

2. If saving and investment take place in the amounts indicated by the natural rate of growth:
(1) the ratio of capital to labor in production will rise.
(2) the ratio of capital to output will rise.
(3) the rate of profit or interest will rise.
(4) the share of labor-owners in GNP will rise relative to the share of capital-owners.
(5) none of the above is correct.

3. According to the analysis of the "natural rate of growth," if the economy is actually growing at that rate:
(1) the capital-output ratio will increase, but at a rate less than the natural rate of growth.
(2) technological change will be taking place at a steady rate, and the rate of return on capital will be maintained at a steady level by this technological change.
(3) there will be a widening of capital but no deepening of capital.

(4) there will be a deepening of capital but no widening of capital.
(5) none of the above is correct.

4. "Balanced growth," as the term is used in Harrod-Domar models, involves essentially a balance between:
(1) saving and investment.
(2) investment and the capital-output ratio.
(3) total capital and total labor.
(4) investment and the distribution of income between capital and labor.
(5) saving and population growth.

5. The principal concern of "warranted-rate-of-growth" analysis is with the:
(1) rate of increase in the labor force needed to just match the scheduled increase in investment spending.
(2) rate of saving needed to just balance against the rate of increase in the labor force.
(3) rate of interest that will attract a volume of investment just sufficient to maintain full employment.
(4) maximum rate of growth in output that is possible without setting off inflationary price increases.
(5) rate of investment spending needed to just balance against the fraction of income which the public wishes to save.

6. Which alternative in question 5 would be correct had that question referred, not to the "warranted rate," but to the "natural rate" of growth?
(1).
(2).
(3).
(4).
(5).

7. The results attributed to "capital deepening" (without technological change) are those produced by:
(1) the law of diminishing returns.
(2) a fixed capital-output ratio.
(3) balanced growth.
(4) the warranted rate of growth.
(5) a decrease in the K/L ratio.

8. A Leontief input-output system records, with respect to the total output of any one industry:
(1) only that part going to households, since to include the part going to other industries would be double counting.
(2) only that part going to other industries, since its purpose is to record input-output relationships.
(3) that part going to households and the part going to other industries as well, but the latter on a value-added basis to avoid double counting.
(4) both the part going to households and the part going to other industries, in full.
(5) none of the above, since for industries it records inputs, not outputs.

CHAPTER 37

THE ECONOMICS OF DEVELOPING COUNTRIES

Twenty percent of the world's population, more than 1 billion people, live at or below the subsistence level. Only about 25 percent of the world's population earn the equivalent of $3000 per year or more. Nonetheless, the average per capita income of people living in the advanced market economies of North America and Western Europe exceeds $11,000 per year. A list of alarming statistics like this can be extended almost indefinitely, but the point is clear. There exists, across the globe, a disparity in standards of living that boggles the mind. And it is this observation that raises a litany of questions which could turn out to be *the* critical questions for survival through the twenty-first century. What, first of all, could possibly be the source of this disparity? Second, what can be done by the developing countries to correct it? And finally, is there anything that the developed world can do to help? Without some attempt to answer these questions, the growing gap between the wealthy and poor nations of the world could foster economic, political, and military conflict that could destroy the planet.

These are the questions raised in Chapter 37. For our purposes, though, they will turn out to be, to one degree or another, almost unanswerable, and the text is modest in advancing solutions and answers only in their most general form. The focus of the chapter is, instead, to ponder the ability of economic analysis to provide insight into possible answers. Only if we understand the sources of inequity can we begin to work to correct it. And only if we sort out false strategies from productive strategies will progress be made. The major objective of the chapter is, therefore, an understanding of the dimension of the problem. As you develop that understanding, you will also achieve the following more specific objectives.

LEARNING OBJECTIVES

1. Outline the theory of population and its implications for economic growth as it has evolved from the original Malthusian view, through its most recent incarnations and into the transition model of modern theorists.

2. Identify the four "wheels of development" and relate the problems faced by less developed countries in getting each one "rolling uphill."

3. Describe the vicious circle of underdevelopment facing economic planners and development economists who try to improve the living standards of the world's less developed countries.

4. Explain (*a*) the takeoff theory of development, (*b*) the backward hypothesis, and (*c*) the balanced-growth theory of development. Indicate the path of development that each implies and contrast each to the reality described by Simon Kuznets.

5. Explain the various strategies of development and identify the pitfalls associated with each one.

The world's less developed countries are characterized by per capita income levels that are well below the worldwide average. Associated with low incomes are, moreover, human problems like poor health, widespread illiteracy, poor housing, poor diets, and demoralizing underemployment. Question 1 asks you to refer to Table 37-1 in the text to record quantitative measures of these problems.

1. Compared with the high-income market economies, countries on the bottom of the development scale display the following characteristics:

a. Population growth rates that are (*twice as high / about the same / almost 3 times as high*).

b. Per capital levels of GNP that are (*about 50 percent lower / about 90 percent lower / over 90 percent lower*).

c. Literacy rates that are (*25 percent lower / 50 percent lower / 75 percent lower*).

d. Life expectancies that are *(25 percent lower / 33 percent lower / 50 percent lower)*.

e. Employment rates in agriculture that are *(5 times higher / 8 times higher / over 11 times higher)*.

---

a. almost 3 times as high   **b.** over 90 percent lower   **c.** 50 percent lower   **d.** 33 percent lower   **e.** over 11 times higher

2. Compared with the Malthusian view of population growth that predicted *(gradual / geometric / logarithmic)* growth in population and *(increasing / constant / decreasing)* growth in food production, modern population theorists espouse a transition model of growth and development. They identify four stages in the transition; list them in order in the spaces below.

a. _____

b. _____

c. _____

d. _____

As countries proceed through the transitions, history suggests that high birth and death rates give way first to lower *(death / birth)* rates and second to correspondingly lower *(death / birth)* rates before converging to a final stage of *(growing / stable / declining)* populations. During the second stage, though, the birth rate *(exceeds / falls short of)* the death rate and the population can be expected to *(climb / fall / remain stable)*.

---

geometric; decreasing;   **a.** preindustrial stage   **b.** early development stage   **c.** later development stage   **d.** maturity; death; birth; stable; exceeds; climb

3. The characteristics of a nonsocialist "developed economy" are well understood. A country in this category has a large supply of capital goods per capita. Members of its population accept the principle of division of labor, and they are trained in skills adapted to that principle. Money is almost universally employed in place of barter, and money is used for the hiring of labor. There is an active "entrepreneur class," and the making of money is not frowned upon or treated with scorn. There are well-organized money and credit markets. There is general acceptance of the authority and trustworthiness of a central government which passes laws, imposes taxes, and enforces execution of private contracts. The laws are in general obeyed and the tax levies paid (which is not to say, of course, that there is no cheating at all on taxes). Ordinarily, it is not necessary to bribe government officials to have them carry out their ordinary jobs (which, again, is not to say that bribery and corruption are completely absent).

The developed economy accomplishes new things because of its entrepreneur class, its use of the money market mechanism, and its refusal to accept unquestioningly the dictates of tradition or custom as to how things should be done. As a result,

it produces high material living standards for its members and a greatly increased life expectancy.

Since the characteristics described are common to all developed societies, it is agreed that they explain the higher material living standards and increased life expectancy. But the problem remains of *how* these characteristics were acquired. This is the central problem for planners in less developed societies. It is also agreed that most citizens of these less developed nations want the benefits of development. (The argument that such peoples are probably happiest as they are now, and best "left alone," has little application. Whether or not they are "happy" is an unanswerable question. They will not, most certainly, be "left alone" in a world in which methods of communication and transportation have been changed and increased so dramatically.) "The theory of development" thus becomes an attempt to explain how the characteristics of developed societies emerged, or how they can be fostered.

a. Some of these explanations have emphasized wholly, or in the main, one single factor—for example, geography. Here the view is usually that a cool, temperate climate is conducive to vigorous activity and hence to growth. The text *(accepts / accepts with qualifications / rejects)* the view that geography is a vital consideration.

b. Another factor emphasized is culture. The text *(accepts / accepts with qualifications / rejects)* the view that some cultures have properties which impede growth.

Two questions are raised by the problem of cultures that seemingly oppose economic development: (1) Can established culture patterns be altered by planners for development? (2) Even if they can be broken, should they be?

There is a partial answer to the first of these questions. What appear on the surface to be well-established culture patterns sometimes break up quite easily, and without evidence of any great distress appearing among the people involved.

A more positive answer exists for the second question. No country can avoid the worldwide impact of economic development, so that proposals to "protect" an established culture are becoming less popular. In their place are suggestions about how to integrate the essentials of a unique culture into a modern economy.

---

a. rejects   **b.** accepts

4. a. Max Weber disagreed with the view, attributed to Marx, that all determining forces in history are economic in origin. Weber felt that cultural elements were of at least equal importance, and that in Europe's economic development, religion had been a critical element. The name given to summarize Weber's views here is:

_____

b. Many economists speak of *the preconditions for economic growth*—a kind of foundation that must be laid before any significant growth can begin. In general terms, this means the development of a reasonably well-knit and cooperative society, establishment of tolerable stability in that society, and the acceptance of some degree of central authority.

We can be a bit more specific as to these preconditions. They find expression in "external economies." These are economies which facilitate production (and so reduce cost) for the individual firm, but are outside the control of any such firm (hence "external"). They would include such things as development in transportation facilities, health measures to improve the productivity of labor, and establishment of a system of law which makes contracts enforceable. The point about such external economies is that an individual firm *(can / cannot)* undertake them. They *(must / can, but need not necessarily)* be undertaken by government. Any individual firm which tackled such an external-economy project would find *(it worthless / that most of the benefit accrued to other firms who bore no part of its cost)*.

c. Suppose we try to focus even more closely upon the preconditions for growth. Such growth means substantially the creation of tools, machinery, and equipment—i.e., "capital formation." In terms of income received, and the disposition of that income, growth requires:

_____ .

---

a. the "Protestant ethic"   **b.** cannot; must; that most of the benefit accrued to other firms who bore no part of its cost   **c.** saving (on the part of some fraction of the population) out of income

5. The text speaks of the four economic fundamentals in terms of which the problems of development must be reviewed and understood: population, natural resources, capital formation, technology.

a. Regarding *population*, the big question is (pick one):
(1) As economic development begins, will it bring about the population increase required for further development?
(2) Is it possible to improve health habits to control disease and bring about a longer life span?
(3) Will development bring about a population increase such that real income per capita is no higher than before?

b. Concerning the second fundamental, *natural resources*, circle as many of the following as correctly indicate problems or difficulties in this area.
(1) Many less developed countries are resource-poor, so far as is known. How then are they to develop?
(2) Land reform is necessary for development in many countries, since land is not being used to the best advantage because individual holdings are too small.
(3) Land reform is necessary for development in many countries, since land is not being used to the best advantage because individual holdings are too large.

c. With respect to the third fundamental, *capital formation* (or the process of saving and investment), again circle as many statements as seem correct.

(1) Less developed nations find it very difficult to save (to refrain from consumption) to free resources for investment activity.
(2) The social customs in some less developed countries are such that rich people prefer to hoard their savings or use them in nonproductive ways; they are not used to finance investment projects that would raise the national product.
(3) The desire for development and the example of the developed nations have noticeably increased the amount of saving out of income in many less developed countries.
(4) In many poor countries, investment expenditure tends to go heavily into housing, an investment form which does not have the highest priority in development.
(5) The amount of private lending for financing investment activity by citizens in developed areas to those in less developed areas is greater than it was in the nineteenth century, both absolutely and relatively.

d. With respect to the fourth fundamental, *technology*, again circle as many as seem correct.
(1) Less developed countries have the advantage that imitation of techniques already worked out is easier than the development of new and sometimes sophisticated techniques.
(2) Efforts by developed countries to export advanced "technological know-how" are frequently unsuccessful.
(3) Some advanced technologies are "capital-saving," and these are likely to be particularly well suited to adoption in less developed countries.

---

a. (3)   **b.** (1), (2), (3)   **c.** (1), (2), (4)   **d.** (1), (2), (3)

6. a. Higher savings will be useless and productive investment will not take place in any country unless it has a class of

vigorous, creative _____ .

b. Sometimes it is said that the recurring problem with which a developed country must cope is that of *(too much / too little)* saving and hence *(not enough / too much)* demand for goods. By contrast, the problem of the less developed country is that of *(too much / too little)* saving and hence *(not enough / too much)* demand for goods.

---

a. entrepreneurs   **b.** too much; not enough; too little; too much

7. Figure 37-1 displays the growth trends of three different countries that are implied by the three different and modern theories of development outlined in the text. One is the takeoff theory, which envisions a leading sector catching fire, creating profits, encouraging investment, increasing the capital stock, increasing wages and incomes, and generally providing the initial momentum for consistent growth. The second is the backward hypothesis that suggests that developing countries have it easier today than they did a century ago because technology and markets already exist. The third contemplates a balanced-growth approach that is slow but steady once it starts. Label each panel with the theory that it portrays. The work of

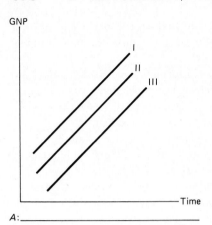
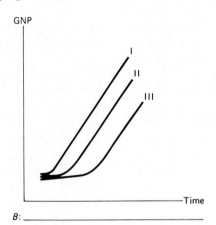
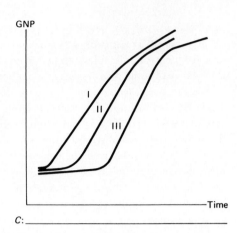

Figure 37-1

Simon Kuznets, for which he won a Nobel Prize, suggests that

_____ is the most accurate discription of historical development trajectories.

---

panel (*A*): balanced growth; panel (*B*): takeoff theory; panel (*C*): backward hypothesis; balanced growth.

8. Strategies for development must confront at least three general questions. First of all, is it more worthwhile to concentrate on industry or agriculture in initiating growth? Investment in industry might provide a few high-paying jobs, but investment in agriculture might support industrialization by (*increasing the productivity of city workers / increasing the productivity of the farms and thereby releasing labor for industrial jobs / creating large agricultural surpluses that can replace imports*).

Second, it is important to decide whether or not to promote exports to generate growth supported by the worldwide marketplace or to protect import-competing industries to generate growth in domestic markets. Care should be taken in considering the second alternative because protection can (*increase / decrease*) domestic prices, (*increase / decrease*) real incomes, and (*stimulate / retard*) investment at home and from abroad.

Finally, many developing countries find themselves over-specialized and vulnerable to the whims of the world market for their good. The key to avoiding this difficulty is _____. The question is how to do that.

---

increasing the productivity of the farms and thereby releasing labor for industrial jobs; increase; decrease; retard; diversification

9. One particularly troubling problem that beset the developing countries of the world in the late 1970s and 1980s was the debt crisis. Borrowing by developing countries from private banks had grown by $(*25 / 500 / 1000*) billion from 1972 to 1983, and these debts were denominated in dollars. Many countries, particularly in Central and South America, began to

have trouble meeting their debt obligations in the early 1980s because (pick as many as apply):
(1) American interest rates were so high.
(2) The value of the dollar was so high.
(3) The price of oil had climbed so high in the late 1970s that higher than expected debt was required.
(4) The crisis added risk premiums to the interest rates charged by private banks, particularly on refinancing agreements.
(5) The price of oil stopped rising so that the revenues that were expected to cover the debt were lower than anticipated. The crisis seems to be under control, at least to a some degree, but any disturbance that causes massive default (*could / could not*) create a major, worldwide banking crisis. To bail defaulting countries out with grants and income transfers would, however, dramatically increase the world's money supply and could therefore cause significant worldwide (*deflation / inflation*).

500; all apply; could; inflation

10. Figure 37-2 illustrates the vicious cycle of underdevelopment. Identify the boxes of the cycle in the spaces provided.

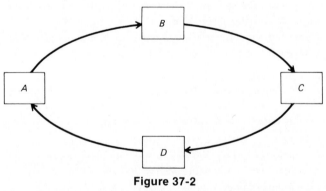

Figure 37-2

A: _____

B: _____

C: Low productivity.

D: _____

A: low saving and investment; B: low rate of capital accumulation; D: low average income

11. A less developed country is undertaking a large-scale development program and asks you to supply information on the following points. (Under each point, circle the number which you think furnishes the best answer.) It is 1985.

a. Change in population to be expected:
(1) Both the birth rate and the death rate are likely to remain high for some time.
(2) Both the birth rate and the death rate are likely to remain low for some time.
(3) Both the birth rate and the death rate are likely to fall substantially in the next few years.
(4) The death rate is likely to fall, and the birth rate to remain at its present high level for some time.

b. Capital-formation policy:
(1) In view of the post–World War II experience, primary reliance can be placed on borrowing and aid from abroad.
(2) The primary problem will be better allocation of existing saving rather than increasing total saving.
(3) Historical experience suggests that the percentage of national product put into personal saving and into capital formation will have to be increased.
(4) "Borrowing technology" will enable development at existing levels of saving.

c. Investment allocation:
(1) The government should make sure that it is undertaking adequate investment in social overhead capital with external economies.
(2) Private entrepreneurs can be relied upon to properly allocate available saving.
(3) Although inflation tends ultimately to discourage saving, it also tends to better allocate available saving.
(4) Modern technology makes heavy use of capital in production and hence should be avoided.

d. Change in foreign trade:
(1) Imports are likely to fall as domestic manufactures replace foreign manufactures.
(2) Imports are likely to rise because of the need for foreign capital goods, and possibly for food and fuel.
(3) Exports of primary products should be pushed, since this is where comparative advantage must lie.
(4) Exports should fall as the demand of developed countries for raw materials continues to decline.

---

a. (4)   **b.** (3)   **c.** (1)   **d.** (2)

QUIZ: Multiple Choice

1. One area of economic development in which the country's government must take the initiative and also participate, according to the text, is that of:
(1) maintaining balanced growth.
(2) promoting heavy industry.

(3) transferring resources needed in the shift from agricultural predominance to industrial predominance.
(4) providing social overhead capital.
(5) none of the above, because there are no areas in which such government involvement is always needed.

2. The main reason population growth has spurted ahead so rapidly in many less developed countries in recent years is that:
(1) birth rates have increased sharply with improvements in nutrition.
(2) great strides have been made in keeping older people alive an extra 5 or 10 years.
(3) infant mortality and mortality due to epidemics have been drastically lowered.
(4) large-scale immigration has occurred into many countries since World War II.
(5) birth rates have risen markedly as the natural result of widespread reductions in the customary age of marriage.

3. Four of the following five statements more or less repeat what the text identified as a problem of economic development. One is false and runs counter to what the text says. Which one?
(1) Developing economies often have reasonable prospects of looking to "increasing returns to scale" as they expand their total output.
(2) Ordinarily, individual firms cannot undertake investment in social overhead capital, no matter how important such projects may be.
(3) Entrepreneurship and innovation are vital for the success of any developing economy.
(4) The principle of protecting import-competing industries is not necessarily a wise one for a developing nation to follow.
(5) In a probable majority of the less developed nations, excess saving is a significant problem.

4. "Disguised unemployment" refers to a situation in which:
(1) deficiencies in population statistics give a faulty picture of the labor force that is actually available.
(2) workers who actually are effectively self-employed claim to be in need of work.
(3) a country, having reached a certain stage in development, finds difficulty in recruiting workers for industrial jobs because of their reluctance to leave traditional occupations.
(4) demand for finished consumer goods is insufficient.
(5) for most (or all) of the year, the marginal productivity of labor in agriculture is actually very low.

5. As a country develops economically and builds its own industry, one of the following usually does not occur, Which one?
(1) It imports less and less from other developed and industrialized countries.
(2) Its total exports tend to rise.
(3) It imports more and more from other industrialized, highly developed countries.
(4) It imports more from less developed countries.
(5) Its total imports tend to rise.

6. "Social overhead capital" is:

(1) the money investment required before any return is obtainable from a particular natural resource.

(2) a particular form of "external economy."

(3) investment in those projects considered to have the highest net productivity.

(4) projects which must be financed by the nation itself, as distinct from those financed by external aid.

(5) any capital investment the amount of which does not vary as the quantity of national output is increased.

7. An absolute "precondition for growth" is the:

(1) development of some excess of income over consumption.

(2) creation of a surplus labor force for employment in manufacturing.

(3) discovery and exploitation of some internal economies.

(4) cultural acceptance of free enterprise principles of economic behavior.

(5) development of manufacturing to the point where it can begin to supplant agriculture.

8. Four of the following five statements more or less repeat what the text identifies as a problem of economic development. One is false and runs counter to what the text says. Which one?

(1) In some less developed countries, considerable investment takes place, but goes into items that are of low priority or even are undesirable from the standpoint of national economic development.

(2) The development of adequate "social overhead capital" is usually essential if there is to be much economic development.

(3) In history, political revolutions have often taken place *after* some economic progress has been achieved.

(4) Most of the less developed countries are known to have substantial unexploited natural resources, if only the capital needed to bring them into effective use were available.

(5) In poor countries, especially rural ones, often a large part of the labor pool does almost nothing because there is nothing for it to do.

9. Less developed countries have lower per capita incomes than developed countries. The text suggests that the gap between the two income levels is:

(1) diminishing as to the "free enterprise" less developed countries, widening as to the socialist-oriented ones.

(2) almost incapable of measurement, because of differences in cultures, tastes, and climates.

(3) perceptibly diminishing, evidently as the result of foreign-aid programs.

(4) diminishing with respect to those countries which have concentrated their investment upon social overhead capital.

(5) not perceptibly diminishing, and in some areas may even be widening.

CHAPTER 38

INTERNATIONAL TRADE AND THE THEORY OF COMPARATIVE ADVANTAGE

Chapter 38 begins a three-chapter excursion into the fundamentals of international economics—the issues surrounding the conduct of international trade and finance. The first two chapters introduce the real factors involved in trade and describe how differences in resource endowments, tastes, and technology can generate the potential for gleaning substantial welfare benefits from trade abroad. The problems associated with that trade and the restraint of its proliferation by tariffs and quotas are thus central to the discussion. Chapter 39, in fact, focuses on these issues almost exclusively. In the meantime, the end of Chapter 38 presents a brief survey of how international trade accounts are kept. The details of the monetary mechanisms that support international trade, including exchange-rate determination and other current issues of international finance, occupy Chapter 40.

The details of international economics are extremely complex, and an introductory course can only scratch their surface. Nonetheless, the fundamental welfare implications of international and interregional trade are easily presented and understood. Chapter 38 starts the presentation and puts you on the way to achieving this general learning objective. In the process, you will also achieve the following more specific objectives.

LEARNING OBJECTIVES

1. Distinguish between "absolute advantage" and "comparative advantage." (Do this by making a comparison between two different countries, using labor-hours as the sole measure of productive cost and efficiency.)

2. Explain briefly why, using a simple two-commodity case, a country can increase its real income by specializing in production upon the commodity in which it has a comparative advantage, and importing the commodity as to which it is at a comparative disadvantage.

3. State the one situation in which, using a two-country and two-commodity example, neither country has a comparative advantage in either commodity. Cite two reasons why, despite this lack of comparative advantage, international trade might still be mutually profitable to the two countries.

4. Explain why (assuming zero transport cost) the establishment of the equilibrium price ratio common to both countries (after trade has been fully developed) is essentially a supply-and-demand problem.

5. List the major "simplifying assumptions" that are made in order to reach the comparative-advantage conclusions of this chapter.

6. Outline the basic accounting procedure with which the world keeps track of its international accounts. Define current account, capital account, official settlements, and statistical discrepancy in this context. Note, as well, that a credit is recorded in any account whenever a transaction produces foreign currency, and a debit is recorded for any transaction that expends foreign currency.

7. Trace the usual development of a nation from a young, debtor nation to a mature, creditor nation.

The fundamental result of Chapter 38 is that foreign trade can improve welfare (i.e., the standard of living) of most nations, even if they are most productive in producing everything. There are, of course, political problems that frequently stand in the way of countries' exploiting this potential: problems of reciprocal trade restriction in the face of "unfair" trading practices by trading partners; problems of national security and overreliance on foreign suppliers of critical commodities; and so on. There can, moreover, exist problems caused by the multiplicity of currencies across the world. Still, the welfare result that produces the potential gains from trade is robust and widely known. Chapter 38 produces it for you in the simple context of the Ricardo model, and the Study Guide explores it further. The numbers are different here, for the sake of variety and to avoid "puppeting" rather than "thinking" answers; but the point is the same: international trade can improve the welfare of everyone involved by expanding the consumption possibilities of everyone involved.

1. The trend in the United States over the past half-century has been to (open / close) its economy to foreign trade. The usual measure of openness, the ratio of _____

and/or _____ to GNP has, in fact, (risen /

fallen) to _____ percent. This is a percentage that is,

however, (higher / lower) than the _____ percent that characterizes most of the economies of Europe.

It is important to note that although the simple Ricardo model implies compete specialization by bilateral trading partners, reality seldom achieves that extreme condition. The pattern of trade (in fact shows that / does, however, show that) the United States (frequently / never) imports and exports the same general commodity within the same year.

_____

open; imports; exports; risen; 10; lower; 50; in fact shows that; frequently

If the United States has no domestic sources of tin, then surely it must import the tin it needs. What is not so obvious is why the United States, or any other country, should import a commodity which it *could* and does produce.

The basic message of this chapter is that a nation should import some goods which it is capable of producing at home if it wants to use its resources to the best advantage. Each country should move toward specializing in the production of those commodities it is best equipped to make, given its own resources, and given those available to other countries. It should export part of what is has produced, receiving in exchange other goods (imports) which it is less well equipped to make.

The "model" used in this chapter is intended to drive home this point in the simplest possible form. Based on the model, most of the chapter concentrates on a review of some *wrong* ideas about international trade. One such incorrect idea holds that when a highly efficient country can outproduce another country in every line of activity, then profitable trade between them is impossible. Part of David Ricardo's great contribution to this subject was to show that even if a country is relatively inefficient in all lines of production, this predicament shows up in a lower living standard at home and not in an impossible bargaining position in international trade. The efficient and inefficient countries can still trade to mutual advantage, provided there are some differences in their *relative* costs of producing different goods. Both the text and the review questions following develop this point at length. A few

qualifications to the model and the conclusions are voiced, but this major message is strong and cannot be dismissed.

Before trying to understand why certain ideas about international trade are mistaken ideas, you must grasp the basic *comparative-advantage* idea: why, in real income terms, it pays each nation to specialize in production, to export, and to import.

The first group of questions below deals with a nation's situation before it engages in foreign trade. The idea is first to identify the country's before-trade real-income position, and then to show how foreign trade, when it begins, can increase real income.

The same simplifying assumptions are employed as in the text chapter. There are only two countries: "America" and "Europe." Only two commodities are involved: food (*F*) and clothing (*C*). All costs of producing *F* or *C* can be measured in hours of labor. For some reason or reasons, such as differences in climate or in skills, the yields from an hour of labor, in the making of both *F* and *C*, differ across international boundaries. (The specific productivity figures used here are different from those employed in the text chapter.)

2. The quantities of *F* and of *C* yielded by 1 hour of labor effort in America and in Europe are as follows:

Yield of 1 Labor-Hour	Units of *F*	Units of *C*
In America	20	6
In Europe	10	8

They translate into the following input requirement data:

	Minutes of Labor Required to Produce	
	1 Unit of *F*	1 Unit of *C*
In America	3	10
In Europe	6	7.5

Assuming that "1 hour of labor effort" means the same thing in both countries, these figures indicate that, for some reason, America is more productive in (*F / both F and C / C / neither F nor C*). Europe is more productive in (*F / both F and C / C / neither F nor C*).

In an 8-hour day, a worker in America can produce either 160 units of *F* or (*10 / 48 / 64 / 80*) units of *C*. In Europe, in an 8-hour day, a worker can produce either 64 units of *C* or (*10 / 48 / 64 / 80 / 160*) units of *F*.

_____

F; C; 48; 80

3. **a.** This chapter assumes that all costs of producing either commodity in either country are solely labor costs, and that all revenue from sale of the commodity goes to that labor. Hence, if the market price of a unit of *F* in America is $1, the hourly wage earned by an American worker producing *F* will be $*(0.05 / 0.10 / 1 / 10 / 20)*.

If, instead, *F*'s price in America were to be $0.05 (5 cents), the corresponding hourly wage for an *F*-worker would be $*(0.05 / 0.10 / 1 / 10 / 20)*.

Similarly, if *C*'s price per unit in America were to be $2, the hourly wage of a *C*-worker would be $*(0.30 / 0.60 / 2 / 10 / 12)*.

b. If in Europe the price per unit of *F* is £1, the hourly wage of an *F*-worker there will be £*(1 / 4 / 6 / 8 / 10)*. If *C*'s price in Europe is £1, the corresponding hourly *C*-wage will be £*(1 / 4 / 6 / 8 / 10)*.

---

a. 20; 1; 12 **b.** 10; 8

---

4. **a.** Suppose that, for some unspecified reason, the prices of *F* and *C* in America were both $1. A worker, free to choose either occupation, would earn more by going into *(F / C)* production. Specifically, in *F* production, earnings per hour would be $*(1 / 6 / 8 / 10 / 20)*, and in *C* production $*(1 / 6 / 8 / 10 / 20)*.

Given freedom of labor to enter either occupation (and with no other preference between them), the prices noted above (both $1) *(could / could not)* characterize an "equilibrium" situation in America. If such prices did prevail—say the government tried to enforce them by law—then ultimately *(only F would / only C would / both F and C would continue to)* be produced.

b. In Europe, if the prices of both *F* and *C* were somehow £10, then (again assuming no barrier to movement between occupations) *(all workers would move into F / all workers would move into C / such prices would not affect F and C)* production.

c. The point here is that unless the prices of *F* and *C* stand in the proper relation to one another, the entire resource supply (here, the entire labor force) will shift away from production of the "underpriced" commodity. If in America the price of *F* were $3, then, if both *F* and *C* are to continue to be produced, *C*'s price must be $*(1 / 3 / 8 / 10 / 12)*. If *C*'s price in America were $2, then *F*'s price should be $*(.30 / .60 / 1 / 1.50 / 2)*. Prices of $2.40 for *F* and $9 for *C* *(would / would not)* constitute an equilibrium relationship.

Relative prices are what matter here. In America, the ratio between p_F and p_C must be *(1:1 / 3:10 / 5:10 / 10:3)* because that pair of figures matches the underlying ratio of production costs, measured in labor time needed to produce 1 unit of each commodity. (The absolute level of prices will be governed by such factors as the quantity of money circulating within the country.)

If prices of *F* and *C* somehow got stuck at $2.40 and $9, respectively, workers would move away from *(F / C)* production and into *(F / C)* production.

d. In Europe the same requirement holds, except that the relationship must match productive conditions there. If the price of *F* in Europe were £4, then, for an equilibrium in which both commodities were produced, the price of *C* would have to be £*(1 / 2 / 3 / 4 / 5 / 6)*. More generally, Europe's ratio p_F/p_C must be *(3:10 / 5:10 / 4:5 / 5:4)*.

---

a. *F*; 20; 6; could not; only *F* would **b.** all workers would move into *F* **c.** 10; .60; would not; 3:10; *F*; *C* **d.** 5; 4:5

The questions thus far have assumed that there is no international trade between America and Europe. Now, suddenly, the opportunity of such trading opens up. For simplicity, the costs of shipping goods from one region to the other are assumed to be so small that they can be considered zero. The prices of *F* and of *C* in America are, respectively, 60 cents and $2.

5. **a.** You are a shrewd, wealthy American entrepreneur. To be more specific, you have $9 in cash, and are the first to notice that *F*'s price in Europe is £4, and that *C*'s price is £5. Given such prices, how can you convert your $9 into $24? Describe the necessary operations in four steps; the first step is provided to get you on your way.

Step 1: <u>Buy 15 *F* for $9</u>

Step 2: _____

Step 3: _____

Step 4: _____

b. If you were an entrepreneur in Europe with a capital of £15 and a similar desire to improve your financial and social standing, what would you do, and what would the result be?

Step 1: _____

Step 2: _____

Step 3: _____

Step 4: _____

---

a. 2: Sell the 15 *F* in Europe for £60; 3: Buy 12 *C* for £60; 4: Sell the 12 *C* in America for $24 **b.** 1: Buy 3 *C* for £15; 2: Sell the 3 *C* in America for $6; 3: Buy 10 *F* for $6; 4: Sell the 10 *F* in Europe for £40

---

6. **a.** As a result of this difference in price ratios between the two countries, the two commodities will accordingly begin to move internationally. Specifically (pick two alternatives), *(F moves from America to Europe / F moves from Europe to America / F moves in both directions / C moves from America to Europe / C moves from Europe to America / C moves in both directions)*.

A quick rule of thumb for determining what country will export which commodity in such circumstances is this: write down the two before-trade price ratios as fractions, and take the smaller of the two, noting the country to which it belongs. (In question 5, the p_F/p_C fractions would be ³⁄₁₀ and ⁸⁄₁₀; America's ³⁄₁₀ is the smaller.) The numerator of that fraction indicates that country's export commodity. (The numerator is 3, and that 3 pertains to food price; so America will export food.) The other country will export the other commodity.

b. Had America's F and C prices been 30 cents and $1, respectively, rather than 60 cents and $2, the results described in part **a** *(would / would not)* have changed. Had Europe's F and C prices been £8 and £10, respectively, rather than £4 and £5, this *(would / would not)* have changed the results described.

---

a. F moves from America to Europe; C moves from Europe to America
b. would not; would not

7. a. In America (and in Europe) the pretrade domestic "equilibrium" has been disrupted. For example, in the United States, domestic supplies of C are supplemented by imports. Thus C's price should *(rise / remain unchanged / fall)*. This in turn means that the ratio p_F/p_C will *(rise / remain unchanged / fall)*.

b. We know from questions 3 and 4 that if America's ratio p_F/p_C is anything other than 3:10 (or .3), workers will leave the "underpriced" occupation. In this case, workers will move from *(F / C)* to *(F / C)* production. Because of America's new export trade, more workers are needed in this commodity.

c. In Europe which imports what America exports, there will *(be a / not be any)* corresponding change in domestic prices. There, the ratio p_F/p_C will *(rise / remain unchanged / fall)*. The price of F will fall, as imports of this commodity arrive from America. The price of C will rise, since there is a new demand for C from those exporting it to America. Workers will leave *(F / C)* production, moving instead to production of Europe's export commodity.

---

a. fall; rise **b.** C; F **c.** be a; fall; F

8. a. The before-trade price ratios were 3:10 in America and 4:5 (or 8:10) in Europe. Clearly, such different ratios allow you to make a financial killing, when trade opens up, by going through the trading process of question 5. The profit you make would be one of "arbitrage."

These arbitrage profit opportunities will not last. They are in fact a symptom of disequilibrium. As question 7 indicated, when goods begin to move in volume between the two countries, prices are affected. Specifically (to repeat question 7), America's before-trade p_F/p_C of 3:10 will *(rise / fall)* and Europe's ratio of 4:5 (or 8:10) will *(rise / fall)*. That is, the two ratios move *(closer together / farther apart)*.

Suppose that America's ratio rises from 3:10 to 4:10, and Europe's falls from 8:10 to 7:10. There is *(no longer / still)* an

arbitrage profit to be made; it persists so long as any difference at all persists between the two ratios. But as more and more people discover this opportunity, the trade volume keeps increasing. This increase in turn pushes the two ratios even *(closer together / farther apart)*. In the case here assumed, that of literally zero transport cost, the two ratios must finally meet at a common figure, the same in both countries. A possible common figure would be 5:10. (It would be any figure between 3:10 and 8:10, but leave the matter of determination of the exact common ratio for a later question.)

b. Alas, when this common ratio is reached, your chances of getting rich quickly are ended; the arbitrage opportunity vanishes. Does this mean that international trade will stop? Not at all; it means only that the trade volume will stop increasing. Thereafter, a food producer in America gets the same return whether the output is sold in America or in Europe; the same is true of a clothing producer in Europe. An international equilibrium is established, comparable to the separate equilibria formerly prevailing in the two countries. The new equilibrium is one in which America produces only food, Europe only clothing.

If the trade volume were somehow greatly disrupted (say, by serious and persisting shipping difficulties), the price ratios in the two countries would *(still remain at a common figure / draw apart again)*.

Introduce some transport cost, and the two price ratios will continue to differ somewhat—but by just enough to reflect that transport cost and not by enough to allow for any enduring arbitrage profit.

---

a. rise; fall; closer together; still; closer together **b.** draw apart again

9. The result of this international exchange is that both countries enjoy an increase in real income. Specializing in F production, America will have available for consumption more of F than it did before, and more of C also. The same holds for Europe, which concentrates on C production.

This point is illustrated by looking at the labor cost to America of the two methods of getting C—domestic production, or export-import.

America can produce 6 units of C per hour; thus each unit costs 10 minutes of labor time. What will that unit cost if C is obtained by producing F, exporting it, and bringing back C in exchange?

Assume, as in question 8, that the international price ratio, p_F/p_C, is 5:10. That is, a unit of clothing costs twice as much as a unit of food. Or in barter terms, $2F$ exchange for $1C$. America can produce 20 units of F in 1 hour. If this is sent to Europe (with transport cost still assumed zero), America can get *(5 / 6 / 10 / 20 / 40)* units of C in exchange. Since 1 hour of labor effort was involved, each of those C units costs *(5 / 6 / 10 / 20 / 40)* minutes of labor. This is *(not as good as / better than)* obtaining C through domestic production.

Thus, international trade produces for America a result equivalent to development of a new technology greatly improving labor productivity in the *C* industry. The same is true for Europe, but for the *F* industry instead of the *C* industry.

The introduction of transport cost would somewhat reduce this real-income gain. If such cost were sufficiently high, there would be no point in trade, and no real-income gain.

10; 6; better than

10. The points of questions 2 through 9 can all be illustrated

graphically. Take the input requirements listed in question 2 as given, and suppose that Europe and America are both endowed with 10 hours of labor (not very realistic, to be sure, but a convenient number around which to build some illustrative geometry). Suppose further that both countries start in the absence of any trade by dividing their labor resources equally between *F* and *C*.

a. Draw, in panel (a) of Figure 38-1, the production-possibility frontier for America, and identify the initial production mix as

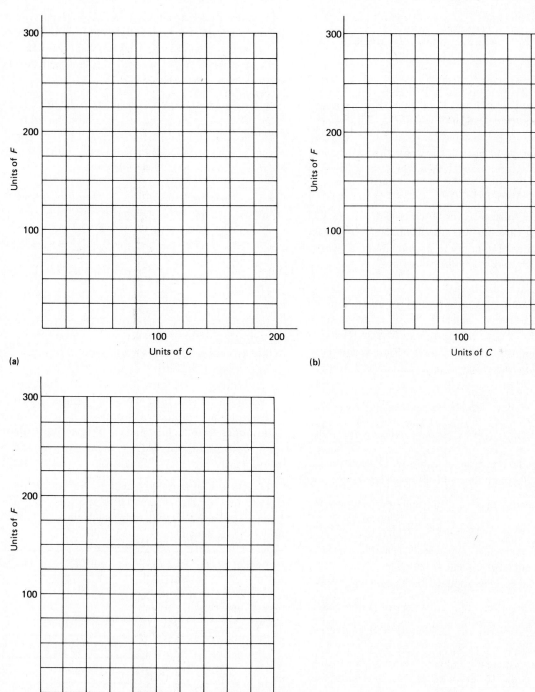

Figure 38-1

point *A*. Draw the corresponding frontier for Europe in panel (b) and identify the initial production mix as point *B*. The slope of the American frontier, equaling _____ in magnitude, represents the relative domestic price ratio of food to clothing in the United States. The corresponding slope of the European frontier, equaling _____ in magnitude, is similarly the relative domestic price ratio in Europe. Let's begin with America, which produces _____ units of *F* and _____ units of *C*; Europe begins producing _____ units of *F* and _____ of *C*. Total production of *C* is _____ units; total production of *F* is _____ units.

b. Suppose now, for the sake of argument, that America were to choose to specialize in *F* and trade with Europe at the European domestic price ratio to generate its desired consumption of *C*. Draw a budget constraint indicating the possible points of consumption given this strategy. If America were to continue to consume the original 30 units of *C*, then she could increase her consumption of *F* from 100 units to _____ units by selling _____ units of *F* for 30 units of *C*. Welfare in America, assuming a smooth transition from a 50-50 labor split to 100 percent concentration in the production of *F*, would therefore necessarily *(fall / stay the same / rise)*.

c. Now play the same game from the other side of the Atlantic. Assume that Europe decides to specialize completely in the production of *C* and buys as much *F* as is desirable given the American price ratio. Draw the appropriate budget constraint in panel (b). If Europe were still interested in consuming 40 units of *C*, it could not increase its consumption of *F* from 50 units to _____ units by selling 40 units of *C* for _____ units of *F*. European welfare would, in this second case, also *(climb / remain the same / fall)*, making the same assumption of continued full employment.

d. The world production frontier can now be constructed. Suppose, first of all, that both countries specialized in *F*; production of *F* would equal _____ units in America and _____ units in Europe, for a total of _____ units; the production of *C* would equal _____ units. Plot this combination in panel (c) and label it point *D*.

Now reverse the specializations of both countries. Total *F* production would then equal _____ units with *C* production, climbing to a maximum of _____ units. Plot this point and label it *E*.

Halfway between these extremes are two intermediate cases of mixed specialization. If Europe specialized in *C* and America specialized in *F*, then _____ units of *F* would be produced with _____ units of *C*. Denote this point *G* and plot it

in panel (c), as well. If the specializations were reversed, though, _____ units of *F* would be produced by Europe and _____ units of *C* would be produced in America. This point, plotted and labeled *H* in panel (c), *(would / would not)* be on the frontier because production levels of *(F / C / neither F nor C / both F and C)* are lower at *H* than at *G*.

The world frontier is now at hand. A straight line connecting points *D* and *G* would correspond to specialization by *(America / Europe)* in the production of *(F / C)* and some intermediate combination of *F* and *C* production in *(America / Europe)*. Similarly, points along a line connecting points *G* and *E* would correspond to specialization in *(America / Europe)* in the production of *(F / C)* and some intermediate combination in *(America / Europe)*.

e. Finally, plot the pretrade initial production combination; it *(is / is not)* on the frontier. The point chosen by free trade outlined above would be *(D / E / G / H)*. It *(would / would not)* be on the frontier and it would, for both countries, be superior to the initial, pretrade position.

---

a. Panel (**a**): straight line from ($C = 0; F = 200$) to ($C = 60; F = 0$); $A = (C = 30; F = 100$); Panel (**d**); straight line from ($C = 0; F = 100$) to ($C = 80; F = 0$); $B = (C = 40; F = 50$); 3/10; 5/4; 100; 30; 50; 40; 70; 150 **b.** Straight line from ($C = 0; F = 200$) to ($C = 250; F = 0$); 162.5; 37.5; rise **c.** Straight line from ($C = 0; F = 266\frac{2}{3}$) to ($C = 80; F = 0$); 133.3; 133.3; climb **d.** 200; 100; 300; 0; 0; 140; 200; 80; 100; 60; would not; both *F* and *C*; America; *F*; Europe; Europe; *C*; America **e.** ($F = 150; C = 70$); is not; *E*; would

---

The preceding questions have concentrated on an example in which Europe and America both held absolute advantages in the production of one good; America was more productive in food and Europe was more productive in clothing. The theory of comparative advantage stresses, however, that an even distribution of absolute advantage is not necessary for trade to be mutually beneficial. The next few questions will concentrate on this possibility—the real power of the Ricardo result.

11. Now change the productivity figures. Double America's yield per labor hour in the production of both commodities (leaving the figures for Europe unchanged). Thus, the tables in question 2 become:

Yield of 1 Labor Hour	Units of *F*	Units of *C*
In America	40	12
In Europe	10	8

	Minutes of Labor Required to Produce	
	1 Unit of *F*	1 Unit of *C*
In America	1.5	5
In Europe	6	7.5

The critical difference is that American labor is now assumed more productive than European labor in the production of *both* commodities. We do not ask what background factors would result in such differences. We simply accept the fact that there are now "high-productivity" and "low-productivity" countries, so that we may ask the Ricardo question: is trade that would be profitable to both participants possible in such circumstances?

In America's previous pretrade situation (questions 2 through 4), its ratio p_F/p_C was 3:10. In the new situation—still pretrade—that ratio will be *(higher / unchanged / lower)*. (The two absolute prices may of course be different.)

Question 5 examined the trading opportunity arising out of the opening up of international trade. With the changed productivity figures introduced in this present question, this trading opportunity will *(no longer exist / be exactly as it was before)*. Why? Because domestic, pretrade prices are unchanged. The dimensions of the transactions identified in question 5 might have changed, but the *directions* have not.

---

unchanged; be exactly as it was before

---

12. Let America be endowed with 5 hours of labor and Europe be endowed with 10; suppose that the production possibilities of both countries are accurately described by the tables recorded in question 10. Plot, in panels (a), (b), and (c) of Figure 38-2 the production-possibility frontier of America, or Europe, and the world, respectively.

Indicate in panel (c) the point toward which free trade would lead the two countries, if they would only trade with one another at some price ratio between $(10/3) = (20/6) = (40/12)$ and $(10/8) = (5/4)$. At that point, world production of F would equal _____ units and world production of C would equal

_____ units because Europe would specialize in producing (F / C), exporting (F / C), and importing (F / C); America would do the reverse.

They are identical to those of question 10; point G at the corner; 200; 100; C; C; F

---

13. The point, then, is that a "low-productivity" country should still be capable of dealing profitably with a "high-productivity" country; both should gain in real income from international trade. The cost of low productivity is a low per capita income within that country, not an inability to cope with international exchanges.

The essential factor upon which an opening up of trade (and profitable trade) *does* depend is a difference in the pretrade price ratio as between the two countries.

a. Below are three sets of pretrade price figures (each quite different from anything used earlier). In the right-hand column, indicate the proper conclusion by this code: (1) America would export F, Europe C. (2) America would export C, Europe F. (3) No opportunity for any trading gain here.

America		Europe		
P of *F* in \$	*P* of *C* in \$	*P* of *F* in £	*P* of *C* in £	**Answer**
1	2	3	4	
1	2	3	6	
1	2	3	8	

(To answer, use the question 5 technique—which between-country transfer of goods would earn you a profit?—or the rule of thumb suggested in question 6.)

b. All the foregoing may indicate why it was thought necessary to introduce such terms as *absolute advantage* (or disadvantage) and *comparative advantage* (or disadvantage).

America has an *absolute* advantage over Europe if her productive conditions are such that, domestically, she can produce the commodity in question at less real cost (which in this chapter means simply labor cost) than Europe can. (If America needs 1 hour to produce 1 unit of F, and Europe needs $1\frac{1}{2}$ hours, then America has the absolute advantage with respect to F).

Look back at the question 11 tables. They indicate that America has the absolute advantage in *(F alone / both F and C / C alone)*. Yet this circumstance does not prevent Europe from exporting good C, despite the absolute advantage of American producers. Thus it is said that Europe, regardless of its absolute disadvantage, still has a comparative advantage in production of good *(F / C)*. (In terms of question 11 data, America is decidedly the high-productivity country. Yet, in comparative terms, its productivity shows up less prominently with respect to good C.)

In two-country, two-commodity examples like the ones used here, it is necessary to examine and compare the prices of both commodities *(in that one country alone / in both countries)* to determine who has a comparative advantage in what.

---

a. 1; 3; 2   **b.** both F and C; C; in both countries

---

14. At what exact level will the common, posttrade price ratio be established? This is essentially a supply-and-demand question. The trade process described earlier is just an exchange of one good for another. Indeed, for purposes of understanding how the common intermediate ratio is reached, it's easiest to think of this trade as simple barter. The exact quantities exchanged are settled by working out a barter rate which both countries find, in terms of the amounts exchanged, satisfactory.

Start with the same pair of pretrade p_F/p_C ratios used earlier: 3:10 in America, 4:5 (or 8:10) in Europe. If the price of F in America is, say, \$3, then the price of C is \$10. One unit of C costs $3\frac{1}{3}$ times as much as 1 unit of F. In barter terms, it takes 10 units of F to match 3 units of C. Similarly, Europe's 4:5 p_F/p_C ratio means that *(4 of F equals 5 of C / 5 of F equals 4 of C)*.

When trade opens up, these two pretrade ratios (recall

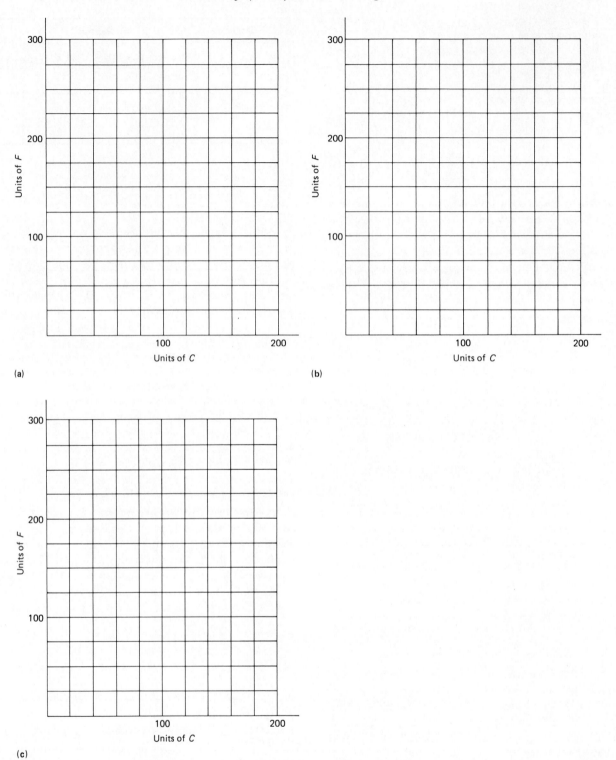

Figure 38-2

questions 7 and 8) are pushed closer together. Consider any intermediate ratio, picked at random—say, 1:2 (or 5:10). At that ratio, there will be a particular quantity of F which America would wish to export, and a corresponding quantity of C it would want to import. If the desired F-export quantity were 100 units daily, the quantity of C that America would want in exchange (remember, the 1:2 ratio is expressed in p_F/p_C terms, as before) would be *(50 / 100 / 150 / 200 / 250)* units daily.

At that same 1:2 ratio, there are particular quantities of C and F which Europe would wish to export and import daily, respectively, but these quantities may not match the American ones. If they did not, then 1:2 would not be an "equilibrium" common ratio.

The intermediate and common ratio finally established is one at which the two countries' wishes (in terms of *F* and *C* quantities as exchanged) *do* match. The better the barter terms America is offered—the more the old 3:10 ratio moves upward—the *(more / less)* it will want to exchange. Europe, by contrast, will want to trade more extensively, the more that its pretrade ratio of 4:5 moves *(up / down)*. Somewhere between the two differing pretrade price ratios, there should be a common price ratio that is mutually satisfactory.

---

5 of *F* equals 4 of *C*; 50; more; down

15. The principal basis for mutually profitable international trade is a difference in relative production costs and prices. The case in which a country imports a commodity which it cannot produce at all is simply an illustration of the extreme case of such differences-in-production-cost trade. It does not matter what factors account for these relative cost differences (e.g., climate, differences in labor education and skill, differences in capital equipment); they must simply emerge in the form of differences in relative prices.

Differences in "factor endowments" are usually cited as the principal source of such differences in relative production costs and prices (although this explanation is of the kind which may raise as many questions as it answers).

The text mentions briefly two other possible sources of mutually beneficial international trade. They are:

a. _____

b. _____

---

a. Decreasing cost (*Note:* In this case, we assume that the pretrade cost ratio between commodities *F* and *C* is the same in country A as in country E. But if A specializes in production of *F*, this may lower the per unit cost of producing *F*. Here, trade is still based on a difference in costs, but this difference emerges only *after* trade has begun) **b.** Differences in tastes between the two countries

16. The analysis of Ricardo depends upon an implicit assumption of full employment. That is to say, when a country moves from producing a mix of goods to specializing more heavily in a few goods, resources must flow freely from the production of one good to the other. Labor *(must be / need not be)* included in this flow—labor which may or may not like the idea. If it does not, then serious opposition to free trade can arise, as labor asks its government for *(unemployment compensation / protection from foreign competition)*. Even though total welfare might improve with trade, it therefore is possible that some individuals would be forced to endure short-term pain sufficient to lobby against it. There could, moreover, be a long-term loss to some if the distribution of relative wages were to shift with the move toward specialization.

All is not barter and roses in the world of multilateral trade. The world is full of currencies and floating exchange rates that complicate international transactions almost beyond belief. The costs of foreign business offices, foreign exchange hedging, and insurance certainly lead to the conclusion that the Ricardo assumption of zero transportation (read transactions) cost is far from reality. Profit margins have to be large to make international trade worth the effort.

---

must be; protection from foreign competition

17. A country's balance of payments is the official record of all its transactions with foreign countries for some specified period of time—usually 1 year. There are four main categories; list them in the spaces provided.

a. _____

b. _____

c. _____

d. _____

The key to entries in any of these categories is the effect that it has on domestic holdings of foreign currencies. If a transaction generates foreign currency, then it is recorded as a *(debit / credit)*; it if costs currency because a foreign citizen (or institution) requires payment in his or her (or its) own currency, then it is a *(debit / credit)*.

---

a. Current account; **b.** Capital account; **c.** Statistical discrepancy; **d.** Official settlements; credit; debit.

18. A less developed nation is typically one which borrows abroad to the full extent of its line of credit. A mature, developed nation is typically one which lends to other countries. As a nation develops over a long time period, it may change from borrower to lender, and this shift will affect its BP position. The sequence outlined below (and in the text)—*young debtor, mature debtor, new creditor, mature creditor*—is an attempt to describe the likely BP changes involved.

a. The less developed nation is likely to try to build up its stock of capital goods through sales of its IOUs to more developed countries. On its BP, these security sales will be recorded as a *(credit / debit)*. The import of capital equipment or other goods purchased with security-sale proceeds will appear on the "merchandise" line as a *(credit / debit)*. This country has *(a "favorable" / an "unfavorable")* balance of trade. These facts make it a "young debtor" nation.

b. As time passes, this country ceases to borrow, or borrows in smaller quantities. It still pays interest and dividends on earlier years of bond and stock financing, but its exporting capacity has increased. It now shows a surplus of merchandise exports over imports, or an excess of *(credits over debits / debits over credits)*. This *("favorable" / "unfavorable")* balance of trade is matched, or approximately so, by a surplus of debits on the BP investment income account. The "mature debtor" stage has been reached.

c. In further time, this country may begin not only to repay its own earlier borrowings but to lend to other countries itself. This means a surplus of *(credits over debits / debits over credits)* in the BP capital section. If this is matched, or approximately so, by a surplus of merchandise exports over imports, the "new creditor" stage has been reached.

d. Ultimately, the "mature creditor" stage may be attained. Such a country may still be lending capital abroad, but its inflow of interest and dividend payments is more than sufficient to offset this lending. On the BP merchandise account; therefore, there is a surplus of *(credits over debits / debits over credits)* and the balance of trade is *("favorable" / "unfavorable")*. This balance is supported by the *(debit / credit)* balance on the investment income account.

---

a. credit; debit; an "unfavorable" **b.** credits over debits; "favorable" **c.** debits over credits **d.** debits over credits; "unfavorable"; credit

QUIZ: Multiple Choice

1. In terms of comparative advantage, the most correct explanation of why bananas are imported instead of being grown commercially in the United States is that:
(1) bananas cannot be produced in the temperate zones.
(2) it would take a great deal of effort to produce bananas in the United States.
(3) bananas can be produced with less effort in other countries than they can in the United States.
(4) United States resources are better employed in producing other commodities, and tropical-country resources are better employed in banana production than in other things.
(5) the United States climate does not lend itself to banana production.

2. David Ricardo's theory of comparative advantage, or comparative cost, is intended to show that trade between two countries will be mutually beneficial. An assumption made in this analysis, to which some objection might be raised on the ground that it influences and perhaps alters the conclusions reached, is the assumption that:
(1) comparative advantage, not absolute advantage, is the important element in trade.
(2) each country, in consequence of such trade, will specialize in the commodity it exports.
(3) full employment is at all times maintained in both countries.
(4) no tariffs exist in either of the two countries.
(5) the pretrade ratio of prices within each country has no part to play in the determination of trade flows.

3. Before international trade begins, a country will have an equilibrium ratio of prices (determined by relative production costs) between any two commodities. If trade with another country begins, involving these commodities, this price ratio will ordinarily be altered:
(1) only if a change in production costs results within the country.

(2) in all cases (excepting only the one where the volume of international trade proves to be too small to affect it).
(3) only in cases where the volume of international trade is small.
(4) not at all, since it is an equilibrium relationship.
(5) only in cases where the volume of international trade is exceedingly large.

4. The output of labor (assumed to be the only input involved) in production of wine and of cloth in two countries, Upper Utopia and Lower Utopia, is as follows:

Production per Hour	Upper Utopia	Lower Utopia
Yards of cloth	5	15
Quarts of wine	10	20

Comparing the two countries and contemplating trade between them on the basis of production advantages, it would be correct to say that Upper Utopia has:
(1) an absolute advantage in cloth production.
(2) an absolute advantage in wine production.
(3) a comparative advantage in cloth production.
(4) a comparative advantage in wine production.
(5) a comparative advantage in neither commodity.

5. Initially, there is no trade between the two countries of question 4; each lives in isolation. In Upper Utopia, the currency unit is the "up"; in Lower Utopia, it is the "down." The prices of cloth in Upper and Lower Utopia in their pretrade situations are, respectively, 20 ups and 60 downs. For an equilibrium in which each country continues to produce both commodities, the corresponding wine prices would have to be:
(1) 5 ups, 20 downs.
(2) 40 ups, 45 downs.
(3) 10 ps, 45 downs.
(4) 10 ups, 80 downs.
(5) 40 ups, 80 downs.

6. If trading opportunities were to be opened up, given the data of questions 4 and 5 (international transport cost assumed to be zero or negligible), then we should expect Lower Utopia to:
(1) import wine.
(2) export wine.
(3) import both commodities.
(4) export both commodities.
(5) neither export nor import, since her productive situation is such that there is no prospect of profitable trade with Upper Utopia.

7. Before the trading opportunity of question 6 emerged, each country had its own price ratio, reflecting domestic production costs. If trade develops between Upper and Lower Utopia, this ratio—specifically, the ratio of cloth price to wine price—will:

(1) rise in Upper Utopia, fall in Lower Utopia.

(2) fall in Upper Utopia, rise in Lower Utopia.

(3) rise in both.

(4) fall in both.

(5) not change in either country, except perhaps during a short transitional period before equilibrium is reestablished.

8. When international trade has become established, in the circumstances of questions 4 through 7, and a new equilibrium has been reached, the ratio of cloth price to wine price (transport cost still assumed zero) might reasonably be:

(1) 1.2 in both countries.

(2) 1.8 in Upper Utopia, 1.5 in Lower Utopia.

(3) 1.6 in both countries.

(4) 2.1 in Upper Utopia, 1.3 in Lower Utopia.

(5) 2.3 in both countries.

9. Given the price ratio or ratios set out in question 8, if we know that the total of cloth exports is 500 yards daily, then the daily wine exports must be:

(1) 600 quarts, from Upper Utopia.

(2) 600 quarts from Lower Utopia.

(3) 800 quarts, from Upper Utopia.

(4) 800 quarts, from Lower Utopia.

(5) 1150 quarts, from Upper Utopia.

10. The gain from trade is illustrated by the position of the wine-importing country (either Upper or Lower Utopia). Question 4 shows hourly output of wine if that wine is produced at home. If the country specializes in cloth production and gets its wine via imports, then—at the price ratio of question 8, transport cost still assumed zero—the number of quarts of wine resulting from 1 hour's labor is:

(1) 16.

(2) 20.

(3) 24.

(4) 28.

(5) 32.

11. Differences in comparative production costs are usually cited as the principal basis for international trade. Another (and different) possible source of such exchanges is:

(1) differences in climates.

(2) fixed foreign exchange rates.

(3) differences in transport costs.

(4) differences in labor skills.

(5) economies of mass production.

12. Trade between countries comparable size with different standards of living will be:

(1) profitable to the country of lower living standards at the expense of the one of higher standards.

(2) profitable to both as long as price ratios differ in the two countries, but of no profit to either once a common price ratio has been established.

(3) profitable in some degree to both, even after a common price ratio has been established.

(4) unprofitable to both because one country would be at an absolute disadvantage in all products.

(5) profitable to the country of higher living standards at the expense of the one of lower living standards.

13. A "favorable balance of trade" means:

(1) an excess of merchandise exports and other current account credits over merchandise imports and other current account debits.

(2) an excess of foreign currency received by the home country over domestic currency received by foreigners.

(3) an excess of merchandise exports over merchandise imports.

(4) an excess of total credits over total debits in the entire balance of payments.

(5) a situation in which the value of total imports exceeds the value of total exports.

14. The five transactions listed below are all entries to be made on the U.S. balance of payments. For balance-of-payments purposes, four of the five are fundamentally similar. Which is the different one?

(1) The Federal Reserve Bank of New York receives gold from the Bank of England.

(2) An American tourist on vacation spends francs in Paris.

(3) A South American Government sells long-term bonds in New York.

(4) A British shipping firm is paid to carry an American export commodity abroad.

(5) An American investor receives a dividend check from a West German steel company.

15. A mature debtor nation is one whose balance of trade is:

(1) unfavorable, the import surplus being paid for by borrowing.

(2) unfavorable, thanks to the interest which is received from abroad.

(3) favorable, the interest on past borrowing being paid out of the surplus of exports.

(4) favorable, being made so by interest received from abroad.

(5) not correctly identified by any of these descriptions.

CHAPTER 39

PROTECTIVE TARIFFS, QUOTAS, AND FREE TRADE

The case for free trade has been made. The comparative-advantage results of Chapter 38 were produced in a simplified environment, to be sure, but they are strong and robust. It is now time to turn the coin over to look at its opposite side. If, in particular, free trade is so beneficial, then why do we see so many barriers to free trade in the real world?

To answer this question, it is essential to see how trade barriers work. Only then can their effects be delineated and their merits evaluated. Chapter 39 tends to this task in its initial sections. With the effects of protection firmly in hand, the various arguments for and against protection are then critically reviewed. Having completed your work on this chapter, therefore, you will have accomplished the following objectives.

LEARNING OBJECTIVES

1. Use supply-and-demand analysis to outline the economic effects of protection. Show, in particular, that a tariff can be expected to (*a*) promote inefficient domestic production, (*b*) cause uneconomical reductions in domestic consumption, and (*c*) generate some extra revenue for the government.

2. Outline the noneconomic arguments for trade restrictions and evaluate their validity.

3. Outline the false economic arguments for trade restrictions and indicate where they fall short.

4. Outline the dynamic economic arguments for trade restrictions and evaluate their validity.

5. List a few non-tariff barriers to trade that have been employed by the United States over the past few years.

Three principal reasons (often working in combination) explain most of the actual or proposed restrictions on foreign trade: (1) the country fears unemployment, and regards imports as generators of unemployment be-

cause they substitute for domestically produced goods; (2) the country is short of foreign exchange reserves; and (3) there are always particular groups which benefit from protection, and they bring (or try to bring) political pressure accordingly.

In a period of heavy unemployment, for example, it is hard to preach comparative advantage and free trade to legislators and businesspeople. They may argue that a reduction in imports would raise domestic employment, and so they advocate an increase in protective tariffs.

Such an attempt to "export unemployment" may be canceled out when other countries retaliate with similar tariff increases aimed at the initiating country. It would be wrong to insist that import restrictions can never reduce unemployment, nor raise GNP. The proper objection is that use of fiscal and monetary policies, as discussed in Parts Two and Three of the text, is far more effective. Moreover, these policies avoid the dubious ethics of trying to foist off your unemployment onto other nations; hence they do not incur the danger of retaliation.

Other arguments exist against free trade. Given reasonable assurance that unemployment can be handled by methods other than tariff or quota protection, most people in large, developed countries find it fairly easy to accept the free-trade principle. Those who live in a less developed country may be more hesitant. They look at the world's most prosperous nations; they hope that in due course their own country will enjoy equally high standards of production and income. And they wonder if some restriction on the import of particular goods may not be needed in order to widen productive and employment opportunities, and to foster their nation's industrial growth.

To evaluate the validity of these basic motives behind trade protection, it is essential to understand precisely how a tariff works. The first few questions explore their operation in a simple supply-and-demand model.

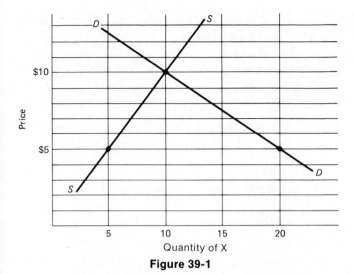

Figure 39-1

1. Consult Figure 39-1. Curve SS drawn there represents a domestic supply curve for some good X; if X is a competitive industry, SS represents the horizontal sum of the marginal cost curves of many firms. Curve *DD* represents domestic demand for the same good. It is implicitly assumed that consumers do not care where the good was made; they simply want to buy the indicated quantities at the indicated prices.

a. The market clearing price in the absence of trade is $_____;

_____ units of X are demanded and supplied domestically at that price. If the world price of $5 were allowed to prevail, though, _____ units of X would be demanded, _____ units would be supplied domestically, and _____ units would be imported.

b. Now suppose that the domestic government has been convinced somehow to restrict imports by 50 percent. A tariff of $_____ per unit imported would do the trick, but it would raise the domestic price to $_____. At that price, _____ units would be demanded, _____ units would be supplied domestically, and _____ units would be imported. The effect of the tariff, therefore, is to *(raise / lower)* prices, *(raise / lower)* domestic production and employment, and *(raise / lower)* imports.

c. Given the tariff of part **b**, the government would collect $_____ in revenue; this is revenue that would be collected above and beyond the revenue that it collected from its domestic tax base. The higher domestic price would, however, promote *(less / more)* efficient production at home, and produce an efficiency *(loss / gain)* of $_____. The marginal cost of producing X at home would, quite simply, increase to a level 50 percent higher than the marginal cost incurred by the rest of the world. The domestic economy would, in other words, be wast-

ing resources in the production of X that would have been employed more efficiently somewhere else. Consumer surplus would, moreover, be *(reduced / increased)* by $_____. Total spending on X would, in fact, climb in the case drawn, so that income effects on the demand for other goods across the economy should be expected.

d. If the government chose to impose a quota rather than a tariff, then it would award licenses to import up to _____ units of X. If these licenses were given away, then importers would earn excess profits of $_____ by buying X abroad and selling X domestically. If the government auctioned the licenses, though, the total revenue generated by the auction would be $_____.

e. If there were no tariff, but if it cost $2.50 per unit to transport X from the world marketplace into the domestic economy, then your answers to part **b** *(would / would not)* be altered. The revenue that part **c** identified as going to the government *(would / would not)* simply go to the transport company.

a. 10; 10; 20; 5; 15 **b.** 2.50; 7.50; 15; 7.5; 7.5; raise; raise; lower **c.** 18.75; less; loss; 3.12 (=½ × $2.50 × 2.5); reduced 6.25 (=½ × $2.50 × 5) **d.** 7.5; 18.75; 18.75 **e.** would not; would

2. Often it is argued that a high tariff (*a*) brings revenue for the government, and (*b*) protects the domestic industry against competition. There is an inconsistency in using both of these arguments. Why?

The more revenue brought in, the less protection; and vice versa. A tariff sufficiently high to keep out all imports brings in zero revenue

3. Several noneconomic arguments for tariff protection have been advanced. One suggests that protection is necessary to preserve national security. The notion here is that foreign sources of supply are unreliable, and that domestic production of certain strategic goods should be guaranteed even if it is inefficient. Protection, if it is awarded in response to this reasoning, should *(be total / be large enough to satisfy only minimum and essential consumption needs / be permanent and growing)*. If the commodity is a raw material, then perhaps _____ sufficient emergency supplies would be more efficient. If the commodity is a production good, then internal protection by

_____ would be better than external protection by trade restraint.

Second, some argue that protection is needed to preserve a way of life—a culture or a unique characteristic of an economy.

_____ is again a more reasonable alternative than tariff protection.

_____

be large enough to satisfy only minimum and essential needs; storing; subsidy; Subsidy

4. a. The *mercantilist* approach to international trade argued that a nation should try to have *(exports / imports)* in excess of *(exports / imports)*—hence the phrase *favorable balance of trade.* The surplus so obtained would be used to acquire *(merchandise / gold).* The mercantilist position was thus strongly disposed toward *(protectionism / free trade).* It was a convenient argument for many *(producer / consumer)* groups seeking protection against foreign competition.

The underlying mercantilist philosophy was that a nation ought to apply the same principles of prudence appropriate for a family. It is prudent for a family to try to save part of its income. The nation, mercantilists said, is just the family on a larger scale. And they equated saving, at the national level, with the accumulation of gold.

The argument is not totally fallacious. Any nation will find it desirable to have reserves of gold (or foreign exchange) to cope with changing events which may produce balance-of-payments deficits. But even at the family level, the argument for "prudence" is wrong if interpreted as meaning that all families must hoard their money. Saving which is not allowed to flow into investment spending leads only to depression and to a fall in saving.

b. It would be quite *(possible / impossible)* for every nation to practice mercantilism successfully, since it is *(possible / impossible)* for every nation to have a surplus of exports. A general attempt to practice this philosophy, by trying to expand exports and restrict imports, would lead to a major *(rise / fall)* in *(exports / imports / both exports and imports).*

_____

a. exports; imports; gold; protectionism; producer **b.** impossible; impossible; fall; both exports and imports

5. a. In a country such as the United States, a protariff argument sometimes put forward is that American producers cannot compete against "cheap foreign labor." The free-trade response to this argument is that (pick one):

(1) Such cheap labor is simply a particular illustration of the international cost differences on which mutually profitable trade can, in principle, be based.

(2) The cheap-labor argument is sometimes a valid reason to impose a tariff, but it has often been used to excess.

(3) Where cheap foreign labor does threaten the domestic industry, the proper remedy is a subsidy or quota, not a tariff.

b. If the United States were to impose a tariff on imported industrial goods, it would reduce U.S. exports of, say, agricultural goods if (pick one):

(1) But only if, foreign nations retaliate with a countertariff against such agricultural goods.

(2) Foreign earnings of American dollars are reduced by this tariff to the point that other nations can no longer buy the agricultural goods, regardless of the imposition or nonimposition of a countertariff.

c. The "escape clause" provision in U.S. tariff legislation comes into play when import volume harms a domestic producer. The text's verdict as to a tariff so imposed is that (pick one):

(1) It is valid where national security is involved.

(2) On economic grounds, the industry ought to be exposed to that competition even to the point of possible extinction.

d. If another country harms us by erecting a tariff against our goods, our own position *(will / will not)* normally be improved if we impose a retaliatory tariff.

e. If a country happens to be economically powerful, and also important in international trade, it may find that a moderate tariff improves its real-income position, due to a change in the

_____ .

_____

a. (1) **b.** (2) **c.** (2) **d.** will not **e.** terms of trade

_____

6. a. The text concedes that the "national-survival" argument for tariff protection for a particular industry may be valid—although it is one to be viewed with some skepticism, since it has so often been used by special-interest groups. The text's suggestion is that where concern for national survival (particularly in wartime) does seem to warrant protection for some domestic industry, the best remedy is a *(quota / tariff / subsidy).*

b. The text notes also that there may be a valid argument for imposition of tariffs in the case of the *(less developed / richer)* nations, because such tariffs *(may be one of the few sources of revenue for government that are administratively feasible / are almost the only effective means of protecting domestic employment in time of recession).*

c. The *infant-industry* argument is one often invoked within the less developed nations. It is that the domestic industry needs protection when it is young and inexperienced, hence unable to stand up to the competition of mature foreign producers. The text's verdict on this argument is that (pick one):

(1) It has at least some validity in principle, although in practice many industries have proven perpetual infants, never able to survive without protection.

(2) It has no validity at all, since international trade is founded on natural cost advantages.

Tariff arguments such as the infant-industry suggestion move us from the realm of static economic analysis to that of dynamic analysis. (Chapter 38, on comparative advantage, is a good example of static analysis. Such material puts its emphasis upon equilibrium, and the properties of equilibrium positions.

Dynamic analysis deals with change—e.g., with growth—and with the process of change.) In general, the text's position is that economic arguments for protection are probably stronger in the *(static / dynamic)* region of analysis.

---

a. subsidy **b.** less developed; may be one of the few sources of revenue for government that are administratively feasible **c.** (1); dynamic

7. Much has been made recently of domestic content legislation for American-built automobiles. Under this legislation, a fixed percentage of the parts used to produce a car built in the United States would have to be built in the United States. It is argued by labor that this would protect American jobs and increase employment in the United States. This question will explore the validity of that claim under the (reasonable) assumption that domestic content restrictions would limit the quantity of parts imported from abroad (if that were not the case, why bother?).

Let some good Y be produced from some combination of inputs including both labor and good X of question 1. Content legislation would amount to placing a quota on imports of X, so Figure 39-1 shows that the price of X should *(rise / fall)* and quantities demanded should *(rise / fall)*. At the same time, though, domestic production of X should *(climb / fall)* and domestic employment in that industry should *(climb / fall)*.

It is now clear that the marginal cost of producing good Y should *(increase / decrease)*; illustrate this effect assuming perfect competition in Figure 39-2 by drawing a new supply curve for Y. The price of Y must therefore *(climb / fall)*, the output of Y must correspondingly *(climb / fall)* as the economy moves along the *(demand curve / old supply curve / new supply curve)*, and employment in the production of Y must follow suit—it must *(climb / fall)*, as well.

The result, if you add things up, is ambiguous. The claim that domestic content legislation will help the employment picture in the United States is premature. Its employment effect will depend upon the elasticity of demand for automobiles (good Y), and it is by no means certain that it will be positive.

---

rise; fall; climb; climb; increase; draw a new supply curve above and to the left of S_YS_Y; climb; fall; demand curve; fall

QUIZ: Multiple Choice

1. One argument for tariffs is that they should be imposed to help a domestic producer to compete when the level of foreign wages is significantly below the level of domestic wages. This argument:
(1) is conceded by most economists to be correct, although sometimes exaggerated in order to justify some level of tariff protection.
(2) is fallacious because there are almost no instances in which there is any real difference between the level of foreign and domestic wages.
(3) ignores the fact that differences in relative costs constitute the principal basis for international trade.
(4) may be correct with respect to money wages at home and abroad, but is not correct with respect to real wages.
(5) is not correctly described by any of the preceding.

2. Country A imposes a new tariff on Country B's products. Country B is considering a retaliatory tariff on A's goods. On economic grounds, B should:
(1) reject the idea of a tariff increase.
(2) make the retaliatory tariff less than A's tariff.
(3) make the retaliatory tariff more than A's tariff.
(4) impose the retaliatory tariff only if B is in a situation of full employment.
(5) adjust the price of its currency relative to B's currency.

3. The policy of the mercantilists with respect to foreign trade held that:
(1) imports should exceed exports—i.e., the country should "get more than it gives"—in order to increase real income at home as much as possible.
(2) exports should exceed imports in order to bring in gold.
(3) since this trade represented commerce, it should be encouraged to the greatest possible degree—i.e., there should be free trade.
(4) exports should be kept in balance with imports, and at the lowest possible level of both.
(5) trade in agricultural products was more important than trade in industrial goods.

4. The principal reason high-wage American labor should not require tariff protection from lower-paid foreign labor is because:
(1) no American labor would be thrown out of work even if there were no tariffs.
(2) the high per-worker-hour productivity of American labor in many industries is an offset to the lower cost of foreign labor.

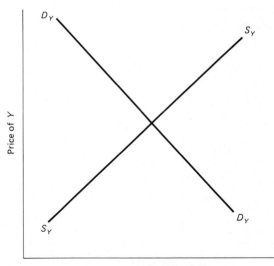

Quantity of *Y*

Figure 39-2

(3) American consumers tend to buy American-made goods in preference to foreign-made goods.

(4) a high-wage American industry can be presumed to have a comparative advantage over foreign competitors.

(5) of none of the preceding reasons.

5.   The argument by workers in a protected industry in the United States that free trade would worsen the income position of American labor is:

(1) not valid even for workers in that industry after allowance is made for the improvement in real income afforded by cheaper imports.

(2) not valid even for workers in that industry after allowance is made for the employment effect of increased exports.

(3) valid for workers in that industry but probably not valid for American labor as a whole.

(4) valid for workers in that industry and probably valid for American labor as a whole.

(5) probably valid for workers in that industry but unquestionably invalid for American labor as a whole.

6.   From a purely economic point of view, the best level at which to set a tariff (under static assumptions) is:

(1) the prohibitive point.

(2) the amount needed to bring the level of foreign costs up to the level of domestic costs.

(3) zero.

(4) a level sufficiently low so that it is not likely to invite retaliation by other countries.

(5) the level at which revenues from the tariff will be at a maximum.

7.   One argument for tariff protection is that a tariff would improve the terms of trade in dealing with other nations. This argument:

(1) is a refinement of the mercantilist argument that a nation's exports should exceed its imports.

(2) may be valid if the tariff-imposing country is a relatively large one, and the tariff is a relatively small one.

(3) is a refined version of the infant-industry argument, hence has no validity.

(4) may be valid if the tariff-imposing country is unimportant in world trade for the commodity or commodities involved.

(5) may be valid if it is applied to all the country's imports, without or almost without exception.

8.   It may be argued that a tariff should be imposed on a commodity if that commodity is considered essential to material well-being and if it is suspected that the foreign suppliers thereof might use their supply control for purposes of political blackmail—as in the case of oil. The text's verdict on this argument is that:

(1) if the commodity is deemed really essential, the tariff is justified.

(2) if the commodity is deemed really essential, a subsidy would be preferable to a tariff.

(3) the best remedy for threats of political blackmail is to insist on all-around free trade.

(4) although the imposition of a tariff might be used as a threat, political moves should be met by political countermoves (even to the threat of war), not by economic moves.

(5) if the commodity is deemed really essential, its domestic production should be nationalized.

9.   If we reduce the flow of import goods by imposing heavy tariffs, our exports are likely to be affected as follows:

(1) They will be reduced if other countries retaliate by imposing tariffs against those exports (as is likely), but not otherwise.

(2) There is little reason to expect that they will be affected at all, since retaliatory tariffs have usually proved ineffective.

(3) They will be increased, since other countries will find it necessary to buy more from us to compensate for the higher cost of the goods they sell us.

(4) They will be increased if the tariff raises the level of employment and national product at home, but not otherwise.

(5) They are likely to be reduced in all or almost all circumstances.

10.   A valid counter to the argument that a tariff results in increased money wages in the protected industry is that:

(1) workers in that industry will in all probability suffer a loss in real wages.

(2) workers in other industries will suffer a loss in real wages.

(3) the increase in money wages in the protected industry will cause unemployment.

(4) tariffs cannot increase money wages in any industry.

(5) any increase in real wages is likely to lead to inflation.

11.   Arguments cited in favor of a protective tariff are that such a tariff (*a*) protects the domestic industry against foreign competition and (*b*) brings revenue for the government to offset the higher domestic price. In response to these arguments, it may be said that:

(1) the tariff reduces rather than increases the sales of the domestic industry.

(2) if the industry in question enjoys an absolute advantage in production, it stands in no need of such a tariff.

(3) the emphasis on government revenue may lead to a tariff per unit much higher than the domestic industry needs for protection.

(4) an effective tariff may actually bring in no government revenue at all.

(5) none of these statements is correct.

12.   A difference between a tariff on an imported good and a quota on such a good is:

(1) that a quota can never be made to yield revenue for the government, whereas a tariff can.

(2) that a tariff can never be made to yield revenue for the government, whereas a quota can.

(3) that a quota can be used to shut off all, or virtually all, the inflow of the imported good, whereas tariff cannot.

(4) that a tariff can be used to shut off all, or virtually all, the inflow of the imported good, whereas a quota cannot.

(5) not correctly stated by any of these descriptions.

CHAPTER 40

EXCHANGE RATES AND THE INTERNATIONAL FINANCIAL SYSTEM

This concluding chapter focuses attention on the workings of the international financial system. Coverage begins with one essential fact of life: there exists, in the world today, a multitude of currencies that all function as money in one place or another. To conduct transactions on an international level is to deal in foreign exchange markets. Flowing immediately from this fact of life is the consequent necessity for the world community to prescribe some sort of standard of monetary exchange that sets down the rules of the game. Be it the gold standard and its fixed-exchange-rate regime, the marketplace and its pure-flexible-exchange-rate regime, or the intermediate managed float mechanism and its goal to minimize inefficient exchange-rate variability, the rules of the game must be clearly understood by all the players. The first part of Chapter 40 reviews these issues.

Subsequent sections outline the effects of changes in imports, exports, and exchange rates on macroeconomic variables. It is a two-way street, to be sure, and the effects depend critically upon the monetary rules set forth by international agreement and/or custom. This dependence is clearly outlined. Finally, a description of the evolution of the international financial system from the Bretton Woods agreement of 1945 to the managed float regime of the 1980s is provided as background for a critical review of the major issues of contemporary international finance. Significant here, of course, is the impact of the overvalued dollar on the United States and the rest of the world.

These are all complicated topics that draw on your understanding of much of what has gone before. Micro concepts are exercised as well as macro concepts. Having completed your work on this chapter, therefore, not only will you have accomplished the following objectives, but you will also have accomplished an integrated review of many of the fundamentals of economic analysis.

LEARNING OBJECTIVES

1. Define precisely what is meant when someone quotes an exchange rate, and differentiate carefully between devaluation, depreciation, and appreciation.

2. Differentiate the fixed-exchange-rate system of the gold standard from the pure-float alternative. Describe the intermediate managed float that characterizes the international financial system of the 1980s.

3. Explain the equilibrating mechanism advanced by David Hume to counter mercantile impressions of appropriate behavior under fixed exchange rates.

4. Describe precisely the two sides of a foreign exchange market and how they interact to produce an equilibrium exchange rate under the flexible regime.

5. Define purchasing-power parity and indicate how it can be used to determine if a currency is overvalued or undervalued.

6. Outline the sequence of events through which tight monetary policy can lead to an overvalued currency, the worldwide effects of such an overvaluation in a large economy like that of the United States, and the various means by which the overvaluation can be corrected under fixed and managed exchange rates. Indicate why calls for protectionism frequently accompany overvaluation.

7. Sketch a brief chronology of the evolution of the international financial system from the construction that emerged from Bretton Woods to today's regime of managed floating.

8. Describe the pros and cons in the debate over whether or not to reestablish the gold standard.

1. a. The earliest exchanges in human history were barters— goods exchanging for goods. These were succeeded by what we ordinarily call "money transactions"—those everyday swaps in which goods were exchanged for money. When we investigate international transactions, though, we are discussing transactions in which one money exchanges for another money.

In a sense, therefore, we are back to barter again. If we refer to the exchange market between dollars and pounds, we can speak equally well of the price of the pound sterling in (*dollars / pounds sterling*), and of the price of the dollar in (*dollar / pounds sterling*).

b. Suppose, for example, that the rate of exchange between

U.S. dollars and British pounds sterling were £1 = $2. This means that (pick one or both):

(1) The price of the pound sterling is $2.

(2) The price of the dollar is £0.50, or one-half a pound sterling.

c. As a further consequence of the money-for-money property of foreign exchange transactions, note that the participants can be identified as "demanders" or as "suppliers" only by identifying one of the two monies as the good that is bought and sold. If you want to buy pounds sterling, you think of yourself as a demander of pounds, but it would be equally correct to describe yourself as a *(supplier of pounds / demander of dollars / supplier of dollars)*.

---

a. dollars; pounds sterling   **b.** (1) and (2)   **c.** supplier of dollars

2.   Left to its own devices, a foreign exchange rate will move up and down under the pressure of changes in supply and demand. The exchange rate is a price; it is subject to the same influences as any other price. However, governments rarely leave the foreign prices of their own currencies entirely free to *float*. To a greater or lesser degree, they try to manage foreign exchange rates. Any nation heavily engaged in exporting and importing finds the price which its currency can command on the foreign exchange markets to be a matter of the highest importance.

Until 1971, most governments tried to keep the prices of their own currencies in foreign monies fixed, or very nearly so. Fixed rates were altered only under the strongest pressure for change.

The great advantage of a fixed exchange rate is that everyone knows exactly what a foreign purchase will cost and what a foreign sale will bring in domestic money. The demands for a fixed rate (commonly heard among bankers and business firms especially) are further bolstered by the fact that in the past, nations have often relied on a particular technique for maintaining fixed rates: *the gold standard.*

A country goes on the gold standard by declaring that gold is the basis or standard for its currency unit. Thus the United States may say that the gold "content" of its dollar is 1/100 of an ounce, but it must back this statement by a declared willingness to buy or to sell gold freely at $100 per ounce.

Suppose that the United Kingdom, also on the gold standard, will buy or sell gold at £50 per ounce. This implies a pound-dollar exchange rate of *(£1 = $7 / £1 = $5 / £1 = $3 / £1 = $2)*.

This £1 = $2 algebraic equality means nothing to exporters or importers unless it affects the rate at which they can buy or sell a currency, but the gold standard does just that. Since a further requirement of this standard is that the country must not restrict the export or import of gold, the system works. If you owe a British firm 100 pounds sterling for goods imported, it would never cost you much more than $200 to pay your bill. If necessary, you could get your £100 via gold. You could *(buy / sell)* gold for $200. Sending that gold to Britain and selling it to the British government, you would receive *(pounds / dollars)*

in exchange. (In practice, of course, banks and other such agencies would handle the gold part of the transaction in bulk, but the effect is the same as if you did it yourself.)

£1 = $2; buy; pounds

3.   Suppose that a widespread taste for Scotch whiskey develops in the United States. This means an increase in demand for *(dollars / pounds sterling)*. If the United States is on the gold standard, and if this demand increase is sufficiently large, there will be a flow of gold *(away from / toward)* the United States. If this demand increase persists without countering effect for sufficiently long, the United States might be drained of its entire stock of *(gold / Scotch whiskey)*.

---

pounds sterling; away from; gold

4.   The gold standard keeps exchange rates steady by definition, but demand-and-supply forces are still at work. Why don't some nations, trying to maintain that standard, run out of gold?

A nation must indeed "go off" the gold standard if it loses all or most of its gold because of a major rise in imports (or import prices), or a sufficient drop in exports (or export prices). However, there are some "equilibrating" forces that would operate to brake any such gold outflow.

The first major attempt to describe such an equilibrating mechanism was laid out by David Hume in the eighteenth century: the *gold-flow–price-level mechanism*.

a. Suppose, as in question 3, that the U.S. demand for imports increases. This American demand for foreign currencies pushes *(up / down)* their prices to the gold *(import / export)* point. According to Hume's gold-flow–price-level analysis, the resulting gold flow *(out of / into)* the United States *(increases / decreases)* the U.S. money supply, causing the price level to *(rise / fall)*.

b. In one or more foreign exporting countries, the *(same / reverse)* situation occurs. The gold which has left the United States flows into these countries, increasing their money stock and so causing their prices to be *(higher / lower)*. Since American prices have gone down while foreign prices have gone up, *(more / fewer)* American goods will be bought by foreigners, while Americans will tend to buy *(more / fewer)* foreign goods. That is, in America, exports will *(rise / fall)*, imports will *(rise / fall)*, and the rise in the U.S. imports which began the process is offset.

In rough outline, for sufficiently large movements, Hume's analysis may have some validity. But today there is almost no link between a nation's total gold stock and its total money supply. Moreover, Hume's analysis relies heavily on the quantity theory of money and its assumption of full employment. Both of these caveats leave the Hume analysis wanting as a description of modern-day responses to current account imbalance.

---

a. up; export; out of; decreases; fall   **b.** reverse; higher; more; fewer; rise; fall

5. Although the old international gold standard is gone today, its influence persists, particularly in two important respects. First, nations still consider their gold stocks as reserves for settling international balances. (But now they tend to regard gold as an "emergency" reserve; they do not part with gold unless events force them to do so. Here, the United States was one of the last to yield. Until 1971, America stood ready to give gold to any nation which had accumulated dollars and wanted them swapped for gold; today, it will no longer do so.)

Second, the desire for relative stability in exchange rates persists. The gold standard is not the only possible mechanism to this end. You can hold the price of your currency steady by simply maintaining a sufficently large inventory of foreign monies.

a. Canada, for example, relies heavily on exports to, and imports from, the United States. Suppose the Canadian authorities (to whom the exchange rate is consequently important) decide that for trading purposes it would be desirable to keep the price of the U.S. dollar at $(Can.)1.15. If the price of the U.S. dollar begins to drift below this figure, Canada will enter the foreign exchange market and support the price by *(selling / buying)* U.S. dollars. For this purpose, it will supply (sell) *(Canadian / American)* dollars. And if the U.S. dollar's price starts to move above $(Can.)1.15, Canada will *(buy / sell)* U.S. dollars.

b. Alternatively, Canada might choose a modified version of the same plan, keeping the price of the U.S. dollar within a "band of, say, $(Can.)1.12 and $(Can.)1.18. Of course, she cannot keep the exchange rate indefinitely at a level not justified by supply and demand. If the price of the U.S. dollar keeps chronically trying to push $(Can.)1.18, in due course Canada will *(accumulate too many / run out of)* U.S. dollars.

---

a. buying; Canadian; sell   **b.** run out of (Use supply-and-demand geometry to see that these answers are correct)

6. The great problem with fixed exchange rates, then, is that they grow outdated when they are maintained too long under changing world conditions. Some nations then run dangerously low on their reserves of foreign currencies and gold; others pile up excess reserves. (It is, however, a most unusual nation that will concede that its reserves are excessive.")

At the close of World War II, the international mood strongly favored fixed rates that were to be altered only with changes in "fundamental conditions." This mood reflected a desire to regain, if possible, the stability which had characterized the old pre–World War I gold-standard days. Moreover, during the worldwide depression of the 1930s (after the gold standard had broken down), a "currency price war" had begun; some countries deliberately allowed their currencies to depreciate in price to gain a competitive advantage in world markets for their exporters. The rules of the International Monetary Fund, created after World War II, therefore reflected a desire for fixed rates. Thereafter, until the early 1970s, exchange-rate revisions were probably made too slowly. Some nations clung to overvalued rates, others to undervalued ones.

This disposition to stick to a fixed rate is understandable. Such a rate removes uncertainty. Moreover, any hint of a revision, whether upward or downward, will provoke strong opposition. Reduce the price of your currency, and there results *(upward / downward)* pressure on your domestic price level, since the domestic prices of all imported goods go *(up / down)*. Moreover, you suffer at least some loss of international prestige. In effect, you are admitting that you can't sell enough of your nation's merchandise for as high a price as you used to get. (In the early 1960s, for example, it became increasingly apparent that the British pound was overvalued. Yet for several years the British government clung to its $2.80 value, in the process losing foreign currency reserves, borrowing abroad, and diverting the energies of government officials from critical domestic issues.)

On the other hand, if you increase the price of your currency, then prices of all your export goods, as foreigners see them, automatically go *(up / down)*. Any suggestion of such an increase will provoke howls of protest from exporting firms that such a price rise will destroy that tiny selling edge they have over their foreign competitors. (Japan appreciated the yen in 1972 because foreign pressure was so strong that she had to; but she did so by much less than some other nations thought appropriate in the light of her trade and reserve position.)

By the early 1970s, the consensus was that the price of maintaining fixed rates (the threat to reserves of gold and foreign exchange) had grown too high. In December 1971, all the major trading nations shifted to *floating rates*. The West German mark and the Swiss franc thereupon rose notably; the U.S. dollar fell.

Thus far, the floating-rate system seems to have worked fairly well. It has been described as a "managed float," i.e., not a totally free supply-and-demand one, but rather, a situation in which central banks still move in periodically, for what they consider to be good reasons, to check particular rises or falls in the price of their own national currencies.

The fixed-rate system still has strong advocates. While usually conceding the need for an interim period of floating in turbulent conditions, they insist that (1) in the longer term, fixed rates are necessary for stable, large-scale international trade; (2) in conditions of recession or depression, floating rates degenerate into a "very dirty float" of competitive currency depreciation; and (3) such floating rates only invite currency speculation, hence needless ups and downs in the foreign exchange markets. (Floating-rate proponents reply that fixed rates do not stop speculation, they just give speculators a periodic free ride. Thus when it becomes evident that a currency is undervalued and due for fixed-price revision, then the speculators need only buy that currency, sit back, and await its new and higher price.)

A country which, for good reasons or bad, wants to maintain a fixed price for its currency in foreign-money terms but is losing foreign currency reserves or gold reserves in the attempt thereat, may consider alternatives other than giving up and letting the price fall. It may impose new tariffs, set even stronger restrictions on imports by establishing quota limits, or even ban the import of "nonessential goods." These moves provoke strong resentment among other nations, and invite retaliation. Alternatively, the country may follow what international bankers consider "the rules of the game": raise interest rates and make fiscal policy more restrictive.

---

upward; up; up

---

7. In a period of floating rates, when the exchange rate between two currencies keeps shifting up and down, one wonders: Isn't there some way of penetrating beyond these day-to-day fluctuations, to discern, at least approximately, the real rate at which the two monies should exchange? One attempt to answer this question is Gustav Cassel's idea of *purchasing power parity*.

Consider for example the exchange rate between the U.S. dollar and the Swiss franc. How do the *domestic* purchasing powers of these two currencies compare? Take some appropriate bundle of commodities produced and widely consumed within both countries. This bundle costs in total, say, $100 if purchased within the United States. It costs 300 Swiss francs when bought in Switzerland. By the measure of this package of goods, the purchasing power of one U.S. dollar is *(3 / 2 / 1 / ½ / ⅓)* times that of one Swiss franc. That is $1 should equal *(3 / 2 / 1 / ½ / ⅓)* francs. Or to turn the exchange rate around, the franc's price should be $*(3.00 / 2.00 / 1.00 / .50 / .333)*.

This approach disregards completely such factors as transportation costs and tariffs. Moreover, the result obtained will vary with the particular bundle of goods selected. However (continuing with the same example), suppose that choice of various bundles of goods indicates purchasing-power exchange rates varying from 30 to 50 cents (to 1 Swiss franc). If the current (although fluctuating) *market* price of the franc were 60 cents, then these figures would suggest that the market was *(overvaluing / undervaluing)* the franc.

If the American price level were to double, then the purchasing power of the dollar would be *(halved / doubled)*. If the Swiss price level were unchanged, then at 60 cents the market would be *(overvaluing / undervaluing)* the franc.

3; 3; .333; overvaluing; halved; undervaluing

---

8. a. The word "devaluation" goes back to the gold-standard days described in question 2, in which the currency unit allegedly had a "gold content," and gold consequently had an "official price" per ounce. Devaluation meant a government-decreed *(reduction / increase)* in that gold content—i.e., *(a reduction / an increase)* in the official price. President Roosevelt's 1933 declaration that the dollar's gold content would be reduced from ¹/₂₁ to ¹/₃₅ of an ounce would *(be / not be)* an instance of devaluation. With the dissolution of the gold standard, "devaluations" no longer take place. The U.S. government may still sell gold from time to time, but there is nothing "official" about the price it obtains.

b. *Depreciation* (in the foreign exchange markets) means a change in the price of a currency relative to other monies. It occurs when the price of the currency falls. Suppose that the price of the Canadian dollar were 90 U.S. cents. If this price were to drop to 85 U.S. cents, then the Canadian dollar would be worth, in U.S. funds, *(more / less)*; this would be an instance of depreciation. If the price were to rise from 90 to 95 U.S. cents, this would be *(depreciation / appreciation)* of the Canadian dollar.

c. Any depreciation of a foreign currency (relative to the U.S. dollar) makes that foreign country's goods appear *(cheaper / dearer)* to Americans. To residents in that other country, in terms of their own currency, American goods appear *(cheaper / dearer)*. When a country's currency is depreciated, therefore, this move tends to *(increase / decrease)* the volume of its exports, and to *(increase / decrease)* the volume of its imports.

---

a. reduction; an increase; be **b.** less; appreciation **c.** cheaper; dearer; increase; decrease

---

9. Taking the viewpoint of the United States for illustrative purposes, most international transactions fall into two categories: (*a*) export and exportlike items whose effect is to bring foreign money to the United States and (*b*) imports and importlike items whose effects is to send American money abroad. If the total money volume in category (*a*) exceeds that in (*b*) then under a fixed-exchange-rate system, U.S. reserves tend to increase. Under a floating-rate system, the same excess of (1) over (2) tends to drive up the U.S. dollar price, expressed in any foreign money.

Assume a floating-rate system. For each of the following, indicate whether its effect would be to increase (*I*) or to decrease (*D*) the dollar's price in foreign-currency terms.

a. American demand for imports increases. . . . . *(I / D)*

b. Foreign demand for U.S. goods decreases. . . . . . *(I / D)*

c. A recession in the United States results in falling GNP, employment, and imports. . . . . *(I / D)*

d. The rate of inflation in foreign countries is more rapid than that in the United States. . . . . *(I / D)*

e. Americans decide to invest less abroad—i.e., their demand for foreign IOUs decreases. . . . . *(I / D)*

f. Foreign firms increase their dividend payments, and some of the shareholders are Americans. . . . . *(I / D)*

g. Foreigners decide to hold fewer U.S. dollars. . . . *(I / D)*

---

a. *D* **b.** *D* **c.** *I* **d.** *I* **e.** *I* **f.** *I* **g.** *D*

---

10. Below is a demand schedule for francs, at various dollars-and-cents prices. Convert it into a supply schedule for dollars, at various franc prices. [NOTE: Although this is not a simple problem, it is an interesting one. A "straight-line" demand schedule results in a supply schedule of quite unexpected shape. Convert in this way: if the price of 1 franc is 90 cents, then 1 franc = 90 cents, and so $1 = 100/.90 francs (i.e., the price of $1 is about 1.1 francs). The schedule below says that when the price of the franc is 90 cents, 100 francs will be demanded; i.e., $90 will be supplied to buy them. In sum, when the dollar's price is 1.1 francs, $90 will be supplied. Work out other points on the supply schedule similarly.]

P of Francs (in $)	Q of Francs Demanded	P of Dollar (in Francs)	Q of Dollars Supplied
$1.00	0	_____	_____
0.90	100	_____	_____
0.80	200	_____	_____
0.70	300	_____	_____
0.60	400	_____	_____
0.50	500	_____	_____
0.40	600	_____	_____
0.30	700	_____	_____
0.20	800	_____	_____
0.10	900	_____	_____

(fr. 1.00, 0), (fr. 1.11, 90), (fr. 1.25, 160), (fr. 1.43, 210), (fr. 1.67, 240), (fr. 2.00, 250), (fr. 2.50, 240), (fr. 3.33, 210), (fr. 5.00, 160), (fr. 10.00, 90)

11. The exchange rate between U.S. dollars and French francs is a floating one. What effect, if any, is each of the following events likely to have on the price of the franc in dollars?

Put (*U*) in the space if the effect should be to push the price of the franc (in dollars) up; (*D*) if down; (*N*) if there is no reason why the price of the franc should be affected.

a. French corporations have a large interest payment to make, in dollars, to American bond-holders .... (_____)

b. French corporations have a large interest payment to make, in francs, to American bond-holders .... (_____)

c. France emerges from a recession, and with this increase in incomes, the French people want to buy more American merchandise .... (_____)

d. American residents decide to buy French bonds .... (_____)

e. The French government ships gold to the United States .... (_____)

f. French corporations sell bonds to Americans. They borrow in dollars and in New York because the interest rate is lower there; but the proceeds of the bond issue are to be spent on French labor and materials .... (_____)

g. Foreign exchange speculators decide that the price of the dollar in francs is going to fall ......
.... (_____)

h. The taste of American gourmets for French wine is replaced by a taste for California wine
.... (_____)

i. The French government decides that American movies are immoral and refuses to admit them into France .... (_____)

j. An American citizen sends a package of merchandise to her French relatives as a gift .... (_____)

k. An American citizen sends a remittance of dollars to his French relatives as a gift .... (_____)

l. A French bank, in possession of a dollar bank account, decides to convert these dollars into gold
.... (_____)

m. A French bank, in possession of a dollar bank account, decides to convert these dollars into francs .... (_____)

a. *D* b. *D* c. *D* d. *U* e. *N* f. *U* g. *U* h. *D* i. *U* j. *N* k. *U* l. *N* m. *U*

12. a. Experience before the Depression of the 1930s seemed to indicate what you should now expect: loans made by the United States to foreign countries (*increased / decreased*) American employment and GNP, because the dollars so supplied led to (*an increase / a decrease*) in American (*exports / imports*).

b. During the Depression, many of these foreign borrowers defaulted on their loans. The problem here (in part) is that if a country is to pay principal or interest on a loan in dollars, it must earn dollars. During the 1930s, the United States (*increased / decreased*) its tariffs, thus making it (*easier / harder*) for foreigners to earn the dollars needed. (Of course, the low level of American incomes and production in those years meant that it would have been more difficult to sell goods in the United States even without the tariff increase.)

c. In a depression, the incentive to "protect employment at home" by (*encouraging / discouraging*) imports is strong. But if you succeed in reducing imports (say, by higher tariffs), the foreign nation which formerly sold you those imports must suffer; you would be "exporting your unemployment." This constitutes a *beggar-my-neighbor* policy.

The text's verdict is that a depression-level GNP should be remedied by (*tariff increases / tariff decreases / fiscal and monetary policies*). But even if the nature of this remedy is generally understood (in the 1930s, it was not), it may be difficult to put into practice if depression is virtually worldwide, as was true in the 1930s. If you adopt this policy while your neighbor countries do not, the increase in your GNP might *(increase / decrease)* your imports, and so may cause you to *(lose / gain)* some of your stimulus through import leakage.

---

a. increased; an increase; exports   **b.** increased; harder   **c.** discouraging; fiscal and monetary policies; increase; lose

---

13.   The vulnerability of reserves of gold and foreign monies is most serious if you are trying to hold a fixed value for your own currency in the foreign exchange markets. Remember the experience of the 1930s—a period in which the maintenance of fixed exchange rates was still considered very much a part of good international behavior. This emphasis upon fixed rates drew on past experience. It was in large part a heritage of the old gold standard. The full gold standard, with all its requirements, had largely disintegrated after 1931, but its influence persisted even through Bretton Woods.

By the 1930s though, it was clearly understood that if you stuck to a fixed exchange rate but were losing reserves in the process, there was no automatic mechanism that would go into action to check this reserve loss in full. Hence, as part of the good-behavior code, there had evolved the notion of "the rules of the game."

a.   The first of these rules said that, if losing reserves, you should adjust the level of your domestic interest rates (particularly short-term rates) to attract foreign monies. That is, you should *(lower / raise)* interest rates. There are large amounts of "footloose" worldwide money capital; it is highly interest-rate sensitive, and will move rapidly from one country to another—provided the nation which has raised its interest rates has good capital markets and is considered a stable country. This international liquidity, seeking your higher rates, shows up as a foreign demand for your domestic currency. You have been using foreign reserves to maintain the fixed international value of that currency. Now your need to do this is ended or diminished. The practice of raising short-term interest rates in order to cope with a fall in the price of your currency in the foreign exchange markets is widely used even today.

Up to a point, this policy works. If the reserve loss is minor, and if only a small *(increase / decrease)* in your interest rates is needed, the problem may be resolved with little impact on the domestic economy. However, if the interest-rate change must be pushed further, then clearly you are implementing *(an easier / a tighter)* monetary policy. This may be in keeping with your domestic needs—or it may not. Should your country happen to be in recession at the time, then you want *(an easy- / a tight-)* money policy. That is, in the matter of monetary policy, there arises the possibility of a clash between domestic needs and foreign needs.

b.   Perhaps you may be able to reconcile this conflict by using the tighter monetary policy to improve your foreign-reserve position and, concurrently, using an easier *fiscal* policy to cope with your recession. But as you pull out of recession, the rise in GNP affects your imports: they probably will go *(up / down)*. This will *(add to / diminish)* the pressure on your exchange rate; it will *(improve / worsen)* your foreign-reserve position.

Moreover, a stronger interpretation of "the rules of the game" was possible—one especially favored by some central banks and commercial banks with large international dealings. In this view, any nation experiencing a continuing loss of gold or foreign exchange was overspending its income and ought to use both fiscal and monetary policies to restrain or reduce its GNP. Reducing incomes would *(cut down-on / increase)* import spending. It should free *(less / more)* of the nation's resources for export sales. Thus the foreign-balance position should be *(worsened / improved)*.

Under full-employment conditions, it often makes good sense to insist that a nation with persistent reserve-loss troubles is spending beyond its income. But in conditions of deep depression (like the 1930s), when it is obvious that the nation should try to develop more employment for its labor force, the notion that incomes should be reduced is abhorrent. In such situations, if you are trying to abide by "the rules of the game," you face a truly serious clash between domestic needs (to increase employment) and foreign needs (to maintain the value of your currency). The so-called good-behavior game rules then become stupid rules, by both domestic and international standards.

Hence, in the 1930s, some nations disposed of the problem of adhering to "the rules of the game" by dropping out of the game. That is, they allowed their currencies to depreciate in the foreign exchange markets. And these countries recovered domestically *(more / less)* rapidly than those others which held to the vestiges of the gold standard by trying to maintain a stable price for their currencies.

---

a. raise; increase; a tighter; an easy-   **b.** up; add to; worsen; cut down on; more; improved; more

---

14.   At the close of World War II, the Western nations created two new international agencies: the International Monetary Fund (IMF), and the World Bank. The IMF was the agency principally concerned with the issues discussed in questions 12 and 13.

The intended goal behind the IMF's formation was this: there were to be, so far as possible, stable exchange rates. But no nation would have to push itself deliberately into recession or depression just to maintain a steady international value for its currency—as strict application of "the rules of the game" mentioned in question 13 might sometimes have required it to do.

Each participating nation deposited with the IMF a supply of its own currency (and, in some cases, gold). These deposits established a "lending pool," from which any nation could borrow if temporarily losing reserves as a consequence of maintaining a fixed rate. It was of course understood that persisting reserve losses indicated some form of "fundamental disequilibrium" which could not be sustained by continual borrowing. A nation could depreciate its currency value by up to 10 percent if it wished. Further depreciation required "consultation with the fund"—in effect, international approval.

Today, with emphasis leaning strongly toward the need for "floating rates," it may seem odd that so much effort should have gone into establishment of a maintenance-of-fixed-rates system. But remember that there are valid arguments for steady rates as well as for floating ones.

In the course of time, it became evident that the IMF's "lending pool" of national currencies—dollars, pounds sterling, francs, etc.-was *(insufficient / excessive)* and in need of *(reduction / supplement)*. A new "international money"—although one to be used only in settlements between governments or central banks—was created. Its name was

_____.

The prime movers behind this new money were those who felt that gold should be eliminated (or its status reduced, at least) as an international reserve. Thus an alternative and more

colloquial name for these SDRs was "_____."

These SDRs are created just as commercial banks create money through their lending activity. The maximum amount of their creation each year is settled by vote of IMF members. The extent to which any nation can draw SDRs is governed by its quota participation in the IMF.

_____

insufficient; supplement; Special Drawing Rights; paper gold

For 25 years, the IMF operated successfully. Its rules were, in general, respected. In the middle of the 1960s, though, the strains of maintaining the system grew more and more apparent. Nations began to undertake more frequent changes in the international values of their domestic currencies with and sometimes without IMF approval. The system was sick and finally, in 1975, the IMF concluded that floating exchange rates were essential in times of extreme turbulence. Quoting from my daughter Mari's latest book relating her most recent visit to the Mystic Aquarium, "We went to see Alex the Whale, but he was sick. He is thirty years old. If you ask me, that is old for a whale. It sure is. He died last Friday." Thirty years is a pretty long time for an international arrangement that affects the everyday lives of billions of citizens of a multitude of countries to survive, too.

15. Why all this turbulence, after a considerable period of relative stability? To answer, we must return again to the early post–World War II period.

a. At that time, the United States was not only the world's industrial giant; it was a nation whose productive capacity had emerged from the war unscathed. Consequently, there was a 10-year period of acute "dollar shortage." The dollar was the only currency that could buy much-needed U.S. goods. Had the period been a floating-rate one, the dollar's exchange-market value would have greatly *(depreciated / appreciated)*.

This dollar shortage was considerably relieved by the Marshall Plan, created by the United States to assist the war-ravaged nations in economic reconstruction. It was to the interest of the United States that these nations should once again become prosperous trading partners. Fear that they might turn communist also played its part. Nevertheless, by international standards, it was a notably generous act.

The war-damaged nations (especially those in Western Europe, and Japan) regained economic health with remarkable speed. The process began with the Marshall Plan. Thereafter, in Europe, development of the Common Market was a major contributing factor. With recovery, the dependence of these nations on American goods was reduced. Indeed, with much-improved output capacity, their products became *(increasingly / less)* competitive with those American goods in world markets. The dollar shortage dwindled. In time, it became converted into a "dollar glut."

b. Many factors contributed to this turnaround in the dollar's standing. First of all, most of the big American corporations were attracted by the postwar opportunities for new markets abroad (mainly in Europe, but elsewhere in the world as well). They built new plants abroad; they bought up foreign corporations and many of them became "multinationals." Since foreign monies were needed for this activity, the effect was to *(depress / increase)* the demand for foreign currencies—i.e., to *(depress / increase)* the supply of dollars offered.

Moreover, these corporations brought to their new foreign plants much American technology. This expertise improved foreign productivity, and with it, foreign ability to compete against American-produced goods.

Nevertheless, the dollar's shift from strength to glut cannot be explained solely in terms of a shift in relative productivities and competitive standings. What had happened, beginning in the early postwar years, was that the U.S. dollar had become the world's money. (Before the war, the pound sterling had played this role. Postwar Britain was so weakened that the burden had to be transferred. Tradition was strong, though, and the pound was still quite extensively used as a world money, even though its position was now decidedly second to that of the dollar.)

The international community needs a money stock to carry on its trading, just as the domestic economy needs one. Only central banks and governments dealt with the IMF. Commercial banks, corporations, and other concerns involved in international trade and finance kept substantial deposits of dollars just in order to settle their accounts with one another.

The all-essential requirement in a money is confidence. So long as the dollar remained strong, it functioned well. But when evidence began to appear that changes in productivity and competitive positions had made it a little less strong than before, some dollar holders began to *(reduce / increase)* their holdings. They started to switch to German marks, Swiss francs, Dutch guilders, and so on. In the money community, news spreads fast. There arose the danger of a kind of international "bank run," in which the dollar's value might have been driven fantastically (*above / below*) the value which a comparison between American and foreign price levels have indicated to be appropriate.

This bank-run threat was averted because foreign central banks, aware of the major crisis it would have brought about, (*bought up / sold*) the dollars which nervous private holders wanted to unload even though their purchases left some of those central banks with dollar holdings so large that they may not have been entirely happy about holding them.

c. By the mid-1960s, it was common knowledge that the dollar's position was weak, if only because of the big dollar overhang in foreign central bank holdings. The British pound was weak for more fundamental reasons. Some currencies were overvalued, others undervalued. Widespread speculation on prospective rate changes began. In the crises of the late 1960s and early 1970s, it became evident that much of this "speculation" was the activity of multinational corporations which handle many currencies, sometimes in huge amounts. To the treasurers of such companies, it was only the most elementary prudence, if any currency seemed in danger of falling in value, to shift (*into / out of*) that currency. By their actions, they (*intensified / diminished*) the prospect that the currency would fall in value.

The stable-rate system persisted for several years after the dollar's weakness had become apparent. Why? Because the nations knew they needed an international currency unit, and the dollar had become that unit. They feared the consequences of abandoning stable rates and consequently depreciating the dollar. But by the early 1970s, it had become apparent that the established system was increasingly producing both overvalued and undervalued currencies. There was a sudden switch to floating rates with consequences much less catastrophic than had been feared. The new rates, to be sure, were often managed floats in which central banks (*still / refuse to*) intervene(d) against what are considered to be unnecessary or undesirable rate fluctuations. But in 1975, the IMF gave reluctant and qualified approval to the floating-rate system.

---

a. appreciated; increasingly   **b.** increase; increase; reduce; below; bought up   **c.** out of; intensified; still

16.   a. The text cites many contributing factors to the gradual deterioration of the U.S. dollar's postwar international status and to the associated worsening of the United States' balance-of-payments position. Three of these factors have just been discussed: heavy investment abroad by American firms; the gradual postwar improvement in foreign productivity, especially in Western Europe and in Japan; and a loss of confidence abroad in the secure value of the U.S. dollar.

The five-item list below includes four other factors. One item is inappropriate. Which one?
(1) A quadrupled price of foreign-produced petroleum
(2) Too much domestic inflation, especially after the Vietnam war

(3) Large deficits incurred by federal and state governments within the United States
(4) Persisting remnants of foreign discrimination against the sale of American goods
(5) Generosity on the part of the United States in the matter of economic and military aid

---

(3)

17.   The World Bank's task, in brief, is to channel money from the richer nations to less developed ones. In slightly more detail, the bank's function is to (*make short-term loans / make long-term loans / provide foreign exchange for balance-of-payments shortages*) to the world's poorer countries. It provides funds for a less developed nation (*even if that nation can / only if that nation cannot*) borrow privately at a reasonable interest rate.

The World Bank can make loans (pick one):
(1) Only from its capital, subscribed by member nations.
(2) From its capital, or by floating bond issues with principal and interest payments guaranteed by member nations.

In its early years, the bank was rather (*liberal / conservative*) in its loan policies, but when Robert McNamara became its president (in 1968), it (*expanded / curtailed*) the scope of its activity. McNamara's plan for the World Bank in the 1980s was to focus especially upon the (*more rapidly developing / poorest*) nations.

---

make long-term loans; only if that nation cannot; (2); conservative; expanded; poorest

18.   Movement toward free floating exchange rates has substantially reduced the need for large national reserves. Yet some reserves must still be kept; there are still international settlements to be made. What should be the role of gold in such settlements, and in reserves?

Opponents of gold consider it a barbarous relic left over from the early days of money—a relic which has already disappeared from domestic monies, which is overdue for removal from the international scene. Gold is inflexible in supply; its quantity cannot be increased so as to match smoothly the expanding needs of international commerce and finance.

This supply inflexibility could be overcome by periodic increases in the price of gold. Doubling its price would, for example, make the same physical quantity of gold stand for (*half / twice*) as much money value, but this price-increase technique has disadvantages. It would be an open invitation for speculation in future gold-price movements. Moreover, benefits would accrue unduly to the few major gold-producing nations, notably the Soviet Union and South Africa.

There is a third objection to the flexible-price idea—indeed, by far the strongest objection, in the view of those who want their nation's domestic money supply to be based on gold. They want this base in order to prevent the government from generating price inflation by overissue of paper money. They want, that is, the very feature that gold's opponents consider to be its major fault: inflexibility. If a government is free to raise the price of gold whenever it feels so disposed, it has as much freedom to increase the money supply as if there were no link to gold at all.

At this stage in the debate, gold's opponents are likely to point out that, for international settlements, Special Drawing Rights have now been developed. They can be issued, and increased, as dictated by the needs of international trade. And gold's advocates will respond that SDRs are "paper gold," subject to the same danger of overissue as any other form of paper.

The conviction that gold is a necessary base for stable domestic money (and hence for a stable system of foreign exchange rates) derives powerfully from the belief that gold has "inherent" or "intrinsic" value. Economists have grown skeptical of phrases like "inherent value." Experience has taught them that (cold-blooded commercial transactions, at any rate) "value" reduces to the price which the item in question will fetch in the marketplace; it emerges as a balance between the strength of demand and the strength of supply.

The world's total gold supply vastly exceeds the quantity usable for jewelry, dentistry, and industrial applications. Gold is valuable mainly because people *think* (and for a long time have thought) that it is valuable. Still, this belief is no worse than the belief (or convention) that a piece of paper money carrying the seal of some government or the name of a central bank is valuable. Indeed, by past experience, confidence in gold is more solidly based. There are many instances in history (European history especially) when people who held gold as their asset fared well (because gold is inflexible in supply), whereas those who held paper money fared badly. Note that we are here drifting into a different topic. The subject of this question is: Ought gold to be used as the base for the domestic money supply, or as the commodity to be used in international settlements? It may be eminently sensible for you, as an individual, to hedge against inflation by converting part or most of your assets into gold. Perhaps you will thereby beat inflation much more successfully than others who chose different policies. Yet even if you do succeed, that success does not logically carry to the conclusion that your government should sensibly base its money supply upon gold, or use gold for all its international settlements.

The crucial rule for success in any money medium—be it gold, paper, or china beads—is this: neither underissue nor overissue the unit of account and the store of value. When the Spaniards brought back huge quantities of Inca gold from South America in the sixteenth century, the resulting inflation in European prices was the same as would have been produced by a vast increase in paper money.

A compromise view would run as follows: it is impossible to rely solely on gold for international settlements (for reasons such as those cited at the beginning of this question). Neverthe-

less, the belief that "gold has value" is still widespread—even among some governments. (The strength of a government's advocacy of gold tends to be correlated with the amount of gold that government has stored in its vaults. France under de Gaulle was a particularly strong advocate.) This traditional confidence in gold may be misplaced. But confidence is always a vital element in money; there is no point in seeking to violate a traditional belief so long as that belief does no great harm. Of course, there is some inequity in the use of gold, in that benefit accrues particularly to those few nations which happen to have large quantities of gold-bearing ore beneath their ground. Still, the international reserves can have two components: gold and SDRs. Needed increases in this money stock should be created by increases in the *(total of SDRs / price of gold)*.

Gold's opponents are not happy with this compromise. They believe that gold's retention sustains the myth of its "inherent value." This makes SDRs the *("second-class" / "first-class")* international asset—in circumstances when the international trading world must rely increasingly on a regulated supply of such "paper gold," just as national economies have had to make increasing use of bank-deposit money, rather than stick exclusively to coins and paper bills.

---

twice; total of SDRs; "second-class"

---

19. One of the most significant problems of international finance in the early 1980s was the overvaluation of the dollar, estimated by some to have been *(10 / 25 / 50)* percent from 1981 into 1984. The scenario that produced this overvaluation begins with the *(tight / loose)* monetary policy and *(stimulative / contractionary)* fiscal policy under the Reagan administration that drove real interest rates in the United States *(up / down)*. Foreign investment therefore flowed *(into / out of)* the United States, *(increasing / decreasing)* the demand for dollars and thus causing the dollar to *(appreciate / depreciate)* in money markets all around the world. United States exports thus became *(more / less)* expensive while foreign imports into the United States became *(more / less)* costly. Net exports *(expanded / contracted)* by nearly *($50 billion / $140 billion / $250 billion)*, as a result, and created an enormous *(deficit / surplus)* in the current account. This discrepancy was, though, almost canceled by a *(deficit / surplus)* in the capital account, so the overvaluation persisted and drove interest rates abroad *(up / down)*. The result was a tendency for foreign economies to move into *(recession / boom)* and for *(depressed / overextended)* export- and import-competing industries in the United States to call for *(free trade / protection and subsidy)*.

Under fixed exchange rates, the only way to relieve overvaluation is to endure a *(recession / boom)* to generate *(higher / lower)* domestic prices. Under flexible exchange rates, the correction is supposed to be automatic, but it can be retarded by capital account flows. Under a managed float of the type now in place, the government of the United States can help things along by *(selling / buying)* dollars in the world marketplace. The Reagan administration (*pursued this policy vigorously / claimed that the dollar was not overvalued and undertook little official intervention*).

50; tight; stimulative; up; into; increasing; appreciate; more; less; contracted; $140 billion; deficit; surplus; up; recession; depressed; protection and subsidy; recession; lower; selling; claimed that the dollar was not overvalued and undertook little official intervention

QUIZ: Multiple Choice

1. If we say that a country's currency has been devalued, we mean specifically with respect to that country that:
(1) it has gone off the gold standard.
(2) the domestic purchasing power of its currency unit has fallen.
(3) its government has increased the price it will pay for gold.
(4) it is experiencing an unfavorable balance of trade.
(5) the prices of at least some foreign currencies, as expressed in that country's domestic currency, have fallen.

2. To be fully on the gold standard, the government of a country must:
(1) set a fixed price at which it is prepared to buy or sell gold in any quantity without restriction.
(2) be prepared to buy or sell gold at any time without restriction, but at a price which it is free to vary from day to day as it chooses, provided the same price (or almost the same price) applies to both purchases and sales.
(3) be prepared to buy gold in any quantity without restriction at a fixed price, but not necessarily to sell it.
(4) be prepared to sell gold in any quantity without restriction, but not necessarily to buy it.
(5) maintain a fixed gold content in its money unit, but not necessarily be prepared to buy or sell gold at any fixed price or without restriction.

3. In a stable exchange-rate situation, if the price of the French franc is 25 U.S. cents, and the price of the U.S. dollar is 600 Italian lire, then the price of the French franc in Italian lire must be:
(1) 90 lire.
(2) 150 lire.
(3) 200 lire.
(4) 300 lire.
(5) 600 lire.

4. The exports of Country A to Country B increase substantially. Both A and B operate on the gold standard. According to David Hume's gold-flow–price-level mechanism:
(1) A's domestic price level will fall; B's domestic price level may or may not change.
(2) A's price level may or may not change, but B's will fall.
(3) A's price level will rise; B's will fall.
(4) A's price level will fall; B's will rise.
(5) none of the above will happen.

5. If the exchange rate between Swiss francs and U.S. dollars changes from Sfr. 4 to the dollar to Sfr. 3 to the dollar, the franc's price has:
(1) risen from 25 to 33 cents, and the dollar has appreciated relative to the franc.
(2) fallen from 33 to 25 cents, and the dollar has depreciated relative to the franc.
(3) risen from 25 to 33 cents, and the dollar has been devalued relative to the franc.
(4) risen from 25 to 33 cents, and the dollar has depreciated relative to the franc.
(5) fallen from 33 to 25 cents, and the dollar has appreciated relative to the franc.

6. If American corporations make large dividend payments (in dollars) to foreigners:
(1) the effect on the price of the U.S. dollar, if any, will be to depreciate it.
(2) the effect on the price of the U.S. dollar, if any, will be to appreciate it.
(3) gold will tend to flow into the United States to compensate for the U.S. money going abroad.
(4) imports into the United States will tend to increase to compensate for the U.S. money going abroad.
(5) none of the above will be true.

7. If the exchange rate between Canadian and U.S. dollars is a floating one, and if the demand for Canadian dollars increases, then:
(1) the supply of Canadian dollars has decreased or will decrease.
(2) the price of the Canadian dollar in U.S. currency will fall.
(3) the supply of U.S. dollars has decreased.
(4) the price of the U.S. dollar in Canadian currency will fall.
(5) the U.S. dollar has been devalued.

8. A substantial fall in the price of the dollar in foreign currencies (e.g., the price of the dollar in francs) could be expected to affect physical quantities of exports from the United States and imports into the United States as follows. To:
(1) increase both exports and imports.
(2) increase exports, decrease imports.
(3) decrease both exports and imports.
(4) decrease exports, increase imports.
(5) have no perceptible effect on either imports or exports.

9. When Countries A and B are both fully on the gold standard, the exchange rate linking their currencies is fixed, or almost so:
(1) in the sense that there is a mechanical relationship between the currencies of A and B, but not in a sense that is useful for exporters or importers.
(2) because as a necessary part of being on the gold standard, Country A must supply B's currency on demand at a fixed price, and vice versa.
(3) because residents of A can always get B's currency at a fixed price through shipment and sale of gold to B, and vice versa.

(4) because being fully on the gold standard requires both countries to use the same currency unit, so that there is really no foreign exchange problem.

(5) in some circumstances, but not necessarily; the fact that A and B are both on the gold standard does not of itself imply any fixed-exchange-rate relationship.

10. If a country depreciates the foreign exchange value of its currency, the results will typically be as follows:

(1) Its imports will seem cheaper (from the viewpoint of its own citizens), and its exports will seem more expensive (from the viewpoint of foreigners).

(2) Its imports will seem more expensive (from the viewpoint of its own citizens), and its exports will seem cheaper (from the viewpoint of foreigners).

(3) Both its imports and its exports will seem cheaper (from the viewpoint of both its own citizens and foreigners).

(4) Both its imports and its exports will seem more expensive (from the viewpoint of both its own citizens and foreigners).

(5) None of the above, since there is no reason why the prices of either imports or exports should be affected.

11. The "foreign-trade multiplier" is a factor which determines:

(1) the amount by which exports increase as GNP rises.

(2) the amount by which imports increase as GNP rises.

(3) the amount by which GNP can increase as exports increase.

(4) the amount by which GNP can rise as imports increase.

(5) the amount of "leakage" to be expected from induced imports as GNP rises.

12. The two items paired below have the same characteristics in terms of their multiplier consequences and their impact on the level of domestic GNP. A:

(1) rise in imports and a rise in domestic investment.

(2) rise in saving and a rise in exports.

(3) fall in the propensity to save and a rise in exports.

(4) rise in the propensity to consume and a rise in imports.

(5) rise in imports and a rise in exports.

13. The "gold-flow–price-level mechanism" was part of the traditional account of the gold standard's functioning. One of the following did not have any part to play in its account of how a gold inflow or outflow would tend to be self-correcting, namely, the:

(1) gold outflow that would follow any large increase in imports.

(2) reduction in quantity of imports to be expected following significant price rises abroad.

(3) rise in money prices that might result from a large increase in exports.

(4) increase in exports that might well follow upon a fall in the domestic price level.

(5) rise in real and money incomes due to a rise in exports, and the consequent disposition to import more.

14. A nation's exports rise by $5 billion. In terms of the effects on GNP and imports to be expected therefrom, a reasonable and normal set of consequences might be to find (in billions):

(1) GNP up by $12, imports up by $15.

(2) GNP up by $12, imports up by $2.

(3) GNP up by $12, imports down by $2.

(4) GNP up by $4, imports up by $2.

(5) GNP up by $2, imports up by $5.

15. If GNP falls in the United States, and exchange rates are floating:

(1) imports will tend to decrease and the price of the U.S. dollar to increase.

(2) imports will tend to decrease and the price of the U.S. dollar to decrease.

(3) imports will tend to increase and the price of the U.S. dollar to increase.

(4) imports will tend to increase and the price of the U.S. dollar to decrease.

(5) none of the preceding statements will be true.

16. American corporations have large investment projects to undertake in Europe (involving European labor, materials, and equipment). They finance these projects by floating bond or stock issues in the United States. The short-run or immediate effect, if any, upon the international position of the dollar will be this:

(1) The dollar will tend to weaken in price, or the United States to lose gold or foreign exchange reserves.

(2) The dollar will tend to strengthen in price, or the United States to gain gold or foreign exchange reserves.

(3) The United States may gain gold or foreign exchange reserves, but there is no reason why the dollar's price should strengthen.

(4) The dollar's price may well strengthen or rise, but there is no reason why the United States should gain gold or foreign exchange reserves.

(5) Neither the dollar's price nor the U.S. gold or foreign exchange position is likely to be affected in any way.

17. The projects described in question 16 have a significant effect in lifting Europe out of a recession. Should this occur, which alternative in question 16 would correctly describe the resulting effect, it any, upon the international position of the dollar?

(1).

(2).

(3).

(4).

(5).

18. International trade and finance grew rapidly after the close of World War II. The resulting need for greater international liquidity (particularly during the 1950s, and up to the mid-1960s) was met principally by:

(1) new gold production.

(2) gold released by the Soviet Union.

(3) the credit-creating facilities of the World Bank.

(4) Special Drawing Rights.

(5) gold released by the United States plus increased foreign holdings of dollars.

19. One factor which contributed significantly to the balance-of-payments deficits experienced by the United States during the 1960s was:

(1) the activity of U.S. corporations in expanding their plants and operations abroad.

(2) a large excess of interest and dividends paid foreigners over similar investment income received.

(3) a substantial excess of merchandise exports over merchandise imports.

(4) the export of gold.

(5) very heavy imports of miscellaneous "services" (other than travel).

20. A country is at full employment and is experiencing an undesirable degree of price inflation. Its reserves of gold and foreign exchange are gradually being reduced as a result of balance-of-payments deficits. Particularly if this country wants to postpone any decision on changing the foreign price of its currency, the monetary policy indicated is:

(1) a tighter policy concerning domestic prices, but an easier policy concerning foreign reserves.

(2) a tighter policy as it concerns both domestic prices and foreign reserves.

(3) an easier policy as it concerns both domestic prices and foreign reserves.

(4) an easier policy concerning domestic prices, but a tighter policy concerning foreign reserves.

(5) a tighter policy as it concerns domestic prices, but no special policy as to foreign reserves, since domestic interest rates have no part to play in this problem.

21. Change the conditions of question 20 in one respect only: the country is experiencing heavy unemployment but not an undesirable degree of price inflation. Which alternative in question 20 then becomes correct?

(1).

(2).

(3).

(4).

(5).

22. The principal task assigned to the International Monetary Fund at the time of its organization was to:

(1) serve as a partial substitute for the gold standard in maintaining stable exchange rates.

(2) try to maintain a high level of employment within member countries, so as to avoid any danger of competitive depreciation policies in the foreign exchange markets.

(3) make loans to private companies in any country where the funds could not otherwise be borrowed at any reasonable interest rate.

(4) facilitate the development of free trade "regions" similar to the European Common Market.

(5) coordinate the views of the larger and more developed nations concerning exchange-rate and trade problems.

23. It could also be said that the principal task assigned to the International Monetary Fund was to:

(1) act as the world's banker in matters of both short-term and long-term credit.

(2) make direct long-term loans to less developed nations when necessary, so as to assist in their economic development.

(3) control international credit sufficiently to enable member nations to maintain their price levels at reasonably noninflationary levels.

(4) help bridge short-run disequilibrium in any member nation's balance of payments.

(5) work toward the gradual reduction of tariffs and elimination of protectionist policies among nations.

24. Which alternative in question 23 would be correct had that question referred to the World Bank, not to the International Monetary Fund?

(1).

(2).

(3).

(4).

(5).

25. A disturbance in its balance of payments may cause any nation to lose gold or foreign exchange reserves. This danger of loss is most acute whenever that nation:

(1) increases its exports.

(2) seeks to maintain a flexible exchange rate.

(3) seeks to maintain a fixed exchange rate.

(4) increases its borrowing from other nations.

(5) experiences a drop in GNP—i.e., whenever any recession or depression occurs.

26. The text speaks of action by a country which should increase its domestic employment, but at the possible expense of employment abroad. An example of such action by Country A, to "export its joblessness" to Country B, might be:

(1) an appreciation of A's currency relative to B's.

(2) a decrease in loans made to country B.

(3) a depreciation of A's currency relative to B's.

(4) a reduction in tariffs levied on imports from B.

(5) an increase in the price of A exports—i.e., making buyers in B pay more for what they buy from A.

27. A "managed float" means:

(1) an increase in the protectionist policies by some device other than a tariff increase.

(2) refusal by a nation to allow its currency to appreciate even though its reserves are large and increasing.

(3) a beggar-my-neighbor policy.

(4) introduction of a split exchange rate—a fixed rate for some transactions, a floating rate for others.

(5) periodic intervention by a central bank to check excessive fluctuation in an otherwise-floating exchange rate.

ANSWERS TO QUIZ QUESTIONS: Multiple Choice

Chapter 2
1. 4	**9.** 2
2. 4	**10.** 5
3. 4	**11.** 3
4. 2	**12.** 1
5. 2	**13.** 3
6. 1	**14.** 2
7. 5	**15.** 3
8. 4	**16.** 1

Chapter 3
1. 1	**9.** 5
2. 5	**10.** 1
3. 2	**11.** 3
4. 3	**12.** 2
5. 5	**13.** 5
6. 3	**14.** 5
7. 2	**15.** 4 (or 1)
8. 2	

Chapter 4
1. 4	**10.** 5
2. 4	**11.** 2
3. 1	**12.** 5
4. 1	**13.** 2
5. 2	**14.** 5
6. 1	**15.** 2
7. 5	**16.** 3
8. 4	**17.** 1
9. 3	**18.** 3

Chapter 5
1. 5	**7.** 2
2. 3	**8.** 4
3. 4	**9.** 3
5. 5	**10.** 1
5. 1	**11.** 2
6. 3	**12.** 4

Chapter 6
1. 3	**7.** 2
2. 4	**8.** 1
3. 5	**9.** 1
4. 4	**10.** 4
5. 3	**11.** 1
6. 3	**12.** 5

Chapter 7
1. 4	**12.** 3
2. 5	**13.** 5
3. 1	**14.** 2
4. 2	**15.** 4
5. 1	**16.** 4
6. 5	**17.** 3
7. 2	**18.** 5
8. 3	**19.** 4
9. 4	**20.** 1
10. 2	**21.** 2
11. 1	

Chapter 8
1. 5	**12.** 3
2. 5	**13.** 5
3. 5	**14.** 1
4. 3	**15.** 5
5. 2	**16.** 4
6. 4	**17.** 2
7. 5	**18.** 4
8. 5	**19.** 2
9. 1	**20.** 4
10. 4	**21.** 4
11. 3	**22.** 2

Chapter 9
1. 5	**12.** 4
2. 5	**13.** 3
3. 3	**14.** 5
4. 2	**15.** 3
5. 4	**16.** 5
6. 3	**17.** 3
7. 5	**18.** 1
8. 5	**19.** 4
9. 5	**20.** 1
10. 1	
11. 2	

Chapter 10
1. 4	**10.** 2
2. 3	**11.** 4
3. 2	**12.** 1
4. 5	**13.** 2
5. 5	**14.** 3
6. 2	**15.** 4
7. 5	**16.** 5
8. 5	**17.** 3
9. 4	

Chapter 11
1. 3	**7.** 5
2. 1	**8.** 3
3. 2	**9.** 2
4. 1	**10.** 1
5. 3	**11.** 5
6. 2	

Chapter 12
1. 5	**8.** 1
2. 1	**9.** 5
3. 5	**10.** 4
4. 1	**11.** 2
5. 5	**12.** 4
6. 3	**13.** 1
7. 2	

Chapter 13
1. 3	**9.** 1
2. 1	**10.** 1
3. 2	**11.** 1
4. 5	**12.** 3
5. 2	**13.** 4
6. 5	**14.** 5
7. 2	**15.** 2
8. 4	

Chapter 14
1. 5	**15.** 2
2. 2	**16.** 4
3. 1	**17.** 3
4. 3	**18.** 4
5. 5	**19.** 3
6. 1	**20.** 2
7. 1	**21.** 1
8. 1	**22.** 5
9. 5	**23.** 5
10. 5	**24.** 4
11. 1	**25.** 5
12. 5	**26.** 3
13. 5	**27.** 4
14. 2	**28.** 4

Appendix
1. 3	**5.** 3
2. 1	**6.** 1
3. 5	**7.** 2
4. 4	**8.** 4

Chapter 15
1. 5	**7.** 4
2. 4	**8.** 5
3. 2	**9.** 3
4. 3	**10.** 2
5. 1	**11.** 1
6. 1	**12.** 2

13. 3   **16.** 4
14. 1   **17.** 5
15. 5   **18.** 5

Chapter 16
1. 4   12. 5
2. 4   13. 3
3. 2   14. 5
4. 5   15. 4
5. 5   16. 1
6. 1   17. 2
7. 5   18. 3
8. 3   19. 1
9. 2   20. 2
10. 5   21. 5
11. 1   22. 5
Appendix
1. 4   6. 1 or 2
2. 1   7. 5
3. 3   8. 3
4. 3   9. 5
5. 2

Chapter 17
1. 1   9. 2
2. 3   10. 5
3. 3   11. 3
4. 4   12. 4
5. 5   13. 1
6. 4   14. 4
7. 3   15. 5
8. 3   16. 1
Appendix
1. 5   8. 2
2. 2   9. 4
3. 4   10. 3
4. 2   11. 4
5. 1   12. 3
6. 4   13. 1
7. 2   14. 2

Chapter 18
1. 5   13. 4
2. 4   14. 1
3. 2   15. 4
4. 3   16. 5
5. 2   17. 2
6. 1   18. 2
7. 3   19. 4
8. 2   20. 2
9. 4   21. 1
10. 1   22. 3
11. 1   23. 1
12. 1   24. 5

Appendix
1. 2   9. 2
2. 3   10. 1
3. 1   11. 1
4. 1   12. 1
5. 3   13. 1
6. 2   14. 2
7. 3   15. 1
8. 4   16. 1

Chapter 19
1. 4   10. 1
2. 1   11. 4
3. 2   12. 3
4. 4   13. 4
5. 1   14. 5
6. 5   15. 1
7. 1   16. 1
8. 3   17. 2
9. 2   18. 2
Appendix
1. 5   4. 5
2. 4   5. 5
3. 4

Chapter 20
1. 2   11. 1
2. 1   12. 5
3. 3   13. 2
4. 2   14. 2
5. 2   15. 1
6. 4   16. 3
7. 1
8. 1
9. 2
10. 2
Appendix
1. 3   9. 5
2. 3   10. 2
3. 2   11. 5
4. 2   12. 3
5. 1   13. 4
6. 3   14. 1
7. 4   15. 3
8. 4

Chapter 21
1. 4   6. 4
2. 4   7. 1
3. 5   8. 4
4. 3   9. 1
5. 1   10. 5

Chapter 22
1. 4   16. 3
2. 2   17. 3
3. 4   18. 1
4. 5   19. 2
5. 4   20. 5
6. 2   21. 5
7. 5   22. 3
8. 3   23. 1
9. 3   24. 3
10. 5   25. 4
11. 1   26. 5
12. 2   27. 5
13. 4   28. 4
14. 4   29. 2
15. 1   30. 1

Chapter 23
1. 5   12. 5
2. 3   13. 1
3. 1   14. 2
4. 3   15. 4
5. 1 or 3   16. 3
6. 3   17. 1
7. 3   18. 5
8. 3   19. 3
8. 5   20. 5
10. 1   21. 3
11. 2   22. 3

Chapter 24
1. 5   11. 3
2. 2   12. 1
3. 4   13. 5
4. 1   14. 3
5. 2   15. 2
6. 3   16. 2
7. 1   17. 2
8. 5   18. 4
9. 4   19. 1
10. 1   20. 2

Chapter 25
1. 5   9. 2
2. 2   10. 3
3. 4   11. 1
4. 3   12. 2
5. 3   13. 3
6. 2   14. 4
7. 4   15. 2
8. 3   16. 4

Chapter 26
1. 3   11. 1
2. 4   12. 3
3. 4   13. 5
4. 3   14. 2
5. 4   15. 2
6. 5   16. 3
7. 4   17. 4
8. 3   18. 3
9. 5   19. 5
10. 1
Appendix
1. 3   7. 5
2. 4   8. 4
3. 4   9. 5
4. 2   10. 3
5. 1   11. 3
6. 1   12. 2

Chapter 27
1. 3   7. 5
2. 1   8. 5
3. 1   9. 1
4. 2   10. 3
5. 4   11. 5
6. 1   12. 2

Chapter 28
1. 2   10. 1
2. 1   11. 3
3. 5   12. 2
4. 5   13. 1
5. 3   14. 1
6. 2   15. 5
7. 4   16. 2
8. 3   17. 3
9. 5   18. 3

Chapter 29
1. 5   11. 2
2. 4   12. 4
3. 3   13. 5
4. 3   14. 3
5. 2   15. 1
6. 4   16. 4
7. 2   17. 1
8. 5   18. 4
9. 3   19. 1
10. 4   20. 5

Chapter 30
1. 4   3. 2
2. 3   4. 1

5. 3	17. 1
6. 4	18. 3
7. 4	19. 4
8. 3	20. 5
9. 2	21. 2
10. 5	22. 4
11. 3	23. 5
12. 1	24. 4
13. 4	25. 2
14. 3	26. 3
15. 1	27. 4
16. 4	28. 1

Appendix

1. 4	5. 5
2. 5	6. 3
3. 3	7. 3
4. 5	

Chapter 31

1. 2	5. 5
2. 5	6. 4
3. 2	7. 2
4. 4	

Appendix

1. 2	3. 4
2. 1	4. 4

Chapter 32

1. 3	11. 5
2. 2	12. 5
3. 2	13. 1
4. 2	14. 2

5. 5	15. 5
6. 5	16. 4
7. 2	17. 3
8. 1	18. 5
9. 4	19. 1
10. 3	20. 2

Chapter 33

1. 3	14. 5
2. 2	15. 1
3. 2	16. 4
4. 1	17. 2
5. 4	18. 5
6. 3	19. 5
7. 2	20. 2
8. 5	21. 1
9. 2	22. 5
10. 2	23. 3
11. 5	24. 4
12. 3	25. 2
13. 2	26. 1

Chapter 34

1. 5	11. 5
2. 2	12. 1
3. 5	13. 5
4. 4	14. 5
5. 4	15. 1
6. 3	16. 3
7. 3	17. 2
8. 5	18. 5
9. 4	19. 5
10. 3	20. 1

Chapter 35

1. 3	10. 2
2. 3	11. 3
3. 5	12. 4
4. 4	13. 3
5. 1	14. 5
6. 4	15. 3
7. 1	16. 2
8. 3	17. 1
9. 1	18. 5

Chapter 36

1. 1	7. 5
2. 3	8. 1
3. 2	9. 5
4. 5	10. 1
5. 2	11. 4
6. 4	12. 5

Appendix

1. 1	5. 5
2. 5	6. 2
3. 3	7. 1
4. 5	8. 4

Chapter 37

1. 4	6. 2
2. 3	7. 1
3. 5	8. 4
4. 5	9. 5
5. 1	

Chapter 38

1. 4	8. 3
2. 3	9. 3
3. 2	10. 3
4. 4	11. 5
5. 3	12. 3
6. 1	13. 4
7. 2	14. 5
	15. 3

Chapter 39

1. 3	7. 2
2. 1	8. 2
3. 2	9. 5
4. 2	10. 2
5. 3	11. 3
6. 3	12. 5

Chapter 40

1. 3	15. 1
2. 1	16. 1
3. 2	17. 2
4. 3	18. 5
5. 4	19. 1
6. 1	20. 2
7. 4	21. 4
8. 2	22. 1
9. 3	23. 4
10. 2	24. 2
11. 3	25. 3
12. 3	26. 3
13. 5	27. 5
14. 2	